DISTURBING ARGUMENT

This edited volume represents the best of the scholarship presented at the 18th National Communication Association/American Forensic Association Conference on Argumentation: the biennial conference that brings together a lively group of argumentation scholars from a range of disciplinary approaches and a variety of countries. *Disturbing Argument* contains selected works that speak both to the disturbing prevalence of violence in the contemporary world and to the potential of argument, itself, to disturb the very relations of power that enable that violence. Scholars' essays analyze a range of argument forms, including body and visual argument, interpersonal and group argument, argument in electoral politics, public argument, argument in social protest, scientific and technical argument, and argument and debate pedagogy. Contributors study argument using a range of methodological approaches, from social scientifically informed studies of interpersonal, group, and political argument to humanistic examinations of argument theory, political discourse, and social protest, to creatively informed considerations of argument practices that truly disturb the boundaries of what we consider argument.

Catherine H. Palczewski, Ph.D., is a Professor of Communication Studies and Affiliate Faculty in Women's and Gender Studies at the University of Northern Iowa, USA, where she also served as the Director of Debate from 1994–2009. She received her B.S., M.A, and Ph.D. from Northwestern University where she also competed in policy debate. She was a member of the 1987 US team, and in 1999 served as coach of the team, that participated in the Committee on International Discussion and Debate tour of Japan. She recently completed her term as co-editor for the American Forensic Association journal *Argumentation and Advocacy*. Her work has appeared in that journal, as well as in the *Quarterly Journal of Speech, Communication Studies, NWSA Journal*, and *The Southern Communication Journal*. She received the Francine Merritt Award for Outstanding Contributions to the Lives of Women in Communication, the Iowa Regents Award for Faculty Excellence, the University of Northern Iowa College of Humanities and Fine Arts Faculty Excellence Award, the George Ziegelmueller Outstanding Debate Educator Award, and the Rohrer Award for the Outstanding Publication in Argumentation. Her work tends to focus on how marginalized groups rhetorically construct their messages to gain access to, and be legible in, the dominant public sphere.

Selected Works from the 18th NCA/AFA Alta Conference on Argumentation

DISTURBING ARGUMENT

Edited by Catherine H. Palczewski

LONDON AND NEW YORK

First published 2015
by Routledge
2 Park Square, Milton Park, Abingdon, Oxon, OX14 4RN, UK

and by Routledge
711 Third Avenue, New York, NY 10017, USA

Routledge is an imprint of the Taylor & Francis Group, an informa business

British Library Cataloguing in Publication Data
A catalogue record for this book is available from the British Library

Library of Congress Cataloging in Publication Data
  NCA/AFA Conference on Argumentation (18th : 2013 : Alta, Utah)
  Disturbing argument / Edited by Catherine H. Palczewski.
     p. cm.
  Includes bibliographical references and index.
  ISBN 978-1-138-79029-2 (hbk : alk. paper) — ISBN 978-1-315-76396-5 (ebk : alk. paper)   1. Persuasion (Rhetoric)—Congresses. 2. Debates and debating—Congresses.   3. Communication in politics—Congresses.   4. Reasoning—Congresses.   5. Forensics (Public speaking)—Congresses.   I. Palczewski, Catherine Helen, editor.   II. Title.
  P301.5.P47N365 2013
  168—dc23

                                                                                        2014020172

ISBN: 978–1–138–79029–2 (hbk)
ISBN: 978–1–315–76396–5 (ebk)

Typeset in Bembo by RefineCatch Limited, Bungay, Suffolk

Cover photo: Catherine H. Palczewski

Disclaimer
Every effort has been made to contact copyright holders for their permission to reprint material in this book. The publishers would be grateful to hear from any copyright holder who is not here acknowledged and will undertake to rectify any errors or omissions in future editions of this book.

CONTENTS

Contents

Interpersonal and Group Argument

Argument in Electoral Politics

Contents

Contents

Public Argument

Argument in Social Protest

Contents

Argument and Debate Pedagogy

Contents

ACKNOWLEDGEMENTS

Being asked to direct the 18th National Communication Association/American Forensic Association Conference on Argumentation and edit its selected works is, quite simply, an honor. My first time attending this conference was in 1993, when I presented at the 8th biennial conference as a young assistant professor. Over the last two decades worth of conferences, time in the mountain air has provided me the chance to watch and work with a range of skilled conference directors, and to spend time with mentors, colleagues, and fellow scholars. And, I called on many of them to help me as I directed the conference. The connections I developed over the years were essential; I could not have directed this conference without the help of people I consider my Alta/argument family.

The Steering Committee members were always supportive, helpful, and willing to offer reminders. For their vote of confidence and encouragement, I offer thanks to: David Zarefsky (chair), Jim Klumpp (treasurer), Carol Winkler (AFA representative), Harry Weger (NCA representative), Danielle Endres (local host), Robin Rowland (Director, 2011), Dennis Gouran (Director, 2009).

Robin Rowland and Dennis Gouran, directors of the last two conferences, compiled an extremely helpful "directing document" and were always available with speedy, and unfailingly helpful, advice. To Robin and Dennis, I offer thanks for their experience and guidance.

Jim Klumpp and Jeff Jarman also deserve thanks for their work on the Alta websites, Jim for the permanent portal and Jeff for working with me on the electronic submission site for the conference. I thank the both of them for pretending that I sometimes make sense when I talk about all things digital.

The editorial board gave their time and expertise to review both the initial submissions and the essays submitted for publication consideration – always on a very tight schedule. For their promptness and insight, I thank: Jarrod Atchison, Wake Forest University; Dan Brouwer, Arizona State University; Jon Bruschke, California State University – Fullerton; Danielle Endres, University of Utah; Leo Groarke, University of Windsor; Dale Hample, University of Maryland; Dale Herbeck, Boston College; Jeff Jarman, Wichita State University; Casey Kelly, Butler University; Susan Kline, Ohio State University; Randy Lake, University of Southern California; Damien Pfister, University of Nebraska – Lincoln; and Mary Stuckey, Georgia State University.

After the conference, a hearty few remained for an editing "boot camp" – two days of intense editing, debates, and discussions. This faithful crew assisted me in making the decisions about which essays to include. In addition, they helped draft the editorial letters that offered advice to those essays that needed revisions. For their engaging conversations, hearty appetites, incredible work ethic, and ability to have far too much fun even when laboring, I thank: Daniel Brouwer, Danielle Endres, Casey Kelly, Susan Kline, and Damien Pfister. This is a crew who takes their work very seriously, but not themselves. This volume, quite simply, would not have been possible, or as good, without their joyful assistance and advice.

At this point, you have now read Danielle Endres's name multiple times. She really does deserve multiple, if not endless, thanks. As local host, she took care of all the details relating to food, the hotel, rooms, AV equipment, and the list goes on and on. Her assistant, Brain Cozen, did the layout for the program. These two really made the job of directing incredibly easy. I thank them for the vast range of gigabytes we used up in their email accounts and for their always sunny dispositions.

A number of institutions provide support for this conference. The National Communication Association and the American Forensic Association sponsor the conference and the University of Utah is the local host. Folks at the University of Northern Iowa also helped with financial and other support. Dean Joel Haack of the University of Northern Iowa's College of Humanities, Arts and Sciences and Dean Michael Licari of the Graduate College provided the monetary support for my editorial assistant. Chris Martin, interim head of the Department of Communication Studies, provided unwavering moral support and any service or material support I requested.

Finally, I owe special thanks to my editorial assistant and helper extraordinaire: Laura Bartelt (University of Northern Iowa) and Ryan McGeough (Upper Iowa University). Laura developed the system to track submissions and created every bizarre form of table and spreadsheet I requested in my ongoing attempts to organize the conference. And, when there were times when I was out of commission, I knew I could give her instructions and everything would be in order when I resurfaced. Without her, the processing of both the conference and publication submissions would not have happened as expeditiously as they did. Ryan consistently volunteered to help in any way he could – and I ended up being extremely thankful for his willingness to help. I was a bit under the weather as a result of unexpected, but routine, surgery that was happening right as the editorial reviews of the conference submissions were coming in. Laura got everything organized and Ryan gave up one of his Saturdays to come in to my office to work with me and Laura to process all the reviews and panel all the papers. Their assistance with this process helped make the conversations at the conference as lively as they were. They helped me see connections between papers and topics, and they made sure I did my math right when computing acceptances. With helpers like these, it was easy to play through the (post-surgical) pain.

Finally, I owe thanks to Arnie Madsen, who came out of academic retirement to attend the conference. Arnie was the person who originally encouraged me to start attending this conference, telling me it would be my chance to "meet my footnotes" and a place where I would find an academic home. He was right. Twenty years later, I am glad I have made a home at this conference, and with him.

NOTES ON CONTRIBUTORS

Luis M. Andrade, California State University, Fullerton, USA

Satoru Aonuma, Tsuda College, Japan

Lauren Archer, University of Washington, USA

R. Jarrod Atchison, Wake Forest University, USA

Ruth J. Beerman, Bloomsburg University, USA

Jennifer L. Bevan, Chapman University, USA

Matthew Bost, Willamette University, USA

Alexandra Boulger, Chapman University, USA

Brett Bricker, University of Kansas, USA

Matthew P. Brigham, James Madison University, USA

Daniel C. Brouwer, Arizona State University, USA

Stephen Howard Browne, The Pennsylvania State University, USA

Jon Bruschke, California State University, Fullerton, USA

Derek Buescher, University of Puget Sound, USA

David Cratis Williams, Florida Atlantic University, USA

Alexis Della Ripa, Chapman University, USA

David R. Dewberry, Rider University, USA

Aaron Dimock, Minnesota State University, Mankato, USA

Valeria Fabj, Lynn University, USA

Lisa A. Flores, University of Colorado, USA

John Fritch, University of Northern Iowa, USA

Kathleen M. Galvin, Northwestern University, USA

Matthew G. Gerber, Baylor University, USA

Ryan Gillespie, University of Southern California, USA

G. Thomas Goodnight, University of Southern California, USA

Dennis S. Gouran, The Pennsylvania State University, USA

Leo Groarke, University of Windsor, Canada

Jeremy R. Grossman, University of Georgia, USA

Leslie A. Hahner, Baylor University, USA

Heidi Hamilton, Emporia State University, USA

Eileen Hammond, Florida Atlantic University, USA

Dale Hample, University of Maryland, USA

Kelly E. Happe, University of Georgia, USA

Heather Ashley Hayes, Whitman College, USA

Alexander Hiland, University of Minnesota, USA

Linda Diane Horwitz, Lake Forest College, USA

Amanda L. Irions, University of Maryland, USA

Jeffrey W. Jarman, Wichita State University, USA

John M. Jones, Pepperdine University, USA

Casey Ryan Kelly, Butler University, USA

Susan L. Kline, Ohio State University, USA

James F. Klumpp, University of Maryland, USA

Randall A. Lake, University of Southern California, USA

Brian Lain, University of North Texas, USA

Danielle Levine, Chapman University, USA

Marcin Lewi ski, Universidade Nova de Lisboa, Portugal

Esther Liu, Northwestern University, USA

Arnie Madsen, Mad Cat Antiques, USA

Joan Faber McAlister, Drake University, USA

Megan D. McFarlane, The University of Utah, USA

Danielle Dick McGeough, University of Northern Iowa, USA

Ryan Erik McGeough, Upper Iowa University, USA

Gordon R. Mitchell, University of Pittsburgh, USA

Dima Mohammed, Universidade Nova de Lisboa, Portugal

Junya Morooka, Rikkyo University, Japan

William Mosley-Jensen, University of Georgia, USA

Marylou R. Naumoff, Florida Atlantic University, USA

Meredith Neville-Shepard, University of Kansas, USA

Ryan Neville-Shepard, Indiana University-Purdue University Columbus, USA

Denise Oles-Acevedo, Iowa State University, USA

Kathryn M. Olson, University of Wisconsin – Milwaukee, USA

Kent A. Ono, University of Utah, USA

Catherine Helen Palczewski, University of Northern Iowa, USA

Edward Panetta, University of Georgia, USA

Marcus Paroske, University of Michigan-Flint, USA

Sarah T. Partlow-Lefevre, Idaho State University, USA

Samuel P. Perry, Baylor University, USA

Damien S. Pfister, University of Nebraska-Lincoln, USA

Barbara A. Pickering, University of Nebraska at Omaha, USA

Jessica M. Prody, St. Lawrence University, USA

John J. Rief, University of Pittsburgh, USA

Robert C. Rowland, The University of Kansas, USA

William O. Saas, Louisiana State University, USA

Kazuhiko Seno, ThinkHard, Inc. Japan

Brian J. Schrader, Regis University, USA

Susan A. Sci, Regis University, USA

Vesta T. Silva, Allegheny College, USA

Chelsea Simmons, Chapman University, USA

L. Paul Strait, University of Southern California, USA

Mary E. Stuckey, Georgia State University, USA

Noriaki Tajima, Kanda University of International Studies, Japan

Erika M. Thomas, California State University, Fullerton, USA

Sarah S. Topp, Trinity University, USA

Philip Tschirhart, University of Missouri – Columbia, USA

Aryn Tuazon, Chapman University, USA

Scott J. Varda, Baylor University, USA

Jean H. M. Wagemans, University of Amsterdam, The Netherlands

Don Waisanen, Baruch College, City University of New York, USA

Benjamin R. Warner, University of Missouri – Columbia, USA

Rachel Avon Whidden, Lake Forest College, USA

Carol Winkler, Georgia State University, USA

Kaori Yamada, University of Wisconsin – Milwaukee, USA

David Zarefsky, Northwestern University, USA

Kate Zittlow Rogness, Monmouth College, USA

DISTURBING ARGUMENT

An introduction to the selected works from the 18th National Communication Association/ American Forensics Association Alta Conference on Argumentation

Catherine Helen Palczewski

UNIVERSITY OF NORTHERN IOWA, USA, WRITTEN IN CONVERSATION WITH DANIEL BROUWER, DANIELLE ENDRES, CASEY KELLEY, SUSAN KLINE, AND DAMIEN PFISTER

This selected works volume represents the best of the scholarship presented at the 18th National Communication Association/American Forensic Association Conference on Argumentation. Also known as the Alta Argumentation Conference, given its locations in the mountains of Alta, UT, the conference happens every other summer and brings together a lively collection of argumentation scholars from a range of disciplinary approaches and a variety of countries.

When I was invited to plan this conference, I knew almost immediately the theme I would use: Disturbing Argument: as in argument that disturbs, contains disturbing words or images, or is about disturbing topics; as in argument that disturbs relationships of power; as in theories and approaches that disturb traditional approaches to argument; as in examples of argument that disturb what we think we already know about the processes of argumentation. So, quite intentionally, the theme invited people to submit scholarship that was *disturbing*, in all its polysemous and polyvalent (if not wholeheartedly equivocal) glory. Although *disturbing* often carries negative connotations, it need not always. That which disturbs can agitate, disquiet, startle, and perturb. Now, if one likes things settled and unchanging (if not calcified), one might find being disturbed to be a distressing experience. But, if one recognizes the contingency, fluidity, and malleability of life, theories, and argument, then disturbation becomes inevitable, if not welcome (given complete rigidity might be a sign of rigor mortis).

Like the effect of tossing a pebble into a still pool (or Cecret Lake), the result of the disturbance to the water is that images refract, what was surface and transparent becomes interior and opaque, and the margins of the body of water expand and contract. Similarly, the essays in this volume represent considerations of what happens when one considers disturbing argument. What one sees and studies, the boundaries of argument, what matters in argument is disturbed. Carol Winkler's keynote address essay that opens this volume disturbs in every way possible. She disturbs what bodies we see when we think of arguers, she engages with disturbing images, she disturbs what counts as argument, and she disturbs existing theories of argument. She shakes us up, and likely perturbs many, which is precisely what a good argument should do.

The result of the invitation to argumentation scholars to consider disturbing argument is a collection of essays that speaks both to the disturbing prevalence of violence in the contemporary world (most vividly illustrated by the many essays about U.S. drone policy) and to the potential of argument, itself, to disturb the very relations of power that enable that violence. Argument, rather than being a tool of power, was offered as a gift, as love, as community, or as the very grounds on which community is built. For those who assemble in the mountains of Utah, argument is an infinite game, the purpose of which is to keep playing. However, argument in this sense is possible only if it is structured in a way that invites others in, rather than repels or excludes them.

As one might expect of a conference that convenes experts on argument, as well as expert arguers, the essays, themselves represent a series of dialectical tensions – not stalemates or protracted altercations, but productive tensions that illuminate the stakes, grounds, and functions of argument. To name just a few, you will see essays that navigate: constraint v. openness of society, constraint v. agency of the individual, public v. private, structure v. agency, optimism v. pessimism, stability v. transformation, permanence v. change, discursive v. material. The scholars' willingness to open themselves to argument, and to open themselves and their arguments to being disturbed, means this argument conference produced dialectical tensions and debates that generate conversations rather than close off discussions. It also means these selected works provide a way for those arguments to continue, to sustain that infinite game. Three central dialectics deserve a bit of further commentary.

First, the tension between realism and idealism in the assessment of argument's utility. Many essays in this volume consider whether argumentation as a democratic capacity can save those governed from the governing apparatus of the state and corporations, or if the state and corporations are public relations machines that churn out argument to generate disingenuous controversies. Scholars will leave you asking if argument, as a technique to make decisions in a world of contingency and probability, is moribund, merely a cynical ploy used to induce people to believe they live in a democracy, or if there is hope that argument can offer a way to make better, if not good, decisions.

Second, the tension between normative and descriptive analyses of argument. Many essays offer ways to normatively judge which arguments are better. Others, however, describe how actually existing argument functions. In some, if not many, cases, the actually existing arguments that occur fall far short of the normative measures of good argument. Yet, there appears to be an enduring commitment to teaching, students in particular and people in general, ways to judge when assent is warranted and ways to produce arguments that sidle more closely to the normative ideal.

Third, the tension between whether argument is a farce, or should be farcical. Many essays noted we live in dubious times, and argument is merely a farce meant to distract. However, others argued that precisely *because* we live in dubious times, the farcical possibilities of argument should be deployed. Given traditional rational argument seems to fail (especially for those with the least power), what can advocates do? Answers included: argue sideways, argue ironically to make evident the absurd reality in which we live, argue with an orientation to community, argue with their bodies, argue with masses of bodies, argue about the body.

Ultimately, as Stefon of *Saturday Night Live* fame might have opined, "This conference had everything." A range of argument forms was studied, including body and visual argument, interpersonal and group argument, argument in electoral politics (both in the U.S. and in

Egypt), public argument, argument in social protest, scientific and technical argument, and argument and debate pedagogy. Scholars studied argument using a range of methodological approaches, from social scientifically informed studies of interpersonal, group, and political argument to humanistic examinations of argument theory, political discourse, and social protest, to creatively informed considerations of argument practices that truly disturb the boundaries of what we consider argument. The book section that grew out of the spotlight panel on perspectives on argument over fiscal policy, organized by Robin Rowland, exemplifies the range of approaches one can take to argument and exposes what each approach can offer critics of argument.

Ultimately, all of the essays in this volume speak to a central question, either explicitly or implicitly: What is the role of the argument critic? Is it to explain arguments as they happen or model arguments as they should happen? In what cases should the critic intervene? When the critic chooses to intervene, how best can it be done and what does it mean?

And, these essays accomplish all this within rigorous word limits: 3700 words for the spotlight essays and 3200 words for the remainder of the essays. The result is essays that are focused, concise, and tightly argued scholarship that speak to a range of intellectual communities, including the young scholars of argument who populate our classes. The vivacity and focus of the arguments contained in these essays, ultimately, is what gives credence to a faith in argument. The scholars published here show what argument can do, should do, and can be, all the while leaving open the possibility that the conclusions they draw, themselves, may be disturbed in the face of future argument.

CHALLENGING COMMUNITIES

A perspective about, from, and by argumentation

Carol Winkler

GEORGIA STATE UNIVERSITY, USA

Given the high regard I have for the argumentation scholars here today, for the people from the University of Utah whose hard work and commitment sustains this unique conference, for the daunting list of past keynote speakers, and for this year's incomparable conference director, I am truly honored, if not a bit overwhelmed, to address you today. In line with the intriguing conference theme, I'll start by breaking from Alta convention in two ways. First, I want to thank Georgia State University doctoral students – Stephen Heidt, Houda Abadi, Andrew Barnes, and Sara Baugh – for their hard work and ideas in helping me prepare for this address. If I disturb you today, be assured it was not of their doing. Having the opportunity to work with them, knowing they will emerge as insightful colleagues, and hoping that they will remain life-long friends is important to me. Second, I need to issue a warning. Viewer discretion is advised. However else you may remember my speech in the future, I believe it may go down as the first R rated Alta keynote address.[1] So, let's get started.

Two colleagues and I recently examined whether middle school participation in urban debate leagues improved school engagement. Using student data from the year before partici-pants entered the debate program, we created a group of non-debaters matched for demo-graphic, socio-economic, academic achievement, and academic risk factors. The debaters scored between .47 and .63 standard deviations higher than the non-debate students on stan-dardized test scores in science, reading, social studies, math, and language arts. On average, after only one year in the league, the debaters posted one-third fewer annual school absences and 1.4 fewer annual disciplinary incidents than their non-debate peers. All of the study's results were statistically significant.

Today, my point in recounting these findings is not to suggest that, given growing demands for educational accountability, our field has a pedagogical approach suited to aid academic progress across academic subject areas (although I do wholeheartedly applaud the National Association of Urban Debate League's goal of doing so). Instead, my point is that educators, both in and outside our field, would never have understood the far-reaching value of debate pedagogy had scholars not examined its impact within urban communities. We might never have asked whether debate participation improved student conduct, because we assumed the White, suburban students, who served as the subjects of our early studies, rarely, if ever, expe-rienced suspensions from school. Likewise, debate's impact on standardized test scores might have gone overlooked, given the assumption that high school debaters were destined for success in their college application processes. Finally, we might have missed debate's positive impact on middle school children altogether had we not wanted to know whether debate could reach African-American and Hispanic children who, in far too many cases, fall behind academically or drop out of school altogether in the 9th grade (Neild, 2009; Stillwell & Sable, 2013).

Recent world events highlight the need for us to explore how argumentation functions in non-dominant publics. The Obama 2012 presidential campaign's micro-targeting of young voters, African-Americans, Latinos, and single women helped drive the president's successful election-day turnout, despite a multi-year sluggish economy, a controversial health care law, and a $1 billion Republican campaign counter effort. Further, disempowered citizens in the Middle East, moved in part by the online circulation of arguments, sparked the dramatic leadership and constitutional changes we now know as the Arab Spring. The list of examples could go on and on, but the central insight would remain the same: Argumentation studies needs to focus more on analyzing the strategies of nondominant, networked publics to expand contemporary understandings of argument and to heighten our relevance across academe and beyond.

From my own perspective, Cate Palczewski's theme, "disturbing argument," provides a space, if not an open invitation, to embark on such a project. One standard definition of "disturb" is "to break up or destroy the tranquility or settled state of" (*The Free Online Dictionary*, n.d.). Applied to theoretical studies of our field, the theme challenges us to rethink our preconceived notions of argument spheres, fields, rules, and contexts, to name but a few. Applied to particular case studies, it dares us to move outside our field's dominant focus on the arguments of "the public" and examine the strategies of those who seek to intrude, interrupt, or interfere with such logics in an effort to build and maintain their own. While the recent strong collection of essays on Buddhist argument in *Argumentation* serves as an exemplar of the value of such efforts, much, much more is needed. Whether one is interested in creating, sustaining, or disrupting established orders, more attention to how publics define and challenge argumentative norms provides a lens for revitalizing our field's earlier insights, for revising our theories, and for re-imagining new approaches for the study of argument.

I believe a good starting point would be Greene's (2002) insightful critique of Warner's (2002) discussion of publics and counterpublics. If we consider the field of argumentation studies to work "like a post office assembling and circulating subjects capable of recognizing themselves as a subject of, by, and for a public" (Greene, 2002, p. 441), our field's central importance in the rapidly changing age of new and social media becomes difficult to ignore. In short, circulating constellations of argumentative practices work to constitute groups of strangers who form, and subsequently function as, sub-national or transnational collectives. In a world where each month, more than a billion unique viewers access *YouTube* (YouTube, 2012) and more than a billion people use *Facebook* (Associated Press, 2013), aggressive pursuit of such a scholarly agenda is sorely needed. While current work in computer science is rapidly refining methods for how to track social networks and retrieve their discourse sharing practices, argumentation studies provides a critical foundation for understanding why such networks both form and retain their currency.

To illustrate the value of such a focus for argumentation studies, today I will analyze the videos that were found in the possession of individuals prosecuted for terrorism-related offenses in U.S. courts between September 11, 2001, and December 31, 2011. I have multiple reasons for focusing on those particular videos. First, those who engage in jihad now form an active and growing online global network that seemed directly on point to our conference theme. A recent study by University of Arizona researchers revealed the network's vitality. It reported on the communication content of 29 related online forums that produced more than 14 million messages written by more than 350,000 individuals (Chen et al., 2011). Second, the videos represent the shared discourse of those motivated to act. Of the 56 cases prosecuted during the 2001 to 2011 time period, a full half referenced videos that were in the defendant's possession at the time of arrest. Finally, the videos offer a rich source of both the discursive and the nondiscursive arguments pitched to the target audience. By examining the argumentative practices embedded in the discourse of those who wage jihad, I hope to demonstrate how studies of networked publics can provide a critical lens for re-visioning three important theories that undergird our field.

Re-visioning Constitutive Rhetoric and Argument

In his foundational article crediting insights from McGee and Althusser, Charland (1987) introduced the concept of "constitutive rhetoric." His expressed goal for writing the article was to expand scholars' conventional understandings of ideographs and arguments from simple vehicles of persuasion into ways of seeing them account for "the very nature of the subjects that rhetoric both addresses and leads them to be" (p. 148). He identified three ideological effects of constitutive rhetoric – constituting a collective subject, positing transhistorical subjects, and the illusion of freedom – that function in tandem to transform interpellated subjects into active agents. The process of that transformation, Charland insisted, occurs either through constitutive narratives or aesthetic frameworks.

Adopted by many as a useful theoretical construct for their work, constitutive rhetoric gained adherents quickly in studies of public argument. Greene (1998) identified four values of the approach: It provides a limitless range of objects to study; it refocuses studies of democracy onto argumentative practices; it reinterprets disagreement into a way of better understanding regulation, invention, and circulation; and it revises judgment into an aesthetic-ethical process whereby arguments speak for and about places, persons, and events. Farrell (2008) added that it helps critics better understand how history functions within new collectivities, how audiences co-participate in the development of their historical identities, and how ongoing historical episodes will function in the future within the plots of discourse. Lee (2006) offered that it explains the coherence of seemingly disparate and disjointed communities over sustained periods of time, while Stuckey and Hoffman (2006) showed how, by tracking the way U.S. leaders constitute polities, scholars better understand the ways they shape national policy debates.

Despite the growing, accepted value of the perspective, constitutive rhetoric has nevertheless spawned some debate and refinement. Haskins (2005) and Chase (2009) reminded scholars that the roots of constitutive rhetoric should be traced back to Isocrates. Others, like Sweet and McCue-Enser (2010), added that, in certain contexts, interpellated subjects in public discourse are never fully constituted; instead, they rhetorically remain in the process of constitution. Finally, Leff and Utley (2004) warned against drawing sharp dichotomies between the constitutive and instrumental functions of rhetoric based on their demonstration of how Martin Luther King simultaneously and fluidly performed both functions in his "Letter from Birmingham Jail."

Viewed from the perspective of the videos in the possession of those who practice jihad, constitutive rhetoric again emerges as a valuable approach. I would argue that the videos qualify as some of the early defining discourse of the networked group's presence online. Given an information environment where cameras and editing equipment are now cheap and the Internet is easily accessible, such groups are no longer dependent on broadcast news media to filter their messages to the broader public (Dauber, 2009). Nevertheless, one of Charland's core assumptions, namely that constitutive narratives and aesthetic approaches are the only available methods of transforming interpellated subjects to action, needs reexamination.

To explain why, I need to briefly return to Perelman and Olbrechts-Tyteca's (1997) concept of *loci communes*. Borrowing from Aristotle's (1997) concept of *topoi*, but wanting to emphasize an exclusive focus on general, rather than specific, lines of argument, they define *loci communes* as "storehouses for argument" (p. 83) that function as inventional and grouping resources for attempts to establish and defend value hierarchies. Examples of *loci communes*, such as quantity, quality, order, the existent, the essence, and the person, help reveal a public's cherished values, as well as the intensity with which group members adhere to them.

The videos I will examine today rely heavily upon one particular instance of the locus of quality – the irreparable – to constitute widely dispersed individuals around the globe as a public. Theorized more than three decades ago, Cox (1982) described the *locus* of the irreparable as "a *forewarning*, an opportunity to act in appropriate ways before it is too late" (p. 232). He explained that, "its use calls attention to the *unique* and *precarious* nature of some object or state of affairs, and stresses the *timeliness* of our relationship to it" (p. 229). In the context of the videos of those who engage in jihad, the irreparable sets the framework for the three ideological effects Charland identified as the defining characteristics of constitutive rhetoric.

Charland's first ideological effect, *constituting a collective subject*, occurs when the videos use the irreparable to portray the *ummah*, or put another way, the Muslim nation. Those worshipping within the Islamic faith are *unique* because, as the audio track of *The Expedition of Sheikh Umar Hadeed* (2007) surmised, "there is none worthy of being worshipped except Allah." Bin Laden echoed the exceptional position of Muslims in *State of the Ummah, Part I* (2007) when he maintained, "There is no Power or Might except with Allah, the Most High, the Supreme." The videos argued for the *precarious* position held by members of the faith by recounting historical and ongoing foreign assaults against Muslims in Bosnia, Afghanistan, Tajikistan, Chechnya, Kashmir, Palestine, Iraq, Lebanon, the Philippines, Somalia, and Indonesia. As the *Martyrs of Bosnia* (2000) video insisted, "the Muslims are being slaughtered . . . The Muslims are being expelled from their homes . . . Each day more than a thousand Muslims are killed." Bin Laden sounded the *timely need for urgent action* when he argued:

> It is incumbent on the Muslims, especially those in leadership positions from among the faithful soldiers, honest businessmen, and heads of the tribes to migrate for the cause of Allah, and find a place where they can raise the banner of Jihad, and revitalize the Ummah to safeguard their religion and life; otherwise, they will lose everything.
>
> *(State of the Ummah Part 1, 2007)*

Charland's second ideological effect, *positing a transhistorical subject*, occurs when the irreparable characterizes the individuals who wage jihad in the videos. The producers present those who choose to train and die for the cause as *uniquely* pious. *The Martyrs of Bosnia* (2000) explained, "the Martyr is the one who has borne the greatest testimony for Allah and with it he reaches the pinnacle of Islam." Positioning the uniqueness into a transhistorical context, a compatriot speaking about the martyr Usama al Hamawi in *Winds of Paradise, Part I* (2007) noted, "I look at him and it is as if a Muslim knight or Salahuddin has come back to us once again." The *precarious* position of those who seek martyrdom stems from the possibility they might not be chosen. As *Martyrs of Bosnia* argued, "the rank of martyrdom is very high and not everyone can reach it, except those whom Allah chooses and those whom Allah wishes to bestow this Honour [sic] upon." The need for *timely action* results from the desire to have time to achieve eternal salvation. As martyr after martyr appears onscreen, the narrator of *The*

Martyrs of Bosnia (2000) reiterated the future that awaits those who wage jihad: "I am in the Gardens of Eternity, I did not die. I have become a new creation in the Gardens. So I am here, still alive, by my Lord and living happily in the care of God."

The irreparable produces Charland's third ideological effect, *the illusion of freedom*, through its relationship with the viewer position. The viewers' *uniqueness* stems from the small percentage of the total Muslim population who view the circulating videos. Out of 1.6 billion Muslims worldwide (Desilver, 2013), only a few thousand view any one of the videos, and that figure includes those who fall outside of the target audience. Viewers hold *precarious* positions because their lives on Earth could end before they have properly prepared themselves for the afterworld. The *Expedition of Sheikh Umar Hadeed* (2007) insisted that, "you are sinning if you do not join jihad." Bin Laden in *State of the Ummah Part I* (2007) foretold the consequences: "If you march not forth, [Allah] will punish you with a painful torment." The *timely need* for the individual to take immediate action stems from the possibility of death at any moment. The narrator of the *Hoor Al Ayn Winds of Paradise Nasheed* (2007) asked, "Doesn't my death come only once in my life. So why not make its ending my martyrdom?"

Despite the demonstrated relationship between argument and the ideological effects shown above, Charland still ultimately discarded argument as the basis for becoming a constituted member of the public. Instead, he insisted the essence of the person's being leads him or her to be oriented toward action. But, in the videos found in the possession of those prosecuted for terrorism, the characteristics of the fighters' beings derive from the strategic considerations of the irreparable. Returning to Cox (1982) for a moment, he outlined four strategic implications of the irreparable for deliberation and decision making: "(1) an expansion of the time frame in which choices are considered, (2) heightened information-seeking, (3) invocation of a minimum condition rule, and ironically (4) the warranting of extraordinary measures" (p. 234).

Cox's four strategic implications of the irreparable map directly onto how the videos present the character of those who die for the cause of Islam. The videos presented a series of personal narratives that adopt a common form: They introduced where a martyr has come from, where he migrated to in order to fight (as all martyrs in the video sample were male), a description of the individual's character, and a witnessing of how the martyr died. In the portion of the videos focusing on the character of the individual martyrs, a common litany of character traits replayed, with rare to no mention of how one martyr differs from another. Instead, the videos repeatedly praised the martyrs for their patience, a character trait consistent with Cox's strategic implication of demonstrating a willingness to expand the time frame before action. The videos admired the martyr's devotion to the study of Qur'an, echoing the heightened information seeking implicated by the irreparable. Martyrs are remembered as those who never argue, suggesting such individuals consider alternatives as irremediable under the minimum condition rule. Finally, the videos' repetition of the martyr's state of sublime happiness brought on by the decision to give their Earthly lives in defense of Allah suggested an acceptance of the warrant for extraordinary action.

In sum, Charland's decision to exclude argument as one of the ways constitutive rhetoric transforms interpellated subjects to action seems premature. The irreparable defines the essence of the subject by implication and does the ideological work of constituting the subject as a member of a public, defining the transhistorical subject that will model beliefs and behaviors, and offering the subject the illusion of freedom. Rather than relegate argument to the role of good reasons supportive of constitutive narratives that function to interpellate subjects into active agents, scholars of argument should recognize that the narratives, instead, may be functioning to warrant constitutive lines of argument.

Before I leave the topic of the constitutive rhetoric, I want to revisit and reiterate Leff and Utley's (2004) conclusion that constitutive and instrumental functions of discourse can operate simultaneously. Returning briefly to the individual character traits of martyrs featured in the videos (i.e., patience, a focus on the Qur'an, a willingness not to argue, and acceptance of extraordinary actions), I would also maintain that the traits serve a dual instrumental function of disciplining the conduct of group members. Many of the videos describe numerous rewards awaiting those who give their Earthly lives in jihad. Such promises include: having their sins forgiven, escaping the torment of the grave, living throughout eternity as neighbors of prophets and other martyrs, offering redemption to members of their families, having access to beautiful virgins, and being crowned with dignity (e.g., *Hoor Al Ayn Winds of Paradise Nasheed*, 2007; *Winds of Paradise I*, 2007). As interpellated subjects might be motivated to act quickly in an effort to achieve such outcomes, the character traits simultaneously prompt viewers to remain patient, to embrace a commitment to their religious studies, to follow the directives of their leaders, and not to act precipitously in ways that might prove consequential to the group.

Re-visioning Controversy and Argument

While the video's discursive arguments certainly help constitute and sustain the public, the nondiscursive should not be overlooked. Palczewski (2001) made a compelling case for why when she observed, "the nondiscursive can be an argument(1), can be part of an argument(1), can function as a response to a discursive argument, and can participate in an argument (2)" (p. 5). Further, recognition that the video's target audience – the global Muslim population – speaks many languages and has varying levels of literacy heightens the need to understand the role of the nondiscursive.

Given the growing body of work analyzing why particular images circulate and re-circulate within collectives, I thought I should start by accessing the previous insights to explain the role of nondiscursive argument within the videos. I thought I might find iconic images similar to those Hariman and Lucaites (2007) showed could perform the deliberative function of helping citizens to "negotiate the trade-off between individual autonomy and collective governance" (p. 14). Or perhaps, if I were really lucky from a purely self-interested point of view, I would find one more example of a visual ideograph that, through its use as a representative form, "rhetorically identifies and delineates the ideals of the body politic" (Edwards & Winkler, 1997, p. 295). If not, I hoped Finnegan's (2005) image vernaculars would help me define the nature of the public, the uniqueness of its character, and the boundaries of its morality. At the very least, I assumed that videos about jihad would include instances of Zelizer's (2010) about-to-die trope, where images have resiliency due to their ability to evoke contingent meanings over time, to invite the audience to use their imaginations to fill in the events before and after the frozen moment in the picture, and to arouse a range of unpredictable emotional reactions.

As expected, the about-to-die trope does characterize three images that re-circulate in the videos. The "hooded man on the box" photograph snapped by U.S. military personnel at Abu Ghraib prison, the al-Durrah image filmed by France2 TV during an Israeli-Palestinian battle of the second intifada, and the burning World Trade Center towers all share the defining characteristics of the about-to-die trope. Within the context of the videos, however, the producers incorporate those three images into visual litanies of hundreds of other images demonstrating how civilian populations fare in the war on terror, and even within those litanies, the recurrence of the three images is infrequent.

While I was intrigued that the videos utilized the about-to-die trope to characterize Muslim civilian populations rather than fighters for jihad, I chose, alternatively, to analyze a representative visual form that circulated across the entire video sample. The videos routinely displayed what I will call "*the blissful martyr image*," a form that metonymically represents a smiling head of a martyr's corpse. The videos' blissful martyr images showed fallen fighters with various amounts of blood, grime, and other outward signs of battle engagement. But in every instance of the form's usage, the facial expression of the corpse visually evoked the fighter's serenity, if not apparent pleasure, with the afterlife. As a representative form, the blissful martyr image is not a single, iconic shot of an individual fighter; instead, it includes shots of numerous martyrs that share the notable visual elements just described. As a habitually recurrent form, the blissful martyr image appears more central to understanding the ideological work of the videos within the online community.

As I considered why the blissful martyr image circulated so frequently, none of the earlier explanations that visual argument scholars had offered seemed appropriate. Beyond the obvious question about whether any of the findings from studies of images in the U.S. context should be generalized, the blissful martyr image certainly could not employ the about-to-die trope, as its subject had already passed on to the afterworld. Further, the shared characteristic of visual icons and ideographs, namely that each relies on the image having a flexible, adaptive meaning, also seemed ill suited. As I will discuss more in a moment, the blissful martyr image makes a specific, non-flexible argument about life throughout eternity for those who die in defense of Allah. Image vernaculars offered the most help, as the blissful martyr image has enthymematic associations related to publics, character, and morality, but even that explanation seemed incomplete.

What became a more fitting explanation for why the blissful martyr image circulates relates back to Olson and Goodnight's concept of social controversy. From my memory of his keynote address, Goodnight (1991) ignited this group by introducing *controversy* as a phenomenon with an astonishing range of application and a complete lack of theoretical reflection. Olson and Goodnight (1994) subsequently defined social controversy as "an extended rhetorical engagement that critiques, resituates, and develops communication practices bridging the public and personal spheres" (p. 249). They insisted that both discursive and nondiscursive arguments have important roles to play within social controversies, while maintaining that the two function in unique ways. In their words, "Whereas the discursive arguments work to block enthymematic associations by contesting the means of establishing 'accepted' opinion, the nondiscursive arguments work – in the new, 'free' space of reassociation – to redefine and realign the boundaries of private and public space" (Olson & Goodnight, 1994, p. 252).

While I have little doubt that Olson and Goodnight are correct in their conception of how most images function *within* social controversies, I believe we should also recognize that certain image forms also function as visual markers *of* social controversies. To begin to qualify as a marker of social controversy according to Olson and Goodnight's conception, the blissful martyr image would need to encapsulate an extended social engagement. The image form was present in virtually all of the 24 video segments in my decade-long sample and appeared 70 times alone during a single 6-minute portion of one of the videos. Beyond the resiliency it garners from its frequency of circulation, I would argue the blissful martyr image has ongoing currency due to its representative form. The representative form functions not as a frozen iconic moment, but as vehicle capable of encompassing an endless supply of images memorializing those killed in jihad around the globe. The time and place of the battle may change, but the blissful martyr image works as an extended social engagement for attendant viewers.

To be eligible as a marker of social controversy, the blissful martyr image would also have to bridge the personal and public spheres. To explain how the image meets this criterion, consider how the body of the Prophet Muhammad was handled after his death and recognize that those practices still guide members of the Islamic faith today. In brief, Muslims move quickly to wash and prepare the bodies of their dead for burial outside of public view. Those serving as corpse washers are respected, trustworthy individuals who complete the process discretely with the understanding that they would never reveal anything they discover, such as rapid decomposition, which might signal harm to another Muslim as they move into the afterworld. After the purification of the body is complete, corpses are then shrouded and the head customarily covered (Halevi, 2007). Preparation of Muslim bodies for burial, then, works as a private process held outside of public view.

By sharp contrast, the corpses of the blissful martyrs are not handled with discretion in private, whether in the videos or the broader societal context. Martyrs' heads are uncovered, their bodies are unwashed, and they are on display for indiscriminate viewing. The blissful martyr image freezes the moment where the individual moves from the personal sphere of the rank-and-file's burial practices into the public sphere of the martyr's burial, allowing it to replay again and again at the viewer's discretion.

To meet the definitional requirements of social controversy, the blissful martyr image must also critique, develop, and resituate communicative norms. Initially, the recurrent form elevates eyewitness testimony over authoritative testimony as the appropriate evidentiary standard for resolving competing views of Islamic clerics as to the current moral obligation of Muslims to engage in jihad. The image does so reflexively through what Atkinson (2012) described as a simultaneous "record of a past event and as present-tense performance of that event" (p. 675). The blissful martyr image invites viewers to infer from what they see that those who move onto the afterworld in the practice of jihad follow the path of the Prophet Muhammad and ascend to the highest levels of heaven. The peaceful smile on the blissful martyr's face is simply inconsistent with the immediate torments that await those who commit suicide or even the more common levels of anxiety associated with the process of afterlife questioning by the archangel. Rather than suggest that those who die in jihad suffer punishments of the tomb or find final placement in either the lower levels of heaven or into the dreaded fire (Rustomji, 2009), the blissful martyr image invites viewers to infer that Allah will forgive their sins and welcome them in the afterworld if they become martyrs for the cause.

A second way that the blissful martyr image marks the moment of revised argumentative practice involves identifying who has the authority to make arguments. For the most part, the only individuals in the videos who speak are the narrators, the groups' spiritual leaders, and those martyred. The exception occurs when no image is available to demonstrate that the martyr has been killed. Sometimes accompanied by a textual apology crawling across the screen for not having an image to show, the videos include comments by unidentifiable compatriots who bear witness to the martyr's character, how he fought in the defense of Allah, and how he moved on into the afterworld. The videos position martyrs to speak through the use of pre-recorded interviews and interactions videotaped during their training for jihad. The videos include the martyr's name to identify him as an authority for the public, a privilege denied to members of the group still planning to fight in the future.

To serve as a visual marker of controversy, the blissful martyr image would finally have to assume both roles Olson and Goodnight assign to discursive and nondiscursive arguments. To do otherwise would make the representative form simply a partial marker. By describing how the transition to the afterworld shifts from a private to a public event, I have already

11

demonstrated how the blissful martyr image performs the nondiscursive role of re-associating the boundaries between the personal and public spheres. The representative form, however, also performs the function of discursive argument by blocking enthymematic associations that contest the means of establishing accepted opinion. With only a small minority of the global Muslim population responding to the current call for jihad, the moral legitimacy of the fight is central to the controversy. Accepted opinion by many, then, is that the fighters' choice to kill themselves is an act of suicide, rather than a legitimate act of a warrior fighting in defense of Allah. Members of the Islamic faith believe that those who commit suicide suffer immediate punishments of the tomb (Smith & Haddod, 1981) and are denied Allah's mercy (Halevi, 2007). In such a context, the serenity captured in the blissful martyr image works to block the enthymematic association that the fight is illegitimate, the fighter has committed suicide, and the fighter's life in the afterworld will be one of torment.

By this quick examination of how image recirculation operates in the discourse of those who practice jihad, I hope to have elevated the concept of visual controversy to the status of icons, visual ideographs, image vernaculars, and specific tropes as cultural markers of networked publics. By utilizing Olson and Goodnight's definitional components of social controversy as a rubric for identifying visual controversy, we can better understand what nondiscursive arguments circulate within networked publics, as well as how and why they do so. By understanding what they portend for communicative norms, scholars should be able to refine argumentative practices in ways that could facilitate more productive interactions with networked audiences.

Re-visioning Narrative and Argument

In the mid–1980s, Fisher (1984) reconsidered the role of argument in public discourse by noting, "human communication should be viewed as historical as well as situational, as stories competing with other stories constituted by good reasons, as being rational when they satisfy the demands of narrative probability and narrative fidelity, and as inevitably moral inducements" (p. 2). In response to Gronbeck's (1984) point that stories did not constitute argumentative frames, Fisher (1989) clarified that narration should be understood as a multi-faceted concept: "narration(1) – individuated forms such as depiction, anecdote, and characterization; narration(2) – generic forms such as argumentation and narration; and narration(3) – a conceptual framework, like dramatism, for understanding human decision, discourse, and action" (p. 56).

A number of scholars have since theorized a typology of narratives that attempts to address the challenge of understanding how multiple publics and individuals interface with narration. Examples include polysemic narratives where ambiguity allows different listeners to have multiple interpretations of their meaning (Fiske, 1986), polyvalent narratives where those who hear the narration understand it in similar ways but evaluate it differently (Condit, 1989), multivalent narratives where contradictory value structures within the narrations compel listeners to reconstruct their meaning and potentially accept new views (Stroud, 2004), and meta-narratives where a single over-arching perspective frames how listeners will understand and respond to competing societal narratives (Lyotard, 1979).

Under theorized, from my point of view, is how argumentation functions to help produce the acceptance of one narrative over another in a multi-public sphere. Scholars of narrative have long understood that narratives "mediate between alternative notions of what the moral order should consider" (White, 1981, p. 794) and they function in an environment where the meaning of one narrative emerges from its relationship to others (Gibson, 1996). Ormison and Sassower (1989) rightly observed that, in many contexts:

narratives intend to replace one another — their fiction is designed to subvert the power of others. Moreover, this subversion is a move towards dominating the form and style of discourse, the field of discourse, as well as legitimating itself and the field it fabricates.

(p. 109)

Yet, besides frequent demonstrations of how Fisher's useful, general concepts of narrative probability and fidelity function within specific contexts, and Bex and Veheij's (2012) recent exploration of how dialectic employed through critical questions can help evaluate argumentation schemes, story schemes, and hybrid schemes in court cases, argument scholars still lack a well theorized perspective of how argumentation helps explain why publics accept one narrative over another.

To me, a reasonable starting point is to identify how other competing narratives strive to define networked publics. The narrative context can be complicated, given that more than one competing public may exist and each one of those may posit more than one counter-narrative. In the context of those who engage in jihad, for example, both the west and the global Muslim public (at a minimum) operate in significant ways within the discourse environment; further, western leaders alone incorporate both crime and war narratives into their public discourse about terrorism (Winkler, 2006). My point today will be to focus on how the videos use argumentation practices to navigate through such a swirling narrative context and to draw implications from those strategies for the broader topic of narrative and argument.

To begin, the video producers merged the west's crime and war narratives about terrorism, treating them as an indivisible whole within their own narrative. The videos presented western military soldiers and their allies in the region as committing crimes against humanity and crimes against God. The focus of the crimes against the humanity involved the treatment of Muslim civilians. The focus of crimes against Allah featured encroachments on Muslim lands and culture. By including both types of crimes, the videos directly responded to the two historical instantiations of the crime narrative that former U.S. presidents have utilized in their public talk about terrorism (Winkler, 2006).

The producers then applied what Perelman and Olbrechts-Tyteca's (1969) identified as philosophical pairs to dissociate themselves from the criminal behavior of the western military forces and its allies. Their chief strategy of dissociation was use of the appearance/reality pair Perelman and Olbrechts-Tyteca draw from Plato. In short, the videos presented the criminal behavior of foreign militaries and their allies as real. The *State of the Ummah Part I* exemplified the approach when it argued, "For America claims that is the guardian of human rights and democracy and the protector of human freedom. All of this while it imposes on the Muslim regimes absolute tyranny and total corruption and ultimate subjugation of its people." Repetitive use of photographic evidence documented foreign military offenses against Muslim citizens, foreign presence on sacred Muslim lands, and violations of Muslim culture.

The videos also presented as real the willingness of Muslim leaders, past and present, to take bribes and to participate in other forms of corruption involving the west. Images, showing Muslim leaders from Egypt, Saudi Arabia, Jordan, Afghanistan, and Pakistan celebrating, dancing, and laughing with western military and political leaders, functioned to document the authenticity of the alliances. Shots of formal state dinners attended by Muslim leaders and their western allies focus viewer attention on alcoholic beverages to underscore the threat such alliances pose to the long-standing values of the Muslim culture.

The videos used the appearance half of the dyad to depict all criminal behavior alleged against those who participate in jihad. While some of the video images placed the fighters for

Allah in prisons at Abu Ghraib and Guantanamo Bay, the textual and audio context for those images insisted that Allah, not the western courts, will serve as final judge. In a repeated line of assurance that occurs with slight variations in many of the videos, the *Martyrs of Bosnia* (2000) offered the first of the seven favors that Allah promises martyrs, namely "He is forgiven his sins with the first spurt of his blood." From the point of view of the videos, those who fight in the cause of Allah commit no crimes and any appearance to the contrary is deceiving.

Another dyadic pair that recurs in the videos is that of duration/eternity, which Perelman and Olbrechts-Tyteca drew from Spinoza. For the west and their allies, rewards have a short duration, limited to their time of life on Earth with no eternal promise of salvation. For pious Muslims who fight in the cause of Allah, the situation reverses. The short-term sacrifices on Earth, be they torture, imprisonment, denial of worldly goods, or migration from home, will all be replaced with an eternal life of bliss in the highest levels of heaven. As *The Martyrs of Bosnia* (2000) explained:

> But death, i.e., to die and to be killed can occur in one of two types: either through striving in the Path of Allah or not. In one of these types there is forgiveness and mercy from Allah, and also there is something better than all the things that people amass for in this world.

To reinforce the point through visual argument, martyrs' heads surrounded by each martyr's name float against backdrops of clouds or other scenes that suggest heavenly ascendance.

Through visual argument the videos strove to make the merger of the crime and war narratives, as well as the two related dyadic pairings, understandable to the widest possible audience. In *Expedition of Sheikh Umar Hadeed* (2007), for example, the camera panned through various empty cells of a western jail, coming to a final resting point in one corner cell. Only the (presumably male) viewer, through his subject position as a not yet actualized member of the forces of jihad, emerges as an occupant of a cell seated at a table with only a Qur'an and lamp on its surface. The camera shot moves up the cell wall to a poster of a foreign military tank with its main gun pointing straight at a Muslim civilian and, simultaneously through the camera's positioning, at the viewer of the video. The video superimposes multiple images of foreign military forces harming Muslim citizens, rotated one after the other in the center of the poster. Throughout the sequence of the superimposed images, the tank remains partially visible, rendering it the frame for all of the depicted atrocities. The layered images served as visual evidence of the crime/war narrative merger. Sympathetic Muslim viewers, by contrast, stand falsely accused but, through their faith, will ultimately have rewards from Allah.

Taken together, the strategies of dissociation grounded in the video's philosophical pairings unsurprisingly reinforce the oppositional stance of those who engage in jihad vs. the west and its allies. More interesting is how the video producers reconciled their character portrayals of the west and its allies within the narrative context of the broader Muslim community. If the video producers characterized members of the ummah yet to join the forces of jihad as criminals bound for eternal damnation (in a manner similar to how they depict Muslim leaders who ally with the west), the group's potential recruits might take offense and withhold their participation.

Instead, the video producers changed the narrative content implicated by their strategies of dissociation, while still relying on the same dyadic pairs. They used the appearance/reality pair to divide pious Muslims from those who only appear to be so. The *Hoor Al Ayn Winds of Paradise Nasheed* (2007) illustrated the strategy:

O Brother don't complain and cry about the humiliation. Until when will you keep crying and complaining? Will a soul be pleased that my ears flow like the mourners who weep? Do you think that crying will bring back honor? Glory has become mere poems and wishes.

The producers used the duration/eternity pair to divide those who will demonstrate a willingness to forego worldly goods and pleasures in pursuit of long-term salvation from those who will not. The *Martyrs of Bosnia* (2000) maintained that, "The primary characteristic that Allah grants a person such that he is qualified for the rank of martyrdom is that they attach a higher priority to matters of the Hereafter than to the affairs of the World."

By utilizing the same dyadic pairs to evaluate all characters within the videos' narratives while applying them in differential ways based on the character's identity, the producers reinforced their preferred moral choice within a complex narrative environment. The repetition of the two dyadic pairs provided the internal consistency necessary to establish narrative probability. Yet, differential application of the two dyads contributed to the narrative fidelity by avoiding tensions that could arise between those the video producers want to cooperate with and those they want to oppose.

Parting Thoughts

In sum, argument has a primary role in constituting publics and sustaining them over time. As networked publics will continue to grow and the need to understand their communicative practices becomes more acute, argumentation scholars should prioritize the examination of how arguments work within such contexts. While endeavors to do so may interrogate our existing theories, disrupt our common assumptions, and expand our methodological approaches, I have no doubt that our community is certainly up to the challenge.

Note

1. To review the images described in this address, see *The Expedition of Sheikh Umar Hadeed*. (http://www.youtube.com/watch?v=yOi9hLBizc0), *Winds of Paradise, part I* (http://www.liveleak.com / view?i=e35_ 1189033423), *State of the Ummah, part I* (www.youtube.com/watch?v=bfuiAj9Mdos), *Hoor al Ayn Winds of Paradise Nasheed* (http://www.youtube.com/results?search _query=Hoor+al+ ayn+winds+of+paradice), and *The Martyrs of Bosnia* (http://www.youtube.com/watch?v= mUW4obPxvTo). Please note that at any time these videos may be removed from the liveleak.com or the youtube.com websites because of their content.

References

Al-Qaidah Network in the Land of the Two Rivers. (2007). *The expedition of Sheikh Umar Hadeed.* Retrieved from http://www.youtube.com/watch?v=yOi9hLBizc0

Aristotle. (1997). *Topics books I and VII: With excerpts from related texts.* (R. Smith, Trans.). New York, NY: Oxford University Press. (Original work published 350 B.C.E.)

As-Sahab. (2007). *Hoor al ayn winds of paradise nasheed* [Video file]. Retrieved from http://www.youtube. com/results?search_query=Hoor+al+ayn+winds+of+paradice

As-Sahab. (2007). *State of the ummah, part I* [Video file]. Retrieved from www.youtube.com/ watch?v=bfuiAj9Mdos

As -Sahab. (2007). *Winds of paradise, part I* [Video file]. Retrieved from http://www.liveleak.com/ view?i=e35_ 1189033423

Associated Press. (2013). Number of active Facebook viewers over the years. *Yahoo News.* Retrieved from http://news.yahoo.com/number-active-users-facebook-over-230449748.html

Atkinson, N. (2012). Celluloid circulation: The dual temporality of nonfiction films and its publics. *Rhetoric and Public Affairs*, *15*(4), 675–84.

Azzam Publications. (2000). *The martyrs of bosnia* [Video file]. Retrieved from http://www.youtube.com/ watch?v=mUW4obPxvTo

Bex, F., & Verheij, B. (2012). Solving a murder case by asking critical questions: An approach to fact-finding in terms of argumentation and story schemes. *Argumentation*, *26*(3), 325–353.

Charland, M. (1987). Constitutive rhetoric: The case of the *Peuple Quebecois*. *Quarterly Journal of Speech*, *73*(2), 133–150.

Chase, K. R. (2009). Constructing ethics through rhetoric: Isocrates and piety. *Quarterly Journal of Speech*, *95*(3), 239–262.

Chen, H., Denning, D., Roberts, N., Larson, C. A., Ximing, Y., & Huang, C. (2011). The Dark Web forum portal: From multi-lingual to video. *Proceedings on the 2011 IEEE International Conference on Intelligence and Security Informatics* (pp. 7–14). Beijing, CN: ISI.

Condit, C. M. (1989). The rhetorical limits of polysemy. *Critical Studies in Mass Communication*, *6*(2), 103–22.

Cox, J. R. (1982). The die is cast: Topical and ontological dimensions of the locus of the irreparable. *Quarterly Journal of Speech*, *68*(3), 227–239.

Dauber, C. (2009). *YouTube war: Fighting in a world of cameras in every cell phone and photoshop on every computer*. Carlisle, PA: Strategic Studies Institute.

Desilver, D. (2013). World's Muslim population more widespread than you might think. *Pew Center for Research Fact Tank*. Retrieved from http://www.pewresearch.org/fact-tank/2013/06/07/worlds-muslim-population-more-widespread-than-you-might-think/

Disturb. (n.d.) *Free Online Dictionary*. Retrieved from http://www.thefreedictionary.com/disturb

Edwards, J. L., & Winkler, C. K. (1997). Representative form and the visual ideograph: The Iwo Jima image in editorial cartoons. *Quarterly Journal of Speech*, *83*(3), 289–310.

Farrell, T. B. (2008). Rhetoric in history as theory and praxis: A blast from the past. *Philosophy and Rhetoric*, *41*(4), 323–336.

Finnegan, C. A. (2005). Recognizing Lincoln: Image vernaculars in nineteenth-century visual culture. *Rhetoric and Public Affairs*, *8*(1), 31–57.

Fisher, W. R. (1984). Narration as a human communication paradigm: The case of public moral argument. *Communication Monographs*, *51*(1), 1–22

Fisher, W. R. (1989). Clarifying the narrative paradigm. *Communication Monographs*, *56*(1), 55–58.

Fiske, J. (1986). Television: Polysemy and popularity. *Critical Studies in Mass Communication*, *3*(4), 391–408.

Gibson, A. (1996). *Towards a postmodern theory of narrative*, Edinburgh, GB: Edinburgh University Press.

Goodnight, G. T. (1991). Controversy. In D. Parsons (Ed.), *Argument in Controversy: Proceedings of the Seventh SCA/AFA Conference on Argumentation* (pp. 1–13). Annandale, VA: Speech Communication Association.

Greene, R. W. (1998). The aesthetic turn and the rhetorical perspective on argumentation. *Argumentation and Advocacy*, *35*(1), 19–30.

Greene, R. W. (2002). Rhetorical pedagogy as a postal system: Circulating subjects through Michael Warner's "Public and Counterpublics." *Quarterly Journal of Speech*, *88*(4), 433–444.

Gronbeck, B. E. (1984). Storytelling as a mode of moral argument: A response to Professor Fisher. In D. Zarefsky, M. O. Sillars, & J. Rhodes (Eds). *Argument in Transition: Proceedings of the Third Summer Conference on Argumentation* (pp. 463–469). Annandale VA: Speech Communication Association.

Halevi, L. (2007). *Muhammad's grave: Death rites and the making of Islamic society*. New York, NY: Columbia University Press.

Hariman, R., & Lucaites, J. L. (2007). *No caption needed: Iconic photographs, public culture, and liberal democracy*. Chicago, IL: University of Chicago Press.

Haskins, E. V. (2005). Philosophy, rhetoric, and cultural memory: Rereading Plato's Menexenus and Isocrates' Panegyricus. *Rhetoric Society Quarterly*, *35*(1), 25–45.

Lee, M. J. (2006). The populist chameleon: The people's party, Huey Long, George Wallace, and the populist argumentative frame. *Quarterly Journal of Speech*, *92*(4), 355–378.

Leff, M., & Utley, E. A. (2004). Instrumental and constitutive rhetoric in Martin Luther King Jr.'s "Letter from Birmingham Jail." *Rhetoric and Public Affairs*, *7*(1), 37–51.

Lyotard, J. (1984). *The postmodern condition: A report on knowledge*. (G. Bennington & B. Massumi, Trans.). Minneapolis: University of Minnesota Press. (Original work published 1979)

Neild, R. C. (2009). Falling off track during the transition to high school: What we know and what can be done. *The Future of Children, 19*(1), 53–76.

Olson, K. M., & Goodnight, G. T. (1994). Entanglements of consumption, cruelty, privacy and fashion: The social controversy of fur. *Quarterly Journal of Speech, 80*(3), 249–276.

Ormiston, G. L., & Sassower, R. *Narrative experiments: The discursive authority of science and technology.* Minneapolis: University of Minnesota Press.

Palczewski, C. H. (2001). Argument in an off-key. In G. T. Goodnight (Ed.), *Arguing Communication and Culture* (pp. 1–23). Washington, D. C.: National Communication Association.

Perelman, C., & Olbrechts-Tyteca, L. (1969). *The new rhetoric: A treatise on argumentation.* (J. Wilkinson & P. Weaver, Trans.). Notre Dame, IN: University of Notre Dame Press. (Original work published in 1958)

Rustomji, N. (2009). *The garden and the fire: Heaven and hell in Islamic culture.* New York, NY: Columbia University Press.

Smith, J. I., & Haddod, Y. Y. (1981). *The Islamic understanding of death and resurrection.* Albany: State University of New York Press.

Stillwell, R., & Sable, J. (2013). *Public school graduates and dropouts from the common core of data: School year 2009–10, 309.* Retrieved from http://nces.ed.gov/pubs2013/2013309/index.asp

Stroud, S. R. (2004). Narrative as argument in Indian philosophy: The Astavakra Gita as multivariate narrative. *Philosophy & Rhetoric, 37*(1), 42–71.

Stuckey, M. E., & Hoffman, K. S. (2006). National identity under William H. Taft and Richard M. Nixon. *Congress and the Presidency, 33*(2), 69–94.

Sweet, D., & McCue-Enser, M. (2010). Constituting "the people" as rhetorical interruption: Barack Obama and the unfinished hopes on an imperfect people. *Communication Studies, 61*(5), 602–622.

Warner, M. (2002). Publics and counterpublics (abbreviated version). *Quarterly Journal of Speech, 88*(4), 413–428.

White, H. (1981). The narrativization of real events. *Critical Inquiry, 7*(4), 793–798.

Winkler, C. (2006). *In the name of terrorism: Presidents on political violence in the post-World War II era.* Albany: SUNY Press.

YouTube (2012). Statistics. Retrieved from *www.youtube.com/t/press_statistics*

Zelizer, B. (2010). *About to die: How news images move the American public.* New York, NY: Oxford University Press.

INTRODUCTION

Perspectives on argument over fiscal policy

The spotlight panel, organized by Robin Rowland, continued the conversations across disciplinary approaches started at the 2011 Alta Conference. The essays here include work by leading researchers in the areas of pragma-dialectics, informal logic, social science, pragmatic approaches, and academic debate. They spoke about a common topic – recent economic debates over fiscal policy – to demonstrate what each approach uniquely offered to the study of argument. As a collection of essays, they offer readers a chance to compare and contrast what different approached to argument can offer.

1

ECONOMIC RATIONALITY, TWENTY-FIRST CENTURY STYLE

A critical examination of its realism, pragmatic value, and ethical consequences

Dennis S. Gouran

THE PENNSYLVANIA STATE UNIVERSITY, USA

In 2011, U.S. Congressional figures engaged in a protracted debate focusing on the debt ceiling, the disposition of which portended dire consequences in the minds of both those arguing the need to raise it and the opponents of doing so in the absence of corresponding spending cuts if their respective positions failed to prevail (Newton-Small, 2011; Rogers, 2011). The debate unfolded intermittently from early January to August 2 ("Timeline," 2011), which was the date on which Treasury officials anticipated that the extant debt ceiling on borrowing would be reached, with the United States thereafter having to default on loans from its creditors (Murse, 2011) and to face economic difficulties the country certainly did not need.

With the last-minute agreement of August 2, the worst fears of those taking part in the debate failed to materialize (Davidson, 2011) even though the subsequent Standard and Poor's (S&P) unprecedented downgrading of the U.S. credit rating from triple A to double A did send ripples of concern throughout an economy that at best was in a fragile state of recovery at the time (Murse, 2011). Not coincidentally, within days of the S&P action, approval of Congress matched its then-historic low of 13% (Jones, 2011).

While averting what could have been a much more serious crisis, the parties involved in the debate nevertheless did harm and in the process engaged in argument, much of which MarketWatch commentator Rex Nutting (2011) characterized as "silly," "ridiculous," and even "crazy." In a spirit of somewhat greater charity than Mr. Nutting displayed, I would posit that the parties' inability to do better stemmed in large part from a basic misconception, if not downright corruption, of the concept of economic rationality and collateral pursuit of a set of negotiation strategies and practices that severely limited the prospects for arriving at not only a mutually acceptable settlement, but a beneficial one as well. I have taken the elaboration of this view as my principal task. In so doing, I think it important to note that my purpose is to examine behavior of elected officials that seems to fly in the face of generally understood notions of economic rationality, not to offer a critique of the concept itself.

Economic Rationality

Economic rationality, often referred to as "classical economic theory," in its most pristine sense is an idealization of the process by which individuals choose among alternative modes of addressing problematic situations in ways that maximize positive outcomes related to the material well-being of those involved. Although characterized in various formulations, the process typically has the person or persons choosing carefully: defining the nature of the problematic situation, identifying all of the pertinent criteria for assessing choice options, weighting the criteria in terms of their perceived relative importance in specifying conditions in need of satisfaction, generating the possible options, assessing each option in terms of each criterion, and endorsing the one that apparently best satisfies the criteria (see, for instance, Bazerman & Moore, 2013, pp. 2–3). Others have appropriated such characterizations and applied them to non-economic situations (e.g., Gouran & Hirokawa, 1996), even though some would question the propriety of such extensions (Zafirovski, 2003).

Thanks to Herbert Simon (1955), as a description of how individuals choose, whether in the narrower or broader sense, economic rationality's adequacy, except for the most restrictive of choice situations, is subject to serious reservation if not outright repudiation (Beach & Connolly, 2005; Frame, 2013; Singal, 2013). Within limits, however, there is reason to believe than one can increase the likelihood of making positive consequential choices by behaving generally in line with the logic of classical theory, but within the framework of what Simon (1982) came to refer to as *bounded rationality*.

An assumption underlying the conception of economic rationality is that those confronting a problematic situation ostensibly requiring choice have the single motive of maximizing desired outcomes. Obviously, this is not always the case. People frequently find themselves in situations involving mixed motives – one stemming from a desire to optimize personally rewarding outcomes and another directing them to focus on the necessity of making concessions to others involved if there is to be a settlement, as with the debt-ceiling debate. However, this does not preclude acting in a manner consistent with the maximization of joint outcomes. In fact, to do so is to behave rationally in the classical sense, but the process in such a domain entails negotiation, not unilateral action. For this context, the perspective that Howard Raiffa (1982, 2001) has developed is both informative and better suited for examining rationality in the debate of interest.

The process for maximizing joint outcomes under conditions in which one finds oneself having to deal with other parties having different preferences is known as "decision analytic" (Bazerman & Moore, 2013, p. 176). It entails a number of characteristics that presumably are evident when those taking part in negotiations are behaving "rationally" in the more realistic sense of Simon's (1982) conception of bounded rationality. Within such a framework, a rational negotiator either does, or at least should, consider three factors: (1) the parties' alternatives to a negotiated agreement, (2) their respective interests, and (3) the relative importance of those interests (Raiffa, 2001).

The first consideration influences the determination of the parties' respective aspirations, or desired outcomes, and reservation prices, or the minimum acceptable outcomes. Levels of aspiration are typically explicit, whereas reservation prices are not and are, therefore, sometimes open to serious over- or underestimation. If one's best alternative to a negotiated agreement (BATNA) is favorable, one's level of aspiration is apt to be high and the reservation price fairly close to the level of aspiration. If the reservation price falls between that of the other party and that party's level of aspiration, a "positive zone of agreement" exists, and the number of possible mutually acceptable agreements is proportional to the width of the zone (Beach & Connolly,

2005, p. 121). When this condition does not exist, the zone of agreement is negative, and no settlement is possible unless at least one of the parties adjusts his or her reservation price.

The second and third considerations relate to how negotiators are apt to interact in their efforts to reach an agreement or settlement concerning the matters in dispute. Parties often enter negotiations by claiming initial value, that is, making known their professed levels of aspiration and offering justifications for why their preferences should have priority. Levels of aspiration, however, are not necessarily accurate reflections of interests, as when an employee seeking a raise in compensation would find greater personal leave time more to his or her liking because the actual interest is increased opportunities for leisurely pursuits. Negotiations are rarely about single issues and their relative importance likewise can affect how one pursues a settlement in a dispute. In the preceding illustration, the employee might want both a raise and more leisure time but, because the latter is of greater personal importance, would be willing to accept a smaller raise if accompanied by an appropriately compensatory reduction in workload.

When the parties to a dispute have done well in dealing with the three considerations noted, their prospects for achieving integrative settlements are much better than if they have not (Raiffa, 1982, 2001). They succeed at what Bazerman and Moore (2013) called "creating value" (p. 180), whereby mutual gain – also known as a "Pareto-superior agreement" (p. 189) – is the outcome. The reasons that such outcomes do not materialize more frequently are numerous and varied, with many being beyond the scope of this essay. In the remainder, I discuss several influences that appear to have been operative in the debt-ceiling debate of 2011, and how they contributed to the parties' inability to manifest behavior consistent with the principles of economic rationality, even though they may have viewed themselves as eminently rational. As Matthew Hancock and Nadhim Zahawi (2013) have noted, in a recent survey, 48 percent of respondents from a general population reported themselves as always acting rationally. One presumes that elected officials would see themselves as so acting in much greater proportions. The particular influences on which I have chosen to focus are cognitive ones that Bazerman and Moore (2013) discuss at some length: the fixed-pie mentality, framing, the escalation of commitment, and anchoring.

The Fixed-Pie Mentality

The view that disputes necessarily reduce to conflicting interests fosters a distributive approach to negotiation and decision making in mixed-motive situations. This approach, in which the parties view the activity as a zero-sum game, unfortunately, is fairly common (Beach & Connolly, 2005). In addition, it encourages both parties to devalue their adversaries' concessions (Curhan, Neale, & Ross, 2004). This further reduces the possibilities for the maximization of joint outcomes.

The debt-ceiling debate of 2011 revealed evidence of both tendencies. Although the matter of primary interest, raising the debt ceiling or having to default on loans beyond a certain date, appeared to be clear, some in Congress seized on the opportunity the issue presented to tie the action to spending cuts. Others saw this as holding a necessary action hostage and, while nevertheless receptive to some such requirement, were unreceptive to the amounts and types of cuts proposed by those seeking to attach strings to the actions. Thus commenced the seven-month trek toward what some justifiably perceived as very serious economic contingencies and longer-range adverse consequences, as those in adversarial roles became increasing entrenched in keeping "the other side" from realizing its aspirations – prevailing, if you will. This is clearly inconsistent with, if not antithetical to, the view that Howard Raiffa's (1982, 2001) decision-analytic approach to negotiation embodies.

Framing

Another factor that often contributes to decision makers' inability to behave in a manner consistent with the precepts of economic rationality is the way in which they frame the outcomes of the choice options they are considering. A substantial number of framing effects have received attention in scholarly literature relating to decision making. Of most interest in the context of the debt–ceiling debate of 2011 perhaps is the framing of outcomes as gains and losses. The human tendencies in this regard are not always apparent to agents, as both Dan Ariely (2010) and Max Bazerman and Ann Tenbrunsel (2011) have aptly noted.

Spawned by the pioneering work of Nobel Prize Laureate in Economics Daniel Kahenman and his long-time colleague Amos Tversky (see Kahneman, 2011), scholarly inquiry into the framing of outcomes related to choice options has revealed a consistent tendency for decision makers to be risk-averse in the case of gains and risk-prone in the case of losses, or, more accurately, in their avoidance. For instance, a person earning $1000 in supplemental income for which the income tax bite is, say, $250, might decide to avoid incurring the certain cost by not reporting the income and, in the process, risking having to pay much more in a combination of the tax, delinquency penalties, legal fees, and the like. Such behavior is putatively irrational.

It appears from the evolution of the debt–ceiling debate of 2011 that advocates on both sides of the dispute, especially the part centering on the magnitude and categories of spending cuts, were caught up by the impulse to avoid loss in respect to the positions they had staked out and, thereby, took the consequent risk of losing far more. In fact, in holding out as long as they did, this appears to be precisely what occurred. If one considers opportunity costs, that is, those the competing parties incurred by pursuing given courses of action during the seven-month debate at the expense of potentially more profitable ones (e.g., figuring out in specific ways what cuts in spending were actually necessary and desirable, as well as how they might have been best implemented, or possibly looking to the longer range and attempting to determine how to honor the "partnership between the generations" of which Edmund Burke spoke – see Ferguson, 2013, p. 14), it seems virtually certain that those participating in the debate could have achieved something of greater legislative merit than they did. It is hard to imagine their achieving anything less than they did.

The Escalation of Commitment

A constraint on possibilities for behaving as much in line with the canons of economic rationality as we might is sunk-cost thinking (see Bazerman & Moore, 2013), or the tendency to make current decisions as a way to rationalize past ones that have produced less-than-desired, if not clearly unwanted, outcomes. When this type of mentality sets in, it can lead to an escalation of commitment that may persist over long periods, not only to the detriment of the decision makers involved, but also to those affected by their decisions (Arkes & Blumer, 1985; Staw, 1981; Staw & Fox, 1977).

The escalation of commitment is by no means exclusively an individual phenomenon. It clearly is in evidence in multi-party contexts, of which negotiation is one. In such contexts, one may have an even greater inclination to escalate than when acting alone. Bazerman and Moore (2013) have identified four reasons why one might escalate commitment in one's interactions with others who are party to a negotiation, including "perceptual bias," "judgmental bias," "impression management," and "competitive irrationality" (pp. 128–131). As to the debt-ceiling debate of 2011, the final two may be particularly apropos.

In the debate, the participants, of course, not only were addressing one another but external audiences as well. Motivated by a desire to fare well in the eyes of these other audiences, whether consciously or not, it makes sense that one would argue and defend prior positions on issues in the interests of projecting strength and, thereby, currying favor with the members. Primary season, after all, was not that far off, and certain voting blocks were of importance. This, however, does not fully accommodate the excesses in commitment that "competitive irrationality" seems to capture. Once one has gone so far down the escalation path, the motivation can shift, becoming less a matter of wanting to prevail as a strong desire to avoid coming across as a loser. What might appear to some as mere intractability or rigidity of personality when an individual escalates commitment makes more sense perhaps when one considers it as the consequence of a shift in motivation. This makes the behavior no less irrational, however, in the sense of one's moving further and further from being able to achieve any outcome other than failure.

Anchoring

Anchoring is often the source of biased, if not always poor, judgments. It reflects a tendency to use arbitrary, possibly irrelevant, reference points in making assessments of probability and value, which are the two indispensible elements in models of rational choice (Bazerman & Moore, 2013). A good, and common, example occurs when an employer bases salary increases on extant salaries, irrespective of the performance of those being considered for them. Hence, those with the lowest salaries may receive the lowest increases even though in some cases they may have contributed more to the success of the organization than have their better-compensated counterparts.

In the context of negotiations, parties may have difficulty even reaching an agreement, let alone a mutually beneficial one, because of the anchors that are operative. As an illustration, the asking price for a home or automobile can strongly influence what the parties see as the value of the acquisition (Northcraft & Neale, 1987) and, therefore, are willing to settle for. If the seller is overly reliant on asking price, he or she could fail to accept a reasonable counteroffer from a prospective buyer. Similarly, if the buyer becomes too committed to the price at which he or she would like to secure the purchase, he or she also might pass on a reasonable counteroffer. What is the consequence in such a case? The seller is stuck with the product, and the buyer leaves the negotiation empty-handed.

In the debt-ceiling debate of 2011, the disputants' difficulty in agreeing on cuts in government spending appears to have been a result of setting their reservation prices too close to their aspiration levels and, from time to time, seemingly making no distinction between the two. In so doing, they came dangerously close to having no positive zone of agreement and, hence, no possibility of a settlement. Recall that for such a zone to exist, parties' reservation prices have to fall between those of the other parties and their respective levels of aspiration. Choosing rationally in negotiations requires that the parties involved all have some possibility of gain, not just those representing one viewpoint. Some interesting research involving so-called ultimatum games makes this necessity exceptionally clear (see Bazerman & Moore, 2013; Beach & Connolly, 2005; Ochs & Roth, 1989).

Conclusion

Examination of the debt-ceiling debate of 2011 reveals evidence of an approach to resolving differences at such variance with Howard Raiffa's (1982, 2001) decision-analytic perspective that it would be inappropriate to dignify it with the label rational. Nor is there much basis for concluding that the eventual settlement has had much in the way of pragmatic value. Serious economic conditions continue to plague the country, and those individuals who had such difficulty dealing with the debt-ceiling crisis seem to be doing no better on other economic fronts, primarily because the reasoning system in use is what Peter Senge (1990) refers to as "political" rather than "rational" (p. 60). Understandably, members of Congress and other elected officials do and should serve political interests, but only to a point, which is where the ethical implications of the exploration herein come into play.

In the debt-ceiling debate of 2011, it seemed that only political interests were driving the interaction and attempts at negotiation to the neglect of the public good. In 2011, the country was in trouble and in 2013 still is. Under such conditions, one would think that those we empower to make decisions on our behalf would recognize their moral responsibility to place the collective well-being uppermost in their priorities. However, the lesson from the debt-ceiling debate and its aftermath suggests that this prospect currently is far from reality.

References

Ariely, D. (2010). *Predictably irrational: The hidden forces that shape our decisions* (Rev. ed.). New York, NY: Harper Perennial.

Arkes, H., & Blumer, C. (1985). The psychology of sunk cost. *Organizational Behavior and Human Decision Process, 35*, 124–140.

Bazerman, M. H., & Moore, D. A. (2013). *Judgment in managerial decision making* (8th ed.). Hoboken, NJ: Wiley.

Bazerman, M. H., & Tenbrunsel, A. E. (2011). *Blind spots: Why we fail to do what's right and what to do about it.* Princeton, NJ: Princeton University Press.

Beach, L. R., & Connolly, T. (2005). *Decision making: People in organizations* (2nd ed.). Thousand Oaks, CA: Sage.

Curhan, J. R., Neale, M. A., & Ross, L. (2004). Dynamic valuation: Preference change in the context of active face-to-face negotiations. *Journal of Experimental Social Psychology, 40*, 142–151.

Davidson, P. (2011, July 28). A primer on the debt-ceiling debate. *USA Today.* Retrieved from http://www.usatoday.com

Ferguson, N. (2013). *The great degeneration: How institutions decay and economies die.* New York, NY: Penguin Press.

Frame, J. D. (2013). *Framing decisions: Decision making that accounts for irrationality, people, and constraints.* San Francisco, CA: Jossey-Bass.

Gouran, D. S., & Hirokawa, R. Y. (1996). Functional theory and communication in decision-making and problem-solving groups: An expanded view. In R. Y. Hirokawa & M. S. Poole (Eds.), *Communication and group decision making* (2nd ed., pp. 55–80). Thousand Oaks, CA: Sage.

Hancock, M., & Zahawi, N. (2013). *Masters of nothing: Human nature, big finance and the fight for the soul of capitalism* (Rev. ed.). London, England: Biteback.

Jones, J. M. (2011, August 16). Congressional job approval ties historic low of 13%. *Gallup® Politics.* Retrieved from http://www.gallup.com

Kahneman, D. (2011). *Thinking, fast and slow.* New York, NY: Farrar, Strauss & Giroux.

Murse, T. (2011, August 6). How the debt ceiling debate hurt America: Credit rating downgrade follows gridlock over debt ceiling. *C-SPAN.* Retrieved from http://www.c-span.org

Newton-Small, J. (2011, June 30). A guide to the debt-ceiling debate: What each faction wants. Retrieved from http://swampland.time.com/2011/06/30/a-guide-to-the-debt-ceiling-debate-what-each-faction-wants/

Northcraft, G. B., & Neale, M. A. (1987). Expert, amateurs, and real estate: An anchoring and adjustment perspective on property pricing decisions. *Organizational Behavior and Human Decision Processes, 39*, 228–241.

Nutting, R. (2011, July 25). 10 craziest things about the debt-ceiling crisis; Commentary: Pay debts? Throw world into recession? I can't decide. Retrieved from http://www.marketwatch.com/story/10-craziest-things-about-the-debt-ceiling-crisis-2011-07-25

Ochs, J., & Roth, A. E. (1989). An experimental study of sequential bargaining. *American Economic Review, 79*, 355–394.

Raiffa, H. (1982). *The art and science of negotiation.* Cambridge, MA: Belknap Press.

Raiffa, H. (2001). *Collaborative decision making.* Cambridge, MA: Belknap Press.

Rogers, D. (2011, July 18). Debt ceiling debate turns "scary." Retrieved from http://www.politico.com

Senge, P. M. (1990). *The fifth discipline: The art & practice of the learning organization.* New York, NY: Currency Doubleday.

Simon, H. A. (1955). A behavioral model of rational choice. *Quarterly Journal of Economics, 69*, 99–118.

Simon, H. A. (1982). *Models of bounded rationality.* Cambridge, MA: MIT Press.

Singal, J. (2013, July/August). Which eggheads should run DC? *Pacific Standard*, pp. 25–26.

Staw, B. M. (1981). The escalation of commitment to a course of action. *Academy of Management Review, 6*, 577–587.

Staw, B. M., & Fox, F. V. (1977). Escalation: The determinants of commitment to a chosen course of action. *Human Relations, 30*, 431–450.

Timeline of events in debt ceiling debate. (2011, August 1). *C-SPAN.* Retrieved from http://www.c-span.org

Zafirovsky, M. (2003). Human rational behavior and economic rationality. *Electronic Journal of Sociology, 17*, 1–34. Retrieved from http://www.sociology.org

2

INFORMAL LOGIC TO THE RESCUE?

Politics and logic in U.S. fiscal debates

Leo Groarke

UNIVERSITY OF WINDSOR, CANADA

I am pleased to have the opportunity to help demonstrate how argumentation theory can illuminate our understanding of a specific case of contemporary argumentation: the U.S. fiscal cliff debate. As a commentator who is not from the United States, I jump into the debate with some trepidation, but in the hopes that I can use this as an opportunity to show how one branch of argumentation theory can contribute to the analysis of public argument.

Informal Logic: A *Thick* Theory

One might describe informal logic (IL) as an attempt to extend traditional logic so that it can be applied to the kinds of arguments that characterize ordinary discourse. A move in this direction is already evident in Copi (1953), but IL as we know it is rooted in the work of Johnson and Blair at the University of Windsor in the 1970s. It is their work that initiated the evolution of informal logic as a distinct field with its own canon and scholarly tradition (see Johnson, 1996).

As a representative of informal logic as a field, it behooves me to say that it would be a mistake to speak of it as though it were characterized by a single methodology. In a manner in keeping with IL's roots in philosophical discussion – philosophers seldom agreeing with one another – informal logicians often approach the subject in different ways. In a forthcoming book on the methods of informal logic, Hansen emphasizes the point that scholars might best speak of informal logic*s* and the different methodologies this implies.

These differences being noted, there are two features of informal logic that characterize all its variants. One is a focus on argument in the premise-and-conclusion sense (so called "argument$_1$"). A second is a commitment to argument critique. To this end, IL's goal is a set of techniques that provide scholars and ordinary people with ways to judge whether the arguments they consider are strong, weak, plausible, implausible, and so on. The practice of IL is in this way determinedly judgmental, though it recognizes that assessments of argument are inherently open to debate.

Elsewhere I have described the IL that I practice as a *thick* rather than a *thin* theory of argument (Groarke, 2013). By this I mean that it is committed to methods of analysis that apply to a broad range of arguments which includes arguments that occur in public debate, in inter-personal communication, and in legal and scientific controversy.

In moving in the direction of a thick theory, informal logic has frequently borrowed from other argumentation traditions, notably from dialectics (and especially pragma-dialectics) and rhetoric. Already in Groarke and Tindale (1987), one finds an attempt to incorporate rhetorical analysis within informal logic. Today, informal logicians frequently incorporate notions of ethos and pathos, dialectical obligation, and dialogical frameworks into their analyses. In an attempt to understand multi-modal arguments which employ pictures, images, and other non-verbal means of communication, they may employ the principles of communication one finds in pragma-dialectics. This kind of cross pollination has made the difference between IL and other argumentation traditions less significant than it once was.

I will summarize the IL methodology I employ as an attempt to analyze and assess an argu-ment (in the premises and conclusion sense) by answering the following six questions:

Q1. Is the language used in presenting the argument appropriate or misleading?
Q2. What are the argument's premises and conclusion?
Q3. Can the argument's premises be accepted without further support?
Q4. Is the inference from the argument's premises to its conclusion strong or questionable?
Q5. Can any issues with the argument's premises or inference be resolved by sub-arguments?
Q6. In what kind of dialogue does the argument occur?

Some aspects of these questions warrant further comment. In asking Q1, I understand the term *language* broadly, so that it includes non-verbal elements of argument like pictures, maps, and graphs. Understanding Q1 in this way raises the important question whether these non-verbal elements are accurate or misleading. In asking Q4, I use the expression *sub-argument* to refer to other arguments that can be used to buttress the premise(s) or the inference of the argument being analyzed.

Though the Q1–Q6 methodology consciously aims at simplicity and straightforwardness, Q5 introduces some considerations that may need explanation. The notion of dialogue it invokes is rooted in pragma-dialectics. Like Walton (2007), I and many other informal logi-cians believe that critical discussion is one important kind of argumentative dialogue but that that there are others which are characterized by different expectations, rules, and norms for argument.

Following Walton, *inquiry dialogue* is an attempt to establish the truth about something – who should be blamed for an accident, whether current theories about the Higgs boson are correct, how to build an office tower that withstands an earthquake, and so on. *Inquiry dialogue* assumes traditional logical norms which require that the evidence for different points of view be collected, assessed, and used as a basis for the strongest conclusions possible.

In contrast, the focus of *negotiation dialogue* is bargaining between two parties with conflicting interests. Here the aim is not truth but some kind of agreement that is accepted by both parties to the dialogue. Bargaining over the price of an eggplant at a market is a case of negotiation dialogue. So is collective bargaining, which is governed by a complex set of rules that establishes who is allowed to bargain, with whom, and how they must proceed. The important point is that negotiation dialogue does not rule out moves that are fallacious in an inquiry dialogue. Appeals to emotion – including emotions like anger and indignation – are an accepted part of negotiation, as are insults and threats (though they are instances of the fallacies *ad hominem* and *ad baculum* in inquiry). The latter is the very essence of collective bargaining, which is ultimately driven by the threat of a strike or lockout.

Arguing the Fiscal Cliff

A cliff is a vertical face of rock or ice. It is a dangerous place because tumbling over it can lead to serious injury, even death. The U.S. "fiscal" cliff is rooted in an impasse between Democrats and Republicans that occurred in 2011, when the government's debt ceiling had to be raised to accommodate more borrowing. The Act that resolved the impasse established a joint committee on deficit reduction which was charged with finding a way to decrease the U.S. deficit by $1.2 trillion over ten years. It included the proviso that tax cuts would expire and substantial cuts to spending would be implemented on January 2, 2013, if no agreement could be reached. This is the so called fiscal cliff that the U.S. was in danger of falling over.

For reasons Lakoff (2013) has explained, the fiscal cliff is a compelling metaphor which has captured the imagination of the public. Trying to capitalize on its popularity, a Detroit television advertisement defined a "personal" fiscal cliff as the imminent demise of one's personal finances. The fiscal cliff metaphor is popular with political cartoonists, who have reveled in exaggerated depictions that ridicule the U.S. economy, taxpayers, Republicans, Democrats, Obama, Boehner, and others. These cartoons are a notable feature of ongoing debate about U.S. fiscal policy, not only because they demonstrate the debate's multi-modal character, but because some of the cartoons represent incisive attempts to summarize the argumentation it contains.

The initial issues that prompted talk of a fiscal cliff were resolved by the American Taxpayer Relief Act of 2012, which was passed in the U.S. Congress on January 1, 2013. By raising the debt ceiling, it halted the fiscal cliff debate, but only for a short reprieve. The continuing growth of the U.S. federal debt will require further increases in the debt ceiling in 2013 (and probably beyond), and this is likely to produce further iterations of the debate. So long as the U.S. federal debt continues to grow, arguments about the fiscal cliff debate are likely for a long time to come.

In turning to arguments about the fiscal cliff, the first question in the list, Q1, raises the question whether the term "fiscal cliff" is misleading. At this point, it seems to be a term that we cannot easily eradicate, but it can still be criticized as a misleading depiction of the U.S. fiscal crisis, primarily because it places so much emphasis on the management of the U.S. debt ceiling.

There are practical realities that have made the debt ceiling a decision point which is a focal point for debate. They are reinforced by the theatrical appeal of talk about a fiscal cliff, which highlights a dramatic moment full of tension and high drama. The problem is that this focus artificially separates the debt ceiling issue from much broader issues of taxes, spending, debt, and the U.S. economy with which it is inextricably entwined.

Keeping this broader focus in mind, there are two opposed lines of reasoning which are usually taken to be the basis of the standoff that is the fiscal cliff debate. One is associated with Democrats, the other with Republicans. So understood, the impasse this produces is captured in the Legge cartoon below, which features Barack Obama and John Boehner hurtling toward the edge of the fiscal cliff, Obama insisting that the USA turn "LEFT!" Boehner insisting that it turn "RIGHT!"

Putting aside questions that might be asked about the distinction between political "left" and "right", this cartoon captures the basic structure of the Republican/Democrat impasse, but it fails to capture the arguments they use in their debate. One finds a better depiction of the popular understanding of these arguments in the Glenn Foden cartoon, "The War of Tugs," below.

Behind the tug of war that Foden drew is the fundamental challenge that faces any government which continually spends more than it recoups in revenue. The Republican elephant

Figure 2.1. Reprinted by permission of Artizans.com

attempts to remedy the situation by pulling for spending cuts. The Democrat donkey opts for a different strategy, pulling instead for tax hikes. The U.S. citizen is dismembered in the process.

Using argument IL diagrams, these two lines of reasoning can be summarized as follows, where "P" indicates a premise and "C" a conclusion.

THE REPUBLICAN ARGUMENT: (P) Government spending exceeds revenues, *so* (C_R) we should avoid the fiscal cliff by cutting spending (and not raising taxes).

$$P$$
$$\downarrow$$
$$C_R$$

THE DEMOCRAT ARGUMENT: (P) Government spending exceeds revenues, *so* (C_D) we should avoid the fiscal cliff by raising taxes (and not cutting spending).

$$P$$
$$\downarrow$$
$$C_D$$

Like the Foden cartoon, these diagrams are in one important way too simple. Given that Republicans reject cuts to defense spending, and Democrats reject increases to middle and

Figure 2.2. Reprinted by permission of Artizans.com

lower class taxes, we can better identify the Republican conclusion (C_R) as the proposition that the U.S. government should avoid the fiscal cliff by cutting spending *to social programs*; and the Democrat conclusion (C_D) as the proposition that the U.S. government should avoid the fiscal cliff by raising taxes *for the rich*.

Identifying the premise and conclusion in the Republican and Democrat argument in this way provides a general answer to the second question in IL methodology (Q2). The next three questions, Q3-Q5, ask us to evaluate arguments by considering the strength of their premises and the inferences they depend upon.

Q3 asks whether the premises in an argument can be accepted without further support. In analyzing the fiscal cliff debate, I have purposely presented the arguments in a way that makes them both rely on the same generally accepted premise. Doing so recognizes that the (huge) imbalance between government revenue and spending in the United States is not a point of contention in the debate and can be legitimately accepted as a premise in arguments that address it.

More problematic issues are posed by Q4, which asks whether the inference in an argument is problematic. The same premise cannot lead to contradictory conclusions, so the inferences in the arguments I have identified are clearly questionable. From the point of view of IL, this makes an analysis of their strength turn on an answer to Q5, which asks whether the issues this raises can be resolved by adding sub-arguments to one or the other side of the debate.

In a short essay, it is impossible to fully analyze all the sub-arguments that might be employed in a public debate as complex as the one that surrounds U.S. fiscal policy, but there are good reasons to be pessimistic about their ability to resolve the disagreement which characterizes the Republican and Democrat points of view. In some cases, it seems impossible to resolve this disagreement because opposed arguers back their views by embracing contradictory values that oppose economic liberty to concerns about the welfare of the disadvantaged; or, trust in (big) government to distrust. This is a deep problem because disagreements about such fundamental values are notoriously difficult to resolve.

In other cases, Democrats and Republicans appeal to sub-arguments that depend on opposing answers to key causal questions. In an Ed Hall cartoon on the 2013 Budget Sequester that suspended the operations of the U.S. government, the standoff between the two parties is summarized as a dichotomy between a decision to "SLASH TAXES" or "SOAK THE RICH." This dichotomy is, however, the result of very different views of the causal consequences of cutting taxes or taxing the rich. Untangling the issues this raises would require a complex understanding of the ways in which government spending, lower tax rates, and taxes on the rich affect the economy and the government balance sheet. And this is an understanding that is hampered by the inherent uncertainty of predictions about the future consequences of government policy. In looking at the past, one can find specific instances in which spending or tax cuts are correlated with economic growth but correlation does not equal cause, and there are so many variables present in real historical situations that arguers are almost always able to attribute positive or negative correlations to other causes.

Such issues make the sub-arguments one might use to settle the fiscal cliff debate inherently controversial. This does not prevent politicians from presenting them with a rhetorical air of certainty, but it is difficult to find a firm argumentative footing which can be the basis of a clear answer to the question whether one should favor the Democrat or the Republican argument.

It can be said that almost all independent authorities agree that tax increases *and* spending cuts are needed to resolve the fiscal issues that underlie the fiscal cliff debate, but there are two general problems why this has not resolved the split between Democrats and Republicans. First, because the two parties strongly emphasize contradictory sides of this dichotomy, typically with arguments founded on premises which are acceptable to their own partisans rather than a *universal audience* made up of individuals who have competing points of view, the result is many arguments that beg the question instead of resolving the debate. Second, and more seriously, neither the Democrat nor the Republican party has faced up to the magnitude of the fiscal issues the U.S. government faces. Especially in the context of long term debt issues, the concrete proposals on both sides have provided no real answer to the underlying problems. All that proposals have achieved is the raising of the debt ceiling in a manner in keeping with one or the other party's views but this is, at the end of the day, a short term measure that compounds rather than alleviates the underlying fiscal problem (by allowing more debt to accumulate).

When all is said and done, the situation is stark. The U.S. government is spending vastly more than it is generating in revenue. There is no reason to believe that this will stop. Servicing this debt will exacerbate the issue. And demographic trends mean that some costs will increase dramatically. In a lengthy search of discussions of the issues, I have not been able to find any analysis that discounts the conclusion that the ratio of U.S. debt to GDP will continue to rise substantially.

Figure 2.3. Reprinted by permission of Artizans.com

A Negotiation Dialogue?

In the wake of this negative assessment of the central arguments that make up the fiscal cliff debate, there is one question, Q6, left in the IL list. In answering it, it is possible to try and explain away the shortcomings of fiscal cliff arguments by arguing they should be seen as an instance of negotiation rather than inquiry dialogue. Considered from this point of view, the lapses of logic that seem to characterize exchanges between the Democrat and the Republican parties are not flaws in attempts to provide compelling arguments in inquiry, but attempts to rouse support and prevail in a negotiation that will determine the behavior of the government. In such a context, the point of argument is not so much about truth as success in negotiation.

One might back this view by arguing that some of the fundamental differences between the Democrat and Republican perspectives (the different commitments to egalitarian and libertarian values, for example) are intractable and not open to rational resolution. There are good philosophical reasons for taking such a perspective seriously, but it must be said that accepting them comes at a cost. A decision to reframe the fiscal debate as a negotiation dialogue turns it into a partisan opportunity for political maneuvering, creating the real possibility that there is no rational way to resolve the impasse that has produced it.

Beyond the CR/CD Dichotomy

My IL analysis has suggested that the fiscal cliff arguments standardly associated with Democrats and Republicans are not compelling. This is a negative conclusion but one that

Figure 2.4. Reprinted by permission of Artizans.com

can open the door to other ways of thinking about the issues. In that vein, I want to end by noting a third, more productive, line of argument. I think it is correctly identified by a *New York Times* commentator, Mankiw (2012), who diagnoses the problem on both sides as the shared premise that "Taxes on the middle class must not rise." This is a premise that is key to both Democrat and Republican positions, Democrats pledging to raise taxes only on the rich and Republicans promising to protect tax cuts for the middle class. Looked at from this point of view, the Democrat and Republican positions are, as the cartoon below suggests, more similar than they first appear.

It seems to me that it is difficult to avoid the conclusion that this joint refusal to consider a rise in middle class taxes is a matter of political expediency. While it does carve out political positions that are consciously tailored to the interests of middle class voters, it eliminates the only practical way to manage U.S. spending (by raising revenue). To the extent to which this is the key obstacle to the most promising resolution of the fiscal cliff issue, my attempt to apply informal logic to the arguments I have outlined leads to the conclusion that it is politics, not logic, which is the driving force in the debate.

References

Copi, I. (1953). *Introduction to logic.* New York, NY: Macmillan.

Groarke, L. (2013). A thick theory of argument. In G. Kiši ek & I. Zagar (Eds.), *What do we know about the world: Rhetorical perspectives* (pp. 6–28). Windsor, ON: Windsor Studies in Argumentation. Available at http://windsor.scholarsportal.info/omp/index.php/wsia/catalog/book/8

Groarke, L., & Tindale, C. (1987). Logic and rhetoric: Groundwork for a synthesis. In F. H. van Eemeren, R. Grootendorst, J. A. Blair, & C. A. Willard (Eds.), *Argumentation: Perspectives and approaches* (pp. 274–282). Providence, RI: Foris Publications.

Hansen, H. (forthcoming). An inquiry into the methods of informal logic. Manuscript.

Johnson, R. H. (1996). *The rise of informal logic.* Newport News, VA: Vale Press.

Lakoff, G. (2013, June 30). Why it's hard to replace the "fiscal cliff" metaphor. *George Lakoff.* Retrieved from http://georgelakoff.com/2013/06/30/why-its-hard-to-replace-the-fiscal-cliff-metaphor

Mankiw, N. G. (2012, December 29). Wishful thinking and middle-class taxes. *New York Times.* Retrieved from http://www.nytimes.com/2012/12/30/business/on-middle-class-tax-rates-too-much-wishful-thinking.html

Walton, D. N. (2007). *Dialog theory for critical argumentation.* Amsterdam, NL: John Benjamins Publishing Company.

3

OBAMA ON THE AFFIRMATIVE

Sequester arguments as policy debate

Sarah T. Partlow-Lefevre

IDAHO STATE UNIVERSITY, USA

Academic debate is rarely used as a method to critically examine real-world arguments even though the *topoi* of academic debate theory appear in public. Because of its thorough inter-rogation of arguments, scholars have called for application of academic debate theory to public policy discussions. In this essay, I use academic debate as a method for engaging argu-ments about the 2013 budget sequestration. I use President Obama and Speaker Boehner's statements to construct and evaluate their arguments from an academic debate perspective. I also problematize the role of the decision-making debater in public policy.

Academic Debate as Method

Academic debate is a useful method for policy analysis in two seemingly contradictory ways: Debate theory enables examination of all sides of an issue and debaters are willing to make judgments about the relative quality of arguments. First, Muir (1998) posited that debate theory develops multiple perspectives on an issue: "This conceptual development is a basis for the formation of ideas and relational thinking necessary for effective public decision making, making even the game of debate a significant benefit in solving real world problems" (p. 287). Accordingly, academic debate develops "tolerance and fairness" as ethical practices (Muir, 1998, p. 288). Academic debate as a method incorporates its habits of thought and tools of analysis to juxtapose contradictory arguments in a common forum.

Second, debaters use the tools of analysis developed through academic debate to judge and be judged. Calling for theorists to engage real-world policy, Bruschke (2012) contended, "trained argument professionals . . . should approach significant contemporary debates, care-fully assess the evidence presented by each side of the dispute, and make normative judgments about which side is right" (p. 68). Scholars may give society what it "needs from argumenta-tion," resulting in more relevant scholarly participation in public debates (p. 67). Because "presidents, members of congress, regulators and others are asked to make policy judgments on a host of issues," argument scholars should use "the tools at our disposal" to seek "answers to the question of contemporary public policy disputes" (pp. 68–69). Rowland and Fritch (1989) agreed: "The practice of academic debate may illuminate . . . policy sciences" and such application can produce "much more effective" policy outcomes (p. 457).

Academic debate as a method requires scholars to act as both debater and judge. Scholars should reconstruct arguments on both sides of an issue and carefully evaluate them. Ulrich (1983) wrote, "the debater is expected to search . . . while a judge is expected to develop standards for evaluating competing arguments" (p. 938). Argument critics must also incorporate academic debate skills such as "research, organization, strategy, and technique" (Muir, 1993, p. 286). Such an approach to policy analysis produces results that may be juxtaposed with real world outcomes providing insight into public policy issues.

In this essay, I cast President Obama and Speaker of the House Boehner as debaters engaging the question of what should be done in the face of budget sequestration. To reconstruct the arguments, I reviewed public statements made by President Obama and Speaker Boehner on their respective websites from January through May 2013. I analyzed every statement regarding budget sequestration and constructed affirmative and negative arguments.

Obama's Affirmative

Obama's affirmative answered the question of what to do in the face of a sweeping series of budget cuts designed to automatically go into effect in 2013. Initially, inherency arguments were that in the midst of economic recovery, a budget deal was necessary. Obama maintained job numbers had increased "every month for three years" and the "momentum" should not be lost (2013g). Sequestration would harm economic growth. Obama (2013c) said, "At a time when economists and business leaders . . . have said that our economy is poised for progress, we shouldn't allow self-inflicted wounds to put that progress in jeopardy." Therefore, Obama (2013d) argued that Congress must stop sequestration stating, "Our top priority . . . should be . . . to grow our economy and create good, middle class jobs . . . automatic budget cuts . . . will do the exact opposite." In the midst of economic recovery, Obama had strong arguments for avoiding a disruption.

Next, Obama outlined the impacts of sequestration. Harms would occur in several areas. Initially, U.S. security would be threatened. Subcomponents included limitations on emergency response, border patrol, the FBI, federal prosecutors, and harm to military readiness. Obama (2013c) stated, "this meat-cleaver approach . . . will jeopardize our military readiness . . . It won't consider whether we're cutting . . . a vital service."

Second, Obama (2013b) developed a scientific research and innovation impact tying it into economic growth, stating, "Every dollar we invested to map the human genome returned $140 . . . Now is not the time to gut these job-creating investments in science and innovation." Obama (2013d) argued medical research would be harmed for "a generation."

Third, uncertainty would damage business confidence. Obama (2013e) stated, "the uncertainty . . . is having an effect" as companies anticipate "layoff notices." Giving specific examples, Obama (2013e) argued that the impact would have a "ripple effect" throughout the economy dampening recovery. He (2013f) said:

> The longer these cuts remain . . . the greater the damage . . . we could see growth cut by over one-half of 1 percent . . . Every time that we get a piece of economic news . . . as long as the sequester is in place . . . [it] could have been better if Congress had not failed to act.

Obama's (2013e) preemptive arguments blamed Congress for economic lags under sequestration, declaring the United States "can't keep on conducting its business drifting from one crisis to the next." Obama (2013c) showed empathy for people's economic struggles and argued that growth should be *a priori*, saying, "Our top priority must be to . . . grow the economy and create good, middle-class jobs . . . That's our North Star."

Fourth, cuts to governmental services "could cause delays in airports across the country" (Obama, 2013e). After flight delays began, Congress passed a law allowing the TSA to shift money from an infrastructure modernization account to fund daily operations. Obama (2013h) argued that this would harm economic competitiveness, stating "not a single U.S. airport . . . came in the top 25" in the world and that cutting infrastructure would be akin to "using our seed corn short term." In other words, the money could be used to ensure future growth or be consumed immediately.

Fifth, education funding was at risk. Education cuts would hurt the economy. Obama argued that many students would lose access to financial aid, job training, and early childhood education. In Virginia alone, "more than 2,000 college students would lose their financial aid. Early education . . . would be eliminated for nearly 1,000 children, and around 18,000 fewer Virginians would get . . . the . . . training they need to find a job" (Obama, 2013e). Obama (2013d) articulated an economic impact to early childhood education given "every dollar we invest . . . can save more than seven dollars later" due to "boosting graduation rates, reducing teen pregnancy, even reducing violent crime" (Obama, 2013b).

To solve these problems Obama (2013d) advocated a plan requiring spending cuts, increased revenue, and entitlement reform: "We should . . . build on the . . . deficit reduction we've . . . achieved . . . But . . . in a balanced way – with smart spending cuts, entitlement reform, and tax reform. That's my plan." Developing specifics required democratic compromise. Obama (2013e) clarified, "None of us will get 100 percent . . . we're prepared to make some tough cuts . . . Republicans . . . have to compromise as well." Obama (2013d) argued that asking "more of the wealthiest Americans" was necessary and fair. His plan would "responsibly lower the deficit without laying off workers, or forcing parents to scramble for childcare, or slashing financial aid for college" (Obama, 2013f). His approach had already cut "more than 2.5 trillion" from the deficit and would lead to cuts of "4 trillion . . . that economists and elected officials from both parties say we need to stabilize our debt" (Obama, 2013c). Obama argued that reasonable compromises would produce smart cuts solving for the economy, maintaining services, and reducing the deficit. Obama (2013c) said, "I am willing to cut more . . . programs that aren't working," for example entitlement and tax reform would "save hundreds of billions of dollars" and be "a balanced approach." Such changes would reduce the deficit and limit cuts "that could hurt our economy" (Obama, 2013c).

Finally, the plan would promote education, training, and research and reduce the deficit "by $4 trillion over the next decade" (Obama, 2013a). It would invest in "people and education and job training and science and medical research" to promote growth (Obama, 2013a). Obama (2013e) argued the plan resembled a smart family's budget. Specifically:

> You've got a little less money coming in. Are you going to say . . . we'll cut out college tuition . . . stop feeding the little guy over here, we won't pay our car note even though that means we can't get to work – that's not what you do, right? . . . You prioritize, and you make smart decisions.

Boehner's Negative

Boehner's strategy was a plan-inclusive-counterplan to do part, but not all, of Obama's plan. Boehner advocated budget cuts, Medicaid reform, and no new revenue. Conceding some of sequestration's harms, Boehner (2013c) proposed a balanced budget as key to economic prosperity and contrasted "responsible" cuts in the counterplan with Obama's "tax increases on the American people." Boehner (2013c) argued that taxes would be "on top of the ones the president imposed on families and small businesses through his health care law." Balancing the budget was essential to "grow the economy, expand opportunity and prosperity, and ensure America maintains its leading role in the world with a strong national defense" (Boehner, 2013c).

Initially, Boehner (2013a) said his approach would balance the budget "in 10 years." Boehner (2013e) declared Obama's plan was not "credible" and could never pass because the revenue "debate is now closed." Boehner (2013e) insisted, "spending is the problem" and "the focus." He argued that the sum of evidence was on his side, explaining, "180 economists agree that reining in spending-driven deficits and balancing the budget are key to fueling stronger economic growth" (Boehner, 2013o). Boehner (2013o) also used a family budget metaphor: "hard working moms and dads will gather around their kitchen tables, parsing the bills . . . Americans are making sacrifices to make ends meet." He suggested that the government must make similar sacrifices.

Boehner identified four advantages. First, the Republican plan would "continue focusing on helping Americans get back to work and putting the country on a path to a balanced budget" (Boehner, 2013i). Job creation and spending limits were the keys economic recovery because *"The number one priority for the American people is creating jobs and getting our spending under control"* (Boehner, 2013b). Yet, Obama's plan would undermine these priorities because "his budget never balances, and calls for a $1.1 trillion tax hike . . . America will have run deficits at or near a trillion dollars for five years straight" (Boehner, 2013o).

Second, the Republican counterplan corrected a lack of fiscal restraint. Boehner (2013o) argued that Obama's plan would put "the American dream further out of reach." He personalized this saying, "I want to hand my kids and grandkids the same shot at the American Dream that I had – not some mountain of debt" (Boehner, 2013k). Boehner (2013h) used a soldier as an example of a citizen who "is concerned about . . . demands for additional revenue, and wants meaningful reforms to tackle our debt crisis."

Third, the counterplan would preserve national security and military readiness. Sequestration would force cuts in "Border security, law enforcement, aviation safety" (2013g). The impact would "be devastating to our military" (Boehner, 2013f). The counterplan could put "America on the path to a balanced budget in 10 years, without threatening national security" (Boehner, 2013g).

Fourth, Boehner decried wasteful spending. He said talk of tax increases was uncalled for "when the government is still paying people to play videogames, giving folks free cellphones, . . . buying $47,000 cigarette-smoking machines" (Boehner, 2013g), and "robotic squirrels" (Boehner, 2013j). He argued that many budget cuts could be painless because Democrats were spendthrifts.

Boehner rebutted Obama's case by arguing Obama exaggerated the impacts and could solve sequestration's harms at any time given the desire to do so. Boehner's (2013j) first argument was that Obama's implementation of sequestration was intentionally painful "from shutting down White House tours to spreading fear of long lines at airports." Boehner (2013g) claimed sequestration resulted from Obama's "own failed leadership" and "the sequester is an ugly and dangerous way" to achieve beneficial spending cuts.

Boehner (2013m) argued case turns stating that spending harmed the economy: *"Hundreds of thousands fled the workforce last month and unemployment remains far above what the Obama administration promised when it enacted its 'stimulus' spending plan."* Boehner argued (2013m) Obama's plan didn't balance the budget: "Obama's budget will reduce the deficit by a meager $600 billion over the next 10 years." Boehner (2013n) said, "Washington can't spend its way to prosperity" and the national debt "is draining our economy and threatening our kids and grandkids." He claimed government spending was "crowding out private investment . . . like a wet blanket on our economy" (Boehner, 2013l). Each person in the United States would feel the impact. Boehner (2013d) stated, "Washington has a spending problem that threatens the prosperity of every child, every family, and every small business in America." Ending with a patriotic appeal, he argued, "our people, not our government . . . give us confidence in America's future" (Boehner, 2013d).

Evaluating the Debate

Obama's plan to replace the sequester with additional tax revenue, entitlement reform, and smart budget cuts proved to have several advantages such as maintenance of government services, education, research and development, and economic growth. Obama employed specific examples and statistics explicating the harms. Obama argued that some programs were investments in economic prosperity. Though such programs would be damaged under sequestration, they might be eliminated under the counterplan. Thus, each of these benefits were disadvantages to the counterplan. They also provided independent internal links into economic growth. In each case, Obama justified expenditures economically. Additionally, he suggested a willingness to compromise, essentially combining the best of both sides and then creating a permutation.

The counterplan would replace sequestration, preserve defense spending, and implement sweeping cuts elsewhere. Advantages to the counterplan included maintaining military readiness, the economy/jobs, and the American dream, and eliminating wasteful spending. Boehner rarely gave specific evidence. When he did, his evidence lacked detail or generalizability. Conversely, Obama cited business leaders, economists, and statistics suggesting that public investment had significant economic returns. Boehner's impacts were solved by Obama's plan.

Boehner claimed to bolster military readiness, jobs, and the American dream. The military readiness arguments were not a net benefit to the counterplan because the plan would solve them. Jobs and the American dream were subsets of the economy impact. Thus, whoever won the direction of the internal link to the economy was likely to win the debate. The counterplan strategy was weak because it had no net benefits other than an argument that it would solve for the economy better.

Obama developed multiple internal links into prosperity by identifying the economic impact of each advantage. He used business leaders and job growth to suggest that his strategy empirically solved. Obama's plan was bidirectional, including some spending cuts and investment to produce growth. Boehner's internal links to the economy were much less well defined. His argument that spending was crowding out business investment were answered by Obama's reference to business leaders and the consistent job growth numbers. Boehner's attempt to portray Obama as a spendthrift unwilling to cut expenditures distracted him from adequately answering the permutation. Thus, if I were judging this exchange as an academic debate, Obama would win.

Academic Debate and the Real World

Actually, Obama did not win, gridlock remained, and sequestration took effect. Such analysis highlights differences between policy making and academic debate. Academic debate is an asynchronous method. The arguments analyzed here occurred over time but are presented as a whole requiring reconstruction and injection of the critic into argument creation. Both an advantage and a disadvantage, asynchronicity promotes broad understanding of each side. However, it does not provide real time perspectives and may create bias. Choices about inclusion, focus, etc., influence argument construction. Fortunately, such concerns are countered by the availability of statements from each speaker.

In constructing each perspective, I used a series of statements made over several months. Obama tended to present longer speeches while Boehner's material was shorter and focused on fewer, more compact arguments. Boehner seemed to rely on a few key negative arguments. Additionally, asynchronicity makes it more difficult to trace and analyze the development of arguments over time. For example, Obama used the development of the problems with the FAA and excessive wait times at airports to demonstrate the impact of sequestration. In response, Congress passed a measure to allow the FAA to use modernization funds to avoid furloughs. The subtleties of this development are difficult to articulate using this method.

Another difference is that the impacts are qualitatively different. Obama and Boehner did not develop terminal impacts. In academic debate, economic problems would be linked to depression and war. Public policy debate tends to assume economic growth is positive while the question is more open in academic debate. Indeed, the discussion centered on competing methods of achieving growth. Additionally, there was little prioritizing of impacts. Both speakers agreed that the economy was the primary impact.

In policy discussions, advocates often make decisions. They are decision-making debaters. Such a concept hinders positive outcomes when an advocate is so tied to a specific position s/he is unable to inject reason. The decision-making debater cannot achieve compromise because s/he lacks the habits of ethical debate. For example, the honest engagement of multiple perspectives is necessary to seek the best solution. In the case of Obama vs. Boehner, the debaters were decision makers. Unfortunately, the debaters remained in rigid perspectives encouraging continued gridlock. Advocates who are unwilling to critically engage all sides of an issue and search for compromise endanger the well being of public policy.

Fortunately, academic debate as a method offers hope. If decision-making debaters would honestly engage in debate, they might be able to approach policy making in a more open way. Examining all sides of an issue could result in better, less politicized policies. Perhaps, then, policy judgment would be nuanced and determined through a process of ethical engagement and openness.

References

Boehner, J. (2013a, February 5). Speaker Boehner statement on the president's sequester. Retrieved from http://boehner.house.gov/news/documentsingle.aspx?DocumentID=319013

Boehner, J. (2013b, February 6). President's "sequester" should be replaced with spending cuts & reforms that put us on a path to balance the budget over the next 10 years. Retrieved from http://www.speaker.gov/video/speaker-boehner-president-s-sequester-should-be-replaced-spending-cuts-reforms-put-us-path

Boehner, J. (2013c, February 8). The Obama sequester must be replaced with responsible spending cuts. Retrieved from http://boehner.house.gov/news/documentsingle.aspx?DocumentID=319420

Boehner, J. (2013d, February 12). Speaker Boehner statement on the state of the union. Retrieved from http://boehner.house.gov/news/documentsingle.aspx?DocumentID=319797

Boehner, J. (2013e, February 19). Speaker Boehner statement on the president's sequester. Retrieved from http://boehner.house.gov/news/documentsingle.aspx?DocumentID320444

Boehner, J. (2013f, February 20). Boehner statement on pentagon letter outlining consequences of President Obama's sequester. Retrieved from http://boehner.house.gov/news/documentsingle.aspx?DocumentID=320494

Boehner, J. (2013g, February 20). The president is raging against a budget crisis he created. *Wall Street Journal*. Retrieved from http://online.wsj.com/article/SB10001424127887323495104578314240032274944.html?mod=WSJ_Opinion_LEADTop

Boehner, J. (2013h, March 1). Smarter cuts, not tax hikes, are key to replacing president's sequester. Retrieved from http://boehner.house.gov/news/documentsingle.aspx?DocumentID=321875

Boehner, J. (2013i, March 6). Senate should follow house lead to keep government open. Retrieved from http://boehner.house.gov/news/documentsingle.aspx?DocumentID=322369

Boehner, J. (2013j, March 15). The president's sequester still needs to be replaced. Retrieved from http://boehner.house.gov/news/documentsingle.aspx?DocumentID=324294

Boehner, J. (2013k, March 21). Democrats who reject the goal of balancing the budget are out of step with the American people. Retrieved from http://boehner.house.gov/news/documentsingle.aspx?DocumentID=325049

Boehner, J. (2013l, March 22). A balanced budget would create jobs and expand opportunity. Retrieved from http://boehner.house.gov/news/documentsingle.aspx?DocumentID=325229

Boehner, J. (2013m, April 5). Washington is making it harder for Americans to find work. Retrieved from http://www.speaker.gov/press-release/speaker-boehner-washington-making-it-harder-americans-find-work

Boehner, J. (2013n, April 26). Leading by example, creating a better environment for jobs. Retrieved from http://boehner.house.gov/news/documentsingle.aspx?DocumentID=33185

Boehner, J. (2013o, May 6). Boehner in politico: Republicans are doing more with less to fix the budget. Retrieved from http://boehner.house.gov/blog/?CatagoryID=3943

Bruschke, J. (2012). Argument and evidence evaluation: A call for scholars to engage contemporary public debates. *Argumentation and Advocacy, 49*(1), 59–75.

Muir, S. A. (1993). A defense of the ethics of contemporary debate. *Philosophy & Rhetoric, 26*(4), 277–295.

Obama, B. (2013a, January 14). News conference by the president. Retrieved from http://www.whitehouse.gov/photos-and-video/video/2013/01/14/president-obama-holds-news-conference

Obama, B. (2013b, February 12). President Barack Obama's 2013 state of the union address – as delivered. Retrieved from http://www.whitehouse.gov/state-of-the-union–2013

Obama, B. (2013c, February 19). Averting the sequester and finding a balanced approach to deficit reduction. Retrieved from http://www.whitehouse.gov/photos-and-video/video/2013/02/09/weekly-address-averting-sequester-and-finding-balanced-approach-de

Obama, B. (2013d, February 23). Congress must act now to stop the sequester. Retrieved from http://www.whitehouse.gov/photos-and-video/video/2013/02/23/weekly-address-congress-must-act-now-stop-sequester

Obama, B. (2013e, February 26). Remarks by the President on the impact of the sequester. Retrieved from http://www.whitehouse.gov/photos-and-video/video/2013/02/26/president-obama-speaks-impact-sequester

Obama, B. (2013f, March 1). Statement by president on the sequester. Retrieved from http://www.whitehouse.gov/photos-and-video/video/2013/03/01/president-obama-makes-statement-sequester

Obama, B. (2013g, March 9). End sequester to keep growing the economy. Retrieved from http://www.whitehouse.gov/photos-and-video/video/2013/03/09/weekly-address-end-sequester-keep-growing-economy

Obama, B. (2013h, April 30). Obama, news conference by the president. Retrieved from http://www.whitehouse.gov/the-press-office/2013/04/30/news-conference-president

Rowland, R. C., & Fritch, J. E. (1989). The relationship between debate and argumentation theory. In B. E. Gronbeck (Ed.), *Spheres of Argument: Proceedings of the Sixth SCA/AFA Conference on Argumentation* (pp. 457–463). Annandale, VA: Speech Communication Association.

Ulrich, W. (1983). The influence of the judge on the debate round. In D. Zarefsky, M. O. Sillars, & J. Rhodes (Eds.), *Argument in Transition: Proceedings of the Third Summer Conference on Argumentation* (pp. 938–950). Annandale, VA: Speech Communication Association.

4

THE LIBERAL PUBLIC SPHERE AND THE DEBT CEILING CRISIS

Robert C. Rowland

THE UNIVERSITY OF KANSAS, USA

Although contemporary argumentation theory embraces diverse theoretical perspectives, that diversity emerged from a broad, if partial, consensus that argument was a pragmatic means of problem solving in a democratic society. The faith in pragmatic reason was evident in Brockriede's (1975) definition of argument as "*a process whereby people reason their way from one set of problematic ideas to the choice of another*" (p. 180). A similar perspective was implicit in Gronbeck's (1980) keynote at the first Alta conference, where he called for an effort to "disambiguate our vocabulary, restore a sense of 'publicness' into our speculations concerning argumentation, and reunite theorists with critics" in order to avoid continuing "to dwell in the booby hatch" (pp. 9, 11–14). Most explicitly, Wenzel (1980) "embraced . . . a conception of argumentation as the rationale of critical decision making" (pp. 125–126).

Today, there is much less faith that reason is an inherent good, as reflected in the criticism of Habermas's vision of the public sphere (Calhoun, 1992) and in the attacks on technical reason by Fisher (1984) and Goodnight (1982). In the remainder of this essay, however, I illustrate how a critic infused with a faith in public reason can apply that faith to analyze a recent controversy. Based in a pragmatic justification of rational argumentation and debate as "cognitive principles" justified by "an evolutionary process that favors the fittest methods" (Rescher, 1977, p. 108), I use the lens of the *liberal public sphere* (Rowland, 2005, 2012) to test how well argument is working in U.S. democracy.

The Liberal Public Sphere

Habermas, a German intellectual who labeled himself "the last Marxist," (Habermas, 1992, p. 469), developed public sphere theory. Although Habermas's focus on "impartiality, inter-subjectivity, and rationality" (Phillips, 1996, pp. 233–234) should have been appealing to argumentation theorists, the gap between Habermas's ideals and the reality of the public sphere that excluded groups from deliberation indicated the utter failure of his view of the public sphere. In this context, public sphere research shifted away from the idea of a singular public sphere in favor of multiple public spheres, publics, and/or counterpublics (Asen, 2009, p. 271). At the same time, some issues do arise that relate to the functioning of the whole, where "the impact is universal," and there "must be a single public sphere" (Garnham, 1992, p. 371).

One alternative is to ground a theory of a singular public sphere not in the coffee house culture that inspired Habermas, but in the founding documents of U.S. democracy, especially the writings of James Madison. Madison was well aware of forces that pushed public debate toward partisanship, self-interest, ideology, and irrationality. Rather than a focus on impartial reason, Madison placed his faith in the idea that, over time, even in the process of sometimes unreasonable public disputation, sensible democratic governance could be achieved. Madison (1999) knew that "enlightened statesmen will not always be at the helm" (p. 163), and "public measures are rarely investigated with that spirit of moderation which is essential to a just estimate of the tendency to advance or obstruct the public good" (p. 194) but he still believed that the process of vigorous, though flawed, public debate would ultimately assure that the people were represented and that good policies would be chosen because "a bad cause seldom fails to betray itself" (p. 230). Through vigorous debate, he believed there could be "a republican remedy for the diseases most incident to republican government" (p. 167).

The liberal public sphere is not defined by disembodied public reason, but by argumentative theory about the actual process of democracy. Four primary actors populate the liberal public sphere. First, representatives of the public who should authentically represent the concerns of the community: The public sphere fails if major voices are not fully represented, but it also fails if public discourse is not authentic and is instead based in mere ideological posturing. Second, the public, which is not a symbolically created entity, but composed of all actual citizens and other stakeholders: Although citizen participation is important, liberal public sphere theory realistically assumes that most will have neither the time nor the inclination to do so. At a minimum, citizens need to expose themselves to debate so that they understand the competing positions. Third, the expert community: Their function is to provide the best available data to media and the representatives of the public. The liberal public sphere embraces the need for expert testimony because the world is a complex place and "a certain degree of knowledge of the subjects" (Madison, 1999, p. 306) under discussion is needed in order to make reasonable decisions. Fourth, media: Their role is to present to the public the views of the representatives and background information from the expert community.

The functioning of the liberal public sphere can be tested through five questions:

1. Were the views of all of the relevant stakeholders authentically represented?
2. Was the debate shaped by authentic informed expert opinion?
3. Did media report the dispute in a way that informed the public and its representatives?
4. Did the public gather adequate information to assess the debate?
5. Did the better arguments win out in the end? (In many cases, no principled judgment may be possible, but in instances where there is consensus on policy, failure to act can be seen as a failure of the liberal public sphere.)

Liberal public sphere theorists recognize that real-world debate is often quite messy with extreme, uninformed, and ideological advocacy. Madison believed that even such a flawed debate could still produce effective governance because a process of ideological contestation could reveal the best policy. Like Rescher 170 years later, Madison believed that over time the better argument would win out. The debate over the debt ceiling in 2011 suggests that this faith in pragmatic reason is not always justified.

The Debt Ceiling

The debt ceiling crisis of 2011 is an appropriate test of the liberal public sphere. The resolution of the crisis should have been easy given the debt ceiling had been raised "78 times since

1960" and before 2011 there had never been any serious risk of default (Harwood, 2011, p. A11; Mann & Ornstein, 2012, pp. 5–7). Moreover, consensus emerged that failure to raise the debt ceiling risked economic catastrophe (Woodward, 2012). A broad expert consensus, reflected in several national commissions, agreed that *both* increased revenues *and* entitlement reform were needed to address a long-term deficit problem, but that major cuts should not be made in the short term because of the economic downturn (Mann & Ornstein, 2012, pp. 15–16). Reflecting this consensus, President Obama offered a plan calling for "roughly $3 in spending cuts for every $1 in tax increases," a proposal that some on Obama's team believed "was too reasonable" (Scheiber, 2011, p. 269) because it made major compromises on government spending prior to actual negotiations.

Ultimately, the crisis was resolved in "an appalling spectacle of hostage taking" in a package focused exclusively on cuts, a result that "led to downgrading the country's credit, and blocked constructive action to nurture an economic recovery or deal with looming problems of deficits and debt" (Mann & Ornstein, 2012, p. xii). The deal also produced the sequester that the Congressional Budget Office and Bipartisan Policy Center estimated would cost the economy between 1 million and 1.4 million jobs ("A Million," 2013; see also Rowland, 2013).

The remainder of this essay focuses on a defining moment that reveals a great deal about dysfunction in the liberal public sphere: when Republican leaders and President Obama presented duelling plans for resolving the long-term budget problem. Rising Republican star Paul Ryan authored the Republican plan, *The Path to Prosperity* (2011). Presented as a serious attempt to cut the deficit, the plan also included tax cuts totaling $2.4 trillion that strongly benefitted upper-income people in the United States (Hulse, 2011; Scheiber, 2011). These revenue reductions meant that to achieve the $4 trillion reduction in the deficit, spending would need to be reduced by $6.2 trillion, necessitating huge cuts in both entitlements and other domestic programs.

Liberal commentators labeled the plan as "right-wing lunacy" (Scheiber, 2011, p. 260). Some on the right agreed with this judgment. Bruce Bartlett (2011), a former Reagan administration budget chief, noted that "Ryan's plan puts an exceptionally heavy emphasis on cutting programs like Medicaid and food stamps that primarily aid the poor, while the well-to-do are essentially held harmless." Bartlett also questioned whether the plan would actually "raise 19 percent of GDP" in revenues that Ryan claimed, citing an estimate that the actual figure would be "just 16.8 percent of GDP," meaning that the plan increased, rather than cut, the deficit.

Obama (2011) presented his plan at George Washington University. He began by framing the "debate over budgets and deficits" as "about the kind of future that we want." His approach was consistent with the expert consensus that a combination of increased revenues and cuts in military spending, discretionary domestic spending, and entitlements was needed. After laying out the case for "shared responsibility and shared sacrifice," Obama advocated a "balanced approach" combining one trillion dollars of tax increases on the rich through rate increases and closing loopholes with two trillion dollars of cuts in spending and additional interest savings, producing a net "$4 trillion in deficit reduction over 12 years," an approach that he said was similar to that "of the bipartisan fiscal Commission." He also critiqued the Ryan plan, claiming that it would make major cuts in clean energy, transportation, and education and create "a fundamentally different America." He also attacked the plan for turning Medicare into a voucher program, thereby ending "Medicare as we know it," causing "50 million Americans" to lose their health insurance and, through the additional tax cuts for the rich, threatening "the basic social compact in America." Obama also called for bi-partisan action and made it clear that substantial cuts in entitlements would be needed, arguing that "a progressive vision" requires that we "prove that we can afford our commitments."

Unbeknownst to Obama, Ryan was present in the front row during the speech. The conventional wisdom is that Obama made a major misstep in attacking the Ryan plan with Ryan present. Woodward (2012) concluded that "the speech widened the partisan divide" (p. 106), a conclusion evident in Ryan's comment to an Obama advisor: "You just poisoned the well" (as cited in Calmes, 2012, p. A1). According to Woodward (2012), "He'd expected an olive branch. What he got was the finger" (p. 106). Ryan's reaction convinced Obama that he could not use the speech "as the opening shot in a communications offensive" because, as one Obama advisor noted, "publicly attacking the Republicans would blow up the negotiations" (Scheiber, 2011, pp. 270, 271).

Obama's remarks were not out of the bounds of normal political rhetoric. The language in his speech was harsh, but not nearly as harsh as the language Ryan used to defend his budget proposal. Ryan's (2011) budget plan attacked the Obama administration, declaring "America is drawing perilously close to a tipping point that has the potential to curtail free enterprise, transform its government, and weaken its national identity in ways that may not be reversible." The extremism of the language in the document is evident in the claim that the nation faced:

> two dangers: long-term economic decline as the number of makers diminishes and the number of takers grows and, worse, gradual moral-political decline as dependency and passivity weaken the nation's character and as the power to make decisions is stripped from individuals and their elected representatives and given to non-elected bureaucracies.

Ryan claimed that Obama's budget proposals worsened these problems by "suffocating investment and stifling growth." Ryan's language was much harsher than Obama's. Despite this, Ryan was outraged that the President had criticized him, viewing the attacks as "outside the normal boundaries of partisan discourse" (Woodward, 212, p. 105).

Madison believed that a sharp interchange of ideas was the key to both representing the many factions in the nation and reasonably solving problems. At this moment, Obama recognized that sharp interchange was too risky and shifted to private negotiation. Krugman (2011) was right when he predicted that "given the hysterical Republican reaction, it doesn't look likely that we'll see negotiations trying to narrow the difference" between the budget proposals.

The Assessment

What does this interchange between representatives reveal about the status of the liberal public sphere? Obama and Ryan presented the views of the two primary sides in the dispute. Ryan argued that excessive government threatened U.S. capitalism and demanded both significant tax cuts and major cuts in domestic spending. Obama attacked Ryan's approach, laying out a case for a balanced approach to deficit reduction that was broadly similar to the proposals of several national commissions. It seems clear that Ryan's proposal was not designed simply to resolve the debt ceiling crisis, but to dramatically downsize government itself. Using a negotiation over debt ceiling as a rationale for cutting taxes in a way that primarily benefitted upper-income people appears to be an inauthentic attempt to use a manufactured crisis to benefit the wealthy.

News media reporting on the Ryan budget plan and Obama's response to it focused on a broad description of each proposal and the political implications of the controversy. Reporting on Ryan's plan described its basic outline and cited Republican support and Democratic criticism (Rucker & Fahrenthold, 2011; Wolf, 2011). Conservative commentary was enthusiastic. *The Washington Times* praised Ryan's approach as based on the recognition that "Mr. Obama's Keynsesian borrow-and-stimulate policy has been an utter failure" ("GOP Proposes," 2011). While liberal commentators were broadly critical, the dominant reaction of mainstream news media was that Ryan's plan was "a budget of the grownups" and a "serious proposal to reduce the federal deficit" (Ferris, 2011; "Hard Choices," 2011), judgments that did not reflect the expert consensus.

The dominant theme in news analysis about Obama's speech was that his "partisan tone" had "widened the partisan divide" (Woodward, 2012, p. 106) and that even "some Obama allies" saw the speech as "a tactical error" (Montgomery, 2011). Fact checkers took a pox-on-both-houses approach. Kessler (2011) concluded, "As with President Obama's budget, the Ryan budget plan relies on dubious assertions, questionable assumptions and fishy figures." The norm of presenting an ostensibly balanced treatment of all issues ignored the fact that Obama's approach mirrored the expert consensus, while Ryan's approach was based on such radical assumptions that conservatives such as Bartlett found it reprehensible. In this case, "a balanced treatment of an unbalanced phenomenon is a distortion of reality" (Mann & Ornstein, 2012, p. 194).

What of press commentary? While conservative commentators generally attacked Obama, liberal commentators provided a broader discussion of the controversy. Many observed that Obama combined a call for a bipartisan solution modeled on the work of experts with a "stark, but accurate" critique of Ryan's budget plan (Cohn, 2011; Krugman, 2011; Shear, 2011). Interestingly, liberal commentators did a better job of reporting about the underlying economic issues in the two proposals than did mainstream reporters, precisely because they were not limited to simply presenting what both sides said. At the same time, the liberal credentials of these commentators undoubtedly led many to conclude that they were simply partisans.

Members of the public failed to fulfill their responsibility to minimally inform themselves about the issue. Polling across the years has made evident that on both policy and knowledge about how the government works, the public is woefully uninformed (Pew Research Center, 2010). Moreover, on the deficit the public is largely unwilling to accept cuts in benefits or tax increases, unless those cuts or tax hikes fall on someone else (Pew Research Center, 2011). This combination of lack of information and unwillingness to sacrifice created a situation in which calls for a plan modeled after various national commissions held little appeal. In contrast, misleading arguments or calls for others to sacrifice had much more potential appeal.

What of the expert community? A broad consensus existed in favor of avoiding major cuts in the short-term, while combining entitlement reform with increased revenues and tax reform over the long term. There was disagreement on the ratio of cuts to tax increases, but across the ideological spectrum there was agreement on the outline of needed action. This consensus had almost no effect on the resolution of the crisis. If the debt ceiling is representative of liberal public sphere policy debates, fears of technocratic domination are wildly overstated. The failure to take into account the broad expert consensus is one reason that the resolution of the crisis was a policy debacle.

The Status of the Liberal Public Sphere

The exchange between Obama and Ryan and more broadly the debt ceiling debate of 2011 suggest that the liberal public sphere is not working very well. Of the four primary actors in the public sphere, only the expert community consistently fulfilled its democratic function. An argument can be made that President Obama attempted to authentically present a liberal perspective on resolving the debt ceiling, but it quickly became clear that doing so risked economic catastrophe. His decision to back off public advocacy for several months can be read either as a failure of presidential leadership or a necessary tactical response to an impossible political situation. Other actors in the public sphere largely failed to fulfill their responsibilities. Much of the debate was inauthentic ideological posturing. Most press reporting focused on the political conflict, rather than the underlying policy issues, and the public was both uninformed and unwilling to accept any solution that cut benefits or raised taxes. In the debt ceiling crisis of 2011, it was not just the liberal public sphere that largely failed, but U.S. democracy itself.

References

Asen, R. (2009). Ideology, materiality, and counterpublicity: William E. Simon and the rise of a conservative counterintelligentsIa. *Quarterly Journal of Speech, 95*, 263–288.

Bartlett, B. (2011, April 7). Imbalanced budget: Ryan gives wealthy a free pass. *The Fiscal Times*. Retrieved from http://www.thefiscaltimes.com/Columns/2011/04/07/Wealthy-Get-Fr

Brockriede, W. (1975). Where is argument? *Journal of the American Forensic Association, 11*, 179–182.

Calhoun, C. (Ed.). (1992). *Habermas and the public sphere*. Cambridge, MA: MIT Press.

Calmes, J. (2012, February 27). Obama's deficit dilemma. *New York Times*, p. A1.

Cohn, J. (2011, April 13). Obama makes his stand. *The New Republic*. Retrieved from http://www.newrepublic.com/blog/jonathan-cohn/96645/obama-ryan

Ferris, K. (2011, April 20). Back channels: Have a real debate, Obama vs. Ryan, on federal budget. *Philadelphia Inquirer*, p. D1.

Fisher, W. R. (1984). Narration as a human communication paradigm: The case of public moral argument. *Communication Monographs, 51*, 1–22.

Garnham, N. (1992). The media and the public sphere. In C. Calhoun (Ed.), *Habermas and the public sphere* (pp. 37–401). Cambridge, MA: MIT Press.

Goodnight, G. T. (1982). The personal, technical and public spheres of argument: A speculative inquiry into the art of public deliberation. *The Journal of the American Forensic Association, 18*, 214–227.

GOP proposes real spending cuts. (2011, April 6). *Washington Times*, p. 2.

Gronbeck, B. E. (1980). From argument to argumentation: Fifteen years of identity crises. In J. Rhodes & S. Newell (Eds.), *Proceedings of the Summer Conference on Argumentation* (pp. 8–19). Washington, DC: Speech Communication Association.

Habermas, J. (1992). Concluding remarks. In C. Calhoun (Ed.), *Habermas and the public sphere* (pp. 462–479). Cambridge, MA: MIT Press.

Hard choices on the budget [Editorial]. (2011, April 10). *Tampa Bay Times*, p. 2p.

Harwood, J. (2011, May 16). Frugality is a virtue, but politics rule the debt-limit fight. *New York Times*, p. A11.

Hulse, C. (2011, April 15). House approves Republican budget plan to cut trillions. *New York Times*, p. A1.

Kessler, G. (2011, April 6). Fact-checking the Ryan budget plan. *Washington Post*. Retrieved from http://www.washingtonpost.com/blogs/fact-checkers/post/fact-checking

Krugman, P. (2011, April 15). Who's serious now? *New York Times*, p. A27.

Madison J. (1999). *Writings*. New York, NY: Library of America.

Mann, T. E., & Ornstein, N. J. (2012). *It's even worse than it looks*. New York, NY: Basic Books.

Montgomery, L. (2011, April 15). Obama's tone confounds GOP invitees. *Washington Post*, p. A4.

A million jobs at stake. (2013, February 3). *New York Times*, p. A18.

Obama, B. (2011, April 13). Remarks by the President on fiscal policy. Retrieved from http://Whitehouse.gov

Pew Research Center. (2010, January 28). Public knowledge: Senate legislative process a mystery to many. Retrieved from http://pewresearch.org

Pew Research Center. (2011, April 12). The deficit debate: Where the public stands. Retrieved from http://pewresearch.org

Phillips, K. (1996). The space of public dissension: Reconsidering the public sphere. *Communication Monographs, 63,* 231–248,

Rescher, N. (1977). *Dialectics: A controversy-oriented approach to the theory of knowledge.* Albany: State University of New York Press.

Rowland, R. C. (2005). A liberal theory of the public sphere. In C. A. Willard (Ed.), *Critical Problems in Argumentation* (pp. 281–287). Washington, DC: National Communication Association.

Rowland, R. C. (2012). The battle for health care reform and the liberal public sphere. In F. H. van Eemeren & B. Garssen (Eds.), *Exploring Argumentative Contexts* (pp. 269–288). Amsterdam, NL: John Benjamin.

Rowland, R. C. (2013). The debt ceiling and the liberal public sphere. In D. Mohammed & M. Lewi ski (Eds.), *Virtues of Argumentation: Proceedings of the 10th International Conference of the Ontario Society for the Study of Argumentation.* Windsor: Ontario Society for the Study of Argumentation.

Rucker, P., & Fahrenthold, D. A. (2011, April 5). *Washington Post,* p. A5.

Ryan, P. (2011, April 5). *The path to prosperity.* Retrieved from http://budget.GOP.gov

Scheiber, N. (2011). *The escape artists: How Obama's team fumbled the recovery.* New York, NY: Simon & Schuster.

Shear, M. D. (2011, April 14). Obama speech defends liberal principles. *New York Times.* Retrieved from http://thecaucus.blogs.nytimes.com/2011/04/14/obama-speech-defends

Wenzel, J. (1980). Perspectives on argument. In J. Rhodes & S. Newell (Eds.), *Proceedings of the Summer Conference on Argumentation* (pp. 112–133). Washington, D.C.: Speech Communication Association.

Wolf, R. (2011, April 5). House GOP fiscal plan unveiled to slice off $4.4 T; Many cuts from health benefits, Social Security. *USA Today,* p. 8A.

Woodward, B. (2012). *The price of politics.* New York, NY: Simon & Schuster.

5

ARGUMENTATION FROM EXPERT OPINION IN THE 2011 U.S. DEBT CEILING DEBATE

Jean H. M. Wagemans

UNIVERSITY OF AMSTERDAM, THE NETHERLANDS

On July 29, 2011, within the broader context of the U.S. debt ceiling debate, Republican Representative John Boehner (R-OH, 2011c) made the following remark regarding the Budget Control Act of 2011:

> With this bill, I think we're keeping our promise to the American people that we will cut spending by more than the increase in the debt limit. The Congressional Budget Office has certified this common-sense standard, and it has been backed by more than 150 distinguished economists from across the country.
>
> *(para. 2)*

Viewed from the perspective of argumentation theory, Boehner defended his standpoint by means of *argumentation from expert opinion*. In saying that the idea to "cut spending by more than the increase in the debt limit" had been backed by "more than 150 distinguished economists from across the country," he tried to render the standpoint (more) acceptable, claiming that it was held or asserted by an intellectually trustworthy source.

A common problem concerning the evaluation of argumentation from expert opinion is that someone who is not an expert in the relevant field will not be able to judge the acceptability of the standpoint in a direct way (i.e., on the basis of the internal criteria belonging to the field of expertise at issue). This does not mean, however, that the acceptability of a standpoint supported by argumentation from expert opinion cannot be judged at all. When there is no possibility of verifying directly what the expert claims to know, the assessment of argumentation from expert opinion may take place on the basis of external criteria (Goodwin, 2011).

In this essay, I present an instrument for the assessment of argumentation from expert opinion that is based on such external criteria and illustrate its use by reconstructing passages from the 2011 U.S. debt ceiling debate. Because the instrument is founded on pragma-dialectical insights regarding the reconstruction of argumentative discourse, I begin with some of the starting points of the pragma-dialectical approach. More particularly, I explain how elements that are implicit in the actual discourse, but relevant to its evaluation, can be reconstructed in a theoretically justified way. I then discuss the general characteristics of argumentation from expert opinion and present the argumentative pattern involved. Finally,

I illustrate how the pattern is used as an assessment instrument by reconstructing some concrete examples of argumentation from expert opinion put forward in the 2011 U.S. debt ceiling debate.

Reconstructing Implicit Elements of Argumentative Discourse

When providing a reconstruction of concrete cases of argumentation from expert opinion, the analyst may be confronted with the problem that certain elements of the argumentation are implicit in the actual discourse. Rather than adding these elements on subjective grounds, the analyst should be able to find and justify them on the basis of theoretical considerations. Within the pragma-dialectical approach to argumentation, the addition of implicit elements takes place on the basis of a combination of pragmatic insights regarding the use of language and dialectical insights regarding the aim, structure, and regulation of argumentative exchanges (see van Eemeren & Grootendorst, 2004 for an explanation of the pragma-dialectical approach; van Eemeren, Garssen, & Wagemans, 2011 for an illustration of the pragma-dialectical method of analysis and evaluation; Snoeck Henkemans, in press for an exposition of the pragmatic starting points of pragma-dialectics; and Wagemans, 2010 for an exposition of its dialectical starting points).

The pragma-dialectical reconstruction of argumentative discourse is dialectical in the sense that it takes place in terms of an idealized discussion procedure called the *model of a critical discussion*. Depending on the quality of the discourse at hand, the reconstruction of the discourse in terms of the model may involve several so-called *dialectical* transformations. From a systematic point of view, four such transformations can be carried out: (1) *deletion*: elements of the discourse that are irrelevant to the evaluation are left out; (2) *addition*: elements that are relevant but have remained implicit in the discourse are made explicit; (3) *permutation*: the order of the elements is brought in line with an idealized discussion procedure; and (4) *substitution*: the formulation of the elements is standardized and made more precise.

Of the four dialectical transformations, the *addition* transformation is related to the problem of reconstructing implicit elements of argumentative discourse. The addition transformation can be justified by referring to pragmatic insights regarding the doxastic commitments of language users involved in argumentative exchanges. The commitments are derived from some of the so-called *correctness conditions* for performing the speech act of putting forward a standpoint and those for performing the speech act of putting forward an argument. Starting from the assumption that an arguer who puts forward an argument does so in order to overcome the real or anticipated doubt of the addressee regarding the acceptability of the standpoint, the correctness conditions for performing the speech acts involved include the following:

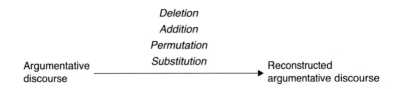

Figure 5.1 Dialectical transformations of argumentative discourse

Correctness conditions for putting forward a standpoint

(I)   The arguer believes that the addressee does not already deem the standpoint acceptable (otherwise, the arguer would perform a superfluous act).

(II) The arguer believes that the propositional content of the standpoint is acceptable (otherwise, the arguer would perform an insincere act).

Correctness conditions for putting forward an argument

(I)   The arguer believes that the argument is acceptable (otherwise, the arguer would perform an insincere act).

(II) The arguer believes that the argument renders the standpoint acceptable (otherwise, the arguer would perform a pointless act).

From these conditions it can be derived that the arguer is committed, not only to the *propositional content* of the standpoint and the argument, but also to the *justificatory force* of the argument (i.e., the belief that the argument renders the standpoint acceptable). The commitment regarding the propositional content of the standpoint and that of the argument can be expressed in terms of a categorical proposition, while the commitment regarding the justificatory force of the argument can be expressed in terms of a hypothetical proposition that has the argument as the antecedent and the standpoint as the consequent. I do not consider the cases in which the propositional content of the standpoint and/or the argument can be reconstructed in terms of a hypothetical proposition. I also refrain from discussing complications concerning the formulation of the hypothetical proposition that expresses the commitment of the arguer regarding the justificatory force of the argument.

In practice, arguers do not always put forward their standpoint and argumentation in a fully explicit way. The account of the correctness conditions (and the related commitments) has a heuristic function insofar as it enables the analyst to find out which elements in the discourse remained implicit, but also has a justificatory function in the sense that it enables the analyst to provide a theoretically motivated reconstruction of the implicit elements of the discourse. When applying these insights to, for example, feminist writer Chloe Angyal's tweet "Murray is indeed the first Brit to win Wimbledon in 77 years unless you think women are people," the analyst may arrive at the following reconstruction (the standpoint is numbered 1, the propositional content of the argument is numbered 1.1, the justificatory force of the argument is numbered 1.1', and the added elements are put in between brackets):

(1)   (Murray is not the first Brit to win Wimbledon in 77 years)
(1.1) (You think women are people)
1.1' If you think women are people, Murray is not the first Brit to win Wimbledon in 77 years

The reconstruction can be justified by explaining that "A unless B" can be substituted by "If B, then not A" and by claiming that this hypothetical proposition expresses the justificatory force of the argument involved.

Arguers may also put forward arguments in support of other arguments. Within the pragma-dialectical approach, such arguments are called *subordinative* arguments. Because the addressee may call into question the propositional content as well as the justificatory force of the main argument, the arguer may put forward subordinative arguments in support of either of the two elements.

As with any argument, the commitments regarding the propositional content and the justificatory force of subordinative arguments can be expressed in terms of a categorical proposition and a hypothetical proposition respectively. The reconstructed elements of the discourse are numbered accordingly (e.g., the proposition expressing the justificatory force of the subordinative argument supporting the propositional content of the main argument is numbered 1.1.1′).

Argumentation from Expert Opinion

Before turning to the actual analysis of some examples of argumentation from expert opinion, I provide a short description of the main characteristics of the type of argumentation based on Wagemans (2011) and Snoeck Henkemans and Wagemans (2012), with some modifications and additional observations.

Whenever an arguer supports her or his standpoint by claiming that the opinion in the standpoint is held or asserted by a trustworthy source, the argumentation can be labeled as *argumentation from authority*. Depending on the degree of detail required, the argumentation may be further specified on the basis of the type of authority involved. As a first step, I propose a distinction between *argumentation from quantitative authority* and *argumentation from qualitative authority*. The distinction is inspired by Aristotle's (1995) definition of a reputable opinion (*endoxon*): "those opinions are reputable which are accepted by everyone or by the majority or by the wise – i.e. by all, or by the majority, or by the most notable and reputable of them" (*Topica* 100b20–25).

The label *argumentation from quantitative authority* applies when the arguer tries to render the standpoint acceptable by claiming that it is held or asserted by a (large) number of people. Depending on their approach to fallacies, scholars may consider this type of argumentation to be fallacious by nature, calling it *argumentum ad populum*, *mob appeal*, or *populist fallacy*.

The label *argumentation from qualitative authority* applies when the arguer tries to render the standpoint acceptable by claiming that it is held or asserted by a qualified source of some kind. This variant can be further divided into subtypes by using the specific type of qualification as a name for the argumentation involved (e.g., *argumentation from invested opinion*, *argumentation from professional expert opinion*, *argumentation from experiential expert opinion*). Depending on their

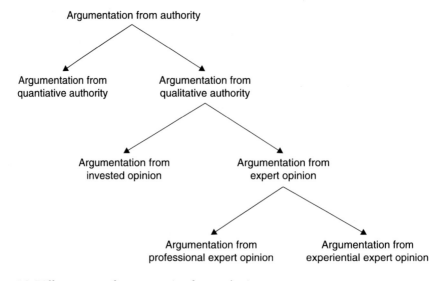

Figure 5.2 Different types of argumentation from authority

approach to fallacies, scholars may refer to the fallacious counterparts of one or more of these subtypes of argumentation from qualitative authority with the term *argumentum ad verecundiam, snob appeal,* or *appeal to inappropriate authority.*

Having placed argumentation from expert opinion in the broader context of argumentation from authority, I now concentrate on the more specific characteristics of the type of argumentation by providing an argumentative pattern that consists of a numbered representation of the standpoint, the main argument, and the subordinative arguments involved.

In technical terms, with O denoting an opinion and E denoting an expert, argumentation from expert opinion is put forward in support of the standpoint "Opinion O is true (or acceptable)" and has as a main argument "Opinion O is held by expert E." As explained in the previous section, the arguer is not only committed to the propositional content of the main argument, but also to its justificatory force, which latter commitment can be expressed in terms of a hypothetical proposition having the argument as an antecedent and the standpoint as a consequent. In the case of argumentation from expert opinion, the hypothetical proposition can be formulated as follows: "If opinion O is asserted by expert E, then opinion O is true (or acceptable)." Further, because the addressee of the argumentation may call into question both the propositional content and the justificatory force of the main argument, the arguer may put forward subordinative arguments in support of both elements. As to the first element, several constituents of the proposition may be doubted by the addressee (e.g., whether E is really an expert in the relevant field and whether E really asserted O and not something else). As to the second element, several factors may have an influence on the justificatory force of the argument (e.g., whether E voiced O from her or his own expertise rather than from her or his personal interest, whether E is able to defend O in a way different from referring to expertise, and whether experts in the same field agree as to the truth or acceptability of O).

All in all, a fully explicit pattern of argumentation from expert opinion consists of the following elements:

1   Opinion O is true (or acceptable)
1.1 Opinion O is asserted by expert E

     1.1.1a   E really is an expert in the relevant field
     1.1.1b   E really asserted O

1.1' If opinion O is asserted by expert E, then opinion O is true (or acceptable)

     1.1'.1a   E did not voice O from his personal interest
     1.1'.1b   E is able to defend O without referring to his expertise
     1.1'.1c   O is consistent with what other (types of) experts assert

Of course, whenever this is necessary for the purpose of providing a reconstruction of the discourse at hand, other elements (e.g., the justificatory force of the subordinative arguments or arguments in support of subordinative arguments) may be added to the reconstruction on the basis of the theoretical considerations expounded in the previous section. On the basis of the pattern, I will now analyze a number of examples of argumentation from expert opinion taken from the 2011 U.S. debt ceiling debate.

Analysis of Examples Taken from the 2011 U.S. Debt Ceiling Debate

The argumentative pattern presented in the previous section can first of all be used in order to reconstruct concrete cases of argumentation from expert opinion. Regarding the case mentioned in the beginning of the paper, for example, the argumentative pattern of argumentation from expert opinion enables the analyst to identify which arguments and subarguments Boehner (2011c) put forth in support of his standpoint that it is a good idea to "cut spending by more than the increase in the debt limit." Because the main argument is that the policy has been backed by "more than 150 distinguished economists from across the country," Boehner may be assumed to have anticipated two types of criticisms that are related to argumentation from expert opinion. By saying that his source consists of "distinguished economists," he tried to address potential doubt about the qualification of the source as experts in the relevant field. And by saying that the experts are "more than 150" in number and that they are "from across the country," he implied that a representative sample of experts agrees on the matter – representative both in terms of number and geographical distribution. According to this reconstruction, Boehner was committed to the following elements from the pattern:

1   Cutting spending by more than the increase in the debt limit is a sound policy
1.1   It has been backed by more than 150 distinguished economists from across the country
1.1.1a   The experts are distinguished economists
(1.1′)   (If a policy is backed by experts, then it is a sound policy)
1.1′.1c The experts are 150 in number and they are from across the country

In addition to the help it provides in reconstruction, the pattern is useful for identifying potential criticisms of specific instantiations of argumentation from expert opinion. In the argumentation reconstructed above, for example, the arguer does not address potential doubt regarding the content of the expert opinion. In which source exactly is it stated that the experts in question believe that cutting spending by more than the increase in the debt limit is a good idea? Neither does the arguer anticipate criticism regarding the expert opinion being potentially biased by personal interest. What if it is easy to find 150 economists from across the country who all vote for the Republican party?

In another passage, dated June 2, 2011, Boehner (2011a) was clearer about the source of the expert opinion he referred to in his argumentation, but left out other aspects of the argumentation:

> I have released a statement signed by more than 150 economists who agree that, to help create jobs, any debt limit increase must be met by an even larger spending decrease. Increasing the debt limit without spending cuts and reforms would send the message to our job creators that we're just not serious about stopping the spending addiction going on here in Washington.
>
> *(para. 4)*

On the basis of the pattern, we may now assume that Boehner anticipated doubt with regard to the source of the expert opinion (he does mention element 1.1.1b). Also, by specifying the elements of the pattern that Boehner omitted to address, we may identify potential criticisms of his argumentation.

In yet another passage, dated July 15, 2011, Boehner (2011b) mentioned two authorities that can be identified as experts on the matter, but left their opinion implicit:

> As Moody's and Standard & Poor's have signaled this week, our nation's economy is literally begging for Washington to take meaningful action to cut spending and reduce the deficit. It is absurd and self-destructive to continue dumping taxpayer

money into a "stimulus" philosophy that has consistently failed to support private-sector job creation in our country.

(para. 2)

A comparison of the elements in this passage with the standard elements of the pattern of argumentation from expert opinion shows that, in this case, there is no further support for the claim that the experts really asserted the opinion defended in the standpoint. On the basis of the reconstruction, which I will not carry out in detail here, one might question whether the opinion mentioned in the standpoint corresponds with the one mentioned in the argument.

Conclusion

Summarizing, the pattern of argumentation from expert opinion as presented in this essay can first of all be used in order to provide a reconstruction of concrete argumentative discourse in which a standpoint is defended by referring to an intellectually trustworthy source. The pattern may not only help the analyst to determine which standard elements of the argumentation have been provided in the specific case, but also to identify implicit elements in the discourse and justify the reconstruction of these elements on the basis of theoretical considerations.

Second, the pattern can be used in order to find out which criticisms are addressed by the arguer (and which criticisms may still be raised by her or his opponents). As is clear from the pattern, some subordinative arguments are assumed to be aimed at taking away the (possible) doubt with respect to the person referred to being a real expert in the relevant field and the accuracy of the representation of the person's opinion. Other subordinative arguments are assumed to be aimed at taking away the (possible) doubt regarding the personal reliability of the expert, the expert's ability to provide further evidence for the acceptability of the opinion, and the consistency of the opinion with what other experts in the field (or even other types of experts) assert.

As to the 2011 U.S. debt ceiling debate, the pattern of argumentation based on expert opinion that I presented in this essay may count as an illustration of how the pragma-dialectical approach to argumentation can be used for analyzing and evaluating the argumentative aspects of the debate. In this particular case, the pragma-dialectical approach may be used (1) to reconstruct instantiations of argumentation from expert opinion within the debate and (2) to identify the specific ways in which such argumentation can be criticized.

The importance of developing a tool for the assessment of argumentative aspects of political debates, in particular when they contain argumentation from expert opinion, derives from the fact that the acceptability of standpoints supported by such argumentation, as I mentioned in the beginning of the paper, can only be judged by people who are an expert in the relevant field, which most voters (and politicians) are not.

References

Aristotle, (1995). *The complete works of Aristotle* (Vols. 1–2, Revised Oxford Translation, J. Barnes, [Ed.], 6th printing, with corrections). Princeton, NJ: Princeton University Press.

Boehner, J. (2011a, June 2). Congressman Boehner: To help create jobs, GOP ready to act on plan ensuring spending cuts exceed debt limit hike. Retrieved from http://boehner.house.gov/news/documentprint.aspx?DocumentID=244439

Boehner, J. (2011b, July 15). Congressman Boehner responds to President Obama's press conference. Retrieved from http://boehner.house.gov/news/documentprint.aspx?DocumentID=252163

Boehner, J. (2011c, July 29). Congressman Boehner remarks on the House floor re: the GOP Budget Control Act of 2011. Retrieved from http://boehner.house.gov/news/documentprint.aspx? DocumentID=254536

van Eemeren, F. H., & Grootendorst, R. (2004). *A systematic theory of argumentation: The pragma-dialectical approach*. Cambridge, UK: Cambridge University Press.

van Eemeren, F. H., Garssen, B. J., & Wagemans, J. H. M. (2011). The pragma-dialectical method of analysis and evaluation. In R. C. Rowland (Ed.), *Reasoned Argument and Social Change: Selected Papers from the 17th Biennial Conference on Argumentation* (pp. 25–47). Washington, D.C.: National Communication Association.

Goodwin, J. (2011). Accounting for the appeal to the authority of experts. *Argumentation, 25,* 285–296.

Snoeck Henkemans, A. F. (in press). Speech act theory and the study of argumentation. In F. H. van Eemeren, K. Budzynska, & M. Koszowy (Eds.), *Pragmatics and dialectics of argument* [Special issue of *Studies in Logic, Grammar, and Rhetoric*].

Snoeck Henkemans, A. F., & Wagemans, J. H. M. (2012, June 1–2). The reasonableness of argumentation from expert opinion in medical discussions: Institutional safeguards for the quality of shared decision making. In J. Goodwin (Ed.), *Between Scientists & Citizens: Proceedings of a Conference at Iowa State University* (pp. 345–354). Ames, IA: Great Plains Society for the Study of Argumentation.

Wagemans, J. H. M. (2010). Dialectics and pragmatics. *Cogency, 2*(1), 95–110.

Wagemans, J. H. M. (2011). The assessment of argumentation from expert opinion. *Argumentation, 25,* 329–339.

6

ARGUING FOR EMPTINESS

Community in the debate over rhetoric and love

Matthew Bost

WILLAMETTE UNIVERSITY, USA
MCGEE OUTSTANDING GRADUATE STUDENT PAPER AWARD WINNER

"Since only lovers risk selves, only lovers can grow" (Brockriede, 1972, p. 10); this much of Wayne Brockriede's essay, "Arguers as Lovers," remains a relevant provocation for scholars of argument. Brockriede (1972) made an ethical distinction between coercive and manipulative arguers relying on "superior power" (p. 2) over the other parties to an argument and willing to use deceit and manipulation to attain their goals, and an ideal arguer as lover who "aims" at "power parity" (p. 7) between the parties in a given situation. Brockriede's discussion highlights the vulnerability and subjective risk provoked by love and links it to philosophical questions of the relationship between self and other in ways that resonate with more recent discussions of these topics as central concerns for scholars of argumentation and rhetoric (e.g., Gehrke, 2009). In what follows, I argue that rethinking the concept of love in conjunction with that of community allows an account of the "risk" gestured at in Brockriede's article. This rethinking contributes to theories of alterity ethics within argumentation and rhetoric.

Since "Arguers as Lovers" was written, the ethical themes it raises have been significantly critiqued. One productive line of scholarship (Palczewski, 1997) drew out the gender/sex-bias implicit in Brockriede's article, arguing that his focus on the intent of the *arguer* to manipulate or engage in dialogue (rather than the co-arguer's reception of the argument as coercive or egalitarian) prevents any truly ethical argumentative exchange, and installs an implicitly masculine subject as the one doing the arguing. In a parallel move, Sonja Foss and Cindy Griffin (1995), following the work of Sally Miller Gearhart (1979), have taken up the insights of radical feminism to offer a view of persuasive models of communication as implicated in patriarchal violence and to call for an alternative to persuasion in a concept of invitation that assumes "equality, immanent value and respect for others" as ethical guidelines and in which rhetors offer their perspectives "without seeking adherence or pronouncing judgments" (p. 15). This perspective, in turn, has been challenged by a number of scholars (Dow, 1995; Fixmer & Wood, 1995). Most germane in the present context is Nina Lozano-Reich and Dana Cloud's (2009) argument that a focus on invitation is problematic because it "assumes a shared interest between oppressors and oppressed" (p. 221) and ignores the degree to which invitations, especially invitations to offer one's perspective without critiquing others', are frequently tools to disempower the less powerful parties involved in an argument.

The above are pressing challenges to Brockriede's argument. In the first place, accounts of argument as love which place the ethical onus on a self-contained agent who decides whether to treat the other party in good faith fall prey to a fallacy of intention that does not truly admit the alterity of the other parties to the situation, perpetuating an implicitly gendered/sexed ethical framework. Additionally, at a larger level, attitudes of openness have their own risks – personal hurt, political disempowerment, and a potentially tenuous grasp of the unequal power relations inherent in an argumentative situation. Both perspectives serve to indict a theory of argument as risk of self. Two more recent engagements with love in rhetorical studies, to which I will now briefly turn, have tried to reestablish love's utility as a political concept in light of these critiques.

Between Fantasy and Techne

Lovers risk selves, but what if the self risked is a fiction? Joshua Gunn (2008) argued that rhetoric should rethink love not around the success of intersubjective communication, but as its (inevitable) failure. Drawing on the psychoanalytic theory of Jacques Lacan, Gunn (2008) argued that "all forms of love" are "fundamentally illusory" (p. 136). This does not mean that love is a useless concept; quite the contrary. In Lacan's logic, love is so important because (unlike the imaginary fantasy of identification with another person) love names the failure of people's intersubjective relationships, insisting through "endless symbolic reminders" that "I am not you, and you are not me" and that any truly intersubjective relationship is impossible (Gunn, 2008, p. 136). This perspective takes invitational rhetoric to task for attempting to "reverse [the] default alienation" characteristic of the human condition (the fact that all identification presumes a corresponding division) in favor of a mythical "pre-linguistic relatability" (Gunn, 2008, p. 148).

Gunn's treatment of love shifts the ground of Brockriede's project. "Arguers as Lovers" relies on the claim that an ethical argument constitutes a "genuine interaction" for which adherence to claims is secured through "free assent" (Brockriede, 1972, pp. 9–10). Implicitly, then, Brockriede participated in the fantasy of pure understanding or identification that Gunn described. A psychoanalytic account of love extends critiques of love or vulnerability as argumentative paradigms complicit with social inequality into an account that sees communicative equality itself as a fantasy. It also provides one way to rehabilitate these paradigms: Love is a fantasy, but one that is potentially constitutive of subjectivity. The reason to embrace "rhetoric's love" lies not in an ideal of fully human or equal communication, but in the work that the fiction of love can do to prop up the risky process of engaging with an Other which can never be known or understood (Gunn, 2008, p. 148). On this account, and in line with some of the earliest readings of Brockriede's essay, love is a tool for effecting the "untiring stretch toward the other" (Corder, 1985, p. 26) necessary for an ethical response to alterity, with argument being one of the primary spaces in which the fiction of this process is created and sustained.

Addressing the question of social change also leads to the most serious objections to Gunn's account. The injunction to embrace the joy that deceit brings presents the same gamble that any irony does: a distinction between a group who is aware of the ironic move and a group who is not (and who is thus duped in quite a different sense than the Lacanian one of affirming love despite/because of its impossibility), once again raising the specter of unequal power relations in the potentially more insidious form of one who knows love is a fiction, but cynically exploits it. Assuming everyone is in on the joke, arguably we all become cynics, performing love even as we recognize its hollow nature. In either case, an ironic affirmation of kitschy, "false" love (Gunn, 2009, p. 149) seems ill-suited to addressing the inequalities of collective power that Lozano-Reich and Cloud discussed, as well as the more specific concern that those asked to assume the risks involved in love reflect gendered/sexed inequalities of power.

Another more recent rhetorical discussion of love attempts to serve as a corrective to these arguable pitfalls. Taking as a departure the concept of multitude advocated most famously by Michael Hardt and Antonio Negri (2005), J. David Cisneros and Eric Jenkins (2012) and, implicitly, Ronald Walter Greene (2010), advanced a theory of love as the substrate of a collective political practice founded upon living labor. This line of thought remains to be expanded upon within rhetorical and argumentation studies, but Negri (2005) offered a succinct definition of love as "the ontological power that constructs being" (p. 210) and which produces the common – a set of capacities and common concerns which form the basis, in Negri's view, of an emancipatory politics. For Negri (2005), love is like a needle pulling common threads through the chaotic tapestry of a constantly changing being, creating "tools, languages and politics" (p. 211) which knit experiences and bodies together in common action. Love is eminently political; the joyful affects of working and living together with others that it generates produce "militancy" against relations of power that would subordinate others and stifle love (Negri, 2005, p. 219). In a mirror to the critique of unmediated or successful communication offered by psychoanalysis, the motor of love is history; it is practiced, not so that it might be completed, but so that it might produce novel ways of living and interacting with others in an ongoing process of experimentation and negotiation.

This approach to love, like Gunn's, presents both possibilities and problems for scholars of argument. On the one hand, Negri's account provides a clearer way to describe where exactly argument fits into rhetorical theories of love. A variety of different technologies of deliberation (Greene, 1998) are produced by love and in turn produce it (along with other politically useful affects), serving to further projects of collective empowerment and agency. This shifts the questions Gunn asked even further onto the terrain of politics, better showing how the process of love (fictional or not) is produced through language and common *techne* and what kinds of social structures it allows to emerge. On the other hand, Negri's (2005) potentially utopian framing of a specifically Christian love as the "location" of politics (p. 204) and the instrumental nature of his theory run the risk of uncritically valorizing identification in the ways that Gunn and Lozano-Reich and Cloud indict. If "all you need is love" is a viable reading of Negri's philosophy, then it is questionable whether it avoids charges of mysticism and utopianism. In order to bypass such charges (and prove its relevance to scholars of argument), the theory Negri offers needs to better account for what the various technologies he described look like and how they work politically. It also needs to be connected to the more robust philosophies of the arguing subject provided in Brockriede's and Gunn's work.

Love and Community

The remainder of this essay begins these tasks through recourse to the concept of community. It is widely assumed that the parties to an argument share some manner of common ground, whether common values or a worldview, the possession of reason by all parties, the basic fact of being human, or some other crucial element. With emphasis on the common, rather than the ground, it seems worth asking what kind of community is suggested by rhetorical discussions of love, and how this community might produce a theory of ethical argument.

Jean-Luc Nancy's philosophy is a useful starting point here. Nancy (2001) took the tension between ironic celebration and skepticism offered in a Lacanian account of love and turns it into an ethical principle. If the exchange in love – the idea that I can give myself fully to another and they to me – is a fiction, then the way out is neither to ironically affirm the fiction nor to despair of its fictional nature, but to affirm fiction and its undoing as parts of a larger productive process. Nancy (2001) wrote that, instead of sharing the symbolic tokens of a continual failure (which is in turn repaired with symbolic thread), love means attempting to embrace our loss for words at its encounter as an opening on a communal outside, and thus "to share" the outside itself.

This idea of shared emptiness lead Nancy to the question of community. In an attempt to recover community from its fruits in fascism and capitalist exploitation, Nancy (2001) rejected the idea of a shared substance between a community's members, or even a shared political project that might one day be complete. Community is still a sharing – but it is a sharing of "the absence of common being," existing in tension between the necessary re-sedimentation of the illusion of perfect communication (or perfect communion), and people's knowledge that such communication is not possible. Nancy's reading thus emerges as a re-thinking of Brockriede's risk of self that dispenses with the idea of risk as a single act committed by one or another party to an argument in favor of risk as an infinitive process – to risk – whereby the ethics lies in the affirmation of commonality as well as irreducible difference, both continually produced.

If community is productive, then of what is it productive? Psychoanalysis would say symbols, a concatenation of substitutes for an originary lack, but this reading, as much as Nancy (2001) might bear it out in some respects, still leaves the same dilemma – irony or cynicism – as before. Adding Negri's (2005) discussion of love to an idea of community as a sharing of nothing provides another, more affirmative answer. Negri argued that love produces tools, the languages and politics of shared collective action. While agreeing that this is certainly the case, Nancy's framework, and that of those who take him as a point of reference, suggests a more fundamental answer, of which these various *techne* are expressions. One risks oneself, without going all in or, at the risk of stretching the metaphor, ever winning the game. The point, instead, is to keep the game going. Love in the context of community building produces affects – trust and a general willingness to gamble on the reciprocal response of whatever Other is in question. In light of Nancy's (1991) caveat that a community founded on a shared project tends to flirt with fascism and exclusionary violence (p. 13), this version of the concept would rather see the process of sharing he described as generative of common languages and political technologies. In sum, what practicing love as community produces is what Roberto Esposito (2010), following Nancy, has called a common *munus* (p. 4): collective obligation, cemented by a repertoire of shared passions, that is the fabric of an ethical relationship with others.

Conclusion

Having sketched the ways in which rhetorical theories of love may productively converse with a theory of community, it remains to outline this conversation's implications for theories of argument. Darren Hicks and Lenore Langsdorf (1999) offered a critique of proceduralist theories of argument that, like Brockriede, theorized the construction of arguing subjects. They critiqued proceduralism (and implicitly, less nuanced precursors that give place to universal reason or shared meaning as foundations of argument), claiming that even the most apparently neutral theory of argument assumes "de facto substantive-ethical commitments" (p. 141) which act to enable or bar participation in a given argumentative situation. Hicks and Langsdorf's framework for these commitments revolves primarily around the form taken by the statements that constitute a given argument, perceptions about the identities of those arguing, and the *fora* in which arguments take place, which leads to a focus on the power relations inherent in various argumentative exchanges. They described an argumentative paradigm that is pervasive (especially in liberal democracy) and that would emphatically (and sometimes violently) exclude the paradigm of community offered here. Reworked in light of the points offered so far, their framework leads to an alternate question: What substantive ethical commitments *should* attend the step of risking ourselves (as opposed to adopting a defensive or confrontational attitude) in interactions with others? Granting that the tools of argument can be deployed to confront other perspectives without lowering our own affective and rhetorical defenses, and that they may also be deployed without such defenses in a spirit closer to that of Nancy's communal sharing, are there situations where community (as opposed to confrontation) is preferable? How might this sharing be articulated as a political tool in a way that also acknowledges its potential for misuse?

Using Hicks and Langsdorf as a starting point, this question may be fleshed out in three main ways. First, an ethics of argument based on love would not evaluate participants on the conformity of their claims to a procedural ideal. Rather than taking the form or idiom of a statement as a marker of legitimacy, it would instead inquire into the statement's context as a marker of power or empowerment, weapon or olive branch. Instead of being a marker of individual agency, statements (at least ethical ones) would be reframed as building blocks of collective agency which would be sustained by and exceed any given set of statements.

Second, taking love as a starting point allows us to rethink rhetorics of confrontation. Given the version of the concept I have proposed, it does us no good, as Brockriede (1972) did, to describe unethical argument in the context of manipulative or deceitful love. Rather, the full repertoire of devices of confrontation and struggle remain appropriate. What such a shift would do is allow an ethics of argument as confrontation, tempered with questions about how groups agitating for social change might deploy argument from within in mutually empowering ways even as confrontation remains an option for rhetorical defense from external oppression.

Third, and finally, such a concept would replace an ethical standard based on identity with one rooted in community. To return to Brockriede one final time, love is not a position consciously taken by one or more parties to an argument. Rather, the risk of self he described names a decision to enter into a larger process of collective composition in which an initial ethical gamble produces narratives, technologies, and other formal routines of argument which ideally, in their turn, generate further relations of mutual empowerment. Such a perspective links the discussion of arguing subjects Brockriede offered with the recognition of those subjectivities' partial and fabricated natures and a desire to explore the various technologies that generate them. All of these components turn around a fundamental ethical imperative to realize, as bell hooks (2004) wrote, that "life is held in common", that "we exist because we exchange, because we move the gift" (p. 244), and that such exchange forms a valuable ethical and political resource.

References

Brockriede, W. (1972). Arguers as lovers. *Philosophy and Rhetoric, 5*(1), 1–11.

Cisneros, J. D., & Jenkins, E. (2012, May). *Love and rhetoric: A 'dear Josh' letter.* Paper presented at the Rhetoric Society of America Biennial Conference, Philadelphia, PA.

Corder, J. (1985). Argument as emergence: Rhetoric as love. *Rhetoric Review, 4*(1), 16–32.

Esposito, R. (2010). *Communitas: The origin and destiny of community* (T. Campbell, trans.). Palo Alto, CA: Stanford University Press.

Foss, S. K., & Griffin, C. L. (1995). Beyond persuasion: A proposal for an invitational rhetoric. *Communication Monographs, 62*, 2–18.

Gearhart, S. M. (1979). The womanization of rhetoric. *Women's Studies International Quarterly, 2,* 195–201.

Greene, R. W. (1998). Another materialist rhetoric. *Critical Studies in Mass Communication, 15,* 21–41.

Greene, R. W. (2006). Orator communist. *Philosophy and Rhetoric, 39*(1), 85–95.

Gunn, J. (2008). For the love of rhetoric, with continual reference to Kenny and Dolly. *Quarterly Journal of Speech, 94*(2), 131–155.

Hardt, M., & Negri, A. (2005). *Multitude: War and democracy in the age of empire.* New York, NY: Penguin Books.

Hicks, D., & Langsdorf, L. (1999). Regulating disagreement, constituting participants: a critique of proceduralist theories of democracy. *Argumentation, 13*(2), 139–160.

hooks, b. (2004). *Communion: The female search for love.* New York, NY: HarperCollins.

Lozano-Reich, N., & Cloud, D. (2009). The uncivil tongue: Invitational rhetoric and the problem of inequality. *Western Journal of Communication, 73*(2), 220–226.

Nancy, J-L. (1991). *The inoperative community* (Christopher Fysk, trans.). Minneapolis: University of Minnesota Press.

Nancy, J-L. (2001). Love and community. Roundtable Discussion at the European Graduate School. Retrieved from http://www.egs.edu/faculty/jean-luc-nancy/articles/love-and-community/

Negri, A. (2005). *Time for revolution* (M. Mandarini, trans.). London: Verso Books.

Palczewski, C. (1997). Bodies that argue: Power difference and argument. In J. Klumpp (Ed.), *Argument in a Time of Change: Definitions, Frameworks and Critiques* (pp. 79–84). Annandale, VA: National Communication Association.

7

THE WILLING CHOICE OF FARM LABOR IN THE UFW "TAKE OUR JOBS" CAMPAIGN

Lisa A. Flores

UNIVERSITY OF COLORADO, USA

"Take our Jobs, Please!" So announced the United Farm Workers (UFW) in their 2010 campaign inviting U.S. citizens to "Take Our Jobs." With a promise to provide training and job placement assistance for interested "American" applicants for jobs in the nation's fields, the UFW's "Take Our Jobs" (TOJ) campaign (2010) challenged people to face a truth: "Agriculture in the United States is dependent on an immigrant workforce." Interested applicants could enter their contact information on the campaign homepage, just below the statement "I want to be a farm worker." Situated explicitly by the UFW (2010) as emphasizing "the need for reforms without which the domestic agricultural industry could be crippled," the TOJ campaign was designed to promote the AgJobs bill, which would have revised the nation's temporary agricultural worker program (H–2A) to provide greater protection and greater access to legal residency status for undocumented agricultural workers. In its infancy, the TOJ campaign received some media attention, likely prompted by its collaboration with Stephen Colbert who featured UFW President Arturo Rodriguez on the *Colbert Report*. In both the design of the campaign and in its collaboration with Colbert, the TOJ campaign relies on irony and satire in its attempt to produce legislative change.

I turn to the mediated coverage of the campaign for the lessons it offers rhetoric and argument scholars interested in immigrant activism and its disruptive potentials. These disruptive possibilities demand critical attention, for in negotiations of citizen and immigrant, and arguments about border and nation, social change is possible. In this essay, I examine the discourse of the campaign and argue that its juxtaposition of absurdity and reality, combined with its shift from the border to the field, disrupt prevalent anti/immigrant discourses in ways that prevent easy association of immigrant with threat/danger/pity while still relying on essentialist notions of migrant-as-other.

Rhetorical Disruptions

Discourses of and around immigration, particularly what is labeled *illegal* immigration, remain mired in historic narratives of danger, threat, and vulnerability (Demo, 2005). These familiar narratives often are premised on well-worn tropes of immigrant danger, emergent in the pervasive and ever-available imagery of floods and swarms (Ono & Sloop, 2002). Prompting an association of chaos with immigrants, particularly those labeled *illegal aliens*, the predominant frame around immigration is menace. Indeed, Ono and Sloop (2002) noted that the metaphors surrounding immigrants animate fears of "pollution" (p. 28) in which immigrants spread disease and disaster, while Cisneros (2008) wrote that immigrants are typically cast as bringing "monumental and threatening changes" (p. 569).

However dominant, the trope of immigrant-as-threat is not complete. Instead, it remains rhetorically malleable, particularly within the hands of immigrants themselves, whose narratives of citizenship disrupt and intervene, offering what Demo (2012) named "competing frames of interpretation that reveal the distortions in media and government accounts" (p. 201). Such disruptions may be linked as well to negotiations around the centrality of the border, both as physical and ideological site. Indeed, Demo (2012) found that the "geography of immigration debates may be shifting" (p. 210). Is it possible that other, potentially disruptive, consequences might also emerge and that satiric and ironic frames might enable such argumentative interventions?

The Ironic Potential of Ridicule

In his interview with Rodriguez, Colbert (2010a) asked about the current status of the UFW, and Rodriguez replied that they are "improving the lives of farm workers." At that moment, Colbert moved immediately into recognizable character and asked, "now why do we need to improve the lives of farm workers. They're mostly *illegal* immigrants, aren't they?" With deliberate and pointed emphasis on "illegal," Colbert signaled the rhetorical problem at play – race/citizenship – as he also offered a possible space for productive discussion. Though it is tempting to view the exaggerated humor as mostly just fun, scholars argue that satire and irony have considerable rhetorical potential (Achter, 2008; Rossing, 2011).

Increasingly, scholars have turned a critical eye toward irony and satire and have argued that seemingly comedic moments can be disruptive and progressive. Noting the prevalence and circulation of highly ironic and satiric texts and rhetors (e.g., Jon Stewart, Stephen Colbert, *The Onion*, and *Saturday Night Live*), rhetorical scholars suggest that within ironic comedy is democratic potential (Hariman, 2007; Waisanen, 2009). In part, the intersections of irony, comedy, entertainment, and news prompt pause and reflection. Within these intersections lie the often exaggerated and the clearly ridiculous, the caricatured and the hyperbolic. These ironic exaggerations call into question the every day and the taken-for-granted in ways that ask, and perhaps expect, audiences to pause and reflect. They are rhetorical texts that engage audiences (Gring-Pemble & Solomon, 2003). Rossing (2011) noted that comic texts require audiences to "scramble to make sense of the world" (p. 424). This scrambling is rhetorically significant, for within it, Hariman (2007) explained, is space for "informed participation, civil speech, and rational argument on behalf of sound public policy" (p. 274). In other words, irony, satire, and comedy provide spaces of reflection and consideration in the service of democratic deliberation. Moreover, irony and satire may enable citizens to discuss productively "socially taboo" topics (Achter, 2008, p. 11). Within the TOJ campaign, the socially taboo is immigration.

The Absurd Reality of Migrant Farm Labor

When the UFW issued their call to Americans to "Take Our Jobs," they indicated their willingness to train and help place interested applicants in agricultural positions. Though its time in the spotlight was short-lived, the TOJ campaign marks a shift in mediated border discourses. Diverting abruptly from the predominant narratives of misery and blame, the campaign situates its argument for immigrant rights at the intersections of absurdity and reality.

This intersection of absurdity and reality is central to the logic of the TOJ campaign, which forwards a narrative grounded in reality that seeks to make visible the multiple truths of farm labor and, thus, of immigration politics. Reality, as the organizing logic, frames how it is that the campaign positions farm work, immigration, and labor in the United States. Rodriguez brought all three together when he discussed the impetus for the campaign: "We're really tired of all the criticism that's been launched against farm workers, immigrants, and saying that we're actually taking their jobs when in fact I don't think people really realize how difficult it is to work in the fields" (as cited in Martin, 2010). Rodriguez named various realities – that immigrants are farm workers, that immigrants don't take jobs, that U.S. citizens won't do farm work. Elsewhere, Rodriguez framed the campaign and the reality more directly: "The reality is farmworkers who are here today aren't taking American jobs away. They work in often unbearable situations. . . . I don't think there will be many takers, but the offer is being made. Let's see what happens" (as cited in Barbassa, 2010). Rodriguez made visible the narrative collapse that occurs in much anti-immigrant discourse in which immigration is framed as a problem because of its impact on jobs. The TOJ campaign reveals the absurdity of that narrative.

The emphasis on reality is evident not just in Rodriguez's framing but across the TOJ coverage. For instance, one account noted "most applicants quickly lose interest once the reality sinks in" (Smith, 2010), while another stated: "Working on farms is a much more dangerous occupation than most people realized" (mtippett, 2010). Indeed, the logic of reality is a logic that I call an *absurd reality*, for what emerges as reality throughout the campaign is also an absurdity. The naming of this absurdity occurs regularly, such as when Rodriguez is asked: "But are you seriously expecting to and willing to and hoping to train people who are unemployed . . . Are you really saying, 'I'm going to train people to do this work?' " (Martin, 2010). Elsewhere, in coverage that announced the campaign as a "dare," a reporter asked: "Because really, forget Census taking – what American *doesn't* want a back-breaking, hot, dangerous (workers get enslaved, poisoned by pesticides, and die from heat stroke) job with no health benefits, paid vacation, or even a living wage?" (Powell, 2010). As these fragments illustrate, the campaign announces, and media coverage highlights, an absurd reality constitutes farm work and immigrant farm labor: "Americans don't want to work in the fields because the conditions are horrid" (Rodriguez as cited in Powell, 2010). The absurd reality that emerges makes visible the implausibility of prominent anti-immigrant arguments, at least as related to farm labor, for it refuses the possibility that immigrants *take* jobs.

In the emphasis on the absurd, both through attention to the details of farm work and to the disparities between the numbers of interested American workers versus needed laborers, the TOJ campaign taps into the rhetorical possibilities of satire and irony. Rossing (2011) explained that conversations on race tend to "ignorantly deny racial realities or devolve into immature finger-pointing and blame games" (p. 423). Comedy, however, provides a space in which racial realities can be named differently. Indeed, the campaign attempts to do just this. Across the campaign is a consistent juxtaposition of the need for labor versus the willingness of Americans to do this labor. This juxtaposition attempts to shift the conversation about immigration and farm labor from the immigrants' alleged taking of jobs to American unwillingness to do the jobs.

The emphasis on "Americans" as unwilling is proven by the numbers of applicants: "at least half a million applicants are needed to replace the immigrant workforce" (Smith, 2010).

Directing attention to unemployment and a struggling economy, accounts juxtapose unemployment rates with interested applicants. Consider this posed question: "In an economy where there are over 14 million Americans out of work, some may ask: Why aren't they scooping up farm jobs?" (Lithiluxa, 2010), and this conclusion: "These numbers demonstrate that there are more politicians and finger-pointers interested in blaming undocumented farm workers for America's unemployment crisis that there are unemployed Americans who are willing to harvest and cultivate America's food" (Weiner, 2010).

With consistent references to "Americans" and the insistence on the reality of farm labor, the mediated accounts of the campaign, and the campaign design itself, situate the collapse of anti-immigrant sentiment with the "taking" of jobs as ridiculous in ways that define "Americans" as wrong or misguided. Here, Colbert becomes particularly significant. In his testimony to congress, Colbert directed attention to the oft-repeated phrase "this is America," a phrase regularly referenced in anti-immigrant arguments and typically followed by some command, such as "speak English." Colbert (2010b) mocked that logic, arguing instead, "this is America. I don't want a tomato picked by a Mexican. I want it picked by an *American*, then sliced by a Guatemalan and served by a Venezuelan in a spa where a Chilean gives me a Brazilian" (emphasis in original). Invoking Americans' eager consumption of the ethnic and the foreign on our own terms – in spas and nail salons – Colbert noted the hypocrisy and indeed ridiculousness of the anti-immigrant sentiment. His exaggerated references, done in typical Colbert-character, revealed the embeddedness of immigrant labor and our complicity in that labor.

In its grounding in absurd reality, the TOJ campaign redefines the problem such that it is not immigration, not a problem that floods through leaky borders into the nation. Instead, the campaign defines the problems as "American" unwillingness to do agricultural labor and "American" hypocritical refusal to admit reliance on cheap labor and cheap products. However, that very redefinition relies upon a narrow timeworn construction of immigrant "illegal" labor.

The Ironic Reinvestment in Racial Essentialism

Typically immigration narratives, almost regardless of political perspective, are located at the border. These border narratives tend to emphasize crossing, either with attention to immigration as illegal and immigrants as criminal and alien or with attention to the danger and death that results from the perils of crossing barren desert. In contrast, the TOJ campaign locates the immigration debates within farm fields. Rhetorically, this move is apparent simply in the carefully delimited parameters of the debate. That is, the campaign directs attention to farm labor and thus asks readers to think about labor conditions and food production, particularly as they implicate immigration policies and practices.

However, perhaps there is an ironic – and troubling – twist to the ironic tone of the campaign. In the move to the field and the emphasis on the absurd reality of farm labor, the campaign participates in an essentialist racial logic. "Americans" won't do this work. Mexicans will do and are doing this work. The location of the debate within the fields and the emphasis on Mexicans as farm workers is rhetorically sensible in part through its articulation with the docile Mexican "*peon*," whose attractiveness as a laborer was grounded in *his* natural suited-ness for such work (Flores, 2003). Some of the coverage relies on images of Mexican workers. These images typically invoke the stock shot of the Mexican *peon*, stooping to pick crops, carrying heavy crates and baskets of fruit, laboring under the hot sun (e.g., Smith, 2010). The endless vistas afforded by such images, in which isolated workers are set against endless rows of crops or stand silently and valiantly in poses that convey fortitude and suffering, situate Mexican workers as the willing and able laboring beasts and perpetuate the divide between essential Mexican – cast as worker – and essential American – unable and, more importantly, unwilling to work (e.g., Mirk, 2010). Grounded in the trope of the immigrant-to-be-pitied, the campaign, for all its disruptions, also tells a familiar narrative of exploitation that relies on othering. Indeed, this may be a danger of the kind of visibility politics that emerges here and in other recent instances of immigrant activism, which continue to invoke "reductionist and stereotypical representations" of immigrants (Sowards & Piñeda, 2013, p. 73).

Conclusion

In his account of *La Gran March*, Cisneros (2011) argued: "While (rhetorical) bordering may be our obsession, it is not totalizing" (p. 27). Instead, activist moments such as the *Take Our Jobs* campaign offer contemporary contestations of narrow and static instantiations of "illegal aliens." In the emphasis on the absurd reality of farm labor, the *TOJ* campaign provides a space – both literal and figurative – that contests anti-immigrant narratives.

At the same time, the campaign itself takes an ironic turn. As it moves from the border to the farm, it forwards the farm laborer, that familiar hard-working and amenable Mexican, stooped over picking tomatoes. This easy reinscription of an all-too-familiar figure is cause for concern. However, I also find at least two disruptive possibilities in this discourse. First, disruption occurs in the visibility politics of the campaign. In the active naming of migrants as migrants and as undocumented, with consistent emphasis on the numbers of undocumented migrants who constitute the farm labor force, the TOJ campaign revises, slightly, the insider/outsider terms of bordering practices. There is a refusal here of the citizen/alien divide. That refusal then suggests the second possibility, which lies in what Carillo Rowe (2005) identified as "differential belonging," a politics of relation that occurs in and through identities. Differential belonging draws attention to complexities; it refuses "the significance of legal citizenship as the only mode for offering rights" (Chávez, 2010, p. 150). In the TOJ campaign, the attention to complexities and the refusal of legal citizenship as the only possibility emerge through the satiric absurd reality of the campaign. If, indeed, satire and irony work through audience engagement (Gring-Pemble & Solomon, 2003) and make possible serious reflection on socially taboo topics, such as race (Rossing, 2011; Waisanen, 2009), then the UFW call to citizens to "Take Our Jobs, Please!" asks them, at least those willing to engage the irony of the plea, to reflect upon their hypocritical complicity and recognize the reality that the campaign repeatedly names: "So much demonizing of immigrants is done by people in air conditioned offices that were completely removed from the reality on the ground of what it's like to do the work that everyone depends upon" (Martin, 2010).

References

Achter, P. (2008). Comedy in unfunny times: News parody and carnival after 9/11. *Critical Studies in Media Communication, 25*, 274–303.

Barbassa, J. (2010, June 24). Colbert, immigrant farm workers challenge pundits and unemployed to "Take Our Jobs." *Huffington Post*. Retrieved from http://www.huffingtonpost.com

Carillo Rowe, A. (2005). Be longing: Toward a feminist politics of relation. *NWSA Journal, 17*, 15–46.

Chávez, K. (2010). Border (in)securities: Normative and differential belonging in LGBTQ and immigrant rights discourse. *Communication and Critical/Cultural Studies, 7*, 136–155.

Cisneros, J. D. (2008). Contaminated communities: The metaphor of "immigrant as pollution" in media representations of immigration. *Rhetoric & Public Affairs, 11*, 569–602.

Cisneros, J. D. (2011). Bordering the civic imaginary: Rhetoric, hybridity, and citizenship in *La Gran Marcha. Quarterly Journal of Speech, 97*, 26–49.

Cisneros, J. D. (2012). Looking "illegal": Affect, rhetoric, and performativity in Arizona's Senate Bill 1070. In D. R. DeChaine (Ed.), *Border rhetorics: Citizenship and identity on the US-Mexico frontier* (pp. 133–150). Tuscaloosa: University of Alabama Press.

Colbert, S. (Producer). (2010a, July 8). *The Colbert Report*. New York, NY: Busby Productions.

Colbert, S. (2010b, September 24). Testimony to congress. Retrieved from http://www.examiner.com

Demo, A. (2005). Sovereignty discourse and contemporary immigration politics. *Quarterly Journal of Speech, 91*, 291–311.

Demo, A. T. (2012). Decriminalizing illegal immigration: Immigrants' rights through the documentary lens. In D. R. DeChaine (Ed.), *Border rhetorics: Citizenship and identity on the US-Mexico frontier* (pp. 197–212). Tuscaloosa: University of Alabama Press.

Flores, L. A. (2003). Constructing rhetorical borders: Peons, illegal aliens, and competing narratives of immigration. *Critical Studies in Media Communication, 20*, 362–387.

Gring-Pemble, L., & Watson, M. S. (2003). The rhetorical limits of satire: An analysis of James Finn Garner's *Politically Correct Bedtime Stories. Quarterly Journal of Speech, 89*, 132–153.

Hariman, R. (2007). In defense of Jon Stewart. *Critical Studies in Media Communication, 24*, 273–277.

Lithiluxa, A. (2010, July 15). United Farm Workers union says "Take Our Jobs." Retrieved from http://www.ynn.com

Martin, M. (2010, July 7). "Take my job" campaign markets agricultural labor [Interview]. Retrieved from http://www.npr.org

Mirk, S. (2010, June 28). Immigrant farmworkers: Take my job, please! *Portland Mercury.* Retrieved from http://www.portlandmercury.com

Mtippett. (2010, June 25). Take my job. Please! Retrieved from http://www.nowpublic.com

Ono, K. A., & Sloop, J. M. (2002). *Shifting borders: Rhetoric, immigration, and California's Proposition 187.* Philadelphia, PA: Temple University Press.

Powell, B. A. (2010, June 26). Farmworkers dare Americans to "Take our jobs!" *Grist Magazine.* Retrieved from http://www.grist.org

Rossing, J. P. (2011). Comic provocations in racial culture: Barack Obama and the "politics of fear." *Communication Studies, 62*, 422–438.

Smith, A. (2010, July 10). Farm workers: Take our jobs, please! *Money Magazine.* Retrieved from http://money.cnn.com

Sowards, S. K., & Piñeda, R. D. (2013). Immigrant narratives and popular culture in the United States: Border spectacle, unmotivated sympathies, and individualized responsibilities. *Western Journal of Communication, 77*, 72–91.

United Farm Workers. (2010). *Take Our Jobs.* Retrieved from http://www.takeourjobs.org

Waisanen, D. J. (2009). A citizen's guide to democracy inaction: Jon Stewart and Stephen Colbert's comic rhetorical criticism. *Southern Communication Journal, 74*, 119–140.

Weiner, R. (2010, September 23). Stephen Colbert to testify on Capitol Hill on "Protecting America's Harvest." *Washington Post.* Retrieved from http://voices.washingtonpost.com

8

YARN BOMBING AND ARGUMENT BY AESTHETIC APPROPRIATION

Leslie A. Hahner

BAYLOR UNIVERSITY, USA

In 2009, authors Mandy Moore and Leanne Prain capitalized on a newly popular trend with the publication of their how-to volume, *Yarn Bombing: The Art of Crochet and Knit Graffiti*. Yarn bombing – surreptitiously covering public fixtures with knitted and crocheted works – has become a chic enterprise among the needle-set. The jacket of *Yarn Bombing* promoted the volume as part of a "covert plan for world yarn domination." The writers elaborated on its artistic merits:

> Yarn graffiti's impermanence and benign nature allow you to produce exciting, eye-catching street art without damaging property or, arguably, breaking the law . . . This impermanence is one of the most important differences between this and other forms of graffiti. However, like traditional graffiti, yarn bombing can be considered a political and subversive medium of communication.
>
> *(p. 29)*

Yarn bombing enthusiasts couch the enterprise as a kind of disturbing visual argument – it is situated as that which upsets the established order. Yet, in order to make this claim, yarn bombers pirate the radical features of paint graffiti and its raced and classed associations. In this way, the truly disturbing aspects of yarn bombing arguments are their aesthetic appropriation of graffiti culture.

Attending to the discursive and visual arguments surrounding yarn bombing, my analysis suggests that yarn bombers traffic in radical democratic aesthetics by borrowing the rebellious ethos of paint graffiti. As such, yarn bombing visually and discursively participates in a mode of argumentation I name *aesthetic appropriation*. These comparative claims poach the anti-establishment aspects of graffiti in order to justify and proliferate guerrilla knitting. Yarn bombing is thus instructive for understanding unique modes of aesthetic argumentation given that bombers argue through juxtaposition. I first describe aesthetic arguments and the possibilities imagined through radical aesthetic style. Next, I analyze the visual practice of yarn bombing and public statements about it in order to tease out the aesthetic comparisons used to oppose guerrilla knitting against paint graffiti. I conclude by illustrating the importance of this analysis for the study of aesthetic forms of argumentation.

Radical Aesthetic Argument

Aesthetic arguments are typically theorized as manifest through the stylistic and ethical components of visual and discursive texts. Hariman (1995) attended to the aesthetic features of political style. He wrote that political style is a set of rhetorical conventions that seek a particular aesthetic reaction for political purposes. For scholars of argumentation, aesthetics operates as one mode of visual argument. In keeping with Birdsell and Groarke's (2007) discussion of visual culture, style functions as argument by focusing on how audience interpretation is limited by norms of representation or conventions of design. Ommen (2005) contended that the features of an image can be read against a larger visual culture in order to understand the arguments at stake. Put more generally, aesthetic arguments operate by using stylistic conventions to prompt a set of audience responses.

Texts that display radical democratic aesthetics argue by disturbing orthodox modes of address. Through his analysis of the Young Lords, Enck-Wanzer (2008) suggested that radical democratic aesthetics attempt to subvert democratic traditions. For him, radical democratic style is best defined "in the negative" (p. 459). If the features of democratic style include "deliberation, representation, consensus, and contestation," radical democratic style both adopts and resists these features in order to set itself against democratic traditions (Enck-Wanzer, 2008, p. 460). Discursive and visual texts fashioned in this mode re-imagine the possibilities of democratic practice by drawing attention to the inherent limitations entailed within the democratic tradition. Critical engagement with radical democratic style suggests that arguments may traffic in a radical aesthetic in order to invite the public to strive for social change.

Although certainly some yarn bombing events participate in radical politics that open up imaginative possibilities for the public, the vast majority of yarn bombing operates by merely trafficking in an ethos of rebellion. That is, bombers often situate their work as revolutionary by appropriating the radical political style articulated to paint graffiti. Such claims adopt the scholarly and popular understanding of graffiti as subversive (Brummett, 2008). As is clear in the revolutionary language employed by Moore and Prain, bombers often position their work as part of the rebellious tradition of graffiti. Yet, much of the discourse about and visual practice of yarn bombing works by argumentatively usurping the radical aesthetic of paint graffiti while simultaneously maintaining the privilege of class and race typically not afforded to paint graffiti artists. In this way, the discourse and practice of yarn bombing demonstrates a novel mode of stylistic argument: aesthetic appropriation. Arguments by aesthetic appropriation do not simply display one style to elicit certain responses, but instead traffic in one style in order to clandestinely secure the virtue of another. These modes of visual argument appropriate by borrowing the ethos of another style. By analyzing the arguments about yarn bombing, scholars of argumentation may better understand the comparative and conflicted articulations inherent to aesthetic claims.

Welcome, Yarn Bombers!

One of the most remarkable differences between yarn bombing and traditional graffiti is that both citizens and municipal authorities frequently welcome yarn-bombing installations. Yarn bombers such as Magda Sayeg are often commissioned by communities to install large-scale yarn bombs. While certainly some graffiti artists (e.g., Banksy) are entreated to grace public sites with their work, the vast majority of commonplace graffiti is criticized as a nuisance that must be eradicated. The public arguments supporting the practice of yarn bombing often rely on this distinction to uphold the virtue of urban knitting. Yarn bombing is said to open the minds of the public by modifying its vision of the city. Indeed, such democratic virtue is set in contrast to paint graffiti, which is described as dangerous, ugly, and aggressive (Conquergood, 1997).

Like paint graffiti, yarn bombing is technically illegal in most locales. Yet, guerrilla yarn that blankets public fixtures is typically not removed and is often embraced by officials. As is evident in Moore and Prain's volume, many of the arguments that support such appreciation insist that yarn bombing is beneficial given that it is only temporary and does not cause damage. Such claims are often leveled in comparison to paint graffiti. Australian bomber Crystal Petch, a member of the Country Women's Association, stated that "yarn bombing is a type of non-permanent graffiti" (as cited in Gropler, 2012). While she noted that yarn bombing is against the law, she insisted that they typically "have permission" to install their works (as cited in Gropler, 2012). Many of these assertions could apply to traditional graffiti – paint is certainly not permanent, is not necessarily damaging, and with a small amount of work can be recovered. Indeed, these claims may even be inaccurate about yarn bombing insofar as wet yarn left on a tree can cause rot, some bombers use industrial adhesive to affix their works, crafts separated from their original roost can clog storm drains, and, depending on one's vantage, knitted works can easily be described as quite ugly. Yet, these arguments explicitly frame yarn bombing as a welcome addition to the public landscape in distinction from paint graffiti.

Proponents of yarn bombing commonly maintain that guerrilla knitting is a form of subversive public art that creates imaginative possibilities for the public while paint graffiti is simply aggressive. In *The Sunday Times* of London, fiber arts teacher Orla Breslin described yarn bombing as similar to graffiti in that both are "illegal," yet suggested that yarn bombing was more beneficial (as cited in Power, 2013). She explained, "Of course, it's very different from graffiti in one respect. Graffiti is aggressive – this is the exact opposite. It's sweet. You can take it down and even bring it home" (Breslin as cited in Power, 2013). A Honolulu reporter engaged in a similar argumentative strategy when she described a commissioned yarn bomb for a local art museum: "In the spirit of street art, yarn bombing marks a public space with knitted or crocheted fiber, rather than paint. It has a more whimsical, less criminal quality, since yarn is easily removed" (Oshiro, 2012). For this reporter, the whimsical quality of yarn expanded the aesthetic possibilities of the cityscape. Both of these claims rely on aesthetic comparison: Yarn bombing is sweet and whimsical while paint graffiti is aggressive and criminal. As bombers demean paint graffiti, they simultaneously traffic in the radical ethos of street art while abjuring the danger and vitriol that often accompanies subversive public art.

Making the Urban Suburban

Fans of yarn bombing commonly employ another comparative claim by pitting the suburban, domestic feel of knitted art against the cold, sterile urban scene. Yarn bombs are often posited as warm and cozy additions to the dour urban landscape. These kinds of arguments are made both discursively and visually. Wool and yarn objects are situated as soothing additions to the harsh angles of the street scene. Much of these claims are undergirded by assumptions about class. The suburban aesthetic – and the associated connotation of comfort – situates a middle-to-upper class sensibility against that of the working class.

Many of the discursive arguments in favor of yarn bombing suggest that it renders urban spaces cozy and warm. Most who laud yarn bombing seem to agree with a reporter from New Mexico who noted that, "yarn bombing represents an attempt to add warmth to and improve urban landscapes . . . Stitchers are regarded as artists rather than vandals because the knit graffiti does not deface objects or property" ("Yarn Bomb," 2012). Indeed, a writer discussing the practice in Toledo proclaimed that yarn bombing was a "kinder, gentler form of graffiti" because "it takes the most matronly crafts [*sic*] knitting and crocheting and transfers them from the comforts of grandma's rocking chair to the concrete and steel surfaces of the urban streets" (Mullen, 2012). In this statement, and for many other bombing enthusiasts, woolen objects soften the hard edges of the city by importing the texture and feel of the domestic. Bombing supposedly adds value by papering the ugly urban landscape in the warmth of the suburban, domestic aesthetic.

The trend attempts a similar form of argument through visual display. Yarn bombers typically select tags based on how the connoted coziness of the yarn contrasts with the object being bombed. Street lamps and meters are often covered with stockings while statues are gifted with leg warmers. These projects emphasize the way the domestic style of the knitted work apparently warms hard surfaces. For instance, stockings on metal poles metaphorically insist that the yarn is heating the cold aluminum. Moore and Prain's volume featured two popular projects that illustrate a similar mode of engagement. Consider the doily tree – a common form of crochet bombing that covers a tree in a series of doilies. The suburban/urban contrast is unmistakable: Grandma's doilies grace the rough wooden trunk. Yet, the visual argument at play suggests that the aesthetic style of the doilies enhances the tree through domestic undertones. Similarly, the front cover of the volume showed a pair of knitted sneakers thrown over an electric line. The bomb mimicked an ostensibly urban practice. A reporter for *The Atlantic* wrote, "ghost shoes are a staple of urban decor; they propagate furiously in inner cities, spreading to nearby trees like ugly sparrows come to roost" (Metcalfe, 2012). Often called shoefiti, the use of knitted sneakers emphasized the way in which yarn bombers layer the domestic over the urban landscape. These shoefitis are art, not "ugly sparrows," because they translated the urban through the suburban. The comparative assumptions of yarn bombs are predicated on the appropriation of raced and classed associations with different modes of public art. Indeed, the implications of these articulations are laid bare in the presumed creators of yarn bombs versus those of paint graffiti.

Knitta, Please

Yarn bombing often attempts to appropriate the radical aesthetic ethos of paint graffiti. Bombers insist that their works are subversive insofar as they warm and brighten the bleak urban landscape. Graffiti knitting, then, invokes a tongue-in-cheek juxtaposition: Yarn bombs are unique additions to the city scene because they radically contrast the domestic to the urban. That notion is bolstered by the personae and bodies associated with both yarn and paint graffiti. As Palczewski (1997) argued, the body is marked and inscribed by argument. In this instance, the visual texts and the discursive arguments about yarn bombing imply the bodies that fashion these claims: White middle-class women and Black urban youth.

Certainly, not all yarn bombers are White middle-class women just as not all graffiti artists are Black urban youth. But, the argumentative claims surrounding yarn bombing discursively and visually mark these bodies as connected to each form of graffiti. Moore and Prain's volume illuminated this logic:

> Because knitted and crocheted items are intrinsically homey, using yarn craft in
> unconventional ways can have a special kind of resonance . . . Many of us have a
> lifetime of memories of sweaters and afghans that are warm, comforting, soft, and
> useful. They were likely made by women, and though a good deal of skill and time
> was used to make them, that skill and time has often been undervalued.
>
> *(p. 23)*

The authors adopted a kind of feminist visibility politics by identifying yarn crafts as
inherently connected to women. For them, yarn bombing values the unseen labor of women
in the suburban home. Setting aside the question of whether or not yarn bombing actually
resignifies women's labor (a query that would comprise an entirely different essay), the point
I highlight here is that yarn bombing becomes primarily articulated to middle-class women
as artists.

The raced aspects of these womanly bodies are rendered visible in the tag names yarn
bombers employ. While some bombers tag their works with crew names including the Ladies
Fancywork Society or Knitted Landscape, a significant number tag their works with names
that connote Black urban bodies. For example, the Knotorious N.I.T., P-Knitty, and Micro-
Fiber Militia all re-use names associated with Black rappers famous for their associations with
New York City. Indeed, the most egregious of these names is "Knitta, Please," the tag for the
internationally celebrated mother of yarn bombing, Magda Sayeg. Trading on the popularity
of a phrase known variously as a song by Jay-Z, an album by Ol' Dirty Bastard, and a Black
colloquialism, Sayeg's tag is at best a flippant joke, and at worst a racially insensitive appropriation of epic proportions.

The use of these names further marks the women performing with the privilege of middle-
class whiteness – they are able to pilfer the names of rappers and racial slurs with little consideration of the implications. As Alcoff (2006) noted, "the core of white privilege is the ability
to consume anything, anyone, anywhere" (p. 217). The arguments fashioned about yarn
bombing mark the bodies of its creators as middle-class White bodies while simultaneously
pirating the radical ethos of the Black urban bodies associated with urban graffiti culture. To
borrow Tate's (2003) phraseology, these so-called rebellious acts of yarn bombing seem to
appropriate "everything but the burden" from Black culture.

Argument as Aesthetic Appropriation

Discourses about yarn bombing and its visual display commonly create arguments that employ
aesthetic appropriation. By borrowing the radical political ethos of paint graffiti, yarn bombers
uphold the value of the craft while simultaneously eschewing the burdens of race and class
placed on paint graffiti artists. The aesthetic claims surrounding the practice traffic in a
radical democratic ethos that claims to open up imaginative possibilities for the public.
However, yarn bombing simply poaches radical democratic aesthetics in order to insist on its
democratic potential while covering over the privilege of its presumed creators. As such,
aesthetic arguments may not simply display one particular style or another but may engage in
comparative juxtaposition. Aesthetic appropriation as a rhetorical mode of argumentation
relies on such opposition to warrant the appeal of a given style. Arguments about yarn
bombing are disturbing arguments in that they proclaim that guerrilla knitting will upset
relations of power, but engage in cultural appropriations that maintain the privilege of
middle-class whiteness. Specifically, the domestic style of the suburban home is valorized as
the litmus test for the radical possibilities of art.

I have provided a brief foray into grasping the argumentative features of yarn bombing. What seems clear about this practice and the discursive claims made about it is that aesthetic appropriation is a particularly pernicious mode of argument when the original style is emptied of its subversive ethos. The radical potential of paint graffiti is found at least partially in the necessarily risky endeavor of illegally tagging monuments, signs, or walls. In many locales, paint graffiti artists risk felony arrest for their craft, and the implicit danger of such an act provides at least part of the acts' provocations. Yarn bombers are not prosecuted for their acts of vandalism and often commended as feminine rebels. Such glorification is not simply the effect of unacknowledged privilege; that privilege is reinscribed through the argumentative practices of yarn bombing. What yarn bombing illuminates about arguments of style is that aesthetic claims often embrace comparative articulations that cover over the power of privilege that accompanies certain aesthetic modes. To grasp the contours of this mode of argumentation requires the critic to disturb or unhinge the interconnectedness of the juxtaposition.

References

Alcoff, L. (2006). *Visible identities: Race, gender, and the self.* New York, NY: Oxford University Press.

Birdsell, D., & Groarke, L. (2007). Outlines of a theory of visual argument. *Argumentation and Advocacy, 43,* 103–113.

Brummett, B. (2008). *A rhetoric of style.* Carbondale: Southern Illinois University Press.

Conquergood, D. (1997). Street literacy. In J. Flood, S. Brice Heath, & D. Lapp (Eds.), *Handbook of research on teaching literacy through communicative and visual arts* (pp. 354–375). Mahwah, NJ: Lawrence Erlbaum Associates.

Enck-Wanzer, D. (2008). A radical democratic style? Tradition, hybridity, and intersectionality. *Rhetoric & Public Affairs, 11,* 459–465.

Gropler, S. (2012, December 6). Age no barrier for CWA. *Stock Journal.* Retrieved from LexisNexis

Hariman, R. (1995). *Political style: The artistry of power.* Chicago, IL: University of Chicago Press.

Metcalfe, J. (2012, April 4). Shoes over telephone wires: This probably doesn't explain it. *The Atlantic.* Retrieved from http://www.theatlanticcities.com/neighborhoods/2012/04/shoes-over-telephone-wires-probably-doesnt-explain-it/1669/

Moore, M., & Prain, L. (2009). *Yarn bombing: The art of crochet and knit graffiti.* Vancouver, BC: Arsenal.

Mullen, R. (2012, April 26). Ohio knitters unravel yarn bombs as art. *AP State and Local Wire.* Retrieved from LexisNexis

Oshiro, J. (2012, July 1). Trio knit and purl fanciful show. *The Honolulu Star-Advertiser.* Retrieved from LexisNexis

Ommen, B. (2005). Iconic visual argument and the potential for a visual dialectic. In C. A. Willard (Ed.), *Critical problems in argumentation* (pp. 496–502). Washington, DC: National Communication Association.

Palczewski, C. (1997). Bodies that argue: Power, difference, and argument. In J. F. Klumpp (Ed.), *Argument in a time of change: Definitions, frameworks, and critiques* (pp. 179–184). Annandale, VA: National Communication Association.

Power, E. (2013, January 6). Knitty gritty. *The Sunday Times.* Retrieved from LexisNexis

Tate, G. (2003). *Everything but the burden: What White people are taking from Black culture.* New York, NY: Random House.

Yarn bomb mystery unraveled. (2012, February 24). *US Fed News.* Retrieved from LexisNexis

9

ARGUING SIDEWAYS

The 1491s' *I'm an Indian Too*

Mary E. Stuckey[1]

GEORGIA STATE UNIVERSITY, USA

The 1491s (n.d.) are a sketch comedy group who offer biting criticisms of the state of indigenous politics. They are equally caustic when it comes to the current state of U.S. politics as those politics impinge on indigenous nations. They have been affectionately referred to as "the bastard children of Manifest Destiny" (Waters, 2012) because of the ways they challenge both the stereotypes of American Indians as humorless, stoic, and tragically doomed and the politics based on those stereotypes.

The 1491s tour the nation, performing at colleges and in areas with significant native populations, and sponsor a series of short videos starring young native people called "Represent," which depict the wide variety of contemporary indigenous experiences. They encourage civic engagement and advocate voting and other forms of political activity. Their work functions, in Gerald Hauser's (2008) terms, as vernacular assertions of agency. All of this sounds like the kind of actions with which most people are comfortable and that are easily placed within mainstream politics. But the 1491s can be anything but mainstream and their more controversial tendencies are the subject of this essay, for those tendencies allow me to both examine the ways in which web-based vernaculars intervene in political discourses and to observe how those interventions might strengthen minority voices in public debates (Hess, 2007; Howard, 2008).

Specifically, I examine one of the 1491s' videos, "I'm an Indian Too" (2012a). Like most satires, this one has disturbing elements: It features nearly all of the negative stereotypes of indigenous people. The title references the Irving Berlin song from the 1946 Broadway musical *Annie Get Your Gun*. The musical, better known for "You Can't Get a Man with a Gun" and "There's no Business Like Show Business," was wildly popular and had long runs on the New York and London stages before becoming a movie in 1950 (Sidney, 1950). The song, "I'm an Indian Too" comes at a moment in the narrative when Annie is officially adopted, by no less a figure than Sitting Bull himself, into the Great Sioux Nation.

There are many ways this treatment of indigenous people could be understood: as a window into the historical moment when the action is set or when the play was written, as an example of the pernicious stereotypes that animate hegemonic understandings of native peoples, and so on. The 1491s take a different approach however and, in September 2012, posted a video on YouTube. They went to the Santa Fe Indian Market, put one of their members (Ryan Red Corn, Osage) in a dish towel breechcloth and a cheap "Indian" feather "war bonnet," painted the word "Hipster" on his bare chest, and filmed him dancing to a recorded version of the song with a variety of people around the market. Images of his dancing are interspersed with various stereotypical representations of Indianness, including the covers of romance novels, the Three Stooges dressed in "Indian" garb, and a cigar store wooden Indian. There are also a number of moments featuring non-native people wearing Indian jewelry or in other ways that suggest the commodification of Indian identity. There are instances of apparently non-natives' discomfort with Red Corn's performance and also of their willing participation in it. He sings with a wide variety of apparently Indian people, who seem to see the performance as both ironic and celebratory. The roughly 4-minute video ends with a group of native and non-native people dancing together at what appears to be a public performance of the 1491s. Within a month, the video received 56,249 hits, 770 likes, 27 dislikes, and 288 comments.

The video enacts a parodic version of the song in ways that confound the problem of how to resist stereotypes without also reinscribing them, what David Cheshier (personal communication, 2007) called the "problem of despicable discourse," and thus warrants analytic attention. Relying on Burke's (1984) theory of perspective by incongruity, I treat this video as an example of argument that disturbs the hegemonic inscription of Indian identity in potentially productive ways. Rather than directly confronting stereotypes, the 1491s come at them sideways, transforming them (Lake & Pickering, 1996). Perspective by incongruity is thus revealed as an argumentative resource for minority groups seeking to enter an argumentative arena characterized by unequal distributions of definitional power (for a discussion of perspective by incongruity as argument, see Klumpp, 1993; Levasseur, 1993). As the commentary on the video reveals, such arguments are enabled by the access associated with web-based media (Hess, 2007; Howard, 2008).

Background

The original Berlin song offends contemporary sensibilities rendering the 1491s' video disturbing. The music, a disco cover of the original, is based on a stereotypical "Indian" drumbeat, and the lyrics begin with a rhythmic chant of "a Sioux/a Sioux." The lyrics evoke every available stereotype concerning American Indians. Indigenous names, religions, customs and practices, clothing, and dance are all caricatured in the music, lyrics, and performance of the original musical and in the cover version used as the soundtrack of the 1491s' video, both of which are caricatured in turn by the 1491s. It is hard to imagine a contemporary audience failing to writhe as witnesses to such treatment of minority peoples.

But this is precisely the point. The 1491s argue here and elsewhere (2012b), that the treatment the dominant culture affords indigenous people is based on the acceptance of such stereotypes. But rather than arguing against these stereotypes, an exercise we know to be unproductive, the 1491s instead attack them sideways by satirically embodying them. In this video they accomplish this in two main ways: by pointing to the sexualization of Indianness and to the commodification of native culture, both of which enable the denigration of indigenous peoples. Rather than merely exposing the fact of hegemonic stereotypes, however, the 1491s also point to a different reality, shared and experienced by contemporary native people. By juxtaposing that reality with the stereotypes that circulate through popular culture, the 1491s potentially disturb the cultural dominance of those stereotypes.

By placing disparate elements next to one another, perspective by incongruity allows the audience to reinvision those elements. As a rhetorical tactic, perspective by incongruity allows rhetors to disturb an argument without also reinscribing it because the argument is placed in a context that renders it absurd. By arguing sideways, the 1491s avoid directly engaging the dominant view and enact a guerilla argument that refutes the idea of argument as direct opposition and allows the audience to think of it in other ways (Lake & Pickering 1996; McPhail 1996).

Sexualized Indians

Eur-americans have a long history of treating Indian peoples as sexual objects (Bird, 2009). Certainly the "Indian maiden" stereotype is a familiar one, appearing most glaringly in films like *Pocahontas* and on commodities such as Land O' Lakes butter. The Indian maiden represents purity, an unspoiled and intimate relationship with nature, and a way for Whites to acquire land through their relationships with these women (Stuckey & Morris, 1999). Indigenous men also frequently are sexualized, although in their case it is more through the vehicle of romance novels rather than actual commodities, and is trickier to deal with, as they cannot be seen as intimate with non-native women. Thus, "Indian" men are often not actually Indian, but are whites who have been adopted into indigenous nations and/or they become involved with White women who have been living as Indians but are secretly White, as in *Dances with Wolves* and *The Last of the Dogmen*. White men may marry indigenous women but indigenous men may not share sexual relationships with White women, for that threatens to upset the hegemonic order.

The 1491s' video centralizes the sexualized Indian. The video opens with Ryan Red Corn doing a bump and grind and includes images of women in bikinis and headdresses and similarly clad men on the cover of novels with names like *Lakota Surrender, Proud Wolf's Woman*, and *Under Apache Skies*. The video shows Red Corn dancing with all kinds of people in an overtly sexual way: bumping, to one apparently White man's dismay, very close to him; with a couple of apparently White women, one of whom is wearing a very cheap feather headdress; and finally, with an apparently White woman who clearly relishes the salacious contact. It is clear that passersby exposed to Red Corn's dancing are often made uncomfortable by it – they quickly walk past; one apparently White man pushes him away and another takes Red Corn's picture and then flees, avoiding physical contact.

Those who appear to be non-Indian are thus portrayed in two ways in most of the video: They are interested in exploiting Indian sexuality, either by attempts to get close to Red Corn or by the mediated versions of Indians, or they are frightened by such sexuality. In both cases, they are revealed as either trying to dominate Indian bodies or as afraid of those bodies. By centralizing the sexualization of indigenous peoples through close encounters with an actual Indian body, the video highlights the dominant culture's relationship with such bodies, and makes proximate the consequences of this relationship. This is the heart of "arguing sideways," which provides rhetors with the opportunity to avoid what Cheshier (2007) calls the problem of "despicable discourse" – such arguments challenge without reinscribing stereotypes. The video accomplishes much the same goal with its treatment of Indianness as a commodity.

Commodified Cultures

The tendency to commodify indigenous cultures is well documented (Castile, 1996). Nowhere is that commodification more obvious than at Indian markets and fairs, which are premised on the authenticity of the items being sold (it is illegal for non-natives to sell Indian goods), and on the assumption that Indianness can be appropriated by non-natives. It is perhaps worth noting in this context that the web site (lyricsfreak.com) where I obtained a copy of the song's original lyrics offers it as a ring tone for my cellular phone.

At issue here is the question of authenticity, of who has the right to sell Indian culture and its artifacts, who has the right to buy these objects, and the nature of the consequences of both practices. It is interesting, for instance, that one of the longest threads in the comments on the YouTube version of the video concerned Red Corn. After someone noted in a post that he was White, others weighed in to claim that he was a member of the Osage nation; or argued that he was also part White and proud of his entire family; or that he had, by virtue of his legal status, the right to speak on issues pertaining to indigenous identity (see thread on youtube.com involving windstorm1000, funnynative, osagedine, and AtiuitzolTiazohtla). The precise nature and parameters of Indian identity are hotly contested (Garroute, 2003); this video reveals some of the parameters of that contestation within indigenous communities. "Looking White" means Indians have to defend their own identities as somehow legitimate; looking and being Indian means they have to defend those identities against those who seek to appropriate them.

Note, for instance, that Red Corn is dressed as a particularly cheap Indian mascot. The feather headdress, combined with a gym towel breechcloth worn over shorts and with black shoes is a clear attempt at highlighting the absurd consequences of combining "Indian" accoutrements with "White" ones. Such accommodation can be accomplished, naturally – this is clear in the various clothes worn by natives in the video, where various people wear beaded earrings or other markers of indigenous identity (tee shirts or caps with native organizations as logos, for instance). But that accommodation goes only in one direction. None of the apparently indigenous people in the video are treating their cultures or cultural artifacts as commodities. They are not "playing Indian" (Deloria, 1999) but are playing with stereotypes of Indians and, in doing so, rob those stereotypes of definitional power.

The apparently non-native people, on the other hand, accept, even embrace, the commodification of Indian identity. They are at the Santa Fe Indian Market, in fact, in order to buy Indian objects. They wear oversized Kokopelli bolo ties and fake headdresses; they treat Indian religious artifacts as costumes and props. They take pictures of the Indians, thus treating the Indians themselves as commodities. Worse, they all seem relatively unconscious of how this must appear to the actual Indians they encounter – at least they are unconscious of this until Red Corn appears.

Commentators on YouTube thanked the 1491s (2012a) for challenging "racist crap" (Cici Minicici) and noted that "real natives have to laugh or we would go crazy" (titocomedy), a choice this writer seemed to associate with stereotypes of his/her people as they circulate through the shared culture. A few people, however, were less happy with the satiric approach, and at least one person took part in a thread focused on his concern that "displaying ignorant views of Natives, and laughing at them does nothing to educate ignorant people who hold those views to have a more actuate [*sic*] and respectful view" (AtiuitzolTiazohtla). Another writer agreed, arguing "Disrespect is disrespect no matter what your intentions are" (Phillip Espinoza). These commenters were concerned about the circulation of stereotypes and feared that the damage contained in that circulation was not, in fact, undone by the satiric nature of the video. At issue, then, are questions of satire, education, and the relationship between them. Perspective by incongruity has the potential to challenge without confronting hegemonic arguments, a potentially productive strategy for those who seek to disturb those arguments.

Arguing from the Margins

This video is not just another example of exposing media stereotypes. We have plenty of such examples, and we understand their function and the mechanisms through which they do their work (Stedman, 1982). This video is interesting because it indicates the absurdity of the stereotypes in question while avoiding reinscribing them. Actual indigenous people are shown in ways that indicate the vastness of the space between stereotypes and lived realities. The 1491s make an implicit argument concerning the ways in which those realities are impacted by the stereotypes in question. That is, the visual juxtaposition of actual indigenous people, wearing jeans and tee shirts, inhabiting the contemporary world, does most of the political work of disturbing the stereotype of Indians as only inhabiting the 19th century. It is the non-natives who wear the oversized bolos featuring Kokopelli; they are the ones in sombreros laden with Indian jewelry; and it is the White people who are flummoxed by Red Corn's behavior. The people who appear to be indigenous are happily dancing with him, laughing at his antics, comfortable with his absurd self-identification as an Indian mascot. The Indians are portrayed as understanding – and laughing at – the incongruity between their own lives and the dominant view of those lives. The non-Indians alternately fear and try to contain and commodify those identities; the Indians confound both the fear and the containment.

The political work of this video is accomplished through the visuals: the presentation of Ryan Red Corn as a low-rent version of an Indian mascot, the contrast between actual indigenous people and the stereotypes of those people, the absurdity of the apparently non-native appropriations of Indian identity, are all conveyed through visual juxtaposition. This, of course, is how perspective by incongruity works. As one person commenting on the video noted, "it would be easier for [my wife] to think deep thoughts about the very real issues this video presents if she could stop laughing long enough" (Satanica65). Perspective by incongruity relies on this humor, this amusement, to do its work, reconciling opposites by admitting the basic opposition. Clearly, too, it is enabled by the medium – Indian agency is facilitated by its circulation in cyberspace (Hess, 2007; Howard, 2008).

The video ends at what appears to be a public performance by the 1491s; members of the troupe are on stage, in front of a copyright notice projected onscreen. The audience, which seems to be comprised of both native and non-native individuals, dances together. No one is wearing clothing or jewelry that is easily identified as "Indian" and everyone is dancing in similar ways. There are old people and younger ones; men and women; and there is a visual sense of unity and community. The music continues, but there are no lyrics – no one in the audience is singing, nor are they dancing to the words, "I'm an Indian too." It would appear that in forsaking stereotypes, in setting aside cultural markers of Indianness, something like shared community is possible. Identity, especially shared identity, does not depend on cultural commodification and exploitation. The Indians in the room know who they are; the non-natives appear to understand who they are not, a recognition that makes communal dance possible.

Note

1. I'm grateful to Cate Palczewski for her wisdom and advice in revising the essay and to David Cheshier for his thoughts on challenging without recirculating negative stereotypes – he is the first person I know of who labeled the issue I address in this essay as the "problem of despicable discourse."

References

1491s (n.d.). About [Facebook page]. Retrieved from https://www.facebook.com/1491s/info
the1491s. (2012a, September 21). I'm an Indian too [Video file]. Directed and edited by Sterlin Harjo. Retrieved from http://www.youtube.com/watch?v=9BHvpWP2V9Y&noredirect=1
the1491s. (2012b, November 9) More Indianer than you [Video file]. Retrieved from http://www.youtube.com/watch?v=SGCCFFS7x74

Berlin, I. (1946, April 15). I'm an Indian too [Song lyrics]. *Lyricsfreak*. Retrieved from http://www.lyricsfreak.com/i/irving+berlin/im+an+indian+too_20259672.html

Bird, S. E. (2009). Gendered construction of the American Indian in popular media. *Journal of Communication, 49*, 61–83.

Burke, K. (1984). *Attitudes toward history* (3rd ed.). Berkeley: University of California Press.

Castile, G. P. (1996). Forum: The commodification of Indian identity. *American Anthropologist, 98*, 743–746.

Deloria, P. (1999). *Playing Indian*. New Haven, CN: Yale University Press.

Garroute, E. M. (2003) *Real Indians: Identity and the survival of Native America*. Berkeley: University of California Press.

Hauser, G. A. (2008) *Vernacular voices: Studies in rhetorical communication*. Columbia: University of South Carolina Press.

Hess, A. (2007). In digital remembrance: Vernacular memory and the rhetorical construction of web memorials. *Media, Culture & Society, 29*, 812–830.

Howard, R. G. (2008). The vernacular web of participatory media. *Crticial Studies in Media Communication, 25*, 490–513.

Klumpp, J. F. (1993). A rapprochement between dramatism and argumentation. *Argumentation and Advocacy, 29*, 148–163.

Lake, R. A., & Pickering, B. A. (1996). Argumentation, the visual, and the possibility of refutation: An exploration. *Argumentation, 12*, 79–93.

Levasseur, D. G. (1993). Edifying arguments and perspective by incongruity. *Argumentation and Advocacy, 29*, 195–203.

McPhail, M. L. (1996). *Zen in the art of rhetoric*. Albany: SUNY Press.

Sidney, G. (Director). (1950). *Annie, get your gun* [Motion picture]. United States: Metro-Goldwyn-Mayer.

Stedman, R. (1982). *Shadows of the Indian: Stereotypes in American culture*. Norman: University of Oklahoma Press.

Stuckey, M., & Morris, R. (1999). Pocahontas and beyond: Commodification and cultural hegemony, *World Communication, 28*, 45–67.

Waters, R. (2012, October 8). The 1491s: Bastard children of manifest destiny [Web log message]. *Coilhouse Magazine and Blog*. Retrieved from http://coilhouse.net/2012/10/1941s-bastard-children-of-manifest-destiny/

10

TONED ARMS OR BIG BUTT?

Michelle Obama's disturbed notions of body, race, gender, and advocacy as *Let's Move!* spokesperson

Ruth J. Beerman

BLOOMSBURG UNIVERSITY, USA

In 2010, First Lady Michelle Obama began her ongoing campaign *Let's Move!*, designed to end childhood obesity. Obama promoted the campaign through speaking engagements, online social media, and guest appearances. However, Obama did not simply work as spokesperson for the *Let's Move!* campaign: Her body, and the discourse surrounding her body, functioned as ways to read the success or failure of the campaign and, correspondingly, herself as a social advocate. This case study builds on scholarship by Quinlan, Bates, and Webb (2012) who argued Obama and her body faced different standards than former First Ladies due to her race and answers their call to perform critical interrogation of discourses surrounding her body (p. 124). Additionally, I extend previous notions of the body as argument (DeLuca, 1999) and display (Prelli, 2006) to argue Obama's body functions as advocacy and display in relationship to gender, race, and weight.

Rhetoric surrounding Obama and her *Let's Move!* campaign fit within two competing yet amplifying images and discourses: "toned arms" and "big butt". Both discourses drew upon themes of fatness and Black image representations to use Obama's body as evidence, either in support or criticism of the program. Advocacy functioned as constituted and enacted through intersections of race, gender, and weight, as both discourses presumed the ideal, fit bodily advocate was a thin person. Ultimately, Michelle Obama disturbed neat conceptualizations of a subject or an object while also solidifying advocacy via the thin body. To demonstrate this, I outline the context of the campaign; examine complexities of subjectivity, objectivity, and agency via the body and Obama's body in particular; and conclude by looking at agency's limits.

Historical Context

Obesity exists as a key health concern in the United States. The Centers for Disease Control (2013b) reported rates of obesity increased in the last thirty years, with the rates for children more than doubling and the rates for teens more than tripling (para. 1). However, the CDC acknowledged (2013a) these rates decreased from 2003–2010. Even with a statistical decrease, advocates label the situation as an obesity epidemic to urge immediate action (Gard, 2011).

One such action includes Obama's public health campaign *Let's Move!* The campaign's mission statement (*Let's Move!*, n.d.) centers on "solving the challenge of childhood obesity within a generation, so that children born today will grow up healthier and able to pursue their dreams" (para. 9). *Let's Move!* demonstrated significant attention by the federal government to citizens' bodily lives.

Bodily Advocacy

Bodies are crafted by communication practices, and public displays of bodies reflect societal values about who counts as worthy or unworthy of representation (Warner, 2002, p. 42) and who can be an advocate (Hesford & Kozol, 2005). Viewing the body as rhetorical provides two important insights: First, bodies function as a means of bringing forth an argument in rhetorics of display (Prelli, 2006) and second, bodies exist as the site and substance of argument (DeLuca, 1999). Much body rhetoric literature (DeLuca, 1999; Hauser, 1999; Kiewe, 1999; Palczewski, 2002) focused on agentic uses of the body, whereby an individual used her/his body as a site of resistance, operating as a subject. Objectification theory, where bodies operate as objects rather than subjects (e.g., Butler, 1993), identifies constraints on agency. Some work interrogated how one's material body can be used in an argument against her/himself (Beerman, 2011; Harold & DeLuca, 2005); however, scholars should pay more attention to the dialectics between subject and object, where one single body serves as a site for struggle between agency and objectification. Obama's bodily discourses disturbed a neat category of subject or object, highlighting the complexities of agency within one corporeal body.

Discourse about Obama's advocacy falls into two contrasting themes. One discourse cast her primarily as a subject: She exhibited toned arms as an example of her commitment to physical fitness. The other discourse cast her primarily as an object: Her big butt, being out of control, proved her gluttony and hypocrisy. By analyzing the two themes, I identify how Obama (and her body) functioned as both subject and object, recontextualizing fatness and fitness within gendered and racialized norms. Although the discourses come to different conclusions, both operate on the same premise: Her body served as the site to judge one's appropriateness for public life and advocacy.

Toned Arms Discourse

The toned arms discourse drew on Obama's physicality and strength, using her body as evidence of success, arguing we can all make changes to our bodies because she managed to find the time to exercise and be physically fit. Focusing on Obama's toned arms extended the lineage of visual images of Black female strength via the physicality of the body. Both Obama and others used such discourse to promote the campaign. As a self-advocate, Obama outlined her personal fitness routine to promote fitness. Activities included daily running, lifting weights, the elliptical, push-ups, sit-ups, and sometimes boxing, kick boxing, or yoga (Knox, 2013, para. 8). The physical prowess and control of her body highlighted her agency; she actively chose to be fit.

Similarly, the campaign promoted fitness images such as Obama dancing, playing basketball, and doing push-ups. One such event highlighted the physicality of her body as she danced along to Beyonce's "Move Your Body" song, did the Dougie dance, some Cha Cha, and the Running Man (DiMargo, 2011, para. 10). By showing Obama dancing in a silk blouse and dress pants, the discourse argued that anyone, at any time, can engage in physical fitness by moving their bodies through dance.

Obama also participated in the toned arms discourses, most evident in her two *Ellen* appearances early in 2012 involving a push up competition. In February, DeGeneres asked Obama about her fitness routine; projected in the background, a photograph displayed the First Lady and her arms in a sleeveless black dress (TheEllenShow, 2012a). Obama's sleeveless look not only functioned as a fashion trend, but served as a statement of physical fitness where the bare arm demonstrated her abilities regarding fitness, strength, and health. But, simply stating Obama worked out daily was not enough. DeGeneres and Obama did a competitive push-up challenge, to the cheers of the audience, with Obama completing more push-ups than DeGeneres. Obama stated "I just stopped," implying she could have done more than the twenty-five she successfully completed. Following the show, news outlets declared Obama the decisive winner, which prompted an April follow-up show (TheEllenShow, 2012b). DeGeneres said, "We should talk about the push up situation." Obama responded "You're still bothered by that huh?" to laughter from the audience. She continued, "You're licking the wounds of defeat." DeGeneres responded by performing more push-ups for the viewers. Obama had already demonstrated her physical fitness; her arms spoke for themselves as evidence of fitness as Obama's arms are seen as "impossibly perfect" (Stark, 2012, para. 11). Magazines such as *Fitness Magazine* and *Ebony* outlined how to achieve such a look: "the Michelle Obama arm workout." Here discourses about her body and self-advocacy work together to cast Obama as a subject in control of her body.

These physical activities demonstrated the moving part of the *Let's Move!* campaign; Obama as self-advocate showcased how she kept her body fit and toned, and was an appropriate advocate for physical fitness. Discourses about her toned arms also utilized the images of her toned physique to argue Obama's physical fitness demonstrates her role as advocate. Not only did she talk the talk, but she danced, basketballed, and push-uped the walk as well. Obama's body drew on a lineage of strength of Black female icons such as Angela Davis, Pamela Grier, and, most notably, Sojourner Truth and her strong arms. Sojourner Truth, in her famous address concerning the role of Black women in society and the need for suffrage, bared her arm to the crowd as evidence of her strength, challenged the idea women are weak, and demonstrated her advocacy of Black women's suffrage. The historical contexts between Obama and Truth vary, particularly regarding class. Truth's strong arms reflect "the back-breaking labor she was forced to do" whereas Obama "has the familiar and professional support to build exercise into her daily schedule" (Cooper, 2010, p. 53). But, both women used their bodies as a form of advocacy, providing visual proof of their prowess. Obama's body stands as representative of her non-weakness by showcasing the body as evidence, visualizing health. However, Obama's bodily advocacy was limited to a particular understanding of an appropriate body; such agency stemmed from hegemonic understandings of the thin body as fit or in control, and extended fat-phobic ideologies (LeBeseco & Braziel, 2001), objectifying Obama's body while also serving as a basis for agency and advocacy.

Big Butt Discourse

The big butt discourse attempted to visually contain Obama's power and strength as a Black female leader and advocate by casting her body as unhealthy. It argued Obama was a gluttonous hypocrite who wanted individuals to change but was unwilling to make changes herself, evidenced by buttocks too big to be considered healthy. Such discourse operated within the larger historical coding of representations of Black women's posteriors as being overly large and, thus, out of control. The specific reading of her butt as "too big" emphasizes her lack of personal control due to her race and positions Obama as a threat to the nation in her role as advocate.

Those who focused on her butt see it as proof of her being out of control – of her body, eating habits, and her behavior as a strong Black woman telling others what to do. A similar contemporary case involved Black physician Regina Benjamin, President Barack Obama's nominee for Surgeon General, who faced criticism of her fitness for political advocacy due to her weight (James, 2009). Writing extensively on images of Black representation, hooks (1992) argued the focus on particular body parts of Black women, such as the buttocks, drew upon discourses from slavery: "Just as the 19th-century representations of black female bodies were constructed to emphasize that these bodies were expendable, contemporary messages . . . give a similar message" (p. 64). Similarly, Hobson (2005) argued contemporary images of Black women exist in the lineage of the Hottentot Venus, particularly as the size of her buttocks stood for the grotesque, leading to "black women's bodies [being] typically ridiculed, not revered" (p. 100). Obama's butt became coded within narratives of dominant fatness rhetorics as well as narratives of Black female otherness. These discourses point to a racialized version of fatness meant to disrupt power.

For example, Wisconsin state representative Jim Sensenbrenner criticized the campaign, stating First Lady Obama "lectures us on eating right while she has a large posterior herself" (as cited in Rothstein, 2011, para. 2). Ann Marsh-Meigs, a fellow church member of Sensenbrenner, told reporters he discussed Obama relative to other First Ladies and their projects, stating, "Michelle Obama, her project is obesity. And look at her big butt" (as cited in Bice, 2011, paras. 6, 7). Sensenbrenner explicitly linked Obama's body with the *Let's Move!* campaign, reading her body as too large to be healthy and thus evidence of the failure of the campaign. Although he later apologized for his comments, the fact that he felt comfortable voicing such comments indicates how others perceived the First Lady's body to be evidence about the campaign and Obama as an advocate.

In a similar critique, Rush Limbaugh (2011) called for Obama to demonstrate her advocacy: "If we're supposed to go out and eat nothing, if we're supposed to eat roots and berries and tree bark, show us how." Drawing on fat-phobic ideologies which link "bad" food consumption to poor physical health, Limbaugh then linked her body to proof of the success of eating and exercising strategies. He stated: "ok fine, show us: haven't seen any evidence here that the advice, if being followed, works." Her body functioned as proof of failure due to its size; Obama's body existed out of control and unable to demonstrate a healthy life-style.

The big butt discourse then focused on what she consumes, particularly what are deemed "poor" food choices. Reports frequently focused on Obama's love for French fries. *Fox Nation* (2011) ran the headline: "Michelle Obama: 'I can't stop eating French fries. But eat your vegetables'." An American Pundit blogger explicitly linked French fries to a lack of self-control and lack of self-advocacy: "The same woman who lectures 300 million people on eating health food and avoiding that unhealthy stuff can't stop eating french fries. She's just like her husband, who wants to control everyone else's health but can't stop smoking himself" (Tawney, 2011, n.p.). Not only was Obama a bad person, but she was also an inappropriate advocate for change given she could not control herself and her love of French fries, her self-declared favorite food. The simple act of eating a particular food visually added on the pounds. Along with her big butt, the food choices showed Obama as out of control as she failed to enact her argument of health. Continuing the logic of these discourses, if she as an individual was out of control, her ability to tell the nation how to live healthy also existed as out of control for her as an advocate, read as stereotypical bossy Black woman.

Conclusion and Implications

The toned arms versus big butt discourses both assumed the First Lady should be a social advocate, but disagreed on her success as an advocate. Obama's corporeal body was the main, if not only, evidence considered. As Obama serves as the United States' first Black First Lady, intense scrutiny over her actions define what it means to be socially appropriate for women in general, and African American women in particular. By analyzing the two themes, these rhetorics showcased how a strong Black leader or social advocate disturbed images of Black women (Hobson, 2005) while it drew upon notions that fatness disturbs a normal healthy order (LeBesco, 2004; LeBesco & Braziel, 2001), reinscribing visualizations of the body as the primary, if not only, way to understand health and health advocacy.

In the United States, where increasing attention is placed on bodies, and particularly bodies within places of power and prestige, individuals must take notice of how they look and present themselves. Michelle Obama demonstrated how the corporeal body stands in as a metonymic representative of appropriate bodily advocacy. Agency operated within a particular bodily interpretation, circumscribed by how individuals read her body. Per the big butt discourse, if Obama had more control, she would not be a fat butt and glutton; she would be an appropriate advocate. Per the toned arms discourse, if Obama had less control, she would no longer be thin/toned but become fat and no longer be an appropriate advocate. Although she demonstrated being both subject and object, and thus disturbed easy categorizations of agency, the focus on advocacy as bodily display limited who can function as an appropriate advocate for change: those bodies deemed physically fit and thin.

References

Beerman, R. J. (2011). Too fat for Hooters? Examining the body as aesthetic evidence. In R. C. Rowland (Ed.), *Reasoned argument and social change: Selected papers from the seventeenth biennial conference on argumentation* (pp. 457–463). Washington, DC: National Communication Association.

Butler, J. (1993). *Bodies that matter.* New York, NY: Routledge.

The Centers for Disease Control. (2013a, January 11). Data and statistics: Obesity and extreme obesity rates decline among low-income preschool children. Retrieved from http://www.cdc.gov/obesity/data/childhood.html

The Centers for Disease Control. (2013b, February 19). Childhood obesity facts. Retrieved from http://www.cdc.gov/healthyyouth/obesity/facts.htm

Cooper, B. (2010). A'n't I a lady? Race women, Michelle Obama, and the ever-expanding democratic imagination. *MELUS, 35,* 39–57.

DeLuca, K. M. (1999). Unruly arguments: The body rhetoric of Earth First!, ACT UP, and Queer Nation. *Argumentation and Advocacy, 36,* 9–21.

DiMargo, C. (2011, May 4). Michelle Obama does the Dougie. *NBC Washington.* Retrieved from http://www.nbcwashington.com/the-scene/events/Michelle-Obama-Does-the-Dougie.html

Harold, C., & DeLuca, K. M. (2005). Behold the corpse: Violent images and the case of Emmett Till. *Rhetoric & Public Affairs, 8,* 263–286.

Hauser, G. A. (1999). Incongruous bodies: Arguments for personal sufficiency and public insufficiency. *Argumentation and Advocacy, 36,* 1–8.

Hesford, W. S., & Kozol, W. (2005). Introduction. In W. S. Hesford & W. Kozol (Eds.), *Just advocacy? Women's human rights, transnational feminisms, and the politics of representation* (pp. 1–29). New Brunswick, NJ: Rutgers University Press.

Hobson, J. (2005). *Venus in the dark: Blackness and beauty in popular culture.* New York, NY: Routledge.

hooks, b. (1992). *Black looks: Race and representation.* Boston, MA: South End Press.

James, S. D. (2009, July 21). Critics slam Surgeon General pick, Regina Benjamin. *ABC News.* Retrieved from http://abcnews.go.com/Health/story?id=8129947&page=1

Kiewe, A. (1999). The body as proof: Franklin D. Roosevelt's preparations for the 1932 presidential campaign. *Argumentation and Advocacy, 36,* 88–100.

Knox, O. (2013, February 28). Michelle Obama: Obesity fight is "generational" campaign. Yahoo! News. Retrieved from http://news.yahoo.com/blogs/ticket/michelle-obama-obesity-fight-generational-campaign-003906872--election.html

LeBesco, K. (2004). *Revolting bodies? The struggle to redefine fat identity.* Amherst: University of Massachusetts Press.

LeBesco, K., & Braziel, J. E. (Eds.) (2001). *Bodies out of bounds: Fatness and transgression.* Berkeley: University of California Press.

Let's Move! (n.d.). Learn the facts. Retrieved from http://www.letsmove.gov/learn-facts/epidemic-childhood-obesity

Michelle Obama: "I can't stop eating French fries. But eat your vegetables." (2011, June 23). *Fox Nation.* Retrieved from http://nation.foxnews.com/culture/2011/06/23/michelle-obama-i-cant-stop-eating-french-fries-eat-your-vegetables

Palczewski, C. H. (2002). Argument in an off key: Playing with the productive limits of argument. In G. T. Goodnight (Ed.), *Arguing communication and culture: Selected papers from the twelfth NCA/AFA Conference on Argumentation* (pp. 1–23). Washington, DC: National Communication Association.

Prelli, L. J. (Ed.). (2006). *Rhetorics of display.* Columbia: University of South Carolina Press.

Quinlan, M. M., Bates, B. R., & Webb, J. B. (2012). Michelle Obama "got back": (Re)defining (counter)stereotypes of Black females. *Women & Language, 35*(1), 119–126.

Rothstein, B. (2011, December 21). Lawmaker says Michelle Obama has "large posterior." *Mediabistro. com.* Retrieved from http://www.mediabistro.com/fishbowldc/lawmaker-says-michelle-obama-has-large-posterior_b59691

Rush Limbaugh: Michelle Obama "doesn't look like" she eats healthy foods. (2011, February 21). *Huffington Post.* Retrieved from http://www.huffingtonpost.com/2011/02/21/rush-limbaugh-michelle-obama-food_n_826092.html

Stark, L. (2012, September 5). Reporter's notebook: The Michelle Obama effect. *ABC News.* Retrieved from http://abcnews.go.com/Politics/OTUS/reporters-notebook-michelle-obama-effect/story?id=17164394#.UHbCzrSSLjA

Tawney, S. (2011, June 23). Michelle Obama: "I can't stop eating French fries. But eat your vegetables" [blog post]. *The American Pundit.com.* Retrieved from http://amerpundit.com/2011/06/23/michelle-obama-i-cant-stop-eating-french-fries-but-eat-your-vegetables/

TheEllenShow. (2012a, February 2). Can Ellen do more push-ups than Michelle Obama? [YouTube video]. Retrieved from http://www.youtube.com/watch?v=OTAIedFfUBU

TheEllenShow. (2012b, April 16). Michelle Obama defends her push-ups [YouTube video]. Retrieved from http://www.youtube.com/watch?v=1Zz9fh54GBI

Warner, M. (2002). *Publics and counterpublics.* New York, NY: Zone Books.

11

THE PROGENIC TRAUMA TATTOO AS RESIGNIFICATION

Auschwitz 157622, A-15510, 4559,...

Linda Diane Horwitz

LAKE FOREST COLLEGE, USA

Daniel C. Brouwer

ARIZONA STATE UNIVERSITY, USA

Addressing a recent and increasingly visible form of disturbing body argument, a September 30, 2012, *New York Times* article featured Israeli grandchildren of Auschwitz survivors choosing to duplicate the notorious numerical tattoos imposed upon the flesh of their grandparents decades ago on their own, progenic skin (Rudoren, 2012). Both the practice and the timing of such traumatic self-stigmatization call for careful analysis of salient political, cultural, and corporeal dynamics. While what we call *trauma tattoos* function as disturbing arguments, as both self-expressive identity construction (for the wearer) and rhetorical reminder to never forget (for the viewer), we are concerned primarily with how the progenic tattoo functions as a specific type of reappropriation, namely resignification.

This essay will unpack the argumentative force of the trauma tattoo once it has been (re)located and (re)presented from the bodies of actual survivors who were forcibly marked in the 1940s in Auschwitz to the bodies of progeny who choose to have their bodies tattooed with the sign. In the contemporary practice under our scrutiny, use of the Auschwitz tattoo disturbs our sense of the direct experiential relationship between the tattoo and the wearer. For Auschwitz survivors, the tattoo indexes a direct experience of Nazi atrocities. For progeny of survivors, wearing the tattoo retains a poignant *but altered* indexical function while newly activating other functions and effects of signification. The progenic tattoo indexes that tattooing was a real practice of Nazi inscription on Jewish bodies and that the Holocaust happened – but not directly to the wearer. This lacuna produces spaces of signification wherein the tattoo makes an invisible identity visible and understandable, insisting upon the continued traumatic effects of the Holocaust, calling upon public vigilance against its recurrence, and more. By retaining the content, style, medium, and familiar placement (on the left forearm) of the sign, yet drastically changing its meaning through the sign's historical circumstance, this contemporary practice demonstrates how resignification can be a powerful argumentative strategy.

We argue that shifting conditions of discourse across time (*chronos*) alter decorum (specifically, *kairos*) about the Holocaust. That is, a third generation of grandchildren participates in and hails others to participate in "never forgetting" in the face of losing the last generation of survivors, yet the manner in which they do so confounds discursive assumptions of a second generation that scarcely could imagine the practice as a legitimate form of memory work. In this sense, the third generation's practice disturbs fundamental expectations about what can be said by whom and in what way.

Trauma Tattoos, Resignification, and Jewish Culture

The Auschwitz tattoo, in comparison to other types and functions of tattoos, should be understood as a *trauma tattoo*. With *trauma* understood broadly as wound, we define the trauma tattoo as an inscription upon the body that signifies a wound. The wound can be individually experienced (e.g., the loss of a partner) or collectively experienced (e.g., stigmatization of HIV/AIDS diagnoses). Importantly, the tattoo can be imposed or chosen. Further, the tattoo can itself be the index of trauma – itself the brutal act (or one of many brutal acts) committed upon a body – or the tattoo can signify, more broadly, a physical, psychological, social, and/or political abuse. Defined in this way, we argue that both the Auschwitz tattoo (a brutally imposed wound inscribed upon unwilling prisoners) and the progenic tattoo (a chosen signifier of collective wound) are *trauma tattoos*, although the conditions for their existence differ radically.

The chosen progenic tattoo of the grandchild, copying the content, style, and placement of the grandparent's Auschwitz tattoo, is an example of a type of appropriation theorized as *resignification*. Broadly conceived, resignification refers to "the capacity to recite language oppositionally so that hegemonic terms take on alternative, counter-hegemonic meanings" (Lloyd, 2007, p. 129). Through familiar examples like *queer* and *bitch*, we see how "hate-speech can be turned against its tainted past; . . . [i]ts interlocutors can 'talk back'; they can resist" (Lloyd, 2007, p. 132). Bodies, too, can be sites of resignification, as scholarship on oppositional deployments of the Hottentot Venus and the slut body suggest (Netto, 2005; Ringrose & Renold, 2012). Traditionally, Jews have not engaged in rhetorical resignification in relation to the Holocaust. However, second and third generation Holocaust survivors have started to engage in the practice (Art Spiegelman's use of mice to depict Jews in *Maus* is a compelling example given the Nazi depiction of Jews as vermin). To clarify why Auschwitz tattoos are disturbing – disturbing to Jewish self-understanding, disturbing to presumptions about how best to practice public memory of the Holocaust, and disturbing to argument theory – we elaborate key dynamics of Jewish tradition in relation to tattoos and key dynamics of Nazi tattooing of Jewish people. Reference to these histories undergirds our argument that shifting conditions of discourse across time (*chronos*) alter decorum (specifically, *kairos*) about the Holocaust.

The use of a tattoo as a medium to practice public memory of the Holocaust can seem strange from at least three directions: the explicit prohibition against tattoos in the Torah; the urban legend that tradition prohibits people with tattoos from being buried in Jewish cemeteries; and the over-determination of the meaning of "Jewish tattoos" via the Nazi experience. Together, these conditions seem to stabilize – more specifically, incredibly *delimit* – the communicative context (and thus, the meanings and the political potentialities) of the progenic Auschwitz tattoo. As we demonstrate below, however, the burial myth is easily dispelled and the Torah's prohibition against tattoos is contested and not vigorously enforced. Nevertheless, important questions about agency via the acquisition of an over-determined sign remain open.

Until recently, tattoos were not a part of Jewish culture. Indeed, the Torah explicitly prohibits body modifications like tattoos: "Ye shall not make any cuttings in your flesh for the dead, nor print any marks upon you. I *am* the LORD" (Lev. 19:28). Rabbi Marshal Klaven, whose thesis at Hebrew Union College focused on Jewish tattoos, argued that "historical context is key. When Leviticus was written, tattooing was largely a pagan practice, done to mark slaves or to show devotion to a pharaoh" (as cited in Torgovnick, 2008). A tattoo, then, marked one as non-Jewish. Rabbi Klaven challenged the integrity of the Torah's seemingly unambiguous and enduring prohibition, suggesting that the rule "may be outdated" (as cited in Torgovnick, 2008). In contrast, Klaven's contemporary, Rabbi Alan Bright, insisted that tattooing should be avoided (Torgovnick, 2008). These positions are emblematic of the fact that the practice of tattooing is contested among Jewish scholars and is not unquestionably prohibited. Rabbi Bright, a representative of the Jewish Funeral Directors of America, was considerably more permissive on the issue of cemetery burials, dismissing the burial prohibition "as a load of rubbish" (as cited in Torgovnick, 2008). He is not alone: Several rabbinical scholars described the perception that being tattooed prohibits burial in a Jewish cemetery as a kind of "urban legend," likely instigated by a specific cemetery's prohibition that then was taken up by some Jewish elders as a way to express opposition to tattoos generally on grounds of "scriptural doctrine" (Torgovnick, 2008).

The fact that tattoos were foreign to Jewish culture is one reason that the forced identifying tattoos of Auschwitz are both so horrible and emblematic of the Holocaust. The U.S. Holocaust Memorial Museum's *Holocaust Encyclopedia* (n.d.) clarified that while the blue tattoos are emblematic of the Holocaust, "concentration camp prisoners received tattoos only at one location, the Auschwitz concentration camp complex" (para. 1). The process and placement of prisoner identifying numbers changed over time, including shifting placement of the tattoo from the left chest to the outer left forearm, to the inner left forearm. Primo Levi offered a poignant personal reading of the tattoos:

> Beginning in 1942 in Auschwitz[. . . ,] prisoner registration numbers were no longer only sewed to the clothes but tattooed on the left forearm . . . [M]en were tattooed on the outside of the arm and women on the inside. . . . The operation was not very painful and lasted no more then a minute, but it was traumatic. Its symbolic meaning was clear to everyone: this is an indelible mark, you will never leave here; this is the mark with which slaves are branded and cattle sent to slaughter, and that is what you have become. You no longer have a name; this is your new name.
>
> *(as cited in Apel, 2001, p. 165)*

Although only a fraction of the people impacted by the Holocaust was forced to endure tattoos, the tattoo has become a representative image of the Holocaust.

Auschwitz tattoos are easily understood outside of the context of 1940s Europe. In fact, they have come to stand in for the atrocities of the Holocaust and for humanity's disapproval of the Nazis' dehumanization and genocide of the Jews. Edwards and Winkler (1997) explained this function in rhetorical terms: "A representative form transcends the specifics of its immediate visual references and, through cumulative process of visual and symbolic meaning, rhetorically identifies and delineates the ideals of the body politic" (p. 295). Along these lines, M. E. Cohen drew a cartoon in response to the 2006 International Conference to Review the Global Vision of the Holocaust, held in Iran. The cartoon entreated, "all those who think the Holocaust is a myth, raise your hand," and depicted a single man raising his hand while leaning on a sign that reads "Holocaust Denial Conference" (Cohen, 2006). The next frame's header requested, "all those with proof that the Holocaust was real, please raise your hand." This frame is filled with six arms raised, all revealing numbers tattooed on the forearm. The cartoon's enthymematic meaning relies on the tattoos' status as proof of the Holocaust.

As the cartoon illustrates, the tattoos were not just a representative image but function as indexical proof of the Holocaust. Indeed, no one volunteered to acquire this specific tattoo. Therefore, until the recent practice of progenic tattooing, the presence of one of these tattoos on a person's arm would be a clear sign that s/he was a Holocaust victim. Such tattoos have been a powerful counter-argument to the claims of Holocaust deniers. As the people who bear these tattoos succumb to old age and engage in tattoo removal, the use of these tattoos in the effort to "never forget" is disappearing.

The Politics and Poetics of Progenic Tattoos

Tattoos in general, however, are becoming more and more common. The Pew Research Center found that, in 2012, 40% of Americans ages 26–40 had at least one tattoo (as cited in Tattoo statistics, n.d.). Jews have not escaped the trend. Andy Abrams, the creator of the documentary "Tattoo Jew," interviewed dozens of Jews with body art. His experience was that many of the tattoos are Jewish-themed: "The people I interviewed are trying to express their Judaism, or connect with God or their Jewish roots . . . They're taking this prohibited act and using it to feel more Jewish" (as cited in Torgovnick, 2008). The young Israelis profiled in the 2012 *New York Times* article are responding to the loss of the generation of survivors by marking their own bodies. Eli Sagir, who has the same tattoo as her grandfather, Yosef Diamant, 157622, explicitly got the tattoo to remind people of the Holocaust: "I decided to do it to remind my generation: I want to tell them my grandfather's story and the story of the Holocaust." She elaborated: "It's shocking when you see the number on a very young girl's hand. It's very shocking. You have to ask, Why?" (as cited in Rudoren, 2012). Ayal Gelles, who copied his grandfather's tattoo, A-15510, on his arm, said: "It's provocative, I guess. Everyone is kind of appalled at first, kind of shocked by it" (as cited in Rudoren, 2012).

The old, faded, fuzzy tattoos on the bodies of survivors, the youngest of whom now would be nearly 70 years old, signify that these people were subject to Nazi dehumanization and were detained, deprived, and scheduled for death, yet managed to survive and live to old age. When the sign is transferred to a new, young body, the sign's meaning changes. This transfer raises compelling concerns about damage to the original sign as an index of trauma. While we believe that transferring the sign alters the indexical meaning of the tattoo, the unfortunate truth is that the generation of survivors is diminishing and will soon be lost. In our view, because the sign is being placed on a body that could not have lived through World War II and the Nazi genocide, there is no concern that people will misread the sign as an index of the wearer's direct experience. Therefore, concern about damage to the original sign should be enjoined, but should not warrant prohibition of its resignification.

In short, shifting conditions of discourse across time (*chronos*) alter decorum (specifically, *kairos*) about the Holocaust, wherein resignification of the Auschwitz tattoo becomes intelligible as an act of public memory. Recognizing that the political valences and efficacies of resignification are never guaranteed in advance, we follow Lloyd's (2007) call to attend to the particular historical conditions that constitute the possibilities for resistance or counter-hegemony through resignification. Here, the specter of loss through the natural deaths of the last remaining Holocaust survivors (their fleshy evidence) produces an exigence. This exigence calls for a set of remembering practices, of kairotic responses, one of which we have featured here. A practice that would be largely unimaginable among second generation survivors becomes intelligible and understandable as a chosen signifier of collective wound, even as it disturbs because of the specter of loss.

In these altered historical conditions, this particular form of resignification works in distinct ways. Progeny understand their tattoos as disturbing, as shocking and provocative, and they report that some who witness their tattoos are appalled. We argue that the tattoos are disturbing in large part because they alter the indexical function of the tattoo while simultaneously validating iconic and symbolic functions. We anticipate that progenic tattoos are most disturbing to those who view the Auschwitz tattoo as so sedimented with meaning, and thus over-determined, by brutal Nazi imposition that it simply is not available for revision through resignification (e.g., Lloyd, 2007, pp. 132–134, 139). Progenic tattoos are an index (that the Holocaust happened); they are iconic (or representative forms); and more broadly, they are symbolic (a possibility opened up by the gap between the Holocaust and the third generation). Importantly, to describe them as symbolic is not to deny their indexicality, nor to suggest entrance into a frictionless field of floating signifiers – the number does not mean just anything, to be sure.

Through their simultaneous management of indexical, iconic, and symbolic functions, the new tattoos carry an argument of their own. The incongruity caused by a young person (who could not have lived through the war, as the sign normally designates) displaying this tattoo is an example of Burke's notion of the argumentative function of irony. For Burke (1945), *irony* is another word for *dialectic*, a presenting of two (or more) sides of an issue in which the audience is invited not to pick one side over the other but to see an enfolding of positions: "true irony, humble irony, is based upon a sense of fundamental kinship with the enemy, as one *needs* him, is *indebted* to him, is not merely outside him as an observer but contains him *within*, being consubstantial with him" (p. 14). In our example, one remembers the Nazi pawn forcibly tattooing a grandparent by choosing to be tattooed with the same image. This corporeal gesture is ironic or dialectical in that, in the tattoo, the viewer sees both the progenic tattoo and the original Auschwitz tattoo. It represents the win and the loss, freedom and control, past and the march to the future, all at the same time, inviting the audience both to remember that the Holocaust happened and to enact a moral imperative to spread the word. Young Jews assert their identity as grandchildren of survivors by marking themselves with the number that replaced their grandparent's name. These grandchildren assert their identity (as someone who would not exist if the Nazis had succeeded) while exposing that their lives, as well as their parents' and grandparents' lives, were altered forever by the Nazis.

As time passes and the eyewitnesses disappear, the Holocaust becomes ancient history. These young people articulate that they are not going to forget, and they are also going to help anyone who witnesses their tattoo in the process of never forgetting. Never forgetting is important enough that it must be permanent, visible, undeniable, and earned painfully. The trauma tattoo is a reminder that, even though the Allies ultimately won the war, the human losses were enormous, and the impact of inhumane treatment, which should never be repeated, is felt generations later. By *choosing* to tattoo themselves with their grandparents' trauma tattoo, these young people are taking on the roles of both agent and object, in the name of humanity. The sign moves from being an example of *inartistic* evidence (in the Aristotelian sense that it is a physical mark and not crafted by the speaker or the wearer) to *artistic* articulation of identity and the beliefs of the body politic. These tattoos also will generate conversation, either internally by the viewer or with the person displaying the tattoo. This conversation is what the grandchildren are hoping will take place, thereby ensuring that the world never will forget what happened in Europe in the 1940s.

References

Apel, D. (2002). Tattooed Jew. In *Memory effects: The Holocaust and the art of secondary witnessing* (pp. 164–186). New Brunswick, NJ: Rutgers University Press.

Burke, K. (1945). *A grammar of motives*. New York, NY: Prentice Hall.

Cohen, M. E. (2006). The Cagle post: Cartoons and commentary. Retrieved from http://www.cagle.com/members/news/holocaustdenial/page/3/

Edwards, J. L., & Winkler, C. K. (1997). Representative form and the visual ideograph: The Iwo Jima image in editorial cartoons. *Quarterly Journal of Speech, 83*, 289–310.

Lloyd, M. (2007). Radical democratic activism and the politics of resignification. *Constellations, 14*, 129–146.

Netto, P. (2005). Reclaiming the body of the "Hottentot": The vision and visuality of the body speaking with vengeance in *Venus Hottentot 2000*. *European Journal of Women's Studies, 12*, 149–163.

Ringrose, J., & Renold, E. (2012). Slut-shaming, girl power and "sexualisation": Thinking through the politics of the international SlutWalks with teen girls. *Gender and Education, 24*, 333–343.

Rudoren, J. (2012, September 30). Proudly bearing elders' scars, their skin says "never forget." *New York Times*. Retrieved from http://www.nytimes.com

Tattoo statistics. (n.d.). *Statistic brain*. Retrieved from http://www.statisticbrain.com/tattoo-statistics

Torgovnick, K. (2008, July 17). For some Jews, it only sounds like "taboo." *New York Times*. Retrieved from http://www.nytimes.com

U.S. Holocaust Memorial Museum. (n.d.). Tattoos and numbers: The system of identifying prisoners at Auschwitz. *Holocaust Encyclopedia*. Retrieved from http://www.ushmm.org/wlc/en/article.php?ModuleId=10007056

12

SMACKDOWN! MICHELLE v. OPRAH

Disturbing pleasures of the black catfight

Joan Faber McAlister

DRAKE UNIVERSITY, USA

Denise Oles-Acevedo

IOWA STATE UNIVERSITY, USA

We open by considering two articles, one from the *New York Post* and one from the *National Enquirer*, each alleging disputes involving former First Lady Laura Bush. The first appeared in 2006 with the headline "A (First) Lady-Like Way to Go on Attack" and reported Laura Bush's response to Hillary Clinton's quip about Republicans running a "plantation" in the House of Representatives, claiming Bush "deftly cut the former first lady down to size" without appearing "shrill" in her "ladylike" rejoinder to Clinton's "ridiculous comment" (Orin, 2006). The second article, titled "Feuding First Ladies!," leads with "Nancy Reagan BLASTS Laura Bush's memoir as 'shameful and undignified'" *and* explains that "oh-so-prim and proper Nancy" is "in a snit" over Bush's "unseemly" and "crass bid for publicity," to which Bush reportedly responded that Reagan is a meddling "old biddy" ("Why Nancy," 2010).

Both of these articles use gendered terms to redirect what might have been an exchange of differing positions on politics and ethics into the familiar drama of the "catfight," "a staple of American pop culture" revitalized by the news media (Douglas, 1994, p. 222). Susan Douglas (1994) described the catfight as "a spectacle: two women . . . locked in a death grip" (p. 223) which propagates the notion that "successful women can't get along with each other; they 'clash,' 'butt heads,' and 'fight,'" particularly over scarce resources: attention and decent men" – a scenario repeated in media depictions that redirect adult "female agency" into "high school" drama (Douglas, 2010, p. 258). Reinke (2012) analyzed the catfight as a stereotypical and sexualized medium of containment for women's bodies that infantilizes, eroticizes, and even invents agonistic encounters between women.

Although the sensationalistic and sexist spectacle of the catfight is already on display in the Bush-Clinton-Reagan articles, we can imagine even more titillating versions of these scandalous portraits of First Ladies. What if the *New York Post* depicted jealousy coming between close friends, described Laura's rage and suspicion that her husband is too intimate with her saucy rival, a fear fueled by the president's tendency to phone Nancy late at night? What if the *National Enquirer* declared a WAR! between Laura and Hillary, reported wounding remarks Laura made about Hillary's weight and public humiliations she cruelly visited upon this former friend, a powerful ally now heartlessly shoved aside as she pursued her career ambitions? What if these stories were spiced up with violent metaphors and a play-by-play format, illustrated with intimate photographs of the two friends embracing in happier times and later giving each other sidelong glances in glamorous evening attire, eyebrows arched and tension in the air?

These creative alterations to the original articles would amp up the drama and sex appeal of the alleged disputes, turning a catty exchange into a fleshy fight with more visceral appeal – replacing "ladylike" rejoinders with jealous rage, civility censures with a romantic rivalry, a "snit" with a war – and raising the stakes by bringing intimacy and intrigue into the conflict. Our hypothetical versions of articles about Laura Bush, Hillary Clinton, and Nancy Reagan might seem to go beyond the pale or sink below the belt (even for the *New York Post* and *National Enquirer*), but they were inspired by actual articles in these very publications – stories that took *precisely* this turn when reporting on an alleged dispute between First Lady Michelle Obama and talk show host Oprah Winfrey in May of 2012. We aim to examine how this dramatic heightening of aesthetics and erotics, aggression and intimacy, and physicality and emotionality provide particular pleasures in the spectacle of the Black catfight.

Analogies between representations of Michelle Obama and any former First Lady (or between Oprah Winfrey and any other media figure) are not easily drawn. However, we are not convinced that conventional concepts in argument theory are equipped to analyze the particular conditions shaping public representations of the character and rhetorical performances of Michelle Obama and Oprah Winfrey. Johanna Schmertz (1999) has challenged the application of the traditional abstract categories of character, charisma, and credibility because they do not get at established prejudices that audiences may project onto engaged interlocutors. Similarly, Carolyn Skinner (2009) argued that traditional understandings of ethos are inattentive to the role that *bodily* politics play in the performance of argument. Moreover, we are informed by Catherine Palczewski's (1998) observation at the 1997 Alta Conference on Argumentation that the "body is already always present in our theory whether we recognize its presence or not" and we are heeding her call to attend more carefully to the role of the body in the production of argument (p. 179).

Because arguments are em*bodied* and bodies are marked by differences that register to impede or assist ethos, we aim our inquiry directly at the patterns of prejudice at play in public performances of argument by profiling a specific case evidencing a mass-mediated cultural projection onto bodies, a fantasy fight developed out of agonistic exchanges that may or may not have taken place. Examining a popular, sensationalized version of a disagreement between two prominent Black women allows us to attend to the pleasures such staged performances offer to audiences, helping us to consider *how* and *why* the Black catfight sells papers. Although we find the spectacular portraits of Michelle Obama and Oprah Winfrey locked in combat to be disturbing, we are even more troubled by traditional argument studies' inattentiveness to the patterns that produce them and the pleasures they offer audiences. This is a trend we hope to disturb.

Birth of a Media Event

Edward Klein's (2012a) sensational book on Barack Obama, *The Amateur*, attributed a host of failures and flaws to a president in the midst of a re-election bid. It is comprised of 22 chapters exposing Obama's "dark side," including revelations that he "is inept in the arts of management and governance," promotes "policies that make our economy less robust and our nation less safe," and "discards old friends and supporters"(p. 2). U.S. tabloid print periodicals, online news services, and blogs generated a media event coinciding with the book's May release focused not on the male political leader disparaged in the book's title, but on a small section of the text describing a dispute between Michelle Obama and Oprah Winfrey. The many tempting and scandalous avenues down which election-year coverage of Klein's (2012a) book might travel (including the allegations that President Obama bribed Jeremiah Wright and that Bill Clinton was the source for its derogatory title) were barely explored as popular journalism gravitated toward a single chapter. These nine pages provided fodder for dishing out a catalog of clichéd personal insults and eroticized struggles invoking the spectacle of two estranged girlfriends battling over a man.

This "catfight" between the First Lady and the talk show host was illustrated through crude headlines, scandalous descriptions, and suggestive images, and cast two leading media stars in the roles of sexualized and demonized caricatures engaged in a disturbingly fleshy fight. Our analysis shows that the text and images used to create this spectacle offered visceral pleasures that are closely tied to cultural logics of sexism and racism. John Gabriel (1998) argued that the "populist style of engagement" tabloid media employ contributes to their particular significance as "sites for the articulation of racialised themes and imagery" making for a "distinctive role vis-à-vis ideologies of whiteness and the wider context from which whiteness both draws inspiration and invites an identification" (p. 41). Inspiring invitations to identify with whiteness (and reinscribe its caricatures of gender and racial difference) are evident in the spectacle of the Black catfight.

In May of 2012, eye-catching headlines appeared on the covers of the tabloids and the home pages of online popular news services and celebrity gossip blogs carrying stories of a conflict between Michelle Obama and Oprah Winfrey. Given space and time limitations, we analyze just six examples in order to illustrate shared themes and devices. The *New York Post* headline read "Michelle Obama's 'Jealousy' and 'Resentment' Led to Rift with Oprah" (Klein, 2012b), while the *National Enquirer* proclaimed "MICHELLE OBAMA WAR WITH OPRAH WINFREY!" in stark white capital letters surrounded by a black box. Likewise, *Newser* declared "It's Over Between Oprah, Michelle" (Gastaldo, 2012), and *The Blaze* sold the story with the headline "MICHELLE OBAMA VS. OPRAH? NEW BOOK CLAIMS JEALOUSY (AND FATNESS) MADE THEM GROW TO 'DESPISE' EACH OTHER" (Ritz, 2012). Perez Hilton's (2012) headline simultaneously sensationalized and questioned Klein's story with "Oprah And Michelle Obama HATE Each Other?! Bogus Reports Surface Suggesting Feud!" and the Black celebrity blog *Bossip* led with "Girl Fight: Explosive New Book Claims Michelle Obama And Oprah Were Beefin' And Fighting Over Barack" (2012). Each headline invoked the "catfight" with aggressive and violent terms making use of physical metaphors, with half of the headlines feminizing the conflict by implying that the women are battling over a man. Four of the six headlines suggested Michelle Obama is the aggressor or instigator, in keeping with the "Angry Black Woman" figure scholars have consistently found in media portrayals of the First Lady (Cooper, 2010; Madison, 2009; Lugo-Lugo & Bloodsworth-Lugo, 2011; Walley-Jean, 2009).

Each story placed prominent photographs of the First Lady and media icon close to the headlines. The *New York Post* printed a large color image of the First Lady beside Winfrey, their bodies pressed close together, bosoms nestling to form an s-curve at the center of the frame (Klein, 2012b). Obama wears a wide (but tense) grin and a dark pink sheath dress, appears at least six inches taller than Winfrey, and has one arm draped around Oprah's shoulders and the other exposed and fully inside on the left the frame.[1] Winfrey smiles slightly in a light peach sweater with a ruffled and flowered collar that is snug and only partially buttoned, her right arm around Obama's torso and her left side expanding beyond the right border of the image. The color scheme, height difference, and cropping assist a tall and athletic Obama to visually dominate Winfrey's relatively wide, passive, effeminate, and pale form. The *National Enquirer* is illustrated with a large color photograph of Obama and Winfrey seated together in formal attire. The bright lighting reflects off of the First Lady's glistening forehead and gold metallic gown, her heavy layer of cosmetics noticeable as she looks sideways under arched brows toward an out-of-focus Winfrey who faces forward in a navy-blue ruffled dress. The First Lady's right bicep is again fully visible, while Oprah's arms are hidden by Obama's body and expand beyond the frame, the angle accentuating their intimate distance. *Newser* provided the same photograph in the *Enquirer* story, but included a frame from the same sequence that captured Oprah laughing as Obama whispered into her ear (Gastaldo, 2012). *The Blaze*'s image placed President Obama between the First Lady and Winfrey (backed by a Christmas tree) where he stands closer to the talk show host than to his wife (Ritz, 2012). The First Lady wears a dark-purple, low-cut gown and smiles with arched brows. President Obama wears a wide grin over a dark suit and a deep red tie matching Winfrey's ruffled blouse and sweater. Perez Hilton juxtaposed two unflattering headshots of the talk show host and the First Lady: Neither is smiling but Obama's face is glistening and seen in semi-profile with a chin that juts forward, an anxious look in her eyes ("Oprah and Michelle," 2012). *Bossip* used the same image from the *National Enquirer* article, captioning Obama's sideways glance at Winfrey with the phrase "LET'S GET READY TO RUUUUUUUUUUUUUMBLE!" ("Girl Fight," 2012).

A repeated element in these images includes the First Lady's visual dominance in relation to Winfrey's passive poses and effeminate attire. The physical proximity and visible disengagement is heightened by bodily positions, facial expressions and the direction of their gazes – the First Lady looks "askance" or even covertly at the talk show host while the latter looks away in most images. Connotations of physical antagonism and intimacy are amplified by written descriptions enhancing the aggressive and sexual themes. The *New York Post* (2012b) article (taken from excerpts of Klein's book) reads like a blow-by-blow account of a fight, Winfrey was "shoved aside" but "struck back" and caused the First Lady to "stumble," while descriptions of Obama as "jealous" and suspicious after her husband's "late night calls" to Winfrey offer dramatic motive. *National Enquirer* reported that Obama and Winfrey "clashed repeatedly" in an "unseen war" after the First Lady "rudely pushed Oprah aside," repeated the phone calls detail, and quoted a remark from the First Lady about Oprah's "huge girth" with Winfrey declaring "Michelle hates fat people." *Newser* cited Winfrey's previous "closeness" to the Obamas and explained the "deteriorating" relationship with the jealously claims and weight comments (Gastaldo, 2012) while *The Blaze* depicted Obama and Winfrey "engaged in a subtle 'Mean Girls' style battle" (Ritz, 2012). Perez Hilton (2012) reported the questionable claim that these "two powerful women have been 'at war'" and expressed doubt (but nonetheless entertained the prospect) that "these strong women would . . . call each other fat and fight over a boy!" *Bossip*'s Black celebrity blog described "two female powerhouses" in an "ugly beef" during which the First Lady "rudely pushed Oprah aside." Transitioning between plot points with "But wait it gets nastier!!" and "DAYUM," *Bossip* added the playful phrases "calling Oprah a chubby lumpkins behind her back," "trying to late night creep with" the president, and "high school drama" ("Girl Fight," 2012).

These examples demonstrate the visual mode of the Black catfight, a spectacle evoked through sensational descriptions and evocative images providing pleasurable proof of characters preemptively ascribed to certain bodies. Media representations of Black women in the U.S. have long followed familiar formulas now identified by critical race scholars, including the Jezebel and Bitch figures. Patricia Hill Collins (2004) argued that these popular cultural stereotypes discipline as they "defeminize and demonize Black women" (p. 123). Though the stereotypes shift and adapt, their historical origins are still apparent (Lugo-Lugo & Bloodsworth-Lugo, 2011). Emerging during the slave era, the Jezebel is a Black woman who is "sexually promiscuous and immoral" (Walley-Jean, 2009, p. 70). Collins (2004) argued that the Jezebel figuration works to label Black women as "sexually aggressive," (77) while the more recent "Bitch" stereotype "draw[s] upon American sexual scripts of Black women's wildness" (p. 126). Images of "sexualized Black Bitches" are ubiquitous on billboards, television shows, and music videos. Moreover, films, websites, and magazines promising images of Black women fighting are mass-marketed and easy to find. If the "pissing contest" features the phallus, the catfight stars its unmentionable other. The catfight is always already a sexual spectacle.

Implications of the Black Catfight for Argument Studies

Our study analyzes popular media stories from 2012, but it is grounded in an important set of critiques of argument studies launched long before this event. Both feminist scholars (Bruner, 1996; Palczewski, 1997) and critical race scholars (Collins, 1998; Tomlinson, 2013) argued that body politics mediate argument performance, and our analysis shows that their concerns are still relevant nearly two decades after they were introduced. The spectacular fantasy fight projected onto these two famous Black women – influential leaders in U.S. public culture – indicates that certain patterns of prejudice are appealingly associated with particular bodies, even if the pleasures these associations promise are too polite to mention in a political culture permeated by "postracial" rhetoric. Indeed, Patricia Hill Collins (2004) has convincingly argued that bodily containment via media depictions is particularly urgent when Black women assume positions of leadership that may be seen as a threat to White and masculine privilege. Her warning is applicable to agonistic engagements between interlocutors whose eloquent speech acts may be disturbing for audiences accustomed to seeking different forms of entertainment from Black female bodies.

We close with the observation that an important chapter in the etymology of the term *interlocutor* concerns its historical association with a central figure in minstrel shows. It is the disturbing pleasures offered by what we have come to see as a mass-mediated minstrel show that we seek, most urgently, to disturb.

Note

1. Carmen R. Lugo-Lugo and Mary K. Bloodsworth-Lugo (2011) and Joan Faber McAlister (2009) address how media representations of the First Lady's bare arms help to render her body non-normative through tropes of masculinity, class, and race.

References

Bruner, M. (1996). Producing identities: Gender problematization and feminist argumentation. *Argumentation and Advocacy*, *32*(4), 185.

Collins, P. H (1998). It's all in the family: Intersections of gender, race and nation. *Hypatia 13*(3), 62–82.

Collins, P. H. (2004). *Black sexual politics: African American, gender, and the new racism*. New York, NY: Routledge.

Cooper, B. (2010). A'n't I a lady?: Race women, Michelle, Obama, and the ever-expanding democratic imagination. *MELUS*, *35*(4) p. 39–57.

Douglas, S. J. (1994). *Where the girls are: Growing up female with the mass media.* New York, NY: Times Books.

Douglas, J. (2010). *Enlightened sexism: The seductive message that feminism's work is done.* New York, NY: Times Books.

Gabriel, J. (1998). *Whitewash: Racialised politics and the media.* London, UK: Routledge.

Gastaldo, E. (2012, May 14). It's over between Oprah, Michelle: Winfrey-Obama relationship breaks down, Edward Klein alleges. *Newser.* Retrieved from http://www.newser.com/story/145952/its-over-between-oprah-michelle.html

Girl fight: Explosive new book claims Michelle Obama and Oprah were beefin' and fighting over Barack. (2012, May 14). Retrieved from http://bossip.com/585356/girl-fight-explosive-new-book-claims-michelle-obama-and-oprah-were-beefin-and-fighting-over-barack

Klein, E. (2012a). *The Amateur: Barack Obama in the White House.* Washington, DC: Regency.

Klein, E. (2012b, May 12). Michelle Obama's "jealousy" and "resentment" led to rift with Oprah. *New York Post.* Retrieved from http://www.nypost.com/p/news/national/jealous_michelle_vs_oprah_wDXXjFfq75tZRro1jy1AtK

Lugo-Lugo, C. R., & Bloodsworth-Lugo, M. K. (2011). Bare biceps and American (in)security: Post-9/11 constructions of safe(ty), threat, and the first black First Lady. *Women's Studies Quarterly, 39*(1–2), 200–217.

Madison, D. S. (2009). Crazy patriotism and angry (post)black women. *Communication and Critical/Cultural Studies, 6*(3), 321–326.

Michelle Obama War with Oprah Winfrey! (2012, May 14). *National Enquirer.* Retrieved from http://www.nationalenquirer.com/celebrity/michelle-obama-war-oprah-winfrey

Oprah and Michelle Obama hate each other?! Bogus reports surface suggesting feud! (2012, May 14). Retrieved from http://perezhilton.com/2012–05-14-oprah-and-michelle-obama-hate-each-other

Orin, D. (2006, January 19). A (first) lady-like way to go on attack. *New York Post.* Retrieved from www.nypost.com/p/news/item_GjDiBOSIfWd2Su8bzASHSM

Palczewski, C. (1998). Bodies that argue: Power, difference and argument. In J. Klumpp (Ed.), *Argument in a Time of Change: Definitions, Frameworks, and Critiques* (pp. 179–184). Annandale, VA: NCA.

Reinke, R. (2010). Catfight: A feminist analysis. *Chrestomathy, 9*, 162–185.

Ritz, E. (2012, May 13). Michelle Obama vs. Oprah? New book claims jealousy (and fatness) made them grow to "despise" each other. Retrieved from http://www.theblaze.com/stories/2012/05/13/michelle-obama-vs-oprah-new-book-claims-jealousy-and-fatness-made-two-of-americas-most-powerful-women-despise-each-other/

Schmertz, J. (1999). Constructing essences: Ethos and the postmodern subject of feminism. *Rhetoric Review, 18*(1), 82–91.

Skinner, C. (2009). "She will have science": Ethos and audience in Mary Gove's lectures to ladies. *Rhetoric Society Quarterly, 39*(3), 240–259.

Tomlinson, B. (2013). To tell the truth and not get trapped: Desire, distance, and intersectionality at the scene of argument. *Signs, 38*(4), 993–1017.

Walley-Jean, C. J. (2009). Debunking the myth of the "angry black woman": An exploration of anger in young African American women. *Black Women, Gender & Families, 3*(2), 68–86.

Why Nancy Reagan hates Laura Bush's guts. (2010, May 17). Retrieved from http://www.nationalenquirer.com/celebrity/why-nancy-reagan-hates-laura-bushs-guts

13

STARVING TO LIVE

Self-mutilation as public argument in the Colombian hunger strikes

Ryan Erik McGeough

UPPER IOWA UNIVERSITY, USA

Danielle Dick McGeough

UNIVERSITY OF NORTHERN IOWA, USA

On August 1, 2012, Jorge Parra carefully applied sterilizer to his mouth and the area surrounding his mouth before piercing his lips with a needle and systematically sewing his mouth shut. Exactly one year prior, former General Motor (GM) employees began picketing the U.S. embassy in Bogatá, Colombia to protest having been fired after suffering debilitating injuries on the job. Many of the injuries reported by former employees of GM Colmotores outside Bogotá "stem from repetitive movements, lifting excessive weights, harmful body postures, and an accelerated work pace on the assembly line" (Luft, 2012). Such injuries make it difficult for ex-GM employees to find work elsewhere, thus leaving the ex-workers and their families without electricity, water, food, or a home. Following a year of picketing in relative anonymity, thirteen men initiated a hunger strike. Seven of them recorded themselves sewing their mouths shut, as they proclaimed that they are "totally prepared to die" (Cavaliere, 2012). The video shows the workers puncturing their lips with needles and methodically pulling thread through their lips to seal their mouths shut. Images of the sewn workers' faces quickly circulated through both Colombian and international media. Within three weeks, the images and a video produced by the strikers had prompted solidarity hunger strikes throughout the Americas and Europe, and played a role in compelling GM to begin negotiations with the strikers.

Be it hunger strikes, self-immolation, or chopping off one's fingers, photographing images of deliberate self-harm is an extreme approach to obtaining social or economic redress. Underlining DeLuca's (1999) claim that bodies are "a pivotal resource for the cultural practice of public argumentation" (p. 10), this essay explores the hunger strike by the Association of Injured Workers and Ex-Workers of General Motors Colmotores (ASOTRECOL). Michelle Murray Yang (2011) argued that rhetorical artifacts, such as photographs of extreme communicative acts, "can function as a resource for future rhetorical acts in varying contexts" (p. 4). Re-appropriating previous methods of public protest, ASOTRECOL's decision to sew their mouths shut as part of their hunger strike created a spectacle intended to shock and affect viewers. Such self-inflicted violence is "a means of performing a visual embodiment of violence done by an 'other'" (Yang, 2011, p. 2). The photographic capture, remediation into video, and circulation across communication networks of the sewn mouths of ASOTRECOL members registers and preserves this violence. Deliberate self-harm – self-immolation, chopping off one's fingers, or, as we argue, hunger strikes – are extreme communicative acts designed to draw attention to situations needing redress. Maud Ellmann (1993) suggested "the feature that distinguishes a hunger strike from other forms of self-starvation is the statement that supplements the wordless testimony of the famished flesh" (p. 17). In the ASOTRECOL images, the recently sutured strikers are not yet starving. However, by displaying the impossibility of eating, the images simultaneously portray a body already in pain and index the entire process of the hunger strike, enthymematically suggesting the potential for workers to starve.

As the ASOTRECOL images present the viewer with the potential death of the workers, the verbal cues that accompany the images – whether the captions under the images, the information on the ASOTRECOL website, or the verbal testimonies offered on the ASOTRECOL-produced video – present death as inevitable unless General Motors agrees to negotiate with the workers. In a statement released with the images, ASOTRECOL stated that "to symbolize their commitment to this hunger strike and to the justice that they are seeking, they will be sewing their mouths closed and plan to carry out the hunger strike to the death" (Luft, 2012). The combination of the disfigured workers and accompanying verbal cues indicating their likely death makes the images a unique subset of what Barbie Zelizer (2010) has coined *about to die* images. Zelizer noted that about to die images present:

> a range of ambiguous, difficult, and contested public events, which are shown by depicting individuals facing their impending death. Focusing on intense human anguish, [they offer] a simplified visualization of death-in-process in events as wide-ranging as natural disaster, crime, accidents, torture, assassination, war, illness, and acts of terrorism.
>
> *(p. 24)*

The images thus serve a metonymic role, as the depicted bodies at risk offer corporeal representations of the complex events leading up to and following the image. Images offer a powerful tool for shaping public argument and moving publics (Hariman & Lucaites, 2007). About to die images are particularly powerful in this regard. Zelizer (2010) located the power of the about to die image in its ability to suspend the moment just before death and break from the denotative "as is" typically associated with photographs to the subjunctive "as if" (p. 15). In fixing the moment before death, about to die images shape public discourse by creating a space for the viewer to imagine alternative possibilities.

Examples of about to die images include Zelizer's (2004) analysis of people jumping from the burning World Trade Center, Hariman and Lucaites's (2007) consideration of iconic images including those from the Vietnam War and Kent State Massacre, Zelizer's (2010) analyses of about to die images from Afghanistan and Iraq, and Yang's (2011) essay on Malcolm Browne's photograph of the burning monk. In each case, the images were taken by bystanders (typically photojournalists) and, as Zelizer (2010) noted, circulated to a public who generally knew what happened immediately after the photographs were taken.

In these regards, the ASOTRECOL images are different from most about to die images. Members of ASOTRECOL produced the images in an attempt to gain public recognition and support in their struggle with Colomotors. The remainder of this essay analyzes how the ASOTRECOL images function rhetorically by focusing on three central strategies of the images: 1) depicting disturbing body argument, 2) offering a representation of impending – but preventable – death, and 3) providing agency to viewers by combining the images with discursive calls to engage in specific actions in order to prevent the workers from starving to death.

Disturbing Body Argument

The positions once held by the former General Motors workers required workers with healthy, strong bodies. By lifting heavy equipment and spending long hours on the assembly line, GM workers used their bodies as a resource to provide for themselves and their families. However, over time, the repetitive movements and the quickness with which employees were expected to work took a toll on workers' bodies. Now injured, the workers were unable to perform their jobs as they once did, thus justifying General Motors' decision to fire the injured workers. Disabled, jobless, and homeless, the ex-workers once again called upon their bodies, this time using their vulnerable bodies as public argumentation to attract media and to provide visual and physical evidence to their claims.

From the time the former General Motors' employees began to strike, their bodies were at risk. The AFL-CIO reported that Colombia is one of the most dangerous countries in the world for labor unions, estimating the murder of roughly 4,000 Colombian trade unionists in the past 20 years (Cavaliere, 2012). The threat of violence from others was not enough to gain notice, as the strikers received little media attention until they initiated the hunger strike and threaded their lips shut. The photographs of the workers' sewn lips and the accompanying video of the workers sewn lips are viscerally disturbing. In the video, Parra's skin turns a sickly yellow as he applies sterilizer. He grimaces as the needle punctures his skin and reluctantly slides through his lips, a procedure that is repeated several times before the task is done. Upon completion, Parra's mouth is yellow and pink and swollen, with two x's sealing his mouth shut. Parra does not need to tell his audience that he is in constant pain or weak. He does not need to explain how dire the situation has become. He does not need to say, as he later does through his sewn lips, that "We're practically dead, you know, seeing our families like this" (as cited in Detroit, 2013).

The strikers' vulnerable bodies not only attract media attention, they also provide visual and physical evidence to support their claims. In the video "Kicked to the Curb" (Luft, 2012), former GM employees share stories about how they acquired their injuries. For example, one man in the video displays his scarred and disabled hand for the camera as he tells about an accident in which his hand was caught in a machine and skewered (Luft, 2012). However, the GM workers' bodies are not the only bodies that suffer from General Motors' actions. In the video "GM Generating Misery" (Luft, 2012), a father explains that his family does not have electricity due to his loss of job. His children have burned themselves on candles, as that is all with which they have to light their home. Another child shows a severe leg injury that must be treated with home remedies because her family has no money for medical treatment. The ex-workers and their families' weakened, scarred, and disabled bodies serve as evidence of GM's unethical practices. The strikers' sewn lips visually demonstrate what is otherwise invisible: the ex-workers are starving. Thus, the images "visually demonstrate the human consequence of the violent acts in question" (Birdsell & Groarke, 2007, p. 109).

Images of Impending But Preventable Death

The disabled and starving bodies depicted in the ASOTRECOL images vividly suggest the potential of the hunger strikers' impending deaths. These images, like all about to die images, function as a visual enthymeme – not actually depicting death itself, but rather providing evidence and asking viewers to supply a conclusion. In traditional media representations, about to die images work through enthymeme by necessity – Zelizer (2010) noted that significant public backlash typically accompanies depiction of actual death. Instead, by depicting the moment preceding death, about to die images testify to death but still allow viewers the possibility of imagining alternative possibilities. In these images it is too late to save the dead, but the images still function to inspire collective action to avoid repetition of the circumstances that led to death.

The ASOTRECOL images differ from traditional about to die images in that although it is difficult to look at them and not recognize the impending starvation of the workers, the moment of death is further in the future. The images do not just suspend the moment before death; they also index the totality of the hunger strike process. The regular updates posted to the ASOTRECOL website supplement the images by offering visitors information on the progress of the strike. Updates include one malnourished worker being hospitalized and an accompanying video depicting one worker with only enough space between his lips to drink water through a small straw (Farrell, 2006, p. 66).

The ASOTRECOL images also are unique in that they allow for the possibility of saving the people depicted. Zelizer described the power of about to die images as their tie to the subjunctive, the "what if" moment in which death is suspended, and the viewer is able to look at the image and imagine an alternative ending – what if the Vietcong general did not execute the hostage, what if firefighters rescued the burning monk, what if the people jumping from the burning towers somehow landed safely, etc. Zelizer described these responses as illogical or fanciful, as viewers generally know what happened after the photograph was taken. Yet the ASOTRECOL website supplements the images by making clear the complete contingency of the hunger strike: If Colmotors continues to ignore the workers, they will starve; if Colmotors negotiates with the workers, they will live. In an interview prominently linked on the ASOTRECOL website, hunger strikers speak through sewn lips about the possibility of their impending deaths. Yet, the ASOTRECOL site also makes clear the workers' desire to lift the strike if Colmotors would negotiate with them. Both the images and accompanying videos and text suggest that though the workers and their families face death, their lives may yet be saved.

Providing Agency to Viewers

Zelizer (2010) and Yang (2011) both noted that about to die images provide resources for collective action and future rhetorical acts. Such images offer rhetorical resources to motivate collective action to prevent similar events from recurring. Those depicted in about to die images metonymize "the groups who can most easily carry the symbolic message they embody – children, babies, the elderly, and prison guards, relief workers, soldiers, members of militias" (Zelizer, 2010, p. 128). As viewers we might not be able to save those falling from the World Trade Center, but perhaps we can work to prevent another similar disaster from occurring.

In the case of the ASOTRECOL images, however, the accompanying videos and website (with its prominent "Como Ayudar – How To Help" tab) not only indicate the very real possibility of preventing the workers and their families' deaths, but encourage the viewer to engage in specific actions that can help prevent these impending deaths. Here, then, is where images of impending but preventable death differ most clearly from traditional about to die images. The stretched temporality of impending but preventable death images, coupled with

ASOTROCOL's verbal and written calls to action, position viewers in a way that allows them to affect what comes next. Viewers are offered agency through the calls to engage in very specific actions to help ASOTRECOL. This possible agency converts the subjunctive "what if" (e.g., What if Colmotors negotiated with the workers?) into "what if I" (e.g., What if I contacted the Columbian embassy?). The How to Help page includes a number of ways viewers can aid the strikers, including a donation link; phone numbers and email addresses for the United States embassy in Columbia, the Columbian embassy in Washington, D.C., and the U.S. Bureau of International Labor Affairs; Twitter links for U.S. President Barack Obama, Colombian President Juan Santos, and General Motors; and multiple Facebook sites. Juxtaposed against this information is an image of four of the ASOTRECOL workers with their lips sewn shut.

The ASOTRECOL website also asks visitors to donate to support the families of the starving workers and to post links about the hunger strike. Thus, visitors are offered an active role in compelling Colmotors to negotiate with the workers, supporting the workers' families, and helping to spread word (and images) of the strike. As noted, this strategy works because the ASOTRECOL images suspend deaths that are impending but preventable. By tapping into the sympathy created by an image of starvation and providing agency for viewers, the hunger strike has not only mobilized international support for the workers but has led to support in other ways as well. Dozens of sympathizers have used social media to distribute their own videos and images of solidarity hunger strikes. Strikers have also picketed General Motors headquarters with signs including images of the Columbian hunger strikers.

Conclusion

Within three weeks of circulating these images, officials from Colmotors agreed to meet with the strikers. We argue that the power of this hunger strike results from the production and dissemination of images of the strikers as well as accompanying information that allowed viewers to complete the visual enthymeme. As a form of visual enthymeme, impending but preventable death images differ from traditional about to die images in at least two ways. First, the moment of death is further in the future in impending but preventable death images, and thus the possibility of saving the particular person in the image remains. Second, though viewers of about to die images know with certainty what happens next, about to die images are open in terms of possibilities for how one might respond. Impending but preventable death images, by contrast, are combined with text to call for a much more specific response. Because the stakes are not preventing future deaths, but saving the lives of the particular people depicted, images of impending but preventable death offer a powerful rhetorical tool to move viewers toward particular actions to aid those who need help dealing with their specific material circumstances. By combining images of their starving bodies with discourse calling for particular actions, the ASOTRECOL images ask viewers to prevent the deaths of future workers and the discourse invites them to help the hunger strikers and their families by providing supporters with specific ways to help save the lives of the strikers. Negotiations continue, but the disturbing images of the hunger strikers have provided a powerful visual argument and ensured they will no longer be ignored.

References

Birdsell, D. S., & Groarke, L. (2007). Outlines of a theory of visual argument. *Argumentation and Advocacy, 43*, 103–113.

Cavaliere, V. (2012, August 15). Ex-GM workers in Colombia sew shut mouths, open third week of hunger strike. *Daily News*. Retrieved from http://www.nydailynews.com/news/world/ex-gm-workers-colombia-sew-shut-mouths-open-week-hunger-strike-article-1.1136973

DeLuca, K. M. (1999). Unruly arguments: The body rhetoric of earth first!, ACT UP, and queer nation. *Argumentation and Advocacy, 36*, 9–21.

Detroit. (2013, January 27). Jorge Parra, hunger striker, speaks out about injured Colombian workers. *Critical Moment*. Retrieved from http://critical-moment.org/2013/01/27/jorge-parra-hunger-striker-speaks-out-about-injured-colombian-workers/

Dicker, R. (2012, August 20). Ex-GM workers on hunger strike in Colombia sew mouths shut to protest firings. *The Huffington Post*. Retrieved from http://www.huffingtonpost.com/2012/08/20/gm-hunger-strike_n_1812561.html

Douglas, M. (1966). *Purity and danger: An analysis of concept of pollution and taboo*. New York, NY: Routledge.

Ellmann, M. (1993). *The hunger artists: Starving, writing, and imprisonment*. Cambridge, MA: Harvard University Press.

Farrell, J. M. (2006). The horrible spectacle: Visual and verbal sketches of the famine in Skibbereen. In L. J. Prelli (Ed.), *Rhetorics of display* (pp. 66–89). Columbia: University of South Carolina Press.

Hariman, R., & Lucaites, J. L. (2007). *No caption needed*. Chicago, IL: University of Chicago Press.

Luft, A. (2012, August 2). Colombian workers sew their mouths together to protest GM plant firing tactics. Retrieved from http://gmauthority.com/blog/2012/08/colombian-workers-sew-their-mouths-together-to-protest-gm-plant-firing-tactics/

Nicholas, J. (2008). Hunger politics: Towards seeing voluntary self starvation as an act of resistance. *Thirdspace: A Journal of Feminist Theory & Culture, 8*(1), Retrieved from http://www.thirdspace.ca/journal/article/viewArticle/nicholas/215

Sturken, M. (1997). *Tangled memories*. Berkeley: University of California Press.

Wee, L. (2004). "Extreme communicative acts" and the boosting of illocutionary force. *Journal of Pragmatics, 36*, 2161–2178.

Yang, M. M. (2011). Still burning: Self-immolation as photographic protest. *Quarterly Journal of Speech, 97*, 1–25.

Zelizer, B. (2004). The voice of the visual in memory. In K. R. Phillips (Ed.), *Framing public memory* (pp. 157–186). Tuscaloosa: University of Alabama Press.

Zelizer, B. (2010). *About to die*. New York, NY: Oxford University Press.

14

DISTURBANCES TO CERTAINTY

A rhetorical analysis of the legality of the "Pregnant Man"

Marylou R. Naumoff

FLORIDA ATLANTIC UNIVERSITY, USA

Erika M. Thomas

CALIFORNIA STATE UNIVERSITY, FULLERTON, USA

Since antiquity, the need to address issues of the contingent (what is possible and also probable) provided early rhetoricians with a drive to develop and study discursive strategies. When approaching contingency, a common assumption is that rhetoric and argument reduce or eliminate uncertainty. For example, the notion that exigencies occur that require a rhetorical response (Bitzer, 1968) or that argument is "the practice of justifying decisions under conditions of uncertainty" (Zarefsky, 2001, p. 32) speak to this presumed tendency in both rhetoric and argumentation. Perhaps individuals tend to privilege the predictable because, as Burke (1966) argued, humans are "goaded by the spirit of hierarchy (or moved by the sense of order" (p. 16), incentivizing and requiring predictable, tidy outcomes. However, theorists have also celebrated the creation of uncertainty, such as G. Thomas Goodnight (1991) and Charles Willard (1986). Goodnight's endorsement of controversy and Willard's promotion of dissensus show that the generation of certainty is not always the most productive function of argument. To sustain disagreement and controversy at the expense of delaying consensus and the restoration of certainty forces individuals to ask questions and think critically about issues in a way that is often not possible when there is a need to reach a consensus quickly.

U.S. society is experiencing a crisis of consensus over sex identity. One example contributing to this dissensus is the emergence of improbable figures making claims to sex categories that seem inconsistent with our traditional notions governed by the male/female binary. For many, Thomas Beatie made the impossible a reality when he became a pregnant man. This essay uses the case of the "Pregnant Man" to explore how the rhetor, Thomas Beatie, benefited from making the choice to actively exacerbate contestations over his sexual identity. By stressing his legal designation as man, Beatie challenged his detractors to not only question how they define him, in particular, but also how they define sex, in general. This analysis reveals how definitional arguments can actually serve as a way to unsettle, rather than promote, consensus/certainty.

Definitions typically gain power by fixing that which is contingent and fluid. In a similar way to how rhetoric and argument are frequently used to limit the improbable in the face of a world made up of contingent relations, definitions are used to stabilize and limit conditions of possibility by providing rules of classification. Definitions ensure that if something is to count as one thing, then it must possess the defining qualities of said thing. A definition, then, is an "instrument of naming reality, namely the aspect of shared knowledge allowing one to give a name to a fragment of reality" (Walton & Macagno, 2009, p. 83). Thus, the ability to define an individual or thing is not neutral and ultimately influences understandings of reality.

Definitions also carry power as arguments because they stabilize the contingent and attempt to limit the meaning of a term regardless of the situation. Of course, definitions are themselves contingent, but their power comes from the fiction that they are not and that they fix the contingent element of the thing defined. As Brian McGee (1999) stated, "all definitions in the end are contingent, given that they are continuously subject to revision as the discursive terrain shifts and perceptions of material reality are altered" (p. 153). Thus, definitional claims invite contingency perhaps more so than other forms of argument because of their indeterminate and changing nature.

Furthermore, Zarefsky (1997) explained that definitions used in argumentation can rarely reflect or describe permanent qualities because "what is really being defined is not a term but a situation or a frame of reference" (p. 5), thereby further highlighting the contingent nature of arguments by definition. Because definitions are unstable, like the situations they define, they require constant maintaining and negotiating. In the following case study, we trace Beatie's use of definitional argument. We argue that he breaks with traditional conceptions of definitional argument as a way to fix meaning or create rules that should be followed. Beatie's rhetorical strategy is to reference his legal designation as male to destabilize understandings and assumptions about the moniker *man*.

In his memoir, *Labor of Love*, Beatie (2008c) shared his story. Beatie was born Tracy Lagondino in 1974 and was raised as a girl. He recalled being mistaken for a boy by his classmates in elementary school. Despite conflicted feelings, Tracy identified as a woman and lesbian as a young adult. In 1998, Tracy met her current wife, Nancy. Shortly thereafter, Tracy began to question her identity, again. She started to identify as transgender and began the process of transitioning through hormone therapy. In 2002, Tracy applied for a legal sex change and legally became Thomas Trace Beatie. In 2003, after the sex change was legal, Thomas and Nancy were married in Hawaii. Beatie and Nancy wanted to have children, but Nancy was unable to conceive due to a hysterectomy. At age 34, Beatie decided to use his uterus to "father" his children. He stopped testosterone hormone treatments, was artificially inseminated with donor sperm and, during his pregnancy, announced his condition to the public. On March 25, 2008, *The Advocate* published Beatie's story, which explained that he was currently living as the "first" legally pregnant man (Beatie, 2008a).

Two constituting elements make Beatie's claim to being a pregnant man possible: the legal designation *man* and the claim of possessing an essence of manhood. Both claims are interrelated definitional arguments.

The moniker *man* is not only a way to categorize an individual, but also a way to establish criteria of what can be expected of such individuals and their position in society. Society takes comfort in the predictable categorization of bodies so that they remain readable. As more transgender individuals make the transition from one sex to another, in some ways, the male/female binary becomes solidified rather than challenged. When making this transition, individuals are then permitted and expected to act in accordance with the performances of that sex. Beatie in many ways defies this promise by not acting in accordance with the definition of man. Grounded in premises of disruption and uncertainty, Beatie's arguments become a way to resist traditional arguments in public debates and a means to justify and define a new identity.

Transgender individuals' primary claim to obtaining sexual reassignment surgery is that their interior self does not match their exterior self and, therefore, a correction is necessary to render them whole. This is not to say transgender individuals or the medical community view identity as fixed and essential, but a certain overstating and overperforming of the claim is necessary to garner the legitimacy needed to receive sexual reassignment surgery and the change in their legal sex status. The notion of being born "in the wrong body" stems from the *Diagnostic and Statistical Manual of Mental Disorders* (*DSM*), which:

> subscribes to forms of psychological assessment which assume that the diagnosed person is affected by forces he or she does not understand. It assumes that there is a delusion or dysphoria . . . that certain gender norms have not been properly embodied.
>
> *(Butler, 2004, p. 77)*

John Sloop (2004) explained that heterosexuality and gender normativity are often maintained through a transgender/sexual claim to an essential identity:

> There is an articulation of gender identity as based in the "soul" or brain, and of the preoperative body as birth defect . . . there is an overall argument that the transition to the "other" gender was made because the person was already essentially the other, that only a "defect" kept one from one's natural body . . .
>
> *(p. 138)*

Furthermore, traditional dictionary definitions of the word *transsexual* emphasize the notion of desire for an opposite identity. MacKenzie (1994) surveyed several entries for "transsexual" and noted that these definitions include the following: "a person having a strong desire to assume the physical characteristics and gender role of the opposite sex" and "a person who has undergone hormone treatment and surgery to attain the physical characteristics of the opposite sex" (p. 12).

Beatie's attempt to redefine his own identity/body disrupts the previous definitions cited by members of the transgender community, located in legal and medical literature. Beatie used the discourses available to him, available largely due to the work of the transgender community, to inhabit a body that feels authentic to him and to have that body recognized as legitimate by the law. Beatie can be viewed as breaking a promise by choosing to craft an identity that is not explicitly masculine. An example of this can be found in the following claims: "Who I am today is who I always was" and "I had exactly the body needed for my life" (Beatie, 2008c, pp. 81–82). A similar sentiment is found in his interview with Oprah: "And I realized that I wanted to be free again like I was when I was younger, when I didn't see the world as male or female. I just wanted to be myself . . . It wasn't something that I analyzed" (Beatie, 2008b, p. 7). Rather than describing himself in accordance with a sex, he often referenced his identity as "me." He asserted that he was simply living as it felt natural, implying that there is a truthfulness to his embodiment.

According to Butler (2004), discourse like Beatie's is fairly risky, especially when attempting to gain a DSM-IV diagnosis:

> You would be ill-advised to say that you believe that the norms that govern what is
> a recognizable and livable life are changeable . . . you cannot explicitly subscribe to
> a view that changes in gendered experience follow upon changes in social norms.
>
> *(p. 81)*

Beatie strategically attempted to undue the conditions that produce various forms of certainty
through the use of definitional claims that violate the established transgender rules. These
rules dictate that one is seeking to lead a life that is consistent with social and cultural understandings of sex. Beatie problematized the definitions and characteristics that determine who
is a male and who is a female and how individuals are required to live their lives. Beatie
accomplished this in two ways. First, he illustrated that notions of sex are inherently unstable.
Beatie in effect challenged his audience to question the constituting elements of their
definition of *man*. In one passage in his book, Beatie (2008c) factually described the complexity
of sex. He discussed intersex individuals who are born with mixed chromosomes and
hormones, rhetorically asked whether a man who loses his penis in an accident is any less of
a man, explained that reproductive organs are not a conclusive characteristic, and described
various biological sex conditions in populations. Finally, he stated: "For me, the answer to the
question 'What makes a man a man?' is this: There is no scientific answer. It is a personal
conviction – it is how you feel inside when you wake up in the morning" (Beatie, 2008c,
p. 259). These claims demonstrate how Beatie attempted to displace the definition of
man based on empirical fact and replace it with a notion that man be defined by one's own
conviction. He also privileged his definition of manhood as based on conviction rather than
biological sex as he vehemently claimed, in an interview appearing in the documentary about
his life, that he is his child's father, not mother:

> I would say that 99, 100% of people when you see someone and you see someone
> that looks like me, I'm going to be called male. People are now calling me female
> because I decided to use my reproductive organs – what if I had gotten a surrogate,
> you know, what if we adopted you know, if we adopted a child I'd be the child's
> father. I would be, right? Isn't that what most people would see our family as?
> Father, mother . . . but for some reason, a lot of people have a problem seeing me as
> male. So does a penis make a man?
>
> *(as cited in Kozak & Lazarus, 2008)*

In this passage, Beatie exposed the assumptions grounded in U.S. society. He attempted to
use facts about biology as a way to unravel people's preconceived notions of sexual difference,
genitalia, and reproduction, or characteristics that Sloop (2004) identified as "visible cultural
marker(s)" (p. 61). Rhetorically, Beatie questioned the cultural discourse that iterates strict
sexual binaries by selecting arbitrary traits that define maleness and femaleness.

The second way that Beatie disrupted certainty is by referencing his legal claim to manhood
to craft his identity. Beatie consistently referenced and cited his legal status as male to expose
the abstract nature of sex. In other words, each time Beatie cited the legality of his sex change,
audiences are faced with questioning which are the most legitimate expressions of one's true
sex identity: the law or concrete gender/sex performances? This perspective is represented in
the documentary, *Pregnant Man*, when the narrator explained, "Thomas's decision not to have
his womb and his ovaries removed has caused many to question whether he can really be
considered a pregnant man" (Kozak & Lazarus, 2008). As Beatie further clarified, "One of the
major criticisms is that I'm not a man, you know, why is the media continually perpetuating

the story as a pregnant man . . . it followed by calling me by my first name, my former name, Tracy . . . No one is recognizing my legal status as male" (as cited in Kozak & Lazarus, 2008). By citing the law, Beatie explicitly disrupted pregnancy as a cultural marker of womanhood. In much the same way, he disrupted attempts of some individuals to categorize him as a lesbian. In his memoir, Beatie (2008c) explicitly denied that he can now identify as a lesbian:

> It's strange to me when people ask me if Nancy and I aren't just two lesbians. By definition, a lesbian is a woman who is sexually attracted exclusively to other women. Therefore, because I am legally male and identify as male, I am not a lesbian. Years ago, before I decided to transition, I lived my life as a woman, and I was attracted to other women. But even then I knew inside I was a man.
>
> *(p. 311)*

In this passage, Beatie referenced constituting elements of his manhood – definition, legal designation, and conviction – to render illogical claims that he is a lesbian. Beatie insisted that he is a man despite his reproductive organs and his choice to become pregnant. Beatie (2008c) explained:

> I am our baby's father . . . I was the one who gave birth to our child, and existing definitions equate "birth parent" with "mother" – but that is only because no one like me has ever come around before. By those same definitions, all mothers are female – and I am legally and unequivocally a male; therefore, I can't be a mother.
>
> *(p. 310)*

This is Beatie's most explicit deferral of biological sex as the defining quality of whether one is man or woman. Even in light of giving birth, he still adamantly privileged his conviction of being male as *the* defining element of his identity.

The privileging of an internal sense of one's sexual identity trumped biological markers of sex as ever-present elements of Beatie's discourse. Surprisingly Beatie is only able to create this separation through the referencing of his legal status as male. Ordinarily, legal designations of sex seek to guarantee certainty by rigidifying definitions of sex. Isaac West (2011) noted that the Kansas Supreme Court chose to define sex based on the ability to procreate to avoid the messy case of a transgender women obtaining half of her late husband's estate. To minimize confusion and to avoid disrupting conventional notions of womanhood, the court defaulted to understandings of sex based on a biological function rather than an internal conviction. This led West to encourage transgender advocates to "undo cultural attachments to binary, immutable sex categories" (p. 175). This is precisely what Beatie's discourse achieved when he gave accounts of his identity as male. Interestingly, he primarily achieved this rhetorical feat through the use of his legal status as male, a legal definition that ultimately functions to prevent such actions from occurring. Beatie proved to be a savvy rhetor, indeed, as he shifted the function of legal definitions and the law and consequently used them to serve a purpose antithetical to producing order and certainty.

Ultimately, Thomas Beatie and his rhetorical strategies serve as a useful case study for both argument and rhetorical studies. The twenty-first century has proven to be a time of contestation over many types of identity and there does not seem to be a tidy terrain of certainty emerging any time soon. As individuals continue to disrupt conventional notions of identity and performativity, critics who study discourse should consider the potentiality of the exacerbation, rather than the elimination, of uncertainty.

References

Beatie, T. (2008a, March 25). Labor of love. *The Advocate*. Retrieved from http://www.advocate.com

Beatie, T. (2008b, April 3). Interview by O. Winfrey [Transcription]. First TV interview: The pregnant man. *The Oprah Winfrey Show*. Harpo Productions, Chicago, IL.

Beatie, T. (2008c). *Labor of love: The story of one man's extraordinary pregnancy*. Berkeley, CA: Seal.

Bitzer, L. (1968). The rhetorical situation. *Philosophy and Rhetoric*, *1*(1), 1–14.

Burke, K. (1966). *Language as symbolic action*. Berkeley, CA: University of California Press.

Butler, J. (2004). *Undoing gender*. New York, NY: Routledge.

Goankar, D. (2001). Contingency and probability. In T.O. Sloane (Ed.), *Encyclopedia of rhetoric* (pp. 151–166). New York, NY: Oxford University Press.

Goodnight, T. (1993). Controversy [Keynote address]. In D.W. Parson (Ed.), *Argument in Controversy: Proceedings of the 7th NCA/AFA Summer Conference on Argumentation* (pp. 1–13). Washington DC: National Communication Association.

Kozak, S., & Lazarus, S. (Producers), & MacDonald, E. (Director). (2008). *Pregnant man* [Documentary]. United Kingdom: September Films.

McGee, B. R. (1999). The argument from definition revisited: Race and definition in the progressive era. *Argumentation and Advocacy*, *35*, 141–158.

MacKenzie, G. O. (1994). *Transgender nation*. Bowling Green, OH: Bowling Green State University Popular Press

Sloop, J. M. (2004). *Disciplining gender: Rhetorics of sex identity in contemporary US culture*. Boston: University of Massachusetts Press.

Walton, D., & Macagno, F. (2009). Reasoning from classifications and definitions. *Argumentation*, *23*(1), 81–107. DOI: 10.1007/s10503–008-9110–2

West, I. (2011). What's the matter with Kansas and New York City? Definitional ruptures and the politics of sex. *Argumentation and Advocacy*, *47*, 163–177.

Willard, C. A. (1986). Valuing Dissensus. In F. H. van Eemeren, R. Grootendorst, J. A. Blair, & C. A. Willard (Eds.), *Argumentation: Across the lines of discipline: Proceedings of the Conference on Argumentation* (pp. 145–158). Providence, RI: Foris Publications.

Zarefsky, D. (1997). Definitions [Keynote address]. In J. F. Klumpp (Ed.), *Argument in a Time of Change: Proceedings of the 10th NCA/AFA Summer Conference on Argumentation* (pp. 1–11). Annandale, VA: National Communication Association.

Zarefsky, D. (2001). Directions in research in argumentation theory. In G. T. Goodnight (Ed.), *Arguing Communication and Culture: Proceedings of the 12th NCA/AFA Summer Conference on Argumentation* (pp. 32–39). Washington, DC: National Communication Association.

15

DJANGO UNCHAINED AND THE UNDISTURBED FRONTIER HERO ARCHETYPE

Samuel P. Perry

BAYLOR UNIVERSITY, USA

The opening of Quentin Tarantino's *Django Unchained* features a Western ballad playing as slave traders atop horses lead slaves on foot through the desert terrain of Texas. The Western theme music and topography foreshadow the transition of the title character, Django, from chattel slave to gun slinging frontier hero. So begins the "bloody live action cartoon" (Scott, 2012, p. C1) and Tarantino's (2012) self-described quest to "deconstruct *Birth of a Nation*" through a re-articulation of spaghetti Westerns and Blaxploitation films. *Django Unchained* attempts to deal with the ugliness of slavery through graphic representations of violence endured by slaves and by creating a Black character capable of revisiting that violence on a plantation owner and his underlings. Along the way, Tarantino invites audiences to witness brutal Mandingo fights, the devouring of a slave by ravenous dogs, threatened castration of the title character, and other violent actions accompanied by steady deployment of the "N" word. The movie's themes and representations of violence make it a complicated text. Tarantino (2012) justified his creative choices during an interview with Henry Louis Gates, Jr., promoting the release of *Django Unchained* by arguing: "It's like, look, the stuff that we show is really harsh, and it's supposed to be harsh, but it was [actually] a lot worse." Tarantino's comment suggested he thinks the violence of the film is necessary to convey a particular message about the evils of slavery. Many interpretations of the violence and representation of slavery are available. Jamie Foxx, Kerry Washington, and Samuel L. Jackson, the film's African American stars, found the film a unique and productive representation and retelling of slavery (Tarantino and Cast, 2012).

While *Django Unchained* offers potentially liberating readings of racial violence, when read a certain way, the film engages in what Jean Baudrillard (1993) referred to as "operational whitewash" (pp. 44–45). Operational whitewash is the process by which "everything which is unable to relinquish its own identity is inevitably plunged into a realm of radical uncertainty and endless simulation" (Baudrillard, 1993, p. 45). *Django Unchained* sanitizes historical structures by failing to address larger systemic issues of slavery and White supremacy that precluded slave revolts and ensured that African Americans, freed or enslaved, never got the chance to live out revenge fantasies akin to the one in the film.

The film forgoes critical reflection on the circumstances of slaves in antebellum United States because Django is cast as a mythological frontier hero. Janice Hocker Rushing (1991) argued that because the "frontier myth is a powerful and value-laden embodiment of the [U.S.] cultural identity, it is important for the rhetorical critic to trace its changes" (p. 244). Rushing (1989) argued the static nature of frontier heroes remains predicated on patriarchal notions of "conquest" (p. 21). Inflexible adherence to the frontier hero role in situations or locations incommensurate with the frontier myth often creates rhetorical or ethical problems (Perry, 2012, p. 265). While Helene Shugart (1997) aptly pointed out that appropriation of the frontier myth is possible (pp. 214–220), *Django Unchained* falls short of critical appropriation of the frontier myth in this reading.

Ultimately, *Django Unchained* fails to make the arguments about race through the creation of a new Black hero because Django's perpetration of violence within the frontier hero construct becomes his only means to power to the extent that the "exercise of power implies the insignificance of those who exercise it" (Baudrillard, 1993, p. 50). Operational whitewash takes place as Tarantino's spaghetti Western revenge fantasy absconds with the film's emancipatory potential. Django becomes a one-dimensional rehash of frontier heroes past.

The first step in operational whitewashing takes place in forging Django into a frontier hero. Frontier heroes engage in conflict in limited ways. Django adheres to the typical model of conflict prescribed the frontier hero. Ron Carpenter (2006), building on Rushing's work, wrote that frontier heroes inevitably follow a path that leads to the hero exterminating "evil personae with 'consummate gunmanship'" (p. 180). Django learns the tricks of the frontier trade from King Schultz, a white German bounty hunter, played by Christoph Waltz. The unlikely union of Schultz and Django takes the two men to a plantation in Mississippi where Calvin Candie, played by Leonardo DiCaprio, holds Django's wife, Broomhilda, played by Kerry Washington. The intrepid frontier heroes attempt to secure Broomhilda's freedom through guile adhering to the notion that, at least until the final showdown, the frontier hero "avoid[s] violence for as long as possible" (Carpenter, 2006, p. 180). However, Django fulfills his frontier hero destiny by killing Candie, all of his associates, and blowing up the Candie plantation. The frontier hero mythos is maintained with striking faithfulness, a fact Tarantino (2012) repeatedly pointed out in his interview concerning the movie with Gates.

Such adherence throws the film into a loop regarding the potentially liberating role of Django. For all the genre fusion and Tarantino's willingness to disturb the audience with casual usage of the "N" word and graphic images of violence toward slaves, he forgoes a willingness to manipulate the generic conventions of the frontier hero beyond giving him a Black identity, which rather than being original functions as Tarantino's nod to Blaxploitation films (Tarantino, 2012). Django as the frontier hero *qua* frontier hero falls into the same conventional limitations that make such a hero deeply problematic in terms of inculcating that hero in a mythology of ever-expanding and never-ending violent, zero-sum conflict (Slotkin, 1973, p. 5). This means that conflicts that arise from slavery, or any other racial inequity, can only be addressed through violence – an argument new to no one with an inkling of historical knowledge regarding Black militancy and its heroes.

Further, the frontier hero model generally establishes a hero apart from the community. The loner arrives just in time to solve a problem and rides westward into the setting sun once the problem ceases to exist. Rushing (1991) wrote that frontier heroes often spend most of their existence on the periphery of society (p. 246). Django remains on the edges of society throughout the film, forming a bond only with King Schultz. Django's development into a frontier hero apart from society proves problematic from the standpoint of creating a slave hero and fully addressing the evils of slavery from an institutional standpoint. Salamisha Tillet

(2012) aptly explained the problem: "And yet his exceptionality comes at a price: Unlike 'Amistad's' Cinque or 'Beloved's' Sethe, he [Django] seems to exist in a vacuum. Most of the slave characters he meets are not his equals … they barely dent racial stereotypes." The movie's brutal representations of violence carry little critical weight because the protagonist remains aloof and isolated from the other Black characters in the film with the exception of his wife, Broomhilda. So even as the film breaks ground through postmodern critiques of genre in regard to the ever sensitive subject of U.S. slavery, the genre transgressions do little to tie the violence of slavery, or the violence Django commits, to a critical framework that interrogates the historical structures that propagate actual racial violence. Django's violence is an aesthetic expression of the genre. While references to films like *Mandingo, Goodbye Uncle Tom*, and Sergio Corbucci Westerns complicate the violent aesthetic, they may not account for Django's own detachment from the struggle against slavery.

Django's detachment takes center stage in a scene where a prize fighting slave, D'Artagnan, from Candie's plantation runs away only to fall back into the hands of Candie's minions. Simultaneously, Candie, Candie's entourage, King Schultz, and Django happen upon the hopelessly trapped D'Artagnan. Treed by dogs and surrounded by captors, Candie orders D'Artagnan to descend the tree in order to speak with him. After a brief conversation with Candie, D'Artangan receives a death sentence. In a detailed, disturbing scene, the audience bears witness to dogs tearing apart a still living D'Artagnan. Tarantino, comparing the scene to violent spaghetti Westerns directed by Sergio Corbucci, explained, "And with that in mind, this violent, pitiless Corbucci West: What would be the American equivalent of that – that really would be real – that would be an American story? It was being a slave in the antebellum South" (Tarantino, 2012). Tarantino drives home the point that chattel slavery allowed slave owners to act violently, with impunity, toward slaves. Two things stand out here. First, in Tarantino's rush to find a point of comparison to make sense of the violence represented in his film, he forgoes the possibility that the violence in the West, though brutal, shares little in common with the violence faced by Blacks held in slavery in the antebellum United States. The point of comparison falls apart when one realizes that the violence of the slave trade resulted from a highly structured legal system that explicitly approved of violence toward African Americans, while the violence of the American West as represented in Westerns occurred largely in the absence of legal structures that might have prevented it. Secondly, the graphic representation of a Black man being eaten alive by dogs causes serious distress that motivates violent retribution on the part of only one character.

The scene creates a moment of reflection not for Django, but instead for King Schultz. The scene marks a turning point in the film. Django, perhaps desensitized from violence he witnessed as a slave, perhaps because of a singular focus on rescuing his wife, is less affected by the scene than Schultz. Django assumes the role of the leader in the film from this point on because he retains the ability to separate his goal of saving Broomhilda from the practice of slavery itself. Schultz's concern ends up his undoing in the final showdown with Candie, and it is Schultz's empathizing with D'Artagnan that leads to his demise. Schultz relinquishes his frontier hero title and Django's frontier hero role takes on epic proportions because Schultz attaches himself to the idea that he cannot maintain his integrity in a world where slavery dominates the landscape.

The construct of the frontier hero hews the edges off the Django character and weakens his connection to other slaves. Django stands in a long line of characters and historical figures made less complex through frontier mythology. Rushing (1989) explained in her analysis of *Alien* and *Aliens* that the frontier myth often coopts its heroes into "patriarchal archetypes" (p. 24). Leroy Dorsey (2007) argued that while the frontier myth sometimes offered a proving ground for minority groups to establish American identity, all too often that identity required dropping distinctive characteristics of the previously held identity (p. 67).

The frontier hero persona assumed by Django focuses him singularly on securing his wife's freedom. No solidarity between Django and other slaves exists outside of his love for Broomhilda, with the exception of one moment during a gun fight when confronting the henchmen who captured D'Artagnan, Django yells, "D'Artagnan, Mother Fuckers!" before dispatching the henchmen with precision marksmanship and deft theatricality. In this highly stylized exhibition of violence, Tarantino's conformity to the frontier identity plunges into cycles of endless simulation and exaggeration by entering into an "indifference to content," marked by "operational, performative" (Baudrillard, 1993, p. 48) uses of violence. The violence loses connection to the struggle faced in slavery, despite the exhortation of the fallen slave's appellation. Tarantino's explanation of the violence that takes place in the movie from this point in the plot forward is telling:

> . . . on one hand I'm telling a historical story, and when it comes to nuts and bolts of the slave trade, I had to be real and had to tell it the right way. But when it comes to more thematic things and operatic view, I could actually have fun with stylization – because it is taking parts from a spaghetti Western. And I am taking the story of a slave narrative and blowing it up . . . to operatic proportions . . .
>
> *(Tarantino, 2012)*

Putting aside the question of whether Tarantino exposes the "nuts and bolts of the slave trade . . . the right way," and focusing on the operatic expression of the spaghetti Western, it seems Tarantino is willing to foreground the genre's aesthetic of violence to the detriment of contextualizing the violence of the film within historical trappings of the slave trade – a move that would have provided all the dramatic material Tarantino needed. Recall Tarantino's earlier comment regarding the violence of slavery: "the stuff that we show is really harsh . . . but it was [actually] a lot worse" (Tarantino, 2012). The violence suffered by Blacks in the movie, though graphically and sometimes realistically portrayed, cannot thoroughly represent the violence suffered by slaves. However, Tarantino tries to portray violence visited on slaves realistically. This stands in stark contrast to violence visited on Whites in the film, which operates on a level consumed with simulating the films within the spaghetti Western genre from which Tarantino takes the "parts" of the movie. Django's bullets cut people in half, gunshot wounds explode with blood, and some antagonists are literally blown off the screen. Whites suffer fantastic and unrealistic harm, and never experience trauma at the level that Blacks in the movie face on an almost scene-by-scene basis. The violence against African Americans reaches stomach-churning levels of graphicness, while Tarantino dares the audience to laugh at the violence doled out to Whites by Django. The oscillation between poles of graphic realism and whimsical fantasy suggests the very real violence suffered by African Americans remains and rends the possibility of Whites suffering comparable violence comical. These representations of violence are a far cry from the intended "deconstruction of *Birth of a Nation*."

The transposing of the frontier hero onto a plantation in the U.S. South continues the process of operational whitewash. A frontier hero makes little sense within the confines of a highly structured and stratified society. Mississippi in 1858 hardly fit the definition of a frontier; the frontier hero, much less a Black frontier hero, served little purpose in this milieu. In addition to local customs and laws, the Dred Scott decision and Fugitive Slave Act fortified a culture that denigrated Black humanity in order to prop up White superiority. In 1852, some six years prior to the time *Django Unchained* is set, Frederick Douglass (1998) argued, "For black men there is neither law nor justice, humanity nor religion. The Fugitive Slave *Law* makes mercy to them a crime; and bribes the judge who tries them. An American judge gets ten dollars for every victim he consigns to slavery . . ." (p. 261). Ironically, Django's race places a much more easily fetched bounty on his freedom within the setting of the film than any bounty that Django collects through the course of the film. The social and legal controls of slavery preclude the free movement of Django through Mississippi, Texas, and Tennessee, the three named slaveholding states through which Django travels under the pretense of his bounty hunting occupation.

The banality of evil represented by Candie would not have been most evident in his personal acts of cruelty and terrorism in the singular, isolated location of his plantation, but in the fact that he operated within a network of slaveholders whose estimations of Black humanity so pervaded the cultural mindset of the United States that the Fugitive Slave Act and the Dred Scott decision stood as the legal standard operating procedure. The showdowns staged within the frontier mythos involve mostly unconnected communities with little communicative immediacy from one outpost to the next. The geographic relocation of the frontier hero to the plantation removes any chance of addressing the systemic issues that precluded slave resistance and rebellion. The violent quelling of slave rebellions took place not only at the local level, but through sweeping regional retribution such as the kind following the 1831 Nat Turner Slave Rebellion in Virginia. Black resistance to slavery, other than through the actions of Django, disappears into the ether of Tarantino's revenge fantasy. At one point, Candie questions why slaves never killed Whites, and answers his own question using phrenology to explain Blacks' genetic predisposition to submissiveness – a point so glossed in the movie that one might not stop to recall instances of active and organized Black resistance to slavery. As reviewer Andy Boyd (2013) pointed out, "Tarantino's revenge fantasy depicts acts of black resistance to slavery as just that, a fantasy." Not only the failure to place Django's character within the context of organized Black resistance, but going out of the way to contextualize him within the violence of the slave trade, only make more prominent the operational whitewashing of historical Black heroes who resisted and protested the violence and injustice of slavery. Professor Jelani Cobb (2013) stated in his review for *The New Yorker*, "with the exception of the protagonist and his love interest – [slaves] are ciphers passively awaiting freedom." Tarantino's supposition that Django's willingness to fight slavery at any cost made him 1 in 10,000 undercuts the argumentative potential that fantasized violence against slaveholders in the film might provide.

Django Unchained conforms to the frontier myth in ways that ignore realities of U.S. slavery and cleanse the structural violence propagated within U.S. slavery. Django's detachment from other slave characters in the movie erases the bulk of moral and racial dilemmas regarding slavery. Django's laconic frontier hero attitude flattens the depth of the character in ways that trivialize the violence against slaves in the film. The stylized exaggerations of violence intended to punish the movie's antagonists proffer the points that Tarantino wishes to make through the creation of a Black Western hero moot.

References

Baudrillard, J. (1993). *The transparency of evil: Essays on extreme phenomenon* (J. Benedict, trans.) London, UK: Verso.

Boyd, A. (2013, February). Django Unchained: Quentin Tarantino's new film reinforces racist beliefs. Retrieved from http://www.policymic.com/articles/23809/django-unchained-quentin-tarantino-s-new-film-reinforces-racist-beliefs

Cobb, W. J. (2013, January 2). Tarantino unchained. *The New Yorker.* Retrieved from http://www. newyorker.com/online/blogs/culture/2013/01/how-accurate-is-quentin-tarantinos-portrayal-of-slavery-in-django-unchained.html

Dorsey, L. (2007). *We are all Americans, pure and simple: Theodore Roosevelt and the myth of Americanism.* Tuscaloosa: University of Alabama Press.

Douglass, F. (1998). What to a slave is the fourth of July? In P. S. Foner & R. Branham (Eds.), *Lift every voice: African American oratory 1787–1900* (pp. 246–268). Tuscaloosa: University of Alabama Press.

Tarantino and cast talk: Why make Django Unchained? (2012, December 19). *MTV Buzz.* Retrieved from http://movies.mtv.co.uk/news/tarantino-and-cast-talk-why-make-django-unchained/n8i3rn

Tarantino, Q. (2012). Tarantino "Unchained" Part 1–3 [Interview by H. L. Gates]. Retrieved from http://www.theroot.com/views/tarantino-unchained-part-1-django-trilogy?page=0,4

Perry, S. (2012). Douglas MacArthur as frontier hero: Converting frontiers in MacArthur's farewell to congress. *Southern Communication Journal, 77,* 263–286.

Rushing, J. H. (1989). The New Frontier in *Alien* and *Aliens*: Patriarchal cooptation of the feminine archetype. *Quarterly Journal of Speech, 75,* 1–24.

Rushing, J. H. (1991). Frontierism and the materialization of the psyche: The rhetoric of *Innerspace*. *The Southern Communication Journal, 56,* 243–256.

Scott, A. O. (2012, December 25). The black, the white, and the angry. *New York Times,* p. C1.

Shugart, H. (1997). Counterhegemonic acts: Appropriation as a feminist rhetorical strategy. *Quarterly Journal of Speech, 83,* 210–229.

Tillet, S. (2012, December 2012). Quentin Tarantino creates an exceptional slave. Retrieved from http://inamerica.blogs.cnn.com/2012/12/25/opinion-quentin-tarantino-creates-an-exceptional-slave/

16

DISTURBING IMAGES

Medical photography of the bodies of intersex individuals

Sarah S. Topp

TRINITY UNIVERSITY, USA

Medical photographs have been used for the education of medical professionals and as part of medical records. Offering important visual information, images have an integral role in improving treatment and teaching doctors (Creighton, Alderson, Brown, & Minto, 2002). However, in the case of intersex individuals, medical photographs may do more harm than good. Ostensibly created for educational purposes and to improve treatment, the images function to demonstrate deviation from the *norm*. The photographs depict unwanted physical manifestations of intersexuality. Their realism makes them seem neutral; however, they are embedded within specific cultural contexts. As such, the medical photographs of intersex individuals are best understood by investigating the context of contemporary medicine.

Within the unique visual culture (Evans & Hall, 2004) of the medical arena, photographs of intersex individuals function as a form of disciplinary surveillance, transforming the subject of the photograph into the object of the observer's gaze (Twigg, 1992). I posit that photographs reify unequal power relations, elevating doctors as legitimate authorities able to speak about, and for, intersex people in the absence of the people about whom they speak. Further, the photographs serve as medical enthymemes for why surgery is supposedly necessary in intersex cases. Understood by doctors as displaying disordered bodies, medical photographs legitimize corrective surgery for what is perceived as different and wrong. As long as bodies are trumpeted as aesthetically displeasing and disturbing to binary sex/gender norms, the only appropriate response is surgical change. Finally, the photos function as dangerous figural resources for those outside of the medical field.

To build this case, I define intersexuality and give a brief description of the typical practice of medical photography. This, along with studies and the narratives of adult intersex individuals, helps to explain why the photographs are medically unnecessary and dangerous for the photographed individuals. Their stories offer compelling support for their calls to limit, if not end, the medical photography of intersex children. Many intersex individuals express a desire to maintain ownership of the visual representation of their bodies and differentiate medical photographs from other images used by intersex individuals for self-empowerment.

Although their demands should be sufficient justification for reform of the practice, I construct a supplementary case that details the problems of the medical field's photography of intersex children.

What Is Intersex?

Intersexuality refers to variations in sex characteristics, including chromosomes, hormones, gonads, and/or genitalia. It is an umbrella term for a host of "congenital conditions in which the development of chromosomal, gonadal, or anatomical sex is atypical" (Lee, Houk, Ahmed, & Hughes, 2006, p. 488). People who are intersex may not fit traditional definitions of male or female (OII, 2013). Morland (2005) added, "Intersex bodies have . . . configurations that cannot be adequately apprehended by hegemonic discourses . . . Their genitalia have tended to be called 'ambiguous', which does not mean that they intermittently change shape. . . . Instead, [they] are difficult to understand" (p. 335). "Confusing to all the adults in the room" (Dreger as cited in Bloom, 2003, p. 103), the newborn's genitals are distressing to doctors, who understand the child's body to be abnormal. Thought to be pathological, the perceived deviant body justifies medical interventions, including genital surgeries, hormone regimens, and medical photography to map the body.

Acknowledging problems with the use of medical photography of intersex individuals, doctors from the United Kingdom suggested new standards for good practice. Despite widespread reference in medical journals and a decade's time, little evidence exists proving the adoption of the standards (Creighton et al., 2002). A similar doctrinal shift was suggested in the United States at a 2005 medical conference. The resulting publication limited the rush to surgery and updated other standards of care (Hughes et al., 2006; Lee et al., 2006); however, it remained silent on the issue of photography.

The Photographic Process

Genital photography typically occurs at the first meeting of a doctor with an intersex youth (Brain et al., 2010) and is repeated regularly throughout maturation into adulthood (Preves, 2003). Intersex individuals are "classically photographed naked" (Creighton et al., 2002, p. 67). Reflecting on her childhood, an adult with intersex variation Complete Androgen Insensitivity Syndrome (CAIS) remembered, "They made me be naked in a room and take pictures of me . . . [W]hy did they make me stand in a room and have pictures taken with no clothes on and humiliate me like that without saying anything to me" (as cited in Creighton et al., 2002, p. 69). The shame felt by this individual is replicated many times, as privacy safeguards commonly fail and the photograph is circulated.

Although medical images are now covered by the Health Insurance Portability and Accountability Act, there is little that stops any health care employee from using the images, especially because most are digital and hard to track (Creighton et al., 2002). Similarly, although informed consent is supposed to be obtained every time a photograph is taken and used, there is little enforcement, scant evidence that people follow informed consent procedures, and age restrictions that mean children cannot consent for themselves (Wall, 2010). One adult learned that naked pictures were taken of her without her mother's consent and another, who was searching for information about CAIS, was surprised to find a photograph of herself as a child published in a medical text. She explained, "I was shocked when I saw it . . . not as shocked as my mom though! . . . My mom had no idea he would publish them" (as cited in Creighton et al., 2002, p. 70).

The practice has been found to be psychologically traumatic. Numerous studies have shown medical photography can lead to symptoms that correlate closely with those who have survived the trauma of child sexual abuse (ISNA, 2005; Money & Lamacz, 1987), including dissociation (Young, 1992) and symptoms related to post traumatic stress disorder (Goodwin, 1985). Brain et al. (2010) found long-term psychological stress from the dissemination of the photographs.

Photographs tend to be of two varieties: either close-ups of "children's genitals or full body shots of naked children standing next to a ruler on a wall . . . and their identities obscured by a single black line concealing their eyes" (Preves, 2003, p. 69). Dreger (2000) argued there is not any true anonymity as individuals are easily identifiable even with a bar across their eyes. Prominent Intersex activist Cheryl Chase, herself photographed as a child, said the only thing the black bar accomplishes is keeping the viewer from being stared back at (as cited in Koyama, 2006).

Calling medical photographs "exploitative," many Intersex Initiative activists, like Chase (Chase & Coventry, 1997) and Koyama (2006), bloggers like Childs (2009b), and scholars like Costello (2013), demand an end to the practice of medical photography. Recognizing the importance of creating positive frames, they also call for reclamation of photography, where intersex people control the imagery. Developing the difference between the two genres, Costello (2013) wrote:

> [T]here is a real need for a collection of cruelty-free, nondistorted images of intersex people's bodies, including our genitals . . . [I]llustrations would be best. There may be people . . . willing to be photographed by a respectful ally . . . but I suspect most people, like myself, would be very wary . . . Drawings would avoid the issues of shaming . . . They could be warm rather than clinical, human rather than dehumanized.
>
> *(para. 14)*

Mindful of this distinction, I focus on medical photography of intersex children. Using visual rhetorical theory, I supplement the activists' perspectives with analysis of the visual culture of medical photographs of intersex youth. Aiming to honor the requests of these individuals, I analyze the culture that surrounds and produces the clinical photographs rather than look at the photographs themselves.

The Visual Rhetoric of Intersex Photography

Scholars have noted that the increasing pervasiveness of visual symbols demands investigation (e. g., Foss, 2004; Hariman & Lucaites, 2007; Olson, 2007). Accordingly, scholarship in the field of visual communication has increased in recent years. Much work has focused on establishing theories for analyzing individual images to understand how individual symbols shape identities and ideologies (e. g., Barbatsis, 1996; Finnegan, 2001; Shelley, 1996). As studies continue, it may be productive to identify limits to the analysis of specific visual artifacts. Certain cases, such as medical photographs of intersex persons, may be ethically problematic. Thus, it is useful for rhetoricians to criticize the construction or practice of image creation – the visual culture – rather than only evaluating the images themselves. Because analyzing individual photographs may reproduce the trauma experienced by the people in the images, I analyze the culture to shift the focus to the dangerous practices undertaken in the medical field while avoiding creating a spectacle through analysis of individual people in the photographs.

A move from individual photograph to photographic practice places the photographs in a larger cultural setting. Birdsell and Groarke (1996) explained, "There is no reason to assume that a visual image must conduct its contributions to argument in perfect isolation" (p. 5). Instead, images are created and exist within specific visual cultures. Analysis of visual culture emphasizes moving beyond the image to question the power relations surrounding it. This approach recognizes that asking how and why the image was created, and by and for whom, produces insights that analysis of an isolated image may not. This is because the meaning of images, especially photographs, "relies upon the contingencies of . . . use and . . . embedded-ness within a particular context" (Evans & Hall, 2004, p. 132). Meaning is not situated within the image, but realized through the practices of looking and interpretation (Evans & Hall, 2004). These practices are routinized over time with some interpretations gaining dominance over others. This can be seen in the medical arena.

Medical photographs appear neutral and transparent. Their realist nature erases the "complex web of signification" (Twigg, 1992, p. 306) in which they exist. The photographs are situated in a visual culture of medicine, which is a culture of surveillance that uses photo-graphs to write the body "into a manageable system of signification that flattens human experience into categories of knowledge" (Twigg, p. 308). This can be seen historically; photography "advanced the scientific quest to categorize . . . human beings, distinguishing between male and female, sick and healthy, criminal and law-abiding, along with racially inferior and superior" (Ferutta, 2008, p. 3). The process of categorization continues today through the photographing of intersex individuals.

Photography operates within a variety of complex power relationships, including doctor/patient and normal/atypical. The dualistic pairs lay bare that doctors, and the cisbodied, are allowed dominance due to their respective expertise or congruence with the norm. Always devalued is the individual purportedly in need of fixing. In a very Foucauldian sense, the composition of the images positions the person in the photograph "as a powerless object laid open to the 'clinical gaze'" (Wall, 2010, p. 81). Shown naked with their eyes covered by a black line, the bodies of the subjects in the photographs are used by doctors under the auspices of improving medical care. Although a noble objective, the use of the photographs, especially without consent, is done in the literal absence of intersex individuals. The clinician thus has authority to control the public narrative of the intersex individuals' bodies. Robbed of the agency to tell their own stories, intersex individuals become spectacles for interested medical professionals.

The presence of the photographs shapes diagnosis and limits treatment options. Hester (2004) argued that we tend to understand doctors' diagnoses as "an objective series of . . . decisions based upon empirical evidence" (p. 11). However, the exchange is much more of "an inventional process within a disciplinary context constraining the use . . . of certain evidences, governed by . . . values that give weight to certain sets of data . . . over other sets" (Hester, 2004, p. 11). The photographs offer a strong form of data on which to base treatment plans because there is strong evocative power to visual elements that verbal constructions may not capture (Blair, 2004). The presence of visual data demonstrating the unintelligibility (Butler, 2004) and the non-conformity of an intersex body to a cultural gender norm serves to prove to doctors and parents the need for physical intervention. This is because:

> the visual makes an argument in the sense of adducing . . . reasons in a forceful way. It might contain or present a didactic narrative . . . But, it does not permit the complexity of such dialectical moves as the raising of objections in order to refute or otherwise answer them.
>
> *(Blair, 2004, p. 52)*

The photograph's composition thus functions enthymematically; it offers the premise that a body is atypical. The only possible conclusion for doctors to reach once that premise is evident is that surgical efforts that encourage conformity to the norm are essential.

When seen by doctors, the photographs operate as proof of the need for surgery. When seen by the public, the photographs become a spectacle, connoting freakishness. Disseminated from medical contexts to websites, the photographs are figural resources (Hariman & Lucaites, 2002) that fulfill curiosity. Childs (2009a) wrote:

> My website, which features my writing . . . on intersex, has always gotten the majority of hits via people searching for pictures of intersex people's genitals . . . . With very few exceptions nearly every . . . search sending people to my site was for pictures of intersex people's bodies and . . . their genitals. . . . [T]hat people think they have a right to access the bodies of . . . intersex people is the direct result of many years of . . . medical abuse of intersex people.
>
> *(para. 4)*

Medicine has thus enabled a larger culture of spectatorship. The gaze upon intersex people is not isolated to medical texts and exam rooms, but is expanded to society at large.

Conclusion

Wary of medical photography, there have been calls for a ban on the practice. Troubled by objectification in medical images, some suggest there are alternatives for presenting intersex bodies. From illustrations to humanized images, there are ways to reclaim subjectivity and challenge the dominant gaze. Currently, however, the medical arena continues to use photographs to surveil and categorize, marking intersex bodies as abnormal and in need of change. The photographs reify doctors' authority, justify surgery, and are circulated for public consumption as part of spectator culture.

In addition to illuminating the implications of medical control of visual discourses surrounding intersexuality, my study hopefully also encourages careful attention to visual culture as a way to avoid re-inscribing trauma felt by subjects of photographs. Analysis of individual photographs, including but not limited to those of intersex individuals, raises ethical questions about where scholars focus their gaze. By critiquing the creation and dissemination of visual forms, we hopefully can avoid reifying the surveilling gaze of dominant culture in a way that is attuned to the needs of the subjects of our work.

References

Barbatsis, G. S. (1996). "Look, and I will show you something you will want to see": Pictorial engagement in negative political campaign commercials. *Argumentation and Advocacy, 33*(2), 69–78.

Birdsell, D. S., & Groarke, L. (1996). Toward a theory of visual argument. *Argumentation and Advocacy, 33*(1), 1–10.

Blair, J. A. (2004). The rhetoric of visual arguments. In C. A. Hill & M. Helmers (Eds.), *Defining visual rhetorics* (pp. 41–61). Mahwah, NJ: Lawrence Erlbaum Associates, 2004.

Bloom, A. (2003). *Normal: Transsexual CEOs, crossdressing cops, and hermaphrodites with attitude*. London, UK: Bloomsbury.

Brain, C. E., Creighton, S. M., Mushtaq, I., Carmichael, P. A., Barnicoat, A., Honour, J. W., . . . Achermann, John C. (2010). Holistic management of DSD. *Best Practice & Research Clinical Endocrinology & Metabolism, 24*, 335–354. doi: http://dx.doi.org/ 10.1016/j.beem.2010.01.006

Butler, J. (2004). *Undoing gender*. New York, NY: Routledge.

Chase, C., & Coventry, M. (1997). Chrysalis. Retrieved from http://www.isna.org/books/chrysalis/from_the_editors

Childs, C. P. (2009a). Caitlin Childs. *Masculine Femininities Zine, 3*. Retrieved from http://masculine-femininities.wordpress.com/2009/11/19/masculine-femininities-issue-3/

Childs, C. P. (2009b). To all people searching for pics of intersex genitals. Retrieved from http://caitlinpetrakischilds.com/2009/04/30/to-all-people-searching-for-pics-of-intersex-genitals/

Costello, C. G. (2013, February 20). Hypospadias: Intersexuality and gender politics [Web log message]. *The Intersex Roadshow*. Retrieved from http://intersexroadshow.blogspot.com/

Creighton, S., Alderson, J., Brown, S., & Minto, C. L. (2002). Medical photography: Ethics, consent, and the intersex patient. *BJU International, 89*(1), 67–71. doi: http://dx.doi.org/10.1046/j.1464–410X.2002.02558.x

Dreger, A. D., (2000). Jarring bodies: Thoughts on the display of unusual anatomies. *Perspectives in Biology and Medicine, 43*(2), 161–172.

Evans, J., & Hall, S. (2004). *Visual culture: The reader.* Thousand Oaks, CA: Sage.

Ferutta, P. (2008). The Hermaphrodite as a monster: The photographical genesis of the scientific discourse on Intersexuality since the 19th century. Retrieved from http://www.inter-disciplinary.net/ati/Monsters/M6/Ferruta%20paper.pdf

Finnegan, C. A. (2001). The naturalistic enthymeme and visual argument: Photographic representation in the "skull controversy." *Argumentation and Advocacy, 37*(3), 133–149.

Foss, S. K. (2004). Framing the study of visual rhetoric: Toward a transformation of rhetorical theory. In C. A. Hill & M. Helmers (Eds.), *Defining visual rhetorics* (pp. 303–313). Mahwah, NJ: Lawrence Erlbaum.

Goodwin, J. (1985). Post-traumatic symptoms in incest victims. In S. Eth & R. S. Pynoos (Eds.), *Post-Traumatic Stress Disorder in Children* (pp. 155–168). Washington, D.C.: American Psychiatric Press, Inc.

Hariman, R., & Lucaites, J. L. (2002). Performing civic identity. *Quarterly Journal of Speech, 88*, 363–392.

Hariman, R., & Lucaites, J. L. (2007). *No caption needed: Iconic photographs, public culture, and liberal democracy.* Chicago, IL: University of Chicago Press.

Hester, J. D. (2004). Intersex(es) and informed consent: How physicians' rhetoric constrains choice. *Theoretical Medicine and Bioethics, 25*(1), 21–49. doi: http://dx.doi.org/10.1023/B:META.0000025069.46031.0e

Hughes, I. A., Houk, C., Ahmed, S. F., Lee, P. A., LWPES Consensus Group, & ESPE Consensus Group. (2006). Consensus statement on management of intersex disorders. *Archives of Disease in Childhood, 91*(7), 554–563.

Intersex Society of North America. (2005). The medical management of intersexed children: An analogue for childhood sexual abuse. Retrieved from http://www.isna.org/articles/analog

Koyama, E. (2006). From "Intersex" to "DSD": Toward a queer disability politics of gender. *Intersex Initiative*. Retrieved from http://www.intersexinitiative.org/articles/intersextodsd.html

Lee, P. A., Houk, C. P., Ahmed, S. F., & Hughes, I. A. (2006). Consensus statement on management of intersex disorders. *Pediatrics, 118*(2), e488–e500. doi: http://dx.doi.org/10.1542/peds.2006–0738

Money, J., & Lamacz, M. (1987). Genital examination and exposure experienced as nosocomial sexual abuse in childhood. *The Journal of Nervous and Mental Disease, 175*(12), 713–721.

Morland, I. (2005). "The glans opens like a book": Writing and reading the intersexed body. *Continuum, 19*(3), 335–348. doi: http://dx.doi.org/10.1080/10304311500176586

Olson, L. C. (2007). Intellectual and conceptual resources for visual rhetoric: A re-examination of scholarship since 1950. *Review of Communication, 7*(1), 1–20. doi: http://dx.doi.org/10.1080/15358590701211035

Organisation Intersex International. (2013, April 6). What is intersex and how common is it? OII-USA. Retrieved from http://oii-usa.org/1128/intersex/

Preves, S. E. (2003). *Intersex and identity: The contested self.* New York, NY: Rutgers.

Shelley, C. (1996). Rhetorical and demonstrative modes of visual argument: Looking at images of human evolution. *Argumentation and Advocacy, 33*(2), 53–68.

Twigg, R. (1992). The performative dimension of surveillance. *Text and Performance Quarterly, 12*, 305–328.

Wall, S. (2010). Humane images: Visual rhetoric in depictions of atypical genital anatomy and sex differentiation. *Medical Humanities, 36*, 80–83. doi: http://dx.doi.org/10.1136/jmh.2010.005702

Young, L. (1992). Sexual abuse and the problem of embodiment. *Child Abuse Neglect, 16*(1), 89–100.

17

THE PERSONAL IS NOT POLITICAL

A public argument for privatizing women's sexuality

Kate Zittlow Rogness

MONMOUTH COLLEGE, USA

Studies on counterpublics have largely focused on how discourses of subordinated groups widen the public sphere so as to be more inclusive, suggesting that inclusivity, as a precondition of equality, is contingent on publicity (Felski, 1989; Fraser, 1992; Warner, 2002). Asen and Brouwer (2001) warned scholars, however, that an emphasis on counter discourses that expand the public sphere may "draw critical attention only to those movements from margin to center, thus neglecting the ways in which dominant or public topics are rendered marginal or private" (p. 9). Although Asen and Brouwer suggested that moves to marginalize or privatize dominant or public topics may not reflect a *counter* discourse, their observation hinted that scholars may hold a bias toward the value of inclusion in counterpublic studies. Asen's (2000) directive to focus on the discursive quality of counterpublics in order to avoid reducing counterpublics to persons, places, or topics further indicated that the study of counterpublics may not be as neat as scholars might wish.

The contemporary Slutwalk protests offer argument scholars an opportunity to explore the messiness of counterpublics and the exciting challenges this dis-order evidences for counterpublic scholars as we study arguments for social change. This essay will engage this inquiry by progressing through three sections. I begin by outlining a brief history of counterpublic studies, directing specific focus to the demarcation between the public and private as it relates the role of power and overviewing the history and argument of Slutwalks. I then discuss what we might glean about the study of counterpublics from a case study of Slutwalks before presenting concluding remarks on future directions in counterpublic studies.

Overview of Counterpublic Studies

Counterpublic studies are the critical corollary to public sphere theory. Argumentation scholars found attractive Jürgen Habermas's theory of the public sphere because it echoed the civic values and democratic principles that mark the tradition of Communication Studies (Hauser,

1999). Habermas (1962/1991) conceptualized the bourgeois public sphere as a metaphorical space wherein citizens assembled to deliberate issues of common interest and, through that deliberation, generate public opinion to influence public policy. Generalizing from Habermas's historically specific account, scholars have characterized a healthy public sphere as a metaphorical space of ideal democracy, where members are assured equality by bracketing their specific identities, have open access to information, and direct their arguments towards the common good rather than their particular interests (Goodnight, 1982). The scope and norms of the public sphere are constituted in and through discourse that, in turn, shapes the material conditions of society. As both a philosophical and conceptual theory, public sphere theory has made intelligible the rhetoricity of the "public" (Gaonkar, 2002, p. 412).

According to Warner (2002), a public "comes into being only in relation to texts and their circulation" (p. 66). Warner's definition indicates a common constituency, one generated out of the uptake of texts, suggesting that publics are inherently a communicative phenomenon. Communication scholars have expanded Warner's focus from text to discourse, demonstrating that publics are not limited by medium, but pervade across written, oral, mediated, visual, and performance-based contexts (Deluca & Peeples, 2002; Pezzullo, 2003; Olson & Goodnight, 1994). Publics are both constituted and perpetuated by discursive norms, which encompass content, style, form, and practice. Necessarily, norms set limits of inclusion; they are invented, applied, appropriated, and reinforced in order to sustain a sense of productive civility (as determined by a public).

The public is, according to Asen and Brouwer (2001), "accessible to, relevant to, known to, directed to, and/or constituted by members of a political community" (p. 1). Invoking the political, Asen and Brouwer brought the public into relation with the state, indicating that while some publics may be more extracurricular, there are those that have political import. While all publics have symbolic consequence, those publics with political import have very real, material consequences for both their constituents and those who are implicated by their influence.

The public stands in relationship to the private. Many scholars have described the difference between the public and the private as a dichotomy – a relationship of negation: What is private is not public and vice versa. Private, or personal, opinions may be translated into public arguments when participating in a public conversation and, thus, are dependent on perceptions of an audience (Goodnight, 1982; Guttman & Thompson, 1998). The private may be something that could or should be protected, as one might a secret, as it holds an individual's (or group's) identifying features (Gunn, 2008); the private may be that which is or should be protected from both the state's intrusive arm and public adjudication (Cohen, 1996). The difference between the public and private may also be perceptual and symbolic, in that one might identify with the common identity of a public (stranger-sociability) or as a unique individual (Warner, 2002). At times, the common public identity and one's individual identity may overlap; other times, they stand in stark contrast. Privacy, in this sense, may be defined as a "sense of control over one's identity, over access to oneself, over which aspects of oneself one will present at which time and to whom, along with the ability to press or to waive territorial claims" (Cohen, 1996, p. 204). Finally, the distinction between what is public and private may be "preconceptual, almost instinctual, rooted in the body and common speech" (Warner, 2002, p. 23).

This broad review suggests that the understanding of what is public or private, whether it is scholarly or popular, is simultaneously theoretical, political, and phenomenological. To further complicate, "none of these terms [for public] has a sense that is exactly parallel to or opposite of private. None are simple oppositions or binaries. Because the contexts overlap, most things are private in one sense and public in another" (Warner, 2002, p. 30). It is in this relationship where scholars may observe power's critical function.

That which is deemed public is both common and appropriate, whereas that which the public has deemed private may protected, such as a "zone of privacy," or inappropriate (sometimes both). According to Fraser (1999), the public and private are not "straightforward designations of societal spheres; they are cultural classifications and rhetorical labels . . . they are powerful terms frequently deployed to delegitimate some interests, views, and topics and valorize others" (p. 131). Breakdown in the public sphere occurs when discursive norms prove to exclude individuals by silencing styles of speech, limiting or preventing participation, or prohibiting the deliberation of a specific topic. These exclusions typically reinforce an unequal distribution of power, evoke norms of publicity and privacy, and have both material and symbolic consequences.

Counterpublics emerge in response to perceived exclusionary discursive norms that result in some combination of subordination, marginalization, and resource disparities (Brouwer, 2006; Fraser, 1999; Warner, 2002). Fraser (1999) described counterpublics as "parallel discursive arenas where members of subordinated social groups invent and circulate counter discourses to formulate oppositional interpretations of their identities, interests and needs" (p. 123). Scholars generally agree that the purpose of counterpublics is to address exclusions by expanding the public sphere, transforming that which previously has been characterized as private as public. As per Benhabib (1999), "all struggles against oppression in the modern world begin by redefining what had previously been considered private, nonpublic, and nonpolitical issues as matters of public concern, as issues of justice, as sites of power that need discursive legitimation" (p. 84). Fraser (1999) similarly advocated for widening discursive contestation. Even Asen (2009) valued the expansion of discursive space, as it "would entail recognizing the potential for value conflicts in a pluralist society, and welcoming the adjudication of these conflicts through public engagement" (p. 282). This review suggests that the progression towards equality in the public sphere relies on expanding the scope of what may be considered public, or at least engaged and deliberated by the public. This further presumes that inclusivity is contingent upon and evidenced by publicity.

A (Brief) History of Slutwalks

In January 2011, a law enforcement officer in Toronto suggested that women might "avoid dressing like sluts in order not to be victimized" during a crime prevention assembly at York University in Toronto, Canada (Rush, 2011). Four months later, in April 2011, individuals marched from Queens Park to the Toronto Police Headquarters to protest the officer's statements in what would become the first Slutwalk. Following this protest, Slutwalks became an international phenomenon, with walks taking place on nearly every continent. Slutwalks protest rape culture, which is communicated through the discursive norms of slut shaming and victim blaming and results in the very material consequence of sexual assault and rape.

Simply put, slut shaming is the act of criticizing someone for acting like who society considers to be a slut. A slut is someone who is, or has the appearance of being, sexually promiscuous. The notion of promiscuity is highly subjective and contextual. One may define it liberally, as having casual sexual encounters with multiple partners, or more conservatively, as having sexual intercourse for reasons other than procreation. Slut shaming is typically directed towards females, though males have also been subjected to its derogatory effects.

Slut shaming evolved out of norms that govern appropriate, or so-called normal, gender performance. According to Butler (1999), "gender is produced through the stylization of the body, and hence, must be understood as the mundane way in which the bodily gestures, movements, and styles of various kinds constitute the illusion of an abiding gendered self" (p. 179). To be a woman is to dress and act in ways that generally conform to normative standards of femininity (as these standards are inflected by race, class, sexuality, and nationality). Normative standards of femininity are thus historically and contextually situated in publics; that which is considered feminine in the United States may be vastly different from that in Brazil or India. In the United States, women's sexuality has been fixed to virtue and morality, and is inflected by race, class, sexuality, and nationality (Zittlow Rogness & Foust, 2010). To slut shame a woman is to call her morality into question, which has symbolic implications for her civic agency, as was demonstrated by the Limbaugh/Fluke controversy in 2012; a slut has no authority from which to speak because she is deemed ethically deficient. Slut also designates a form of social leprosy; women are less likely to associate with a woman who has a reputation of being a slut (Vrangalova, Bukberg, & Rieger, 2013).

Slut shaming leads to victim blaming. Victim blaming suggests that a survivor of sexual assault or rape is somehow complicit in, or in some cases completely responsible for, the assault or rape. Like slut shaming, normative standards of gender are evoked to assess whether or not the survivor is at fault. To what ends did she put herself at risk by appearing to transgress gendered norms of virtue and morality?

During Slutwalks, women dressed in provocative, intimate apparel, carrying placards with subversive phrases like "Sluts say yes," "It shouldn't be this hard to be easy," and "Sorry, did my dress make you feel like a rapist today?", march alongside conservatively dressed women who hold placards that read "This is what I was wearing, was I asking for it?", "It wasn't my fault," and "my body, my rules." Their message is two-fold, addressing the interlocking forces of slut shaming and victim blaming that enforce rape culture. First, they argue that women's sexuality has no implicit social or political relevance because a woman's sexuality is not a barometer of her virtue. Second, they argue that perpetrators should be held solely responsible for sexual assault and rape. This message, however, does not fit neatly into the parameters of counterpublic studies described above. Instead, it disrupts the theoretical bias toward the value of inclusion in counterpublic studies.

Counterpublicity of Slutwalks

Slutwalks' advocacy of women's sexuality challenges those discursive norms of gender that have functioned to marginalize, subordinate, and justify the resource disparities that make up rape culture. The rape culture Slutwalks protest is reflected in what Berlant (1997) termed the *intimate public sphere*. According to Berlant (1997), "the intimate public sphere of the U.S. present tense renders citizenship as a condition of membership produced by personal acts and values, especially acts originating in or directed toward the family sphere" (p. 5). Warner (2002) similarly warned that the "personal is political" mantra of 20th century feminist movements contained the potential to metastasize because "'the personal is political' means not that personal life could be transformed by political action but that politics should be personalized" (p. 34). This reversal of the feminist dictum "has resulted in an anti-political nationalist politics of sexuality whose concern is no longer what sex reveals about unethical power but what 'abnormal' sex/reproduction/intimacy forms reveal about threats to the nation proper/the proper nation" (Berlant, 1997, p. 178). In this sense, the public and the private have subsumed each other. In the intimate public sphere, private values have become legitimate public arguments. As it has been fixed to virtue, women's sexuality is a relevant topic for public deliberation and an act that may be policed by both public sentiment and political legislation. Women's sexuality has thus been incorporated into public debates about healthcare, welfare, education, poverty, and even the national debt. To these ends, the crisis Slutwalks are responding to is not one of exclusion, per se, but of inclusion. The inclusion of women's sexuality into public debate has had social, political, and material consequences for women (and men). One of these consequences is the symbolic exclusion of those participants whose ethics have been called into question. In other words, an exclusionary norm is the effect of an inclusionary norm.

Rather than arguing that women's sexuality be politicized, incorporating it into the scope of the public sphere so that it may be publicly deliberated, Slutwalks assert that women's sexuality be *removed* from the public sphere. Yet, their argument is not so simple as to merely narrow the scope of what is public. To do so would not address those private values that inform the resource disparities that shape the social and material conditions of women's lives; it might even cement those values by protecting them with a veil of privacy. Their argument instead suggests that the conditions of the *private* sphere be transformed. They advocate that sex acts be decoupled from virtue, so as to redistribute power among intimate encounters. Thus, they believe that the resource disparities of the public sphere might be resolved by addressing the conditions of the private sphere. This move reflects Cohen's (1996) claim: "the right to inviolate personality protected by privacy rights articulates intersubjectively recognized personal boundaries that are the sine qua non for the establishment and maintenance of autonomous identities" (pp. 204–205). The body is decoupled from property, sexuality from virtue.

Conclusion

As described above, counterpublic studies have emphasized the value of inclusion in the public sphere. This study of Slutwalks is not meant to invert this emphasis, but instead disturb the scholarly bias towards the value of inclusivity and public deliberation – particularly in relation to social change and "poetic world making" (Warner, 2002, p. 114). The emancipatory potential of Slutwalks' argument relies on expanding the scope of the private sphere and transforming the conditions of the private sphere by redistributing power in order to address resource disparities in the public sphere. This case study demonstrates that the study of counterpublics may not be as neat as scholars may wish, as widening the scope of the public sphere may lead to devastating effects. Norms of inclusion (as with appropriate topics for public deliberation) may lead to norms of exclusion (as with participation). This turn suggests that scholars remain vigilant to the relationship between the public and the private, inclusivity and exclusivity, and work to decouple publicity from progress, inclusion from equality.

References

Asen, R. (2000). Seeking the "counter" in counterpublics. *Communication Theory, 10*(4), 424–446.

Asen, R. (2009). Ideology, materiality, and counterpublicity: William E. Simon and the rise of a conservative counterintelligentsia. *Quarterly Journal of Speech, 95*(3), 263–288.

Asen, R., & Brouwer, D. (Eds.) (2001). *Counterpublics and the state.* Albany: State University of New York Press.

Benhabib, S. (1991). Models of public space: Hannah Arendt, the liberal tradition, and Jürgen Habermas. In C. Calhoun (Ed.), *Habermas and the public sphere* (pp. 73–98). Cambridge, MA: MIT Press.

Berlant, L. (1997). *The queen of America goes to Washington City: Essays on sex and citizenship.* Durham, NC: Duke University Press.

Brouwer, D. C. (2006). Communication as counterpublic. In G. J. Shepherd, J. St. John, & T. Striphas (Eds.), *Communication as . . . perspectives on theory* (pp. 195–208). Thousand Oaks, CA: Sage Publications.

Butler, J. (1999). *Gender trouble: Feminism and the subversion of identity.* New York, NY: Routledge.

Cohen, J. (1996). Democracy, difference and the right of privacy. In S. Benhabib (Ed.), *Democracy and difference: Contesting the boundaries of the political* (pp. 187–217). Princeton, NJ: Princeton University Press.

DeLuca, K. M., & Peeples, J. (2002). From public sphere to pubic screen: Democracy, activism, and the "violence" of Seattle. *Critical Studies in Media Communication, 19*(2), 125–151.

Felski, R. (1989). *Beyond feminist aesthetics.* Cambridge, MA: Harvard University Press.

Fraser, N. (1991). Rethinking the public sphere: A contribution to the critique of actually existing democracy. In C. Calhoun (Ed.), *Habermas and the public sphere* (pp. 73–98). Cambridge, MA: MIT Press.

Gaonkar, D. P. (2002). Introduction [The forum: Public and counterpublics]. *Quarterly Journal of Speech, 88*, 410–412.

Greene, R. W. (2002). Rhetorical pedagogy as a postal system: Circulating subjects through Michael Warner's "Publics and Counterpublics." *Quarterly Journal of Speech, 88*, 434–443.

Goodnight, G. T. (1982). The personal, technical, and public spheres of argument: A speculative inquiry into the art of public deliberation. *Journal of the American Forensic Association, 18*, 214–227.

Gunn, J. (2008). Death by publicity: U.S. Freemasonry and the public drama of secrecy. *Rhetoric & Public Affairs, 11*(2), 243–277.

Gutmann, A., & Thompson, D. (1998). *Democracy and disagreement: Why moral conflict cannot be avoided in politics and what should be done about it.* Boston, MA: Belknap Press.

Habermas, J. (1991). *The structural transformation of the public sphere* (T. Berger & F. Lawrence, Trans). Cambridge, MA: MIT Press. (Original work published 1962)

Hauser, G. A. (1999). *Vernacular voices: The rhetoric of publics and public spheres.* Columbia: University of South Carolina Press.

Olson, K. M., & Goodnight G. (1994). Entanglements of consumption, cruelty, privacy, and fashion: The social controversy over fur. *Quarterly Journal of Speech, 80*(3), 249–276.

Pezzullo, P. C. (2003). Resisting "National Breast Cancer Awareness Month": The rhetoric of counterpublics and their cultural performances. *Quarterly Journal of Speech, 89*(4), 345–365.

Rush, C. (2011, February 18). Cop apologies for "sluts" remark at law school. *The Star.* Retrieved from http://www.thestar.com/news/gta/2011/02/18/cop_apologizes_for_sluts_remark_at_law_school.html

Vrangalova, Z., Bukberg, R. E., & Rieger, G. (2013). Birds of a feather? Not when it comes to sexual permissiveness. *Journal of Social and Personal Relationships,* 1–21. Retrieved from http://spr.sagepub.com/content/early/2013/05/16/0265407513487638

Warner, M. (2002). *Publics and counterpublics.* New York, NY: Zone Books.

Zittlow Rogness, K., & Foust, C. R. (2010). Beyond rights and virtues as foundation for women's agency: Emma Goldman's rhetoric of free love. *Western Journal of Communication, 75*(2), 148–167.

18

AN EXPLORATION OF THE EXTENT TO WHICH SERIAL ARGUMENT THOUGHTS AND BEHAVIORS ARE RELATIONALLY DISTURBING

Jennifer L. Bevan

CHAPMAN UNIVERSITY, USA

Alexis Della Ripa

CHAPMAN UNIVERSITY, USA

Alexandra Boulger

CHAPMAN UNIVERSITY, USA

Aryn Tuazon

CHAPMAN UNIVERSITY, USA

Chelsea Simmons

CHAPMAN UNIVERSITY, USA

Danielle Levine

CHAPMAN UNIVERSITY, USA

Serial arguments are ongoing, unresolved conflicts about a specific topic that take place over time, are associated with a variety of goals (Bevan, Hale, & Williams, 2004), and occur in multiple contexts and relationships (e.g., Bevan, 2010; Hample & Kruger, 2011; Trapp & Hoff, 1985). Though serial argumentation research has been expanding knowledge in this research area, little systematic attention has been paid to how cognitive and communicative components of these ongoing arguments could be associated with disturbances to the romantic relationships in which they occur. Such an approach would be valuable, as it would align serial argument research with more general conflict scholarship, where relationship satisfaction (or dissatisfaction, which represents a specific form of relational disturbance) is a frequent and primary indicator of how much relational disturbance can be attributed to interpersonal conflict processes (e.g., Caughlin, Vangelisti, & Mikucki-Enyart, 2013; Segrin, Hanzal, & Domschke, 2009). Further, as relationship satisfaction often predicts dissolution and divorce (Caughlin et al., 2013), determining which thoughts and behaviors in serial arguments are related to relationship satisfaction could improve the long-term outlook of the romantic relationship. As such, this study examines the associations between relationship satisfaction, defined as the "positivity of affect or attraction to one's relationship" (Rusbult, 1983, p. 102), and the conflict strategies, goals, and rumination that emerge in serial arguments.

Conflict Strategies

Elements of relational disturbance have been examined in the serial argument context in two distinct forms: harm and dissatisfaction. For example, for those resisting engaging in a serial argument episode, the more argument episodes, the greater the relational harm (Johnson & Roloff, 2000b). Further, relational harm is negatively related to the serial argument's perceived resolvability and is less likely with relationally confirming behaviors and when there was no hostility (Johnson & Roloff, 1998, 2000a). Relationship satisfaction is also positively associated with both positive and negative argument tactics in intercultural serial arguments, suggesting that "simple participation in a serial argument episode had positive implications" (Hample & Cionea, 2012, p. 441). However, in another recent study, relationship satisfaction (as a statistical covariate) is positively linked to constructive argument outcomes, but unrelated to mutual hostility, number of arguments, and demand/withdraw patterns (Reznik & Roloff, 2011). To be consistent with general conflict research, the integrative (i.e., direct, constructive), distributive (i.e., direct, destructive), and avoidance conflict strategies are examined here. Based on the general pattern of findings described above, hypothesis one states:

H1: Relationship satisfaction is positively related to: (a) integrative communication, and negatively related to (b) distributive and (c) avoidant conflict strategy usage in serial arguments.

Goals

According to Canary and Lakey (2013), seeking to achieve multiple goals is a primary characteristic of serial arguments; accordingly, serial argument research has centered on Bevan et al.'s (2004; Bevan, Finan, & Kaminsky, 2008) positive (e.g., positive relational expression) and negative (e.g., dominance/control) goal typology. To date, no known research has examined serial argument goal importance (i.e., which goals are most primary to individuals in serial argument episodes) in relation to any form of relational disturbance. However, Johnson, Averbeck, Kelley, and Liu (2011) found that two of five serial argument functions (i.e., reasons) positively predicted relational harm: solving behavior incompatibilities and giving or gaining knowledge. Thus, understanding how goal pursuit is associated with relationship satisfaction is important to better clarify how serial argument processes can impact relationships. Based on research that generally finds that positive concepts such as perceived resolvability and integrative strategy usage are positively related to positive goals and negatively linked to negative goals (e.g., Bevan et al., 2007; Bevan, in press; Hample, Richards, & Na, 2012), the second hypothesis predicts:

H2: Relationship satisfaction is positively related to: (a) positive goal importance, and negatively related to (b) negative goal importance in serial arguments.

Rumination

Rumination, or ongoing, unwanted, and conscious thought in reaction to disturbing events or unaccomplished goals or plans (Gold & Wegner, 1995), represents another cognitive aspect of serial argumentation. A serial argument, as an interpersonal event that involves frustrated goals and unfolds over time, tends to arouse rumination, and serial argument-specific rumination has been found to occur at moderate levels (Bevan et al., 2008; Carr, Schrodt, & Ledbetter, 2012). Further, rumination is negatively related to relationship satisfaction in romantic jealousy situations (Elphinston, Feeney, Noller, Connor, & Fitzgerald, 2013) and in depressed individuals (Kuehner & Buerger, 2005; Pearson, Watkins, Kuyken, & Mullan, 2010), suggesting a similar association in the serial argument context. Hypothesis three thus states:

H3: Relationship satisfaction is negatively related to rumination in serial arguments.

Finally, to determine which cognitive or communicative serial argument components are the most informative in understanding romantic relationship satisfaction, a research question asks:

RQ: Which serial argument variables are the best predictors of relationship satisfaction?

Method

Participants and procedures

The study included 198 adults in either current (81.8%) or former (17.7%) romantic relationships, who averaged 26.2 years (*SD* = 9.52, *range* = 18–65), and were predominantly female (65.2%, 34.8% male), Caucasian (67.8%, Asian 12.6%, bi/multi-racial 6.1%, Hispanic 5.6%, Black/African-American 1.5%, Native American .5%, other .5%), and heterosexual (89.4%, homosexual 2.5%, bisexual 2.5%). Relationship length averaged almost five years (*SD* = 83.03 months, *range* = 2–552 months), and a variety of romantic relationships were included (exclusive dating 47.0%, married 28.3%, living together 6.6%, engaged 6.6%, non-exclusive dating 6.1%, other 1.0%). Percentages do not add up to 100% because some participants did not complete all of the demographic items, which were at the end of the surveys.

Respondents were recruited via undergraduate classes at a small private university in the western United States, email, and social networks in two separate data collections. The first (*n* = 86) was part of a larger survey study (Bevan, in press) examining heterosexual romantic couples' serial arguments. To not violate the independence assumption, a sex was first randomly selected, and alternating male and female members of each couple were then chosen for this sample. The remaining participants (*n* = 112) were part of an anonymous, larger online survey study (Bevan & Love, 2013) comparing non-serial and serial arguments. Only individuals randomly assigned to the serial argument condition were included here. All survey directions and items relevant to the current study were identical, allowing the datasets to be combined.

Measures

The three conflict strategies were measured via Bevan's (in press) Likert–type measure (1 = Not at all, 7 = To a great extent): (a) integrative communication (6 items, e.g., I found out what my partner was feeling; $M = 4.65$, $SD = 1.31$, $\alpha = .86$), (b) distributive communication (5 items, e.g., I criticized my partner's behavior; $M = 3.10$, $SD = 1.60$, $\alpha = .87$), and (c) avoidance (6 items, e.g., I avoided my partner; $M = 2.09$, $SD = 1.35$, $\alpha = .88$).

Bevan et al.'s (2008) Likert–type scale assessed serial argument goal importance (1 = Not at all important, 7 = Very important): the two positive goals of mutuality (3 items, e.g., to reach a mutual agreement; $M = 5.08$, $SD = 1.48$, $\alpha = .76$) and positive relational expression (3 items, e.g., to keep our relationship going; $M = 4.82$, $SD = 1.67$, $\alpha = .82$), and the four negative goals of expressiveness negative (2 items, e.g., to release my frustration; $M = 4.21$, $SD = 1.89$, $\alpha = .81$), dominance/control (2 items, e.g., to not lose the serial argument; $M = 3.24$, $SD = 1.78$, $\alpha = .65$), hurt partner/benefit self (7 items, e.g., to get revenge; $M = 1.34$, $SD = .66$, $\alpha = .82$), and relationship termination (3 items, e.g., to terminate our relationship; $M = 1.25$, $SD = .72$, $\alpha = .75$). The change target goal was excluded from hypothesis testing because the scale was not reliable ($\alpha = .55$).

Cloven and Roloff's (1991) 7-point, semantic differential scale measured rumination: (5 items, e.g., 1 = Did not worry at all, 7 = Worried very much; $M = 4.39$, $SD = 1.46$, $\alpha = .89$).

Relationship satisfaction was measured using three items from Hendrick's (1988) Likert–type scale (e.g., In general, how satisfied are you with your relationship? 1 = Not at all, 7 = Very; $M = 5.50$, $SD = 1.35$, $\alpha = .79$).

Results

Bivariate, one–tailed partial correlations that controlled for three variables: (1) the type of sample (0 = dyadic, 1 = serial versus non-serial arguments), (2) relationship status (0 = former, 1= current), and (3) number of arguments (which were each significantly related to relationship satisfaction, $r = -.31$, $p < .001$, $r = -.60$, $p < .001$, and $r = -.13$, $p < .05$, respectively) tested the three hypotheses. Relationship satisfaction was unrelated (at $p < .05$) to the positive relational expression (partial $r = .07$, $p = .16$) and mutuality (partial $r = .04$, $p = .28$) goals, but positively linked to integrative communication (partial $r = .13$, $p < .05$), supporting H1a, but inconsistent with H2a.

Relationship satisfaction was negatively related to avoidance (partial $r = -.31$, $p < .001$), the expressiveness negative (partial $r = -.19$, $p < .01$) and relationship termination (partial $r = -.21$, $p < .01$) goals, and rumination (partial $r = -.24$, $p < .001$), but unrelated to distributive communication (partial $r = -.12$, $p = .05$), the dominance/control (partial $r = -.07$, $p = .16$) and the hurt partner (partial $r = -.03$, $p = .36$) goals, supporting H1c and H3, partially supporting H2b, and not supporting H1b.

To answer the research question, a two–step multiple regression analysis was used. Type of sample, relationship status, and number of arguments were in the first step, and the five serial argument variables that were significant in the partial correlation tests were in the second step. The multiple regression was significant, $F (8, 186) = 26.48$, $p < .001$, adjusted $R^2 = .51$. In the second regression model, avoidance ($\beta = -.20$, $p < .001$), rumination ($\beta = -.18$, $p < .01$), integrative communication ($\beta = .16$, $p < .01$), and the relationship termination goal

($\beta = -.15$, $p < .05$) were (in order) significant serial argument predictors of relationship satisfaction. Expressiveness negative goal importance was not a significant predictor in this model ($\beta = -.06$, $p = .28$). The relationship status ($\beta = -.46$, $p < .001$) and number of arguments ($\beta = -.12$, $p < .05$) covariates were also significant negative predictors of relationship satisfaction, but type of sample was not ($\beta = -.11$, $p = .06$).

Discussion

These findings indicate that multiple positive and negative serial argument cognitive and communicative characteristics are related to romantic relationship satisfaction. Further, when considered together, using the avoidance conflict strategy and ruminating about the serial argument were the aspects of serial arguments that were most strongly associated with disturbance to one's romantic relationship.

Consistent with the bulk of interpersonal conflict research (Segrin et al., 2009), greater romantic relationship satisfaction was associated with decreased avoidance and more integrative communication (H1a, H1c) in serial arguments. Our findings that relationship satisfaction was negatively (though only marginally at $p = .05$) related to distributive communication (H1b) are also consistent with this trend. As relationship dissatisfaction can predict dissolution and divorce (Caughlin et al., 2013), this reflects an important similarity between serial argument and general conflict research that can assist in understanding the possible long-term consequences of serial arguments, an area in need of future research.

With specific regard to conflict avoidance, our findings are illuminating. Specifically, avoidance's role in the serial argument process has been difficult to pinpoint in previous research (Bevan et al., 2007, 2008; see Hample & Kruger, 2011 for an exception in the classroom context). Here, it was the strongest predictor of relational disturbance, suggesting that usage of conflict avoidance in serial arguments might best be understood via relationship variables, rather than the cognitions (i.e., goals, rumination, and perceived resolvability) that it has traditionally been examined in relation to.

In terms of cognitions, the two negative goals (expressiveness negative and relationship termination, H2b) and rumination (H3) were negatively related to relationship satisfaction. However, both positive goals (H2a) and the dominance/control and hurt partner goals (H2b) were unrelated to relationship satisfaction. The finding for rumination is consistent with previous research (e.g., Elphinston et al., 2013) and extends the rumination-satisfaction link to the serial argument context. The positive goal finding may be because romantic partners view the overall serial argument process as primarily negative, thus reducing the size of the association between the importance of these goals and relationship satisfaction. Alternately, the finding that only two serial argument goals were related to relationship satisfaction suggests that communication variables (e.g., conflict styles and patterns) may be more primary in understanding serial argument goals than more distal outcomes such as relationship satisfaction. Finally, similar to Avivi, Laurenceau, and Carver (2009), considering partners' goal mutuality and perception of goal progress in serial arguments may result in a better link between goals and relationship satisfaction.

Limitations and Conclusion

This study has a number of limitations. First, consistent with the bulk of general interpersonal conflict research (e.g., Segrin et al., 2009), we treated relationship satisfaction as an outcome variable when answering our RQ, although relationship satisfaction also could conceivably predict serial argument thoughts and conflict strategy usage. This is especially the case for serial arguments, which can span months or even years. Second, though our sample was drawn from two different datasets, it was still relatively homogenous with regard to sex, ethnicity, and sexual orientation. Our sample was also exclusively from the United States, limiting generalizability. Consistent with Hample and Cionea (2012), future serial argument research should strive to span cultures and ethnicities.

In conclusion, serial argument research is fairly isolated from general interpersonal conflict research, even though both tend to examine ongoing, important conflict experiences between close relationship partners (Bevan & Love, 2013). This study began to bridge these related research areas by examining relationship satisfaction, a common outcome variable in conflict research, in relation to serial argument cognitions and communication strategies. Findings generally revealed that, as in interpersonal conflict research, relationship satisfaction can be a useful variable for understanding how serial argument processes can impact romantic relationships. Thus, to better understand the role of serial argumentation in relational disturbance, we recommend expanding the commonly studied serial argument characteristics – which tend to be individual in nature – to consistently include relationship variables such as satisfaction and harm.

References

Avivi, Y. E., Laurenceau, J-P., & Carver, C. S. (2009). Linking relationship quality to perceived mutuality of relationship goals and perceived goal progress. *Journal of Social and Clinical Psychology, 28*, 137–164.

Bevan, J. L. (2010). Serial argument goals and conflict strategies: A comparison between romantic partners and family members. *Communication Reports, 23*, 52–64. doi: 10.1080/08934211003598734

Bevan, J. L. (in press). Dyadic perceptions of goals, conflict strategies, and perceived resolvability in serial arguments. *Journal of Social and Personal Relationships.* doi: 10.1177/0265407513504653

Bevan, J. L., Finan, A., & Kaminsky, A. (2008). Modeling serial arguments in close relationships: The serial argument processing model. *Human Communication Research, 34*, 600–624. doi: 10.1111/j.1468-2958.2008.00334.x

Bevan, J. L., Hale, J. L., & Williams, S. L. (2004). Identifying and characterizing goals of dating partners engaged in serial argumentation. *Argumentation and Advocacy, 41*, 28–40.

Bevan, J. L., & Love, A. (2013, November). *An exploration of differences in cognitive and communicative components of romantic serial versus non-serial arguments.* Paper presented at the annual meeting of the National Communication Association, Washington, DC.

Bevan, J. L., Tidgewell, K. D., Barkdull, K. C., Cusanelli, L., Hartsern, M., Holbeck, D., & Hale, J. L. (2007). Serial argumentation goals and their relationships with perceived resolvability and choice of conflict tactics. *Communication Quarterly, 55*, 61–77. doi: 10.1080/01463370600998640

Canary, D. J., & Lakey, S. (2013). *Strategic conflict.* New York, NY: Routledge.

Carr, K., Schrodt, P., & Ledbetter, A. M. (2012). Rumination, conflict intensity, and perceived resolvability as predictors of motivation and likelihood of continuing serial arguments. *Western Journal of Communication, 76*, 480–502. doi: 10.1080/10570314.2012.689086

Caughlin, J. P., Vangelisti, A. L., & Mikucki-Enyart, S. L. (2013). Conflict in dating and marital relationships. In J. G. Oetzel & S. Ting-Toomey (Eds.), *The Sage handbook of conflict communication* (2nd ed., pp. 161–185). Thousand Oaks, CA: Sage.

Cloven, D. H., & Roloff, M. E. (1991). Sense-making activities and interpersonal conflict: Communicative cures for the mulling blues. *Western Journal of Speech Communication, 55*, 134–158

Elphinston, R. A., Feeney, J. A., Noller, P., Connor, J. P., & Fitzgerald, J. (2013). Romantic jealousy and relationship satisfaction: The costs of rumination. *Western Journal of Communication, 77*, 293–304. doi: 10.1080/10570314.2013.770161

Gold, D. B., & Wegner, D. M. (1995). Origins of ruminative thought: Trauma, incompleteness, nondisclosure, and suppression. *Journal of Applied Social Psychology, 25*, 1245–1261. doi: 10.1111/j.1559-1816.1995.tb02617.x

Hample, D., & Cionea, I. A. (2012). Serial arguments in inter-ethnic relationships. *International Journal of Intercultural Relations, 36*, 430–445. doi: 10.1016/j.ijintrel.2011.12.006

Hample, D., & Krueger, B. (2011). Serial arguments in classrooms. *Communication Studies, 62*, 597–617. doi: 10.1080/10510974.2011.576746

Hample, D., Richards, A. S., & Na, L. (2012). A test of the conflict linkage model in the context of serial arguments. *Western Journal of Communication, 76*, 459–479. doi: 10.1080/10570314.2012.703361

Hendrick, S. S. (1988). A generic measure of relational satisfaction. *Journal of Marriage and Family, 50*, 93–99.

Johnson, A. J., Averbeck, J. M., Kelley, K. M., & Liu, S-J. (2011). When serial arguments predict harm: Examining the influences of argument function, topic of the argument, perceived resolvability, and argumentativeness. *Argumentation and Advocacy, 47*, 214–227.

Johnson, K. L., & Roloff, M. E. (1998). Serial arguing and relational quality: Determinants and consequences of perceived resolvability. *Communication Research, 25*, 327–343. doi:10.1177/009365098025003004

Johnson, K. L., & Roloff, M. E. (2000a). Correlates of the perceived resolvability and relational consequences of serial arguing in dating relationships. *Journal of Social and Personal Relationships, 17*, 676–686. doi: 10.1177/0265407500174011

Johnson, K. L., & Roloff, M. E. (2000b). The influence of argumentative role (initiator vs. resistor) on perceptions of serial argument resolvability and relational harm. *Argumentation, 14*, 1–15. doi: 10.1023/A:1007837310258

Kuehner, C., & Buerger, C. (2005). Determinants of subjective quality of life in depressed patients: The role of self-esteem, response styles, and social support. *Journal of Affective Disorders, 86*, 205–213. doi: 10.1016/j.jad.2005.01.014

Pearson, K. A., Watkins, E. R., Kuyken, W., & Mullan, E. G. (2010). The psychosocial context of depressive rumination: Ruminative brooding predicts diminished relationship satisfaction in individuals with a history of past major depression. *British Journal of Clinical Psychology, 49*, 275–280. Doi: 10.1348/014466509X480553

Reznik, R. M., & Roloff, M. E. (2011). Getting off to a bad start: The relationship between communication during an initial episode of a serial argument episode and argument frequency. *Communication Studies, 62*, 291–306. doi: 10.1080/10510974.2011.555491

Rusbult, C. E. (1983). A longitudinal test of the investment model: The development (and deterioration) of satisfaction and commitment in heterosexual involvements. *Journal of Personality and Social Psychology, 45*, 101–117.

Segrin, C., Hanzal, A., & Domschke, T. J. (2009). Accuracy and bias in newlywed couples' perceptions of conflict styles and the association with martial satisfaction. *Communication Monographs, 76*, 207–233.

Trapp, R., & Hoff, N. (1985). A model of serial argument in interpersonal relationships. *Journal of the American Forensic Association, 22*, 1–11.

19

DISTURBING ARGUMENTS

Treatment decision making when a female adolescent confronts fertility-threatening cancer

Kathleen M. Galvin

NORTHWESTERN UNIVERSITY, USA

Esther Liu

NORTHWESTERN UNIVERSITY, USA

In 2013, approximately 11,630 U.S. children will be diagnosed with cancer before their 15th birthday (American Cancer Society, 2012). Concurrently a small group of parents will receive additional disturbing news that their adolescent daughters have been diagnosed with fertility-threatening cancer. Such messages upend family life, as members confront the complicated and terrifying realm of treatment(s), often including radiation, chemotherapy, and/or surgery, and their side effects. Some parents learn that an experimental, fertility-preservation minor surgery, completed before cancer treatments commence, may protect their daughters' fertility. Whereas cancer treatment decisions are heavily influenced by the medical team, fertility preservation decisions that address the patient's potential future quality of life tend to be made by parents.

The fertility preservation decision triggers disturbing family conversations related to the risk of postponing cancer treatments, the patient, and possible significant expenses. Fertility preservation procedures further challenge the medical decision-making roles of parents and their affected daughters. Disturbing arguments may surface due to the seriousness of inter-twined topic(s), the need for immediate decision making, and the sensitive nature of the discussions.

In addition to addressing the cancer treatments, many parents and their newly diagnosed daughters encounter complex medical information regarding potential fertility preservation procedures. Whereas adolescent males are able to bank sperm before cancer treatment commences, females face a more invasive procedure because the oocytes (eggs) must be "retrieved surgically, [are] available in limited numbers, and will be at varying degrees of maturity on the time of the menstrual cycle" (Woodruff, 2010, p. 466). *In vitro* maturation of immature follicles combined with oocyte (egg) vitrification has resulted in the birth of four healthy babies (Woodruff, 2010).

Little is known about how adolescents facing cancer treatments comprehend fertility threats or possible treatment alternatives in order to make reasoned decisions (Eiser, 2004). When a female adolescent's cancer diagnosis involves potential fertility loss, her decision-making role in fertility preservation efforts raises disturbing issues. Often medical personnel discuss fertility preservation options only with parents, because minors need parental consent before undergoing a surgical procedure. Research on sperm banking when male adolescents face fertility-threatening cancer treatments reveals that some parents avoid discussing fertility preservation with their sons (Nieman et al., 2006). In other cases, a parental decision reflects consultation with medical staff and the patient. Such conversations would be exceptionally disturbing for adolescents whose parents have not discussed sex with them (Galvin & Clayman, 2010).

To understand the growing involvement of adolescents in medical decision making, the following issues must be considered: (1) changes in medical decision-making practices related to minors, (2) factors that complicate minors' involvement in medical decision making, and (3) potential contributions of argumentation scholars. As the medical profession moves toward more scientific, rigorous decision-making models and process models (shared decision making and informed decision making), the physician's role has changed (Makoul & Clayman, 2006). Both models reflect informed and ongoing communication among family members and health care professionals.

Changes in Medical Decision-Making Practices for Adolescents

Until recently, parents would make any treatment decision on behalf of their minor child, regardless of age, severity, or desirability of treatments. Yet medical decision making may be envisioned along two decision axes: *mundane to highly consequential* and *desirable to undesirable* (Botti, Orfali, & Iyengar, 2009). Irreversible medical decisions are frequently characterized as highly consequential. In cases of childhood cancer, the decision to commence treatment would fall in the desirable and highly consequential quadrant because the child is likely to survive with minimal to serious long-term effects. If the proposed treatment potentially threatens fertility, the highly desirable and consequential decision shifts to the moderately to highly undesirable quadrant.

Recently, incorporating flexibility in medical decision making has become more common when the patient is an adolescent and proposed medical procedures are desirable but may produce highly consequential outcomes. Adolescents now have decision-making autonomy regarding treatment for sexually transmitted diseases or reproductive care. Characterizing the laws relating to children's health decision making as undeveloped, unsettled, and incoherent, Rosato (2008) argued for a more comprehensive and coherent development of laws regarding minors' medical decision making, while stressing the need to give older adolescents more authority particularly for decisions that affect their futures.

Key decisional questions raise disturbing issues for medical professionals: "What should be the scope of parental autonomy over their children?" and "What autonomy (if any) should children have to make their own decisions?" (Rosato, 2008, p. 195). For example, high-stakes medical decisions become extremely complicated when adolescent and medical providers oppose parental decisions. Increasingly medical providers argue for greater involvement of adolescents in their care decisions, according to their prior experiences, maturity level, and cognitive and emotional capabilities. Adolescent patient involvement in medical decisions, such as providing *assent*, is particularly crucial when "the clarity of the 'right choice' fades, and where treatment preferences are based upon personal values and 'quality of life' issues" (McCabe, 1996, p. 506). A pediatric oncology decision-making model reflects this position. It attempts to delineate circumstances in which a child, parent, or clinician should have decisional authority (Whitney et al., 2008).

Ideally, consequential medical decision making involving adolescents includes active family communication among all invested parties. Foreman's (1999) Family Rule Approach argued that children's informed consent "should be regarded as shared between children and their families, the balance being determined by implicit, developmentally based negotiations between child and parent – a 'family rule' for consent" (p. 491). This approach identified a five-step process for ensuring that the child has enough information necessary to give rational consent and five conditions that health care providers (HCPs) may encounter as they attempt to balance respect for the child's autonomy with respect for the variable (diffuse) nature of a child's right to consent.

The concept of crisis frames how families manage communication standards, decision making, and argument, given the challenges of difficult choices. Factors that characterize crisis family decisions include: "topic, duration, intrusiveness, urgency, and scope of involvement" (Ketrow & DiCioccio, 2009, p. 82). Each factor surfaces when addressing adolescent fertility preservation. Parents confront the need to discuss potentially volatile issues such as religion, death, adoption, money, and the extent to which the adolescent patient should be involved in all treatment decisions within a very short time period. Therefore, when adolescents are diagnosed with fertility-threatening cancer, families of young females face a "high-stakes, emotionally-charged, time-sensitive, nested decision with long-term implications" (Galvin, 2009, p. 98). Because this decision falls in the highly undesirable quadrant, most medical professionals will tend to involve the adolescent patient in decision making.

Complications of Involving Minors in Medical Decision Making

Health risk information confounds laypersons (Murphy-Knoll, 2007). Frequently medical information addressing treatment risks, benefits, and secondary effects appears as percentages and probabilities filtered through the lens of medical experts. Thus, parents and adolescents may struggle to understand medical terminology and the implications of "Hodgkin's lymphoma" or side effects of infertility or cognitive impairment.

Multiple factors influence family decision making. Adult decision makers may include multiple parental figures with various backgrounds. Although medical consent literature reflects heavy reliance on biological or legal parents as sole decision makers, a high percentage of children live with parental figures who do not fit this description. A study of childhood cancer decision making in single-parent and re-partnered family forms revealed that any involvement of non-traditional parental figures depended on their familial position (i.e., custodial, nonresidential, and stepparent; Patterson Kelly & Ganong, 2010). Ongoing parental disagreements serve to raise the patient's anxiety and silence her voice. In addition to such stressors within complex family forms, family members may engage in disturbing arguments about fertility treatments that challenge their religion/faith (Lipstein, Brinkman, & Britto, 2012) or cultural beliefs (Lee & Mock, 2005). Parental education levels may further confound decision making (Stewart, Pyke-Grimm, & Kelly, 2005).

Mature minors, those able to understand the nature and consequences of medical treatments (Kuther, 2003), represent a special decision-making category. Some medical practitioners argue that mature minors should have the right to refuse life-sustaining medical treatment. Derish and Vanden Heuvel (2000) called for involving certain adolescents in end-of-life decision making, asserting that mature minors are particularly vulnerable to receiving end-of-life medical care that was not fully explained or that they did not choose to accept. Decrying the lack of communication among parents, children, and medical or legal professionals, they argue that "adolescents, with some exceptions, are capable of making major health decisions and giving informed consent" (p. 113). Increasingly mature minors are becoming involved in their medical decision making.

Argumentation Scholars and Minors' Medical Decision Making

Involving minors in high-stakes medical decision making necessitates greater research focused on family medical decision making when a child is diagnosed with a life-threatening or serious quality-of-life-threatening medical condition. Such involvement increases the possibility that an adolescent and her parent(s) will find themselves in a "deep disagreement," a controversy characterized by "no shared framework that can serve the arguers as a common standard or point or reference" (Zarefsky, 2012). An example involves parent-daughter disagreement about whether to postpone cancer treatment in order to remove an ovary for cryopreservation. Due to the time-sensitive, irreversible nature of this decision, both parties may focus on the incompatibility of their existing frameworks rather than consider new decision-making paradigms. Adolescent patients may express strong desires to learn about treatment effects on fertility but feel uncomfortable discussing such issues with healthcare providers in the presence of their parents (Crawshaw & Sloper, 2006). Allowing patients to more freely engage in dialogue with health care professionals about personal thoughts and emotions toward fertility preservation (Hershberger, Finnegan, Pierce, & Scoccia, 2013) may create space for a new decision-making paradigm.

Decision aids "prepare people to participate in close call decisions that involve weighing benefits, harms and scientific uncertainty" (O'Connor et al., 2009, p. 1). Argumentation scholars have much to contribute to interdisciplinary research focused on the adolescent's role in high-stakes medical decision making and the development of medical decision aids designed for minors and their parents. The following related issues warrant attention: (a) established family interaction patterns (e.g., persuasion and decision-making norms) and family characteristics (e.g. religion, ethnicity/culture) that inform decision-making practices when circumstances require high-stakes decisions and (b) the development of decision aids designed to engage adolescent patients (ages 12–18) in high-stakes decision making related to their medical treatment.

Communication scholars with expertise in decision-making processes, argument, persuasion, and family typologies/interaction patterns could bring new perspectives to medical decision-making research. Key decision points arise during treatment phases: initial treatment options, initial treatment effects management, and long-term care management. Family communication patterns may shift during each phase affecting the locus of control and coping strategies. Control reflects family environments that affect the level of family and patient distress; cohesive and low conflict families experience less distress than high conflict or detached families (Weihs & Politi, 2006). The use of problem-focused coping strategies results in higher appraisals of control than emotion-focused coping, particularly during adolescence (Sorgen & Manne, 2002). Koerner and Fitzpatrick's (2006) research on family communication patterns and family types can contribute greatly to health professionals working with family members confronting a young relative's cancer diagnosis and treatment. Increasingly adolescent patients are involved in decision making related to enrollment in medical trials, nature of medications, and a shift to palliative care. In such cases, evidence, reasoning, and arguments displayed in decision aids contribute to the decision-making process.

Traditional medical decision aids prepare parents of affected offspring to make decisions, often with their medical providers, that reflect deliberative, personal choices among multiple options. Well-designed decision aids present an array of information to assist family members, including adolescent patients, to reach a decision consistent with their beliefs and values. Decision aids present facts about the patient's condition; provide balanced, personalized information about treatment options; support decision making in line with one's life goals (Braddock, 2010); clarify the outcomes that matter most to patients; and guide patients through communication processes in order to reach a decision consistent with their values (O'Connor et al., 2009). Decision aids, used individually or in small group sessions, may be self-managed or professionally administered. Aids appear in multiple forms including print, video, computer disk, and web page.

Most cancer decision aids are designed for adult patients or parents of young cancer patients (Clayman, Galvin, & Harper, 2012); none directly address adolescent female patients. Furthermore, existing decision aids do not reflect family communication styles, ranging from highly open to highly closed (Koerner & Fitzpatrick, 2006), which impact an adolescent's ability to engage in meaningful decision making or provide consent.

Communication scholars, particularly those versed in argumentation, have much to offer as collaborators in the development and assessment of decision aids. Initial stages of collaboration involve developing deliberation flow charts, designed for parent and/or adolescent use, that display probable factors predicted to influence decision making such as family structure, religious beliefs, socioeconomic status, ethnicity/culture, medical language facility, previous parent-child discussion of sexuality, and an adolescent's sexual knowledge/experience. A potential personalized cost/benefit analysis of factors related to the fertility preservation option may be displayed with adaptations addressing issues such as timing and predicted recovery time. Future research needs to focus on analyzing subsequent patient, family, and medical providers' interactions after decisions have been reached and on developing aids adapted to various families' decision-making practices.

The growing trend of interdisciplinary health care research and practice will benefit from the expertise of communication scholars, representing areas of argumentation, health communication, and family communication. Decision aids designed for adolescent patients would support informed decision making in circumstances involving high-stakes medical interventions of an immediate nature, especially when the disturbing nature of the illness or treatment raises difficult issues. Hopefully the critical communication immediately following diagnosis, involving HCPs, adolescent cancer patients, and family members, will result in medically sound, family- and patient-endorsed decisions, consonant with family members' beliefs and values.

References

American Cancer Society. (2012). *Cancer in children*. Atlanta, GA: American Cancer Society. http://www.cancer.org/cancer/cancerinchildren/detailedguide/cancer-in-children-key-statistics

Botti, S., Orfali, K., & Iyengar, S. S. (2009). Tragic choices: Autonomy and emotional responses to medical decisions. *Journal of Consumer Research, 36*, 337–352.

Braddock, C. H. (2010). The emerging importance and relevance of shared decision making to clinical practice. *Medical Decision Making, 30*, 5S–7S.

Clayman, M., Galvin, K. M., & Harper, M. (2012). *Learning about cancer and fertility: A guide for parents of young children*. (Oncofertility decision aid for parents of girls facing fertility-threatening cancer). Northwestern University Medical School.

Crawshaw, M., & Sloper, P. (2006). A qualitative study of the experiences of teenagers and young adults when faced with possible or actual fertility impairment following cancer treatment. York: University of York. http://www.york.ac.uk/inst/spru/pubs/pdf/fertility.pdf

Derish, M. T., & Vanden Heuval, K. (2000). Mature minors should have the right to refuse life-sustaining medical treatment. *Journal of Law, Medicine & Ethics, 28*, 109–124.

Eiser, C. (2004). *Children with cancer: The quality of life.* Mahwah, N.J.: Lawrence Erlbaum Associates.

Foreman, D. M. (1999). The family rule: A framework for obtaining ethical consent for medical interventions from children. *Journal of Medical Ethics, 25*(6), 491–500.

Galvin, K. M. (2009). Deliberation in a contested medical context: Developing a framework to aid family decision making when an adolescent son faces fertility-threatening cancer treatment. In D. S. Gouran (Ed.), *The Functions of Argument and Social Context* (pp. 98–106). Washington, DC: National Communication Association.

Galvin, K. M., & Clayman, M. L. (2010). Whose future is it? Ethical family decision making about daughters' treatment in the oncofertility context. In T. K. Woodruff, L. Zoloth, L. Campo-Engelstein, & S. Rodriguez (Eds.), *Oncofertility: Ethical, legal, social and medical perspectives.* (pp. 429–445). New York, NY: Springer.

Hershberger, P. E., Finnegan, L., Pierce, P. F., & Scoccia, B. (2013). The decision-making process of young adult women with cancer who considered fertility cryopreservation. *Journal of Obstetric, Gynecologic, & Neonatal Nursing, 42*(1), 59–69.

Ketrow, S. M., & DiCioccio, R. L. (2009). Family argument: A model of family communication in crisis. In D. S. Gouran (Ed.), *The functions of argument and social context: Selected papers from the 16th NCA/AFA Conference on Argumentation* (pp. 241–249). Washington, D.C. National Communication Association.

Koerner, A. F., & Fitzpatrick, M. A. (2006). Family communication patterns theory: A social cognitive approach. In D. O. Braithwaite & L. A. Baxter (Eds.), *Engaging theories in family communication: Multiple perspectives* (pp. 50–65). Thousand Oaks, CA: SAGE.

Kuther, T. L. (2003). Medical decision making and minors: Issues of consent and assent. *Adolescence, 38*(150), 343–358.

Lee, E., & Mock, M. R. (2005). Asian families: An overview. In M. McGoldrick, J. Giordano, & N. Garcia-Preto (Eds.), *Ethnicity and family therapy* (3rd ed., pp. 269–289). New York, NY: Guilford Press.

Lipstein, E. A., Brinkman, W. B., & Britto, M. T. (2012). What is known about parents' treatment decisions? A narrative review of pediatric decision making. *Medical Decision Making, 32*(3), 246–258.

McCabe, M. A. (1996). Involving children and adolescents in medical decision making: Developmental and clinical considerations. *Journal of Pediatric Psychology, 21*(4), 505–516.

Makoul, G., & Clayman, M. L. (2006). An integrative model of shared decision making in medical encounters. *Patient Education and Counseling, 60*(3), 301–312.

Murphy-Knoll, L. (2007). Low health literacy puts patients at risk: The Joint Commission proposes solutions to national problem. *Journal of Nursing Care Quality, 22*(3), 205–209.

Nieman, C. L., Kazar, R., Brannigan, R. E., Zoloth, L. S., Cahse-Lansdale, P. L., Kinahan, K., et al. (2006). Cancer survivors and infertility: A review of a new problem and novel answers. *The Journal of Supportive Oncology, 4*(4), 1–8.

O'Connor, A. M., Bennett, C. L., Stacey, D., Barry, M., Col, N. F., Eden K. B., & Rovner, D. (2009). Decision aids for people facing health treatment of screen decisions. http://www.ncbi.nlm.nih.bov/pubmed/19588325

Patterson Kelly, K., & Ganong, L. (2010). Moving to place: Childhood cancer treatment decision making in single-parent and repartnered family structures. *Qualitative Health Research, 21*, 349–364.

Rosato, J. L. (2008). Foreword. *Houston Journal of Health, Law & Policy, 8*(2), 195–205.

Sorgen, K. E., & Manne, S. L. (2002). Coping in children with cancer: Examining the goodness-of-fit hypothesis. *Children's Health Care, 31*(3), 191–207.

Stewart, J. L., Pyke-Grimm, K. A., & Kelly, K. P. (2005). Parental treatment decision making in pediatric oncology. Supplement 2 Seminars in Oncology. *Nursing, 21*(2), 89–97.

Weihs, K., & Politi, M. (2006). Family development in the face of cancer. In D. R. Crane & E. S. Marshall (Eds.), *Handbook of families and health: Interdisciplinary perspectives* (pp. 3–18). Thousand Oaks, CA: Sage.

Whitney, S. N., Holmes-Rovner, M., Brody, H., Schneider, C., McCullough, L. B., Volk, R. J., & McGuire, A. L. (2008). Beyond shared decision making: An expanded typology of medical decisions. *Medical Decision Making, 28*(5), 699–705.

Woodruff, T. K. (2010). The Oncofertility Consortium – addressing fertility in young people with cancer. *Nature*, 7, 466–474.

Zarefsky, D. (2012, June). On deep disagreement. Unpublished paper presented at the Venice Conference on Argumentation, Casa Artom, Venice, Italy.

20

LESSONS FROM LEADERSHIP THEORY AND RESEARCH FOR MAXIMIZING THE VALUE OF ARGUMENT IN DISCUSSIONS OF DECISION-MAKING AND PROBLEM-SOLVING GROUPS

Dennis S. Gouran

THE PENNSYLVANIA STATE UNIVERSITY, USA

Inspired by John Dewey's (1910) exploration of reflective thinking, those in communication studies interested in group discussion as an instrument of deliberation have treated this activity as a form of inquiry having as its paramount goal discovery. They offered a model of discussion that discouraged efforts by participants to convince one another of the merits of competing choice options by means of argument; that purportedly was the domain of debate (see, e.g., Ewbank & Auer, 1941). The dominant feeling was that discussion, conducted properly by individuals trained and skilled in reflective thinking, would serve to reveal the appropriate answers to questions of fact, conjecture, value, and policy, as well as lead to the identification of workable solutions to all manner of problematic situations.

The intellectual landscape has since changed. Currently, it appears that most proponents of the use of discussion by groups to make decisions and solve problems recognize the artificiality and impracticality, if not impossibility, of treating this as a mode of discovery in which advocacy and other forms of social influence are unwelcome intrusions. Despite growing acceptance of argument and arguing as not only inescapable aspects of interaction in groups, but when conducted properly also as valuable, perhaps even critical, instrumentalities for enhancing, if not maximizing, prospects for choosing appropriately (Gouran, 1988) or rationally (Habermas, 1996), argument scholars remain deficient in our understanding of how best to succeed. For guidance, we would be well advised to look to scholarship relating to leadership.

In this document, I have undertaken the task to make clear respects in which different social-scientific perspectives on leadership offer useful insights into enhancing the value of argument in discussions of decision-making and problem-solving groups. In so doing, I have been mindful of the concerns that Barbara Kellerman (2012) recently voiced about the so-called "leadership industry" (p. xiii) and the overly simplistic ways in which those identified with it frequently encourage others to think about the exercise of influence.

Rationale

Peter Northouse (2013a) defined leadership as "a process whereby an individual influences a group of individuals to achieve a common goal" (p. 4). Argument, in Daniel O'Keefe's (1977) second sense of the term, is also a process whereby one person attempts to influence one or more others to accept an argument in his first sense of the term, that is, a disputable claim. Although those who study leadership are not necessarily concerned with argument in this sense, a leader who attempts to influence others is, in one way or another, engaging in argument in both senses in which O'Keefe uses the term. The individual seeks to gain acceptance (argument$_2$) of a claim (argument$_1$) concerning what is true, probable, acceptable, or in need of doing.

What directs my attention to scholarship relating to leadership for indications of how we might increase the value and impact of argument in discussions of decision-making and problem-solving groups is that those studying leadership as a process of influence have, it seems, devoted far more attention to determining what accounts for success than have those in communication studies who are concerned about the role of argument in the two types of choice-making contexts noted. Among the views of leadership that have evolved since social scientists first began studying it as a process, three having direct relevance for purposes of the exploration herein are the Trait Perspective, the Transformational Leadership Perspective, and the Authentic Leadership Perspective.

The Trait Perspective

The oldest of the social-scientific views of leadership, many of its critics have been dismissive of the Trait Perspective's value in accounting for the successful exercise of influence in groups and organizations more generally (Northouse, 2013b). Repeated declarations of its moribund condition, if not outright demise, notwithstanding, the perspective is, in fact, very much alive and transcends the other two I address in this essay. From the Trait Perspective, the key to success in the exercise of influence, not to mention the acquisition of positions of leadership, is the possession of particular personal qualities. Such traits, in early thinking, were genetic in origin. With the genetic basis for understanding influence largely discredited (Bass, 2008), proponents of the perspective began shifting their attention to acquired traits in the latter part of the 1900s and in the process created a good deal of renewed interest in the relationship of personal qualities to the enactment of influence.

If one remains within the realm of acquired personal qualities, several that people reveal in their communicative behavior and that appear to contribute to their ability to be influential in their interactions are self-confidence, determination, integrity, and sociability (Northouse, 2013b). Northouse includes intelligence in the list, but not everyone might see it as acquired. In fact, most of those who have studied this trait seem to have had in mind native ability. Viewed more in the sense of practical knowledge one accumulates and utilizes in communicative exchanges, however, it might qualify as acquired (Sternberg, 1997). Whether inherited or acquired, intelligence is manifested in overt behavior, but it may not be as much an asset when it comes to influence as one likely expects (Hunter & Jordan, 1939). Perhaps more obviously acquired and more significant is what Daniel Goleman (1995) referred to as *emotional intelligence*, or the empathic sensitivity people show toward others. Finally, there is a set of personal attributes that Goldberg (1990) originally identified as the "Big Five": non–neuroticism, extraversion, openness, agreeableness, and conscientiousness. Neuroticism (or its opposite), extraversion, agreeableness, and conscientiousness appear to be similar to self-confidence, sociability, emotional intelligence, and integrity.

From this overview, one can construct a profile of predominantly acquired personal qualities that appear to contribute to one's ability to influence others in such social structures as decision-making and problem-solving groups, and in respect to gaining others' acceptance of arguments in particular. One formulation is that a participant in a decision-making or problem-solving group is apt to be more successful in advancing arguments and gaining acceptance of them by displaying confidence in their merits, determination to make the most appropriate choices, personal integrity in advancing positions on issues central to the matter(s) in need of resolution, a lack of personal antagonism toward others, understanding of the complexity and nuances of the issues, empathy, and openness to other points of view.

With the rise of corporate celebrities, such as Steve Jobs, Donald Trump, and Jack Welch, interest has arisen concerning whether or not narcissism is a useful personal quality to possess in efforts to influence others. Michael Maccoby (2003, 2007) has done much to advance the notion that what he referred to as *productive narcissists* can be forces for good. Although it may be that narcissists succeed in exercising influence generally, and by implication would in respect to gaining acceptance of their arguments, at the group level in a decision-making context, a recent study by Nevicka, Ten Velden, De Hoogh, and Van Vianin (2011) points to a different conclusion. Three-person groups performing a hidden-profile task having an objectively best choice if the members shared all of the information in their collective possession performed far less successfully when the designated leader had a narcissistic personality. If the function of argument is to increase the likelihood of warranted choice, this finding is not good news for those who feel that narcissism may be an asset in the performance of decision-making and problem-solving groups. From what we know about the characteristics of narcissists (see Rosenthal & Pittinsky, 2006), it is difficult to believe that they would contribute to argument in the sense that Habermas (1996) had in mind.

The Transformational Leadership Perspective

The concept of *transformational leadership* originated with James MacGregor Burns (1978) as an outgrowth of his efforts to account for why some people in positions of leadership seem to be able to influence others, even in the millions, without resorting to such common measures as rewards, promises, punishments, and threats. Those leaders who do he dubbed as *transactional* and characterized as behaving in line with exchange-based views of social interaction. Burns's book subsequently attracted the attention of organizational theorists and researchers – most notably Bernard Bass and Ronald Riggio (2006), who devoted considerable time and energy to the formulation and development of a model of transformational leadership applicable to understanding how managers could become more successful in having impact on subordinates that would improve their performance, increase their sense of satisfaction, and otherwise facilitate progress toward the achievement of organizational goals.

The Transformational Leadership Perspective has in common with the Trait Perspective the view that certain personal qualities separate those who qualify as "transformational" from their less successful "transactional" and "*laissez-faire*" counterparts. There are two important differences, however. First, the profile of transformational leaders is uniform, as well as limited in the number of relevant distinguishing features. The applicable categories consist of "Idealized Influence" (charisma), "Inspirational Motivation" (vision), "Intellectual Stimulation" (the capacity to induce in others recognition of the need to be innovative, creative, and critical, especially in respect to buying into the leader's vision), and "Individual Consideration" (showing special attention to followers' needs for both achievement and growth) (Bass & Riggio, 2006, pp. 6–7). Second, genuinely transformational leaders seem to be skilled in eliciting in others the motivation to look beyond themselves and to contribute to the collective well-being of the social entities to which they belong. In so doing, these "others" undergo positive moral change, as does the agent responsible for awakening in them the desire and willingness to behave in such a manner. Of particular relevance to argument and the enhancement of one's influence while engaging in it are the second, third, and fourth components of transformational leadership.

In respect to inspirational motivation, or vision, the lesson from research relating to trans-formational leadership is that ideas, to gain acceptance, require articulation at a level of clarity that (a) ensures that they are not beyond the grasp of those to whom they are directed, and (b) enables them to understand and appreciate the positive consequences that can accrue from their endorsement (Barge, 2003). It is not enough, however, that one be able to articulate the virtues of particular points of view with cogency and coherence to gain acceptance of them. Consistent with Persuasive Arguments Theory, those to whom a source is targeting what he or she wants them to find acceptable, to some extent, have to convince themselves of the merits of subscription (see Burnstein, 1982; Meyers & Brashers, 2003).

A hallmark of transformational leaders is challenging targets to think critically and not to accept what others tell them or encourage them to believe and do at face value (Kouzes & Posner, 2012). By implication, an arguer is apt to improve prospects for being influential by engaging others at a dialectical level, admitting to the possibility of his or her being wrong in upholding or advancing a given point of view, and making clear the willingness to retreat from it should counterarguments provide sufficient grounds.

In adopting this sort of argumentative posture, one not only improves the potential for exercising influence, but also for displaying the final of the four defining components of transformational leadership, that is, individual consideration. Admitting to the possibility of erroneous or deficient judgment while at the same time acknowledging a desire to find the most defensible positions on matters of mutual interest in the discussions of decision-making and problem-solving groups, even if they are in opposition to one's own views, represents a demonstration of respect that ostensibly would serve to improve the climate of interaction and receptivity to a participant's other attempts at influence. Such exhibitions must be sincere, however, not strategic, and certainly not manipulative – attributes that are more closely iden-tified with pseudotransformational leadership. For them to be otherwise would be to incur the risk of creating mistrust and perceptions of patronization even if that is not the immediate reaction.

The Authentic Leadership Perspective

Tied to the Transformational Leadership Perspective in several respects is one of fairly recent origin that goes under the heading of the Authentic Leadership Perspective (presumably because of the number of people who have in recent years been using the term "authentic leadership" in their publications). The perspective has been an outgrowth of the developing angst in large segments of the population stemming from corporate and political corruption, disservice, and other forms of malfeasance among far too many people in positions of authority and leadership. As in the case of pseudotransformational leaders, there is an abundance of inauthentic leaders who can fool others for a time, but they are eventually outed. With each such revelation, the already widespread feeling that U.S. institutions are failing and that U.S. leaders have let us down intensifies, as does the consequent public thirst for trustworthy leadership at all levels of society (Northouse, 2013c). From this perspective, successful influence depends on the genuineness and trustworthiness of the source, not merely one's interpersonal skills or even general competence.

Individuals with backgrounds in business, such as Bill George (2003) and Robert Terry (1993), have attempted to identify the constituent elements of authentic leadership from a practitioner's standpoint, but there appears to be greater clarity and applicability to the context of argument in decision-making and problem-solving discussions deriving from the social-scientific efforts of Fred Walumbwa and his associates (see Walumbwa, Avolio, Gardner, Wernsing, & Peterson, 2008; Walumbwa, Wang, Wang, Schaubroeck, & Avolio, 2010), who consider it as a developmental process subject to the influence of a number of different factors, all of which contribute to others' perceptions of one's trustworthiness.

Authenticity is a reflection of certain psychological capacities (confidence, hope, optimism, and resilience), moral reasoning, and critical life events, which combine in ways that invest one over time with a high degree of self-awareness, a well-honed internal moral perspective, objectivity in the assessment of information, and transparency in relationships (Northouse, 2013c). The clear implication of research concerning authentic leadership is that, to the extent one acquires these four behavioral dispositions as a result of the antecedent factors noted and reveals them in his or her overt behavior, the trust others, as a consequence, place in the person likely will enhance the prospects for success in attempts to influence others' attitudes, values, beliefs, feelings, and behavior and, in the context of argument more specifically, receptivity to the claims he or she seeks to have them accept.

Conclusion

I am confident that there are other lessons from scholarly literature accumulating in the study of leadership beyond those I have drawn from my brief excursion into the Trait, Transformational Leadership, and Authentic Leadership Perspectives. Their identification awaits only the willingness for some party or parties interested in how to improve his/her/their ability to engage in argument in the discussions of decision-making and problem-solving groups to seize the initiative and extract those that become apparent. On the other hand, there is no particular virtue to extending the list of possibilities simply for the sake of doing so. Of possibly greater potential utility at this point would be efforts to translate the implications from the three perspectives concerning how one might behave into specific practices for doing so. It is one thing to note considerations involved in attempting to become more effective in the art of arguing in discussions of decision-making and problem-solving groups and another to know precisely what enactments are most apt to lead to the desired outcomes. If this essay facilitates scholarly activity having such a character, I believe that it will have served a useful function.

References

Barge, J. K. (2003). Leadership as organizing. In R. Y. Hirokawa, R. S. Cathcart, L. A. Samovar, & L. D. Henman (Eds.), *Small group communication theory & practice: An anthology* (8th ed., pp. 199–213). New York, NY: Oxford University Press.

Bass, B. M. (2008). *The Bass handbook of leadership: Theory, research, & managerial applications* (4th ed.). New York, NY: Free Press.

Bass, B. M., & Riggio, R. E. (2006). *Transformational leadership* (2nd ed.). New York, NY: Psychology Press.

Burns, J. M. (1978). *Leadership*. New York, NY: Harper & Row.

Burnstein, E. (1982). Persuasion as argument processing. In H. Brandstätter, J. H. Davis, & G. Stocker-Kreichgauer (Eds.), *Group decision making* (pp. 103–124). New York, NY: Academic Press.

Dewey, J. (1910). *How we think*. Boston, MA: Heath.

Ewbank, H. L., & Auer, J. J. (1941). *Discussion and debate: Tools of a democracy*. New York, NY: Appleton-Century-Crofts.

George, B. (2003). *Authentic leaders: Rediscovering the secrets to creating lasting value*. San Francisco, CA: Jossey-Bass.

Goldberg, L. R. (1990). An alternative "description of personality": The big-five factor structure. *Journal of Personality and Social Psychology, 59*, 1216–1229.

Goleman, D. (1985). *Emotional intelligence*. New York, NY: Bantam.

Gouran, D. S. (1988). Group decision making: An approach to integrative research. In C. H. Tardy (Ed.), *A handbook for the study of human communication: Methods and instruments for observing, measuring, and assessing communication processes* (pp. 247–267). Norwood, NJ: Ablex.

Habermas, J. (1996). *Between facts and norms: Contributions to a discourse theory of law and democracy* (W. Rehg, Trans.). Cambridge, MA: MIT Press.

Hunter, E. C., & Jordan, A. M. (1939). An analysis of qualities associated with intelligence among college students. *Journal of Educational Psychology, 30*, 497–509.

Kellerman, B. (2012). *The end of leadership*. New York, NY: Harper Business.

Kouzes, J., & Posner, B. (2012). *The leadership challenge: How to make extraordinary things happen in organizations* (5th ed.). San Francisco, CA: Jossey-Bass.

Maccoby, M. (2003). *The productive narcissist: The promise and peril of visionary leadership*. New York, NY: Broadway.

Maccoby, M. (2007). *The leaders we need and what makes us follow*. Boston, MA: Harvard Business School Press.

Meyers, R. A., & Brashers, D. E. (2003). Influencing others in group interactions: Individual, subgroup, group, and intergroup processes. In R. Y. Hirokawa, R. S. Cathcart, L. A. Samovar, & L. D. Henman (Eds.), *Small group communication theory & practice: An anthology* (8th ed., pp. 109–121). New York, NY: Oxford University Press.

Nevicka, B., Ten Velden, F. S., De Hoogh, A. H. B., & Van Vianin, A. E. M. (2012). Reality at odds with perceptions: Narcissistic leaders and group performance. *Psychological Science, 22*, 1259–1264.

Northouse, P. G. (2013a). Introduction. In P. G. Northouse (Ed.), *Leadership: Theory and practice* (6th ed., pp. 1–17). Thousand Oaks, CA: Sage.

Northouse, P. G. (2013b). Trait approach. In P. G. Northouse (Ed.), *Leadership: Theory and practice* (6th ed., pp. 19–42). Thousand Oaks, CA: Sage.

Northouse, P. G. (2013c). Authentic leadership. In P. G. Northouse (Ed.), *Leadership: Theory and practice* (6th ed., pp. 253–285). Thousand Oaks, CA: Sage.

O'Keefe, D. J. (1977). Two concepts of argument. *Journal of the American Forensic Association, 13*, 121–128.

Rosenthal, S. A., & Pittinsky, T. L. (2006). Narcissistic leadership. *Leadership Quarterly, 17*, 617–633.

Sternberg, R. J. (1997). *Successful intelligence*. New York, NY: Plume.

Terry, R. W. (1993). *Authentic leadership: Courage in action*. San Francisco, CA: Jossey-Bass.

Walumbwa, F. O., Avolio, B. J., Gardner, W. L., Wernsing, & Peterson, S. J. (2008). Authentic leadership: Development and validation of a theory-based measure. *Journal of Management, 34*, 89–126.

Walumbwa, F. O., Wang, P., Wang, H., Schaubroeck, J., & Avolio, B. J. (2010). Psychological processes linking authentic leadership to follower behaviors. *Leadership Quarterly, 21*, 901–914.

21

ARGUMENT ENGAGEMENT UNDER INVITATIONAL VERSUS DEMANDING CONDITIONS

Dale Hample

UNIVERSITY OF MARYLAND, USA

Amanda L. Irions

UNIVERSITY OF MARYLAND, USA

Interlocutors must decide to engage in an interpersonal argument for the interaction to be recognizable as an argument at all. One person can complain, or challenge, or assert, but only if this conversational move is understood as creating a slot for an argumentative response can interlocutors see an opportunity for arguing. The second person's response is what joins, and thereby creates, an interpersonal argument. The pragma-dialectical theory of argumentation (van Eemeren & Grootendorst, 2004) specifies that a completed critical discussion will have had four stages: confrontation, opening, argumentation, and concluding. The first stage involves the mutual recognition that the two parties have different positions and the second stage negotiates the method of arguing and deciding about the issue. From there, the participants argue and finally conclude. Even though the four stages are present in a completed episode, there is no necessity that participants actually move through the whole system. They can abandon the process at any point. This essay addresses what is perhaps the first key decision: the second party's choice of whether to engage in an argument or not, given that s/he perceives that one is possible.

In common with a recent line of thought, we conceive of the engagement decision as being based on anticipated costs and benefits. General research on conflict management has shown that costs, benefits, and the balance of costs and benefits are key elements in predicting the likelihood or nature of conflict among children (Ram & Ross, 2008), adolescents (Laursen & Collins, 1994), and adults (Louis, Taylor, & Douglas, 2005). Argument theorists have also turned to this framework (Paglieri, 2009; Paglieri & Castelfranchi, 2010), proposing that people consider the consequences of a possible argument when contemplating their possible involvement in it. Paglieri's ideas have been implemented in a program of empirical research (Cionea, Hample, & Paglieri, 2011; Hample, Paglieri, & Na, 2012; Richards & Cionea, 2012). This paper is the fourth in that series.

The merit of this research is not in proposing that costs and benefits are relevant consider-ations in the decision to engage, because that is a theoretical frame that can be imposed on nearly any voluntary human behavior. Rather, the value is in specifying exactly what the key considerations might be, and which are weightier. Based on Paglieri's (2009) theory, several candidate considerations were developed: the effort of arguing (including cognitive work and emotional exposure), the possible rewards of arguing (utilitarian gains and personal satisfac-tions), the other person's anticipated reasonableness (openness to evidence and argument), the anticipated civility of the encounter, the appropriateness of arguing (on that topic, at that time, with that person), the likelihood that the argument can be resolved at all, and the likeli-hood that the person would win the argument. Hample, Paglieri, and Na (2012) found that of these potential considerations, the most consistently important were appropriateness and the likelihood of winning, although civility, other's reasonability, effort, and rewards also played some role in the engagement decision. Using a Romanian sample, Cionea et al. (2011) replicated the results for winning and appropriateness, and also reported contributions from civility and other's reasonability. Richards and Cionea (2012) also replicated several of these basic results, underscoring the importance of the likelihood of winning, benefits, and expected resolvability. These investigations have differed in several ways: whether the sample was drawn from the U.S. or Romania, what relationships were specified among the arguers (close friends or romantic partners), and what sort of argument topics were proposed (public, personal, or workplace; see Johnson, 2002). The prior studies also included measures of argu-mentativeness (Infante & Rancer, 1982) and verbal aggressiveness (Infante & Wigley, 1986), with uneven results. Hample et al. (2012) found that argument-approach had some small effect, but only for public topics; Cionea et al. (2011) reported that argument-avoidance had some effect, but only for romantic partners; and Richards and Cionea (2012) reported that both argumentativeness and verbal aggressiveness interacted with several of the cost/benefit variables, but inconsistently across topic types. The role of these traits is certainly unresolved at this point, but further efforts are warranted.

In all the previous empirical studies, respondents were exposed to vignettes that invited but did not require an argumentative response. The stimuli made a slot for an argumentative rejoinder, but it was entirely plausible to avoid argumentation in response to it. The present essay includes that condition ("invitational") but also adds a condition ("demanding") that more forcefully calls out argumentation in response. This was done by adding a sentence to the end of each vignette: for instance, "Your friend says, 'You're being a total idiot about this,' and it's obvious that s/he is being very aggressive and wants a verbal fight." By changing the nature of the slot – from invitational to aggressively demanding – we explored whether the same cost/benefit considerations still assert themselves in deciding whether or not to engage.

This new argumentative response condition ("demanding") allows us to determine what happens when people are confronted with aggressive speech, which we understand to be a challenging and/or aversive stimulus. Gray's (1964, 1987; Gray & McNaughton, 2000) rein-forcement sensitivity theory has been conveniently summarized and evaluated by Corr (2004). The theory explains that humans have three systems controlling their behavior in response to stimuli. The first is the Fight/Flight/Freeze (FFFS) system, which mediates behavioral responses (typically avoidance or escape) to aversive stimuli. The second, Behavioral Activation System (BAS), mediates humans' approach toward rewarding stimuli. The third is the Behavioral Inhibition System (BIS), which works to resolve conflicts when FFFS-avoiding behaviors and BAS-approaching behaviors are simultaneously activated. These systems are relevant because people seem to respond to aggressive communication along the divisions suggested by reinforcement sensitivity theory. Our "demand" conditions are confrontative. Some will take that experience as aversive, but others may see opportunity for improvement in personal or workplace relationships by accepting the challenge to argue.

When confronted with aggression, the literature indicates that individuals make both avoidant (e.g., Caughlin & Vangelisti, 1999; Christensen & Heavey, 1993; Heavey, Christensen, & Malamuth, 1995) and approach (e.g., Glomb & Liao, 2003; Hample & Dallinger, 1995; Hample et al., 2010; Infante & Rancer, 1982) responses. Personal and situational factors that might mediate the avoid/approach impulse have not been decisively identified. This study combines several situational features (topic type and estimates of costs and benefits) with several likely individual differences (argumentativeness and verbal aggressiveness). It thereby aims to shed light on when invitation force calls out avoidant or engaging responses.

This is an initial study on the force of argument invitations. Our thinking suggests the importance of answering these research questions.

RQ1: Do invitations versus demands to argue affect respondents' intention to engage in interpersonal argument?
RQ2: Do argumentativeness and/or verbal aggressiveness affect respondents' intentions to engage in arguing?
RQ3: How do estimates of possible costs and benefits affect respondents' intentions to engage in arguing?

Method

Respondents were 211 students enrolled in undergraduate communication classes at our institution. Most (65%) were women. Many were first-year (41%), followed by 16% sophomores, 22% juniors, and 20% seniors. The most common self-reported ethnicity was Euro-American (51%), with notable numbers of Asian-Americans (11%), Asians (8%), and African-Americans (7%). The mean age was 19.9 years ($SD = 2.36$).

Participants were randomly assigned to one of six conditions, with cell sizes ranging from 29 to 41. The six conditions reflected three topics (personal, public, and workplace) and two levels of engagement pressure (invited and demanded). The three topics were those used in Hample et al. (2012). The public topic, for example, focuses on a discussion about music with a friend. The invitation condition invites, but does not require, an argumentative response: "One day when you're just spending a little time together, your friend makes a remark about how good the sort of music s/he likes is, and says that the kind of music you like is awful." For the demand condition, a sentence was added to express a verbally aggressive comment by the other person: "Your friend says, 'That crap you listen to is just stupid,' and it's obvious that s/he is being very aggressive and wants a verbal fight."

The standard verbal aggressiveness and argumentativeness instruments were used (Infante & Rancer, 1982; Infante & Wigley, 1986). Cronbach's alphas were .87 for argument-avoid, .86 for argument-approach, .84 for verbal aggressiveness (prosocial), and .86 for verbal aggressiveness (antisocial).

The Hample et al. (2012) instruments were used to assess engagement intention and the various costs and benefits estimates. Cronbach's alphas were calculated separately for public, personal, and workplace topics with these results: engagement intention (.73, .73, and .78, respectively), resolvability (.76, .81, and .81), civility (.77, .76, and .78), other's reasonability (.75, .83, and .78, all with items 2 and 5 omitted), costs (.78, .82, and .81), likelihood of winning (.77, .83, and .82, all with items 3 and 6 omitted), appropriateness (.89, .87, and .84), and benefits (.82, .88, and .81).

Results

Did the manipulation of invitation force affect respondents' intention to engage in arguing? For the personal topic, the demand created a greater intention to engage ($M = 4.20$ v. 4.48; t (209) $= 2.54$, $p < .05$, $r^2 = .03$). This was also the case for the workplace topic ($M = 4.49$ v. 4.78; t (209) $= 2.43$, $p < .05$, $r^2 = .03$). However, there was no effect for the public topic (t (209) $= .90$, *ns*). For our situations, the decision to engage in a public topic argument was independent of how forcefully the invitation was made, but for both the personal and workplace topics a more forceful invitation resulted in greater intention to argue.

Did the subscales of argumentativeness and verbal aggressiveness (along with the manipulation) affect intention to engage? The manipulation was coded (0, 1), with the demand condition coded as "1." For the workplace topic, adj. $R^2 = .06$, $p < .01$. The manipulation was significant ($\beta = .17$, $p < .05$) and the approach subscale of argumentativeness was nearly so ($\beta = .16$, $p = .06$). For the public topic, adj. $R^2 = .09$ ($p < .001$). This result was due only to the effect of argument-approach ($\beta = .23$, $p < .01$). For the personal topic, adj. $R^2 = .07$ ($p < .001$). Argument-approach was a significant predictor ($\beta = .23$, $p < .01$), as was the invite/demand manipulation ($\beta = .16$, $p < .05$). In short, argument-approach and invitation force were important in influencing the decision to engage. A consistent null result was that the verbal aggressiveness subscales were always unrelated to engagement intentions.

Finally, what situation-specific elements predicted the decision to engage for each type of topic? We estimated multiple regressions for each topic type, using the manipulation and all the cost and benefit measures as predictors. For simplicity, we report only the terms with significant standardized coefficients. For public topics, adj. $R^2 = .30$ ($p < .001$), for personal topics, adj. $R^2 = .29$ ($p < .001$), and for workplace topics, adj. $R^2 = .27$ ($p < .001$). Here are the equations:

BIPublic = .31 Win + .43 Appropriate

BIPersonal = .22 Effort −.23 OtherReason + .21 Win + .21 Approp + .22 Reward + .14 Manip

BIWorkplace = .36 Resolv + .37 Effort + .21 Win + .22 Approp

Two predictors approached statistical significance. For the public topic, resolvability was almost significant ($\beta = -.12$, $p = .08$). For the workplace topic, the manipulation nearly achieved significance ($\beta = .11$, $p = .08$).

These regressions indicate that the expectation of winning and the estimate that arguing is appropriate were important considerations that increased the intention to engage for all three topics. Interestingly, high levels of expected effort actually increased the likelihood of engagement for personal and workplace matters.

Discussion

This essay has provided further evidence for the cost-benefit theory of argument engagement initiated by Paglieri (2009). Several of the present results replicate earlier ones. The most consistent and important predictors of the intention to engage in arguing were the estimate that the participant would win the argument and the sense that an argument would be appropriate in the circumstances described. These results also appeared in Hample et al. (2012), Cionea et al. (2011), and Richards and Cionea (2012).

For the most part, positive expectations increased the intention to engage and negative expectations reduced it, as the cost/benefit theory suggests. However, there was one exception to this pattern: For both personal and workplace topics, the more effort that seemed to be required, the greater was respondents' intention to argue. Similar findings appeared in Richards and Cionea (2012) and Hample et al. (2012). Johnson (2002) showed that personal topics have higher stakes than public ones, and we speculate that workplace topics may also be more consequential than public ones. Consider the seriousness of losing an argument about what baseball team is best (public), who needs to devote more effort to a friendship (personal), and who is the less productive worker in the office (workplace). For consequential matters, higher stakes may require more effort. Argument stakes should be more explicitly integrated into the cost/benefit theory instead of just being indirectly represented by the topic type manipulations.

Argumentativeness had some effect on the engagement decision but verbal aggressiveness did not. These variables have not had much explanatory value in this research program.

Our most substantial innovation was the introduction of invitational force. Prior studies used stimuli that did little more than create a slot for an argumentative reply. Here, we added a more forceful instigation to argue, which we labeled the demanding condition. Our review of literature noticed support for contradictory predictions: that a demand would cause responsive aggression (increasing intention to argue), but also that a demand would cause withdrawal (reducing intention to engage). We found that the demand condition increased intention to engage for the personal and workplace topics, but not for the public one. Again, we notice that these results could be explained by stakes: Only consequential demands must be taken up. Although space limitations prevented a full report, analysis of our data showed that the invite/demand manipulation affected the cost and benefit estimates as well as the engagement intention. For all three topics, civility was estimated to be higher in the invited condition. Demands resulted in higher expected effort (personal and workplace), a lower estimate of other's reasonability (workplace), and lower expected rewards (workplace).

Future work should move in several directions. More topics need to be added to the three used here and in prior work. Our manipulation of invitational force resulted in a dichotomy, and surely force is well suited to be a continuous variable. Argument stakes need to be worked into the theory, with predictions as to stakes' effects on estimates of costs and benefits. And invitational force should be integrated as well, with similar attention to how the insistence with which an argumentative response is called out might affect cost/benefit estimates.

References

Brehm, J. W. (1966). *A theory of psychological reactance.* New York, NY: Academic Press.

Case, D. O., Andrews, J. E., Johnson, J. D., & Allard, S. L. (2005). Avoiding versus seeking: The relationship of information seeking to avoidance, blunting, coping, dissonance, and related concepts. *Journal of the Medical Library Association, 93,* 353–362.

Caughlin, J. P., & Vangelisti, A. L. (1999). Desire for change in one's partner as a predictor of the demand/withdraw pattern of marital communication. *Communication Monographs, 66,* 66–89. doi: 10.1080/03637759909376463

Christensen, A., & Heavey, C. (1993). Gender differences in marital conflict: The demand/withdraw interaction pattern. In S. Oskamp & M. Costanzo (Eds.), *Gender issues in contemporary society* (pp. 113–141). Newbury Park, CA: SAGE.

Cionea, I. A., Hample, D., & Paglieri, F. (2011). A test of the argument engagement model in Romania. In F. Zenker (Ed.). *Argument Cultures: Proceedings of the 8th International Conference of the Ontario Society for the Study of Argumentation* (OSSA), May 18–21, 2011. Windsor: Ontario Society for the Study of Argumentation.

Corr, P. J. (2004). Reinforcement sensitivity theory and personality. *Neuroscience and Biobehavioral Reviews, 28,* 317–332. doi: 10.1016/j.neubiorev.2004.01.005

Dillard, J. P., & Shen, L. (2005). On the nature of reactance and its role in persuasive health communication. *Communication Monographs*, *72*, 144–168. doi: 10.1080/03637750500111815

van Eemeren, F. H., & Grootendorst, R. (2004). *A systematic theory of argumentation: The pragma-dialectical approach*. Cambridge: Cambridge University Press.

Glomb, T. M., & Liao, H. (2003). Interpersonal aggression in work groups: Social influence, reciprocal, and individual effects. *The Academy of Management Journal*, *46*, 486–496. doi: 10.2307/30040640

Gray, J. A. (1964). *Pavolov's typology*. Oxford: Pergamon Press.

Gray, J. A. (1987). *The psychology of fear and stress*. Cambridge: Cambridge University Press.

Gray, J. A., & McNaughton, N. (2000). *The neuropsychology of anxiety: An enquiry into the functions of the septo-hippocampal system*. Oxford: Oxford University Press.

Hample, D., & Dallinger, J. M. (1995). A Lewinian perspective on taking conflict personally: Revision, refinement, and validation of the instrument. *Communication Quarterly*, *43*, 297–319. doi: 10.1080/01463379509369978

Hample, D., Han, B., & Payne, D. (2010). The aggressiveness of playful arguments. *Argumentation*, *24*, 405–421. doi: 10.1007/s10503-009-9173-8

Hample, D., Paglieri, F., & Na, L. (2012). The costs and benefits of arguing: Predicting the decision whether to engage or not. In F. H. van Eemeren & B. Garssen (Eds.), *Topical themes in argumentation theory: Twenty exploratory studies* (pp. 307–322). New York, NY: Springer. doi: 10.1007/978-94-007-4041-9_20

Heavey, C. L., Christensen, A., & Malamuth, N. M. (1995). The longitudinal impact of demand and withdrawal during marital conflict. *The Journal of Consulting and Clinical Psychology*, *63*, 797–801. doi: 10.1037/0022-006X.63.5.797

Infante, D. A., & Rancer, A. S. (1982). A conceptualization and measure of argumentativeness. *Journal of Personality Assessment*, *46*, 72–80. doi: 10.1207/s15327752jpa4601_13

Infante, D. A., & Rancer, A. S. (1996). Argumentativeness and verbal aggressiveness: A review of recent theory and research. In B. R. Burleson (Ed.), *Communication Yearbook 19* (pp. 319–351). Thousand Oaks, CA: SAGE.

Infante, D. A., & Wigley, C. J. (1986). Verbal aggressiveness: An interpersonal model and measure. *Communication Monograph*, *53*, 61–69. doi: 10.1080/03637758609376126

Johnson, A. J. (2002). Beliefs about arguing: A comparison of public issue and personal issue arguments. *Communication Reports*, *15*, 99–112. doi: 10.1080/08934210209367757

Laursen, B., & Collins, W. A. (1994). Interpersonal conflict during adolescence. *Psychological Bulletin*, *115*, 197–209. doi: 10.1037//0033-2909.115.2.197

Levine, T. R., & Boster, F. J. (1996). The impact of self and others' argumentativeness on talk about controversial issue. *Communication Quarterly*, *44*, 345–358. doi: 10.1080/01463379609370022

Louis, W. R., Taylor, D. M., & Douglas, R. L. (2005). Normative influence and rational conflict decisions: Group norms and cost-benefit analyses for intergroup behavior. *Group Processes and Intergroup Relations*, *8*, 355–374. doi: 10.1177/1368430205056465

Paglieri, F. (2009). Ruinous arguments: Escalation of disagreement and the dangers of arguing. In J. Ritola (Ed.), *Argument cultures: Proceedings of OSSA 09*, CD-ROM (pp. 1–15). Windsor, ON: OSSA.

Paglieri, F., & C. Castelfranchi (2010). Why argue? Towards a cost-benefit analysis of argumentation. *Argument & Computation*, *1*, 71–91. doi: 10.1080/19462160903494584

Ram, A., & Ross, H. (2008). "We got to figure it out": Information-sharing and siblings' negotiations of conflicts of interests. *Social Development*, *17*, 512–527. doi: 10.1111/j.1467-9507.2007.00436.x

Richards, A. S., & Cionea, I. A. (2012, November). *To argue or not to argue: Predictors of the decision to engage in interpersonal arguments*. Paper presented at the annual meeting of the National Communication Association, Orlando, FL.

Shen, L. (2010). Mitigating psychological reactance: The role of message-induced empathy in persuasion. *Health Communication Research*, *36*, 397–422. doi: 10.1111/j.1468-2958.2010.01381.x

22

NARRATIVE ARGUMENT AS MULTIPLE GOAL MESSAGES IN INTERPERSONAL DELIBERATION

Susan L. Kline

OHIO STATE UNIVERSITY, USA

Although interpersonal argument is usually studied in overt conflict situations (e.g., marital conflict or family discussion), managing disagreement and doubt can be embedded in other speech activities as well. Such is the case when friends discuss their personal problems for the purpose of deliberating over options and obtaining support. Features of "troubles talk" have been documented as a cultural form of North American speech (Goldsmith, 2004; Philipsen, 1992). In these conversations, providing good reasons can be difficult because overt disagreement can be face threatening and not legitimate the interlocutor's perspective. While interpersonal scholars have focused mostly on effective emotional support in these types of situations, some have begun to identify specific argument practices at work in troubles talk messages (MacGeorge, Feng, Butler, & Budarz, 2004). Continuing this line of work, this essay seeks to identify narrative argument practices in these interpersonal messages. The focus here is on messages that address self-doubt in esteem-threatening situations.

Troubles talk is particularly challenging in esteem-threatening situations where the aim is to arrive at a consensus that facilitates the other's adoption of positive internal and stable self-attributions. Doubt about one's capabilities may be entrenched and linked to negative self-beliefs that are difficult to give up. Overt disagreement can convey disrespect, producing a boomerang effect deepening, rather than reversing, self-doubt. Yet existing research has documented a role for argument in messages produced to help others in these situations.

For instance, effective emotional support often contains explicit person–centered reasoning: messages that describe, legitimate, and reason about the basis of the other's feelings from a broader perspective (Burleson & McGeorge, 2002). Effective support also provides advice with an explicit and comprehensive argument structure for justifying advice as relevant, feasible, and without limitations (Feng & Burleson, 2008). Effective esteem support also is associated with extensive and realistic reasoning about advocated actions (Holdstrom & Burleson, 2012). Whether or not troubles talk messages employ narrative argument practices is not known, but it is likely that narrative forms are used by speakers to describe their personal experiences or to describe the other's experiences or qualities to help the other remove self-doubt.

Long recognized by rhetoricians (Fisher, 1987), narrative forms of communication are important in persuasion and for understanding life domains like health (Columbia University Medical Center's Program in Narrative Medicine is an apt illustration). Narrative is generally conceptualized as a representation of connected events and characters that is bounded in time and space, with an identifiable structure and an expressed viewpoint about the topic (Bruner, 1986; Kreuter et al., 2007). Entertainment, education, journalism, literature, testimonials, and storytelling are narrative forms capable of facilitating information gain, attitude change, understanding of emotional issues, and social connections (Kreuter et al., 2007). Although some scholars view narrative as inferior because of its reliance on single examples, persuasion and argument researchers find narrative persuasive and acceptable for certain argument types (Hoeken & Hustinz, 2009), and discourse analysts show how narratives make arguments, perform speech acts, develop viewpoints, engage in self-presentation, and do relational work (Tracy, 2002).

My contention is that narrative argument practices are present in discussions about interpersonal problems. Narrative reasoning can occur when speakers offer their own experience as a model for the other to reason with. Speakers can also produce altercasting narratives by articulating their knowledge of the other's past accomplishments and present qualities. Theoretically, past experiences and present qualities narrative argument practices (referred to as NAPs) may function to invite others to accept new beliefs about themselves in two ways: (1) through argument schemes that facilitate narrative fidelity, probability, and coherence, and (2) through simultaneously enacting identity and relationship aims along with the primary aim of removing the other's self-doubt.

Perelemen and Olbrechts-Tyteca's (1969) analysis of argument schemes may help scholars understand how NAPs function in esteem-threat discussions to solidify the fidelity, probability, and coherence of the narrative. They categorize argument schemes into four categories: quasi-logical schemes, arguments based on the structure of the real (e.g., cause–effect, act–essence), arguments that aim at establishing the structure of the real (e.g., examples, models, analogies, metaphor), and dissociation. Speakers may use examples or concrete instances of a general principle to create a new reality structure. Speakers may also describe qualities to signify the essence of the other as a capable person or past experiences to demonstrate existing cause–effect principles, both of which indicate structures of the real. Finally, speakers may employ dissociation by disengaging the other from self-doubt and articulating an alternative identity.

A second feature of NAPs that may explain their function in esteem-threat situations is that NAPs can better manage the actors' multiple goals in the discussion. Interaction goals can be interpreted from the context and include task, relationship, identity, and process aims. They can be easy or difficult to attain and align with the other's aims, with integrative message forms seen as superior to messages that prioritize single aims (Kline, 1991; O'Keefe & Delia, 1982). A speaker's own story about a similar situation may display caring in its telling and build common ground while inviting the other to consider alternative reasoning. Narratives may also frame the other's qualities to altercast the other in a positive image that also displays caring and commitment, along with inviting the other to consider alternative reasoning. Such NAPs offer plausible reasons for the other to accept the speaker's standpoint and attain his/her identity and relationship goals.

Given the lack of knowledge about narrative argument practices in troubles talk, a first aim was to identify what narrative argument practices may occur in these types of messages:

> RQ1: What narrative argument practices may occur in interpersonal messages that address esteem–threats?

A second aim was to examine the social cognitive capacities undergirding the use of narrative argument practices. Waldron and Applegate (1994) have documented three qualities of planning that are associated with integrative conflict management: specificity of plans (presence of behavioral steps identified to attain each goal); complexity of plans (the number of goals, actions and contingencies); and the quality of plans (how plans address the situation and future conditions). Given a multiple goal account, I expected that the use of narrative argument practices in esteem-threatening situations would also require sophisticated planning:

H1: Planning sophistication (i.e., specificity, complexity, quality) is positively associated with the use of narrative argument practices to address self-doubt in esteem-threat situations.

Method

Participants were 102 students enrolled at a large Midwestern university. Most (61%) were women with a mean age of 22 years (SD = 4.45). Over 80% were Caucasian with middle class backgrounds, and all received extra credit for participating in the study.

Participants produced two messages to randomly ordered scenarios that involved a friend who either had self-doubt about taking an upcoming career examination or self-doubt about starting a challenging new job. The situations were pilot tested and evaluated as realistic (Kline, Rooney, & Jones, 2012). Participants wrote what they would say to their friend "to think well of him/herself, and have a better self-concept." The messages were unitized into expressed thought units and categorized into idea types following Saeki and O'Keefe's procedures (1994). Over 90% of the thought units were classified, resulting in 62 and 65 idea types for the exam and new job situations. Using two coders, unitizing reliability on 35 messages was acceptable, $r = .94$, as was categorizing reliability on idea types, $ks = .66 -.86$.

I constructed two NAP measures from the idea types: past experience and present quality NAPs. The past experience NAP measure elaborated on past experiences to justify removing the other's self-doubt. Idea types that described the message producer's similar experiences, how the message producer's friend had succeeded in the past, how the friend's past experiences resulted in specific accomplishments, and how the friend had overcome challenges were summed together to form the first NAP measure. The second NAP measure elaborated on present experiences, perspectives, and their outcomes to justify removing self-doubt. Idea types that described the friend's attractive qualities; what the friend knows, loves, or desires; how the friend's qualities will enable him/her to succeed; and how the friend can handle the present situation and feel better were added together.

After participants completed their second message, they analyzed it with procedures similar to cued-recall tasks used to study conversational cognitions (e.g., Waldron & Applegate, 1994). Participants numbered each separate thought, strategy, or sentence in their message that they intended "to have an effect on your friend." On a separate sheet, participants were asked to indicate "what you were thinking at the time you wrote each part of the message" including objectives, motives, and actions they had in mind to achieve their objectives (Kline et al., 2012).

Following Waldron and Applegate's (1994) procedures, participants' thought listings were used to form three planning measures. *Plan specificity* coded and summed each numbered response for whether it reflected no planning, undifferentiated planning, function-level planning, or implementation-level planning (1–4, $M = 19.37$, $SD = 9.32$). *Plan complexity* summed general communicative goals and specific behaviors ($M = 11.29$, $SD = 7.32$). *Plan quality* summed each plan for whether it was a stock plan not adapted to the situation, a plan that reacted to immediate situational features, or a proactive plan that advanced the other or situation (1–3, M = 11.68, SD = 7.01). Interrater reliability for plan specificity, complexity, and quality on 30% of the data was acceptable at .89, .87, and .87, using Scott's *pi*. For the regressions, an overall planning index was formed by summing standardized scores for each planning measure.

Results

What is the prevalence of NAPs in messages that address another's self-doubt in esteem threatening situations? Past experience NAPs regularly occurred in 48% of the new job messages (M = 1.00, SD = 1.52, *range* = 0–8) and in 71% of the upcoming exam messages (M = 1.36, SD = 1.31, *range* = 0–7). Present quality NAPs occurred in 61% of the job messages (M = 1.22, SD = 1.42, *range* = 0–6) and 62% of the exam messages (M = 1.31, SD = 1.59, *range* = 0–10).

Each NAP was expressed in several ways, invoking distinct argument schemes to justify removing self-doubt. Four NAPs forms recurred. First, past experience NAPs represented the other's accomplishments, invoking relations of succession schemas to show the operation of cause-effect or act-consequence principles:

> These past few years you have worked extremely hard! You have received excellent grades and are at the top of your class. I have no doubt that you are going to do very well.

> Think of how many exams that you did so well on in college. Every time that you study so much and review you do great. It is highly unlikely that you have come this far and know so much inside that you are going to do bad on this exam.

The message producers' telling of their own experiences often established the validity of forecasting success by using themselves as models and/or employing analogy:

> I remember when I first started my job, I felt just like you do now. Look at me now, I'm doing okay for myself and I know you are like me, so I know you will do great.

By contrast, present quality NAPs used articulated descriptions with relations of coexistence schemas to show the friend's essence or they used examples to establish a particular case:

> You are a wonderful person who is going to excel because of your great attitude, personality and willingness to work hard.

Present quality NAPs also engaged in dissociation by disengaging the other from self-doubt with counter-arguing and then articulating the other's empowering qualities, resulting in replacing the friend's doubting appearance narrative with a more uplifting narrative. Dissociation was sometimes laminated with other schemes like metaphor and illustration to establish a new reality for the other without self-doubt. Examples of these variations were:

> You're very focused when you take on a project with a deadline, you always are able to budget your time to do a good job. And don't worry about the quality of your work, you're a perfectionist, and it shows, just look at your grades on class projects and demonstrations.

I would first sing the chin-up song from Charlotte's Web – "Chin up, chin up everyone loves a happy face, wear it, share it, it will brighten up the darkest place, twinkle, sparkle, let a little sunshine in-you'll be on the right side – looking at the bright side with your chinny chin-chin-UP! laughing . . .

Turning to the hypothesis, NAPs were predicted to be positively associated with planning sophistication, which was assessed with Pearson correlation and regression analyses. As expected, past NAPs were significantly correlated with planning specificity, complexity, and quality, respectively: for exam, rs = .30, .27, .28, all p < .01; for new job, rs = .29, .42, .24, all p at least < .05. Present quality NAPs were also associated with planning specificity, complexity, and quality: exam situation, rs = .44, .40, .39, all p < .001; and job situation, rs = .19, p < .05, .18, .18, p < .08. Of note is that the findings were weaker for the job situation. In subsidiary analyses, across the two situations the two NAPs were moderately intercorrelated, r = .40, p < .001. The planning measures were highly intercorrelated, from .78 to .91, all p < .001, consistent with Waldron and Applegate's findings (1994).

H1 was examined further with hierarchical regression analysis. For each analysis situation type and plan index were entered first, followed by the interaction term for situation type by plan index. The regression on past NAPs was significant, R = .46, Adjusted R^2 = .19, F (3,102) = 8.73, p < .001, with plan index and situation type significant predictors, βs = .37, p < .001, .22, p < .05. Planning was more strongly associated with past NAPs in response to the exam situation. There was no significant interaction between plan index and situation type. The second regression on present quality NAPs was also significant, R = .44, Adjusted R^2 = .17, F (3, 102) = 7.72, p < .001, with plan index a significant predictor, β = .33, p < .001. However, there was a significant planning by situation type interaction, β = .76, p < .001, which indicated that planning was only associated with present quality NAPs in the messages addressing the exam situation.

Discussion

This essay provides evidence that narrative argument practices do occur in interpersonal messages responding to another person's esteem-threat. Two general types of NAPs were identified: narrative arguments in which speakers elaborated on their own or the other's past experiences and present quality narratives in which speakers articulated how the other's qualities would enable success. Both NAPs were associated with planning specificity, complexity, and quality. There was one limitation in that the association with planning and present quality narratives only occurred in messages that addressed the upcoming exam situation. Different esteem-threatening situations should be further examined to see if these NAPs are consistently related to planning competency.

The findings contribute to both argumentation theory and the interpersonal support literature by extending argumentation theory to troubles talk. A next step could examine more types of NAPs and their perceived effectiveness in facilitating changes in the other's self-doubt. Mediating conditions important in narrative persuasion could be examined, such as perceived believability of the narrative and identification with the speaker.

More important is the need to examine the two accounts of NAPs proposed earlier, multiple goals integration, and argument schemes. Interpersonal arguments on personal topics have been found to have higher stakes than arguments on public topics (Johnson, 2002). Discussions about another's self-doubt are difficult to manage because it takes effort to manage the seemingly conflicting goals of preserving desired identities and the relationship with the speaker's desire that the other change his/her viewpoint (O'Keefe & Delia, 1982). NAPs may provide a means to integrate these multiple interaction goals. On the other hand, NAPs employ particular argument schemes, like dissociation or establishing new structures of the real, both of which may be more effective in contexts of self-doubt than schemes that merely reflect current structures of the real. NAPs using dissociation, for instance, may be more effective because they use a rhetorical design logic to create an alternative identity and situation that transcends the other's self-doubt. Thus, both accounts of NAPs could be further studied.

Finally, future work could extend narrative argument practices to other interpersonal support, deliberative, and conflict situations. Eliciting NAPs in interpersonal discussions would provide more naturally occurring data to analyze. Using conversation and discourse analysis to unpack how NAPs operate in conversation could help scholars understand how uptake and mutual alignment are achieved. Finally, a competence theory could be more fully developed to understand the individual and situational factors that predict the use of narrative argument practices.

References

Bruner, J. (1986). *Actual minds, possible worlds.* Cambridge, MA: Harvard University Press.

Burleson, B. R., & MacGeorge, E. (2002). Supportive communication. In M. Knapp & J. Daly (Eds.), *Handbook of interpersonal communication* (pp. 374–424). Thousand Oaks, CA: Sage Publications.

Feng, B., & Burleson, B. R. (2008). The effects of argument explicitness on responses to advice in supportive interactions. *Communication Research, 35,* 849–874.

Fisher, W. R. (1987). *Human communication as narration: Toward a philosophy of reason, value, and action.* Columbia: University of South Carolina Press.

Goldsmith, D. J. (2004). *Communicating social support.* Cambridge: Cambridge University Press.

Hoeken, H., & Hustinx, L. (2009). When is statistical evidence superior to anecdotal evidence in supporting probability claims? The role of argument type. *Human Communication Research, 35,* 491–510.

Holmstrom, A. J., & Burleson, B. R. (2011). An initial test of a cognitive-emotional theory of esteem support messages. *Communication Research, 38*(3), 326–355.

Johnson, A. (2002). Beliefs about arguing: A comparison of public-issue and personal-issue arguments. *Communication Reports, 15,* 99–112.

Kline, S. L. (1991). Construct differentiation and person-centered regulative messages. *Journal of Language and Social Psychology, 10,* 1–27.

Kline, S. L., Rooney, M., & Jones, E. (2012, May 23–28). *A multiple goals perspective on edifying and esteem support.* Paper presented at the International Communication Association Conference, Phoenix, AZ.

Kreuter, M. W. Green, M. C. Cappella, J. C., Slater, M. D., et al. (2007). Narrative communication in cancer prevention and control: A framework to guide research and application. *Annals of Behavioral Medicine, 33*(3), 221–235.

MacGeorge, E. L., Feng, B., Butler, G. L., & Budarz, S. K. (2004). Understanding advice in supportive interactions: Beyond the facework and message evaluation paradigm. *Human Communication Research, 30*(1), 42–70.

O'Keefe, B. J., & Delia, J. G. (1982). Impression formation and message production. In M. E. Roloff & C. R. Berger (Eds.), *Social cognition and communication* (pp. 33–72). Beverly Hills, CA: Sage.

Perelman, C., & Olbrechts-Tyteca, L. (1969). *The new rhetoric: A treatise on argumentation* (J. Wilkinson & P. Weaver, Trans.). Notre Dame, IN: University of Notre Dame Press.

Philipsen, G. (1992). *Speaking culturally: Explorations in social communication.* Albany: SUNY Press.

Saeki, M. & O'Keefe, B. J. (1994). Refusals and rejections: Designing messages to serve multiple goals. *Human Communication Research, 21,* 67–102.

Tracy, K. (2002). *Everyday talk: Building and reflecting identities.* New York, NY: Guilford Press.

Waldron, V. R., & Applegate, J. L. (1994). Interpersonal construct differentiation and conversational planning: An examination of two cognitive accounts for the production of competent verbal disagreement tactics. *Human Communication Research, 21,* 3–35.

23

THE STRUCTURE OF THE PIVOT

Disturbing argument through strategic question avoidance in presidential debate

Aaron Dimock

MINNESOTA STATE UNIVERSITY, MANKATO, USA

Misdirection and distraction are part of a magician's repertoire for creating a convincing illusion. A similar statement could be made about presidential candidates' strategies for convincing audiences that they have answered a question. By telling a story or adding an example, candidates can disturb the flow of argument and shift the issues under contention. Debate consultants teach candidates to perform what strategist Brett O'Donnell called "the pivot" and reporters called "dodging the question" (as cited in Spiegel, 2012). Candidates can use pivoting to shift the ground of a debate, avoid responding to challenging questions, and address their own talking points. Scholars, reporters, and the public have not failed to notice this practice, but in the course of the presidential debates, candidates continually use their "magic" to pivot away from questions they don't like and toward the answers they prefer to provide. I use Action-Implicative Discourse Analysis (Tracy, 1995) to examine the use of these pivots by President Obama and former Governor Romney in the 2012 presidential debates. Both candidates used a number of practices to attempt to shift grounds and control the topics of the debate. The control of those topics has important implications not only for avoiding topics, but also for creating a clear(er) clash of issues, refuting opposing positions, and attacking an opponent's credibility.

Much of the current research on questions and answers in political interviews or debates assumes the pivot is a problem (e.g., Bull, 2008; Rogers & Norton, 2011). My discourse analytic approach explains how pivots work to fulfill the role of an answer both structurally and logically. From this perspective, pivoting is not simply about dodging, but about managing the burden of relevance to make concise arguments for and against positions and opponents. By examining the pivots both candidates made in the 2012 presidential debates, this analysis identifies the types of pivots and the strategies used to supply relevance and attempt to avoid being challenged. By better understanding the methods used to argue in naturally occurring discourse, scholars can better assess how the pivot "disturbs" typical argument practices.

Not Answering Questions

Avoiding questions has been a subject of dispute since disputations were first addressed. Plato's classic dialogue, *The Gorgias*, begins with Socrates criticizing Polus's response to his inquiry with the praise, rather than the definition, of rhetoric. This tendency to resist answering questions as asked has been the subject of much scholarship on news interviews and political debates (Agne & Tracy, 1997; Clayman & Heritage, 2002; Rogers & Norton, 2011). Accusations that politicians are simply being slippery or obstinate operate on the assumption that the purpose of an interview is exclusively to elicit information in a straightforward manner. Analyses have demonstrated, however, that the complex demands of interviews frequently force interviewees to respond in ways that protect information (Agne & Tracy, 1997) or defend their face (Bull, 2008). Bull's (2008) work on evasion found that journalists' questions are "anything but straight, and that equivocation by politicians is very much associated with the high proportion of conflictual questions posed in broadcast interviews" (p. 337). Taking into consideration the fundamental challenges germane to the presidential debate, candidates not only have to manage the questions from the interviewers, but acclaim and defend their own policies and character while attacking their opponent's (Benoit, 2003).

Despite these conflicting demands and goals, there is still a strong orientation to the interviewing norm that interviewees are supposed to answer the questions posed to them. Not answering a question risks being labeled as avoiding or equivocating, negatively affecting a candidate (Clayman & Heritage, 2002; Rogers & Norton, 2011). Answering or not answering a question is, however, more difficult to explain than it may appear. Bull (2008) approached "not answering" as evasion that introduces ambiguity into one or more of four message dimensions: sender, content, receiver, or context. This approach lends itself to an analyst's perspective, but the participants are the ones who determine whether or not a question has been answered. Although the audience of a presidential debate may be the final arbiter, there are ways of identifying and explaining how speakers stave off accusations of dodging or side-stepping questions.

As Clayman and Heritage (2002) noted, answering does not have a clear discursive marker in the way that questioning does. Because answers can take many different forms, interlocutors must monitor responses for their relevance as answers. In political interviews, interlocutors may do so actively and occasionally aggressively. Relevance can be understood as a negotiated feature of a response: a characteristic that speakers build into an utterance that is subject to challenge by the other parties to the interaction. Grice (1975/1999) theorized that communication could be understood in terms of a cooperative enterprise where each speaker, even if at odds, designed utterances in order to be understood. Grice's "Cooperative Principle" entails four categories: quantity, quality, relation, and manner. Under relation, Grice (1975/1999) included only one seemingly simple maxim that could serve as a mantra for interviewees: "Be relevant" (p. 79). Being relevant, however, is argumentatively constructed in discourse. Interviewees attempt to make their answers relevant by adhering to either local or global forms of relevance (Tracy, 1984) while simultaneously attempting to address their other goals.

By examining President Obama and former Governor Romney's responses in their 2012 presidential debates, I identify how their pivots attempt to manage those conflicting goals while being designed to meet the burdens of relevance.

Analyzing the Presidential Debates

The Commission on Presidential Debates (CPD) sponsored three 90-minute debates between candidates Barack Obama and Mitt Romney. Each followed a similar question and answer

Table 23.1 Distribution of Questions

Debate	1st Debate: Domestic Policy	2nd Debate: Town Hall	3rd Debate: Foreign Policy
Moderator	Jim Lehrer	Candy Crowley	Bob Schieffer
Topic Questions	5	11	6
Follow-up	14	22	24
Totals	19	33	30

format where a topic question was asked by either the moderator or, in the town hall debate, a citizen; each candidate was allowed a two minute response; then the moderator asked follow-up questions in a more loosely organized discussion that focused on more specific aspects of the topic question. A total of 22 topic questions and 60 follow-up questions were asked over the course of the debates for a total of 82 speaking turns that directed a candidate to respond to a specific question (see Table 23.1). In the course of the debates, speakers did not necessarily wait to be prompted to speak to a point, so some questions elicited multiple responses. Each question, given the norms of interviews, established the bounds for relevant responses.

I used the transcripts provided by the CPD in coordination with the video recordings provided on C-SPAN to examine and analyze each speaker's message. Transcripts were amended to match the recording in cases where there was a lack of clarity or the transcript was in error. Following the Action-Implicative Discourse Analytic method (Tracy, 1995), analysis proceeded by identifying the situated goals of the participants in the interactions, inductively identifying the types of pivoting associated with those goals, and identifying the strategies used to supply relevance when making a pivot. The analysis proceeds by identifying the types of pivots and examining the strategies used to supply relevance.

Pivot Types and Forms

Speakers may go about making answers fit as the second part of a question–answer adjacency pair in a number of ways (see Hutchby & Wooffitt, 1998). Questions are designed to make particular responses relevant and the key feature of the pivot is that, in order to be a recognizable answer, it must be designed to have *prima facie* relevance as an answer to that question. Sequentially, rules of local relevance dictate that answers are limited to the issues and topics of the prior turn. A pivot can be understood as a unit of talk that deviates from the rules of local relevance to more globally relevant concerns (issues that have come up in the debate or campaign that are related to the current topic).

Each point where a response deviated from the topic of the question to introduce new issues or topics was identified as a pivot. This could happen more than once in a response if speakers introduced a topic then introduced a different topic later in the same response. In the three debates, 92 separate pivots were identified. Each type of pivot created an opportunity to raise issues that could be constructed as more or less relevant to the context of the question. Three categories of pivots were inductively established based on how they connected to the surrounding discourse: giving yourself permission, linking to other issues, and identifying a position (see Table 23.2).

Table 23.2 Types of Pivots

	1st Debate	2nd Debate	3rd Debate
Giving Yourself Permission	9	7	5
Linking to Other Issues	9	22	26
Identifying a Position	5	6	3

The first category, *giving yourself permission*, has the same form as what Clayman and Heritage (2002) called a "token request," requesting permission to address a different topic in such a way that no response was required for the turn to continue. Candidates used this strategy 21 times and the pivot had very little variation in its form. Candidates generally led such pivots with some version of "Let me . . ." as a token request, followed by a phrase that indicated what sort of response was coming, like ". . . talk specifically about" or ". . . mention one last point," and then continued their turn, introducing another topic. A typical example is from the third initial topic question in the first debate (codes identify the debate with a Roman numeral, topic question, and follow-up question):

I.3.0
Lehrer: Do you see a major difference between the two of you on Social Security?
Obama: You know, I suspect that, on Social Security, we've got a somewhat similar position. Social Security is structurally sound. It's going to have to be tweaked . . . But it is – the basic structure is sound. But – but I want to talk about the values behind Social Security and Medicare, and then talk about Medicare, because that's the big driver of our deficits right now . . .

Lehrer had introduced the category of the topic as the third question on the economy and specifically entitlements. His question then restricted the topic to social security and more specifically to the difference between their positions. Obama's answer initially addressed the question directly, then at the point of the pivot (marked by an arrow), he made a bid to shift the topic by broadening the issue, then shifting to a different aspect of entitlements, then dropping social security from his response entirely.

The second category, *linking to other issues*, was by far the largest and contained the most variation. A total of 57 of the pivots, well over half of the 92, were made by creating some kind of link to a related issue. A common variation included comparing or contrasting positions, such as, ". . . but our production is going up, and we're using oil more efficiently. And very little of what Governor Romney just said is true . . ." (II.2.1 Obama). This allowed the speaker to recall a previously stated point and reintroduce it as a topic, or introduce a new topic that could provide an opportunity to shift the discussion onto other grounds. In this case, it opened up an opportunity for Obama to refute criticisms Romney had raised prior to the current question. Other means of *linking to other issues* involved relating consequences of other policies and introducing examples to establish a trend, as in the following:

II.8.1
Romney: → And this calls into question the president's whole policy in the Middle East. Look what's happening in Syria, in Egypt, now in Libya. Consider the distance between ourselves and – and Israel, the

president said that – that he was going to put daylight between us and Israel. We have Iran four years closer to a nuclear bomb. Syria – Syria's not just a tragedy of 30,000 civilians being killed by a military, but also a strategic – strategically significant player for America.

The question involved the State Department's decisions about security prior to the attack on the embassy in Benghazi. Romney had responded by criticizing the administration's response and not identifying it as a terrorist attack, then he created a series of examples to establish the trend. His response became a claim that Obama's whole Middle East policy was suspect, not simply his security decisions before the Benghazi incident.

The third and final category, *identifying a position*, refers to those pivots that were initiated through the statement of a position and was used only 14 times. This involved a particular statement of belief or experience that then served as a starting point to talk about that issue or means of avoiding talking about the issue targeted by the question. For instance Romney resisted a hypothetical question, where Crowley asked: if too little tax revenue was generated, would he reconsider his plan to lower tax rates? Before she could complete the question, he cut her off, refusing the question's grounds on the basis that "I was someone who ran businesses for 25 years, and balanced the budget" (II.3.3). From there he elaborated on his own record before refuting the president's record, bypassing the question entirely. Other forms of this type of pivot involved stating what one's own position had been, what "the people" believed, and what one's opponent had said or done.

Supplying and Challenging Relevance

The type of pivot used creates a discursive space, akin to an expansion slot, which allows a speaker an opportunity to pivot or adjust the matter under consideration. Such discursive moves do not necessarily achieve their goals. Although the public audience's response is not available in this data, there were a number of occasions (25) where pivots were challenged or reprimanded by the interlocutors present, the moderator and the opposing candidate. More importantly, creating such an opportunity to pivot was not the only work the speakers did in order to accomplish their goals. They used numerous strategies to attempt to present their pivots as relevant to the issue currently under discussion or protect it from objection. Many of the strategies used were similar to those identified in other research on political interviews noted by Clayman and Heritage (2002): justifying the shift, unmarked and stepwise transitions (that move on to another topic as though it were related), or repeating key words and phrases from the question.

There were three strategies that were commonly used in these debates to great effect. One common approach was to generalize the question or particularize issues to shift to other issues or introduce different topics. The example in I.3.0 above shows how generalization can work to establish a topic's relevance. The speaker expands the issue in the question to include other issues of a similar nature, and then can focus on other topics within that category that would otherwise be outside the bounds of the question. Working the other direction, speakers could particularize and address only part of an issue, for instance "you're absolutely right about part of that, which is I want to bring rates down" (Romney II.3.0).

A second strategy used commonly by both candidates was the use of a narrative or example at the preface of a question to create a new local context from which to pivot. An excellent example of this practice was in a question in the town hall debate on pay inequality (II.4.0). Obama started his answer by talking about the passage of the Lily Ledbetter law, then spoke generally about his advocacy for women and his opponent's lack thereof. Romney similarly told a story about building his cabinet as governor and from there addressed women's jobs in his economy. Neither made any proposal for how the wage gap could be closed.

A final strategy, used primarily by Obama, structurally bookended a pivot. In this case the speaker surrounds a less relevant argument, like a more direct criticism, with arguments that are on topic. The relevance may come with association or merely allow the speaker to return to the topic before a challenge can be issued. In the midst of an explanation of his military budget decisions, Obama opened an opportunity to renew criticism of Romney's tax plan:

III.3.5

Obama: . . . And that's the budget that we've put forward. But, what you can't do is spend $2 trillion in additional military spending that the military is not asking for, $5 trillion on tax cuts. You say that you're going to pay for it by closing loopholes and deductions, without naming what those loopholes and deductions are. And then somehow you're also going to deal with the deficit that we've already got. The math simply doesn't work. But when it comes to our military . . .

Obama linked the criticism to Romney's tax strategy in general then immediately pivoted back to the military budget topic.

Conclusions

Politicians are as likely to directly answer exactly what they are asked as magicians are to explain each of their illusions. Audiences, however, come to magicians to be tricked and politicians for answers. It is a mistake, though, to assume that the proper way to evaluate questioning and answering is to attempt to construct an objective standard. Such attempts ignore the situated nature of answering questions in a debate and the negotiated nature of relevance. Pivots, as demonstrated in this analysis, are discursive devices that create opportunities for speakers to expand, alter, and shift topics and challenge the constraints of questions. As speakers, interlocutors, and audiences negotiate relevance, it is important to consider how these discursive moves not only disturb a line of argument, but create opportunities for new lines of argument.

References

Agne, R., & Tracy, K. (1997). Not answering questions: A police chief's strategies in a sensationalized murder. In J. F. Klumpp (Ed.), *Argument in a time of change: Definitions, frameworks, and critiques* (pp. 238–242). Annandale, VA: National Communication Association.

Benoit, W. L. (2003). Topic of presidential campaign discourse and election outcome. *Western Journal of Communication, 67*(1), 97–112.

Bull, P. (2008). "Slipperiness, evasion, and ambiguity": Equivocation and facework in noncommittal political discourse. *Journal of Language and Social Psychology, 27*(4), 333–344.

Clayman, S., & Heritage, J. (2002). *News interview: Journalists and public figures on the air.* Port Chester, NY: Cambridge University Press.

Grice, H. P. (1975/1999). Logic and Conversation. In A. Jaworski & N. Coupland (Eds.), *The discourse reader* (pp. 77–88). New York, NY: Routledge.

Hutchby, I., & Woffitt, R. (1998). *Conversation analysis.* Cambridge: Polity Press.

Rogers, T., & Norton, M. I. (2011). The artful dodger: Answering the wrong question the right way. *Journal of Experimental Psychology: Applied, 17*(2), 139–147.

Spiegel, A. (2012, October 3). How politicians get away with dodging the question. *NPR Morning Edition*. Retrieved from http://www.npr.org/2012/10/03/162103368/how-politicians-get -away-with-dodging-the-question

Tracy, K. (1984). Staying on topic: An explication of conversational relevance. *Discourse Processes*, 7(4), 447–464.

Tracy, K. (1995). Action-implicative discourse analysis. *Journal of Language and Social Psychology*, *14*(1–2), 195–215.

24

POLYSEMIC ARGUMENT

Mitt Romney in the 2012 primary debates

Alexander Hiland

UNIVERSITY OF MINNESOTA, USA

In the 2011–2012 Republican primary debates, Mitt Romney was placed in the awkward position of having to campaign against the national version of a policy he supported as Governor of Massachusetts. The passage of the Affordable Care Act (ACA) combined with Romney's frontrunner position in the Republican primary created a complex rhetorical demand that required Romney to simultaneously defend his record while opposing a policy that mirrored the one he created. I argue that Romney used a polysemic argument strategy to simultaneously affirm the value of his healthcare policy while rejecting the similar policy implemented by President Obama.

Analyzing how Mitt Romney deployed polysemic argument in the Republican primary debates offers a way to understand how arguments with multiple meanings can be effective in deliberative debate argumentation. My analysis of the debates serves three important functions. First, it illustrates specific techniques used in debates to create strategic ambiguity. Second, it demonstrates the way polysemic argument can be used to simultaneously accept and deny responsibility for policies to maximize the appeal of a candidate's record across multiple audiences. Third, it demonstrates how rhetors can argue in a manner consistent with their views while simultaneously criticizing policies associated with those views.

Romney's Ideological Commitment to Healthcare

Despite the Republican Party's staunch opposition to the national healthcare system passed under the Obama administration, Romney historically has demonstrated an ideological commitment to government healthcare systems. This commitment was demonstrated by his decision while Governor of Massachusetts to champion a piece of legislation that is almost identical to the ACA. During the primary debates this created a significant problem for Romney in that his personal commitment to government-operated healthcare was at odds with the political view of his party. This forced Romney to appear to be opposed to the ACA, regardless of his personal views on the value of a national healthcare system. To place the arguments made in these debates in context, a brief discussion of Romney's ideological attachment to healthcare is necessary.

Romney's Mormonism is responsible for a significant part of his support for healthcare programs. As David Frum (2012) noted, the Church of Jesus Christ of Latter-day Saints (LDS Church) operates an immense social welfare program (p. 45). The LDS Church emphasizes the role of the Church as a community and support system for its members on the condition that they be accountable for giving back to the Church. While total fidelity to this principle would make healthcare an unpopular option, the idea that organizations should provide leadership and material assistance to their members would be comfortable for Romney as a faithful LDS Church leader.

Romney's political views were also significantly influenced by his family's experience. Romney first became actively involved in politics in 1970 when his mother ran for one of the Michigan Senate seats. As Gellman and Dias (2012) noted, the failed campaign that his mother Lenore Romney ran would affect Mitt for the rest of his life. He was greatly influenced by the political positions his mother took, including her support for a national healthcare and insurance plan (Gellman & Dias, 2012, p. 31). His mother became known for being extremely moderate as a Republican, so much so, in fact, that members of the press associated her on several occasions with the women's liberation movement (Gellman & Dias, 2012, p. 31). It seems reasonable that the more moderate approach to Republican policies taken by Mitt's mother influenced his values, giving credence to the idea that Romney supports government run healthcare programs.

During Romney's term as Massachusetts governor, he demonstrated his support for government healthcare with his passage of a statewide healthcare system. Romney's support for a healthcare program that covered all citizens was a precursor to, and formed the basis of, the policy enacted under the Obama administration. At the core of the Massachusetts law was the individual mandate that all people be covered under some healthcare program (Stephenson, 2011). As Stephenson (2011) noted, initially Romney defended the policy as representing core Republican values (p. 21). Romney himself claimed, "It's the ultimate conservative idea, which is that people have responsibility for their own care, and they don't look to government to take [care] of them if they can afford to take care of themselves" (as cited in Greenberger, 2005, p. 1). This defense demonstrates Romney's particular ideological commitments. He is willing to support government-run healthcare programs, so long as they are tied to individual responsibility.

The decision to advocate the individual mandate on the grounds that it compels people to be responsible for themselves falls well within a popularized Republican perspective. As James Taranto (2011) reported after one of the primary debates, the individual mandate is based on a policy developed by the Heritage Foundation, a conservative think tank. Taranto (who was one of the authors of a Heritage Foundation policy brief in favor of the mandate) affirmed that some forms of the mandate are better than others. It is no small matter that the Heritage Foundation later reversed its position on the individual mandate well before Romney passed his own version (Taranto, 2011, para. 4–10), indicating that Romney stands in opposition to mainstream conservative views on national healthcare.

The 2012 Presidential Primary Debates

The 2012 Republican primary was a volatile primary season with a large number of contenders, significant shifts in leads, and some dramatic changes in the landscape created by sudden additions and subtractions from the field. The result was that maintaining a consistent strategy was difficult, especially during the debates. As new candidates entered and left, significant voting blocs shifted their loyalties. To be able to reach newly available voting groups, or prevent currently loyal groups from defecting, the candidate had to be able to rapidly shift campaign strategy. In 2012, the early removal of weaker challengers such as Tim Pawlenty and the late additions of Rick Santorum and Rick Perry forced Romney into adopting flexible and easily modified strategies. This directly influenced the way issues were debated as each new candidate brought a distinct perspective on the healthcare debate.

In the early debates, Michelle Bachmann and Newt Gingrich both featured prominently on the healthcare issue. Bachmann, a social conservative from Minnesota, challenged Romney on the constitutionality and legitimacy of the individual mandate (Murphy, 2011, para. 2–5). Gingrich joined Bachmann in demanding the repeal of the ACA and specifically targeted Romney for his support for that same piece of legislation (Crowley, 2011, para. 3–5). The change in both tone and policy proposals offered by Herman Cain and Ron Paul forced Romney to make significant adaptations over the course of the debates. Subsequently Rick Perry and Rick Santorum both quickly gained ground and directly attacked Romney on the merits of his Massachusetts plan rather than simply for its similarities to the ACA. This again required Romney to revamp his debate strategies to address this new line of criticism.

Polysemic Argument as a Debate Technique

The rapidly changing field of competitors and arguments Romney faced required an argument strategy that was flexible and could be adapted to changes in arguments offered by opponents. It also required an argument strategy that enabled audiences to read arguments in the most favorable light. To do this, there must be some slippage between what was uttered and how the audience perceived the utterance.

Ceccarelli's (1998) article, "Polysemy: Multiple Meanings in Rhetorical Criticism," presented a number of different theories regarding the ability of language to have multiple meanings. She used the notion of polysemy to describe the possibility for utterances or symbols to have many meanings. Ceccarelli identified several distinct types of polysemic uses of language that are tied to different notions of rhetorical agency. My analysis focuses on her discussion of strategic ambiguity, where the rhetor presents a text in such a way that it is open to multiple interpretations allowing a text to appeal to a dominant audience while simultaneously preventing the text being rejected by a marginal audience (Ceccarelli, 1998, p. 404).

As Ceccarelli (1998) described, strategic ambiguity "is likely to be planned by the author and result in two or more otherwise conflicting groups of readers converging in praise of a text" (p. 404). The author purposefully constructs the text so that it remains open to multiple interpretations. As Ceccarelli (1998) argued, rhetors can deploy strategic ambiguity in three ways depending on their goals: first, as a way to make subversive arguments communicable in the face of a dominant power; second, by dominant powers to prevent outright rejection by a minority group; and third, to increase the general popularity of a text (pp. 404–405).

I argue that there is a fourth way that strategic ambiguity can be used. Rhetors can use strategic ambiguity to argue in a manner that affirms their personal views while appealing to those who hold opposing viewpoints. The distinction here that matters is the relationship between the rhetor and her or his argument. In Ceccarelli's (1998) article, there is an unspoken sense that the argument is at the service of the rhetor when polysemy is being deployed. I contend that polysemy can play a strategic role in arguing one's personal viewpoint in the face of skepticism and criticism.

In the following analysis, I show that Romney used two distinct argumentative strategies to create strategic ambiguity. First, Romney used a co-option strategy to adopt all or part of his opponent's position. Second, Romney used a policy creep argument to defend a minimal policy change that can easily absorb the positions taken by other candidates.

Romney in the Primary Debates

The debates I selected for analysis are representative of the two techniques I argue Romney used to create polysemic arguments. They are not representative of all argumentative techniques used over the course of the primary debates, nor are they representative of the total argumentative trajectory of the primary debates. My aim is to illuminate what I consider to be the important argumentative techniques of polysemy and the circumstances under which they can be used to enhance the effectiveness of argument.

The first debate took place on June 13, 2011, and would be the first opportunity for Romney to outline his stance on health care in a competitive forum. The moderator John King brought Romney into an ongoing healthcare discussion by referring to a recent comment from Pawlenty that compared Obama's Affordable Care Act to Romney's Massachusetts health care plan, concluding that there was no meaningful difference (as cited in Peters & Woolley, 2011a). The moderator offered Romney the chance to respond to this characterization. Romney responded by saying, "First, if I'm elected president, I will repeal Obamacare, just as Michelle [Bachmann] indicated. And also, on my first day in office, if I'm lucky enough to have that office, I will grant a waiver to all 50 states from Obamacare" (as cited in Peters & Woolley, 2011a). In so doing, Romney made an ideological commitment to oppose the ACA, but not necessarily a government-run healthcare system. By claiming he would adopt the position taken by Bachmann and repeal the ACA, the other candidates lost the ability to gain ground with primary voters by appearing to be more conservative than Romney. This response demonstrates the co-option approach where the rhetor takes advantage of the argumentative work done by another candidate.

The waiver system Romney advocated is distinct from repeal in that a state theoretically would be able to decline the waiver, leaving ACA in place. This allowed Romney the flexibility to take a more moderate position later in the primary debates or in the general election by arguing that states should have the choice to opt in or out of a national health care system. Here the audience was afforded two different positions. For those opposed to government-run healthcare, it appears that Romney would repeal ACA. More moderate members of the audience would notice that the 50-state waiver option would leave ACA in place for the states that desire it. A third reading is also possible, where the audience may recognize that there is tension between these two positions, but when both positions open the possibility of ACA being eliminated, they are less likely to read the argument in a negative way.

Romney then began the complicated work of delineating between the healthcare system he had instituted in Massachusetts and the ACA. He made two arguments: First, the Massachusetts plan was far cheaper than the ACA and, second, state-level healthcare is better than a national healthcare plan (Peters & Woolley, 2011a). The problem being identified was not so much the idea that governments should provide healthcare, but rather that it should be limited to state governments so that it could be run at an affordable cost. Given the advocacy for a 50-state waiver, it becomes clear that Romney wanted to appear to be supportive of the idea of some government-run healthcare system, but wanted to clearly oppose the ACA.

In this debate, Romney used two significant techniques. The first is co-option of the positions taken by the opposition. By co-opting the policy outlined by Bachmann, Romney was able to gain credibility as a conservative with Bachmann supporters. At the same time, the very minimal policy outlined by Romney was difficult to criticize because it had such a minimal description and is, itself, such a small policy to defend that criticism is difficult. This is the basis of the second technique, using policy creep. By starting with a very small and minimally interventionist policy, Romney was effectively able to adopt other policies in later debates without appearing to contradict himself and lose credibility.

This approach became a recurring theme throughout the debates. The debate on October 11, 2011, marked the first attempt to challenge Romney on his Massachusetts plan. Romney began the debate on healthcare by agreeing with Rick Santorum's demand that the ACA be repealed and subsequently proposing the same 50-state waiver program that he had featured in previous debates. Perry then engaged Romney on his Massachusetts plan, arguing that it had raised the cost of insurance for small business. Romney responded by making two points. First, there were many uninsured children in his state who deserved healthcare. Second, his plan only affected 8 percent of the Massachusetts population and would not change anything for the other 92 percent of the population (as cited in Peters & Woolley, 2011b).

In this debate, Romney made an important switch in how he discussed healthcare by offering examples for who should receive healthcare and describing how it can be done in a limited manner that does not create the problems that more conservative candidates associated with the ACA. This marked the beginning of more active appeals to voters who may support a government-run healthcare plan. However, it is important to note that he never advocated a national healthcare plan during this debate, and he continued to agree with the other candidates who advocated a repeal of the ACA.

This debate demonstrated the value of polysemic argument. The co-optation technique allowed Romney to adopt the positions of the other candidates, making it difficult for them to criticize him. At the same time, Romney began to creep toward more involved government policies by defending some government-run healthcare systems. Thus, Romney was able to make appeals to both conservative voters and moderate to liberal voters who might be opposed to ACA but in favor of a government-run healthcare program.

On January 19, 2012, Romney demonstrated the end point of the policy creep and co-option approach. In response to a question about healthcare for persons with pre-existing conditions, Romney reversed his stance on a national healthcare plan entirely, switching from a simple repeal or waiver to a "repeal and replace" position with the replacing bill specifically providing healthcare for persons with pre-existing conditions (as cited in Peters & Woolley, 2012).

This demonstrates the utility of the policy creep approach. Over the course of the primary debates there was a subtle, but important shift taking place. As Romney addressed new competitors, he rapidly adopted the positions they advocated which, due to the small and narrow nature of the policy advocated by Romney, is not contradictory. By adopting these new policies and changing his stance over time, Romney was able to remain ambiguous until, at the end of the debate cycle, he was able to advocate what is functionally the opposite of his standard policy positions.

Conclusion

By co-opting the arguments and positions made by his opponents, Romney was effectively able to avoid criticism for his past support of government-run healthcare programs. At the same time, the minimal policy changes he defended enabled him to adopt these policies without contradicting himself, allowing him to subtly creep his way toward more expansive policies until, at the end of the primary, he was defending the creation of a new national healthcare bill. These two techniques allowed him to be ambiguous. Rather than answer questions by defending his own policies, Romney advocated what other candidates had already defended, effectively muting criticism and allowing him to slowly advance his own argumentative agenda. During these debates, he was able to use polysemic argument to appear opposed to ACA while maintaining, advancing, and arguing in the interest of his own ideological commitment to government-run healthcare programs.

References

Ceccarelli, L. (1998). Polysemy: Multiple meanings in rhetorical criticism. *Quarterly Journal of Speech*, *84*(4), 395–415.

Crowley, M. (2011, November 28). The new new new Newt. *Time*, *178*(21), 5. Retrieved from Academic Search Premier

Frum, D. (2012, March 26). A tale of two Romneys. *Newsweek*, *159*(13/14), 46–50. Retrieved from Academic Search Premier

Frum, D. (2012, June 18). It's Mormon in America. *Newsweek*, *159*(25), 44–50. Retrieved from Academic Search Premier

Gelmann, B., & Dias, E. (2012, June 4). Dreams from his mother. *Time*, 179(22), 26–35. Retrieved from Academic Search Premier

Greenberger, S. (2005, June 22). Romney eyes penalties for those lacking insurance. *Boston Globe*. Retrieved from http://boston.com/news/local/articles/2005/06/22/romney_eyes_penalties_for_those_lacking_insurance/

Murphy, M. (2011, July 11). The Bachmann boomlet. *Time*, *178*(2), 9. Retrieved from Academic Search Premier

Peters, G., & Woolley, J. (2011a, June 13). Presidential candidates debates: Republican candidates debate at Saint Anselm College in Manchester, New Hampshire. *The American Presidency Project*. Retrieved from http://www.presidency.ucsb.edu/ws/?pid=90513

Peters, G., & Woolley, J. (2011b, October 11). Presidential candidates debates: Republican candidates debate in Hanover, New Hampshire. *The American Presidency Project*. Retrieved from http://www.presidency.ucsb.edu/ws/?pid=96894

Peters, G., & Woolley, J. (2012, January 19). Presidential candidates debates: Republican candidates debate in Charleston, South Carolina. *The American Presidency Project*. Retrieved from http://www.presidency.ucsb.edu/ws/?pid=98936

Stephenson, D. L. (2011). Health insurance reform rhetoric's two-valued orientation. *ETC: A Review of General Semantics*, *68*(1), 21–32.

Taranto, J. (2011, October 19). Obamacare's heritage. *Wall Street Journal*. Retrieved from http://online.wsj.com/news/articles/SB10001424052970204618704576641190920152366

25

A DISTURBING CONCLUSION

The irrelevance of evidence

Jeffrey W. Jarman

WICHITA STATE UNIVERSITY, USA

Reliance on rationality and reason, especially the appeal to evidence, is a hallmark of argumentation (Rybacki & Rybacki, 2000). An informed public, applying basic skills of argumentation, is a basic necessity of a vibrant public sphere. The need to protect citizens from misinformation inspired journalists to begin fact checking controversial statements made by politicians. Thus, "ad watches are premised on the assumption that prospective voters will use information about misleading ads to discount their claims and turn away from candidates whose ads lack veracity" (Frantzich, 2002, p. 35). The question is: Does fact-checking influence the public?

Scholars initially attempted to answer this question by studying the effectiveness of broadcast news adwatches. Ansolabehere and Iyengar (1996) determined adwatches fail because "the candidate who was scrutinized by the media enjoyed increased support among those who watched an ad-watch report" (p. 82). Pfau and Louden (1994) found mixed results with increased support for one candidate but reduced support for another. Jamieson and Cappella (1997) criticized both studies for errors in their design. In contrast, some studies have concluded that adwatches can be effective (e.g., Cappella & Jamieson, 1994; O'Sullivan & Geiger, 1995). Unfortunately, most previous research on adwatches has two shortcomings. First, most studies have focused on reactions to the *candidates* (as either those attacked or those attacking). When reaction to the *ads* was studied, it typically was to determine the audience reaction to the advertisement as a form of negative campaign communication. Prior studies have not attempted to gauge the audience reaction to the content of the *adwatch*. Second, most research did not control for partisan bias. But, "there is some evidence that ad watch evaluations are in the eye of the beholder" (Frantzich, 2002, p. 55). As such, it is unclear if the successes or failures of prior adwatches are due to the quality of the report or a simple partisan influence.

A growing body of research, predominantly from political science and social psychology, has investigated the likelihood that people will revise their opinions in the face of contrary evidence. This area of research is useful and underutilized by those in argumentation studies. Unfortunately, the results have been mixed. On one hand, scholars have drawn on theories of motivated reasoning to document how individuals process information in a biased manner (e.g., Bullock, 2006; Edwards & Smith, 1996; Lord, Ross, & Lepper, 1979; Nyhan & Reifler, 2010; Taber, Cann, & Kucsova, 2009; Taber & Lodge,

2006). Accordingly, information that is consistent with the pre-existing attitude is perceived to be stronger than evidence that is inconsistent with it. Similarly, individuals are likely to reject evidence that disconfirms a prior opinion. In some cases, the pre-existing attitudes are made stronger after exposure to contradictory evidence. As Peffley and Hurwtiz (2007) made clear:

> Research on motivated reasoning has shown that when individuals with strong prior beliefs on a topic are presented with contradictory evidence or arguments, they tend to seize on consistent information with little scrutiny while subjecting challenging information to withering skepticism in ways that allow them to maintain or bolster their prior attitudes.
>
> *(p. 998)*

On the other hand, there is some evidence that people respond favorably to the presentation of evidence designed to correct their misperceptions (e.g., Gilens, 2001; Howell & West, 2009; Kuklinski, Quirk, Jerit, Schwieder, & Rich, 2000). In these cases, the research has documented a change in attitude after presentation of the correct information. For instance, as Kuklinski et al. (2000) documented, people exposed to the actual level of spending on welfare programs after stating their preferred levels (which were higher) were more likely to support welfare spending than those who were not previously exposed to the information. They concluded that when you provide information to people that "hits them between the eyes" (Kuklinski et al., 2000, p. 805) it can influence their opinions.

This project extends the current research in two important ways. First, this project is applied to a new context: political fact checking. Most of the research in this field has presented the correction in the context of a newspaper article. Although newspaper articles can be a valuable source of information, their purpose is to provide balanced coverage. Corrections in this context are consistent with journalistic neutrality. Fact checking, however, is designed to be one-sided, definitive, and persuasive. This does not mean it should be biased or subjective, but it clearly is a different style of writing than news reporting. Second, using a fact-check analysis will ensure the corrections are longer and more detailed. Most current studies provide a weak correction: They often use a single sentence or simple quotation in a newspaper article to correct a potential misperception. This study reports on the effectiveness of decisive correction. The material used is lopsided and the conclusion to reject the initial statement is obvious. As such, this study attempts to provide further investigation into the effectiveness of corrections that "hit people between the eyes." Therefore, the following hypotheses guided the project:

> H1: Evaluation of the strength of the initial argument will be influenced by initial evaluation of the speaker, attitude toward the topic, and political affiliation, with congruent arguments rated higher.
>
> H2: Evaluation of the strength of the fact-check analysis will be influenced by initial evaluation of the speaker, attitude toward the topic, and political affiliation, with congruent arguments rated higher.
>
> H3: Final evaluation of the strength of the argument will be influenced by initial evaluation of the speaker, attitude toward the topic, initial evaluation of the argument, and political affiliation, with congruent arguments rated higher.

Methodology

Procedure

Respondents initially completed a series of basic demographic questions, including age, sex, level of education, amount of news consumption, political affiliation, and level of political interest. Respondents also completed a feeling thermometer (0–100) to express their level of support for both President Obama and the National Rifle Association (NRA). In addition, some respondents (n=114) completed a series of six questions using a 7-point Likert scale (ranging from strongly agree to strongly disagree) to assess their level of support for gun control measures.

The main experiment involved three steps. First, respondents watched a 30–second advertisement by the NRA opposing additional gun restrictions and recorded their evaluation of the strength of the argument using a semantic differential scale (explained later). Then, respondents were shown a lengthy refutation of the argument (371 words) by a non-partisan fact-checking organization and recorded their evaluation of the strength of the refutation using the same scales. Third, respondents were asked to re-evaluate the strength of the original claim using the same scales. Respondents concluded the study by reporting their post-test evaluation of Obama and the NRA using the feeling thermometer.

Scales

A 6-item semantic differential scale was used to assess opinion about the quality of the arguments made by the NRA and the fact-check analysis. The pairs included: correct-incorrect, valuable-not valuable, unsound-sound, poorly reasoned-well reasoned, logical-illogical, and reasonable-unreasonable. Some pairs were provided in opposite order. Those pairs were recoded so that the negative element received the lowest score. Items were summed together to create an evaluation score for the arguments. Lower scores indicate opposition to the argument while higher scores indicate support for the argument.

Attitude toward gun restrictions was measured using six statements (drawn from Taber & Lodge, 2006) related to gun control using a 7-point Likert scale (strongly agree to strongly disagree). Some statements favored restrictions while others opposed restrictions. Answers favoring restrictions were recoded. The scores were summed to create a composite attitude toward gun control with higher scores indicating stronger opposition to gun control measures.

Participants (N=217) were recruited from several communication classes (in exchange for course credit/extra-credit) and from Amazon's Mechanical Turk service (receiving payment of $0.80 to complete the survey). Participants ranged in age from 18 to 66 years of age (M=30.86). A majority was male (n=132). Most participants had an education beyond a high school diploma (n=192). Over a third of the participants (39.1%) reported either an extremely high or very high interest in information about government and politics. About a quarter of the participants (22.6%) reported only some interest or no interest in similar information. Almost half of the participants reported a political affiliation consistent with the Democratic Party (48.4%). Republican (18.9%) and other affiliations (32.7%) made up the rest of the sample. Samples drawn from Mechanical Turk are reliable (Buhrmester, Kwang, & Gosling, 2011). The sample includes more Democrats, and fewer Republicans and others, than the national average. However, the differences are less meaningful in this study because most of the statistical tests are comparisons of the average scores between the groups.

The semantic differential scales used in the survey were reliable. Cronbach's alpha for the scales were: initial evaluation of the NRA's argument (α=.969), evaluation of fact-check analysis (α=.971), re-evaluation of the NRA's argument (α=.975), and 6-item gun control attitude (α=.896).

Results

The first hypothesis suggests that people will be influenced by their prior attitudes when judging the initial strength of the argument made by the NRA. There was overwhelming support for the hypothesis. A one-way ANOVA of political affiliation was conducted on initial evaluation of the strength of the statement by the NRA and produced a statistically significant result (see Table 25.1). Post hoc LSD tests revealed significant differences between Republicans (who rated it strongest) and both Democrats (who rated it weakest) and others (see Table 25.2). A series statistically significant simple linear regression also confirms the hypothesis (see Table 25.3). Increasing scores on the feeling thermometer for the NRA predicted higher initial evaluations of the strength of their argument. Increasing scores on the feeling thermometer for Obama predicted lower initial evaluations of the strength of the

Table 25.1 One-way ANOVA Results for Political Affiliation

Initial evaluation of argument	$F(2,214)$=23.767, p<.001, η^2=.182
Evaluation of fact-check	$F(2,214)$=9.416, p<.001, η^2=.081
Final evaluation of argument	$F(2,214)$=20.323, p<.001, η^2=.160

Table 25.2 Mean Evaluations for Argument Strength by Political Affiliation

	Initial	*Fact-check*	*Final*
Democrats	20.267	33.352	13.829
Republicans	32.585	25.390	26.171
Others	21.845	21.704	17.268

Table 25.3 Regressions of Feeling Thermometer on Evaluation of the Arguments

	Adj R²	*F*	*DF*	*Sig.*	*β (std)*
Obama Thermometer (pretest)					
Initial evaluation of argument	0.296	91.651	1,215	p < .001	−0.547
Evaluation of fact-check	0.145	37.587	1,215	p < .001	0.386
Final evaluation of argument	0.290	89.213	1,215	p < .001	−0.542
NRA Thermometer (pretest)					
Initial evaluation of argument	0.559	275.209	1,215	p < .001	0.749
Evaluation of fact-check	0.157	41.082	1,215	p < .001	−0.401
Final evaluation of argument	0.514	229.607	1,215	p < .001	0.719
Gun Control Attitude					
Initial evaluation of argument	0.418	82.086	1,112	p < .001	0.650
Evaluation of fact-check	0.118	16.088	1,112	p < .001	−0.354
Final evaluation of argument	0.524	125.179	1,112	p < .001	0.726

Table 25.4 Regressions of Initial Argument Evaluation on Final Evaluation of Argument

Adj R²	F	DF	Sig.	β (std)
0.654	408.558	1,215	p<.001	0.809

NRA argument. Increasing scores on the gun control attitude survey predicted higher initial evaluations of the strength of the NRA argument.

The second hypothesis suggests that people will be influenced by their prior attitudes when judging the strength of the analysis provided by the fact-checking organization. There was modest support for this hypothesis. A one-way ANOVA of political affiliation was conducted on the evaluation of the strength of the fact-check analysis and produced a statistically significant result (see Table 25.1). Post hoc LSD tests revealed significant differences between Republicans (who rated it weakest) and both Democrats (who rated it strongest) and others (see Table 25.2). A series of statistically significant simple linear regressions also confirms hypothesis 2 (see Table 25.3). Increasing scores on the feeling thermometer for the NRA predicted lower evaluations of the fact-check analysis. Increasing scores on the feeling thermometer for Obama predicted higher evaluations of the fact-check analysis. Increasing scores on the gun control attitude survey predicted lower evaluations of the strength of the fact-check analysis.

The third hypothesis suggests that people will continue to be influenced by their prior attitudes. There was strong support for this hypothesis. A one-way ANOVA of political affiliation was conducted on the final evaluation of the NRA's argument and produced a statistically significant result (see Table 25.1). Post hoc LSD tests revealed significant differences between Republicans (who continued to rate it strongest) and both Democrats (who continue rate it weakest) and others (see Table 25.2). A series of statistically significant simple linear regressions also confirms the hypothesis (see Table 25.3). Increasing scores on the feeling thermometer for the NRA predicted higher final evaluations of their argument. Increasing scores on the feeling thermometer for Obama predicted lower final evaluations of the NRA's argument. Increasing scores on the gun control attitude survey predicted higher final evaluations of the NRA's argument. In addition, a statistically significant simple linear regression found that higher initial evaluations of the NRA's argument predicted higher final evaluations of the same argument (Table 25.4).

Discussion

The result of the experiment reported in this essay provides additional support for the theories of motivated reasoning and confirmation bias. In the context of a definitive fact check, partisan bias influenced the evaluation of the original claim, the assessment of the fact check, and the final evaluation. Instead of providing additional information for citizens to use when forming their opinions, it seems more likely that prior opinions influenced the interpretation of the new information. Fact checking appears to have made almost no difference in the final assessment of the original text. Contrary to Kuklinski et al. (2000), this study "hit people between the eyes" and it resulted in only a modest attitude change that continued to be marked by a strong partisan interpretation.

Three important objections need to be addressed. First, it would be easy to conclude that fact checking was effective given the final evaluations were lower than the initial evaluations.

This opinion is rooted in the belief that any attitude adjustment is a sign that people integrated the new information into their opinion. However, the slight decreases in evaluation are not signs of success. Fact checking is effective when partisan influences are reduced. Fact checking assumes partisans can put aside their bias and reach a similar conclusion. "In general, the characteristic pattern of opinion change suggested by the simple Bayesian model is one of converging opinion among people with different prior views" (Bartels, 2002, p. 122). In this case, convergence did not occur. In fact, the gap between Democrats and Republicans *increased*. The enduring conclusion from this data is that partisanship remained a strong predictor of the final evaluation. Moreover, the difference in opinion regarding the quality of the fact-checking analysis is illustrative of bias. There was wide divergence in opinion regarding the quality of the refutation. It is not surprising that a partisan gap remained in the final evaluation of the argument – there was a major partisan gap in assessing the strength of the refutation. Figure 25.1 shows how Democratic (and other) judgments sharply differed from Republican judgments at each point in the process. Clearly, partisan influence was more important than the information provided in the fact-check.

Second, it would be easy to dismiss the conclusion as overly concerned with short-term effects. According to this view, evidence and argumentation can be successful in the long-term. I am hopeful that this conclusion is true. But, the greater danger is that the public sphere demands an answer before the long-term effects of evidence can materialize. In the short term, there definitely is reason to fear that fact checking does not provide a safeguard for informed decision making.

Finally, it could be argued that gun control is a highly emotional issue, inflaming passions brought out both by tragic deaths and constitutional protections. Because of this, some might argue that the topic is not a reasonable test of fact checking. But, fact checking is most important when the controversy is highly charged. The common practice of fact checking is to promote accuracy on topics that are the most controversial. Fact checking would become useless if it were reserved for mundane topics with no interest by the general public. A topic like gun control is the most useful test of effectiveness of fact checking. Fact checking is a valuable enterprise only if it works in the most challenging of cases.

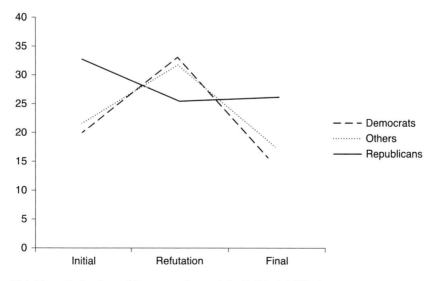

Figure 25.1 Mean Evaluations of Argument Strength by Political Affiliation

Democracy requires citizens have access to accurate information. Unfortunately, democracy also requires citizens who can use the information to update their opinions. Fact checking provides a unique opportunity to educate citizens and improve the quality of public deliberation. Unfortunately, the results presented here portend a serious problem: the irrelevance of evidence in the public sphere.

References

Ansolabehere, S., & Iyengar, S. (1996). Can the press monitor campaign advertising? An experimental study. *Harvard International Journal of Press/Politics, 1*, 72–86.

Bartels, L. M. (2002). Beyond the running tally: partisan bias in political perceptions. *Political Behavior, 24*, 117–150.

Buhrmester, M., Kwang, T., & Gosling, S.D. (2011). Amazon's Mechanical Turk: A new source of inexpensive, yet high-quality, data? *Perspectives on Psychological Science, 6*, 3–5.

Bullock, J. G. (2006). *Partisanship and the enduring effects of false political information.* Unpublished manuscript. Earlier versions of the paper were presented at the 2006 meetings of the Western Political Science Association and the Midwest Political Science Association.

Cappella, J. N., & Jamieson, K. H. (1994). Broadcast adwatch effects. *Communication Research, 21*, 342–365.

Edwards, K., & Smith, E. E. (1996). A disconfirmation bias in the evaluation of arguments. *Journal of Personality and Social Psychology, 71*, 5–24.

Frantzich, S. (2002). Watching the watchers: The nature and content of campaign ad watches. *Harvard International Journal of Press/Politics, 7*(2), 34–57.

Gilens, M. (2001). Political ignorance and collective policy preferences. *American Political Science Review, 95*, 379–396.

Howell, W. G., & West, M. R. (2009). Educating the public. *Education Next, 9*(3), 41–47.

Jamieson, K. H., & Cappella, J. N. (1997). Setting the record straight: Do ad watches help or hurt? *Harvard International Journal of Press/Politics, 2*, 13–22.

Kuklinski, J. H., Quirk, P. J., Jerit, J., Schwieder, D., & Rich, R. F. (2000). Misinformation and the currency of democratic citizenship. *Journal of Politics, 62*, 790–816.

Lord, C. G., Ross, L., & Lepper, M. R. (1979). Biased assimilation and attitude polarization: The effects of prior theories on subsequently considered evidence. *Journal of Personality and Social Psychology, 37*, 2098–2109.

Nyhan, B., & Reifler, J. (2010). When corrections fail: The persistence of political misperceptions. *Political Behavior, 32*, 303–330.

O'Sullivan, P. B., & Geiger, S. (1995). Does the watchdog bite? Newspaper ad watch articles and political attack ads. *Journalism and Mass Communication Quarterly, 72*, 771–785.

Peffley, M., & Hurwitz, J. (2007). Persuasion and resistance: Race and the death penalty in America. *American Journal of Political Science, 51*, 996–1012.

Pfau, M., & Louden, A. (1994). Effectiveness of adwatch formats in deflecting political attack ads. *Communication Research, 21*, 325–341.

Rybacki, K. C., & Rybacki, D. J. (2000). *Advocacy and opposition: An introduction to argumentation* (4th ed.). Needham Heights, MA: Allyn & Bacon.

Taber, C. S., Cann, D., & Kucsova, S. (2009). The motivated processing of political arguments. *Political Behavior, 31*, 137–155.

Taber, C. S., & Lodge, M. (2006). Skepticism in the evaluation of political beliefs. *American Journal of Political Science, 50*, 755–769.

26

DISTURBING ARGUMENT AND SENATOR RICHARD LUGAR'S WARNING AGAINST PARTISANSHIP

John M. Jones

PEPPERDINE UNIVERSITY, USA

On May 8, 2012, after serving in the U.S. Senate for 36 years, Richard Lugar was defeated by State Treasurer and Tea Party champion Richard Mourdock in the Indiana Republican primary. That evening, the defeated Senator delivered a gracious concession speech, reflecting on his years of service and looking to the future with optimism. The following day, however, Lugar released a sharply worded jeremiad that warned that Mourdock and his party must renounce rigid partisanship or face extinction (Lugar, 2012). Although the mainstream media praised Lugar for his statement and his civility (e.g., Dionne, 2012, p. A19; "Goodbye," 2012, p. A18; Kane, 2012, p. A1), the Republican Party failed to heed his warning. Their repudiation immediately could be seen when Mourdock told CNN that his idea of "bipartisanship" was "Democrats joining with Republicans" adding, "you never compromise on principles" (as cited in O'Brien, 2013). Conservative commentators, including Rush Limbaugh (2012) and Charles Krauthammer (2012), echoed Mourdock's sentiments and proclaimed that the era of the moderate Republican was over.

Later that year, Mourdock's campaign self-destructed when he commented that a pregnancy resulting from rape was "something that God intended to happen" (as cited in Jaffe, 2012, p. A30) and he lost decisively to Democrat Joe Donnelly. Since the election, the hardline conservative stance of the Republican-controlled House on issues such as hurricane relief, immigration reform, tax reform, student loans, food stamps, and a host of other issues further indicates that the GOP is nowhere near embracing the bipartisanship of which Lugar spoke (Hernandez, 2013; "The House," 2013; Nakamura & Branigin, 2013; O'Keefe, 2013; Parker & Weisman, 2013). By May 2013, the crisis within the GOP had worsened to the point that former Senate Majority Leader Bob Dole (2013) told Fox News, "I think they ought to put a sign on the [Republican] National Committee that says 'closed for repairs' until New Year's Day next year and spend that time going over ideas and positive agendas." Dole (2013) went on to say "Reagan wouldn't have made it [in today's GOP]. Certainly Nixon wouldn't have made it, because he had ideas. We might have made it, but I doubt it."

However well crafted and prescient Lugar's argument might have been, it did not persuade Republicans to change their course.

In one sense, the failure of Lugar's argument to resonate is puzzling given voter rejection of candidates such as Mourdock, not to mention Barack Obama's reelection over Republican candidate Mitt Romney. Clearly, the party is paying a price for embracing a hard-right ideology. I argue, however, that the result is not surprising when the contrast between two jeremiads, representing two branches of conservatism with two different sets of founding principles, is considered. Mourdock and the commentators mentioned above appealed to a conservative jeremiad while Lugar built an argument in political jeremiad form. Because the appeal of the jeremiad is not primarily based in rational evaluation of evidence, Lugar's political jeremiad had little power when pitted against the conservative (myth-based) ideological system.

The Jeremiad

In this section, I lay out the characteristics of the jeremiad and discuss how this genre was used to represent two opposing variants of conservatism. The jeremiad is a story in which a nation or some other group has strayed from its founding principles and consequently is threatened with disaster, but disaster can be prevented by returning to those principles (Bercovitch, 1978).

The jeremiad functioned in this way for Tea Party conservatives. In fact, one of the dominant reactions to Lugar's call for moderation and reform was an exclamation that conservatives continued to stray from founding principles. For example, Limbaugh (2012) said, "I don't know how conservative he ever really was, but it doesn't matter. To whatever extent he was conservative, he isn't any longer. He became a moderate and then for the most part a Beltway establishment politician." Later in the same broadcast, Limbaugh (2012) posited:

> There's no mystery why Dick Lugar lost yesterday. The American people don't want any more of Barack Obama's domestic or foreign policy, and they don't want any Republicans whose first objective is to "reach across the aisle" and make it easier for Obama to continue on the current path that we are on.

In Limbaugh's view, Lugar and other moderates had strayed to the point that they were practically in the same camp as Barack Obama. Senator Rand Paul (2012) likewise blamed the Lugar defeat on his deviation from founding principles of conservatism, describing the loss as a rejection of the status quo and a strong stand "for issues such as smaller government, constitutional principles, true liberty and the protection of life" (p. 1). The reality that Lugar's views were wildly different from those of Obama made little difference. The power of the myth created what Kenneth Burke (1966) called an "impulse to perfection" (p. 17) that left no room for compromise. It seems clear why many conservatives rejected Lugar's criticisms; they saw his arguments as threatening the basic principles of their conservative covenant.

Lugar's jeremiad followed a similar form as the conservative jeremiad, but also employed argument from example to demonstrate the height from which conservatism had fallen due to its sin of extreme partisanship, the impending doom that could result, and the way back to political and national success. Lugar offered a competing jeremiad that rationally called conservatives back to an alternative form of conservatism. However, as Martha Nussbaum (2013) argued, public emotions "can give pursuit of [the nation's] goals new vigor and depth, but they can also derail that pursuit, introducing or reinforcing divisions, hierarchies, and forms of neglect and obtuseness" (p. 2). The rational political jeremiad of Richard Lugar was limited in that it could only invite people to think through how well the nation was meeting its goals, whereas the public emotions of the Tea Party faction held enormous power to derail not only progressive goals, but any movement toward moderation on the part of Republicans.

Lugar's Political Jeremiad

In this section, I describe how Lugar built his political jeremiad around three arguments: Present Republican policies have become too extreme; this extremism threatens the GOP and the nation; and, finally, this disaster could be averted by recommitting to pragmatic policies and rejection of extremism.

After a brief introduction to his statement, Lugar (2012) moved quickly to confront an environment in which political victory could be achieved only by adhering to strict ideological purity. The defeated Senator wrote of "an unrelenting partisan viewpoint" and an atmosphere in which it is nearly impossible "to hold independent views or engage in constructive compromise." The zeal for ideological purity had been taken to such an extreme that "bipartisanship is equated with centrism or deal cutting."

Later in the statement, Lugar (2012) argued from example to show how far conservatives had digressed:

> I don't remember a time when so many topics have become politically unmentionable in one party or the other. Republicans cannot admit to any nuance in policy on climate change. Republican members are now expected to take pledges against any tax increases. For two consecutive presidential nomination cycles, GOP candidates competed with one another to express the most strident anti-immigration view, even at the risk of alienating a huge voting bloc.

He then continued his argument, citing the example of Richard Mourdock, whose "stated goal" was "to bring more partisanship to Washington" (Lugar, 2012). Lugar offered a detailed description of Mourdock. Mourdock was someone who had embraced an "unrelenting partisan mindset" that Lugar considered "irreconcilable with my philosophy of governance and my experience of what brings results for Hoosiers in the Senate." In Lugar's view, the nominee had promised "a rejectionist orthodoxy" and "rigid opposition to the actions and proposals of the other party." In the face of opposition, Mourdock's solution was "to campaign for more Republicans who embrace the same partisan outlook." This was evident from his ties "to groups whose prime mission is to cleanse the Republican Party of those who stray from orthodoxy as they see it." In such an extreme environment, even someone like Lugar, who "supported Ronald Reagan more than any other senator" (Lugar, 2012) and received a lifetime rating of 77 percent from the American Conservative Union, was an easy target for Tea Party conservatives (Dionne, 2012).

Next, Lugar (2012), having enumerated the transgressions, warned that insistence on complete ideological purity threatened the Republican Party and the nation. He cautioned that unless Mourdock altered his course, he would "achieve little as a senator." He also warned the Republican Party that if it clung unswervingly to its principles with no effort to reach bipartisan solutions, it would be "relegated to minority status" since "parties don't succeed for very long if they stop appealing to voters who may disagree with them on some issues."

Far worse, Lugar (2012) argued, were the consequences for the nation that Mourdock's "orthodoxy" would create at a time when the federal debt needed stabilizing and "millions of baby boomers are retiring." Lugar warned that there would be little progress at such a crucial time "without some degree of compromise." If the rigidity that had come to characterize the modern political scene was not abated, "our government will remain mired in the dysfunction we have witnessed during the last several years." Lugar further warned that "If fealty to these pledges continues to expand, legislators may pledge themselves into irrelevance. Voters will be electing a slate of inflexible positions rather than a leader." Here, Lugar's political jeremiad rationally confronted what the most conservative members of his party in their zeal for purity were unable to see. The pathway that the most conservative Republicans had chosen would lead not only the party, but millions of Americans and perhaps the entire political process, to destruction.

The situation Lugar (2012) described is quite disturbing, not only because of the gridlock that results, but also because it essentially stifles true discussion and debate, which lies at the heart of democracy. When addressing the most vital and complex issues of the day, the best solutions are found by way of argumentation and, presumably, through some level of compromise as both sides are moved from their initial position. But in 2012, when "fealty to pledges" seemed to dominate the political landscape, the kind of argument that typically results in progress was in danger of being rendered powerless. As a consequence, there would be little chance of real solutions to problems such as climate change, immigration reform, or tax reform at a time when U.S. voters needed and desired action. Yet despite the seemingly dire circumstances wrought by extremism and partisanship, the situation was not beyond redemption. Coupled with Lugar's warning was a pragmatic solution that would return bipartisanship, meaningful discussion, and progress to the forefront.

Lugar's solution to the rigidity and dogmatism was to call his party to embrace an alternative form of conservatism based on principled pragmatism. First, Lugar (2012) called Mourdock to reform his ways. In order for Mourdock to be "a good Senator," he would have to "revise his stated goal of bringing more partisanship to Washington." He simply could not govern as he had campaigned and hope to enjoy any semblance of legislative success.

Second, Lugar (2012) argued for both Mourdock and the Republican Party to redefine what it meant to be bipartisan. He did this first by underscoring the need for adherence to principle. "Leaders," he wrote, "should have an ideological grounding and strong beliefs identifiable to their constituents," the very things that he had tried to have "throughout [his] career." But ideological adherence had its limits. To be successful in governance, Lugar understood that "ideology cannot be a substitute for a determination to think for yourself, for a willingness to study an issue objectively, and for the fortitude to sometimes disagree with your party or even your constituents." To reinforce this point, Lugar then suggested that "leaders owe the people they represent their best judgment." This instruction was especially significant because it originated with Edmund Burke, who is recognized by many as the founder of modern conservatism.

With his allusion to Burke, Lugar (2012) re-defined bipartisanship as leadership. True leaders do not blindly follow a pre-determined set of ideological propositions without variation. Instead, they listen to, care for, and respect their constituents, but are willing to act independently of their constituents when it is in the best interest of the public. The bipartisanship that some Republicans would equate "with centrism and deal cutting" was to Lugar the mark of a true leader. To do otherwise was not leadership at all. By implication, Lugar suggested that conservatism could return to prominence if Republicans would but follow the words and example of their most distinguished philosopher.

Having re-defined bipartisanship as true leadership, Lugar (2012) went on to distinguish between selling out one's principles and possessing a true bipartisan spirit:

> Bipartisanship is not the opposite of principle. One can be very conservative or very liberal and still have a bipartisan mindset. Such a mindset acknowledges that the other party is also patriotic and may have some good ideas. It acknowledges that national unity is important, and that aggressive partisanship deepens cynicism, sharpens vendettas, and depletes the national reserve of good will that is critical to our survival in hard times.

Here, Lugar did not call for an abandonment of principle, but rather for a genuine attempt to find common ground, an acknowledgment of the good intentions of the loyal opposition, and a spirit of national unity wherever possible for the good of the country.

Finally, Lugar (2012) called his party back to its hero, Ronald Reagan. After outlining what bipartisanship was, and was not, Lugar wrote, "Clearly this was understood by President Reagan, who worked with Democrats frequently and showed flexibility that would be ridiculed today." The hero of the modern Republican Party, Lugar argued, had compromised with Democrats on a variety of issues, "from assenting to tax increases in the 1983 Social Security fix, to compromising on landmark tax reform legislation in 1986, to advancing arms control agreements in his second term." As with the Edmund Burke allusion, Lugar demonstrated how far the conservative movement had strayed from its first principles and called them implicitly to emulate their hero – not the Ronald Reagan as caricatured by the Tea Party movement, but Ronald Reagan the principled pragmatist. After all, the true Ronald Reagan (1981) made clear that his intention was not "to do away with government," pledging instead to "make it work – work for us, not against us – to stand by our side, not ride on our backs" (p. 2). Furthermore, Ronald Reagan, after first cutting taxes in 1981, subsequently raised taxes on several occasions, embraced an immigration policy that would be considered liberal by modern conservative standards, and actually formed a personal friendship with House Speaker and political adversary Thomas P. "Tip" O'Neill (Hornaday, 2011; Reagan, 1990). In Lugar's (2012) argumentative jeremiad, extreme partisanship had brought the party to the brink of extinction and threatened the political process, but principled pragmatism could provide a return to "great things from my party and my country."

Conclusion

In his written statement, Richard Lugar (2012) presented a powerful political jeremiad, interspersed with argumentative terms. However, the actions of Richard Mourdock, and later House Republicans, demonstrated that his argument, at least in the short run, was not successful. The answer to why his argument failed may lie in the fact that Lugar was attacking a myth-based system with reason. As Rowland and Frank (2002) have observed, mythic systems are largely invulnerable to such attacks. Moreover, when rational argument is used to attack a mythic system, the result is often backlash, which is precisely what Lugar faced.

Lugar's appeal might have been more persuasive had he combined his argument with what Rowland and Frank (2011) called "mythic rectification" (p. 42). This approach affirms mythic identity, yet makes adaptations as times and contexts change. As Rowland and Frank (2011) argued, "Myth-based symbol systems are not always interpreted in a fundamentalist manner. Sometimes the systems can be rectified in order to create space for compromise" (p. 49). Had Lugar appealed in a greater way to the mythic origins of the conservative movement, drawing upon mythic figures such as Abraham Lincoln, Theodore Roosevelt, Dwight D. Eisenhower, and especially Ronald Reagan, but interpreting the mythic tenets of their ideology in a way that was consistent with flexibility and compromise, the statement might have resonated with more conservatives. Instead, Lugar chose a path of logic and reason to confront a system that was deeply rooted in myth. In response, his audience dismissed his pleas, embracing their zeal for purity with even greater tenacity and ensuring that gridlock and inaction would continue for the foreseeable future.

References

Bercovitch, S. (1978). *The American jeremiad.* Madison: University of Wisconsin Press.
Burke, K. (1966). *Language as symbolic action.* Berkeley: University of California Press.
Dionne, E. J. (2012, May 10). Mourdock Republicans. *Washington Post*, p. A19.
Dole, B. (2013, May 26). Interview by C. Wallace. *Fox News Network.* Retrieved from LexisNexis Academic.
Goodbye, partisanship. (2012, May 10). *Washington Post*, p. A18.
Hernandez, R. (2013, January 2). Bill for hurricane aid appears in jeopardy. *New York Times*, p. A17.
Hornaday, A. (2011, February 7). Tearing down walls between Reagan myth and fact. *Washington Post*, p. C1.
The House prefers chaos to order. (2013, May 5). *New York Times*, p. SR10.
Jaffe, G. (2012, November 7). GOP's Akin, Mourdock lose in wake of remarks. *Washington Post*, p. A30.
Kane, P. (2012, May 9). Lugar loses bid to stay in the Senate. *Washington Post*, p. A1.
Krauthammer, C. (2012, May 8). Krauthammer: Generation of right-of-center Republicans coming to an end [video]. *Real Clear Politics.* Retrieved from http://www.realclearpolitics.com/video/2012/05/08/krauthammer_generation_of_right-of-center_republicans_coming_to_an_end.html
Limbaugh, R. (2012, May 9). Lugar became part of the problem. *The Rush Limbaugh Show.* Retrieved from http://www.rushlimbaugh.com/daily/2012/05/09/dick_lugar_became_part_ of_the_problem
Lugar, R. (2012, May 9). Prepared statement of Senator Richard G. Lugar on the Indiana senate primary. Retrieved from http://www.nytimes.com/2012/05/09/us/politics/prepared-statement-of-senator-richard-g-lugar-on-the-concluded-indiana-senate-primary.html?pagewanted=all&_r=0
Nakamura, D., & Branigin, W. (2013, June 1). Obama warns of looming jump in federal student-loan rates. *Washington Post*, p. A2.
Nussbaum, M. (2013). *Political emotions: Why love matters for justice.* Cambridge, MA: Belknap Press of Harvard University Press.
O'Brien, S. (2012, May 9). *CNN Starting Point with Soledad O'Brien.* Retrieved from LexisNexis Academic
O'Keefe, E. (2013, July 12). House passes farm bill without food stamp funds. *Washington Post*, p. A1.
Parker, A., & Weisman, J. (2013, July 11). GOP in House resists overhaul for immigration. *New York Times*, p. A1.
Paul, R. (2012, May 10). Tea Party wins in Indiana; Mourdock sends Lugar, status quo packing. *Washington Times*, p. 1.
Reagan, R. (1981, January 20). Inaugural address. Retrieved from http://www.reagan.utexas.edu/archives/speeches/1981/12081a.htm
Reagan, R. (1990). *An American life: Ronald Reagan.* New York, NY: Simon and Schuster.
Rowland, R. C., & Frank, D. (2002). *Shared land/conflicting identity: Trajectories of Israeli and Palestinian symbol use.* East Lansing: Michigan State University Press.
Rowland, R. C., & Frank, D. (2011). Mythic rhetoric and rectification in the Israeli-Palestinian conflict. *Communication Studies, 62*, 41–57.

27

ARGUMENTATIVE TRAJECTORIES IN THE WAR ON WOMEN

Randall A. Lake

UNIVERSITY OF SOUTHERN CALIFORNIA, USA

Barbara A. Pickering

UNIVERSITY OF NEBRASKA AT OMAHA, USA

The 2012 general election campaign, like many preceding it, reflected elements of ongoing culture wars in the United States. Historically, abortion has been the most hotly contested beachhead in these wars, and on January 22, 2013, the fortieth anniversary of the Supreme Court's codification of abortion rights in *Roe v. Wade* was both celebrated and cursed. Still, the terrain has altered substantially since 1973. One of 2012's most striking features was the drumbeat and reach of some Republicans' opposition to women's health choices, encompassing not only controversial abortion rights but widely accepted rights to terminate pregnancy in cases of rape and incest, to contraceptives (and not only "morning after" forms that arguably are abortifacients), and even to protections from domestic violence.

The War on Women

During the Republican primaries, former Pennsylvania Senator Rick Santorum warned of the "dangers of contraception," which he called a "license" for non procreative sex (as cited in "Taking a Stand," 2012, p. 5A). In Santorum's defense, donor Foster Friess (2012) voiced the opinion that, for an effective, inexpensive contraceptive, "gals" should put aspirin "between their knees." Rush Limbaugh (2012) called the "99%" of American women who use birth control "sluts," elaborating in comments about Georgetown University law student Sandra Fluke's Congressional testimony in favor of insurance coverage for contraceptive services:

> Ms. Fluke is asking to be exempted from personal responsibility. She wants all the sex that she wants all the time paid for by the rest of us. She wants no consequences for it, or to it. She wants a penalty-free, moral-free life where everybody else pays for the mistakes that she makes as a consequence of the way she lives her life.

Subsequently, during the general election, two Republican senatorial candidates made headlines with comments about rape that were widely perceived as insensitive, demeaning, and false. In Missouri, Todd Akin contended in classic Catch-22 fashion that, in cases of "*legitimate* rape," women's bodies have "ways to try to shut that whole thing [pregnancy] down" (as cited in Jaco, 2012; emphasis added). Four years earlier, Akin (2008) had expressed his contempt for women's health care professionals this way: "You find that along with the culture of death go all kinds of other law-breaking: Not following good sanitary procedure, giving abortions to women who are not actually pregnant, cheating on taxes, all these kinds of things." Meanwhile, in Indiana, Richard Mourdock voiced his opposition to abortion even in cases of rape, opining that resulting pregnancies, however "horrible," nonetheless are "something God intended to happen" (as cited in Filipovic, 2012).

Such comments stirred a firestorm of criticism because they seemed to reflect a paternalistic denial of women's capacities for making reproductive (and other) decisions evocative of a time long past (perhaps the stereotypical "Fifties"). Tellingly, Santorum has argued that *Griswold v. Connecticut*, the 1965 Supreme Court decision that protected access to contraception on grounds of a Constitutional right to privacy, should be overturned ("Taking a Stand," 2012). So retrograde did such opinions seem that Democrats and others quickly dubbed them "the war on women," expressing surprise that such views could be taken seriously in the 21st century. More temperate Republicans sought distance from such remarks but were loath to antagonize their party's most conservative wing. Thus, some Republicans, out of genuine disagreement, condemned Akin's remarks as "inexcusable" (Kane & Henderson, 2012, para. 5), "wrong" (Kane & Henderson, 2012, para. 2), "biologically stupid" (Priebus, 2012), and so on. Many others, more out of concern for damage control, called his remarks "inappropriate" (Kane & Henderson, 2012, para. 19) without repudiating them, and urged Akin to resign his candidacy. Many social conservative groups and some politicians continued to support Akin. The Republican reaction to Mourdock was milder. Some called on him to apologize. Presidential candidate Mitt Romney disavowed Mourdock's views but continued running campaign ads on his behalf. John Cornyn, chair of the National Republican Senatorial Committee who had cut off NRSC funding for Akin, accusing him of endangering Republicans' hopes of retaking the Senate, defended Mourdock as merely expressing his belief "that life is a gift from God" (as cited in Filipovic, 2012, para. 3). (These and other responses to the Akin and Mourdock controversies also are recounted in "Rape and Pregnancy," 2012.)

Republican fears of electoral fallout proved well-founded. In August, when Akin made his comments, political analyst Nate Silver gave Republicans a 60% chance of recapturing the Senate ("Rape and Pregnancy," 2012). But Akin and Mourdock – both favored – lost and, in addition to resoundingly re-electing President Obama, Democrats actually increased their margin in the Senate while narrowing their deficit in the House ("2012 Presidential Election," 2012). This electoral thumping – utterly unexpected in Republican circles, in which, even up to election eve, pundits confidently were predicting a GOP landslide (Rove, 2012) – prompted bewildered post-election soul-searching. Many Republicans, who thought that the election should be a referendum on the economy, blamed social conservatives for reigniting the gender gap. Most famously, Louisiana governor Bobby Jindal quipped that Republicans needed to "stop being the stupid party" (as cited in Lavender, 2012). Former Republican National Committee chair Haley Barbour (2012) called Jindal "exactly right." At a post-election retreat, House Republicans were advised, "Rape is a four letter word – don't say it" (Helderman & O'Keefe, 2013).

Which begs the question: What lessons were learned? One reading of national post-election politics suggests: Not many. First, Tea Party Republicans, who had been trying to repeal the Patient Protection and Affordable Care Act (a.k.a. Obamacare) ever since they failed to prevent its passage in March 2010, also stonewalled reauthorization of the heretofore bipartisan Violence Against Women Act until February 28, 2013 ("S. 47," 2013). Then, in June, in yet another direct challenge not only to *Roe* but to state laws prohibiting abortion after fetal viability (around 24 weeks), the House passed a bill prohibiting almost all abortions after 20 weeks ("House Passes," 2013). The House bill mirrors similar efforts in some states (where the nature of state politics may explain their greater success), notably Texas, where Governor Rick Perry had to call a second special session of the legislature after state Senator Wendy Davis successfully filibustered the first attempt ("Texas Lawmakers," 2013).

These well-known developments are the tip of the iceberg. There have been efforts, some successful, in several states (including Wisconsin and Virginia) to compel pregnant women to undergo ultrasounds, whether medically indicated or not (Abdullah, 2013). Meanwhile, former Senator Jim DeMint (2013) defended forced ultrasounds as an "opportunity" that women want. In North Carolina, state senators, using tactics that were condemned even by the state's Republican governor, passed a bill that probably would close all but one of the state's clinics ("North Carolina," 2013). In Ohio, Republican Governor John Kasich signed a budget bill that, among other things, defunds Planned Parenthood clinics while funding anti-choice "crisis pregnancy centers" (Siegel, 2013). Many of these state efforts, known as TRAP (Targeted Regulation of Abortion Provider) laws, are based on boilerplate legislation written by Americans United for Life (Gold & Nash, 2013). Underscoring that the "war on women" is being waged on fronts far removed from reproductive rights and women's health, *Fox Business Report* host Lou Dobbs, Republican radio host Erick Erickson, commentator Juan Williams, and panelist Doug Schoen criticized a Pew Research Report, agreeing that working women could "undermine our social order," are "bad for kids and bad for marriages," and violate the laws of the "natural world," in which "the male typically is the dominant role" (as cited in McDonough, 2013).

Such seemingly counterproductive behavior could suggest that the far right learned little to nothing from the 2012 national election. But some saw a very clear lesson: Conservatives were not conservative *enough*. The Susan B. Anthony List, for example, argued that Republicans would have won had their opposition to abortion been even more vehement and uncompromising (Maddow, 2012). Contrary to those who, perhaps gleefully, view these post-election developments merely as bafflingly self-destructive, we believe that the "war on women" can be explained, and that we ignore its rhetorical dynamic at our peril. Our account of this dynamic takes to heart Leland Griffin's (1984) insight into rhetorical trajectories: We argue that the "war on women" is the foreseeable outcome of the argumentative trajectory launched by the backlash to *Roe v. Wade*.

Argumentative Trajectories

In a memorable essay on the Kennedy assassination, published nearly thirty years ago, Griffin (1984) elaborated a concept of *rhetorical trajectory*, describing a spatial, temporal, ideological, and symbolic curve of development that perfects a moral vision, generates *movement* as motive, and impels action. Griffin argued that JFK's trajectory – a dream of detente between the United States and the Soviet Union – collided with Oswald's trajectory – a dream of violent opposition to both old orders so that the new might emerge – just as surely as their material paths converged in Dallas on November 22, 1963. Griffin argued that Oswald pulled the trigger because, in this space and moment of convergence and collision, he was compelled to enact his dream.

Scholars justly praise this study's inventive extension of Griffin's (1952, 1969) germinal works on the rhetoric of historical movements to imaginary movements. Less remembered, however, is Griffin's important elaboration upon dramatism, particularly Burkeian principles of rhetorical form and their implications.

In an early footnote, Griffin (1984, p. 126 [n. 2]) remarked that a rhetorical trajectory resembles what Burke (1968) called *qualitative progression*, in which "the presence of one quality prepares us for the introduction of another" (p. 125): "We are put into a state of mind which another state of mind can appropriately follow" (p. 125). Qualitative progression, of course, is one species of form, which Burke (1968) described as "the creation of an appetite in the mind of the auditor, and the adequate satisfying of that appetite" (p. 31). The key insight, which animated much of his *oeuvre*, is that form in language generates a certain persuasive momentum, tending toward self-fulfillment. Burke's (1966) famous ontology of humanity, which posited a "principle of perfection," expressed this insight "perfectly": "A given terminology contains various *implications*, and there is a corresponding 'perfectionist' tendency for men [*sic*] to attempt carrying out those implications" (p. 19). Griffin (1984) – who borrowed even the phrase *curve of development* from Burke (1969, p. 32) – explicitly invoked Burke's principle of perfection (p. 129 [n. 99]).

We emphasize Griffin's deployment of this principle of perfection because we believe that the concept of rhetorical trajectory powerfully explains the argumentative arc that extends from opposition to abortion in the *Roe* era to the more contemporary "war on women."

Argumentative Trajectories in the War on Women

Writing in the aftermath of *Roe*, Lake (1986) characterized anti-choice rhetoric of the time along three metaethical dimensions. First, morality is understood in deontological, intrinsicalist, and absolutist terms, as an ethics of duty governed by "universal and immutable moral rules that distinguish right from wrong. Classes of action that violate these rules are intrinsically, inherently, and always wrong," regardless of circumstances, consequences, or intent (p. 487; more generally, pp. 479–487). Second, evil-doing, rather than good, dominates the moral landscape of life (a belief dubbed the "thematic primacy of evil") because ordinary human beings are at best weak, selfish, and callous, and at worst maliciously immoral (p. 489; more generally, pp. 487–490). Third, proper moral reasoning is definitional, hence deductive, and its conclusions are confirmed by unerring conscience; hence, moral ambiguity, neutrality, and compromise when moral principles are at stake (which is always) are anathema because they countenance evil (pp. 490–496). These dimensions are mutually reinforcing. Given the thematic primacy of evil, deontology is an appropriate, even necessary, corrective: People need clear, absolute moral rules to save them from themselves. Moreover, definitional argument is the most appropriate method of applying these moral rules to judge human behavior; in so doing, reason confirms people's innate moral intuitions. Most importantly, these interlocking dimensions create a powerful argumentative trajectory that strives to perfect itself:

> If the injunction against killing is indeed a moral absolute, and the definitional argument concerning the humanity of the fetus is true, there is no *need* for compromise because the anti-abortion position is "right." If humans are essentially self-centered, evil creatures, there is no *basis* for compromise because pro-choice forces are necessarily immoral. If definitional claims are the appropriate form of argument, there is no *reason* to compromise because pro-choice appeals to circumstance and consequence [which ground exceptions for rape, incest, etc.] have no logical force against the irrefutable intuition, confirmed by conscience, that abortion is [always] wrong.
> (*Lake, 1986, p. 496*)

We believe that this metaethical *dynamis* continues to propel the contemporary "war on women," although space allows us only to sketch the trajectory. The recent controversies over contraception and rape exemplify the pressure to perfect at least two, long-standing beliefs: (a) all human life is sacred; and (b) human (especially female) control of reproduction is evil. Thirty-odd years ago, anti-choice advocates dismissed as red herrings charges that a Human Life Amendment would prohibit contraception (for example, see Lake, 1986, p. 492). Santorum, Limbaugh, et al., reveal how the principle of perfection can breach even conception's long-standing, seemingly firm line in anti-choice advocates' reproductive sand (cf. Lake, 1984, p. 436). Akin, Mourdock, et al., reveal the relentless pressure to "round out" these beliefs by eliminating exceptions. Thus could a representative of Personhood USA defend Akin from his own party by distinguishing "Reagan Republicans, who agree with the Republican Party platform on abortion" from "Romney Republicans, a fringe group of *liberals* who *compromise* on human life" when they allow "the death penalty for children conceived in rape" ("Personhood USA," 2012; emphasis added). This does not mean that "imperfect" compromises are impossible; Mourdock himself supports a mother's-life exception (Raju, 2012). But such compromises are inherently unstable because those who have acceded more to the perfecting impulse (and hold their opinions sincerely, no doubt) will find them logically untenable (cf. Lake, 1984, p. 436); even the mother's-life exception is unacceptable to some. Events in Texas illustrate this trajectory perfectly: Governor Perry's ink had barely dried on the law restricting abortions to the first 20 weeks when three state legislators proposed lowering this window to six weeks, knowing that this bill would not get a hearing but wanting to lay groundwork for the 2015 legislative session ("Republicans File," 2013).

The concept of argumentative trajectory explains much about developments in anti-choice rhetoric since the *Roe* era. It also helps explain the Tea Party phenomenon in the Republican Party that has pulled relative moderates, willingly or not, rightward. Finally, this concept may be useful to wider studies of rhetorical extremism. Our study raises the possibility that concordances in public argument (reasonable compromises among competing interests that represent, in some sense, what is possible under the circumstances) may not be genuine and, in any case, are fragile things that the perfectionist tendency to round out the implications of one's own terminology can overwhelm.

References

2012 presidential election. (2012, November 29). *Politico*. Retrieved from http://www.politico.com/2012-election/map/#/House/2012/

Abdullah, H. (2013, July 18). In conservative states, abortion pushback with an eye toward Roe v. Wade. CNN. Retrieved from http://www.cnn.com/2013/07/18/politics/states-abortion

Akin, T. (2008, January 22). Speech–House of Representatives. Retrieved from http://www.c--spanvideo.org/clip/4001030

Barbour, H. (2012, January 25). Barbour to GOP: Shape up. *CBS News*. New York: CBS. Retrieved from http://www.cbsnews.com/8301-505263_162-57565806/barbour-to-gop-shape-up/

Burke, K. (1966). *Language as symbolic action: Essays on life, literature, and method*. Berkeley: University of California Press.

Burke, K. (1968). *Counter-statement* (2nd ed.). Berkeley: University of California Press.

Burke, K. (1969). *A grammar of motives*. Berkeley: University of California Press.

DeMint, J. (2013, June 30). *Meet the Press*. New York, NY: NBC. Retrieved from http://www.nbcuni.com/corporate/newsroom/meet-the-press-clips-transcript-sunday-june-30-2013/

Filipovic, J. (2012, October 25). The real Republican rape platform. *The Guardian*. Retrieved from http://www.guardian.co.uk

Friess, F. (2012, February 16). Foster Friess: Aspirin for contraceptives. *Andrea Mitchell Reports*. New York, NY: MSNBC. Retrieved from http://video.msnbc.msn.com/andrea-mitchell/46417914#46417914

Gold, R. B., & Nash, E. (2013). TRAP laws gain political traction while abortion clinics–and the women they serve–pay the price. *Guttmacher Policy Review, 16*(2), 7–12.

Griffin, L. M. (1952). The rhetoric of historical movements. *Quarterly Journal of Speech, 38,* 184–188.

Griffin, L. M. (1969). A dramatistic theory of the rhetoric of movements. In W. H. Rueckert (Ed.), *Critical Responses to Kenneth Burke* (pp. 456–478). Minneapolis: University of Minnesota Press.

Griffin, L. M. (1984). When dreams collide: Rhetorical trajectories in the assassination of President Kennedy. *Quarterly Journal of Speech, 70,* 111–131.

Helderman, R. S., & O'Keefe, E. (2013, January 17). House GOP told to stop talking about rape. *The Washington Post.* [Web log message]. Retrieved from http://www.washingtonpost.com/blogs/post-politics/wp/2013/01/17/house-gop-told-to-stop-talking-about-rape/

House passes bill restricting abortions. (2013, June 19). *Omaha World-Herald,* p. 6A.

Jaco, C. (2012, August 19). Jaco report: Full interview with Todd Akin. *Fox 2 Now.* KTVI. St. Louis, MO: Fox. Retrieved from http://fox2now.com/2012/08/19/the-jaco-report-august-19-2012

Kane, P., & Henderson, N. (2012, August 20). National GOP pulls funding from Todd Akin's Missouri race. *The Washington Post.* Retrieved from http://www.washingtonpost.com

Lake, R. A. (1984). Order and disorder in anti-abortion rhetoric: A logological view. *Quarterly Journal of Speech, 70,* 425–443.

Lake, R. A. (1986). The metaethical framework of anti-abortion rhetoric. *Signs: Journal of Women in Culture and Society, 11,* 478–499.

Lavender, P. (2012, November 13). Bobby Jindal: GOP should stop being "the stupid party." *The Huffington Post.* Retrieved from http://www.huffingtonpost.com

Limbaugh, R. (2012, March 1). Tell Issa to Condemn Cummings. Retrieved from http://www.RushLimbaugh.com

McDonough, K. (2013, May 30). Fox News: Rise of female breadwinners will destroy society as we know it. Retrieved from http://www.salon.com/2013/05/30/fox_news_rise_of_female_breadwinners_will_destroy_society_as_we_know_it/

Maddow, R. (2012, November 7). *The Rachel Maddow Show.* New York, NY: MSNBC. Retrieved from http://video.msnbc.msn.com/the-rachel-maddow-show/4973643

North Carolina Gov. McCrory signs abortion bill. (2013, July 7). Retrieved from http://www.fayob-server.com

Personhood USA calls on Romney to back Akin in support of GOP platform. (2012, August 22). Retrieved from http://www.personhoodusa.com/news/personhood-usa-calls -romney-back-akin -support-gop-platform

Priebus, R. (2012, August 20). GOP chair: Akin should drop out, skip convention. *Erin Burnett Outfront.* Atlanta, GA: CNN. Retrieved from http://politicalticker.blogs.cnn.com/2012/08/20/gop-chair-akin-should-drop-out-skip-convention/

Raju, M. (2012, October 23). Richard Mourdock under fire for rape remarks. *On Congress: Reporting and Analysis of Capitol Hill.* Retrieved from http://www.politico.com

Rape and pregnancy controversies in United States elections, 2012. (2012). Retrieved from http://en.wikipedia.org./wiki/Legitimate_rape#Todd_Akin:_22legitimate_rape.22

Republicans file "fetal heartbeat" abortion ban, as early as 6 weeks. (2013, July 18). [Web log message]. Retrieved from http://blog.chron.com

Rove, K. (2012, October 31). Sifting the numbers for a winner. Retrieved from http://online.wsj.com

S. 47. (2013, March 7). Violence Against Women Reauthorization Act of 2013. Retrieved from http://www.govtrack.us/congress/bills/113/s47

Siegel, J. (2013, July 1). Kasich signs budget, but veto keeps alive Medicaid expansion. *The Columbus Dispatch.* Retrieved from http://www.dispatch.com

Taking a stand. (2013, February 19). *Omaha World Herald,* p. 5A.

Texas lawmakers reconvene; thousands rally. (2013, July 2). *Omaha World-Herald,* p. 3A.

28

100 MILLION BUTTONS CAN'T BE WRONG

Argument in political pinback buttons

Arnie Madsen

MAD CAT ANTIQUES, USA

John Fritch

UNIVERSITY OF NORTHERN IOWA, USA

At the outset of the U.S. Republic, presidential candidates did not "run" for office. Instead, the office sought them. Early presidential memorabilia was commemorative, focusing on an inauguration, a presidential term, or items mourning a former president (Hake, 1992, p.6; Warda, 1996, p. 13). Not until the 1828 election rematch between Andrew Jackson and John Quincy Adams did candidates begin actively to campaign for the presidency (Hake, 1992, pp. iv, 6). This led to items designed to demonstrate candidates' availability and suitability for office, the causes they would support, and their opponents' inferiority (Sullivan, 1980, p. vii).

Analysis of presidential campaigns generally ignores these items used by candidates, instead focusing on speeches, platforms, and advertisements (Fischer, 1988, p. vii). We broaden the examination of presidential campaign argument, focusing on political pinback buttons.[1] We first discuss the main types of political pinbacks; second, we examine the strategies and functions of the political button; finally, we draw conclusions about the use of buttons in campaigns and their broader role in political argument. Specifically, we argue that buttons play an important role in the creation of identification between voters, candidates, and issues. We also suggest that studies of buttons may provide insight into how meaning is created in Internet memes.

Types of Pinback Buttons

Before the 1896 election, there were no political pinback buttons. Three patents in the 1890s allowed the development of pinbacks, a device involving a piece of paper covered with celluloid, and held in place on a metal frame by a collet and pin (Hake, 1992, p. 7; Warda, 1996, p. 9). Pinback buttons, attached to one's clothing by a pin that is part of the button, are thus different from clothing buttons, which are sewn onto a garment. Over 1000 different pinback

Woodrow Wilson
D - 1912 / 1916

Calvin Coolidge
R - 1924

Theodore Roosevelt
R - 1904

James Cox
D - 1920

Dwight Eisenhower
R - 1952 / 1956

Richard Nixon
R - 1960

Barry Goldwater
R - 1964

Jimmy Carter - D - 1980

Robert F. Kennedy
D - 1968 Hopeful

Richard Nixon
R - 1960

Eugene McCarthy
D - 1968 Hopeful

Jerry Brown - D - 1976 Hopeful

Robert F. Kennedy
D - 1968 Hopeful

William McKinley
R - 1900

Richard Nixon
R - 1968

Adlai Stevenson
D - 1956

Barack Obama
D - 2012

John F. Kennedy
D - 1960

Al Gore
D - 2000

Dwight Eisenhower
R - 1952 / 1956

Harold Stassen - R - 1968 Hopeful

William Jennings Bryan - D - 1896 / 1900 / 1908
Iowa Dairy Cream Separator on Reverse

Dwight Eisenhower - R - 1952 / 1956

designs were used in the 1896 presidential campaign (Fischer, 1988, p. 145), as buttons "became primary emblems of personal and party loyalties" (Melder, 1992, pp. 38–39). During WWI, technological advances led to the development of lithographed buttons, where images and text are printed directly on a piece of tin (Hake, 1992, p. 7).

Collectors of pinbacks identify three primary forms. First are picture buttons. These use a photograph or illustration. In its most common and basic form, the picture button will feature a single person, such as the candidate running for president or vice president, or a member of their family (Hake, 1992, p. 40). The picture may be accompanied by the name of the candidate (the absence of which seems to be most common during elections around 1900). Beyond the candidate's name, this category of button uses only a very limited number of words, such as "Vote for" or "for President." The candidate picture may be accompanied by patriotic or other symbols, such as a flag or the Statue of Liberty. Picture buttons were the most common form of buttons near the turn of the twentieth century, as the voting public seemed to prefer images over text (Hake, 1992, p. 53; Melder, 1992, p. 130).

A variation of the picture button is known as the *jugate*. These again use candidate images, but jugates picture two people (Hake, 1992, p. 33; Warda, 1996, p. 10). Jugates may picture the candidates for president and vice president, the candidate and a family member, or a presidential candidate and the candidate for another office. In the latter case, the candidates for other offices are running on the coattails of the presidential ticket (Hake, 1992, p. 47). As with single picture buttons, jugates may include the names of the candidates, contain brief statements, or feature evocative symbols.

The final, and least common, variation of the picture button are *multigates*, those featuring the images of three or more candidates. A *trigate* is when three candidates appear, while four candidates would be a *quadragate*. Buttons picturing more than four candidates are simply referred to as multigates (Warda, 1996, p. 10). Multigates are again a strategy where other candidates run on the coattails of the presidential candidate (Hake, 1992, p. 47; Warda, 1996, p. 105). Other features of the picture button, such as names and symbols, may appear on multigate examples.

Pinback collectors identify a second type – the name button. Here, the focal point is the name of the candidate(s). A button still is referred to as a name button if it includes a few other words, such as "for President" or "elect." However, a name button does not include a candidate picture. As with picture buttons, name buttons also may include other imagery (Hake, 1992, p. 53). Similar to the photo pinbacks discussed earlier, name buttons may feature one or more names.

Slogans are the third form of pinbacks. The most basic slogan button uses a catchy phrase to draw the attention of voters (Hake, 1992, p. 59). Familiar slogans from the past include Eisenhower's "I Like Ike," or Nixon's "Click with Dick." Political collectors, however, broadly refer to any type of issue pinback as a slogan button. Thus, slogan buttons involve those featuring issue stands supported by a candidate (such as taxation or defense) and the support of a candidate from various groups. Slogan buttons may use the picture of a candidate and also a candidate's name.

Argumentative Strategies of Political Buttons

The first argumentative strategy of political pinbacks is telling the electorate who the candidate is, communicating "tangible evidence of the personalities of leaders," and offering "vivid, appealing, and dynamic depictions of the people who compete for our loyalties" (Melder, 1992, p. 21). At its most basic, this strategy serves to "tell the story" of the candidate, including elements like the candidate's background, family, and professional achievements. For instance, in 1964, a button with the word "Goldwater" inside an arrow pointing to the right shows that his core vision was conservative, wanting to move the nation to the political right. A picture of Robert Kennedy superimposed over the silhouette of John suggests Robert would follow his brother's ideals.

Second, candidates provide arguments regarding campaign issues. "At its best" a button condenses "the barest essence of the central themes and appeals expressed in infinitely greater detail in platforms, position papers, and stump speeches" (Fischer, 1988, p. 304). A candidate might favor an end to war, changes in economic policy, or increased funding for education. The issue discussion might be as simple as McCarthy's "Peace Equality" from 1968, or, like Jerry Brown's 1976 button featuring three bullets points, it might provide a more detailed listing of the candidate or party platform. A visual image might also be used, such as the peace sign formed from the letters RFK in 1968 (Kennedy would seek peace in Southeast Asia) or McKinley's button with the image of a "full dinner bucket" from 1900 (reelecting McKinley would result in broader prosperity than would electing Bryan).

Third, political buttons may emphasize political party, trying to generate party loyalty. "By wearing campaign buttons, loyalists could easily announce their partisan and candidate preferences. . . . In the heat of campaigns, candidate images portrayed on buttons often became the embodiments of partisan affection, bearers of party traditions and virtues" (Melder, 1992, p. 39). Here, the candidates explicitly tie themselves to their party, by referencing the party on the button. The party is not an afterthought that appears in small print or a footnote; it is a central feature. For example, Nixon in 1968 turns a stylized GOP elephant into a map of the United States. Third parties prominently feature the party name on their pinbacks as they try especially to foster party loyalty and allegiance to the platform.

Fourth, buttons create affinities with other groups. Buttons declare "Students for Stevenson," "Students for Stassen for Peace," "Young Americans for Obama," and "Senior Citizens for [John] Kennedy." The AFSCME insignia centered on a button with the words "Gore 2000" around the outer edge demonstrates union endorsement, and "Vets for Ike" suggests support for General Eisenhower. Even products have been used to support presidential candidates, attempting to create favor with the consumers using those products. For example, a William Jennings Bryan button from the turn of the twentieth century features product advertising for the Iowa Cream Separator on its reverse.

Fifth, political buttons may enhance one's campaign by attacking the opposition. Although attacks are not inevitable in campaigns, they are common across U.S. electoral history (Melder, 1992, p. 46). Often "disguised as humor and caricature," negative campaign tactics are deployed to belittle opponents or their ideas, raise doubts about their competence or integrity, or enhance one's own campaign (Melder, 1992, p. 34). In 1940, Willkie loyalists created an extensive series of buttons attacking Roosevelt for various policies, minor scandals, and so on (the title of this paper uses the words from one of these buttons; Hake, 1974, p. 160). Adlai Stevenson was once photographed wearing a shoe with a hole in its bottom. Stevenson attempted to capitalize on this by arguing the hole demonstrated his frugality. Eisenhower tried to turn this against the Democrats with a button featuring a shoe with a hole and the words, "Don't let this happen to you," suggesting Stevenson would cause an economic downturn in which consumers could not afford new shoes.

Conclusions

First, candidates and their campaign structures use buttons and other argumentative strategies to create identification between candidates and the electorate. Burke (1950/1969) suggests identification is created when the interests of people are joined, or when they believe their interests are joined. This merging of interests often is created through repetition of common and daily activities: "We must think of rhetoric not in terms of some one particular address, but as a general *body of identifications* that owe their convincingness much more to trivial repetition and dull daily reinforcement than to exceptional rhetorical skill" (p. 26). With pinbacks, convincingness can be attributed to the commonality of the buttons. Members of the electorate might be persuaded to the extent that the more frequently pinbacks are seen (and seen on a variety of people in a variety of locations), the more common they become. For Burke, this type of repetition and reinforcement are critical factors in the creation of identification.

Identification, for Burkean scholars, is typically seen as occurring between people, focusing on the joining of interests. However, we see identification as happening not only with other people but also with ideas, causes, and political parties. Campaign use of picture and name buttons attempts to create identification with the actual candidate, while slogan and issue buttons create identification with the candidate's positions. Burke (1950/1969, 1937/1984) hints at this possibility of identification between humans and inanimate objects, including the mysticisms of religion, sex, money, crime, drugs, war, corporations, and nations. But, how does this identification take place? The person wearing the button may be the "vessel" allowing for identification with an inanimate object or idea (Burke, 1973/1941, p. 39). In Burke's conception of redemption, the scapegoat serves as a vessel for the redemption of the sinner and allows for reidentification. We suggest that a vessel (or body) can be rethought as providing a basis for identification between a person and an idea or larger group.

At their core, buttons become "shorthand for attitudes and emotions . . . intended to simplify, to soothe and reinforce the party faithful" (Melder, 1992, p. 52). Potential voters can identify with the candidate or the ideas underlying the campaign. Robert Kennedy's pinback featuring his initials in the shape of a peace symbol may have created as much identification for his followers with the anti-war movement as it did with Kennedy himself. While political identification is not limited to the use of pinbacks, identification via buttons seems to be a common enactment of this argument form:

> Buttons make a difference when they personalize a candidate's appeal, trumping ideologies and party lines. Think of Mr. Obama's use of the single word "Hope" or "Yes We Can" in 2008. When someone wears a button like that he [sic] believes he is having an impact on American history larger than a single vote – and he may be right.
>
> *(Fleming, 2012, p. A17)*

When used, buttons (like other forms of advocacy) might help to "stimulate emotions and sensations that are quite diverse, ranging from patriotism to cynicism" (Franklin, 1972, p. 9). While Barack Obama used slogans in a variety of forms throughout the 2008 campaign (speeches, posters, advertisements, etc.), the simple appearance of those phrases on buttons may have helped people identify with a larger connection to U.S. history.

Third, studies of pinbacks may help scholars understand the development of Internet memes and visual argumentation. While memes have been examined as cultural artifacts and in genetics, people using the phrase *Internet meme* seem to borrow little more than the word from such studies. The Urban Dictionary defined *Internet meme* as: "A short phrase, picture, or combination of the two that gets repeated in message boards and Barrens chat for far, far longer than anything ever ought to be" (Internet meme, n.d). A less cynical definition may be that an Internet meme is a viral form of communication in which either the visual or linguistic element of the communication is constant, but the remainder of the communication varies. Memes have been identified as an important part of visual argument (Hahner,

2013). While the study of Internet memes can contribute to an understanding of how meaning and argument are created, the study of Internet memes is in its infancy.

Here, recall the Internet memes of Secretary of State Hillary Clinton texting in dark sunglasses, found on TextsfromHillary.tumblr.com. Thousands created their own versions of this meme. However, each variation depended on the same image of a Clinton wearing sunglasses and texting while aboard a military transport. Pinbacks may function similarly to contemporary Internet memes. The constant in the pinback meme is the button. What changes is how the pinback is deployed – the person who wears it, the combination with other pinbacks on a lapel or bag. Or the variation could be in the use of words or images on a button as the various Willkie buttons demonstrate.

Much as the Internet meme relies on replication of a specific visual or textual component, the pinback depends on constancy for its success. Although campaigns feature numerous pinbacks, the success of an individual button – whether name, image, or slogan – depends on voters' ability to recognize and understand the constancy of the meme. A significant portion of the power of the pinback (and of the Internet meme) occurs when the reader views the constant element in multiple contexts. The power of the pinback is increased as the audience recognizes the pinback in different locations. After a time, the button is recognized instantly and the audience's attention is directed toward the uniqueness, rather than the constancy, of the meme. Similarly, the power of an Internet meme increases as the meme becomes widely recognized. (The Clinton texting meme was so widely spread that Maureen Dowd [2012] wrote a *New York Times* column focusing on it, and Hillary Clinton even contributed her own version.)

Fourth, this brief analysis only begins to study campaign use of pinbacks. Several lines of inquiry could enhance our understanding of pinbacks as political campaign arguments. For example, while buttons might increase understanding of Internet memes, it is possible that study of Internet memes can lend insight to the use of argument in political buttons. Consider the 1940 Willkie slogan buttons. Even though the basic design of the button remained the same (like the essential unchanging picture in the Clinton meme), the specific text changed from button to button, leaving the audience (voters) to wonder what the next Willkie "meme" would be.

We also could examine pinbacks from a traditional perspective. What implications are there for an argument form when there is essentially a claim presented without a warrant? How is electoral meaning constructed within this enthymematic system? Or, how does Burke's (1931) notion of form, especially repetitive form, fit with political pinbacks? The essential nature of pinbacks remains unchanged from their inception in 1896 to 2013. The types of pinbacks are stable across time, as are the overall argument strategies employed in buttons. Can Burke's discussion of form lend additional insight for the argument scholar?

Finally, we cannot claim that pinback buttons in themselves had an impact on actual voting in a specific election:

> It has never been argued . . . that the campaign ephemera produced for presidential hopefuls ever proved a decisive factor at the polls. On the other hand . . . the surviving memorabilia from White House contests can on occasion offer a vividly graphic reflection of the electioneering strategies that caused one to win and another to fail.
>
> *(Voss, 1984, pp. 14–15)*

Pointing to pinbacks as a reason for election victory or defeat would be a difficult task (Fischer, 1988, p. 302). We can argue, however, that pinbacks are symbols of the arguments in a particular election and voter involvement with these arguments. Pinbacks condense "the central themes and appeals expressed in infinitely greater detail in platforms, position papers, and stump speeches" (Fischer, 1988, p. 304) and are some of the most "tangible remains" of presidential campaigns (Melder, 1992, p. 8).

Note

1. All buttons pictured and discussed in this essay are from the personal collection of the first author, and are original buttons, not reproductions. A specific election is noted if we are certain of the attribution. Otherwise, multiple election years may be indicated. At the Conference we examined a number of each type of pinback, but due to space limitations, only a representative example of each form is included here.

References

Burke, K. (1931). *Counter-statement*. New York, NY: Harcourt.
Burke, K. (1969). *A rhetoric of motives*. Berkeley: University of California Press. (Original work published 1950)
Burke, K. (1973). *The philosophy of literary form: Studies in symbolic action*. Berkeley: University of California Press. (Original work published 1941)
Burke, K. (1984). *Attitudes toward history* (3rd ed.). Berkeley: University of California Press. (Original work published 1937)
Dowd, M. (2012, April 10). State of cool. *New York Times*. Retrieved from http://www.nytimes.com
Fischer, R. (1988). *Tippecanoe and trinkets too: The material culture of American presidential campaigns 1828–1984*. Urbana: University of Illinois Press.
Fleming, T. (2012, September 25). How presidential politics fastened onto buttons. *Wall Street Journal*, p. A17.
Franklin, J. (1972). Introduction. In T. Hake, *The button book: An illustrated price guide to 5000 pinback buttons issued from 1896–1972 including listings of buttons issued as sets* (2nd ed., pp. 8–11). New York, NY: Dafron House.

Hahner, L. A. (2013). The riot kiss: Framing memes as visual argument. *Argumentation and Advocacy, 49*, 151–166.

Hake, T. (1974). *Encyclopedia of political buttons: United States 1896–1972.* New York, NY: Dafron House.

Hake, T. (1992). *Hake's guide to presidential campaign collectibles: An illustrated price guide to artifacts from 1789–1988.* Radnor, PA: Wallace-Homestead.

Internet meme. (n.d.). *Urban dictionary.* Retrieved from http://www.urbandictionary.com

Melder, K. (1992). *Hail to the candidate: Presidential campaigns from banners to broadcasts.* Washington, DC: Smithsonian Institution Press.

Sullivan, E. (1980). *Collecting political Americana.* New York, NY: Crown.

Voss, F. (1984). Packaging Presidents. In Hudson River Museum, *Packaging presidents: Memorabilia from campaigns past* (pp. 7–21). Yonkers, NY: Hudson River Museum.

Warda, M. (1996). *100 years of political campaign collectibles.* Clearwater, FL: Galt Press.

29

"THE REVOLUTION MUST CONTINUE"

Strategic maneuvering in post-Mubarak Egypt

Dima Mohammed

UNIVERSIDADE NOVA DE LISBOA, PORTUGAL

Public political arguments in Egypt, since the revolution started there in early 2011, are fascinating. They are intense, daring, and critical, reflecting the prominent revolutionary mood: Nothing is beyond challenge and everything needs to be re-considered. They are also heated and growing increasingly polarized, in a clear indication of the challenges Egyptians are facing and the transformations they are going through. Under the influence of the revolutionary mood, typical characteristics of public political arguments get intensified: Arguers find themselves discussing several issues at the same time and using arguments as discursive means to disturb existing power relationships and structures.

The need to address several issues at the same time, clearly present in Egypt, is common practice in public political argument. Public political arguments are open to participants who have different interests and needs as well as different commitments and positions. Also, participants in public political arguments fulfill different roles with which several different goals can be associated. In order to achieve their goals and to appeal to their heterogeneous audiences, arguers address multiple issues at the same time and craft their arguments strategically so that their position in relation to each of the issues they address is supported.

In order to capture the strategic aspect of argumentative moves that are crafted to address several issues at the same time, an argumentative exchange in which several issues are addressed can be reconstructed as a series of several "simultaneous discussions," each of which is about one of the issues (Mohammed, 2011, 2013b). A discussion, here, is of course not to be understood in the actual sense of a real life exchange that takes place in a specific time and place. Rather, it is a dialectical analytic reconstruction of a discussion, defined in terms of a standpoint and the argumentation advanced in support of it. Two or more discussions that are reconstructed as simultaneous can happen in one and the same real-life exchange. Two or more discussions are considered simultaneous if there is at least one argument, or one argumentative move, that plays a role in more than one discussion, without any of the discussions being subordinate to the other. The reconstruction of one exchange as several simultaneous discussions is meant to capture the specific role that a particular argumentative move plays in the discussion of each of the issues addressed without missing the implications this has for the other issues.

In this essay, I analyze the discursive choices of an Egyptian politician as he crafts his arguments to addresses several issues simultaneously. In the analysis, the concept of *strategic maneuvering* is central. Van Eemeren and Houtlosser (1999) coined the term to refer to arguers' attempts to get their points of view accepted within the boundaries of reasonableness. In order to strike the balance between reasonableness and effectiveness, arguers can be expected to make strategic choices in every move they make. In every move, they make expedient choices from the topical potential available to them, adapt their contributions optimally to the expectations and demands of their audiences, and use the most effective presentational devices in presenting their standpoints and arguments. The topical selection, audience adaptation, and presentational devices are three aspects of strategic maneuvering that are inseparable in practice, but analytically can be distinguished in order to refine the characterization of the strategic function that an argumentative move fulfills (van Eemeren, 2010, p. 93). Taking these three aspects into account when analyzing argumentative moves helps the analyst highlight the specific strategic choices that arguers make in the course of their attempts to reach outcomes that are favorable to them.

A "Letter of Love to the Ikhwan Youth"

The text I analyze was written by Hamdeen Sabahy, a prominent Egyptian revolutionary leader, during the second round of the Egyptian presidential elections of 2012. Sabahy, a long-time opposition activist, was one of the candidates in the first round of the elections. He received 20.74% of the votes, coming third after Mohammed Morsi, the candidate of the Muslim Brotherhood who received 24.78%, and Ahmed Shafiq, the last prime minister under Mubarak who received 23.66%. The scheduling of a second round of elections, in which the two frontrunners would compete, triggered protests and intensified the already heated public discussion. On the one hand, it was difficult to believe that Mubarak's last prime minister could become the president of the post-revolution Egypt. On the other hand, many were growing uneasy with what they saw as the Muslim Brotherhood's pursuit to hegemonize power; at that time, the Muslim Brotherhood had already become a majority in both houses of Parliament and they had a majority in the Constituent Assembly. Many were unhappy with the growing polarization of the political scene between ex-regime loyalists and Muslim Brotherhood supporters, a polarization that was being emphasized by the elections where only candidates of these two currents were represented. While, for some, things became clear – the candidate of the revolution (Morsi) was running against the candidate of the ex-regime (Shafiq) – for many others, things were not so simple. Sabahy's letter, which was announced as a "letter of love to the Ikhwan youth" (the youth of the Muslim Brotherhood), was penned in the middle of all that. It was first published on the official website of his campaign (Sabahy, 2012) and was republished in major newspapers and news sites. It then went viral on social networks and triggered much discussion.

In the letter, Sabahy addressed three main issues.[1] First, he defended his credibility as a revolutionary activist and a political leader, arguing that *I, Sabahy, am a credible leader of the revolution (standpoint 1)*. This was necessary because he was attacked by activists from the Muslim Brotherhood who saw his reluctance to express support for their candidate as a sign of betraying the revolution. The standpoint, as such, was not explicitly expressed, but the arguments that support it cannot be missed. Second, Sabahy addressed the issue of the vote in the second round, arguing that *One should neither vote for Morsi nor for Shafiq (standpoint 2)*. Many, especially his supporters, were waiting for his advice concerning this issue. The advice was not presented in a straightforward manner, though. Sabahy did not express his main standpoint about the vote explicitly. Instead, he argued that *One should not vote for Morsi* (*sub-standpoint 2.1a*) and that *One should not vote for Shafiq* (*sub-standpoint 2.1b*). The analysis to follow shows that leaving the main standpoint about the vote implicit was a strategic choice Sabahy employed to maintain credibility. Third, Sabahy addressed a much broader issue, namely the issue of the revolution in general, arguing that *The revolution must continue* (*standpoint 3*). Sabahy was not the only one to do that. Many voices were at the time re-assessing the revolution and its outcome and discussing the possible next steps. It is interesting to observe that this standpoint was the only one that Sabahy made explicit. This, as the analysis to follow shows, was a strategic choice that allowed him to remain ambiguous when clarity was to his disadvantage.

Strategic Maneuvering in Simultaneous Discussions

Sabahy's two sub-standpoints about the vote reframed the elections debate. Reframing the debate is a common strategic maneuver in political argumentation (Zarefsky, 2008, p. 324). In the case analyzed, the debate was reframed from being about the question of *"Who should become president, Morsi or Shafiq?"* to the question of *"What should Egyptians do in relation to the second round of elections?"* The first question was institutionally set by the electoral system that requires voters in Egypt to choose between two candidates. It enhanced the polarization of the political scene and the dichotomization of the public debate between Muslim Brotherhood supporters and ex-regime loyalists. The second question, raised by Sabahy and other revolutionaries, was an attempt to de-dichotomize the public debate (Dascal, 2008) by extending the range of choices available beyond the two rivals. Two alternative courses of action, called on by political groups and activists, became particularly important: the call on Egyptians to invalidate their votes and the call to boycott the elections altogether.

Sabahy's reframing of the debate redefined the argumentative dispute as a qualitatively multiple one. A *qualitatively multiple dispute* arises when discussants express contrary standpoints (van Eemeren, Houtlosser & Snoeck Henkemans, 2007, p. 22–24, 57). In the qualitatively multiple dispute about the second round of the elections, at least four main contrary standpoints can be identified: *One should vote for Morsi* (+/p1), *One should vote for Shafiq* (+/p2), *One should invalidate his/her vote* (+/p3), and *One should boycott the elections* (+/p4). Re-framing the disagreement as a qualitatively multiple dispute was advantageous to Sabahy as it allowed him to express opposition to standpoints expressed by his opponents without advancing any (positive) standpoint of his own or clearly expressing his position concerning other standpoints in the debate.

In a qualitatively multiple dispute, commitment to one of the standpoints entails commitment to the opposite of the other contrary standpoints. So, for example, if an arguer defends that *One should vote for Morsi* (+/p1), the arguer can be held committed to *One should not vote for Shafiq* (−/p2), *One should not invalidate his/her vote* (−/p3), and *One should not boycott the elections* (−/p4). However, in this type of dispute, opposition to one standpoint does not necessarily entail any commitment to any other contrary one. So, one can be opposed to *One should vote for Morsi* (i.e., express −/p1) without being committed to One *should vote for Shafiq* (+/p2), *One should invalidate his/her vote* (+/p3), or *One should boycott the elections* (+/p4). Framing the disagreement as a qualitatively multiple dispute allowed Sabahy to do exactly that: to argue against the standpoint that *One should vote for Morsi* (i.e., argue that *One should not vote for Morsi*, −/p1) and against the standpoint that *One should vote for Shafiq* (i.e., argue that *One should not vote for Shafiq*, −/p2), without committing himself to anything concerning whether or not *One should invalidate his/her vote* (+/p3) and whether or not *One should boycott the elections* (+/p4).

The ambiguity in Sabahy's position was strategic (Eisenberg, 1984). It was purposefully used to save Sabahy from an unfavorable position. Supporting the standpoint that *One should invalidate one's vote* (+/p3) would have committed Sabahy to participate in the elections, which is something he would rather avoid mainly because he had just publicly asked for alternative measures (namely the presidential council). Similarly, supporting the standpoint that *One should boycott the elections* (+/p4) would have committed him to challenging the legitimacy of the elections, which he would rather not do openly for he would risk being accused of being involved in the elections when he had a chance of winning and going against them after he had lost. Furthermore, by not taking any clear position, either in favor of invalidating one's vote or in favor of boycotting the elections, Sabahy could remain on the same side together with those who thought that Egyptians should invalidate their votes as well as those who thought that Egyptians should boycott the elections altogether. In other words, it allowed him to put himself on the same side with a greater number of revolutionaries than he would have been able to had he expressed a clear position. (Out of the 51 million Egyptian registered voters, 27.3 million did not vote. Out of the 23.6 million who voted, there were 12.4 million voters who did not vote for either Shafiq or Morsi.) This was obviously very useful for Sabahy in the discussion about his credibility. Thanks to this ambiguity, Sabahy could avoid a challenge from the many Egyptian youth, whom he claimed to represent, from different ideological affiliations.

Sabahy's choice to leave implicit his main standpoint about the vote was clearly a strategic choice. If Sabahy had taken the explicit standpoint that *One should neither vote for Morsi nor for Shafiq*, he would have conveyed a challenge to the legitimacy of the electoral system and undermined his credibility. However, Sabahy could not just avoid commitment to the challenge of the legitimacy of the elections by leaving his standpoint implicit. One of the main arguments that he expressed in the letter was that *Neither Morsi nor Shafiq represents the depoliticized and defends their rights and interests*. This argument could very easily be understood as a support to a standpoint like *The elections are illegitimate* and Sabahy would have been considered committed to it, even without explicitly advancing it. In order to make sure that he was not committed to such a standpoint, Sabahy introduced another standpoint that could be supported by the argument that *Neither Morsi nor Shafiq represents the depoliticized and defends their rights and interests*. He explicitly argued that *The political process is not delivering satisfactory outcomes*, and, therefore, *The revolution must continue*. By making the standpoint about the revolution explicit, and bringing it up early in the introductory paragraph of the letter, Sabahy gave prominence to the issue of the revolution, hoping to make the issue of the vote seem secondary. The latter could help him avoid undesirable commitments in relation to the elections.

It is important to realize that it was necessary for Sabahy to explicitly advance a standpoint that can be supported by the argument that *Neither Morsi nor Shafiq represents the depoliticized and defends their rights and interests*. That is to say that he could not have just left the argument without a standpoint that is explicitly advanced, which is something quite common and unproblematic in argumentative discourse. That is because without such an explicitly advanced standpoint, Sabahy would have had (even more) difficulty avoiding the commitment to the standpoint that *The elections are illegitimate* and he would have, consequently, had even more difficulty keeping his position consistent. So, eventually, Sabahy's strategic maneuvering in the discussion about the revolution, namely his choice to explicitly advance the standpoint that *The revolution must continue*, was necessary for his strategic ambiguity in the discussion about the vote to work.

Concluding Remarks

Sabahy maneuvered strategically in between the three issues he addressed. He reframed the argument by de-dichotomizing the elections debate and turning the disagreement about the vote into a qualitatively multiple dispute in which he could afford to remain ambiguous about the question of how to vote. On the one hand, his ambiguity about the vote was necessary for his claim about his own credibility to remain supported. On the other hand, this ambiguity could not have been maintained without addressing the issue of the revolution. Only by making the issue of the revolution the main issue and taking an explicit position about it could he afford to remain ambiguous about the vote and credible in the eyes of his audience.

My analysis of Sabahy's letter shows how what is typical of public political argument, namely addressing multiple issues simultaneously, can become, in revolutionary times, the means to disturb power relations and structures. Sabahy's de-dichotomization of the elections debate would probably not have been as effective in other non-revolutionary times where political institutions are well-established and much harder to challenge. In revolutionary times, where political culture is being reshaped and institutions are being re-built, it becomes possible, if not necessary, to disturb existing power relations and structures. Resorting to claims about the need to *Continue the revolution until its goals are achieved* is particularly powerful in these contexts.

In the Egyptian case, the attempt to de-dichotomize public political arguments and de-polarize the political scene is particularly significant. It reflects a persistent will to create an alternative political current between the Muslim Brotherhood and the ex-regime loyalists. This is still the case, now, one year after the letter analyzed above. Morsi won the second round with a narrow margin (he received 51.8% of the votes and Shafiq received 48.2%). The Muslim Brotherhood's pursuit of hegemonizing power continued, which fuelled continuous popular protests. The protests culminated in the army intervening and removing Morsi from power, one year after he became the first elected president in Egypt. The Muslim Brotherhood and the ex-regime loyalists continue their efforts to polarize the political scene, but there remain strong voices not giving in to this and determined to lead Egypt towards a pluralistic rather than a bi-polar political culture.

My analysis of Sabahy's letter does not provide insights into the Egyptian political scene only. After all, the strategic discursive choices it highlights can be made by any politicians who are addressing multiple issues simultaneously. My analysis shows that the desirable outcomes pursued by certain argumentative choices made by the arguer are not necessarily restricted to the discussion of one issue only. This can be thought as only natural in discourses that address several issues simultaneously. Because, in such discourses, argumentative moves are typically meant to contribute to the discussion of more than one issue at a time, the strategic maneuvering involved in designing them similarly involves the pursuit of desirable effects in relation to the several issues addressed. An important dimension of the strategic design would be lost if the discussions of the different issues were analyzed independently without capturing the strategic maneuvering that occurs between them. The proposal to reconstruct the discourse as a series of simultaneous discussions is meant to prevent this shortcoming, in particular. By analyzing arguers' strategic maneuvering as occurring in between multiple discussions, the choices that are strategic across issues can be highlighted and a more refined analysis of the discourse can be offered.

Note

1. The identification of these issues is based on a detailed argumentative analysis of Sabahy's letter, in which his standpoints and arguments were reconstructed. An English translation of Sabahy's letter, which was published in Arabic, and an elaborate analysis of it can be found in Mohammed (2013a).

References

Dascal, M. (2008) Dichotomies and types of debate. In F. H. van Eemeren & B. Garssen (Eds.), *Controversy and confrontation: Relating controversy analysis with argumentation theory* (pp. 27–49). Amsterdam, NL: John Benjamins.

van Eemeren, F. H. (2010). *Strategic maneuvering in argumentative discourse: Extending the pragma-dialectical theory of argumentation.* Amsterdam, NL: John Benjamins.

van Eemeren, F.H., & Houtlosser, P. (1999). Strategic manoeuvring in argumentative discourse. *Discourse Studies, 1*(4), 479–497.

van Eemeren, F. H., Houtlosser, P., & Snoeck Henkemans, A. F. (2007). *Argumentative indicators in discourse: A pragma-dialectical study.* Dordrecht: Springer Netherlands.

Eisenberg, E. M. (1984). Ambiguity as strategy in organizational communication. *Communication Monographs, 51*, 227–242

Mohammed, D. (2011, May 18–21). Strategic manoeuvring in simultaneous discussions. In F. Zenker (Ed.), *Argumentation: Cognition and Community. Proceedings of the 9th International Conference of the Ontario Society for the Study of Argumentation* (pp. 1–11). Windsor, ON: OSSA.

Mohammed, D. (2013a, January 11–13). Hit two birds with one stone: Strategic manoeuvring in the after-Mubarak era. In A. L. Sellami (Ed.), *Argumentation, Rhetoric, Debate and Pedagogy: Proceedings of the 2013 4th International Conference on Argumentation, Rhetoric, Debate, and Pedagogy* (pp. 95–116). Doha.

Mohammed, D. (2013b). Pursuing multiple goals in European parliamentary debates: EU immigration policies as a case in point. *Journal of Argumentation in Context, 2*(1), 47–74.

Sabahy, H. (2012). Hamdeen Sabahy in a letter to the Ikhwan youth   the official site of Hamdeen Sabahy. Retrieved from http://hamdeensabahy.com/news/[??]/

Zarefsky, D. (2008). Strategic maneuvering in political argumentation. *Argumentation, 22*, 317–330.

30

DISTURBING THE CONVENTIONS OF NATIONAL POLITICAL CONVENTIONS

Crossover addresses and reluctant testimony

Meredith Neville-Shepard

UNIVERSITY OF KANSAS, USA

In 1992, Zell Miller delivered the keynote address at the Democratic National Convention (DNC) in support of Bill Clinton over George Herbert Walker Bush. Twelve years later, he made history as the first politician in modern history to cross over party lines when he delivered the keynote address for the Republican National Convention (RNC). In 2004, and in the exact same location as 1992, Madison Square Garden, Miller endorsed the son of the man he had advocated against in the previous decade. While Democrats bemoaned Miller's choice, Republicans were quite pleased. As Roddy (2004) explained, "Zell Miller [was] a sort of ballistic missile, affixed to the podium of the Republican National Convention and pointed directly at his own party" (p. E1).

Typically, when politicians change their positions (the strongest version of which is to change parties), they are criticized as flip-floppers and their authenticity is called into question. For instance, DeBacker (2008) found that when senators changed their opinions, the "costs to deviating from their past records [was] directly proportional to the size of their change in position" (p. 25). Thus, it would seem logical that few would follow in the footsteps of Miller, whose speech coincided with his exit from politics. However, crossover convention addresses have only become a more regular occurrence since Miller's speech. In 2008, both former Representative James Leach (R-IA) and former Republican mayor Jim Whitaker (of Alaska's Fairbanks North Star Borough) gave speeches at the DNC and former U.S. Senator Joe Lieberman (D-CN) spoke at the RNC. In 2012, former Representative Artur Davis (D-AL) spoke at the RNC and former Republican Florida governor Charlie Crist at the DNC. This trend indicates that, despite the authenticity barrier of being labeled a flip-flopper, something about these speeches is rhetorically powerful enough that politicians are willing to tarnish their political legacy by betraying their entire party.

In this essay, I explore how crossover speakers attempt to bolster their credibility and justify their transition to the new party. I argue that the theory of reluctant testimony provides a window for understanding why these speeches can be particularly persuasive pieces of convention rhetoric. Specifically, I assert that the major strategies these speakers employ revolve around highlighting their reluctance. In other words, crossover speakers are constantly trying to cultivate their credibility by emphasizing that it is actually the consistency of and dedication to their values, which their previous party has abandoned, that has left them no choice but to switch parties. Furthermore, as inside witnesses to the actions of their party, their judgments may be considered more credible, especially to swing voters.

In order to shed light on this unique type of discourse, I begin by elaborating on the connection between reluctant testimony and crossover convention speeches. Based on this connection, I describe the three major rhetorical strategies these speakers generally employ. Second, I analyze the crossover speeches of Miller and Crist as exemplars of this phenomenon. Finally, I end with an evaluation of these speeches and a discussion of implications.

Reluctantly Crossing Over

The importance of the speaker's ethos has always been a central tenet when discussing the success or failure of persuasive discourse. Perelman and Olbrechts-Tyteca (1969) asserted, "The office of a speaker, no less than his [*sic*] person, forms a context which has an undeniable influence" (p. 319). The speaker's identity is of even greater significance when he or she is relying on personal testimony to make an argument. In other words, as Palczewski (2002) argued, "A person's testimony is not the same if repeated by another, and in the very testifying, speakers are asking for others to assent not only to the claims, but also to their existence" (p. 16). The importance of persona in personal testimony is part of what gives crossover addresses the potential to possess great persuasive power. Audiences expect Republicans to speak at the RNC, but when this expectation is violated, people pay attention. A Democrat's personal testimony against the Democratic Party at an RNC carries a special type of authority that Republicans speaking at the RNC could not achieve due to their obvious bias. However, this power may be lost if the audience perceives the crossover speaker as a mere flip-flopper arguing from political expedience rather than from ideological conviction.

One common reason an audience may distrust testimony is because of the perceived bias of the speaker. Benoit and Kennedy (1999) wrote, "A biased source – one who testifies in his or her own selfish interests – should appear suspicious (untrustworthy) to an audience" (p. 380). Conversely, a person who speaks against his or her self-interest, a reluctant testifier, will likely be seen as more trustworthy. Hollihan and Baaske (1994) explained that it is precisely because this type of testimony is "given grudgingly," and "does not serve the motives of the source," that it is perceived as "the most reliable kind" of testimony (p. 104). Furthermore, Benoit and Kennedy (1999) have found empirical evidence that audiences regard reluctant testimony as more trustworthy than biased testimony (p. 385).

Although a crossover speaker is not a true reluctant witness in that he or she voluntarily attends the convention for the express purpose of switching sides, the principle behind what makes reluctant testimony powerful can still apply. Although speakers will most definitely lose the trust of their former party, they can gain the trust of swing voters and rally the base of the party to which they have crossed over. Specifically, they can harness the power of reluctant testimony by depicting themselves as witnesses compelled to speak by their moral principles. Appealing to these two audiences is key in convention rhetoric as two major purposes of the event are to "reach out to undecided voters" and "to solidify [the] political base" (Holloway, 2002, p. 117). This may help to explain why crossover speeches have become more commonplace at recent conventions.

How then does a voluntary speaker go about harnessing the power of reluctant testimony? After analyzing the six crossover speeches that have occurred during the last three presidential election cycles, three major persuasive strategies emerged, all of which partly functioned to emphasize the politicians' reluctance to abandon their parties. First, speakers provided a value-based rationale for switching party allegiance. This rationale was used to illustrate that, in order to remain true to these values, they had no choice but to cross over. It is these values that set up the rest of the speech in which the rhetor provided specific examples of how the previous party violated said values while the candidate of the new party upheld them. Thus, crossover speakers' second strategy was to explain their dissolution from their previous party, and their third tactic was to describe how their new party's candidate was a morally superior alternative. Both of these strategies painted the speakers in a positive light because they implied that, as is true in many cases, the *ethical* choice was not necessarily the *easy* choice.

In order to more clearly illustrate how these strategies were utilized, I analyze Miller's (2004) and Crist's (2012) convention speeches. These two speeches provide a good sample of crossover convention rhetoric for three reasons. First, they span time: Miller was the earliest case and Crist one of the most recent cases. Second, they depict both sides of the political spectrum: Miller spoke at the RNC and Crist at the DNC. Finally, they represent varying intensities: Miller was quite extreme in his condemnation of his former party whereas Crist took a more moderate approach.

Rationale for Switching Sides

Miller (2004) opened his speech by presenting his major reason for switching sides, the value of family. Politics, he argued, "determine what kind of world [children] will grow up in." He even explicitly stated, "My family is more important than my party." The second value Miller appealed to was bi-partisanship. He claimed that Democrats were now "motivated more by partisan politics than by national security" and asked:

> Where is the bi-partisanship in this country when we need it most? Today at the same time young Americans are dying in the sands of Iraq and the mountains of Afghanistan, our nation is being torn apart and made weaker because of the Democrat's manic obsession to bring down our Commander-in-Chief.

Unsurprisingly, bi-partisanship was one of the most popular tropes used by crossover speakers, as they themselves were enacting it. Therefore, describing a lack of bi-partisanship in their speeches not only represented a legitimate value compelling them to switch sides, but also reinforced the notion that, as difficult as it may be, going against the grain of party lines is often necessary for progress.

Crist (2012) discussed the importance of bi-partisanship when recounting advice his father gave him about football. He stated:

> My dad always told me, "Charlie, it takes a cool head to win a hot game." Our country is in the middle of a hot game. We face serious challenges, both at home and abroad. Meanwhile, our politics are defined by discord and discontent.

As evidenced by his willingness to switch sides, Crist embodied the moderation he espoused while also using it as a rationale for crossing over. He exemplified this when he explained, "That's the reason I'm here tonight, not as a Republican, not as a Democrat, but as an optimistic American who understands that we must come together behind the one man who can lead the way forward in these challenging times."

Crist (2012) also emphasized the value of bi-partisanship by quoting Republican icon Ronald Reagan. Crist stated, "Reagan . . . famously said that he didn't leave the Democratic Party; the party left him. I can certainly relate. I didn't leave the Republican Party; it left me." He further appropriated Reagan as a model for justifying his switch by stating, "As my friend Jeb Bush recently noted, Reagan himself would have been too moderate and too reasonable for today's GOP." In comparing his party shift to Reagan's, Crist clearly implied that he did not make an active choice to leave his party. Rather, he argued, they abandoned him, leaving him with little choice but to support the opposing candidate.

Dissolution from the Previous Party

Miller (2004) did not waste much time in his speech before indicting the Democrats and making his dissolution from them quite clear. He posed this question: "What has happened to the Party I've spent my life working in? I can remember when Democrats believed it was the duty of America to fight for freedom over tyranny." Thus, like Crist, Miller tried to bolster his credibility by implying that his party abandoned him, not the other way around.

Miller (2004) continued to angrily criticize his party throughout the speech. He went so far as to warn the Republican Party, "Don't waste your breath telling that to the leaders of my party today. In their warped way of thinking America is the problem, not the solution." Although such a statement may have served to rally the base, it was also a blatant violation of the value of bi-partisanship, which, as shown, was one of the major rationales he presented for leaving the Democratic Party in the first place. Furthermore, Miller immoderately disparaged Democratic candidate John Kerry. He sarcastically remarked, "Listing all the weapon systems that Senator Kerry tried his best to shut down sounds like an auctioneer selling off our national security." By stating that Kerry did not live up to former Democratic ideals, and more generally, American ideals, Miller sought to show that he was not a flip-flopper but a true patriot who valued American freedom and security over petty partisan labels.

Although he was not as severe in his criticisms of his own party as Miller, Crist (2012) also used the values he discussed to show that Republicans no longer lived up to their core principles. For instance, he explained that "today's Republicans" are not capable of bi-partisanship but, rather, are "beholden to 'my way or the highway' bullies, indebted to billionaires who bankroll ads, and allergic to the very idea of compromise." Furthermore, he once again co-opted the virtue of Reagan by contending, "Reagan would not have stood for that." Later in the speech, he appealed to his audience by accusing Paul Ryan and Mitt Romney of hurting key government programs. He explained, "When I look at the Republican ticket today, I see two candidates who would break the fundamental promise of Medicare and Social Security, and cut investments in our middle class which are so important to our economic recovery." These examples of abandoned Republican values reinforced Crist's initial appeal that his party left him (and not the other way around) while also rallying the Democratic base.

Portrayal of the New Party as Preferable

After indicting his own party, Miller (2004) argued that Bush had and would continue to lead the United States effectively. He stated:

> George W. Bush understands that we need new strategies to meet new threats . . .
> President Bush believes we have to fight today's war and be ready for tomorrow's
> challenges. President Bush is committed to providing the kind of forces it takes to
> root out terrorist – no matter what spider hole they may hide in or what rock they
> crawl under.

In this statement, he directly contrasted his claim that Kerry lacked the skills to protect the American family with his description of Bush's experience and dedication. He warned that the "'yes-no-maybe' bowl of mush" message that Kerry sent to terrorists "can only encourage our enemies and confuse our friends." Instead, Miller argued that the country needed someone who had already demonstrated "the courage to stand-up." By depicting Bush as the only nominee who embraced the values necessary to be president, Miller again highlighted that he had no choice but to advocate for the other party's candidate. Toward the end of the speech, he reminded the audience of the importance of having a candidate who would protect family and asserted that Bush was the only candidate capable of that job: "I have knocked on the door of this man's soul and found someone home, a God-fearing man with a good heart and a spine of tempered steel – the man I trust to protect my most precious possession: my family."

Although Crist (2012) admitted in his speech that he did not agree with everything about Obama's policies, the rest of his address is peppered with claims that, unlike Romney, Obama embraced the values Crist held most dear. Crist explained that just like Reagan would not stand for bullies and partisanship, neither would Obama. He also commended Obama on taking action to help the economy. Crist specifically referred to his own personal experience with Obama, stating:

> One of his first trips in office brought him to Fort Myers, where I was proud to
> embrace him and his plan to keep our teachers, police and firefighters on the job . . .
> this president showed his courage, invested in America – and saved Florida.

Crist further explained how Obama saved Florida during the BP Deepwater Horizon oil spill crisis. Calling once again on the value of bi-partisanship, he asserted, "He didn't see a red state or a blue state. He simply saw Americans who needed help. And I once again saw the leader our country needs." Just as Miller showed that he trusted Bush with his top priority, his family, Crist showed that he trusted Obama with his top priority, his home state Florida. Although it was clearly against his personal interest and was likely to tarnish his political legacy, Crist's conscience guided him to support the candidate who represented his values.

Conclusion

The rhetoric of crossover speakers is a unique pocket of discourse that has received little attention in argumentation research. Although these speakers are likely to be labeled flip-floppers, especially by those in their former party, they can cultivate a special type of credibility by justifying their presence at the opposing convention as reluctantly compelled by their conscience. These speeches are likely to be the most influential when the speakers appear sincerely motivated by their political values rather than some sort of personal vendetta or resentment. For instance, Zell Miller may have turned off swing voters by angrily slinging around personal insults and, thus, violating his own tenet of bi-partisanship. Commentator Jonah Goldberg (2004) explained, "If there had been a bit less Southern wrath and a bit more

Southern charm it might have been even more effective" (para. 10). On the other hand, the more moderate Crist came off as a more authentic reluctant witness. This moderation was exemplified by Crist's admission that he did not agree with all of Obama's policies.

In addition to describing this emerging discourse and explaining its appropriation of the power of reluctant testimony, this essay also brings up an important issue concerning argumentation in U.S. democracy. Although democracies are meant to promote independent thought and free expression, politicians are expected to support the presidential candidate chosen by their party. Deviation from this choice results in surprise, backlash, and antagonism. This is perhaps why crossover speeches are most often given by politicians like Miller and Crist, both of whom were exiting their political careers. The controversy created by crossover speeches further highlights one of the problems with the United States' two-party system. As argumentation scholars who hope that people make decisions based on reason and evidence, rather than prior affiliation, the crossover address reminds us that we should continue to be concerned about a system in which many mark a ballot that allows them to vote straight down party lines often without knowledge of each individual's platform. Therefore, despite high ideals of country before party, the two-party system demands a choice, polarizes the electorate, and questions anyone who crosses sides.

References

Benoit, W. L., & Kennedy, K. A. (1999). On reluctant testimony. *Communication Quarterly, 46*, 376–387. doi:10.1080/01463379909385568

Crist, C. (2012, September 6). Charlie Crist Jr. at the 2012 Democratic National Convention [Video file]. *C-Span*. Retrieved from http://www.c-span.org

DeBacker, J. (2008). Flip-flopping: Ideological adjustment costs in the United States. *Munich Personal RePEc Archive*, No. 8735, 1–28.

Goldberg, J. (2004, September 2). Only time will Zell. *National Review Online*. Retrieved from http://old.nationalreview.com/goldberg/goldberg200409022239.asp

Hollihan, T. A., & Baaske, K. T. (1994). *Arguments and arguing: The products and process of human decision making*. New York, NY: St. Martin's Press.

Holloway, R. L. (2002). One nation, after all: Convention frames and political culture. In R. E. Denton Jr. (Ed.), *The 2000 presidential campaign: A communication perspective* (pp. 117–134). Westport, CT: Praeger.

Miller, Z. (2004, September 1). Zell Miller at the 2004 Republican National Convention [Video file]. *C-Span*. Retrieved from http://www.c-span.org

Palczewski, C. H. (2002). Argument in an off key: Playing with the productive limits of argument. In G. T. Goodnight (Ed.), *Arguing communication and culture: Proceedings of the twelfth NCA/AFA conference on argumentation, Alta, August 2001* (pp. 1–23). Washington, D.C.: National Communication Association, 2002.

Perelman, C., & Olbrechts-Tyteca, L. (1969). *The new rhetoric: A treatise on argumentation*. (J. Wilkinson & P. Weaver, Trans.). Notre Dame, IN: University of Notre Dame Press. (Original work published 1958)

Roddy, D. (2004, August 29). Giving 'em Zell, *Pittsburgh Post-Gazette*, p. E1.

31

DISTURBING DEMOCRACY

Argumentative framing and the third party bind in the 2012 presidential election

Ryan Neville-Shepard

INDIANA UNIVERSITY-PURDUE UNIVERSITY COLUMBUS, USA

Prior to the 2012 presidential election, many political analysts predicted that the United States would see the rise of a prominent third party candidate. For instance, Daniel Wood (2011) of the *Christian Science Monitor* argued, "Not only has voter angst created fertile ground for a third-party appeal, there has also been a rise in the number of voters who don't identify themselves with either major party" (para. 5). A Gallup poll from September 2011 reported a record-high 81 percent of people in the United States were dissatisfied with how the country was being governed, and 53 percent had little or no confidence in elected officials (Saad, 2011). Another Gallup poll found that 52 percent of U.S. voters wanted a third party option in 2012 (Jones, 2011). This data led experts like political scientist J. David Gillespie to forecast trouble for the two-party system. "If I were a betting man," Gillespie remarked, "I would say there's a fifty-fifty chance we'll see something this year that will be substantially greater than what Ross Perot was able to do in 1992" (as cited in Knafo, 2012, para. 6). Despite these predictions, third party candidates finished with less than two percent of the popular vote.

The barriers for third party campaigns are not a total mystery. These long-shot candidates face several structural and cultural barriers, including the winner-takes-all electoral system, restrictive ballot access laws, poor campaign financing, neglect from commercial news media, exclusion from presidential debates, and voters' belief that support for third party candidates is a wasted ballot (Gillespie, 1993; Rosenstone, Behr, & Lazarus, 1996). However, this essay advances another explanation for third party failures, grounded in an understanding of a paradox that leads to practices of public advocacy that are seen as too extreme for the U.S. electorate. A significant constraint for third party candidates, I suggest, is a consistent framing by commercial news media depicting such challengers as inevitable losers, with only a hope of succeeding as spoilers marked by extremism both in style and policy. Based on analysis of over 100 mainstream news articles concerning third parties in the 2012 presidential election, I contend that such framing creates a *third party bind* – a forced choice that minor party hopefuls must make to run either as legitimate candidates and go ignored, or as spoilers who receive greater media coverage while confirming negative framing and fueling future antipathy toward the third party. This essay develops a more in-depth description of the third party bind, how it materialized in the 2012 election, and discusses what this means for minor party advocacy.

Understanding the Third Party Bind

The third party bind originates from U.S. legislation in the mid-twentieth century. Although Section 315 of the Communications Act of 1934 guaranteed all political candidates equal access to media coverage, this promise was crushed in 1959 when Congress passed Public Law 86–274 to create exemptions designed to increase presidential news coverage without having to cover all candidates. According to Gillespie (1993), the exemptions placed "broadcasters on firm legal ground when they ignore third parties in newscasts, candidate interviews, and documentaries or give gavel-to-gavel coverage of major party national conventions" (p. 33). Ignoring third party candidates has become common for news media. For example, Stovall (1985) maintained that George Wallace's 1968 campaign received far less coverage than the two major parties and that independent John Anderson faced a similar media blackout in the 1980 campaign. As Zaller and Hunt (1995) summarized, "the press tends to cover candidates in multicandidate races in proportion to how well it expects them to do" (pp. 112–113). Consequently, "Candidates who are ignored by the press never get off the ground" (Zaller & Hunt, 1994, p. 375).

Although communication scholars have not written much on the argumentation of third party candidates, the existing research has highlighted methods they sometimes use to overcome media neglect. Tonn and Endress (2001) summarized Ross Perot's appeal in 1992 as a mastering of perspective by incongruity through which "the oddball Texan reawakened a dormant, more fundamental democratic ideal of government as a partnership of agents" (p. 301). The same could be said of other minor party campaigns that have created perspective by incongruity in a variety ways. Candidates like George Wallace and Ralph Nader have been described as appealing to wider audiences through polarizing and populist forms of argument (Harold, 2001; Hogan, 1984; Lee, 2006; Raum & Measell, 1974), as well as through visual and verbal markers of authenticity (Harold, 2001; Zaller & Hunt, 1994, 1995).

While it appears that third party candidates have ways of adapting to media neglect, their methods demonstrate a difficult catch-22 that has until now only been hinted at in a few case studies. Offering a lesson from Perot's boom-and-bust campaign in 1992, Tonn and Endress (2001) concluded that his perspective by incongruity "not only debunked and altered impressions of certain traditions, but also simultaneously flattered and confirmed political pieties as well" (p. 302). Likewise, Harold (2001) argued that Nader's confrontational argumentation allowed Democrats to effectively cast him "as a contaminating element in an otherwise well-ordered political system" (p. 582). This phenomenon is true for other third party candidates, too. To gain attention requires breaking rules, but breaking rules means violating expectations of presidential decorum and confirming concerns about political outsiders' inability to abide by political norms. Thus, the bind that third party candidates face is the choice of either confirming damaging media portrayals of outsider candidates and making the news, or abiding by political conventions and falling by the wayside.

The 2012 Election and the Third Party Bind

Despite the inclusion of three candidates with significant political experience – including former New Mexico governor Gary Johnson, former Salt Lake City mayor Rocky Anderson,

214

and former United States Representative Virgil Goode – the 2012 presidential election saw another media blockade on news about third party campaigns. Patrick Pexton (2012) of *The Washington Post* acknowledged complaints about this blockade, but announced, "It's not *The Post*'s job to be boosters for any presidential candidate, not even these minor parties' nominees" (p. A13). Paul Singer of *USA Today* similarly argued, "It's not our job to help them become major candidates" (as cited in Powers, 2012, para. 19), contending they deserve coverage only when relevant to a bigger story. However, third party candidates were rarely considered relevant and discussed mostly in stories based around three arguments justifying their exclusion.

First, minor party candidates in 2012 were routinely depicted as inevitable losers. Many journalists, for instance, poked fun at candidates' lack of name recognition. Writing about the Green Party nominee, Saulny (2012) remarked, "When Ms. Stein is introduced on the trail as 'Jill Stein for president,' she is also very likely . . . to be asked, 'For president of what?' " (para. 2). Likewise, Constitution Party nominee Virgil Goode was characterized as "a virtually unknown presidential candidate"(Bomboy, 2012, para. 1). Being portrayed as political nobodies, the third party candidates essentially were depicted as unpresidential. This was especially evident in some journalists' focus on a lack of sufficient pomp in the candidates' public events. Describing the first minor party debate, Powers (2012) wrote that its "setting was a cramped back room of a restaurant-bookstore, not a cavernous college campus arena" (para. 2). Illustrating the consequence of this kind of framing, Hesse (2012) wrote that when Jill Stein was introduced at the Green Party national convention as the next president, the audience "chuckle[d], self-aware, as if unsure about getting too caught up in the dream" (p. C01). For many in news media, then, third party candidates in 2012 were usually not considered important enough to cover.

Second, minor party candidates were routinely portrayed as potential spoilers. Third party hopefuls occasionally became relevant because the race was believed to be so close at times that it could be settled by a few hundred votes. The three top outsider candidates were all portrayed as spoilers in the making. Jill Stein was described as barely appearing in national polls, but still capable of stealing votes from President Obama (Saulney, 2012). Libertarian Gary Johnson's chances of playing spoiler were seen as far greater, especially after "polling between 6 and 9 percent nationally," a number which Ames (2012) called "just large enough to cover most Obama-Romney spreads" (para. 2). With Johnson discussing neglected issues like the legalization of marijuana, Ames added, "If [he] notches his support up to 10 percent, the question won't be if he alters the November outcome, but how" (para. 11). Virgil Goode also was noted for his potential to disrupt the election. Amira (2012) quoted one poll indicating Goode was capable of getting 5 percent in his home state of Virginia, thus making "a difference in what is shaping up to be one of 2012's most pivotal swing states" (para. 1). Sherfinski (2012) echoed, "The president doesn't have to win Virginia to get elected, but there's a good chance Romney does. In that case, Goode could cost Romney the presidency" (p. A4). Although being potential spoilers meant third party candidates actually received press coverage, the coverage they received was far from positive. As Goode was getting characterized as a possible spoiler, one editorial in *The Washington Times* warned, "Voting for a third-party candidate never pays off," and moreover "is rarely the right thing to do" ("Third-Party Votes," 2012, p. 2).

Surprisingly, some minor party candidates were hopeful early on about their chances to emerge victorious. Asked whether he agreed that he was campaigning to siphon votes from Republicans, Gary Johnson argued:

> My candidacy is not about a message of protest. It is about defying conventional
> wisdom and giving a voice to what I believe is a majority of Americans who today
> do not feel comfortable in either the Democratic or Republican Party.
>
> *(as cited in Decker, 2012, p. B1)*

Nevertheless, candidates in 2012 were quick to realize that the media blockade they faced required drastic measures. According to Saulny (2012), Green Party nominee Jill Stein believed that her limited media exposure and resulting exclusion from the debates was "by design, to benefit major parties" (para. 23). Around the same time that she was arrested during a Keystone pipeline protest, Stein argued, "Early in the campaign, a variety of mainstream outlets covered the campaign. They opened their door and then slammed it shut" (as cited in Powers, 2012, para. 28). The arrest "garnered ample press attention," Powers wrote, and was evidence that Stein's strategy was changing (para. 27). As her strategy shifted, however, she was – as were her third party counterparts – falling into the extremist frame perpetuated by the national news media.

Finally, minor party candidates in 2012 were often portrayed as political extremists. Such coverage could be as simple as reporting the extreme tactics such candidates use to gain attention. In particular, the policies that each candidate advocated often came under attack. Commenting on Johnson's lack of public support, Barro (2012) wrote, "When you delve into [his] positions, you can start to understand why" (para. 3). Johnson was "radical all-around," Barro noted, advocating tax policy that "goes far beyond 'fiscally conservative, socially liberal'" (para. 9). Similarly, Young (2012) argued there was neither "a constituency for a drastic shrinking of government programs" (para. 4) nor "majority support for a radical retrenchment on the international front" (para. 5). Virgil Goode's policy positions were similarly disregarded. Lehrer (2012) called the Constitution Party platform "absolutely mad," because it sought to "abolish the patent and trademark office, force the closing of all current banks, abolish the U.S. dollar, and fund the government mostly through huge tariffs on foreign trade" (para. 3). Stein, too, was noted for being a fringe political type. As Stark (2012) suggested, Stein was a bit "dramatic" in proposing to forgive student loan debt, invest billions in clean energy, and drive down health care costs with a single-payer system (para. 2).

Beyond the policies they advocated, third party candidates in 2012 were also portrayed as extremists due to their style of advocacy. Although Jill Stein received significant press coverage for being arrested twice during the campaign in acts of protest, she also turned heads for her shocking claims. For instance, Cass (2012) chronicled how Stein "said many of Obama's supporters are like victims of an abusive relationship, constantly apologizing for the abuser's behavior with statements like, 'I know he really loves me' and 'He didn't mean it'" (para. 8). Gary Johnson was also portrayed as making odd campaign choices. Ames (2012) wrote that the Libertarian was "speaking freely in language unmolested by establishment advisers" (para. 2). Johnson finally let loose when he clearly grasped that he was being ignored by the media. In one intriguing moment, he told viewers of the first minor party debate, "I'm asking everybody here to waste your vote on me" (as cited in Jan, 2012, para. 25). In other moments, Johnson even embraced a somewhat pathetic slogan that went something like, "Once you get to know me, I swear you'll like me" (Merica, 2012, para. 3). By the final minor party debate just before the election, he confessed what he thought the mainstream media left everyone wondering, "Who the hell is Gary Johnson?" (as cited in Lowrey, 2012, para. 22). Such honesty is clearly amusing enough to be picked up by national media, but hardly inspiring to voters.

Conclusion

Tracing the third party bind in the 2012 presidential election, this essay proposes something that should be disturbing to anyone who favors democratic deliberation. The essay suggests that third party campaigns compete in an era without the promise of anything resembling equal or even fair media coverage and thus are bound to fail. Journalists consistently characterize third party candidates as inevitable losers, with only a chance of disrupting the democratic process, who use extreme methods of doing so. This framing leaves third party candidates with few choices. If they insist on running as legitimate candidates, they will likely be ignored. Yet, if they lash out in an extreme style of advocacy, they only seal their fate as an electoral sideshow.

This essay also poses some interesting questions for future investigation. With advancements in social media and candidates' ability to bypass the gatekeepers of mainstream news, one has to wonder if third party candidates have new tools to overcome the bind described in this study. Judging by the quick failure of the Americans Elect movement – the group that tried to create an online primary to find a moderate minor party candidate, but bowed out months before the election – my hunch is that such technologies remain severely limited.

While this study focused on the third party bind as it surfaced in the 2012 election, it would be useful to trace this barrier longitudinally. Third party candidates mustered barely two percent of the popular vote in 2012, but previous candidates like Ross Perot, George Wallace, and John Anderson have done far better. Future research could demonstrate whether the drop in third party candidate performance could be due to their rhetorical bind.

References

Ames, M. (2012, May 6). Don't forget Gary Johnson! How the Libertarian could shake up 2012. *The Daily Beast*. Retrieved from http://www.thedailybeast.com

Amira, D. (2012, May 24). Constitution party candidate Virgil Goode not worried about being a spoiler. *New York Magazine*. Retrieved from http://nymag.com

Barro, J. (2012, August 28). Why is Gary Johnson being ignored? *Bloomberg.com*. Retrieved from http://www.bloomberg.com

Bomboy, S. (2012, August 8). The third party candidate who could derail Mitt Romney. *Yahoo News*. Retrieved from http://news.yahoo.com

Cass, M. (2012, November 2). Presidential candidate Jill Stein brings Green Party message. *The Tennessean*. Retrieved from www.tennessean.com

Decker, B. M. (2012, February 10). Gary Johnson: Five questions with Decker. *The Washington Times*, p. B1.

Gillespie, J. D. (1993). *Politics at the periphery: Third parties in two-party America*. Columbia: University of South Carolina Press.

Harold, C. L. (2001). The green virus: Purity and contamination in Ralph Nader's 2000 presidential campaign. *Rhetoric & Public Affairs*, 4, 581–603. doi: 10.1353/rap.2001.0072

Hesse, M. (2012, July 16). Patiently waiting for the Green light. *The Washington Post*, p. C01.

Hogan, M. J. (1984). Wallace and the Wallacites: A reexamination. *Southern Speech Communication Journal*, 50, 24–48. doi: 10.1080/10417948409372620

Jan, T. (2012, October 27). Third-party candidates could tip vote. *The Boston Globe*. Retrieved from http://www.boston.com

Jones, J. M. (2011, May 9). Support for third U.S. party dips, but is still majority view. Gallup.com. Retrieved from http://www.gallup.com/poll/147461/Support-Third-Party-Dips-Majority-View.aspx

Knafo, S. (2012, January 10). Third-party candidate could rise due to voter dissatisfaction. *The Huffington Post*. Retrieved from http://www.huffingtonpost.com

Lehrer, E. (2012, October 8). The fringe candidate who could cost Mitt Romney the presidency. *Huffington Post*. Retrieved from http://www.huffingtonpost.com

Lowrey, A. (2012, November 5). Another presidential debate, but this time the candidates are much less familiar. *The New York Times*. Retrieved from www.nytimes.com

Merica, D. (2012, September 12). Gary Johnson: An uphill battle to catch a wave, win the presidency. CNN.com. Retrieved from http://www.cnn.com

Pexton, P. B. (2012, October 21). The overlooked names on the ballot. *The Washington Post*, p. A13.

Powers, E. (2012, September). The lonely life of a third-party presidential candidate. Retrieved from www.ajr.org

Raum, R. D., & Measell, J. S. (1974). Wallace and his ways: A study of the rhetorical genre of polarization. *Central States Speech Journal, 25*, 28–35. doi: 10.1080/10510977409367765

Rosenstone, S. J., Behr, R. L., & Lazarus, E. H. (1996). *Third parties in America: Citizen response to major party failure*. Princeton, NJ: Princeton University Press.

Saad, L. (2011, September 26). Americans express historic negativity toward U.S. government. Gallup. com. Retrieved from http://www.gallup.com/poll/149678/Americans-Express-Historic-Negativity-Toward-Government.aspx

Saulny, S. (2012, July 12). Party strains to be heard now that its voice isn't Nader. *The New York Times*. Retrieved from www.nytimes.com

Sherfinski, D. (2012, July 9). Goode's third-party run: Bad news for Romney in Virginia? *The Washington Times*, p. A4.

Simons, H. W. (1996). Judging a policy proposal by the company it keeps: The Gore-Perot NAFTA debate. *Quarterly Journal of Speech, 82*, 274–287. doi: 10.1080/00335639609384156

Stark, J. (2012, October 20). Green Party's Jill Stein offers sweeping vision for planet. *The Bellingham Herald*. Retrieved from http://www.bellinghamherald.com

Stovall, J. G. (1985). The third-party challenge of 1980: News coverage of the presidential candidates. *Journalism Quarterly, 62*, 266–271. doi: 10.1177/107769908506200206

Third-party votes are wasted; Alternative candidates can't solve [Editorial]. (2012, November 1). *The Washington Times*, p. 2.

Tonn, M. B., & Endress, V. A. (2001). Looking under the hood and tinkering with voter cynicism: Ross Perot and "perspective by incongruity." *Rhetoric & Public Affairs, 4*, 281–308. doi: 10.1353/rap.2001.0032

Wood, D. B. (2011, December 20). Why 2012 could be the year of the third-party candidate. *The Christian Science Monitor*. Retrieved from http://www.csmonitor.com

Young, C. (2012, October 22). Young: The Libertarian alternative to Barack Obama and Mitt Romney [Editorial]. *Newsday*. Retrieved from http://www.newsday.com

Zaller, J., & Hunt, M. (1994). The rise and fall of candidate Perot: Unmediated versus mediated politics – Part 1. *Political Communication, 11*, 357–390. doi: 10.1080/10584609.1994.9963046

Zaller, J., & Hunt, M. (1995). The rise and fall of candidate Perot: Unmediated versus mediated politics – Part 2. *Political Communication, 12*, 97–123. doi: 10.1080/10584609.1995.9963057

32

UNQUALIFIED SUPPORT

Joe Biden's disturbing performance of leadership, loyalty, and laughter in the 2012 vice presidential debate

Kathryn M. Olson

UNIVERSITY OF WISCONSIN – MILWAUKEE, USA

"Disturbing" is not a term usually associated with vice presidential debate performances. Certainly there have been disturbing *moments* in televised vice presidential debates, including George H. W. Bush patronizing Geraldine Ferraro on foreign policy in 1984 and Dan Quayle comparing himself to John F. Kennedy to establish his experience in 1988. But generally these performances are *meant* to be reassuring, not disturbing. Among these debates' main purposes are revealing the character and potential presidential tenor of the candidates as well as demonstrating their abilities to defend the values and policies of their respective tickets. Although vice presidential debates' impact on election outcomes is contested (see Benoit & Airne, 2005; Dailey, Hinck, & Hinck, 2008), Carlin and Bicak (1993) argued that such debates "provide one of the best sources for extended exposure to vice presidential candidates and insights into their potential leadership abilities" (p. 122).

While vice presidential debates are sometimes thought to be more "bare-knuckle" confrontations than presidential debates, Dailey et al.'s (2008) longitudinal politeness research empirically demonstrated that there are few differences in face threats between the two contests; in fact, overall, vice presidential debates are *less* face-threatening (pp. 37–39). Debate style rather than actual face threats might account for perceptions of greater aggressiveness (Dailey et al., 2008, p. 42). In a similarly soothing conclusion, Benoit and Airne (2005) found that, while vice presidential debaters do attack opponents more than do presidential ones, they still acclaim their own ticket more than they attack the opposition. Instead of convincing voters to challenge or change their prospective votes, vice presidential debates tend to "help voters confirm their leanings and provide them with a better understanding of why they support a particular candidate" (Carlin & Bicak, 1993, p. 120). They comfort, reassure, and motivate those who already support a ticket.

In his October 11, 2012, debate with Republican challenger Representative Paul Ryan, Vice President Joe Biden seemed under especially intense pressure to reassure. In the general election's first presidential debate a week earlier, Biden's running mate President Barack Obama had underperformed to expectations while Ryan's partner Mitt Romney had

219

exceeded expectations. Romney seemed unusually centrist and leader-like, while Obama lacked energy and failed to articulate his vision (see, e.g., Abdullah, 2012; Cassidy, 2012). The result was a tightening race with few remaining undecided voters in which polls indicated that Romney's debate performance was "peel[ing] off some of Mr. Obama's softer support in addition to gaining ground among undecided voters" (statistician and poll-watcher for the *New York Times* Nate Silver as cited in Knickerbocker, 2012, para. 18). Reversing this development complicated Biden's rhetorical task and framed his disturbing performance.

Biden's Disturbing Performative Norm Violations

Biden's debate performance unambiguously violated numerous norms, which presumably a prudent candidate would avoid, particularly in a tightening race, and resulted in judgments that he acted "unpresidential." Examinations of past presidential campaign debates (e.g., Benoit, McKinney, & Holbert, 2001; Dailey et al., 2008) and experimental research (e.g., Seiter, 1999, 2001; Seiter & Weger, 2005; Seiter, Weger, Jensen, & Kinzer, 2010; Seiter, Weger, Kinzer, & Jensen, 2009) indicated that voters and commentators react negatively to candidates' violations of turn-taking etiquette and nonverbal expressions of disagreement while the opponent is speaking. Such behaviors hurt viewers' perceptions of the violator's sociability, competence, credibility, likeability, and appropriateness and might feed favorable perceptions of the violated candidate. Even when the violator does not audibly interrupt, nonverbal disagreement (e.g., eye-rolling, grimacing, smirking, head-shaking) "constitutes a violation of turn-taking etiquette" (Seiter & Weger, 2005, p. 227). Likewise, Beck (1996) suggested the importance of vice presidential debaters demonstrating their mastery of sophisticated turn-management techniques. Finally, Rhea (2012) declared it "unthinkable" in a presidential campaign debate to use serious discourse to call another a liar; only humor could make such a strong charge "come off as amusing rather than abrasive to the viewing audience" (p. 125).

Yet, based on my comparison of CNN's 2012 split-screen video to NPR's 2012 debate transcript, Biden blatantly and repeatedly violated all of these performative norms. For instance, during Ryan's very first answer, Biden melted into silent laughter, which was replaced by a smirk when Ryan twice claimed that his ticket agreed with the administration on a 2014 military transition from Afghanistan. Biden gave an exaggerated blink of surprise and raised his eyebrows at the second instance. As Ryan answered a follow-up question, Biden shook his head side-to-side, mouthed "that's not true," laughed silently, then smirked and rolled his eyes heavenward. Next Biden verbally interrupted Ryan with "am I going to get to say anything here?" and then interrupted again, before being given permission to speak, only to remark, "With all due respect, that's a bunch of malarkey." When the moderator asked why, Biden categorically stated, "Because not a single thing he said is accurate." On the issue of an Iranian nuclear weapon, Biden called Ryan's answer "a bunch of stuff." Pressed for clarification, Biden stated, "Well, it means it's simply inaccurate." Biden twice more called his opponent's statements "malarkey." He followed this with "I don't know what world you guys are in," then met Ryan's response with "Oh, God," dropping his head, rolling his eyes, and laughing audibly. During Ryan's explanation of his ticket's tax reform and job creation plans, Biden laughed silently, then aloud, shaking his head with eyes squeezed shut as if in utter disbelief. Sometimes Biden chuckled until his shoulders visibly shook or covered his mouth with his hand, as if trying to suppress his derisive hilarity. He dismissed the truthfulness of other Ryan answers with categorical judgments (e.g., "incredible," "come on," "I wish he would just tell – be a little more candid") or incredulous rhetorical questions (e.g., "seriously?", "how's that?").

As the debate proceeded, Biden's talking-over and verbal and nonverbal interruptions of both Ryan and the moderator increased in frequency and intensity. In addition to his disturbing chuckles, scoffs, smirks, and overdrawn facial expressions (e.g., amusement, outrage, annoyance, disbelief), Biden employed repetition as well as exaggerated pausing patterns and vocal emphasis when explaining his points, as if the opponent was too simple to grasp them otherwise/anyway (e.g., "Ninety-seven percent of the small businesses make less than $250,000 a year," "They don't have a weapon to put it into," "That's a bizarre statement, since 49 of our allies – hear me, 49 of our allies signed onto this position, 49"). At times, Biden lectured (e.g., "It's about time they take some responsibility," "These are the most crippling sanctions in the history of sanctions, period, period"). At others, he ridiculed (e.g., "The idea that – that little soliloquy on 47 percent, and you think he just made a mistake, then I think you're – I – I – I – I got a bridge to sell you," "Now they got a new plan [on Medicare and Social Security]. [']Trust me, it's not going to cost you any more[.'] Folks, follow your instincts on this one"). Occasionally Biden dropped or rolled his head helplessly toward his chest, as if despairing of getting his message through despite his elaborate efforts.

Why might a seasoned debater like Biden, with 18 presidential or vice presidential debates to his name (MacQuarrie, 2012), take such a chance with blatant norm violations? Answering requires, as Erickson (2000) argued regarding visual presidential performance fragments, that these performance fragments "be assembled and contextualized to appreciate fully their ideological underpinnings. . . . [The fragments] have multiple and sometimes nonapparent rhetorical objectives" (p. 152). In spite of the risks to his image and the viewers he alienated, Biden's performative choices symbolically displayed his strong loyalty to Obama and the President's leadership and forcefully "righted" the superiority relationship between the two tickets from one approaching equality after the first presidential debate to one that dramatically underscored the incumbents' superiority in status, difference, and distance. Biden's overdrawn performance also seemed calculated to "rally the base and show the American people that the administration still had fire in its belly" (Merkel, 2012, para. 3). Obama's team had told Biden that it was impossible for him "to go too far" (Alter, 2013, p. 329). The next section examines how Biden's seemingly imprudent norm violations might have operated in a rhetorically prudent way, given his situation, but came with rhetorical costs.

The Prudence of Impudence

Biden's boisterous behavior successfully served larger strategic purposes: rallying discouraged Obama supporters sufficiently to get them to the polls (Alter, 2013; Silver, 2012a), diverting public discussion away from the first debate, and buying time for Obama to reel in undecideds with improved second and third debates, goals a more decorous and presidential performance by Biden might not have achieved. Merkel's (2012) comment encapsulated his base's response: "If you're a liberal or a Democrat, you probably loved Joe Biden's performance last night" (para. 1). Biden also needed "to change the story line, to get the press talking about something else so Obama [could] regain his footing" (Marc Landy, a political scientist at Boston College, as cited in MacQuarrie, 2012, para. 21), and his disturbing performance succeeded. Finally, Biden's performance needed to compensate for the perceived weaknesses of his ticket's first debate in order to stop the GOP's rally, especially among the shrinking pool of undecided voters or soft supporters. The vice-presidential debate was "'a continuation of the presidential debate,' said Todd Domke, a Republican consultant who is a political analyst for WBUR. . . . For a vice presidential debate, Domke said, such stakes are unprecedented" (MacQuarrie, 2012, para. 9–10). Instant polls rated the debate a draw, and, perhaps most tellingly, Obama's camp was "ecstatic" with Biden's performance while Romney's complained about it (Alter, 2013, p. 330). Although some polls and pundits favored Ryan (see Merkel, 2012), CBS's poll of *only uncommitted* voters showed Biden winning the debate by 50 percent to 31 percent, a victory beyond the base (Madison, 2012).

Although it is arguable that Biden could have achieved greater individual recognition by playing it straight, as he had in his 2008 vice presidential debate with Sarah Palin (where he was "calm, collected, even presidential," Merkel, 2012, para. 4), his 2012 yuk-it-up performative choices may have helped his ticket more when viewed in the context of compensating for/ rebounding from the first presidential debate. Silver (2012b) opined over the debate results:

> My best guess: perhaps Mr. Biden can be credited with what in baseball statistics would be termed a "hold": something a bit shy of either a win or a save and which will probably seem perfunctory with the passage of time, but which might have done his team a bit of good. However, he won't have relieved Mr. Obama of the burden of needing to improve his performance in next week's presidential debate.
>
> *(para. 11–12)*

The good Biden did his ticket came from performing both enthusiastic loyalty to a foundering Obama and unqualified belief in his ticket's superiority over their opponents in ways that simultaneously made him appear less presidential than, and subordinate to, Obama. Ironically, the reason some gave for thinking that Biden's strategy "backfired . . . horribly" was "he did not come off as 'presidential'" (Merkel, 2012, para. 8).

But, I would argue that seeming loyal and confident yet less presidential than Obama was essential to this performance's strategic value. Biden needed to restore confidence in Obama without outshining his debate-damaged image. Others' experiences show how difficult it is for vice presidential candidates to hit the right balance even in less extraordinary circumstances. For instance, debate performances by Lloyd Bentsen, Joe Lieberman, and Dick Cheney increased the confidence of the public in their candidacies; however their performances, while reflecting well on the decision of their running mates, also compromised the unique appeal of their presidential counterparts as stronger versions of their party's frontrunner (Dailey et al., 2008, p. 32). Via a slightly different double-bind, Al Gore's 1992 vice presidential debate thoroughly demonstrated his command of the issues and presidential potential but arguably hurt his running mate by claiming too equal a "partnership" with him and by failing to refute character charges against Bill Clinton promptly and vehemently enough (Carlin & Bicak, 1993, pp. 127–128).

In light of Obama's lackluster first debate, Biden needed this performance fragment to stimulate viewers' emotional responses (see Erickson, 2000) to ignite passion for giving his ticket another four years in office and to re-shape perceptions of what Romney's surge meant for the race. His combination of performative choices functioned as "nominalist rhetoric" (Erickson, 2000, p. 141) that did not promote himself but named his ticket as featuring the only truly presidential choice in the race: Obama. Biden framed this as the key judgment criterion during his first answer regarding the terrorist attack in Benghazi, Libya, which killed an ambassador and three other Americans:

> When you're looking at a president, Martha, it seems to me that you should take a look at his most important responsibility. That's carrying forward the national security of the country. And the best way to do that is take a look at how he's handled he [*sic*] issues of the day.

Biden then contrasted Obama's, whom he always referred to using his presidential title, actions on national security with Romney's statements and equivocations. He concluded, "The president of the United States has – has led with a steady hand and clear vision. Governor Romney, the opposite." Following up on Benghazi, Biden contrasted the presidential contenders (shifting credit from "we" to Obama alone) and underscored the leadership criterion:

> We – this is a president who's gone out and done everything he has said he was going to do. . . . These guys bet against America all the time. . . . Even before we knew what happened to the ambassador, the governor was holding a press conference – was holding a press conference. That's not presidential leadership.

Biden's exaggerated style repeatedly underscored the wide difference in status, wisdom, and experience between the Republican ticket and his own. If *he* could not take his opponents seriously on an occasion where decorum norms, historical precedents, and high stakes suggested he should, how could voters?

Biden's repeated, unequivocal accusations of the opposing ticket's untruthfulness and amateurish naiveté and assertion of the Democratic ticket's command of the facts and insight, highlighted by his nonverbals, directed viewers to suspect both the integrity of the challengers and the adequacy of their experience, knowledge, and ability to run the country. It painted Obama, by contrast, as a responsible, proven leader making progress on the foreign and domestic messes he had been handed. Intentionally or not, Biden set presidential leadership as the judgment standard, and his performative choices consistently showed Obama as the only contender with true presidential mettle in this race. Biden's performance communicated that he and Obama were both imminently more qualified and knowledgeable about the issues than either Romney or Ryan and demonstrated that Obama was the more presidential of the qualified two because he always played the part with dignity.

The cost of giving his ticket this boost was Biden himself acting unpresidential, in deference to promoting Obama and putting him on a pedestal to a degree that would have been unnecessary had Obama performed to expectations in the first debate. Biden's disturbing performance sacrificed his image and the vice presidential debate's usual goal of demonstrating that the candidate "a heartbeat away" has sufficient presidential gravitas to fulfill the office's highly symbolic duties (e.g., head of state, commander in chief). In fact, Biden's smirking, grinning, and gesticulating like "a southern preacher trying to perform an exorcism" (Merkel, 2012, para. 5) intimated that he lacked the "visual mastery of the mythic presidency" (Erickson, 2000, p. 142) expected of someone who might become president. Yet, for that very reason, the performance pleased some by sharply clarifying the contest, startled the media enough to divert attention from Obama's first performance, and effectively put the race on "hold" so that Obama himself could clinch the "win."

References

Abdullah, H. (2012, October 5). What's next: Can Obama recover or will Romney run up the score? *CNN.com*. Retrieved from http://www.cnn.com/2012/10/04/politics/debate-next

Alter, J. (2013). *The center holds: Obama and his enemies*. New York, NY: Simon & Schuster.

Beck, C. S. (1996). "I've got some points I'd like to make here": The achievement of social face through turn management during the 1992 vice presidential debate. *Political Communication, 13*, 165–180.

Benoit, W. L., & Airne, D. (2005). A functional analysis of American vice presidential debates. *Argumentation and Advocacy, 41*, 225–236.

Benoit, W. L., McKinney, M. S., & Holbert, R. L. (2001). Beyond learning and persona: Extending the scope of presidential debate effects. *Communication Monographs, 68,* 259–273.

Carlin, D. B., & Bicak, P. J. (1993). Toward a theory of vice presidential debate purposes: An analysis of the 1992 vice presidential debate. *Argumentation and Advocacy, 30,* 119–130.

Cassidy, J. (2012, October 4). After Denver: Can Obama bounce back? [Opinion piece]. *New Yorker.* Retrieved from http://www.newyorker.com/online/blogs/johncassidy/2012/10/obamas-big-challenge-can-he-bounce-back.html

CNN. (2012, October 11). Election center: Vice presidential debate. Retrieved from http://www.cnn.com/election/2012/debates/vice-presidential-debate

Dailey, W. O., Hinck, E. A., & Hinck, S. S. (2008). *Politeness in presidential debates: Shaping political face in campaign debates from 1960 to 2004.* Lanham, MA: Rowman & Littlefield.

Erickson, K. V. (2000). Presidential rhetoric's visual turn: Performance fragments and the politics of illusionism. *Communication Monographs, 67,* 138–157.

Knickerbocker, B. (2012, October 7). Latest polls: Romney's uphill fight not as steep. *Christian Science Monitor.* Retrieved from http://www.csmonitor.com/USA/DC-Decoder/2012/1007/Latest-polls-Romney-s-uphill-fight-not-as-steep

MacQuarrie, B. (2012, October 11). Biden, Ryan face high stakes in vice presidential debate. *Boston Globe.* Retrieved from http://www.bostonglobe.com/news/politics/2012/10/10/vice-presidential-debate-looms-important-point-presidential-race/jRH5jV3SrdgYYbnJpKPKrM/story.html

Madison, L. (2012, October 12). Who won the vp debate? Why the polls were so different. *CBS News.* Retrieved from http://www.cbsnews.com/8301-250_162-57531577/who-won-the-vp-debate-why-the-polls-were-so-different/

Merkel, J. (2012, October 12). Who won the vp debate 2012: Paul Ryan wins the polls against laughing Joe Biden. *Policymic.* Retrieved from http://www.policymic.com/articles/16407/who-won-the-vp-debate-2012-paul-ryan-wins-the-polls-against-laughing-joe-biden

NPR. (2012, October 11). Transcript and audio: Vice presidential debate. Retrieved from http://www.npr.org/2012/10/11/162754053/transcript-biden-ryan-vice-presidential-debate

Rhea, D. M. (2012). There they go again: The use of humor in presidential debates 1960–2008. *Argumentation and Advocacy, 49,* 115–131.

Seiter, J. S. (1999). Does communicating nonverbal disagreement during an opponent's speech affect the credibility of the debater in the background? *Psychological Reports, 84,* 855–861.

Seiter, J. S. (2001). Silent derogation and perceptions of deceptiveness: Does communicating nonverbal disbelief during an opponent's speech affect perceptions of debaters' veracity? *Communication Research Reports, 7,* 203–209.

Seiter, J. S., & Weger, Jr., H. (2005). Audience perceptions of candidates' appropriateness as a function of nonverbal behaviors displayed during televised political debates. *Journal of Social Psychology, 145,* 225–235.

Seiter, J. S., Weger, Jr., H., Jensen, A., & Kinzer, H. J. (2010). The role of background behavior in televised debates: Does displaying nonverbal agreement and/or disagreement benefit either debater? *The Journal of Social Psychology, 150,* 278–300.

Seiter, J. S., Weger, Jr., H., Kinzer, H. J., & Jensen, A. S. (2009). Impression management in televised debates: The effect of background nonverbal behavior on audience perceptions of debaters' likeability. *Communication Research Reports, 26,* 1–11.

Silver, N. (2012a, October 10). Biden's debate mission: Whip up Democrats to blunt Romney's gains. *New York Times.com.* Retrieved from http://fivethirtyeight.blogs.nytimes.com/2012/10/10/bidens-debate-mission-whip-up-democrats-to-blunt-romneys-gains/

Silver, N. (2012b, October 12). In polls, Biden gets a hold. *New York Times.com.* Retrieved from http://fivethirtyeight.blogs.nytimes.com/2012/10/12/in-polls-biden-gets-a-hold/

33

THE TIMELINESS OF THE NEW (NETWORKED) RHETORIC

On critical distance, sentiment analysis, and public feeling polls

Damien S. Pfister

UNIVERSITY OF NEBRASKA-LINCOLN, USA

What happens to public argumentation when the pace of communication accelerates? Clay Shirky's (2009) observation that "as a medium gets faster, it gets more emotional" hints at some potential challenges for argumentation in internetworked cultures characterized by rapid circulation of public discourse. Paul Virilio (2005) intensified the point:

> No politics is possible at the speed of light. Politics depends on having time for reflection. Today we no longer have time to reflect, the things that we see have already happened. And it is necessary to react immediately. Is a real-time democracy possible? An authoritarian politics, yes. But what defines democracy is the sharing of power. When there is not time to share, what will be shared? Emotions.
>
> *(p. 43)*

If Shirky and Virilio are correct, what does this mean for public deliberation in digitally networked environments privileging timeliness of response? The accelerated networked media ecology, featuring blogs, wikis, podcasts, viral videos, memes, social networking sites, and nanoblogging sites, thrives on speed. From the 24-hour news cycle hungry to fill time, to blogs that parse and re-parse political moments, to Twitter, Facebook, and Instagram updates about who ate what when, ours is an era that thrives on information-driven events (Xenos, 2008). As opposed to the old rhetoric, which Richard Weaver (1953) characterized as spacious, the new networked rhetoric privileges timeliness. The trajectory away from the spacious oratory that Weaver (1953) traced remains suggestive: "From the position that only propositions are interesting because they alone make judgments, we are passing to a position in which only evidence is interesting because it alone is uncontaminated by propositions. In brief, interest has shifted from inference to reportage" (p. 172). The rage for reportage, represented for Weaver by *Time* magazine's photojournalism, focuses on "impertinences" (p. 179) – "officious details" that "would only lower the general effect" of old oratory (p. 176).

Imagine Weaver's shudder at the state of public discourse in the digitized, culturally pluralized, early networked public sphere. The affordances of networked media – ubiquitous internet connections, instantaneous publication, extensive networks of distribution – fuel reportage. Reportage stimulates an instant reaction culture with endlessly recursive iterations of response and counter-reportage. In this context, timeliness is everything. People are, as Twitter founder Jack Dorsey notes, "as good as your last update. That's what you're currently thinking or doing, or your current approach towards life . . . It's only relevant in the now" (Sarno, 2009). The instantaneous, constant circulation of symbols in networked public culture "disrupts the preferred temporality of rhetorical deliberation" (Greene, 2002, p. 347).

In order to make sense of the timeliness of this new rhetoric for deliberation, I first explore how the rapid circulation of argument through internetworked media reduces the critical distance long appreciated as a resource for invention and judgment. I then examine how the publication of feelings through networked media generates data for sentiment analysis, focusing on the Twindex polls in the 2012 presidential election cycle. Finally, I examine how these "public feeling polls" usefully reflect intensity of opinion, but also pose risks related to the orchestration of affect.

On Critical Distance

Speed, feeling, and argument can be woven together with the concept of critical distance, a spatial and temporal metaphor hinting at removal from instant reaction. Weaver (1953) contended that the perspective provided by distance aids an orator:

> If one sees an object from too close, one sees only its irregularities and protuber-ances. To see an object rightly or to see it as a whole, one has to have a proportioned distance from it. Then the parts fall into a meaningful pattern, the dominant effect emerges, and one sees it "as it really *is*."
>
> *(p. 175, emphasis in original)*

Habermas (1989) faulted the decline in critical distance accompanying electronic mass media for the deflation of the public sphere by noting that:

> radio, film, and television by degrees reduce to a minimum the distance that a reader is forced to maintain toward the printed letter – a distance that required the privacy of the appropriation as much as it made possible the publicity of a rational-critical exchange about what had been read.
>
> *(p. 170)*

The contrast provided by electronic mass media allowed Habermas to retroactively theorize how the slow-moving circulatory matrix of print culture encouraged critical distance crucial to the development of public reason.

Weaver's neo-Platonic epistemology elided how social and historical entanglements shape hermeneutic projects, and Habermas's theory of electronic mass communication is hopelessly naïve. Still, the idea of critical distance is recuperable for rhetorical argumentation. Robert Scott (1967) noted "in substantial arguments, a shift in time always occurs. If a shift in time does not occur, then one is simply reporting what is present, not arguing" (p. 12). Critical distance aids in invention by multiplying different ways of attending to an artifact. Distance makes the critic grow stronger, as a preoccupation with an artifact stimulates, in Burke's

(1931/1968) terms, "exceptional variety" or "exceptional accurateness" (p. 170). Academic commonplaces like "let that idea simmer," "I need to let that marinate," or "that idea is half-baked" all register the importance of time in the inventional process.

Critical distance aids judgment, too, by broadening consideration of the argument's purview. As Hans Blumenberg (1987) eloquently noted:

> Rhetoric [is] a consummate embodiment of retardation. Circumstantiality, procedural inventiveness, ritualization imply a doubt as to whether the shortest way of connecting two points is also the most humane route from one to the other . . . A disproportion has arisen between the acceleration of processes and the feasibility of keeping a "feel" for them, of intervening in them with decisions, and of coordinating them, through an overview, with other processes.
>
> *(pp. 444–445)*

The dimension of time enables attention to the structure of argumentation by moving beyond reportage and toward inferences. Distance yields theoretical insight into the meta- and the macro-, into the structure of argumentation and not just the specifics of an argument itself; only with an appreciation of critical distance does the idea of *reasoned* public opinion make sense. Public deliberation is premised on a series of democratic iterations over time and space, drawing in and synthesizing participation from different perspectives. It is the movement of public argument through time that generates reasonability, as opinion receives critical testing, and publicity, because circulation through space and over time makes arguments legible for opinion-forming publics and "felt" by decision-making publics.

On Sentiment Analysis

There is little question that Twitter accelerates cycles of public argument for political campaigns: "with Twitter, rapid response has an even bigger role, with campaigns needing creative ways – video links, clever hashtags, pithy quips – to push their message, hoping to attract the attention of reporters and supporters" (Parker, 2012). Adam Sharp, head of Government, News, and Social Innovation at Twitter, noted "the shift from a 24-hour news cycle to a 140-character one has dramatically reshaped the rapid-response game. The whole action-reaction-response cycle is compressed to mere minutes" (as cited in Preston & Jaconi, 2012). What happens to the idea of reasoned public opinion in a networked public sphere when the time between iterations of publication shrinks? Following Weaver and Scott, public discourse presumably veers away from inference and back toward reportage. In contemporary digitally networked environments, that reportage is very often about feelings. Twitter, often accessed through mobile devices, affords quick publication in part by constraining extended argument through the 140-character limit on tweets. The more concise the statement, and the quicker the cycle of publication, the more likely it is to convey affective reactions rather than the evidenced and detailed argument forms that prevailed in early print media. This is not to say that, in an age of fast, internetworked media, the critical distance necessary for democratic deliberation inevitably withers. Twitter occasionally features in-depth arguments that span tens of tweets, and of course there is a host of networked media genres with no character constraints and differently punctuated cycles of publication.

In contrast to the public opinion polls made possible by the idea of reasoned public opinion, the publication of feelings through internetworked media give rise to the "public feeling poll." The 2012 election cycle showcased the ability of sentiment analysis, a method of datamining abundant streams of information, to analyze feeling in a political campaign. The most prominent of these public feeling polls was the Twindex, a joint venture between Twitter and the sentiment analysis firm Topsy. The blog post announcing the Twindex described it thusly:

> Each day, the Index evaluates and weighs the sentiment of Tweets mentioning Obama or Romney relative to the more than 400 million Tweets sent on all other topics. For example, a score of 73 for a candidate indicates that Tweets containing their name or account name are on average more positive than 73 percent of *all* Tweets. Just as new technologies like radar and satellite joined the thermometer and barometer to give forecasters a more complete picture of the weather, so too can the Index join traditional methods like surveys and focus groups to tell a fuller story of political forecasts. It lends new insight into the feelings of the electorate, but is not intended to replace traditional polling – rather, it reinforces it . . . the Twitter Political Index helps capture the nuances of public opinion.
>
> *(Sharp, 2012)*

As Twindex launched, Topsy (2012a) released an ethos-bolstering report claiming that, in comparison to "political polls for the past year, the Twitter Political Index was shown to be a valuable leading indicator of public opinion" (p. 2). The Twindex was welcomed by the chattering classes with awe: Matt Buchanan (2012) of *Buzzfeed* wrote "the Twitter Political Index leverages the growing science of sentiment analysis, in which computers – machines! – try to assess what the *meaning* or *feeling* of a piece of writing really is." Chris Cillizza (2012) intoned "ignore the 'Twindex' at your peril." Micah Sifry (2012) tempered this enthusiasm by cynically framing the Twindex thusly:

> Look out, everyone, the web just invented another leaderboard. And now the conversation about politics in America is going to get even dumber, because we have a new magic number to chatter about. Obama is at 34, down 4 from yesterday. Romney is at 25, up 2. Sell Obama! Buy Romney!

Everyday, Twitter's in-house @gov team would release that day's sentiment analysis based on Topsy metrics. As the campaign came to a close, @gov tweeted "Twitter Political Index for November 5, 2012: @BarackObama 66 (+7 since 11/4), @MittRomney 56 (+3)" (tweet, November 5, 2012, 4:33 p.m.). On election day, @gov tweeted "Our last #Election2012 #Twindex Update, for November 7, 2012: @BarackObama 85 (+11 since 11/6), @MittRomney 57 (-2)" (tweet, November 7, 2012, 4:42 p.m.). Lest you think that sentiment analysis perfectly called the election, Twitter also posted sentiment analysis specific to swing states: "On eve of #election2012 @MittRomney leads in #Twindex for 7/12 swing states: Virginia, Colorado, Nevada, Florida, New Hampshire, Ohio, Iowa" (tweet, November 5, 2012, 3:34 p.m.) and "On eve of #election2012 @BarackObama leads in #Twindex values for 4/12 swing states: Michigan, Pennsylvania, New Mexico, North Carolina" (tweet, November 5, 2012, 3:33 p.m.). Obama lost North Carolina and won all the swing states in which the Twindex gave Romney the edge in sentiment.

Peculiarities abound in the Twindex results. In late July, after Romney's botched visit to Israel, positive sentiment for Obama surged above 50, while Romney's languished at 30 (Topsy, 2012b, p. 6). By contrast, when the foreign policy experience of the Romney-Ryan ticket was called into question in mid-August, positive sentiment surged north of 50 for both candidates. After Romney's infamous "47%" comments were leaked, positive sentiment for him surged above 40 (Topsy, 2012c, p. 5). In the wake of Romney's widely panned appearance on *60 Minutes* in late September, in which the vagaries of his economic plan were confirmed to be mathematically impossible, positive sentiment for Romney surged (Topsy, 2012c, p. 4). Even in the first debate, where the consensus was that Obama lost badly, the two candidates virtually tied in positive sentiment in the high 30s (Topsy, 2012c, p. 3). The timeliness of the new networked rhetoric appears to favor uncritical reaffirmation of partisan sentiment in an effort to "rally-round-the-candidate."

On Public Feeling Polls

What the public opinion poll was to mass communication, the public feeling poll appears to be for networked communication: a novel way to measure public attitudes that shapes as it purports to represent, a way to generate insight bound to excite analysts of the political horserace, and a reflection of the broader cultural valuation – or lack thereof – of critical distance. Public feeling polls are increasingly widespread; joining the Twindex in 2012 was a similar Facebook/Politico collaboration and CNN's instant reaction ticker for the presidential debates. The emergence of public feeling polls – as part of a new dashboard of metrics including trending blog and Twitter topics, likes on social networking sites, recommendations on commercial sites, most-read and most-emailed articles, most-viewed videos, and the like – is a welcome destabilization of the hegemony that public opinion polls have exerted over U.S. publics for the last half-century. Moreover, by recentering the affective, public feeling polls recognize that electioneering mobilizes responses beyond the cognitive. Public feeling polls respond to the salient critique that traditional public opinion polls do not capture *intensity* of opinion. They may, too, capture sentiment in a more natural context of unprompted reaction, as opposed to the artificial, dubiously framed interviews that constitute public opinion polls. Most importantly, perhaps, public feeling polls avoid public opinion polls' pretenses of scientific measurement of reasoned opinion. Because the two kinds of polls track so closely, public feeling polls expose how public opinion polls have always, in some ways, basically been about measuring feelings.

Like public opinion polls, public feeling polls have methodological problems. The Twindex, for example, does not randomly sample to account for Twitter users historically trending young and to the political left. Current sentiment analysis is not semantically sophisticated enough to detect sarcasm, like that associated with the #ThanksObama hashtag. Sentiment analysis might be able to identify what is being attended to and what affect is being publicized, but not necessarily the connection between the two. In the case of the Twindex, the sentiment analysis scores were calculated only in relation to the sentiment being reflected in the broader Twitterverse. It is not clear that comparing positive and negative sentiment about Obama or Romney to sentiment about the travails of the Kardashian pregnancy, the fact that Honey Boo Boo is indeed coming, or the popularity of Gangnam Style necessarily tells us anything. Many a sentiment analyst's retort to these methodological qualms is that the sample size, measured in tens of millions of tweets, is big enough to dwarf these problems.

Despite the fact that public feeling polls are methodologically suspect, uncritical, and seemingly unargumentative, they appear destined to shape the future deliberative landscape. How, then, might argumentation scholars intervene in the ongoing conversation about sentiment analysis and public feeling polls? We might consider how public feeling polls change rhetorical processes of invention and judgment. We can neither be nostalgic for the slower circulation of print nor uncritical about the interrelationship between affect and cognition.

Our models of invention and judgment are changing, not evaporating. Inventional processes have shifted from an individual producing *copia* before publication to groups filtering through *copia* produced by many-to-many communication networks after publication. Judgment, too, persists, but within a network of public media networks working on wildly different frequencies (Hartley, 2003). Whether or not these networked modes of invention and judgment meet the demands for creative argument and decision in public deliberation calls for continued interrogation.

Along these lines, argumentation scholars might investigate how campaigns orchestrate affect in order to game the new public feeling polls. There are blunt efforts at orchestrating affect, as when campaigns draw on echo chamber amplification through coordinated campaigns to flood the zone with a specific affectively charged message. There are more subtle efforts, though, that take advantage of how positive affect circulates better than negative affect. For example, Obama's birthday received a Twindex score of 75; by contrast, his highest score at the DNC is 53 (Topsy, 2012b, p. 3). Savvy politicians and their handlers surely learn the lesson that a picture of a candidate hugging their partner, or a cute dog picture, or a vapid feel-good statement gins up positive sentiment. Public feelings as measured by sentiment analysis need not have any connection to issues in the campaign at all. The Romney campaign seemed to learn this lesson when they popularized the #obamadogrecipes hashtag in response to the bad press about strapping his own dog on the roof of the family car, sparking an Obama drop and Romney rise in the Twindex (Topsy, 2012a). The orchestration of public feeling may not be that distant from the orchestration of public opinion – but it calls for more analysis by argumentation scholars interested in the consequences of the new networked rhetoric's timeliness.

References

Blumenberg, H. (1987). An anthropological approach to the contemporary significance of rhetoric. In K. Baynes, J. Bohman, & T. A. McCarthy (Eds.), *After philosophy: End or transformation* (pp. 429–458). Cambridge, MA: MIT Press.

Buchanan, M. (2012, August 1). Twitter launches political index. *Buzzfeed*. Retrieved from http://web.archive.org/web/20130310192303/http://www.buzzfeed.com/mattbuchanan/twitter-launches-political-index-the-twitter-puls

Burke, K. (1968). *Counter-statement*. Berkeley: University of California Press. (Original work published 1931)

Cillizza, C. (2012, August 1). Introducing the Twitter political index [Web log message]! *The Washington Post The Fix* blog. Retrieved from http://www.washingtonpost.com/blogs/the-fix/post/introducing-the-twitter-political-index/2012/08/01/gJQAGniRPX_blog.html

Greene, R. W. (2002). Rhetorical pedagogy as a postal system: Circulating subjects through Michael Warner's "Publics and counter-publics." *Quarterly Journal of Speech, 88*(4), 434–443.

Hartley, J. (2003). The frequencies of public writing. In H. Jenkins & D. Thorburn (Eds.), *Democracy and new media* (pp. 247–270). Cambridge, MA: MIT Press.

Miller, Z. (2012, April 18). How Mitt Romney learned to love Twitter. *Buzzfeed*. Retrieved from http://web.archive.org/web/20120730171720/http://www.buzzfeed.com/zekejmiller/how-mitt-romney-learned-to-love-twitter

Parker, A. (2012, January 28). In nonstop whirlwind of campaigns, Twitter is a critical tool. *New York Times*. Retrieved from http://www.nytimes.com/2012/01/29/us/politics/twitter-is-a-critical-tool-in-republican-campaigns.html?pagewanted=all

Preston, M., & Jaconi, M. (2012, April 13). CNN's gut check for April 13, 2012 [Web log message]. *CNN Political Ticker* blog. Retrieved from http://politicalticker.blogs.cnn.com/2012/04/13/cnns-gut-check-for-april-13-2012/

Sarno, D. (2009, February 19). Jack Dorsey on the Twitter ecosystem, journalism and how to reduce reply spam, Part II [Web log message]. *Los Angeles Times Technology Blog*. Retrieved from http://latimesblogs.latimes.com/technology/2009/02/jack-dorsey-on.html

Sharp, A. (2012, August 1). A new barometer for the election [Web log message]. *Official Twitter Blog*. Retrieved from https://blog.twitter.com/2012/new-barometer-election

Shirky, C. (2009, June 16). Q&A with Clay Shirky on Twitter and Iran [Web log message]. *Ted Blog*. Retrieved from http://blog.ted.com/2009/06/16/qa_with_clay_sh/

Sifry, M. (2012, August 1). Twitter political index launches, but is it actually measuring "voter sentiment"? *TechPresident*. Retrieved from http://techpresident.com/news/22660/twitter-political-index-launches-it-actually-measuring-voter-sentiment#.UBmh29S6sAU.twitter

Topsy. (2012a, August 10). Twindex launch report. Retrieved from http://about.topsy.com/wp-content/uploads/2012/08/Twindex-report1.pdf

Topsy. (2012b, September 9). Twindex supplemental report: July 24-September 9, 2012. Retrieved from http://about.topsy.com/wp-content/uploads/2012/10/Twindex-report-9.9.12-Final.pdf

Topsy. (2012c, October 7). Twindex supplemental report: September 10-October 7, 2012. Retrieved from http://about.topsy.com/wp-content/uploads/2012/10/Twindex-update-report-102312.pdf

Tumulty, K. (2012, April 26). Twitter becomes a key real-time tool for campaigns. *Washington Post*. Retrieved from http://www.washingtonpost.com/politics/twitter-becomes-a-key-real-time-tool-for-campaigns/2012/04/26/gIQARf1TjT_story.html?tid=sm_twitter_washingtonpost

Virilio, P. (2005). *Desert screen: War at the speed of light*. New York, NY: Continuum.

Weaver, R. (1953). *The ethics of rhetoric*. Davis, CA: Hermagoras Press.

Xenos, M. (2008). New mediated deliberation: Blog and press coverage of the Alito nomination. *Journal of Computer-Mediated Communication*, *13*(2), 485–503.

34

SOMETHING FUNNY?

The *Laughing Joe Biden* meme as digital *topoi* within political argumentation

Susan A. Sci

REGIS UNIVERSITY, USA

David R. Dewberry

RIDER UNIVERSITY, USA

Although usually gregarious, Vice President Joe Biden appeared more animated than usual when facing vice presidential candidate Paul Ryan at Centre College in Danville, Kentucky, on October 12, 2012. Throughout the debate, Biden repeatedly smiled, smirked, laughed, and gestured wildly in disagreement and disbelief at several of Ryan's remarks. This performance – whether an embodiment of frustration, aggravation, or mockery – disturbed the normative standards of appropriate demeanor within vice presidential debates (Zak, 2012). Biden's behavior became a focal point in social media discourse and, thus, the perfect subject of Internet memes. The iconic moments when Biden grinned and laughed during the debate were commented on, captured, and widely circulated as divisive (and often hilarious) *Laughing Joe Biden* memes.

This essay theorizes the role Internet memes play within public discourse on social media about political debates by examining Twitter feeds about the 2012 vice presidential debate. We question how and why Internet memes, typically a popular-culture driven form of postmodern play, became an integral part of this political discourse. Generally speaking, the 2012 presidential election and debates were fertile ground for the creation of an array of Internet memes: *Save Big Bird*; *Binders Full of Women*; *Hey Girl, It's Paul Ryan*; *Malarkey*; and, of course, *Laughing Joe Biden*. Consequently, we ask what argumentative significance a meme possesses to make it so prominent in discourse on Twitter.

We analyzed the top tweets from the two main Twitter feeds about the Biden–Ryan debate: #debate and #vpdebate. We also examined fake Twitter handles, gifs, and image macro memes created about the debate that focus on Biden's laughter, smile, smirk, teeth, and/or dentures. Consequently, we argue that the *Laughing Joe Biden* memeplex, or range of memes addressing Biden's behavior, functioned as digital *topoi* in social mediated public discourse about the 2012 vice presidential debate. In argumentation theory, the term *topoi* has been widely contested and there is little consensus on its exact meaning. For this essay, we focus on what Miller (2000) called the "generative potential of the familiar" as an integral characteristic of *topoi* within the digital age (p. 134).

Like Hahner (2013), we are interested in theorizing the connection between memes and the "continued invention of arguments" about them by examining how a meme enables the use of a variety of interpretive schemas (p. 164). While Hahner employed frame theory to conceptualize memes as visual arguments, we have developed a theory of digital *topoi* to explicate how memes are adapted and used to generate arguments on social media sites. To explain this, first, we briefly discuss how the *Laughing Joe Bide* meme was generative on Twitter. Then, we argue that *topoi* as a "scheme of argument" (Rubinelli, 2006, p. 255) can be adapted using an analytic framework of memetics to establish a theory of digital *topoi*. Finally, we explain the findings of our analysis of the top tweets as digital *topoi* before discussing some brief conclusions.

The 2012 Vice Presidential Debate

After President Obama's lackluster performance during the first presidential debate, anxiety ran high among liberals who hoped Biden would play offense by pushing the Democratic ticket and re-energizing the base. Yet given his history of gaffes, many Democrats were concerned that Vice President Biden's penchant for colorful behavior would jeopardize his debate performance. What transpired during the 90-minute debate prompted Jim Messina, Obama's campaign manager, to call Biden a "happy warrior" armed with "facts versus index-card talking points" (as cited in Sonmez, 2012, para. 2). This strength, however, was also a cause for concern.

Biden's seemingly jovial demeanor, in contrast to Ryan's seriousness, became a focal point of viewers' attention. The debate became the "8th most social TV event of all time" with over 4.6 million comments on Twitter (Dowling, 2012, para. 1). Out of those comments, more than 500,000 focused on Biden's smiles and laughter (Phillip, 2012, para. 10). By the end of the debate, there were approximately 22 hashtags and 53 fake Twitter handles referencing Biden's laughter, smirk, smile, teeth, or dentures. With such attention, mainstream news organizations like *The New York Times* and blogs such as Politico and Buzzfeed soon began to report on the meme itself. Clearly, the *Laughing Joe Biden* meme quickly became a prominent part of this public discourse that, we contend, functioned as a digital *topos* for those watching and tweeting the vice presidential debate.

Digital *Topoi*

Not restricted to one ideological system or logic, *topoi* are rhetorical commonplaces among discourses from which disparate and even conflicting claims and reasons can be generated about a subject. As Blinn and Garrett (1993) asserted, *topoi* "function as irreducible concepts from which reasoning proceeds" and can be considered a *loci* of argumentative invention (p. 94). Rubinelli (2006) asserted that within ancient rhetoric *topoi* were used in four main ways: subject matter indicators, schemes of argument, ready-made arguments, and argumentation in general. We focus on *topoi* as schemes of argument which emphasize "the process of inference" that enables rhetors to identify propositions through the relationship between "a certain standpoint" and specific "premises/ conclusions" (Rubinelli, 2006, p. 256).

Topoi, therefore, can help rhetors locate subjects/issues/ideas ripe for debate as well as assist them in generating particular claims by recognizing how the topic can be used from a specific position to reach a desired conclusion. While watching the vice presidential debates, viewers identified Biden's smile and laughter as a loaded topic rife with political and social meaning regarding his image and character. Hence, we focus on a particular schematic form that "leads speakers to focus on interpersonal, emotional and linguistic aspects surrounding the production of arguments" in contexts where "the character of the speakers and the emotions of the audience are driving forces to consider when designing an argument" (Rubinelli, 2006, p. 262).

Gunn (2005) argued that these common sites of reasoning and inference are not limited to discursive forms and theorizes "iconic" *topoi* as "fragments of films or other media texts that are made to signify a number of different things depending on their contextualization" (p. 107). Similarly, we theorize digital *topoi* as taking both discursive and non-discursive memetic forms. The malleability of digital data allows the *topos* of Joe Biden's laughter to quickly transform from more discursive memetic forms (i.e., tweets and fake Twitter accounts such as @LaughingJoeBiden) to more visual ones (i.e., image macro memes such as *Laughing Joe Biden* and *Malarkey*) while still addressing the same common topic but inferring conclusions and articulating claims about Biden's demeanor from a diverse range of subject positions.

Our theory of digital *topoi* utilizes memetics as an analytic framework to conceptualize how common sites of argumentation (i.e., Biden's smile and laughter) quickly and thoroughly spread across social media. In his foundational work, *The Selfish Gene,* Dawkin (1976) coined the term *meme* to describe a small unit of cultural information that is transmitted between individuals, or hosts, enabling cultural survival, inheritance, and evolution. Memes produce thoughts, or memetic ideas, which individuals can discursively and non-discursively communicate to support the meme's survival via mediated circulation. For instance, within only seven minutes of the debate's beginning, four people simultaneously tweeted about Biden's smile and/or laughter and five more top tweets about the same topic were produced, replicating this meme in just two minutes. Distin (2005) argued that memetic evolution relies on the selection, replication, and variation of memes. A meme's evolution is dependent on the socio-cultural environment one encounters it in as well as the individual's cognitive processes and development. Scholars can gain insight into the argumentative significance of a meme as digital topoi by mapping its use and circulation in relation to the socio-cultural environment, details of the memetic text, and the connection between the arguer's position and her/his claim.

Even though the role of human agency has been hotly contested among memetic scholars, we agree with Shifman (2011) who "stress[ed] that human agency should be an integral part of our conceptualization of memes [within the digital age] by describing them as dynamic entities that spread in response to technological, cultural and social *choices* made by people" (p. 189). Simply put, human agency is still relevant due to the role individual choice plays in how one communicates memetic ideas and produces cultural artifacts based upon them. People are continually in contact with an array of memes competing for their attention. During the selection process, successful memes can become manifest in cultural artifacts such as music, art, food, fashion, etc.

"However," Shifman (2011) explained, "only memes suited to their socio-cultural environment will spread successfully" (p. 188). In the vice presidential debates, the meme of Biden's laughter and smile was selected among other debate topics to be manifested within fake Twitter accounts, hashtags, gifs, and image macro memes. We argue that the *Laughing Joe Biden* meme did more than simply survive; it flourished as a digital *topos* from which Twitter users produced arguments regarding Biden's debate behavior that were based on the relation between the user's subject position and the particular conclusions s/he had arrived at about the socio-cultural and political implications of Biden's demeanor on the debate and/or U.S. society.

The *Laughing Joe Biden* Meme as Digital *Topoi*

For our analysis, we favorite'd over 267 top tweets from the Twitter feeds #debate and #vpdebate during the 90-minute Biden-Ryan contest. These tweets inferred or directly referenced Biden's performance by using variations of the terms: smile, smirk, grin, laugh, giggle, giddy, snicker, facial expression, dentures, or teeth. Rather than examine memes individually to assess the ideological meaning of singular tweets, we mapped the movement and use of *Laughing Joe Biden* memes to determine their argumentative significance. Johnson (2007) demanded the use of geographically oriented materialist critique when analyzing memes because they are "sheer surface, and there is nothing to interpret because the meme does not mean anything, or contain anything" (p. 43). That is, the significance of a meme lies in its surface use, not the hidden ideological meaning critics often strive to unearth. By mapping the argumentative use of the *Laughing Joe Biden* meme, we found it was employed to invent claims from four different digital *topoi* categorizes. They are: Good/Bad Strategy, Appropriate/Inappropriate Behavior, Emotional Connection, and Ridicule.

The digital *topos* of Good/Bad Strategy enabled users to make claims concerning the effect Biden's smiles and laughter did or would have on his ability to influence voters. The inferential process focused on Biden's overall demeanor to establish a stance on whether or not the U.S. people would find his laughter appealing. For instance, journalist Bernard Goldberg tweeted, "Every time Biden laughs he gets another vote for Romney. Biden coming off as smug. Americans don't like smug. #debate." Similarly, Ashlee Glenn tweeted, "Uncle Joe is doing a great job but needs to keep those smile and laughs under control. No one likes smug. No one. #VPDebates." In both examples, the user identified Biden's demeanor as an inefficient strategy to gain voters' support. Some tweets included references to past debates (i.e., Gore's sighs in 2000 election) to strengthen their case. This *topoi* assumes a relational dynamic between the Twitter user and Biden as one of armchair pundit/candidate, and a relation of pundit/audience to his/her fellow Twitter users. Consequently, individuals were not invited to debate or question the pundit's claims; rather the arguer used a factual tone that does not validate, or even acknowledge, opposing opinions. Thus, the movement and use of this digital *topos* assumed a network of spectators in which the interactivity of social networking allowing immediate rejoinders is not considered as essential as Twitter's usefulness as a platform from which to announce one's claim.

The second digital *topos* is Appropriate/Inappropriate Behavior. Twitter users often asserted claims regarding the propriety of Biden's smiles and laughter within the context of the debate. Depending on the user's interpretation of Biden's actions, the arguer concluded that Biden was either a "good" or "bad" candidate. For example, user Bradman TV tweeted "If you think Biden being condescending is a good Vice President Trait . . . Please unfollow me. . #VPDebates." On the other hand, Liza Featherstone claimed, "Everyone is hating on the Biden laughter, I think it is a very human response to the b.s. he is listening to. #Biden #debate #VPdebates." In these cases, the users made judgments regarding whether Biden's actions were reasonable given his title or the context, which is the basis of their support or rejection of Biden as vice president. From this *topos*, users established a proponent/opponent relation to Biden and also assumed a relationship based on agreement/ disagreement with other users. While arguments in this category do allow for discussion, a continual debate is uncommon. Rather agreement tended to be expressed in retweeting or favoring a tweet, and disagreement was shown with a mocking reply or in unfollowing someone. By using this digital *topos*, users can activate networks of ideological affiliation (i.e., liberals/conservative) to assist in the circulation of their claims in hopes of influencing public opinion.

Emotional Connection is the third digital *topos*. Arguments in this category posited an affective reaction to Biden's jovial state. There were three common affective reactions exhibited in these tweets: anger, adoration, and frustration. In tweets that exhibited anger, users made statements regarding how irate and/or repulsed they were by Biden's smile and laughter. A strong example is Connor Webb's tweet: "Biden you smug mofo I swear I wanna slap that smirk right off your face! #VPDebates." On the other hand, tweets expressing adoration seemed to revel in Biden's behavior. As user Real World stated, "God, i love Biden's smile/laughter while listening. He reads clear #vpdebate (yeah, I know I said that already- just #loveit." Regardless of whether the user supported or opposed Biden, tweets expressing frustration seem to be driven by a desire to stop Biden's behavior. For instance, Sam Weatherhead asserted, "this isn't fricking comedy hour Biden. stop laughing like a little school girl. I actually want to hear what you have to say #debate." The process of inference for this digital *topos* assumed an intimate, yet mediated, relationship between the user and Biden. Consequently, Biden's actions were seen as a personal affront/pleasure/annoyance and arguments were created based on how the user felt in response to this perception. In doing so, this *topos* created positions of (angry) hater/(adoring) fan/(frustrated) participant between the user and Biden and a dynamic of support/denial with other users depending on each user's own emotional reaction to Biden. Dean's (2010) theory of "affective networks" best describes how these individuals use social media to "produce and circulate affect as a binding technique" to connect users to others in their networks and spark "feelings of community or what we might call 'community without community'" (p. 21–22).

The final digital *topos* was Ridicule, which included tweets that lampooned and mocked Joe Biden *or* Paul Ryan. These tweets used Biden's smile and laughter as a main premise of a joke that ridiculed either debater. These tweets typically took one of three forms: absurdist claims, punch lines, and mocking assertions. Absurdist claims completely decontextualized Biden's actions and used intertextual allusions to develop general arguments regarding the ridiculousness. A humorous example was Ologies's claim, "If Joe Biden were a wrestler, his finishing move would be Devastating Laugh. #debates #teamFbomb." The absurdity here not only called attention to the silliness of Biden's behavior but also the complete decontextualization of his actions suggested that the user did not believe the vice presidential debates need to be taken seriously. The general format of punch lines offered the classic set-up question, "What makes Joe Biden laugh?" and users answered in pithy one-liners that poke fun at either Biden or Ryan (e.g., Josh Hopkins' statement, "Every time Biden smiles, he pictures Ryan wearing a propeller hat. #VPDebate"). Hopkins's use of this *topos* was grounded in ageist humor highlighting the difference in the candidates' experience, positing the vice president as a seasoned elder and Congressperson Ryan as a silly child whom we should not treat seriously. Finally, the last form is mocking assertions. As one of the "most aggressive forms of humor," mocking jeopardizes the subject's reputation "by attacking his or her competence – picking on some mistake in performance, whether spoken, acted, or even merely imagined" (Everts, 2003, p. 374). Scott Monty's tweet, "Joe Biden's foreign policy: laughing, deriding, and a 'bunch of stuff'," is a prime instance of mocking. In each example, a relational dynamic of jester/subject established an unequal relationship between the user and Biden/Ryan based on a sense of superiority over the subject. In this way, the digital *topos* of Ridicule activated a network of entertainment from which users related to one another through the playful engagement with the *Laughing Joe Biden* meme at the expense of Biden and/or Ryan's political character.

Conclusions and Implications

Our analysis highlights how *Laughing Joe Biden* memes functioned as digital *topoi* within social media discourse about the 2012 vice presidential debate. By theorizing memes as digital *topoi*, argumentation scholars can assess a meme's argumentative significance by mapping its movement and use to generate claims about a particular subject (i.e., Biden's laughter). This analysis offers scholars insights into how meme use activates relational networks to circulate one's claim and conceptualizes the dynamic between how individuals position themselves in relation to events, politicians, and other participants to assert specific claims or conclusions. We believe this essay supports Shifman's (2013) stance that while memes "spread on a micro basis, [their] impact is on the macro" (p. 365) via the invention and circulation of arguments.

References

Blinn, S. B., & Garrett, M. (1993). Aristotelian *topoi* as a cross-cultural analytical tool. *Philosophy and Rhetoric, 26*(2), 93–112.

Dawkins, R. (1976). *The selfish gene.* Oxford, UK: Oxford University Press.

Dean, J. (2010). Affective networks. *Media Tropes, 2*(2), 19–44.

Distin, K. (2005). *The selfish meme: A critical reassessment.* Cambridge: Cambridge University Press.

Dowling, E. (2012, October 12). The VP debate breaks into the top ten most social TV events of all time. *Blue Fin Labs.* Retrieved from https://wordpress.blucfinlabs.com/blog/2012/10/12/the-vp-debate-breaks-into-the-top-ten-most-social-tv-events-of-all-time/

Everts, E. (2003). Identifying a particular family humor style: A sociolinguistic discourse analysis. *Humor, 16*(4), 369–412.

Gunn, J. (2005). Prime-time satanism: rumor-panic and the work of iconic *topoi. Visual Communication, 4*(1), 93–120.

Hahner, L. A. (2013). The riot kiss: Framing memes as visual argument. *Argumentation and Advocacy, 49*(3), 151–166.

Johnson, D. (2007). Mapping the meme: A geographical approach to materialist rhetorical criticism. *Communication and Critical/Cultural Studies, 4*(1), 27–50.

Miller, C. R. (2000). The Aristotelian *topos*: Hunting for novelty. In A. G. Gross and A. E. Walzer (Eds.), *Rereading Aristotle's Rhetoric* (pp. 130–48). Carbondale: Southern Illinois University Press.

Phillip, A. D. (2012, October 11). "Laughin' Joe" steals the show at vice presidential debate. *ABC News.* Retrieved from http://abcnews.go.com/blogs/politics/2012/10/laughing-joe-steals-the-show-at-vice-presidential-debate/

Rubinelli, S. (2006). The ancient argumentative game: τόποι and *loci* in action. *Argumentation, 20*(3), 253–272.

Shifman, L. (2011). An anatomy of a YouTube meme. *New Media & Society, 14*(2), 187–203.

Shifman, L. (2013). Memes in a digital world: Reconciling with a conceptual troublemaker. *Journal of Computer-Mediated Communication, 18*(3), 362–377.

Sonmez, F. (2012, October 11). Jim Messina: Biden a "happy warrior" [Web log message]. *Washington Post.* Retrieved from http://www.washingtonpost.com/blogs/post-politics/wp/2012/10/11/jim-messina-biden-a-happy-warrior/

Zak, D. (2012, October 12). Mano a mano, with few holds barred. We want more of this. *Washington Post*, p. A8.

35

THIRD PARTY RHETORIC AND THE CONSTITUTION OF AN AUDIENCE

Philip Tschirhart

UNIVERSITY OF MISSOURI – COLUMBIA, USA

Only twice have general election, nationally televised presidential campaign debates included third party candidates. Of these two times, only once, in the 1992 presidential debate, were both major parties and a third party represented on the same stage. While the 2012 series of prime-time televised presidential debates did not include third party candidates, other networks sought to fill the void, offering debate viewers a third party perspective. In total, the 2012 election cycle offered viewers five third party candidate debates. Only one of these debates included the four leading third party candidates in a traditional podium style debate. The three debates sponsored by Democracy Now streamed online alongside the major party debates and offered candidates the opportunity to respond to the same questions as the major party candidates. Democracy Now's "pause and pretend" format ignored the agenda of third party candidates and constrained candidates' responses.

The debate organized and sponsored by Free & Equal Elections Foundation (FEEF) – the fourth in the series of five – sought to distinguish itself from the others. FEEF's founder and debate co-moderator Christina Tobin promised a debate without "contracts and private interests controlling the questions we ask and the answers the candidates deliver" (Forgrave, 2012). By modifying the familiar podium debate format, this third party presidential debate sought to lend legitimacy to candidates who may be unfamiliar or unknown to their audience. In positioning the debate in contrast to major party debates, the FEEF debate provided candidates an opportunity for an alternative vision to be enacted through debate discourse. Through candidates' contrasting visions, the possibility for an alternative public and future was entertained. These moments of rhetorical exigency allow for an examination of how third party candidates identify and constitute their audiences.

As third party candidates distinguish themselves from one another and the major parties, they are simultaneously challenged to appeal to a broader audience. Third party candidates frequently align themselves with social, environmental, and political movements to mobilize disenfranchised voters. In addition to being a representative of their party's platform, the candidates also recognize their marginalized status as third parties and encourage broader political representation. The FEEF debate provided candidates an opportunity to articulate their party's platform in contrast to both major party candidates and fellow third party candidates. As candidates articulated their vision for the future, they performed a type of social movement maintenance. Through contrasting arguments, the FEEF debate provided an opportunity for candidates to grow their publics. Candidates had to confront viewers' wasted vote concerns while simultaneously opening a space that has become dominated by the impulse to vote for the lesser of *two* evils.

This study seeks to identify those moments in third party debate discourse where an audience is identified, addressed, or called to action in an effort to determine how third party candidates distinguish themselves from one another and the major party candidates. The review of literature seeks to position third party debates as an important site of argumentation scholarship. Next, drawing on the constitutive framework, this study seeks to identify the appeals used to interpellate an audience and transcend subjects' wasted vote or lesser of two evils tension. Finally, my discussion of these appeals seeks to characterize emergent third party discursive strategies and offer recommendations for future study.

Third Party Debates

Political communication scholars have analyzed presidential debates as far back as the first nationally televised presidential debate between John F. Kennedy and Richard Nixon in 1960. As lines of inquiry have developed and scholarship has flourished, various dimensions of political debates have been highlighted. To date, numerous facets of presidential debates have been scrutinized by scholars. Yet, despite a wealth of debate scholarship, third party candidates and their debates remain largely absent from analysis for three significant reasons. First, the sponsorship and organization of third party presidential debates has only emerged since 2004. Second, third party candidates and their debates reach a smaller audience. Third, as a result of their marginalized status, the significance of third party candidates' discourses is easily discounted. In offering an analysis of third party rhetoric, I seek to defend their significance before positioning third party rhetoric as a necessary site for argumentation scholarship.

Although third party candidates have appeared more frequently on local and state debate stages, their national organization is a more recent phenomenon that merits inquiry. Where major party presidential debates are media spectacles, third party debates operate on the margins. The previous three election cycles, however, have facilitated increased debate opportunities for third party presidential candidates. These third party presidential debates have been organized by independent media outlets and candidates seeking additional opportunity for exposure. The 2012 election provided the greatest number of third party presidential debate opportunities to date, with various combinations of candidates appearing for a total of five organized debates. The increasing frequency of these debates may be attributed to the decreased costs of national media dissemination associated with Internet broadcasting channels. However, previous research on third party candidates at the state level suggested a correlation between third party candidate success and dissatisfaction with state government (Lacy & Morgan, 2002; Sifry, 2002). With public opinion polls reporting record-high dissatisfaction with the two-party system, it is possible that voters and independent media outlets may have looked to third parties' presidential candidates to offer alternatives (Mak, 2011).

For political communication scholars, the limited viewership of third party debates may detract from their social, political, and academic significance. However, previous debate research identifies marginalized voters as the most significant audience in regards to political debate effects (McKinney & Carlin, 2008). Third party presidential debates are uniquely positioned to appeal to marginalized or undecided voters. The third party research that does exist suggests that third parties are able to reach and mobilize disenfranchised and uncommitted voters (Green, 2010; Luks, Miller, & Jacobs, 2003; Southwell, 2003). In reaching new audiences and mobilizing alternative publics, third party politicians represent a marginalized voice in the U.S. political system. Regardless of debate viewership, scholars should be listening to these voices and seeking to understand the communicative strategies of marginalized politicians and their publics.

Despite third party candidates' struggle to gain political representation, previous research illustrates their policy success. Kraus (1999) credited third party ideologies for "90% of the ideas that have shaped our democracy," identifying "women's right to vote, abolition of slavery, and the minimum wage" as issues that were injected into the mainstream by third party rhetors (p. 111). While difficult to quantify, the willingness of third parties to tackle unpopular issues is not hard to identify. Ross Perot's focus on and demand for deficit reduction in 1992 was usurped (or blurred) by both major party candidates in 1996, significantly decreasing Perot's platform and appeal but guaranteeing the issue national attention (Green, 2010). Ralph Nader's 2.7 percent of national turnout in 2000 has been associated with somehow "spoiling" the election for Al Gore (Whitmore, 2008); yet Nader has also been given credit for foreshadowing concerns about corporate corruption and the forthcoming financial crisis (Manon, 2011). As third party candidates organize to create social change, communication scholars should resist prioritizing political success as a reason for inquiry and should instead seek to identify significant arguments, appeals, and strategies used by both major party candidates and also those of third party representatives.

Textual Analysis

The FEEF debate was the only opportunity for television viewers to witness all four of the 2012 third party presidential candidates on the same stage. Co-moderated by Christina Tobin and television personality Larry King and broadcast by C-SPAN, Al Jazeera English, Russia Today, and several smaller satellite broadcasters, the FEEF debate offered candidates the opportunity to reach a larger audience than the previous streaming debates. Cognizant that "'mainstream' language also shuts down possibilities for a transformative counter hegemonic politics" (Abbott, 2007, p. 26), this study privileges the voices of four third party candidates who are provided a rare opportunity to constitute a broader audience than previously available.

Even though third party debate viewers exist as an ephemeral audience, the debate format provides candidates with an opportunity to identify and mobilize new supporters. This study seeks to identify the appeals used to interpellate an audience, transcend third party marginalization, and constitute and mobilize an audience. My textual analysis of the debate transcript identifies rhetorical tropes, themes, and narratives used by the third party candidates to identify, address, and persuade their audience. The present criticism seeks to illustrate how third parties attempt to constitute and consubstantiate with a broader audience when given the opportunity to engage in a distinctively third party debate. Together these steps shed light on how marginalized candidates use argumentative strategies to appeal to a wider audience in addition to providing debate theorists an alternative model of third party debate rhetoric.

Interpretive Analysis

The FEEF debate challenged third party presidential candidates to distinguish themselves from more familiar major party candidates. Candidates responded with three concomitant appeals. First, by projecting the collaborative "we" as opposed to the possessive "I," candidates explicitly positioned their constitutive narratives as within the audience's worldview. Second, narratives contrasting the "common person" from "fat cats" created a binary favoring the third party candidate as the righteous choice for representation of the people. Third, as candidates responded to their counter-hegemonic position, they united to attack the status quo and framed major party leadership outside of their audience's ideology. In the analysis that follows, all quotations originate from a verbatim transcript I created based on audio and video recordings of the debate archived on the FEEF webpage (Forgrave, 2012).

As the candidates extended their worldviews, seeking to include the audience, they simultaneously excluded their opposition. Gary Johnson of the Libertarian Party identified himself as one of the people, the collective "we," in an effort to position the audience, *the people*, a collective subject misguided by *our* government:

> I will tell you that regardless of whether or not Romney or Obama gets elected three things are going to happen. We are going to find ourselves with a continued heightened police state in this country. We are going to find ourselves continuing to militarily intervene in the world, which results, has resulted, in hundreds of millions of enemies for this country that would otherwise not exist . . . Lastly, we are going to find ourselves in a continued state of unsustainable spending and borrowing to the point that we are going to experience a monetary collapse unless we fix this.

In positioning their audience as subjects of a hypothetical future world narrative, third party politicians envisioned a government out of control unless we-the-people take back our government. In positioning the audience as actors in the discourse, third party candidates necessitated their subject's future action to avert an Obama/Romney election and its implied dangers.

As counter-hegemonic discourses, third party presidential debates provide candidates a legitimized forum to address their marginalization. By offering ways to re-story the narrative, candidates seek to reconcile the wasted vote concern. Through a variety of ideographs, candidates suggested that it is only through rejecting the corporate interests of major parties and voting for a third party that the people will benefit. Justice Party candidate Rocky Anderson's opening statement exemplified candidates' empathic narrative strategy of framing corporate corruption as preventing real change and effective governance:

> We are at a pivotal moral point in our nation's history. We've all suffered through the sellout of our government to Wall Street. Young people are burdened with crushing record tuition debt, millions of families have lost their homes, retirement accounts have been decimated while Wall Street fat cats who are buying our elections have made out like bandits . . . So if you like the way things are going vote Democratic or republican, if you want real change, vote your conscious, vote justice – economic justice, social justice, and environmental justice.

Where Rocky Anderson articulated "fat cats," Jill Stein of the Green Party suggested "the wealthy few are richer than ever, rolling in more dough than ever and the political establishment is not only *not* making it better, they are actually making it worse." Even conservative candidates Gary Johnson and Virgil Goode of the Constitution Party extended these tropes throughout their narratives. Johnson illustrated a nefarious connection between banks and the federal government and advocated eliminating the IRS and overhauling the Federal

Reserve. Virgil Goode signified a commitment to end super PACs, suggesting the removal of corporate influence "would be one of the best things that would open up our country to more democratic process and the greater voice by the people."

While the FEEF debate presented four candidates of varying political ideologies, candidates largely opted to avoid direct attack on one another. Where disagreement existed, third party attacks on the major party offerings sought to establish unity and a collective subject position. Moreover, the structure of the debate and its journalistic framing contributed to a unified perspective. The first question of the debate concerned ballot access initiatives, a uniquely third party issue. This question served to set the tone of the debate as candidates united to suggest, as Jill Stein did, the independent parties "represent real values." Gary Johnson referred to the voices of the two major parties' candidates as "tweedle dee and tweedle dumb" and Virgil Goode attacked both major parties' economic platforms and used his opening statement to articulate four positions where he deviated from the Obama administration. In projecting a united front of criticism, third party presidential candidates sought to facilitate a joint ideological interpellation creating identification through contrast with a beleaguered two party system.

Discussion and Conclusion

As third party presidential candidates are presented the chance to reach a broader audience through the organization and structure of debate, they are provided an opportunity to hypothetically envision their presidency for a broader audience of subjects. In operating through past, present, and future tenses, these narratives illustrated candidates' marginalized subject position, called for collective mobilization, and constructed an alternative future for their audience. Through narratives, the candidates took turns demonstrating their vision for the future with hypothetical references to themselves as presidents. By offering a re-storied or alternative rhetoric, such narratives sought to mobilize marginalized voters by rearticulating existing tensions so as to contain or resolve experienced contradictions associated with third parties' unique rhetorical exigencies. In this way, use of the first person perspective and hypothetical presidential narrative provided realism and resolution to audience members concerned with wasting their votes.

As third party rhetors positioned themselves in relation to one another, they focused on drawing distinctions between themselves and the major parties. Jill Stein identified the U.S. people as in "crisis," with the global climate in "meltdown" and civil liberties "under attack"; Rocky Anderson posited a pivotal moral point; and Virgil Goode implicated the major parties' monarchy. Continuing the binary construction, Gary Johnson framed the country in "deep trouble" and warned of a "monetary collapse." In presenting audiences with re-storied narratives of the major party candidates, third party candidates recognized audience members' alternative ballot options. However, by framing major party support as the cause of oppression, corruption, and future crisis, subjects were presented with a pre-determined choice. In effect, populism and its "crisis narrative of a 'people' can be popularized and a group can be mobilized" through a narrative of "victimization and redemption" (Lee, 2006, p. 363). However, as previous research illustrates, the exigencies of third party rhetors more often constrain their constitutive efforts. As third party presidential candidates reach out to new audiences, they must establish their unique identity, defend from ideological blur, and overcome subject positions experiencing dialectical constraint. Regardless of their rhetorical methods, third party presidential candidates are challenged to not only interpellate their audience, but also to motivate their audience.

As political argumentation scholarship seeks to analyze political efficacy, issue ownership, and the attack/acclaim/defense strategies of campaign debates, scholars from all paradigms are encouraged to identify those discourses that envision an alternative public. "As institutions that represent the public interests pursue practices antithetical to enabling discourse, communication theorists would do well to preserve the potentiality of this alternative sphere, lest the capacity of all human communication be diminished" (Goodnight, 1987, p. 431). In preserving this sphere, three themes emerge from my analysis to guide future research. First, narrative constitutions of *the people* function to provide the mechanism for investigations of past, present, and future constructions of alternative worldviews. In articulating these interpellated subject positions, boundary issues are identified and their potential for blur or circumvention is explored. Secondly, by framing a crisis, counter-hegemonic politicians draw on populist rhetoric to mobilize an audience. The effects of this populist rhetoric should be explored through quantitative measures and elaborated with qualitative analysis in future research. Finally, dichotomous or binary constitutions seek to transcend persuasion and promote transformation. As third party presidential candidates articulate an alternative ideology, they seek to present a world where no vote is wasted in the effort to mobilize real social change for *the people*. As future third party presidential debates inject themselves into the mainstream political discourse, scholars should value their alternative voice, explore their unique exigency, and articulate their counter-hegemonic subject position.

References

Abbot, B. (2007, November). *From extreme to mainstream, or how to win an election without taking a position*. Paper presented at the National Communication Association Conference, Chicago: IL.

Charland, M. (1987) Constitutive rhetoric: The case of the *Peuple Quebecois*. *Quarterly Journal of Speech*, *73*(2), 133–150.

Charland, M. (1995, August). The Constitution of rhetoric's audience. In S. Jackson (Ed.), *Argumentation and Values: Proceedings of the Ninth SCA/AFA Conference on Argumentation* (pp. 12–15). Annandale, VA: Speech Communication Association.

Forgrave, M. (Producer). (2012). *Free & Equal Elections 2012 presidential debate* [Video file]. Retrieved from https://www.freeandequal.org/2012-presidential-debate

Goodnight, G. T. (1987). Public discourse. *Critical Studies in Mass Communication*, *4*(4), 428–431.

Green, D. J. (2010). *Third party matters: Politics, presidents, and third parties in American history*. Santa Barbara, CA: ABC-Clio.

Kraus, S. (1999). *Televised presidential debates and public policy*. Mahwah, NJ: Lawrence Erlbaum Associates.

Lacy, D., & Monson, Q. (2002). The origins and impact of votes for third-party candidates: A case study of the 1998 Minnesota gubernatorial election. *Political Research Quarterly*, *55*, 409–437.

Lee, M. L. (2006). The populist chameleon: The people's party, Huey Long, George Wallace, and the populist argumentative frame. *Quarterly Journal of Speech*, *92*(4), 355–378.

Luks, S., Miller, J. M., & Jacobs, L. R. (2003). Who wins? Campaigns and the third party vote. *Presidential Studies Quarterly*, *33*(1), 9–30.

McKinney, M. S., & Carlin, D. B. (2008). Political campaign debates. In L. L. Kaid (Ed.), *Handbook of political communication*. Mahwah, NJ: Lawrence Erlbaum Publishers.

Mak, T. (2011, September 26). Poll: 81% unhappy with government. *Politico*. Retrieved from http://www.politico.com

Manon, P. (2011). Ralph Nader: Public health advocate and political agitator. *American Journal of Public Health*, *101*(2), 257.

Sifry, M. L. (2002). *Spoiling for a fight: Third-party politics in America*. New York, NY: Routledge.

Southwell, P. L. (2003). The politics of alienation: Nonvoting and support for third-party candidates among 18–30 year olds. *Social Science Journal*, *40*, 99–107.

Whitmore, A. (2008). Schism on the left: The motivations and impact of Ralph Nader's Candidacy. *Political Quarterly*, *79*(4), 556–559.

36

WHAT "WENT WRONG" IN THE FIRST OBAMA–ROMNEY DEBATE?

David Zarefsky

NORTHWESTERN UNIVERSITY, USA

If your name is Mitt Romney, the answer is "Nothing at all." The first presidential debate of 2012 vindicated the candidate's time-consuming and disciplined preparation and fixed the burden on Barack Obama to defend his record. Evidence of the political benefit came quickly: 70% of respondents to a CBS poll thought Romney had won (Alter, 2013, p. 326), and he stopped or reversed the momentum Obama had developed in almost all of the "swing" states.

If your name is Barack Obama, you did not at first recognize that anything was amiss. In his closing statement, Obama proclaimed that it had been a "terrific debate," but he was soon disabused of that belief. In their post-election retrospective, *New York Times* reporters suggested that the debate led Obama "suddenly [to confront] the possibility of a loss" and "sharply exposed Mr. Obama's vulnerabilities and forced the president and his advisers to work to reclaim the campaign over a grueling 30 days" (Nagourney, Parker, Rutenberg, & Zeleny, 2012, p. P1). Something had gone wrong. Perhaps Obama was rusty, having not participated in debates since 2008. He seemed inattentive and easily distracted during his practice sessions (Nagourney et al., 2012). Maybe the nonverbals were off; Obama spent too much time looking down at his notes. Or perhaps he would not seem "presidential" if he fought harder. Alter (2013) mentioned that Obama's disdain for Romney and the hard-right turn of his primary campaign led him to underestimate his opponent. And then there was the risk that Obama would evoke the negative stereotype of the angry black male if he responded too aggressively.

While there is widespread agreement that something went wrong, and considerable speculation about why, there has been little focus on just *what* went wrong. It is that question that I wish to address. Reading the debate, it seems closer than one recalls (Alter, 2013, p. 325); one can parse the transcripts and find elements of winning arguments. But that exercise would require a far more charitable critic than anyone has a right to expect. If one instead asked the question posed by debate judges, "Who did the better debating?," the polls are correct in reporting a Romney victory. That suggests that Obama's weakness may relate to debate skills and strategy.

Setting the Stage

The debate was held on October 3 at the University of Denver and was moderated by Jim Lehrer. The format was new. The 90-minute debate would be split into six segments of approximately 15 minutes. Each candidate would have two minutes to respond to the moderator's question. Then there would be a discussion, moderated by Lehrer, that would probe more deeply, focus points of disagreement, or prod candidates to answer questions they might have preferred to ignore. There would be no formal allotments of discussion time and no guarantee of equal time. Each candidate also would have a two-minute closing statement.

Things did not work out exactly as planned. The three segments on the economy overlapped and the first one took much longer than 15 minutes. The candidates, especially Romney, repeatedly asked for or simply took additional time, claimed the right to the last word, spoke at length during the free-form discussion period, and resisted Lehrer's attempts to move from one topic to another. Obama was slower than Romney to make these moves (although he spoke for more time), which may have contributed to the perception that he was lethargic or not aggressive enough. By most accounts, Lehrer's performance in getting the debate back on track was ineffectual.

Misstating the Opponent's Position

Within this context, Obama made (at least) three basic debate mistakes. First, he repeatedly misstated his opponent's position. Textbooks often advise that the first step in refutation is to state the opponent's position acceptably to him or her (e.g., Zarefsky, 2014, p. 347). Were it otherwise, one might respond to an argument that the opponent did not advance, committing the straw person fallacy.

In the first segment, Obama characterized Romney's economic plan as cutting taxes for the wealthy and rolling back regulations, and he persisted in that characterization even when Romney explicitly denied that this was his plan. Romney therefore could dismiss much of the president's criticism without answering it. Exasperated, he complained, "virtually everything he just said about my tax plan is inaccurate." (All quotations from the debate are from the transcript posted by the Commission on Presidential Debates at http://www.debates.org/index.php?page=debate-transcripts.) In the second segment, Obama asserted that Romney had ruled out revenue as a partial means of closing the deficit; Romney replied that his position was that new revenue would come from economic growth, not tax increases. In the third segment, Obama characterized Romney's health care proposal as vouchers; this position was not established by Obama and was denied by Romney.

What was the effect of these and other cases of misstating Romney's position? Obama seemed out of touch, unresponsive to the precise arguments in the debate. At one point, ironically, Romney said the president was entitled to "your own airplane and to your own house, but not to your own facts." In Obama's defense, he was attacking positions that Romney had espoused earlier in the campaign. But now the challenger was tacking back toward the center. Later in the campaign, of course, Obama would skillfully ridicule this shift as an attack of "Romnesia." But the only sign in the first debate that Romney was waffling came when Obama said, "for 18 months he's been running on this tax plan. And now, five weeks before the election, he's saying that his big, bold idea is 'Never mind.'"

Compounding Obama's difficulty was that he did not object when Romney misstated *his* position – whether because he thought the public would figure it out, he thought the transgression was trivial, or he did not notice the error. Early in the first segment, Romney characterized Obama's approach as "bigger government, spending more, taxing more, regulating more – if you will, trickle-down government." Even though Jim Lehrer specifically asked him to respond "to what the governor just said about trickle-down," Obama evaded the question, instead talking about his specific proposals. It is customary in political debates for candidates to move well beyond the specific question, using it as a springboard for whatever they wish to discuss. But usually they at least start with the question, pivoting from it to their preferred topic. Obama ignored the question, which did not make for effective refutation.

Handling the "Spread"

Second, President Obama was not strong in his handling of the "spread." Veterans of the intercollegiate debate circuit will recognize the spread as making a series of brief assertions, each of which takes only a few seconds. If the opponent is not able to respond to each of these abbreviated claims, the proponent carries the uncontested position by default. The respondent, therefore, either should say something about each claim, or should group the statements and offer a response that applies to all.

Romney began the spread early in the debate, when he described his five-part economic program: North American energy independence, opening up trade, providing people with "the skills they need to succeed and the best schools in the world," getting to a balanced budget, and championing small business. When his turn came, Obama left Romney's plan standing (except for a comment about education) and, instead, referred to his own ideas. The result was that Romney's proto-arguments carried more weight than they should have, simply because they were not answered. This happened during other debate segments, as well. In debate circles, the spread is not always viewed positively. It can encourage superficiality by focusing on the number of arguments rather than their merit. When delivered at a rapid speaking rate, the spread may be incomprehensible, especially to listeners whose ears have not been trained to follow at a fast clip. These potential difficulties might justify a principled refusal to answer undeveloped assertions. But they do not justify silently ignoring the other candidate's assertions altogether.

Obama also spread sometimes, but where Romney's points were concise and well-formed, Obama's were meandering and often scattershot. In one answer during the second segment, for example, Obama discussed the Simpson-Bowles deficit reduction plan, shifting Medicare to the states, adjustment in some corporate tax rates, oil drilling, and other topics. Romney served notice that it would take him some time to go through such a diverse range of topics. Obama's spread got him no strategic advantage; Romney's did.

Strategically Weak Time Allocation

Third, Obama allowed several questionable assertions to go unchallenged. For example, in the second segment, which concerned the federal budget deficit, Romney put forward a test for spending: "Is the program so critical it's worth borrowing money from China to pay for it?" Obama never took issue with the criterion itself – even though he was calling for revenue increases to mitigate the need for spending cuts or borrowing. In the same segment, Romney asserted that "you'll never balance the budget by raising taxes." Obama let that statement pass too, which undercut his plea to combine revenue increases with spending cuts. Obama also did not respond to Romney's analogy comparing the United States and Spain, both of which, he alleged, were spending 42% of their economy on government. The implication was that both nations were on the path to economic disaster. Obama also had nothing to say about Romney's charge that he had doubled the deficit while pledging to cut it in half, nor to Romney's taunt that the president should have embraced the proposals of the Simpson-Bowles deficit reduction plan.

Why did Obama let Romney "get away with" questionable assertions? Maybe he was not paying attention, although he seemed to be taking copious notes. Neither was he without time to reply. The more plausible explanation is that he simply did not use his time strategically. He repeated answers, he spent excessive time on anecdotes and lengthy illustrations, and he offered dubious precedents.

An instructive example is the fourth segment, concerning Obamacare. Asked why he wanted it repealed, Romney quickly alluded to two people who said they were considering dropping their health insurance – not, apparently, in response to Obamacare – and then he ticked off a series of objections: Obamacare will cost more than traditional insurance, Medicare will be cut to pay for it, unelected boards will have too much discretion, small businesses say they will cut back on hiring, and decisions should be made at the state rather than the federal level (the last, probably an attempt to pre-empt Obama's expected use of the Massachusetts health care system as a model for the country). Now, several of these claims were questionable or potentially misleading, but this was the *prima facie* case Romney had offered for repeal and to which Obama needed to respond. Since the Affordable Care Act was his signature domestic accomplishment and Republicans had made it a centerpiece of the campaign, he should have been prepared for this question.

How did Obama use his two-minute reply? He began by amplifying the problem, referring to the allusions with which Romney began and suggesting that the issue was even more serious:

> It wasn't just that small businesses were seeing costs skyrocket . . . It wasn't just that this was the biggest driver of our federal deficit . . . it was families who were worried about going bankrupt if they got sick . . . If they had a pre-existing condition, they might not be able to get coverage at all. If they did have coverage, insurance companies might impose an arbitrary limit.

By the time Obama embellished each of these points, he had used nearly 75% of his allotted speaking time. And all of this was irrelevant. It would have been pertinent if Romney had argued that health care was not a serious problem. (To be charitable to Obama, perhaps he imputed that view to some portion of the national television audience. But there was no basis for assuming that it warranted 75% of his time.) But Romney had not made that argument; his very brief reference to citizens who told him of their troubles established that he thought it was a problem. Romney's focus was entirely different: that Obamacare was not the right solution. Romney had focused on the stock issues of "cure" and "cost" whereas Obama was replying as if the challenges had focused on the question of "ill" (see Hultzén, 1958/1966). They were making different assumptions about the argument's *stasis*.

Then, realizing that there was considerable public confusion about the Affordable Care Act, the president proceeded to explain "what Obamacare did." He got as far as stating, "If you've got health insurance, it doesn't mean a government takeover" because you can keep your doctor and your insurance. He reassured people that "insurance companies can't jerk you around" and offered several examples. And he had begun to explain that people without health insurance could buy policies on the new exchanges essentially at group rates, saving an average of 18% from the cost of individual policies in the market. At that point, Jim Lehrer announced that Obama's time was up. Obama, protesting that he had five seconds left, added (for about 30 seconds) that the Massachusetts experience was a viable national model.

Even with the additional time, Obama ended his answer having refuted *none* of Romney's arguments against Obamacare, and in one case – the Massachusetts precedent – having made precisely the argument Romney already had pre-empted. When Lehrer prodded Romney to "tell the president directly why you think what he just said is wrong about Obamacare," the governor could reply truthfully, "Well, I did with my first statement." Having a free pass to extend his original answer, Romney took time to distinguish the Massachusetts plan from Obamacare. It was not just that it was a state-level rather than a national plan. It was genuinely bipartisan, it did not raise taxes, it did not cut Medicare, it did not rely on an unelected board for medical judgments, and it did not jeopardize existing insurance.

In his next response, Obama finally began to grapple with the specifics of Romney's argument. Overlooking the fact that Obamacare received no Republican votes in the Senate and almost none in the House, the president insisted that it was bipartisan because it was originally a Republican idea, put forward as an alternative to the Clinton health care proposal during the 1990s. He wished there had been Republican cooperation in Congress like that of the Democrats in the Massachusetts legislature, but nevertheless "we used the same advisers, and they say it's the same plan" as the success there. And as for the unelected board, it consists of "health care experts, doctors, et cetera" to figure out how to reduce the cost of care, because the alternative was to leave people uninsured.

But then the president made another strategic mistake. He spoke favorably and at length about the Cleveland Clinic using a team approach like that of the so-called unelected board and succeeding at reducing the cost of care. Romney turned the tables by making the point that the Cleveland Clinic was private, supporting his contention that "free people and free enterprises trying to find ways to do things better are able to be more effective in bringing down the cost than the government will ever be." Caricaturing the proposed cost control board, he repeated, "That's the wrong way to go. The private market and individual responsibility always work best."

The final exchange of the argument went better for Obama. Asked about how he would replace Obamacare, Romney replied only vaguely, to which Obama urged U.S voters "to ask themselves, is the reason that Governor Romney is keeping all these plans to replace secret because they're too good? Is it – is it because that somehow middle-class families are going to benefit too much from them?" Although Romney pleaded that to disclose details in advance would impair his ability to strike a bipartisan deal, his promise to repeal Obamacare made any such deal highly unlikely and the answer to the president's rhetorical question was fairly obvious. Still, taken as a whole, the health care segment was little short of disastrous for President Obama. This segment is the best illustration in the debate of Obama's strategic error regarding the use of time.

Conclusion

There were other examples of Obama's strategic or tactical weakness. He failed to defend specifically against Romney's attempt to draw distinctions between Obamacare and the Massachusetts health plan. He was too quick to agree with Romney, alleging that they both had similar proposals for Social Security when that was not the case. He failed to exploit Romney's agreement that tax cuts should not result in drops in revenue. And while his challenger asserted himself with the moderator to gain extended discussion periods and additional speaking time, Obama for the most part was passive regarding the rules and procedure. By most accounts, he regained lost ground in the second debate, re-establishing his momentum and throwing Romney back on the defensive. He did so, though, not through substantive arguments but through performative cues. He was more assertive, he spoke directly to Romney, he controlled the time more effectively. For the most part, though, Obama's gain in the second debate came from strategic and tactical blunders on Romney's part (Zarefsky, 2013). By the end of the debate series, the dynamics of the race were about what they had been before the first debate, but that is hardly to say that the debates lacked influence on the campaign.

Few people, of course, obtain their primary or even secondary acquaintance with the debates by reading the transcript; they rely on verbal and visual cues received while watching, supplemented by post-debate "spin" or media analysis. What is interesting, though, is that the textual analysis and the performative cues point in the same direction. This may give scholars more confidence in the intuitive responses of ordinary viewers. This study also reminds critics that the conventions of presidential debates change with the format – as happened in 2012 with the handling of the free-form discussion period. And yet, basic debate skills involving refutation, answering a spread, and strategic time allocation are valuable in presidential debates and offer a lens for viewing and understanding them. I would not be surprised if the frontrunner, whoever he or she may be, takes debate more seriously when preparing for the first debate of 2016.

References

Alter, J. (2013). *The center holds: Obama and his enemies.* New York, NY: Simon & Schuster.

Hultzén, L. S. (1966). Status in deliberative analysis. In D. C. Bryant (Ed.), *The rhetorical idiom* (pp. 97–123). New York, NY: Russell and Russell. (Original work published 1958 by Cornell University Press)

Nagourney, A., Parker, A., Rutenberg, J., & Zeleny, J. (2012). How a race in the balance went to Obama. *New York Times* [national ed.], p. P1.

Zarefsky, D. (2013, May). The "comeback" second Obama–Romney debate and virtues of argumentation. Paper presented at the meeting of the Ontario Society for the Study of Argumentation, Windsor, Ontario.

Zarefsky, D. (2014). *Public speaking: Strategies for success* (7th ed.) Boston, MA: Pearson.

37

NO REGRETS

Public argument and the refusal to apologize

Stephen Howard Browne

THE PENNSYLVANIA STATE UNIVERSITY, USA

The term *regret* finds its ancient origins in the Old Norse *grate,* to weep. It thus designates a capacity as ancient and enduring as the human capacity to effect things worth weeping for. Indeed, implicit in every act, *as act,* is the possibility that it is, or one day will be, regretted. Conversely, an act that carries no such possibility cannot properly be referred to as an act because it entails no imperative to hold the agent responsible. Behavior conducted under force of compulsion, for example, or under conditions of radical abjection, imposes on me no such responsibility to account for myself, to myself, to another, or publically.

Jeffery Olick's (2007) recent work on the politics of regret challenged scholars to examine the propulsive conditions under which certain acts are expected to be acknowledged as acts: acts, more specifically, that require a public accounting and that take the form of an expression of regret. These conditions are political in the primal sense: that is, in contexts constitutive of human community, moral order, and collective identity. Because polity is itself historically contingent, we are given to understand, it must follow that the public performance of regret is similarly contingent. As polity goes, so goes regret. The thesis is not truistic: We do not yet have a history of the wept-for, a genealogy of the lachrymose. That such a history would necessarily include the rhetorical is powerfully illustrated by Bradford Vivian (2012), who observed that it is precisely the function of regret "to educate the public in putative lessons of history and entreats listeners to perpetuate, in classic *epideictic* (or ceremonial) fashion, the civic and humanitarian principles they validate" (p. 7). We thus have in both Olick's and Vivian's work compelling first drafts of what such a history might look like and, as importantly, a rationale for undertaking such an inquiry in the first place.

In what follows, I slant into our subject in a way that I hope seems not perverse, although the phenomenon I examine may well seem so. To this end, I need to take a few steps back and squint again at this peculiar thing we call regret.

Regret is conventionally understood as basic to the work of apologies generally (Goffman, 1971). One is accordingly expected to extend such expressions to include some sense of culpability, of awareness of harms done, and promises not to commit similar acts. Apologies thus presented may be understood as forms of public argument to the extent that they make claims on shared convictions and provide reasons upon which to ground those claims. Apologies, and by extension expressions of regret, may or may not convince, of course, and may be featured as themselves objects of further public debate over questions of motive, timing, or effect.

To say that humans are equipped with the capacity to express regret is not to say that they are always possessed of the will to express regret. And if regret is said to claim a politics of its own, then we are obliged to say that the refusal to express regret also possesses a politics of its own. The reasons we sometimes refuse to regret are of course varied, sometimes convincing, sometimes not. Thus we may deny that a given act even exists to be regretted: say, Turkey's official stance regarding the Armenian genocide. Similarly, we may acknowledge the fact of a regrettable act, but deny responsibility for it: thus recognizing the reality of slavery, but refusing reparations on the basis that the present generation is not to be held in debt to such a past. Again, we may accept that we in some sense participated in a regrettable act, but deny accountability because such participation was coerced: the Nazi prison guard who was following orders on pain of death if he refused to execute his duty. We may in turn refuse to acknowledge the reality of regrettable actions because doing so would exact a cost too terrible to contemplate, in the way Japan turns a blind eye to the "Rape of Nanking." Finally, and here is my particular point of departure, we may acknowledge the reality of an act, indeed accept responsibility for it, but refuse to express regret because we do not think our action to be regrettable.

So to put the matter again: If regretting is a political act, then the refusal to regret is also a political act. The question, then, of which acts are regret-worthy is itself up for grabs, historically contingent, and forged within the crucible of public debate. Times change: Imperial aggression was an expected and sanctioned expression of national sovereignty; now we judge it to be a regrettable chapter in our collective narrative. More specific to my thesis, we can entertain those conditions under which the refusal to express regret for past actions does political work of a particular kind. And while times change, we need only scan the contemporary political landscape to observe how persistent is the recourse not only to apology, but the strategic gains to be had from pillorying those who would so readily profess regret before the world.

What then might be some of these conditions? Three instances stand out: (a) when a collective narrative is under siege, as in the case of imperial Japan; (b) when a collective narrative has been altogether shattered, as in post-war Germany's insistence that it, too, was made victim to the Third Reich; and (c) when the collective narrative is itself in its formative stages. It is with this third situation that I wish to deal in coming to terms with the refusal to regret. History shows us time and again that the bonds of nationhood are forged from resources of public memory. Rituals of shared identity, the symbolics of polity, the invention of tradition: Without these, the prospects of survival among the family of nations are put at risk. There can be little surprise, then, that a nation just getting its feet under itself will cling, if not desperately, then certainly with considerable resolution to the stories it tells about itself. As David Walstreicher (1997) has illustrated so convincingly, politics in the early republic was a "perpetual fete," featuring a rich and varied tableau of Fourth of July orations, parades, toasts, barbecues, and many other official and vernacular celebrations of the United States, arrival on the international scene. Indeed, we may observe that such rituals of collective identity are most conspicuous, most insisted upon, precisely when anxieties about the nation's progress are greatest. And it is in such contexts that the politics of refusal, the public gesture which acknowledges responsibility for an act even as the need to apologize for that act is denied, makes the most sense. In these contexts the public declaration of regret by a leader or representative is most likely to be construed as an act of weakness.

Nowhere is this process more evident than in Jacksonian America. And no one more vividly illustrates the politics of refusal than Andrew Jackson. Few presidents have acted more regrettably, and none have so adamantly refused to apologize. *And Americans loved him all the more for it.* This simple fact may well help us to account for Jackson's rhetorical legacy, and for what might otherwise seem his inexplicable hold on the public affections. He was not an eloquent man. The sixth president was many things to many people: Old Hickory, The General, The Hero, brawler, duellist, scourge of Indian peoples. But eloquent? Hardly. John Quincy Adams was mortified to learn that Harvard College was to bestow upon Jackson an honorary Doctor of Law degree. Refusing an invitation to attend the ceremony, Adams announced that, as "an affectionate child of our Alma Mater," he could not bring himself "to witness her disgrace in conferring her highest honors upon a barbarian who could not write a sentence of grammar and could hardly spell his own name" (as cited in Remini, 1990, p. 258). Jackson's Harvard adventure was soon satirized in the press, wherein it was reported that, having been called upon by the audience to speak a bit of Latin, he proudly announced "E pluribus unum, my friends, sine qua non" (as cited in Remini, 1990, p. 258).

The reasons for such derision in Jackson's own time are not far to seek. He was the first U.S. president to come from outside the genteel circles of either Harvard Yard or the Virginia Squirearchy. His schooling can only with generosity be described as modest. He modeled himself as a man of action, not words. And, of course, he came to political maturity in the golden age of American oratory, when the likes of Henry Clay, John Calhoun, and the redoubtable Daniel Webster were commanding the stage of public life. For that matter, his predecessor in the Oval Office was for a time Boylston Professor of Rhetoric at Harvard College and the author of Lectures on Rhetoric and Oratory (Adams, 1997). Stiff competition indeed.

Historians were wrangling over Jackson's legacy before he was even laid in the grave, and there are today no signs of exhaustion. Entire schools of thought have turned on this or that interpretation of his age, his battles, his banking policy, his Indian wars, his cabinet, his sense of honor. But on one point historians seem to agree: He remains uninteresting as a study in the art of eloquence. In addition to the reasons cited above – largely partisan – we can think of others to explain this phenomenon. For one, historians are not in the main very interested in eloquence and, even if they were, what would they look at? Virtually all of Jackson's state papers were team productions, making attributions of source and intent even more difficult than they already are. The same could be said of Washington, Lincoln, and Roosevelt, of course, but then Jackson claimed no Hamilton, Seward, or Sam Rosenman.

In short, the deck seems stacked high and strong against the following pages. What Jackson's critics did not appreciate was that although they may have been entirely warranted in their convictions about his rhetorical shortcomings, to his supporters, *it did not matter.* Indeed, Jackson's public comportment, verbal and otherwise, was precisely what made the Hero the Hero. Jackson catalyzed a new and distinctly American conception of popular political discourse, and ingredient to that discourse was the staged spectacle of a man refusing to apologize and regretting nothing. His legacy was born at a time when opinion leaders in the early republic were seeking to stake the native ground of American genius. Noah Webster sought it in lexicography, Ralph Waldo Emerson in philosophy and the arts, Melville in the novel. Jackson's claim to the mantle was fastened just because but he so embodied the values associated with what we might call the politics of stubbornness – its essentially American character, its strength, simplicity, and sheer cussedness – that he gave to his fellow Americans a new way of thinking about and practicing the arts of political discourse.

Here I refer to a sitting chief executive of the United States who shot a man dead in a duel over a horse race, who carried with him for the rest of his life three bullets lodged in his shoulder and rib cage from two other duels, including one in a bar room brawl with the Benton brothers, one of whom, Thomas Hart Benton, was a sitting U.S. Senator. I refer to the Hero of New Orleans, who ordered the summary execution of six officers without trial, who, without authority, placed the city under martial law, and then tossed its mayor in jail when he protested. It goes on: Jackson later ordered the execution of two British non-combatants during the invasion of Spanish Florida in 1818, itself also unauthorized. I refer to the chief architect of Indian removal and the "Trail of Tears," during which upwards of 5000 Cherokee perished.

In each instance, cries of alarm were certainly raised, but at no point did Jackson even consider a declaration of regret. Far from it: When pushed about the Florida campaign, he proudly announced that he had "destroyed the Babylon of the South, the hot bed of the Indian war and depredations on our frontier" (as cited in Burstein, 2007 p. 131), and assured his fellow citizens that he had, "in all things," "consulted the public good and safety and security of our southern frontier. I have established peace and safety, and hope the government will never yield it" (as cited in Berstein, 2007, p. 131). So popular was Jackson, in fact, that President Monroe, who had given no permission for Jackson's invasion, told Madison that he would not prosecute the matter because "I have no doubt that the interior of the country would have been much agitated, if not convulsed" (as cited in Brands, 2005, p. 340).

Why would this be the case? Why would Jackson so steadfastly refuse to express one whit of regret, and how could he command such overwhelming popularity in spite of – or, indeed, because of – such a posture? The answer, I think, lies in the culture of honor (Wyatt-Brown, 1982) that shaped so much of the young nation's thinking. To be clear, this "cult of honor," as it has been called, is almost always applied as a description of the White American South (Blight, 2001). It was, to be sure, most evident there, but we mistake its provenance by limiting its appeal geographically. The narrative to which it gave voice in fact appealed to Americans of many types, states, and political leanings. Among its features: the heavy emphasis on masculinized norms of strength, perseverance, valor, and courage; elaborate codes of social comportment, rituals of competition, and military bearing; commitment to nation, state, and family; and standards of honesty, plain speaking, and fair dealing. All of these values cohered into a code of surpassing moral order, the transgression of which was sure to doom the social status of any politician foolhardy enough to attempt it. More importantly, the cult of honor in which Jackson and his fellow Americans thrived meant that those who made a conspicuous display of its values were just as sure to benefit from the approbation of the public.

Within this calculus, in short, the politics of refusal meant that the declaration of regret would be interpreted as a sign of weakness, thus a betrayal of self and country. As a brief exercise in the point, can we identify a single major public figure of the time who in fact undertook to publically profess regret for his actions? Not the young Washington for losing his first battle during the Six Years War; not Jefferson for fleeing Monticello before the advancing British troops; not Burr for killing the former Secretary of Treasury; not Madison for letting the British scorch the Federal City; not Henry Clay for the "Corrupt Bargain." And not Andrew Jackson, for anything, period. At such a time, in such a country, among such a people, there could be no politics of regret. It was *the refusal to regret*, rather, that marked the successful politician, the successful nation, and it is a stance that remains, alas, an available and resonant means of public persuasion.

References

Adams, J.Q. (1997). Lectures on rhetoric and oratory. New York, NY: Scholars Facsimiles and Reprints.

Blight, D. W. (2001). *Race and reunion: The Civil War in American memory*. Cambridge, MA: Harvard University Press.

Brands, H. W. (2005). *Andrew Jackson: His life and times.* New York, NY: Doubleday.

Burstein, A. (2007). *The passions of Andrew Jackson.* New York, NY: Vintage.

Goffman, E. (1971). *Relations in public: Microstudies of the public order.* New York, NY: Basic Books.

Olick, J. (2007). *The politics of regret: On collective memory and historical responsibility.* New York, NY: Routledge.

Remini, R. (1990). *The life of Andrew Jackson.* New York, NY: Penguin.

Vivian, B. (2012). The paradox of regret: Remembering and forgetting the history of slavery in George W. Bush's Goree Island address. *History and Memory, 24,* 5–38.

Waldstreicher, D. (1997). *In the midst of perpetual fetes: The making of American nationalism, 1776–1820.* Chapel Hill: University of North Carolina Press.

Wyatt-Brown, B. (1982). *Southern honor: Ethics and behavior in the Old South.* New York, NY: Oxford University Press.

38

A HERETIC OF LAW

Lieutenant Commander Charles Swift's challenge of executive authority in the War on Terror

Derek Buescher

UNIVERSITY OF PUGET SOUND, USA

Kent A. Ono

UNIVERSITY OF UTAH, USA

One might label the summer of 2013 "the summer of the whistleblower." During this eventful season unauthorized leaks of classified information led to fresh questions about the meaning of the United States as a nation, the possible overreach of presidential power, and the changing role of the military in a time of perpetual war. On June 3, 2013, Bradley Manning's court martial trial began. Among other violations, the court charged Manning with violating the Uniform Code of Military Justice (UCMJ), including espionage and "aiding the enemy," by leaking military documents (to WikiLeaks), undermining efficacy of the War on Terror. In late May 2013, a National Security Agency contract worker, Edward Snowden, leaked information to the press about a governmental surveillance program. In his initial statement, Snowden remarked, "I will be satisfied if the federation of secret law, unequal pardon and irresistible executive powers that rule the world that I love are revealed even for an instant" (as cited in Greenwald, MacAskill, & Poltras, 2013).

Against the backdrop of these whistleblowers, we examine the case of Charles Swift. Given the context and timing of Manning and Snowden's cases, we seek to understand rhetoric surrounding Swift in terms of post-9/11 military and executive branch practices, as well as the prospects for public deliberation. In this way, our study of Swift brings to bear the need for rhetoric and argumentation scholars to attend to the vagaries and limitations of rhetorics of resistance and their challenges to orthodoxy, specifically the potentials and limitations of *heretical rhetoric* that questions existing post-9/11 political *doxa*.

A rhetorical heretic differs from a whistleblower in important ways. Whereas the whistle-blower draws public attention to a leader's or government's wrongdoings and/or illegal actions, the heretic's principle aim is to transform prevailing normative logics as an insider and to embody aspects of those logics s/he deems most important. Whereas the whistleblower seeks to demonstrate what is wrong about the existing logic and/or actions of an authority, the heretic challenges orthodoxy by claiming a truer, authentic, more accurate, or morally pure interpretation of *doxa*. Thus, while both are public rhetorics and both resist existing power and discourse, the whistleblower aims to disprove or discredit authority; in contrast, the heretical rhetor publicly embodies a reimagined *doxa*, one s/he characterizes as having originated from within the existing orthodoxy.

Rhetoric and argumentation scholars' studies of heresy are limited in scope, focusing primarily, but not exclusively, on discourse within a religious domain. In an ongoing effort to understand the potentials and limitations of heretical rhetoric, this essay develops a contemporary application and theorization of heresy within a secular arena, namely the military. We argue that, in this case, the heretic challenges military *doxa* by claiming to embody a better and more complete interpretation of what the *doxa* is, hence advocating a change in *doxa* as a member of the existing secular in-group, and providing an interpretation that necessitates a changed secular process. On the other hand, those opposing the rhetor regard her or his challenges as anathema to military authority and the smooth operation of military process.

In our previous work on heretical rhetoric (Buescher & Ono, 2009), we briefly touched on the case of Lieutenant Commander (LCDR) Charles Swift as a secular heretic. In this essay we expand that analysis and explore Swift in more detail. As co-counsel for Salim Ahmed Hamdan, a Guantanamo Bay detainee from 2002 to 2008, Swift challenged presidential claims to authority in the War on Terror and its "dangerous and unprecedented expansion of Executive authority" (Katyal, 2006b, p. 2). In our initial reading, we concluded Swift's rhetoric failed to meet the basic test of heretical rhetoric: His rhetoric did not call for an alternative interpretation of U.S. Government and military orthodoxy, the *doxa* from which he spoke, but a return to pre-War on Terror military and legal activities. We thought Swift was more of a whistleblower than a native informant and innovator of *doxa*. Here, we return to conduct a more thorough analysis of Swift's rhetoric and interrogate more fully the potential heretical dimension of that rhetoric. We suggest Swift's rhetoric as best understood to be parrhēsiastic, or offering a challenge to authority but not a reinterpretation of the rationale upon which that authority is based. In proposing this distinction between heresy and *parrhēsia,* suggesting that heresy requires a challenge to underlying logics that *parrhēsia* does not, we test the limits of rhetorical theories for their specific applicability. We briefly overview LCDR Swift's case and then discuss secular heresy and its relationship to *parrhēsia*. This brief segue allows us to explore the theoretical limitations of heresy before closing with a more in-depth examination of Swift's rhetoric than previously conducted (cf. Buescher & Ono, 2009)

Swift's Heresy

What we see as Swift's potential heresy occurs in two primary ways. The first is as the Judge Advocate General-appointed attorney in the defense of Salim Ahmed Hamdan. The second are his public statements regarding President George W. Bush administration policies of prisoner detainment generally and at Guantanamo Bay specifically. In the former, Swift and his legal team in *Hamdan* challenged the president's right to rule despite possible breaches of constitutionality. In the "Reply Brief for the Petitioner" in *Hamdan*, the legal counsel wrote, "the President's assertion of absolute dominion over human subjects and trial and punishment cannot be reconciled with the constitutional checks vested in Congress by Article I, and in the courts by Article III" (Katyal, 2006b, p. 1). Further challenging proclamations of presidential authority in times of perpetual war, the brief's opening summary concluded:

> The longstanding restrictions on commissions are not such disposable niceties. Rather, they are the time-tested barriers to the dangerous seepage of martial law

into our civilian order. To fail to enforce these limits would be to allow a dangerous and unprecedented expansion of Executive authority whose legal premise must be that the fight against terrorism justifies a reallocation of constitutional power. There would be no principled way to prevent that precedent from becoming the edifice upon which any number of actions could be grounded, even against U.S. citizens, from surveillance to indefinite detention, on the mere allegation that they are affiliates in that "war."

(p. 2)

Swift's disputation of presidential power – what co-counsel Neal Kumar Katyal (2006a) referred to as "a rare Supreme Court rebuke of the President during armed conflict" (p. 66) – exemplifies his potential heretical action as a U.S. Navy LCDR.

Swift summarizes his own challenge to presidential power in his 2007 *Esquire* magazine article where he wrote, "it's time to close Guantanamo Bay." Swift (2007) challenged the practices of post-9/11 intelligence gathering and the Bush Administration's actions, noting, "we really have arrived at a kafkaesque kind of justice." Swift (2007) made two primary arguments: first characterizing the United States as a nation "bound by the rule of law in our treatment of all people" and second arguing that "part of who we are and what we defend are the Geneva Conventions." Setting aside a history of unequal protection under and within the U.S. legal system, Swift (2007) called attention to a defining orthodoxy of the U.S. as a "nation of laws and not of men," implying an erosion of the U.S. as a nation of men resulting from the pro forma practices and procedures of prisoner detainment and interrogation during the War on Terror. Swift premised his specific condemnation of U.S. actions at Guantanamo Bay, Cuba, on the Bush Administration's use of torture. While such arguments were couched also in the need to protect the nation, its people, and its soldiers from enemy attacks, these arguments offered a revision to increasingly normalized practices in the decade post 9/11. Swift's parrhēsiatic argument centered on his call to return to a prior orthodoxy and his "speaking truth to power." His invocation of torture highlighted a potential heretical turn, echoing Marita Sturken's (2011) claim that "torture is a practice that actively and violently others its victims in its aim to destroy subjectivity, that demands a moral response" (p. 424). Swift's speech, be it heretical or not, called readers' attention to the morality of torture, while challenging the sanctity of presidential power. In the next section, we discuss *parrhēsia* as a way to understand an interpretation of Swift's rhetoric.

Parrhēsia and Heresy

Parrhēsia is a term historically associated with heresy. Originally a Greek term translated as "utterance" or "speech," with "pas" meaning all and "rhesis" meaning word or speech, Demosthenes regarded *parrhēsia* to be sacrosanct,[1] pivotal to Greek citizenship. Demosthenes regarded misuse of *parrhēsia* as socially irresponsible, even while Plato noted its proneness for misuse (*Republic* Book 8.557b). Liddell and Scott's lexicon correlated it with contemporary freedom of speech (*Greek-English Lexicon, New Edition*, p. 1334). In the New Testament, it can refer to the ability and willingness to hold one's ground or interpretation in the face of religious authority. Foucault (2001) significantly expanded *parrhēsia*'s definition, describing it as the necessity of the rhetor to speak truth in the face of consequences. Contemporarily, *parrhēsia* is a personal stance taken out of moral obligation, in which the rhetor seeks truth telling as a means to "improve or help other people" (Foucault, 2001, p. 19) despite possible punishment upon its utterance.

Walzer (2013) reclaimed rhetoric's relationship to *parrhēsia*, drawing upon and criticizing Foucault's theorization of the concept. Walzer (2013) succinctly summarized Foucault's discussion of *parrhēsia* before arguing that Foucault incorrectly separated *parrhēsia* from rhetoric, characterizing rhetoric as "feigned . . . [and] artless" speech (p. 18). Similar to heretical rhetoric, Foucault's *parrhēsia* is "fearless or frank speech" (p. 1). For Walzer (2013), "*parrēsia* is the counselor's obligation and opportunity to speak frankly to a powerful prince [and] is the best way for humanists to influence governing . . . it is an opportunity accompanied by risk" (p. 3). In contrast to *parrhēsia*, as Foucault and Walzer have it, the heretic seeks to restructure the community's status quo interpretation of reason itself. Heresy contrasts principally with orthodoxy; it is not a momentary statement but an embodied position taken contra an interlocutor or even a state. That is, while "the parrhesiast has a primary commitment to state the truth as he or she understands it" (Walzer, 2001, p. 4) to a powerful person such as the president, thereby acting as counsel (as in the statement "speaking truth to power"), the heretic challenges orthodox logics by seeing the truth of *doxa* differently.

We therefore describe Swift as a parrhēsiast and not a heretic. The distinction may seem subtle as both the parrhēsiast and the heretic challenge claims of truth. Even though *parrhēsia* and heresy can share certain conditions of responsibility and consequence to the rhetor, ultimately we view the categories of heretical and parrhēsiast speech as distinct. It is this distinction that may prevent our regarding Swift as a secular heretic. The primary distinction lies in the, ironic perhaps, role of parrhēsiast as counselor. The parrhēsiast counsels the prince or the people about truth but does not do so in the name of upholding a truer orthodoxy. The heretic challenges underlying logics when speaking. Rather than necessarily attempting to right an injustice that ultimately preserves the prince's power, the heretic challenges the potentially conservative reestablishment of princely authority altogether by calling for a fundamental shift in doxastic understanding.

Through the sphere of constitutional law, Swift challenged presidential authority, as Katyal (2006a) put it, in a time of "armed conflict." Of his own actions, Swift (2007) wrote that in other contexts, "when a military officer openly opposes the president, it is called a coup." Arguably, Swift's defense of Hamdan, and even the statements regarding closing Guantanamo Bay, constitute frank speech to the prince and the public in the face of consequences, consequences Swift later encountered when he was inexplicably passed over for promotion and forced out of the Navy due to its "up or out" policy (Totenberg, 2006).

On the one hand, Swift may be a parrhēsiast who speaks a truth but does not challenge the *doxa* of political authority or U.S. legal practices more broadly. For example, Swift (2007) wrote about historical threats to the United States during the Cold War, World War II, and the Civil War, arguing that "none of those grave threats caused us to jettison our most basic idea of justice: that we do not use coercion to get a confession." However, Swift (2007) framed this argument not as a requirement to rethink the U.S. legal system's structural barriers to equal treatment of both foreign detainees and a largely non-White prison population, but instead as a reminder of the very values upon which the War on Terror and its ancillary fronts in Iraq and Afghanistan were predicated: "to keep our country safe from a handful of fanatics." That is, while Swift's statement was, indeed, a frank challenge to presidential authority in a time of perpetual war, it is not a heretical challenge to the assumptions and logics of U.S. hegemony, legal authority, or, ultimately, presidential power. Similar to Manning and Snowden, Swift (2007) counseled the nation about the actions needed to ensure safety and to protect the orthodox assumptions of being "a nation of laws and not of men." One reading of Swift's jeremiad-like call to reposition the United States as a nation of laws is as a conservative lamentation that ensures the nation remain, in keeping with Plato's parrhēsiast, "the shining city upon the hill."

Having considered Swift's rhetoric about presidential authority, we turn now to his assertions of the Bush Administration's use of torture. Although such assertions could be characterized as heretical under the premise that Swift speaks against the post-9/11 normalization of the "state of exception" (Agamben, 2005), we argue his discourse is best understood as parrhēsiastic challenges to authority.

Distinct from but related to its religious counterpart, secular heresy is the dissemination of "false beliefs" by one "from within orthodoxy" through persuasive tactics that challenge the audience's belief structure and place the rhetor at risk of expulsion from the community. Unique to Swift's disapproval of post-9/11 actions is his frank criticism of Bush Administration policies and practices of prisoner detainment and "enhanced" interrogation. As noted earlier, Sturken (2011) argued torture "demands a moral response" (p. 424), and Swift provided one such moral response speaking truth to power.

In his article in *Esquire*, Swift (2007) wrote:

> My fellow Americans ... the real reason the president abandoned 250 years of American jurisprudence was that doing so was the only way to use confessions obtained through physical and mental coercion, and to shield the methods being used to obtain these confessions from public scrutiny.

In a follow-up article, Swift (2008) wrote: "The commissions have been structured to keep the worst government misconduct behind closed doors" and Bush Attorney General Mukasey "announced ... he would not investigate whether any criminal wrongdoing had occurred interrogating these detainees since interrogators had acted pursuant to orders they believed lawful." Although we might read Swift's challenges as fundamentally oppositional to the new post-9/11 norm, where torture and coercive interrogation techniques are standard practice, Swift's challenges merely call the public's attention to a return to pre-9/11 practices outlined in the Geneva Conventions.

Swift speaks truth to power but does not reinterpret law to come up with some more truthful or moral interpretation. Whereas heresy demonstrates an opposition to and corrective course for *doxa*, *parrhēsia* challenges the outcome of a decision. Thus, Swift is at risk, but his risk is not a betrayal or a castigation. Rather, his risk lies with those in power disagreeing with him. Swift provides only a need for the government to defend its interpretation.

Conclusion

People in the United States live in a moment when the means of contemporary information dissemination changes what and how they know public protest. It is unclear whether there is more protest or more news available about protest. Furthermore, the state of perpetual war has affected public discourse. The bearing down on people because of securitization and surveillance technology, de rigueur now post-9/11, makes challenges to established protocols within secular society more pronounced. How do argument scholars assess such discourse? It seems we should pay attention to these resistant rhetorics, whether heretical, vernacular, outlaw, or parrhēsiac to understand their potential for disrupting rhetorics of control. It is the field of rhetoric that is best positioned to document and provide pedagogical commentary on the changes of discourse and their meanings.

By studying heretical rhetoric we are not suggesting that the secular has become religious. We do suggest that the processes of protecting a changed *doxa* – one that embraces the surveillance and disciplining of subjects, one that requires immediate assent to regulation and control, and one that seeks a passive participant in military and governmental fiat – is embedded within normative processes. If scholars are to reenergize public discourse, reanimate the political and cultural possibilities of the *polis* and *civitas*, reinvigorate complex thinking, diversity, and difference, then by necessity scholars need to seek ways to expand tolerance, acceptance, encouragement, and appreciation of speaking, writing, and embodying that does not fit the state's procedural and martial doctrines, with which it assumes each citizen should and will comply. Rather, by identifying both those failed interventions (as we have done here) and those moments that challenge the powerful, felt restriction of creativity, difference in thought and embodiment, as well as the constructed "sacred" power of military and government authority – both right and might – we believe in the potential to reconstitute the grounds for public rhetorical and argumentative possibility.

Note

1. See the *Third Philippic*. We are heavily reliant for this definition on Bill Wenstrom's biblical etymology, in particular his references to Plato, Demosthenes, and Liddel and Scott.

References

Agamben, G. (2005). *State of exception* (K. Attell, Trans.). Chicago, IL: University of Chicago Press.

Buescher, D., & Ono, K. A. (2009, November). *Rhetorical heresy and the content of citizenship*. Paper presented at the meeting of the National Communication Association, Chicago, IL.

Foucault, M. (2001). *Fearless speech*. Los Angeles: Semiotext(e).

Greenwald, G., MacAskill, E., & Poltras, L. (2013, June 9). Edward Snowden: The whistleblower behind the NSA surveillance revelations. *The Guardian*. Retrieved from http://www.guardian.co.uk/world/2013/jun/09/edward-snowden-nsa-whistleblower-surveillance

Hamdan v. Rumsfeld, 548 U.S. 557 (2006).

Liddell, H.G., & Scott, R. (1940). *Greek-English lexicon* (9th ed). Oxford, England: Oxford University Press, p. 1344.

Katyal, N. K. (2006a, November 1). *Hamdan v. Rumsfeld*: The legal academy goes to practice. *Harvard Law Review, 120*(1), 65–123.

Katyal, N. K., et al. (2006b, March). Reply brief for petitioner, *Hamdan v. Rumsfeld*, No. 05–184, (U.S. Mar., 2006). Retrieved from http://www.cja.org/downloads/Hamdan_Reply_Brief.pdf

Sturken, M. (2011). Comfort, irony, and trivialization: The mediation of torture. *International Journal of Cultural Studies, 14*(4), 423–440.

Swift, C. L. C. (2007, March). The American way of justice. *Esquire*. Retrieved from http://www.esquire.com/features/ESQ0307swift

Swift, C. (2008, February 15). Why now? The timing of the Guantanamo trials is not an accident. *Slate.com*. Retrieved from http://www.slate.com/articles/news_and_politics/jurisprudence/2008/02/why_now.html

Totenberg, N. (2006, October 12). Detainee's military lawyer forced out of service. *National Public Radio*. Transcript retrieved from http://www.npr.org/templates/story/story.php?storyId=6256039

Walzer, A. E. (2013). *Parrēsia*, Foucault, and the classical rhetorical tradition. *Rhetoric Society Quarterly, 43*(1), 1–21.

Wenstrom, Bill. (2005). Parrhesia. Retrieved from www.wenstrom.org/downloads/written/word_studies/greek/parrhesia.pdf

39

THE NON-NOMINATION OF SUSAN RICE

Disturbing arguments grounded in race and gender

Heidi Hamilton

EMPORIA STATE UNIVERSITY, USA

On September 11, 2012, an attack on the U.S. compound in Benghazi, Libya, killed four U.S. citizens, including Ambassador Christopher Stevens. Initially, Obama Administration officials described the attack as "spontaneous" not "planned" (Shane, 2012, p. A16). In fact, on September 16, U.S. Ambassador to the U.N. Susan Rice appeared on five Sunday talk shows making this argument. At the time, Rice was widely believed to be President Obama's choice to replace Hillary Clinton as Secretary of State. As clearer information emerged that the attack was both premeditated and involved terrorist elements, Rice increasingly came under scrutiny for her statements. Criticism of her, especially from Senators John McCain, Lindsey Graham, and Kelly Ayotte, threatened to derail her nomination. Over several months, Rice met with senators and issued statements explaining her remarks as based upon "talking points provided by the intelligence community" and not "intended to mislead" (as cited in O'Keefe, 2012, p. A1). Still facing intense negativity, Rice withdrew her name from consideration in December. Examining the mediated discourse surrounding Rice's failed nomination, and particularly the arguments regarding her temperament and lack of diplomatic qualifications, this essay posits these arguments relied upon previously existing images of Black women that function as implicit tropes that perpetuate race and sex discrimination. In doing so, commercial news media discourse contributed to the hostile environment that doomed Rice's possible nomination as Secretary of State.

Tropes about Black Women

Understanding arguments surrounding Rice's testimony requires understanding stereotypes of Black women in U.S. culture and media. This intersection of race and sex positions Black women uniquely. Painter (1992) argued, "As the emblematic woman is white and the emblematic black is male, black women generally are not as easy to comprehend symbolically" (p. 211). The result is a reliance on easily recognizable stereotypes of Black women, functioning as tropes in U.S. society, which can be quickly referenced and drawn upon when needed. These tropes occur in dominant discourse, but do not necessarily reflect Black women's self-understandings (Manning-Miller & Houston, 1995). They are not necessarily blatantly racist, either. As a society, White people like to think they have moved past overt racist images; yet, that does not mean that discourse is stereotype free. Entman (1992) suggested that "stereotypes are now more subtle, and stereotyped thinking is reinforced at levels likely to remain below conscious aware-ness. . . . [S]tereotyping of blacks now allows abstraction from and denial of the racial compo-nent" (p. 345). The belief in a postracial society, one where racial issues have been resolved, perpetuates this denial. Using Obama's election as a heralding event, postracial narratives suggest that race is "an antiquated signifier" (Rossing, 2012, p. 47). Analyzing Tea Party rhet-oric, Wanzer (2011) argued that racial neoliberalism discourages the discussion of race as racism itself, even as racist language pervades U.S. political discourse.

So what tropes exist? Collins (2000) argued that the "dominant ideology of the slave era fostered the creation of several interrelated, socially constructed controlling images of Black womanhood, each reflecting the dominant group's interest in maintaining Black women's subordination" (p. 72). The exaggerated nature of these images – which Collins outlined as the mammy, the matriarch, the welfare mother, and the jezebel – justifies containing the threat that Black women pose. The focus of this essay, the matriarch controls her children and her family within the home (Woodard & Mastin, 2005). The employed Black woman, working outside the home, hurts the family because she is not feminine enough and does not depend on the Black man. Collins (2000) explained how "one source of the matriarch's failure is her inability to model appropriate gender behavior. Thus, labeling Black women unfeminine and too strong works to undercut U.S. Black women's assertiveness" (p. 76–77). Known also as "Sapphire," this portrayal of the Black woman is "an emasculator who is strong, unfeminine, and rebellious" (St. Jean & Feagin, 1998, p. 7).

This image's power comes from the way the Black woman is represented. Because she dominates unrighteously, she is at fault. St. Jean and Feagin (1998) argued that this represen-tation allows the dominant group to blame her both for the negative perception and subse-quent actions against her: "These types of negative imagining have a powerful impact on how black women are viewed and treated by the dominant society, and they can shape when and if black women are included in the distribution of critical societal awards" (p. 13). Furthermore, all gendered identities are implicated as the image of the matriarch provides a symbol of the dangers of challenging patriarchal power (Collins, 2000).

Acting in concert with the trope of the matriarch is the trope of the angry Black woman. Parks (2010) wrote that media often portray Black women, whether mothers, politicians, or celebrities, as angry. Being tough, courageous, and strong becomes anger because "the image says that anger is the black female default emotion, and anytime a black woman is not smiling, she must be angry" (Parks, 2010, p. 115). Parks pointed to communication research that suggests cultural differences in speech patterns that perpetuate this image:

> Sometimes black women do not perform the self-disarming signals that other women do. It is common for women of other racial groups to weaken their speech with disclaimers – "I think . . ." or "I don't mean to . . ." – or they may end a state-ment with the up-tone sound of a question. They may avoid looking the person to whom they are speaking directly in the eye. Often, black women do not do any of these things – I never had to learn to smile when I did not mean it – so black women are perceived as "angry" when they are not.
>
> *(p. 118)*

Parks, who discussed the strong Black woman who is fierce, wise, and nurturing, argued that the image of the angry Black woman "is an insult that seeks to rob black women of emotional nuance and intelligence" (p. 117).

These particular tropes can be found in mass-mediated portrayals of Black women political figures. Manning-Miller and Houston (1995) wrote after Lani Guinier's Assistant Attorney General nomination withdrawal that "as more African American women enter the political arena, both as elected officials and public administrators, the disparity between their own and dominant cultural representations of their motives and actions becomes more apparent and problematic" (p. 34). Media's role in perpetuating negative representations, especially of Black females, has been well-documented (Entman, 1992; Givens & Monahan, 2005; Littlefied, 2008; Quinlan, Bates, & Webb, 2012). Examining print and online media arguments from September to December 2012, I suggest how Rice, as a Black woman rising in the political sphere, was represented demonstrates the continuing power of these tropes.

The Undiplomatic Diplomat: Media Arguments on Susan Rice

Dominant characterizations of Rice align with the matriarch and angry Black woman tropes. To begin, Rice repeatedly is described as "aggressive" (Parker, 2012, p. A21) and her "pugilism" provokes others (Milbank, 2012, p. A25). Later explaining senators' displeasure over the lack of answers, a *Washington Post* article began: "What was supposed to be a make-nice meeting on Tuesday seemed only to make things more contentious between the White House and Senate Republicans" (O'Keefe, 2012, p. A1), implying that she did not make nice and, because that should have been her goal, the contention was her fault. One *Daily Beast* article explained "Rice's personality – or 'temperament,' in the parlance of her Beltway critics – is increasingly front and center. She is frequently described in the press with such adjectives as 'brusque,' 'aggressive,' and 'undiplomatic in the extreme'" (Grove, 2012, para. 5).

The negative characteristics of the tropes explain the emphasis on her communication mannerisms. Roig-Franzia (2012) pointed out that the "meme" about her is that she "is the sharp-elbowed one, the brusque one" (p. C7), terminology that reappears in Milbank's *Washington Post* editorial. She is "outspoken" (Landler, 2012b, p A1), and "sharp-tongued" (Landler, 2012a, p. A1), with "a reputation for brusqueness and bluster" (Rubin, 2012, p. A23). Perhaps most telling is the anonymous quote in a *National Journal* article (later removed from the online version) that indicated Rice is "quite smart but temperamentally unfit for the job . . . Her voice is always right on the edge of a screech" (as cited in Grove, 2012, para. 17). These descriptions point to how Rice is viewed by others through a stereotype's insidious racial and gendered elements. The implication is that she does not act feminine enough, but understandings of that cannot be comprehended apart from her race and judgments about Black women who act "too aggressive."

Her "aggressive" and "sharp" style results in her emasculating men. A *Washington Post* article recounted Rice's experiences at the United Nations:

> Rice can sometimes startle or annoy with her penchant for showing up at meetings and dominating the conversation. She's blunt to a fault sometimes, can lecture to her peers and bugs other diplomats by over-scheduling them, leading them on endless excursions during foreign trips, prompting some to derisively refer to her as the "headmistress." "You're not our schoolteacher and we're not your students," a Security Council diplomat remarked in reference to Rice.
>
> *(Roig-Franzia, 2012, p. C7)*

Using a different metaphor than the family, the representation still fits the matriarch image (if not the particular name). She is described as taking control, dominating colleagues and treating them like children rather than granting them the power they feel they deserve. In multiple accounts, Rice's prior comments about Senator McCain are recounted. For example, "She mocked a McCain trip to Iraq ('strolling around the market in a flak jacket'), called his policies 'reckless' and said 'his tendency is to shoot first and ask questions later. It's dangerous'" (Milbank, 2012, p. A25). While her language is certainly strongly and negatively worded, she is portrayed as "mocking" and "withering" (Landler, 2012a, p. A1) – a gender-loaded term for emasculation. Reporters noted that these comments occurred in 2008; that they occurred as she was speaking on behalf of Obama (campaigning against McCain) and, in the first case, referencing Obama's trip to the Middle East (that he would not be strolling . . .) is rarely mentioned. Readers are left with the characterization of her having "attacked" men (Taube, 2012, p. B3).

Rice also was explicitly portrayed as the angry Black woman. Multiple articles recounted the story of how she "flipped the bird to diplomat Richard Holbrooke during a State Department meeting" (Parker, 2012, p. A21; see also Taube, 2012), without providing context. Roig-Franzia's (2012) article began with "Susan Rice was miffed, all right. Her frequent foil, the Russian ambassador to the United Nations, Vitaly Churkin – an outsize personality whom she might be yelling at one moment, then laughing with the next – was at it again" (p. C7). Being miffed, yelling, and flipping the bird are not activities of an emotionally nuanced woman. Added to the communication mannerisms discussed earlier, this portrayal of Rice further conforms to the trope of the angry Black woman. These characterizations provide simple references to understand the argument regarding Rice's unfitness for diplomatic leadership.

All of these characteristics paint a portrait of Rice as a stereotypical Black woman whose aggressiveness damages those around her, who seeks to emasculate more powerful men, and whose emotional state is one of anger. Nowhere is this more vivid than in the comparisons with Senator John Kerry, the other possible nominee for Secretary of State. Making a direct comparison, after pointing out that she mocks McCain and flips the bird at Holbrooke, Taube (2012) concluded, "Unlike Mrs. Rice, he's a person who knows how to work properly with people across party lines and what it takes to get things done" (p. B3). Although readers do not learn whether she has not gotten things done, they do know that she does not work *properly*, which is coded both in terms of gender and race. Milbank (2012) offered a similar sentiment, suggesting that "in comparison with the other person often mentioned for the job, Sen. John Kerry, she can be a most undiplomatic diplomat" (p. A25).

Those who defended her pointed out that she does not neatly fit in the stereotypes; this further illustrates the reification that mainly occurred in media arguments. For example, "The smiling, gregarious Rice is the one her close associates like to talk about" (Roig-Franzia, 2012, p. C7). The emphasis on smiling attempts to refute that she is brusque and sharp. One commentator pointed out that aggressiveness becomes a negative for Rice, while not a negative for others: "Aggression . . . is rarely considered a flaw in men. . . . Thank goodness Rice didn't tell Holbrooke to go do that which one cannot do to oneself, as Dick Cheney once suggested to Vermont Sen. Patrick Leahy" (Parker, 2012, p. A21). Another article suggested that her approach is similar to the "guys in the locker room," and that "Rice's teachers, though, insist that her bluntness is appropriate [for diplomacy]" (Ioffe, 2012, para. 7). The arguments defending her answer the stereotypes.

Mediated discourse surrounding Rice does not merely reify existing tropes of the Black woman, however. To suggest that she is aggressive would not alone disqualify her for this position. The original stereotype positions the matriarch within the family, suggesting that her independence undermines Black male authority in the household. Although Rice is repeatedly characterized as undiplomatic in her "temperament," she is not characterized as independent from Black male authority (in this case, Obama). She was viewed as "political" (Cohen, 2012, p. A25; Waterman, 2012a, p. A1), shorthand for saying that she played down al Qaeda involvement to not hurt Obama's reelection chances (Waterman, 2012b, p. A1) and calling into question her independence. Senator Corker was quoted saying she has "had every drop of Kool-Aid" (as cited in O'Keefe, 2012, p. A1; Waterman, 2012b, p. A1), implying that she bought into the Administration story without question.

Not only is she too closely aligned with the Administration (Cohen, 2012, p. A25), but Obama's reaction to the attacks against her further undermined her independence. A *Washington Times* editorial, characterizing Rice as a "helpless little lady," framed the situation as Obama "still the tall, dark and handsome prince of feminine fantasy, stepped up manfully to defend the honor of . . . Rice" ("The Little Lady," 2012, p. A4). His actions were "chivalrous" (Marcus, 2012, p. A31), "over-the-top" (Milbank, 2012, p. A25), and had a "virile flare" (Dowd, 2012, p. SR11).

This duality in representing Rice – she's aggressive, but needs to be rescued; she mocks and curses powerful male adversaries, but relies upon Obama's chivalry – presented an interesting double-bind. Theorizing about the matriarch suggests that she can be portrayed positively, as the strong, courageous Black woman. Those defending Rice pointed toward that interpretation of her "aggressive, blunt" approach. However, the addition of arguments casting her as helpless and overly politicized (i.e., dependent) worked to negate that non-dominant interpretation, reinforcing the negative characteristics of the angry Black woman. She is not strong or courageous; she is merely aggressive and emasculating.

Conclusion

Rice's statements on Benghazi appear factually wrong. Whether they were deliberately misleading is open to debate. The political, mediated arguments surrounding these statements, however, provide a complex look into the intersection of race and gender in U.S. society. Collins (2000) argued that "because the authority to define societal values is a major instrument of power, elite groups, in exercising power, manipulate ideas about Black womanhood. They do so by exploiting already existing symbols, or creating new ones" (p. 69). Although some commentators suggested that representations of Rice held either a sexist *or* a racist tone, I have argued that an intersectional look at how mediated arguments exploited cultural tropes of a *Black woman* provides a more complete analysis of Rice's failed possible nomination.

References

Cohen, R. (2012, December 4). It's not about Rice. *Washington Post*, p. A25.
Collins, P. H. (2000). *Black feminist thought: Knowledge, consciousness, and the politics of empowerment* (2nd ed.). New York, NY: Routledge.
Dowd, M. (2012, November 18). Is Rice cooked? *New York Times*, p. SR11.
Enck-Wanzer, D. (2011). Barack Obama, the Tea Party, and the threat of race: On racial neoliberalism and born again racism. *Communication, Culture, & Critique, 4*, 23–30.
Entman, R. M. (1992). Blacks in the news: Television, modern racism, and cultural change. *Journalism Quarterly, 69*, 341–361.
Givens, S. M. B., & Monahan, J. L. (2005). Priming mammies, jezebels, and other controlling images: An examination of the influence of mediated stereotypes on perceptions of an African American woman. *Media Psychology, 7*, 87–106.

Grove, I. (2012, December 12). Susan Rice's personality "disorder." *The Daily Beast*. Retrieved from http://www.thedailybeast.com/articles/2012/12/12/susan-rice-s-personality-disorder.html

Ioffe, J. (2012, December 20). Susan Rice isn't going quietly. *New Republic*. Retrieved from http://www.tnr.com/print/article/politics/magazine/111353/susan-rice-isnt-going-quietly

Landler, M. (2012a, November 18). Diplomat on the rise, suddenly in turbulence. *New York Times*, p. A1.

Landler, M. (2012b, December 14). Under fire, Rice ends bid to succeed Clinton as secretary of state. *New York Times*, p. A1.

The little lady is back in town. (2012, November 16). *Washington Times*, p. A4.

Littlefield, M. B. (2008). The media as a system of racialization: Exploring images of African American women and the new racism. *American Behavioral Scientist, 51*, 675–685.

Manning-Miller, C., & Houston, M. (1995). Toward an understanding of agenda-building discourse by African American women: The case of Lani Guinier. *Women & Language, 18*, 34–36.

Marcus, R. (2012, December 14). Susan Rice, ill-used and abandoned. *Washington Post*, p. A31.

Milbank, D. (2012, November 18). The wrong person to fight for. *Washington Post*, p. A25.

O'Keefe, E. (2012, November 28). Meeting with Rice fails to reassure her GOP critics. *Washington Post*, p. A1.

Painter, N. I. (1992). Hill, Thomas, and the use of racial stereotype. In T. Morrison (Ed.), *Race-ing justice, en-gendering power: Essays on Anita Hill, Clarence Thomas, and the construction of social reality* (pp. 200–214). New York, NY: Pantheon.

Parker, K. (2012, December 5). Susan Rice and the blame game. *Washington Post*, p. A21.

Parks, S. (2010). *Fierce angels: The strong black woman in American life and culture*. New York: One World.

Quinlan, M. M., Bates, B. R., & J. B. Webb. (2012). Michelle Obama "got back": (Re)defining (counter)stereotypes of black females. *Women & Language, 35*, 119–126.

Roig-Franzia, M. (2012, November 30). "Not a typical diplomat." *Washington Post*, p. C7.

Rossing, J.P. (2012). Deconstructing postracialism: Humor as a critical, cultural project. *Journal of Communication Inquiry, 36*, 44–61.

Rubin, T. (2012, November 29). Why Rice is wrong. *Philadelphia Inquirer*, p. A23.

St. Jean, Y., & Feagin, J. R. (1998). *Double burden: Black women and everyday racism*. Armonk, NY: M. E. Sharpe.

Shane, S. (2012, October 18). What happened in Libya? Clearing up a fierce dispute. *New York Times*, p. A16.

Taube, M. (2012, December 19). A better choice for Obama's secretary of state; Kerry more qualified than Rice for top position. *Washington Times*, p. B3.

Waterman, S. (2012a, December 3). Democrats say Rice is not to blame for Benghazi. *Washington Times*, p. A1.

Waterman, S. (2012b, November 28). Senators "troubled" by Rice answers on Libya. *Washington Times*, p. A1.

Woodard, J. B., & Mastin, T. (2005). Black womanhood: "Essence" and its treatment of stereotypical images of black women. *Journal of Black Studies, 36*, 264–281.

40

ABRAHAM LINCOLN AND THE ARGUMENTATIVE STYLE

James F. Klumpp

UNIVERSITY OF MARYLAND, USA
SENIOR SCHOLAR AWARD WINNER

Abraham Lincoln was above all a practitioner of the political arts. Politicians of the nineteenth century, like those today, were required to master several styles of speaking. For example, Daniel Webster, arguably the greatest orator of the early nineteenth century, mastered the styles appropriate to an extraordinarily broad range of speaking venues: the epideictic style of the great civic celebrations, the courtroom style of the small Supreme Court chamber, the electioneering style required by party meetings and rallies, and the argumentative style that dominated debate in the United States Senate. Not every politician achieved success in as many styles as Webster, but each mastered a range of rhetorical styles as their political skills matured.

Lincoln's native style – the one that he mastered first and perhaps most completely – was the frontier stump. In political gatherings and frontier courtrooms throughout Illinois, he excelled. But Lincoln worked to master other styles as well. Lincoln studied oratory through models. His cousin Dennis Hanks reported the teenage Lincoln, after attending church, amused his peers by repeating the sermon from a wilderness stump (Herndon & Weik, 1888/2006, p. 104). We know he borrowed *The Kentucky Preceptor* (Donald, 1995, p. 30; Berry, 1943, p. 834) and *The Columbian Orator* (Cmiel, 1990, p. 59) to study historical examples. Then he experimented. His 1838 "The Perpetuation of Our Political Institutions" (Lincoln, 1838/1953, Vol. I, pp. 108–115) is much admired by conservatives today for its theme, but as an attempt at the high epideictic style there is little to admire. When Lincoln penned his public lecture "On Discoveries and Inventions" (Lincoln, 1858/1953, Vol. II, pp. 437–442) around 1858, he sought to exploit political celebrity to earn lecture fees for lyceum-style speaking. He gave the lecture an undetermined but small number of times in central Illinois before turning down further requests with a note that "I am not a professional lecturer" (Lincoln, 1860/1953, Vol. IV, p. 39). His law partner and biographer William Herndon agreed: "If his address in 1852, over the death of Clay, proved that he was no eulogist, then [the 'Inventions' speech] demonstrated that he was no lecturer" (Herndon & Weik, 1888/2006, p. 271). These efforts, spread over the years of his youth and into early middle age, present a Lincoln seeking to master the speaking arts of his day with mixed success.

During this time, however, Lincoln achieved one of his greatest accomplishments as a speaker, his mastery of the argumentative style, my focus in this essay. I begin by discussing the dynamics of the argumentative style that made it one of the hallmarks of the nineteenth century's age of oratory. Then I trace Lincoln's mastery of the style, and develop my central argument: Lincoln's adaptation of the style gave force to his great achievement at Cooper's Union in the winter of 1860.

The argumentative style rose to prominence in the American rhetorical tradition alongside the epideictic oratorical style. Its great home in the early nineteenth century was the United States Senate. Several characteristics marked the style. First, speeches were structured with an articulated precision of organization. Speakers explicitly identified the claim of their argumentative opponent, closely followed by a clear, concise statement of the speaker's counter-claim. Sometimes the claim was a factual one, often about history, sometimes a moral one. In either case, the elaboration of explanation and proof followed. Multiple reasons supporting the claim were signposted as such. Then, either with a short, crisp repeat of the claim or a forceful projection of the implications of the established claim, the final clinch declared the superiority of the speaker's position.

The style was also reliably marked by characteristic choices for proof. The nineteenth century orator believed that his office was to instruct on great moral issues (Baskerville, 1952, pp. 14–15; Clark & Halloran, 1993, p. 2). History and the classics provided sources for this instruction. By the early nineteenth century the advanced education that had originally been designed to prepare clergy to properly interpret the Bible had been replaced in the country's collegiate system by an education in the classics and practical morality (Clark & Hollaran, 1993, pp. 2–3, 6–7). Quotations, direct and indirect, from the great figures of history rang through speeches, with historical narratives deployed and lessons drawn. Whether in the great epideictic ceremonial occasions or the quasi-deliberative debates of the Senate, the style fully displayed the wisdom of the ancients and of history.

This invoking of a noble past was matched by a logical construction projecting knowledge of the world, knowledge particularly structured with mechanical understanding of practical systems. Sequences of cause and effect linked past and present to future. The argumentative structure of means and ends filled the speeches of the argumentative style. Processes were described, implications traced, predictions generated. This characteristic led to a heavy presence of operationalism in argument. *Reductio ad absurdum* and slippery slope strategies were typical.

Finally, the argumentative style fashioned argument with a human relationship at its heart. An opponent – that is, a counter-arguer – was a necessity. Although ideas may have clashed, the argument was framed as a contest between two reasoning humans. In contrast to the partisan styles current at the time, including the frontier invective that Lincoln mastered, the argumentative style was polite and deferential of character, even as it was sharp in its judgment of the opponent's argument. But the vector of the argument was a human claim that countered the opponent's claim. We might say that, in this regard, the argumentative style featured a portrayal of humans in two dimensions. The first was the dimension of the argument itself. Two worthies were spinning the fabric of argument. The second was the role of argument in human behavior. Human beings were motivated by the strength of reasoning. Thus, at the base of the argumentative style lay a fullness of respect for human reason often absent in other styles.

The argument was often explicitly addressed to the interlocutor, but the orator complicated this simplicity. Often the orator projected greater significance for the argument by recasting his interlocutor as representing a more generalized argumentative voice. Thus, Daniel Webster easily generalized Robert Hayne by conceding "that there are individuals besides the honorable gentleman who do maintain these opinions" (Reid & Klumpp, 1830/2005, p. 354). And the popularity of Senate galleries testified that orators employing the argumentative style not only addressed opponents or their like-minded associates, but performed a debate with appeal to a public audience.

Although the great venue for the argumentative style was the United States Senate, the style was not merely deliberative. It crossed Aristotle's genres of rhetoric. Because of its sharp retort to a counter-arguer and its concern for actions of the past, it carried a forensic quality. The opponent erred and, in the world where argumentative position spawned action, that error misshaped his world. This forensic quality seldom concerned legality and the venue was not the courts, but the great orators were often lawyers who brought skills to the argumentative style from their courtroom practice.

And, at the heart of the argumentative style was a quality of epideictic. The orator's province was didactic. The proper education of the orator required a combining of the *techne* of speaking with moral philosophy. The orator's ethos embodied teaching morality (Baskerville, 1952, pp. 14–15; Clark & Halloran, 1993, p. 2). Specific issues were always in the presence of moral principle. From history and the classics moral principles came down to the present generation. Indeed, with its close cousin the epideictic style that dominated the great civic celebrations of the day, the argumentative style depended for its motivation on moral inheritance: the obligation of the current generation to fulfill the moral charge set by an honored earlier generation. Thus was the pragmatic interest of the deliberative quality of the argumentative style crossed with the moral responsibility to history.

Of course, the emphasis in the argumentative style remained the deliberative. Actions were the focus, but often not specific proposals. In fact, one of the key skills of the argumentative style was converting calls for action into abstract propositions. Thus, targeted opponents were framed as advocates of propositions. These propositions transcended the day's specific topic, transforming the issue into more abstract moral imperatives guiding grand sweeps of history.

The argumentative style was a recognizable form to Americans of the nineteenth century. They admired those like Webster, Calhoun, and Clay who were proficient at the style. And they could anticipate the flow of great speeches. The argumentative style was a form in Kenneth Burke's (1931/1968) understanding of that term: "an arousing and fulfillment of an audience's expectations" (p. 217). Repetitive cultural practice established expectation that carried the argument along and imbued its skillful practitioners with ethos.

As he matured as a speaker, Lincoln developed his facility with this style: from his undistinguished term in Congress in the late 1840s, through the Lincoln-Douglas Debates where he transitioned from the frontier stump to the more formal argumentative style, to the triumph at Cooper Union in the winter of 1860 (Holzer, 2004). Lincoln developed the style, however, in unique ways.

It is often said that Lincoln's argumentative skills were honed in the frontier courtroom of Illinois's eighth circuit (see, for example Lehrman, 2008, p. xvii). But this only partially explains Lincoln's development. John Scott (n.d.), who traveled the circuit and shared cases with Lincoln, described Lincoln's courtroom style as direct and to the point. Lincoln used an abundance of common sense, reasoning through the elements of the case with a measure of principle and a carefulness of narrative. He learned to lay out arguments with a preciseness that permitted even the least sophisticated jury to follow the argument.

The frontier court was not a venue for the argumentative style as I have outlined it. With audiences less trained in the classics and world history, the experiential grounding in common sense was the most powerful source of validation. Of course, the basic framework of common sense logic was also the staple of frontier politics. Lincoln was fond of drawing figures from Shakespeare and the Bible, but the logic that drove his arguments was more likely to be experientially based in ordinary life than in history or the classics. This experientially based forensic demand did not lend itself to the hybrid of epideictic and deliberative demands that were more common in the argumentative style. The ethos of Lincoln's courtroom argument differed from that characteristic of the argumentative style. Indeed, Lincoln brought bemusement with his disparaging of his own education, something that was the opposite of the argumentative style with its emphasis on the orator as a wise man exercising the office of moral teacher.

The explanation for Lincoln's mastery of the style must go to his "passionate yearning to make a mark" (Carwardine, 2006, p. 2). He could admire Webster's "Reply to Hayne" and many of the efforts of Henry Clay, but he knew enough to not bring their argumentative style common to the Senate to the very different venue of the frontier court. He also appreciated the fact that his famous debates with Douglas were a hybrid of argumentative style and frontier stump. In the Cooper Union Address Lincoln reached his fullest expression of the argumentative style.

In the Cooper Union speech (Reid & Klumpp, 1860/2005, pp. 427–441), Lincoln framed his message in a clear, simple, and compelling instantiation of the argumentative style. The speech divided into three parts, with different counter-arguers in each part. In the first, Stephen Douglas was Lincoln's interlocutor. In the second, his ostensible counter-arguers were the Southern people. Lincoln varied from traditional form by failing to identify a particular arguer. The third strayed even further from the argumentative formula, moving toward an advisory tone in addressing an implied voice among his Republican friends. Despite their variation, each of these sections adapted the argumentative style.

In the opening and most famous section of the speech, Lincoln wove actions of and facts about the founders into a near geometric account of their positions on slavery in the territories. He chronicled their votes on the issues before them and projected the votes as voices, founders seemingly back from the dead to comment on contemporary times. Armed with these voices, he proceeded to analyze the opponent's case point-by-point, responding with admirable preciseness, employing observational acuity and logical rigor.

The argumentative foil in this first part was explicitly Stephen Douglas, author of the popular sovereignty doctrine that Lincoln rejected. Lincoln began by quoting Douglas's position directly and explicitly drawing *stasis*: "Upon this, Senator Douglas holds the affirmative, and Republicans the negative" (Reid & Klumpp, 1860/2005, p. 428). Lincoln then became the voice for the Republican position. Having drawn their two positions into sharp opposition, Lincoln replaced Douglas's voice with the voices of the many founders announcing their position on the proposition that Congress possessed the power to regulate slavery in the territories. The proof of history, the votes of each specific founder, refuted the now unnamed Douglas or, more precisely, gave lie to his claim. This proof was not constructed with the common sense of the country bumpkin, but with the ethos of the orator's historical knowledge. The knowledge enhanced the ethos of the knower as its depth and precision enhanced the power of the argumentative case.

As the proof developed, Lincoln invoked operational majoritarianism by counting. "Twenty-three out of thirty-nine fathers" cast explicit votes asserting the power to regulate slavery (Reid & Klumpp, 1860/2005, p. 431). But as he reached the final stage of the argument that marked the style – the clinch – Lincoln refocused the thrust of his assertion. Having demonstrated the proposition of historical fact, he reconstructed the votes as moral imperative. Interestingly, Lincoln evoked Douglas, not with his name, but by repeating his words. Then, he expanded his argumentative interlocutor to "any man at this day" who believed that the federal government had no authority over slavery in the territories (p. 433).

And finally he brought the moral imperative back to his argumentative opponent in a charge worthy of the greatest orators of the day. His opponents have "no right to mislead others, who have less access to history, and less leisure to study it" (p. 433). The charge? His interlocutors had violated the implicit responsibility of the office and ethos of the orator.

He fulfilled that office by shifting from the accusatory to the moral precept: "As those fathers marked [slavery], so let it be again marked, as an evil not to be extended" (Reid & Klumpp, 1860/2005, p. 434). All the motivational power of moral inheritance from the generation of the founders burdened now the issue of the day.

In their classic essay, Leff and Mohrman (1974) argued that the Cooper Union speech's genre is "best characterized as a campaign oration" (p. 347). I believe this claim misses the complexity of genre achieved by the speech's argumentative style. Certainly the speech identified Douglas as its argumentative foil, thus fulfilling a campaign purpose. But it was also deliberative in its strenuous motivational argument against expanding slavery into the territories. And, at heart, it emphasized that the issue was not simply operational – of Congress's Constitutional power – but moral, rooting the founders' assumption of the power in their moral condemnation of slavery. The speech brought the audience to this complex understanding through the energy gathered with the argumentative style.

Although space prevents me from fully commenting on the other two sections of the Cooper Union Address, those sections drew on the same resources of the style, but with variations. In the second – to the Southern people – Lincoln created a generalized interlocutor but still identified and refuted five specific points of *stasis*. A bit more common sense mixed with history in this section: The character of the interlocutor shifted, the ethos toyed with, to adapt the argumentative style to Lincoln's needs. And, in the final part, addressed to his fellow Republicans, Lincoln remained the didact. The counter-arguer as interlocutor was altered as well. To be sure, Lincoln still answered an implied alternative voice, but without the sharp forensic edge typical of the argumentative style. In fact, the relationship here was Lincoln as the advisor to his fellow Republicans. This change illustrates the argumentative style reoriented to a different prospect.

Lincoln mastered some of the styles of his day and failed at others. There can be no doubt, however, that the argumentative was a style that he mastered. His mastery tapped the cultural power of the style to propel the author of Cooper Union into the presidency as a champion of the fight against slavery. Perhaps, his mastery of that style with its sharp edges and moral force contributed to the intolerance with which the South greeted his election and birthed the Civil War that finally ended slavery. It is well to remember that, in its most compelling imperative, argument failed in the antebellum United States. Democracy is a government that seeks to substitute the adjustive powers of argument for the violence of national rupture. The argumentative style did not accomplish that goal. The Civil War came. For better or worse, Lincoln's mastery of the argumentative style thrust the United States' tragic national history forward to its second revolution.

References

Baskerville, B. (1952). Principal themes of nineteenth-century critics of oratory. *Speech Monographs, 19,* 11–26.

Berry, M. F. (1943). Abraham Lincoln: His development in the skills of the platform. In W. N. Brigance (Ed.), *History and criticism of American public address* (Vol. II, pp. 828–858). New York, NY: McGraw Hill.

Burke, K. (1968). *Counter-statement* (3rd ed.). Berkeley: University of California Press. (Original work published 1931)

Carwardine, R. (2006). *Lincoln: A life of purpose and power.* New York, NY: Knopf.

Clark, S., & Halloran, S. M. (1993). Introduction: Transformations of public discourse in nineteenth-century America. In S. Clark & S. M. Halloran (Eds.), *Oratorical culture in nineteenth century America* (pp. 1–26). Carbondale: Southern Illinois University Press.

Cmiel, K. (1990). *Democratic eloquence: The fight over popular speech in nineteenth century America.* Berkeley: University of California Press.

Donald, D. H. (1995). *Lincoln.* New York, NY: Simon and Shuster.

Herndon, W. H., & Weik, J. W. (2006). *Herndon's Lincoln: The true story of a great life.* D. L. Wilson & R. O. Davis (Eds.). Galesburg, IL: Lincoln Study Center. (Original work published 1888)

Holzer, H. (2004). *Lincoln at Cooper Union: The speech that made Abraham Lincoln president.* New York, NY: Simon and Shuster.

Leff, M. C., & Mohrmann, G. P. (1974). Lincoln at Cooper Union: A rhetorical analysis of the text. *Quarterly Journal of Speech, 60,* 546–558.

Lehrman, L. E. (2008). *Lincoln at Peoria: The turning point.* Mechanicsburg, PA: Stackpole Books.

Lincoln, A. (1953) *The collected works of Abraham Lincoln* (Vols. 1–9). R. Basler (Ed.). New Brunswick, NJ: Rutgers University Press.

Reid, R. F., & Klumpp, J. F. (Comps.) (2005). *American rhetorical discourse* (3rd Ed.). Long Grove, IL: Waveland.

Scott, J. M. (n.d.) *Lincoln on the stump and at the bar.* Unpublished manuscript, Abraham Lincoln Presidential Library, Manuscripts Collection, Springfield, Illinois.

41

ARGUMENTATIVE DIMENSIONS OF *PATHOS*

The *Patheme* in Obama's 2012 State of the Union Address

William Mosley-Jensen

UNIVERSITY OF GEORGIA, USA

The contemporary U.S. political climate is characterized by hyperpartisanship with members on the right and the left complaining that reasonable argument is no longer possible. Jim Cooper (D-TN) said of Congress that "members walk into the chamber full of hatred. They believe the worst lies about the other side" (as cited in Nocera, 2011, p. A27), and former Senator Richard Lugar (R-IN, 2013) lamented that "partisanship is out of control." This increasing rancor is not caused entirely by a failure to present *reasoned* arguments for one side or the other. In *The Righteous Mind*, Professor Jonathan Haidt (2013) explained that recent psychological studies suggest reason provides the post-hoc rationalization for the argumentative positions that people find most appealing. The study of rancorous political argument largely has been pre-occupied with the failure of reason, which for some underlies the "problem of faction" (Rowland, 2011, p. 1). Rhetorical and argument studies have incorporated many of the insights of scientists, psychologists, and sociologists in their studies of the emotional effect on the force of discourse (Hariman & Lucaites, 2001; Waddell, 1990). Though this work is exceedingly valuable, it has heretofore relied on traditional rhetorical categories informed by logo-centric analysis and has yet to be fully appreciated for the possible contribution to argumentation through *pathos*. This project theorizes a new object of analysis, the *patheme*, for scholars interested in attending to the effect that emotion plays in shaping and being shaped by rhetorical argumentation.

The case study for the analysis is President Barack Obama's 2012 State of the Union Address. The speech presented a vision of the ideal American as a hardworking blue-collar individual, who is upwardly mobile, politically disconnected, and geographically unfixed. The thesis of my project is that the deployment of "American" in these terms creates a warrant for action by invoking a rhetorical figure of enduring value for which scholars currently have no name. The patheme is most simply defined as an emotionally full signifier and as such can be used to generate support for a policy proposition. Though argumentation has traditionally been understood as the reasoned use of rhetoric advancing a thesis pertaining to a propositional statement (Perelman & Olbrechts-Tyteca, 2008; Toulmin, 2003), this essay attempts to broaden that conceptualization to include advancing a thesis by creating an emotional attachment to the elements of an argument.

This essay proceeds in three parts. The first part outlines the features of the patheme using theories of metaphor and affect to describe the process by which emotional meaning is created. This section highlights the importance of understanding the patheme as a complex operation of factors. The second section analyzes the 2012 State of the Union address, paying particularly close attention to the description of working class values that permeate the speech. This section functions as the case study and application of the concept of the patheme. The third section offers some concluding thoughts on the application of the patheme and seeks to distinguish the patheme from Michael McGee's *ideograph*.

Constructing the Patheme

A patheme is an emotionally full signifier that works by transferring a powerful sentiment through language and people. This rhetorical figure works by combining, in various ways, three modes of meaning making. First, the patheme occupies a non-conceptual space of meaning, activating a fundamental feeling. This is the result of the associational content of a term providing it with emotional meaning. Second, the patheme provides a view of an idealized reality, rather than seeking to authentically describe the world. Emotional meaning is amplified by positive feelings about the ideal. Third, the patheme activates culturally specific myths that reinforce the identity of the group and exclude non-members. A particular patheme's effectiveness will depend on the strength of group identification to generate a common orientation on the part of the audience. These three interrelated mechanics produce a powerful emotionally charged signifier that can be deployed in the service of persuasion, such as with Teddy Roosevelt's "Strenuous Life" or Reagan's "Shining City on Hill."

The first element of meaning making that characterizes the patheme is the non-conceptual origin of emotional content. In other words, the cognitive process engaged is not one that creates a causal linkage between a term and an emotional feeling, whereby the audience members think that they should feel a particular emotion and decide to do so. Rather, the emotions are engaged directly by activating the associational content of a term. A similar process is described by Hans Blumenberg's (2010) *Paradigms for a Metaphorology* as the way that metaphor creates meaning. For Blumenberg, metaphor fills the gap of interpretation because it is a product of the imagination expressing a semantically unified and undistilled meaning. Metaphor creates meaning as it is being expressed, in the moment. Through an analogous process, the operation of a patheme expresses a fundamental feeling through its expression. It creates meaning in the moment, relying on the audience's emotional fluency to create a persuasive force. Signifiers that express themselves in a primarily emotional mode do so through associational, non-cognitive means.

The second element of meaning making that characterizes the patheme is an implicit comparison of the current reality to a more positive ideal. In his 1975 book *The Rule of Metaphor*, Paul Ricoeur outlined a theory of metaphor that describes the mechanics of this process in the linguistic operation of metaphor. For Ricoeur, metaphor "is the rhetorical process by which discourse unleashes the power that certain fictions have to redescribe reality" (p. 5). Ricoeur's account of metaphor provides a valuable orienting function for the patheme as it recognizes the importance of associational content as well. Ricoeur's metaphor functions through association and dissociation of possible meanings. For discourse that evokes a powerful emotion through the deployment of a patheme, there is a process at work not unlike Ricoeur's metaphor. Presenting a view of reality that is idealized creates a sense of similarity to the ideal while also opening up distance from the non-ideal. In this way the patheme constructs a powerful emotional meaning through the creation of positive feelings associated with an inaccessible but hopeful ideal.

The third element of meaning making that characterizes the patheme is the transmission of emotional content. Teresa Brennan's (2004) account in *The Transmission of Affect* provides the theoretical ground upon which to build a theory of the emotional content of the patheme. Brennan argued that emotional states are transmitted between individuals through a complex process involving pheromones and observational data that are filtered through cultural milieu. For Brennan (2004), "[f]eelings are sensations that have found a match in words" (p. 19). Although the patheme is far from a perfect linguistic match for feelings and the circulation of affect, it allows people to fill in the gaps between their conceptual capabilities and their affective experience. The emotional climate is populated by cultural touchstones of great import. As a semantic unit that activates some aspect of this emotional investment in culture, the patheme works by transmission of affect through a culture.

The Patheme in the 2012 State of the Union Address

The State of the Union Address has special significance for argumentation studies. In the modern presidency, the State of the Union Address functions as the public expression of the power of "chief legislator" (Hoffman & Howard, 2006, p. 3). Obama's 2012 State of the Union address exemplifies many of the themes of a speech outlining a legislative program, but it goes beyond a simple layout of his agenda. In the address, Obama constructed a vision of "America" and what it means to be "American" to provide rhetorical force for his particular policy proposals, using "America" or "American" over 100 times in the address. Obama argued that "what's at stake aren't Democratic values or Republican values, but American values." Obama's address challenged U.S. citizens' understanding of the speech as laying out a series of straightforward policy arguments, and it did so by constructing a patheme as the warrant for his policy proposals: Americans' role as workers in a collective.

The first characteristic of a patheme is that it must invoke a fundamental feeling on the part of the audience. Obama's (2012) discussion of the American identity does this as it is rooted in his respect for his grandparents:

> The two of them shared the optimism of a nation that had triumphed over a depression and fascism. They understood they were part of something larger; that they were contributing to a story of success that every American had a chance to share – the basic American promise that if you worked hard, you could do well enough to raise a family, own a home, send your kids to college, and put a little away for retirement.

Two important characteristics create feeling in this example. First, Obama cited his grandparents' contribution to the national effort in World War II, a salient historical example for U.S. citizens, especially elderly ones. Invoking the historic contribution of "America's Greatest Generation" includes a nod to their creation of a thoroughly modern economy and the revivification of society set adrift by the Great Depression. Second, Obama's discussion of the working class promise induced emotion. The pull of working-class values is strong for U.S. citizens, as empirical research has shown (Lucas, 2011). Kristen Lucas (2011) argued that individuals gravitate towards blue-collar family roots, even when those individuals are transitioning into an upper-class lifestyle. This notion of Americans as essentially hard-working lies at the root of Obama's legislative program as well.

The second element of the patheme is the construction of an ideal that is contrasted with the actual, in order to produce a positive affective orientation. The expression of the American identity in terms of its blue-collar roots functions in this manner, connecting the individual and the collective at a fundamental and non-conceptual level. Though the figure may evoke no image for some individuals, that does not deny the powerful feeling that is associated with this class and their importance for American identity writ large. Obama's (2012) discussion of immigration is demonstrative, pointing out that "hundreds of thousands of talented, hard-working students in this country face another challenge: the fact that they aren't yet American citizens. Many were brought here as small children, are American through and through." U.S. citizenship is earned through the hard work that immigrants do while in the United States. They represent the future of the country, which can (and will) be transformed through their hard work.

The third and final characteristic of the patheme is the presentation of salient cultural myths that provide a strong collective affiliation and organizing function. Obama's (2012) understanding of the American character in the address sought to achieve these ends. Obama argued that:

> we can restore an economy where everyone gets a fair shot, and everyone does their fair share, and everyone plays by the same set of rules. What's at stake aren't Democratic values or Republican values, but American values. And we have to reclaim them.

This invokes the American myth of progress and upward mobility, where anyone can achieve the highest levels of success with the humblest of beginnings. Richard Weiss, in *The American Myth of Success: From Horatio Alger to Norman Vincent Peale* (1988), argued that the belief that all people can "exclusively by their own efforts . . . make of their lives what they will has been widely popularized for over a century" (p. 3). Weiss argued that this belief has "a strong hold on the popular imagination" in the United States (p. 3). As a culturally relevant myth, Obama's deployment of the American myth of success established a strong case for American qua "worker" as a patheme.

Obama (2012) began his conclusion of the address with a strong appeal to national identity as service to the country, erasing specific identity relations. Obama argued:

> Those of us who've been sent here to serve can learn a thing or two from the service of our troops. When you put on that uniform, it doesn't matter if you're black or white; Asian, Latino, Native American; conservative, liberal; rich, poor; gay, straight. The success of the United States rests on its people's ability to *work* together.

As Obama suggested, "[n]o one built this country on their own. This nation is great because we built it together. This nation is great because we worked as a team." The identification of the history of the United States served to demarcate its people's national identity from other countries' that may not have been created through a democratic work in progress. The exemplification of U.S. armed forces served to strongly emphasize the collective identification with the nation over and above the individual, as it is the country that Americans are *working* for. Obama's 2012 State of the Union address is thoroughly invested in the patheme of American as "worker", and the United States as the product of its workers' collective labors.

He uses this patheme to move his legislative proposals forward by arguing with pathemes as well as reasons.

Conclusion

In order to be a useful contribution to argumentation theorists' toolbox, the patheme must provide some new or unique conceptual application that other theoretical constructs lack. The most similar (and thus the most in need of disambiguation) is the ideograph (McGee, 1980). The patheme differs from the ideograph in two respects. First, rather than creating meaning through the expression of ideology, the patheme creates meaning through emotional association. Second, rather than being high-order abstractions, pathemes can be expressed through concrete examples.

First, ideographs are the expression of ideology. In his foundational essay, "The 'Ideograph': A Link Between Rhetoric and Ideology," Michael Calvin McGee (1980) sketched out a theory of the ideograph:

> An ideograph is an ordinary language term found in political discourse. It is a high-order abstraction representing collective commitment to a particular but equivocal and ill-defined normative goal. It warrants the use of power, excuses behavior and belief which might otherwise be perceived as eccentric or anti-social, and guides behavior and belief into channels easily recognized by a community as acceptable and laudable.
>
> *(p. 15)*

For McGee, examples of ideographs include terms such as *liberty* and *equality*, and ideographs function through an enthymematic process where the semantic content of the ideograph is provided by ideological conditioning. He argued that the ideograph recognizes a dominant ideology may have its hand in the construction of meaning for key terms in political discourse. In the case of the patheme, the primary mode of its meaning-making function is created through the emotional associations of the term.

Second, while ideographs are high-order abstractions that lack definitive, concrete meanings, pathemes need not be abstract. A patheme could be represented by using the example of someone's parents (or grandparents in Obama's case). The process by which ideographs create meaning is the key difference between an ideograph and a patheme. Where ideographs rely on the logical and enthymematic force of ideology to fill up an otherwise empty signifier, pathemes are terms that are custom-built from the cultural and social circulation of affect and represent a non-rational side of the human experience. In short, ideographs are words that make us think, while pathemes are words that make us feel.

By proposing that argument scholars adopt the patheme as a unit of analysis in their critical efforts, this project could link the study of public argument with some of the theoretical advances in neuroscience and rhetorical studies more generally. Evaluating the role that *pathos* can play in the construction and effectiveness of argumentation could broaden some already existing themes in argument theory. The focus on uncertainty in argumentation and deliberation is a particularly promising point of engagement. David Zarefsky's (1995) keynote presentation at the Third International Conference on Argumentation posited that argumentation is "the practice of justifying decisions under conditions of uncertainty" (p. 43). For Zarefsky, though certainty cannot be achieved, "this does not mean that outcomes are irrational but rather they are guided by rhetorical reason. Warrants are evoked from the cumulative experience of a relevant audience, rather than from a particular structure or form" (p. 45). The cumulative experience of an audience would include its emotional reaction to, and understanding of, cultural myths and potent symbols. This works not only for argument, but also for deliberation. G. Thomas Goodnight (1998) explained, "as deliberation raises expectations that are *feared or hoped for*, public argument is a way to share in the construction of the future" (p. 251, emphasis added). The deliberative construction of the future and the orientation towards that future cannot be based on arguments grounded solely in logical demonstration, as those arguments rely on certainty as their justification. The alternative to the inclusion of reasoning through *pathos* is to simply forget that all deliberative arguments are grounded in uncertainty. Rather than fearing for this uncertain future of deliberative argument, the possibility of a more human form of reasoning should be embraced.

References

Bechara, A. (2004). The role of emotion in decision-making: Evidence from neurological patients with orbitofrontal damage. *Brain and Cognition, 55*, 30–N40.

Blumenberg, H. (2010) *Paradigms for a metaphorology* (R. Savage, Trans.). Ithaca, NY: Cornell University Press.

Brennan, T. (2004). *The transmission of affect*. Ithica, NY: Cornell University Press.

Hariman, R., & Lucaites, J. L. (2001). Dissent and emotional management in a liberal democratic society: The Kent State iconic photograph. *Rhetoric Society Quarterly, 31*, 4–31.

Hoffman, D. R., & Howard, A. D. (2006) *Addressing the state of the union: The evolution and impact of the president's big speech*. Boulder, CO: Lynne Rienner.

Lucas, K. (2011). The working class promise: A communicative account of mobility-based ambivalences. *Communication Monographs, 78*, 347–369.

Lugar, R. (2013, February 12). Terry Sanford distinguished lecture. Sanford School of Public Policy, Duke University. Retrieved from http://news.sanford.duke.edu/sites/news.sanford.duke.edu/files/images/Senator%20Richard%20Lugar_Sanford%20Lecture%c202013.pdf

McGee, M. C. (1980). The "ideograph": A link between rhetoric and ideology. *Quarterly Journal of Speech, 66*, 1–16.

Nussbaum, M. C. (2001). *Upheavals of thought*. New York, NY: Cambridge University Press.

Nocera, J. (2011, September 5). The last moderate. *New York Times*, p. A27.

Obama, B. H. (2012, January 24). Remarks by the President in the State of the Union Address. Office of the Press Secretary. Retrieved from http://www.whitehouse.gov/the-press-office/2012/01/24/remarks-president-state-union-address

Perelman, C., & Olbrechts-Tyteca, L. (2008). *The new rhetoric: A treatise on argumentation*. South Bend, IN: University of Notre Dame Press.

Ricoeur, P. (1975/2004) *The rule of metaphor* (R. Czerny, K. McLaughlin, & J. Costello, Trans.). Taylor and Francis e-Library.

Rowland, R. (2011). Reasoned argument and social change: An introduction. In R. Rowland (Ed.), *Reasoned Argument and Social Change* (pp. 1–4). Washington, DC: National Communication Association.

Toulmin, S. (2003). *The uses of argument*. New York, NY: Cambridge University Press.

Waddell, C. (1990). The role of pathos in the decision-making process: A study in the rhetoric of science policy. *Quarterly Journal of Speech, 76*, 381–400.

Weiss, R. (1988) *The American myth of success: From Horatio Alger to Norman Vincent Peale*. Champaign: University of Illinois Press.

Zarefsky, D. (1995). Argumentation in the tradition of speech communication studies. In F. H. van Eemeren, R. Grootendorst, J. A. Blair, & C. A. Willard (Eds.), *Perspectives and Approaches* (pp. 32–49). Amsterdam, NL: Sic Sat.

42

EXPLAINING LEONARD PELTIER'S FAILED CLEMENCY RHETORIC

Matthew G. Gerber

BAYLOR UNIVERSITY, USA

Denied clemency by President Clinton, and ignored by Presidents Ford, Carter, Reagan, G. H. W. Bush, G. W. Bush, and Obama, American Indian activist and convicted murderer Leonard Peltier spends his time in solitary confinement at a federal prison in Florida. Imprisoned for his role in the 1975 deaths of two federal agents in a shootout on the Pine Ridge Indian Reservation, Peltier has mounted multiple unsuccessful rhetorical campaigns aimed at securing presidential clemency for his crimes. Many varying accounts of the events at Pine Ridge have been offered since the time of the killings. A detailed account of the history of the Peltier case is not possible in a project of this length, neither is it necessary given the arguments I make herein (for exhaustive accounts of Pine Ridge and the Peltier case, see Churchill & Vander Wall, 1988; Matthiessen, 1992).

The purpose of this essay is to offer one potential explanation for the repeated failures of Peltier's campaign for clemency. Specifically, through analysis of Peltier's statements, speeches, and letters written on his behalf, I argue that Peltier's (and his legal and public supporters') strategy of linking his imprisonment and struggle to the broader movement for Indian rights, first elucidated by Endres (2011), failed in two distinct ways. First, Peltier's arguments were not resonant with the public audience, particularly in the face of the rhetorical counter-argument led by the FBI and other law enforcement organizations. Peltier's clemency rhetoric failed to generate enough public support among non-Indians to make it politically palatable for even progressive-leaning Presidents like Clinton and Obama to grant a pardon. Peltier's arguments were not powerful enough, perhaps not confrontational enough, to disturb and disrupt the status quo, a system within which even presidents with virtually unlimited political capital remain beholden to electoral expediency as the ultimate arbiter of action. Second, Peltier was unable to galvanize sustained support even from the internal members of the Free Peltier movement, both Indian and non-Indian alike. A rift between AIM (the American Indian Movement) and Peltier's supporters developed that further undercut the persuasive power of Peltier's clemency rhetoric. Lake (1983) has argued that the supposed failures of Native American orators are only failures when viewed as being directly targeted at White audiences. Internally-directed consummatory rhetoric can often be viewed as effective in terms of its impact on Indian audiences. Certainly Leonard Peltier's rhetoric is no different. Early in his clemency campaign, he was able to generate deep internal support among AIM members but less support from non-Indian audiences in the public (Cuzco, 2001;

Knickerbocker, 1994). While the chances of any president granting a pardon to Peltier were small, I argue that without either a public demand for action, or a strongly unified AIM backing Peltier's campaign, those chances disappeared (Conan, 2012).

Peltier's Rhetorical Linking Strategy

To clearly explain Peltier's failed clemency rhetoric, I briefly revisit prior scholarship that examines historical examples of unsuccessful Indian oratory. In a survey of early Indian eloquence, Morris (1944) offered many examples of situations in which even the most persuasive Indian orator/activists were unsuccessful because of the ideological assumptions of their primarily non-Indian audiences. In his analysis of Chief Red Cloud's Cooper Union address, Ek (1966) argued that Red Cloud was unable to persuade President Grant to protect Sioux trading rights. When Red Cloud delivered a speech in order to generate pressure on the president, it failed to gain sustained traction with the public and Red Cloud came to be seen by his followers as a compromiser for negotiating with White people (Ek, 1966, p. 262). In his analysis of the anti-removal rhetoric of the Cherokee Tribe, Strickland (1982) concluded that the Cherokees failed for two reasons: First, their arguments were not sufficient to overcome a split within the Cherokee tribe over whether to acquiesce or to resist relocation; second, their rhetoric failed because it did not link the protection of the Cherokee people to the broader goal of protection of White rights and interests.

In an examination of Peltier's denied clemency rhetoric, Endres (2011) concluded that the Free Peltier movement attracted many non-Indian members to the movement but ultimately failed because clemency for Peltier was denied. However, Endres also argued that "pressure from non-American Indian members may be particularly persuasive when action from the U.S. federal government is needed to move toward political change" (p. 9). If non-Indian advocates were present in the Free Peltier movement, why did its rhetoric fail to generate the political change the movement sought? I expand on the work undertaken by Endres and others to offer additional insights into the failed clemency rhetoric of this important Indian orator.

Textual analysis of Peltier's clemency rhetoric reveals that his struggle for freedom began to function as a representative anecdote, or synechdoche, for the larger Native American cause of justice. Immediately following his conviction for the murders of FBI agents Coler and Williams, Peltier argued that his imminent imprisonment was symbolic of the long history of unfair treatment of Indians at the hands of the judicial system. Before being led out of the courtroom, Peltier (1977) said "You are and always have been prejudiced against me and any Native Americans who have stood before you" (p. 325). Peltier described his conviction as yet another instance of injustice when he lamented that "after centuries of murder of millions of my brothers and sisters by white racist America, could I have been wise in thinking that you would break that tradition and commit an act of justice? Obviously not" (p. 325). In this way, Peltier's story functioned as a broader narrative of Native American oppression. By explaining the ways in which White America oppressed him personally, Peltier allowed for others to understand the trespasses committed against all Native Americans. In the same way that genocide and subordination were perpetrated on Native Americans as a group, Leonard Peltier was being subjected to the same treatment in microcosm. Burke (1969) argued that political representations, such as those in which Peltier was engaged, often embody "synecdochic form" in that "either the whole can represent the part or the part can represent the whole" (p. 508). In other words, if one understands what was done to Peltier, one also understands the plight of Native Americans as a group, or, if one first understands the oppression of

Native Americans then one might also be able to grasp the individual oppressions visited upon Peltier.

After being sentenced to consecutive life terms in prison, Peltier spent several years exploring his legal options, including an unsuccessful appeal in 1978, an FOIA challenge in the early 1980s that failed to generate public momentum for a new trial, and a denied 1990 Petition for a Writ of Habeas Corpus. His legal options exhausted, Peltier filed a petition for Executive Clemency with President Clinton in November of 1993 (Stockes, 2000, n.p.). Again, Peltier's supporters bombarded the Clinton administration and mass media with the message that Peltier's imprisonment was a symbol of White U.S. injustice toward all Indians. While Peltier's imprisonment was the focal point for this strategy, issues of Indians' equality were foregrounded as a way to create larger symbolic implications for President Clinton. Peltier's case was no longer being argued in legal terms, but was being framed as an issue of Indian rights in general. Dennis Banks, former director of AIM, argued "Peltier has to be the number one human rights issue in this country" and that "it's a question of fairness, a question of justice" (as cited in Kanamine, 1994, p. 13A). By couching Peltier's confinement as inimical to primary U.S. ideals of fairness and due process, Banks and Peltier's supporters should have been able to avoid the pitfalls of the Cherokee rhetoric a hundred and fifty years prior.

In another instance of linking, Peltier's attorney, Ramsey Clark, argued that the shootout at Pine Ridge was actually the last armed conflict between Indian and U.S. forces. When viewed through the lens of the Indian Wars, the shootout at Pine Ridge is substantially rede-fined. In an actual war, enemies are justifiably killed, not murdered in cold blood, as Peltier was accused of doing. From that perspective, Clark reasoned that "for one person to bear the penal burden of that conflict is unfair" (as cited in Kanamine, 1994, p. 13A). In a specific plea to President Clinton, Ernie Stevens Jr., an executive committee member of the National Congress of American Indians, said that "if Clinton rejects that bid, I really think it sets us back in tribal-United States relations" (as cited in Lichtblau, 2000, p. A5). By linking Peltier's clemency to the broader issue of relations between the sovereign tribes and the U.S. federal government, Stevens helped to create pressure on Clinton to follow through on his 1994 promise to consider Peltier's clemency (Clinton, 1994). Endres (2011) argued that Peltier employed a synthesis of instrumental and consummatory rhetoric, a strategy that at once sought to galvanize the Free Peltier movement while also calling upon political leaders to take action. This strategy should have helped to make clemency seem like a politically valuable tool for President Clinton, who was nearing the end of his term in office and was struggling to secure a legacy for himself.

The FBI and a Fractious AIM

Peltier and his supporters provided a blueprint for how the issue could be framed if President Clinton would grant clemency. Peltier's rhetoric seemingly avoided the problems that doomed the persuasive campaigns undertaken by Red Cloud and the Cherokees. Where Red Cloud failed to bring enough sustained public pressure on Grant, Peltier and his supporters had crafted a long-term, large-scale, international social movement that boasted millions of non-Indian members at its zenith (Haga, 2000, p. 1A). While the rhetoric of the Cherokee had been ineffective because it failed to link protection of the Cherokee people to larger issues that affected White people and the justice system, Peltier's rhetoric seemingly *foregrounded* this strategy. Why then, did Clinton deny Peltier's request for a pardon? I argue that as Peltier's movement gained steam in the mid-1990s, the FBI developed and presented a persuasive counter-narrative that disrupted Peltier's clemency bid. Additionally, discord and friction between AIM and Peltier's supporters undercut Peltier's rhetoric.

The FBI counter-narrative was particularly aggressive and FBI Director Louis Freeh argued that no issue was more opposed by the FBI and law enforcement than "the prospect of releasing the murderer of two young FBI agents" (as cited in Gibson, 2000, p. 1A). Another of the FBI's strategies was to discuss the case only in legal terms and to frame Peltier as "hiding behind legitimate Native American issues" (McAuliffe, 1995, p. A1); this effected a rhetorical de-linking because to hide behind means a person is not one of the group behind which s/he hides. Congressperson Michael Oxley (1999) described Peltier as a "thug" and called on President Clinton to "see through this myth that has built up around Leonard Peltier" (p. 1).

Explication of the FBI strategies exposes the ways in which Peltier's rhetoric functioned and why it failed. Lucas (1980) argued that critics can never fully understand the rhetoric of a particular movement without also taking into account the rhetoric of hostile forces. In this case, the arguments of both Peltier and the FBI were geared toward answering the other's claims. Peltier's forces hoped to use the linking strategy to combat the FBI coalition's strategy of de-linking Peltier's case from the broader Indian movement. Sanchez, Morris, and Stuckey (1999) have labeled this strategy "rhetorical exclusion" (p. 27) – a strategy that seeks to rede-fine the identity of those who seek social inclusion as lawless, destructive, and inherently guilty of crimes against the polity (p. 28). Cox (2000) argued that one strategy employed by colonialist storytellers was to create native characters in their plots only so they could "anni-hilate them in their imaginations and texts" (p. 219). Morris and Wander (1990) have argued that political imagery and cultural representations that place Indians as the perpetrators of an "ambush" or a "savage unprovoked attack" are simply a way for "Americans to savor a victory over an evil force" (p. 164). Kelly (2007) labeled the FBI counter-arguments against AIM a "rhetorical counterinsurgency" by which "radical agitation" such as the Free Peltier move-ment is quashed. I argue that despite the support for Peltier's clemency among both Indian and non-Indian people, the competing narrative from the FBI undermined the appeals of the Free Peltier movement by putting Clinton, as the chief enforcer of national law, in an untenable position.

A second potential factor in the explanation of Peltier's failed clemency rhetoric is that at the apex of the movement, from the mid-1980s to the mid-1990s, a rift developed among members of AIM, with both sides accusing the other of collusion with the FBI in the Peltier case (Brennan, 2005). This suggests that Peltier's rhetoric may not have been as effective at generating internal movement support as some have inferred. Like Red Cloud, whose argu-ments failed because he was seen as a "compromiser" with the White man, Ward Churchill, former spokesperson for the Leonard Peltier Defense Committee, was accused of cooperating with the FBI in both the Peltier case and in the 1975 murder investigation of Anna Mae Pictou-Aquash (Gease, 2010, p. 1). Churchill alleged that Anna Mae Pictou-Aquash was murdered by an associate of Peltier because of incriminating information about the Pine Ridge shootout that Peltier had shared with her (Gease, 2010, p. 1).

With rumors swirling, and many within AIM and Indian Country seeking to distance themselves from Peltier and his supporters, doubts must have begun to surface within those people who were charged with considering clemency for Peltier. Like the Cherokee, whose rhetoric failed because of deep internal divisions over strategy and tactics in the face of continued economic subjugation, Peltier's strategy of rhetorical linking was undercut by pervasive finger pointing within AIM regarding cooperation with the FBI. This infighting within AIM likely undercut the persuasiveness of Peltier's rhetorical linking strategy by creating the perception that there was disagreement, even within the Indian audiences, about the validity and authenticity of Peltier's claims. If AIM was not willing to link themselves to Peltier's cause, that strategy was unlikely to be effective. Both the strength of the FBI counter-attack and the split within AIM explain why President Clinton, and now President Obama, both liberal leaders who made campaign promises to work in good faith with Native Americans, have denied Peltier's requests for clemency. Peltier's rhetoric failed for the same reason that Red Cloud and the Cherokees failed: Addressing the Indian problem is not politically expedient for government officials, particularly when faced with a backlash from the FBI and a fractured AIM.

Implications

Scholars of both argumentation and Native Studies can hopefully take away three key ideas sketched out in this brief essay. First, I believe that this study suggests that strong and unified support from one's own in-group is a necessary (if not sufficient) factor in effective clemency rhetoric. I argue that the discord within AIM probably dulled the chances for President Clinton (or those who preceded and followed him) to seriously consider granting Peltier's request for clemency. Second, this study both confirms and enriches prior scholarship on Peltier. Endres (2011) correctly obliterated the assumption that only Indians and/or non-Whites could be a part of the movement. Indeed, millions of White people did support Peltier's campaign. However, I believe this fact further supports my conclusion: Despite a broad-based movement that included both Whites and Indians as key constituents, Peltier's rhetoric could not overcome the political constraints faced by a president who was unwilling to take on the FBI to assuage a splintered AIM movement. While only President Clinton could speak to the exact reasoning behind his denial of clemency, "and he's not talking" (Harjo, 2001, n.p.), it seems reasonable to suggest the aforementioned conclusion. Third, this study adds depth to previous communication research on Indian rhetoric by examining the counter-rhetoric, a frequent omission in the literature on this subject.

References

Brennan, C. (2005, March 26). A player in AIM's internal wars. *Rocky Mountain News*.

Burke, K. (1969). *A Grammar of Motives*. Berkeley: University of California Press.

Churchill, W., & Vander Wall, J. (1988). *Agents of repression: The FBI's secret wars against the Black Panther Party and the American Indian Movement*. Boston, MA: South End Press.

Clinton, W. J. (1994, May 9). Remarks to American Indian and Alaska Native tribal leaders. *Weekly compilation of presidential documents*, *30*(18), 941–945.

Conan, N. (2012, May 3). OWS: A Case study in social movements [Transcript]. *NPR*. Retrieved from http://www.npr.org/2012/05/03/151947678/ows-a-case-study-in-social-movements

Cox, J. H. (2000). All this water imagery must mean something: Thomas King's revisions of narratives of domination and conquest in *Green Grass, Running Water*. *The American Indian Quarterly*, *24*(2), 219–240.

Cuzco, H. (2001, January 8). FBI agents march against clemency for Peltier. *The Militant*, *65*(1), n.p.

Ek, R. A. (1966). Red Cloud's Cooper Union address. *Central States Speech Journal*, *17*(4), 257–262.

Endres, D. (2011). American Indian activism and audience: Rhetorical analysis of Leonard Peltier's response to denial of clemency. *Communication Reports*, *24*(1), 1–11.

Gease, H.B. (2010, April 20). Witness in 1975 AIM slaying trial recalls a fractured AIM, Peltier admission. *The Rapid City Journal*, p. 1.

Gibson, G. (2000, December 16). FBI agents take to the streets. *The Baltimore Sun*, p. 1A.

Haga, C. (2000, November 29). Peltier case at crossroads. *Minneapolis Star Tribune*, p. 1A.

Harjo, S. S. (2001, October 29). Whither the Peltier pardon? *Indian Country Today*, n.p.

Kanamine, L. (1994, July 15). Indian activist Peltier pins hopes on President. *USA Today*, p. 13A.

Kelly, C. R. (2007). Rhetorical counterinsurgency: The FBI and the American Indian Movement. *Advances in the History of Rhetoric, 10*, 223–258.

Knickerbocker, F. (1994, February 3). U.S. is under pressure to ask if justice was done in case against Native American. *The Christian Science Monitor*, p. 1.

Lake, R. A. (1983). Enacting Red Power: The consummatory function in Native American Protest rhetoric. *Quarterly Journal of Speech, 69(2)*, 127–142.

Lichtblau, E. (2000, December 21). Clemency for Peltier likely to fail. *Los Angeles Times*, p. A5.

McAuliffe, D. (1995, July 4). Last stand for Peltier: Clemency drive poses political dilemma for Clinton. *Washington Post*, p. A1.

McBride, J. (2000, April 22). Peltier backers see FBIs lobbying as another example of repression. *Milwaukee Journal Sentinel*, p. A1.

Matthiessen, P. (1992). *In the spirit of Crazy Horse*. New York, NY: Penguin Press.

Morris, M. (1944). Indian oratory. *Southern Speech Communication Journal, 10*, 29–36.

Morris, R. & Wander, P. (1990). Native American rhetoric: Dancing in the shadows of the ghost dance. *Quarterly Journal of Speech, 76(2)*, 164–191.

Oxley, M. G. (1999). Oxley floor statement on convicted murderer Leonard Peltier. Retrieved from http://www.house.gov/oxley/s9911c.htm

Peltier, L. (1977). Statement prior to sentencing, June 1, 1977. In R. Toricelli & A. Carroll (Eds.), *In our own words: Extraordinary speeches of the American century* (pp. 324–327). New York, NY: Washington Square Press.

Sanchez, J., Stuckey, M. E., & Morris, R. (1999). Rhetorical exclusion: The government's case against American Indian activists, AIM, and Leonard Peltier. *American Indian Culture and Research Journal, 23(2)*, 27–52.

Stockes, B. (2000, July 26). Senator Campbell urges decision on Peltier clemency. *Indian Country Today*, n.p.

43

KRISTEVA, REVOLUTIONARY SPEECH, AND THE DISTURBATION OF ARGUMENT

Jeremy R. Grossman

UNIVERSITY OF GEORGIA, USA

Kelly E. Happe

UNIVERSITY OF GEORGIA, USA

In 1984, Julia Kristeva's *Revolution in Poetic Language*, which sought in part to posit a theory of language with a revolutionary logic, was translated into English. Yet, with few exceptions (see, for instance, Ott & Keeling, 2011), the field of rhetoric has largely overlooked her theoretical contributions to the study of both language and politics. Given Kristeva's sustained treatment of what she calls *signifying practice* and its relationship to social change – especially those signifying practices residing between what she calls *sense* and *nonsense* – we find it especially salient to revisit Kristeva's early work on language in order to think through the ways in which she disturbs argument theory and practice as well as helps critics decipher and engage what we here call *revolutionary speech*: collective speech that, through disturbing its own intelligibility, remakes its logics. As we arguably live in revolutionary times, given events from Arab Spring to Occupy Wall Street, theorizing revolutionary speech is a compelling task for argument and rhetorical scholars alike. Theorizing such speech requires rethinking existing frameworks for understanding rhetor, argument, and text. As we shall show, Kristeva offers just such a framework for understanding revolutionary speech today, especially that which resides in the mass protest that characterizes social movement activity around the globe. In view of this conference's theme, in fact, we find it useful to note that the word *disturb* derives in part from the Latin *turba*, "agitation, disorder (of a crowd), hence a crowd either in motion or in disorder, hence a crowd, [especially] of the populace" (Partridge, 1983, p. 742). In defining the relationship between collective speech and political logics, we take up the specific case of the recent street protests in Egypt which entailed the military ouster of the Muslim Brotherhood party president, Mohamed Morsi.

Revolutionary Speech

Social protest has long concerned rhetoric and argument scholars, whether they have endeavored to expand the realm of rhetoric (most recently, see Endres & Senda-Cook, 2011) or think through the relationship between bodies and argument (see DeLuca, 1999). Even with this expansion of the domain of embodied argument, it nevertheless remains difficult to identify the significance of what can only be described as the ineffable qualities of social protest. What role, if any, does speech that does not conform to conventional standards of argument analysis serve? Speech that is called angry and thus perceived to be irrational? Social protest that is unaccompanied by so-called demands (as when Occupy Wall Street was dismissed by the Left and Right alike)? Or social protest that popularly demands the removal of a democratically elected leader and which is elated when what many call a military coup – a word reserved for the forcible overthrow of an elected leader – is the result?

By revolutionary speech, we do not mean slogans, political demands, even utopian narratives, as these speech acts reside in what Kristeva calls the symbolic. The symbolic is the realm of *meaning*, that which is intelligible according to conventional norms. It is therefore not the space where disruption of social codes can take place; drawing on communicative resources within the symbolic necessarily means drawing on the very norms one wishes to move beyond.

The irruption of the drives, however, can disrupt social codes, because they work at the intersection of the sense of the symbolic and the nonsense of what she calls the semiotic. While Kristeva concedes that the suppression of drives is unavoidable, even necessary to function within the realm of the social, the pre- or trans-symbolic – the semiotic – augurs social change insofar as it draws attention to the very process by which the symbolic emerges as an authoritative force (when, for example, socially unacceptable forms of speech present themselves, the process by which people impose standards of intelligibility necessarily draws attention to the way in which the symbolic works, therefore stripping it – even if momentarily – of its force). By laying bare the logic with which demands and arguments make sense, the semiotic applies pressure to the *thetic* boundary between the semiotic discharging of the drives and the capture of this drive energy through language.

The thetic therefore "founds signification's truth capacity" (Kristeva, 1984, p. 53) insofar as it stabilizes semiotic movement on denotative premises. For Kristeva, poetic language is the exemplary case for that which disturbs the space between the semiotic and the symbolic, between sense and nonsense. Poems often occupy this space, as they are neither expository nor completely undecipherable. Yet they also draw attention to their own material aesthetic, as they call upon the reader to attend to the movement, musicality, and rhythm of language. By confronting the seeming stability of denotation, of the unshakable logicality of thesis, position, and argument, poetic language maintains a subject of the symbolic order as open to change precisely because it remains in question. Poetic language consists of the semiotic disturbation of the thetic by troubling the self-evident, that is, by disallowing the truth capacity of thetic denotation and position to cover its origins in the semiotic drives.

Nevertheless, poetic language *must* posit a thesis, or it would remain unintelligible; what it posits, however, is "its own process as an undecidable process between sense and nonsense" (Kristeva, 1980, p. 135). In other words, when one encounters poetic language, one does not merely decipher content (a claim, demand, even an identity), but is also confronted with signification itself. The aesthetic qualities of the words themselves – their arrangement, their musicality – are grounded in the confrontation with signification, *as signification*, thus opening up the possibility for understanding it as a process, unfixed and alterable. Kristeva (1980) described this as the realm of the heterogeneity of meaning and signification:

> The notion of *heterogeneity* is indispensable, for though articulate, precise, organized, and complying with constraints and rules (especially, like the rule of *repetition*, which articulates the units of a particular rhythm or intonation), this signifying disposition

is not that of meaning or signification: no sign, no predication, no signified object and therefore no operating consciousness of a transcendental ego. . . . [The semiotic is] a *distinctiveness* admitting of an uncertain and indeterminate articulation because it does not yet refer (for young children) or no longer refers (in psychotic discourse) to a signified object for a thetic consciousness[.]

(p. 133)

In other words, if and when poetic language operates exclusively in the semiotic, it is unintelligible; it is madness, psychosis, and could not properly be called language at all. Poetic language relies on the symbolic for its intelligibility, but the ground for disturbing momentary stases within this formation is semiotic, rupturing the thetic boundary between sense and nonsense, calling into question meaning and, thus, social norms and arrangements – for it is this boundary that must be the site of disturbance.

The potentially insulated formalism of Kristeva's conceptualization of poetic language risks an attenuated theory of social change, which consideration of the rhetorical function of texts can mitigate against. Here again, Kristeva (1984) is indispensable: In acknowledging the dangers of practicing too near either pole of the semiotic-symbolic dialectic, she encourages a clear critical view of *signifying practice*. For the poetic must be, she said, an "active" or "socialized" form of madness (p. 214). Just as the totalitarian impulse of the symbolic to fix signification once and for all enables hegemonic stases, mere "madness" is not only unintelligible but, worse still, induces a kind of anarchic "delirium" that, in the end, benefits dominant ideologies. Put another way, it has no ethics. In this form of artistic practice, Kristeva (1984) wrote:

A tendency towards "unthinking inertia" arises, which merely reflects the ego's preoccupations and diminishes the opportunities that working with language had provided rejection to give free rein to the violence of its struggles – not to founder under those blows, but instead to carry them into the clash of socio-historical contradictions.

(p. 189)

This art "denies the specificity of 'art,' which is its position between metalanguage or contemplation on the one hand and the irruption of drives on the other" (p. 233). The ethical function of poetic language can be fulfilled only if it avoids such unthinking inertia, and the aesthetic capabilities of poetic language can therefore function rhetorically in ways that other signifying practices cannot.

Extending Kristeva's (1984) conceptual framework, we theorize revolutionary speech through an analysis of recent street protests in Egypt. Rather than examine more conventional texts in social movement (e.g., posters, songs, slogans, even expository texts), we argue that the protesting crowd produces a poetic – and thus rupturously aesthetic – text that functions rhetorically to disturb conventional norms of legitimate political upheaval by working at the edges of argument. We believe such a theoretical move is warranted because, while Kristeva herself examined specific texts (e.g., poems or theoretical tracts about poems), she was nevertheless positing a theory of text more broadly as signifying practice. Texts must evidence socialized madness grounded in history, leave the subject in a state of perpetual critique (its unity is always questioned), possess a language that reveals the "process underlying it," and must "move" (Kristeva, 1984, p. 233). This signifying practice works at the thetic boundary between the *chora*, the realm of the semiotic drives, and their sublimation into language through positing. As such, we are thinking of bodies in the abstract, yet also in their irreducible (though mass mediated) materiality: bodies in streets, acting together in the form of social protest.

Revolutionary Speech in Egypt

In the days leading up to June 30, 2013, the one-year anniversary of Egyptian President Mohamed Morsi's inauguration, an imminent mass protest calling for his resignation dominated U.S. news headlines. Morsi's alleged trampling of the democratic model was to blame: using the elections as a springboard to squashing courts' legitimate checks on executive power and illegally and systematically replacing established members of the administration with members of the Muslim Brotherhood. The economic and social problems of the country, many of which preceded the instatement of a democratic government, were scarcely addressed and/or remedied by the transition to a supposed democracy, it was argued. Finally, the overt presence of religious principles in what many saw as the push towards an Islamist state alienated many religious and nonreligious alike, defying the commitment to populism upon which democratic will rests. And so, on June 30, it was reported that at least 14 million people took to the streets across the country, with Cairo serving as the symbolic center of activity. Specific numbers aside, popular support for the resignation or ousting of Morsi and the Muslim Brotherhood was massive and widespread, and nearly all media attention centered on the street protests. The next day, the Egyptian military issued an ultimatum detailing that, should Morsi fail to resign by July 3, it would forcibly remove him and take control of the Egyptian government. Morsi remained, and he and key figures in his administration were consequently arrested by the military.

For us, the key questions are not what particular grounds supported the demands made by the protesters, whether the scale of protest justified military intervention, or even whether the ousting should be labeled a *coup*. Rather, we are interested in the thetic break, the site at which the aesthetic of the crowd transposes the irruption of bodies onto the streets into a political field of denotation that otherwise recognizes plurality, argument, and demand as the fundamental practices of the people's will. And yet, even as we are uninterested in laying a critic's claim to the appropriateness of the term *coup*, the presence of the question itself undergirds the very need to make sense of the U.S. response to the movement to oust Morsi. On the one hand, convincing suspicions about whether the political uprising was a cover for a more insidious anti-Islamist sentiment function to censure the ouster; on the other, convincing arguments about the overextension of Morsi and the Muslim Brotherhood's political powers mark the subreption of democracy through the sheer façade of the vote and, thus, condone the ouster. Officially, the U.S. government refused to acknowledge Morsi's removal as a coup, which would have legally required halting the $1.3 billion in military aid the United States provides Egypt annually. Whatever the case, the rest of the world has, as of July 2013, not yet intervened politically, economically, or militarily. While the debate over whether cutting such aid would hurt U.S. interests continues alongside the debate over the moral legitimacy of Morsi's removal, and given that the contention over the term should not be seen merely as a debate over foreign policy but also a debate over the importance of naming, a central question for us remains: How does the crowd itself function as a poetic text to seemingly legitimate controversial political action?

Visually, the crowd is almost always marked in news reports by one of two qualities. First, they are portrayed in an impassioned state of exclamation, hands (many with two peaceful, or victorious, digits extended) raised above heads, decrying mouths open, banners and posters filling the empty space between bodies or hoisted to the open sky. Alongside these depictions are images of protesters battling officials in riot gear, praying in vast rows, or climbing aboard the tanks that represent the military, which in turn seeks to represent the people's will. What these photos share, of course, is a sense of the uncapturable in language: No signification quite succeeds in relaying the experience of mass protest, and yet this failure marks the desire for it to succeed. Conversely, aerial shots hope to establish the vastness of the crowd, surveying a gathering of thousands upon thousands of people. Indeed, these seem to be the only two scales available for making sense of the crowd: a small group of bodies that appear to act synecdochally for what is otherwise understood as an unimaginable mass. And yet, the relationship is more complicated than this, for in these two scales we see represented the singular passion of each person alongside – and yet, at odds with – the sterile quantification of the crowd. The crowd whose vastness can only be understood through its numerical aggregation supersedes the emotional fervor of each protester and, at the same time, the visual counter-position of this singular passion belies the crowd's overwhelming size.

Thus, the above question – how does the crowd function rhetorically? – cannot be answered with simple recourse to plurality. News outlets throughout the country were fixated on the 22 million signatures reportedly garnered on a petition by the Tamarod movement asking Morsi to step down. The movement's goal, which it achieved, was to gather more signatures than the number of votes Morsi received in his 2011 election, effectively reconstructing the logic of plurality upon which democratic elections rest. Insofar as the people's will can be represented at the ballot box in strict numerical terms, so, too, as Susan Zaeske (2003) amply demonstrated, can the will of the people be expressed through petitions against the state. The numbers of protesters in the street also were staggering, with at least 14 million people gathered across the country – more than the 13 million votes Morsi won in the 2011 election. These numbers were invoked in news stories aiming to justify the ousting, invariably drawing on a logic of plurality that recognizes the will of the people through various modes of voting. Yet, it is our suspicion that numbers alone cannot a legitimate coup make. It takes bodies in the streets, a crowd of sufficient size *and* passion, a crowd with a certain poetic quality, a signifying practice we are calling revolutionary speech. Insofar as the logic of the people's will can be reordered, such a crowd retains the possibility for social change to the extent that the mass-mediated presence of millions in the streets articulating a demand functions, aesthetically and thetically, to transpose the determinate elements of "the people's will" into something new. If Morsi's regime finds little traction here in its recourse to electoral grounds, it is because of this disturbation.

Thus, as we have just mentioned, because of its reliance on a disavowal of its own semiotic conditions of possibility, a rhetoric of argument and/or demand – even a populism, like Ernesto Laclau's (2005), run through a Lacanian framework and grounded in the demand – is not enough to understand the ambivalent response to the events in Egypt. In the context of social movement and protest criticism, critics would do well to supplement such models with a consideration of the rhetorical function of the aesthetic of the crowd. Inasmuch as a crowd produces, through its very materiality and in its movement, a poetic text that functions as revolutionary speech, the conditions for social change inhere within the signifying practice of the crowd – its rhythm, its scope, its passion, and the other ineffable and uncapturable qualities that mark crowds in protest as fundamentally different than votes and arguments. The rhetorical work that the crowd does supersedes its demands, its size, or the quality of its arguments. By virtue of the passionate and widespread gathering of human bodies around a demand and/or an argument, the aesthetic of the crowd functions rhetorically to disturb the fabric of the symbolic. In this case, it revises a logic of the people's will which, as President Obama has contended, cannot be reduced to popular elections, such that international uproar over the incident appears to us ambivalent at best. Put most simply, the socialized madness of bodies in the streets depicted in the images that frequently convey the crowd's passion disturbs argument by transforming the bases for judgment. As such, ours is a cautionary tale as much as a theoretical meditation on the rhetorical power of the crowd, for the future of Egypt is as yet unwritten, and these protests may well give provisional cover to what could soon be understood uncontroversially as a coup. However this transpires, the crowd remains for us the site of revolutionary speech, bringing its own semiotic motility to bear on the thetic logic with which we must all move through the world, together.

References

DeLuca, K. M. (1999). Unruly arguments: The body rhetoric of Earth First!, Act Up, and Queer Nation. *Argumentation and Advocacy, 36*(1), 9.

Endres, D., & Senda-Cook, S. (2011). Location matters: The rhetoric of place in protest. *Quarterly Journal of Speech, 97*(3), 257–282.

Kristeva, J. (1980). *Desire in language: A semiotic approach to literature and art.* New York, NY: Columbia University Press.

Kristeva, J. (1984). *Revolution in poetic language* (M. Waller, Trans.). New York, NY: Columbia University Press.

Laclau, E. (2005). *On populist reason.* New York, NY: Verso Books.

Ott, B. L., & Keeling, D. M. (2011). Cinema and choric connection: *Lost in Translation* as sensual experience. *Quarterly Journal of Speech, 97*(4), 363–386.

Partridge, E. (1983). *Origins: A short etymological dictionary of modern English.* New York, NY: Greenwich House.

Zaeske, S. (2003). *Signatures of citizenship: Petitioning, antislavery, & women's political identity.* Chapel Hill: University of North Carolina Press.

44

TWEETING THE ARAB SPRING

Argumentative polylogues in digital media

Marcin Lewiński

UNIVERSIDADE NOVA DE LISBOA, PORTUGAL

Dima Mohammed

UNIVERSIDADE NOVA DE LISBOA, PORTUGAL

The point of departure for our analysis is the understanding of argumentation as *reasoning-in-interaction*. This understanding has been extensively and convincingly theorized at least since Aristotle's *Topics* and *Sophistical Refutations* (e.g., Spranzi, 2011). Today, it is a building block of many approaches to argumentation: from "normative pragmatists" (Jackson & Jacobs, 1980), pragma-dialecticians (van Eemeren & Grootendorst, 2004), formal dialecticians (Hamblin, 1970), communication scholars (Hample, Jones, & Averbeck, 2009), informal logicians (Johnson & Blair, 1977), to formal logicians, such as van Benthem (2009), who claim that logic originated as a study of "intelligent interactions" (p. vii). Although the bulk of work in argumentation theory has focused on the task of defining what it means for interactions to be "intelligent" (or rational, reasonable, reasoned, valid, critical), relatively little attention has been paid to how to understand interactions. While for many *reasoning-in-interaction* is basically *reasoning* against conversational background, we work from a perspective where interaction is in the foreground, and reasoning is one of the things that happens there (and a crucial thing if argumentation is to be analyzed).

We admit, though, that the notion of interaction *has* been central to at least one of the chief topics in the discipline: the logic-dialectic-rhetoric divide (Wenzel, 1990) where logic is the study of "the norms of good reasoning" and, as such, applies to all instances of argumentation (Blair, 2012, p. 161); "dialectic is the practice and theory of conversations; [and] rhetoric that of speeches" (Krabbe, 2000, p. 205). A close examination of these distinctions reveals some problematic elements. Dialectical arguments are advanced in interactive exchanges between a few (that basically means "two" – see Lewiński, 2013a) active participants who confront "one or a small set of relatively consistent attitudes" of their interlocutors (Blair, 2012, p. 159). Dialectic so conceived invites a step-by-step (normative or descriptive) study of argumentative procedures built of dyadic action-reaction pairs. By contrast, rhetorical speeches are non-interactive events in which "the rhetorical speaker has to deal with a multiplicity of often inconsistent attitudes among the audience members" (Blair, 2012,

p. 159). This calls for a study of the argumentative process taking place under the contingent opportunities and requirements of the rhetorical situation. One crucial task of a rhetor is to meet the demands of a composite, heterogeneous audience without direct interactive engagement. The view we obtain is schematically captured in Figure 44.1.

Instead of continuing the theoretical debates between these two perspectives on argumentation, we take a different angle opened by constantly evolving information and communication technologies. Communication scholars examining today's Internet-based public sphere picture interaction this way (see Figure 44.2).

Argumentation in such an interactive environment consists of action–reaction elements (note the double arrows), but also requires arguers to address a multiplicity of attitudes and positions – and not just those of a largely silent audience, but rather of active interlocutors arguing with each other in a complex web of discursive relations. The distinctions between rhetorical and dialectical communication appear to collapse here.

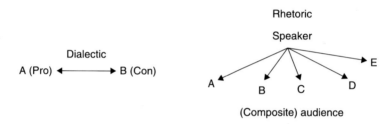

Figure 44.1 Dialectical and Rhetorical Argumentation in the Public Sphere

Note: Arrows indicate communication in the direction of the arrow; thus double arrow = interaction.

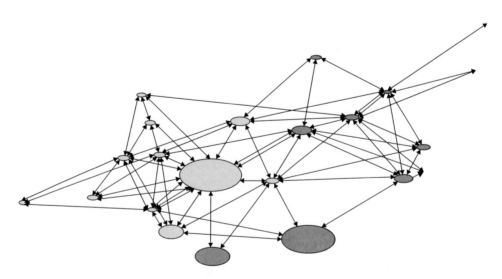

Figure 44.2 Interaction in the Networked Public Sphere

Source: Hsu and Park (2011)

Note: The authors analyzed "Twitter networks" among the members of the 18th (South) Korean National Assembly in 2009.

This short exposition leads us to two points. First, if the novel possibilities of networked communication bring about fundamental changes to interactions (see Bou-Franch, Lorezo-Dus, & Garcés-Conejos Blitvich, 2012; Herring, 1999), then argumentation scholars amicable to the notion of argumentation as reasoning-*in-interaction* should update their understanding of interaction when studying argument in the networked public sphere. Second, the notion of *networked* interaction brings about some explicit challenges to theorizing argumentation, including, but not limited to, the rhetoric-dialectic divide. We confront novel features that do not fit the classical – but still trending – distinctions.

The obvious empirical question arises: What precisely are these new features? In the following section we focus on one element of networked argumentation – the way Arabic-speaking Twitter users manage their disagreement network as they express and discuss their points of view in relation to the multiple issues that are at stake in the context of the Arab Spring.

Managing the Disagreement in a Twitter Interaction

The argumentative interaction on Twitter that we analyze was triggered by a tweet from Bassem Youssef, the host of a popular satirical news program broadcast by a private Egyptian television station (often compared both in terms of style and popularity to *The Daily Show* in the United States). Youssef is a popular Twitter user, with more than 1.7 million followers and over 7,000 posted tweets. His tweets are usually retweeted and often trigger discussions. In the interaction we analyze, his initial tweet, on July 3, 2013, was retweeted 1,881 times, was marked as favorite 1,335 times, and triggered an interaction in which 20 other Twitter users contributed a total of 42 tweets, as of July 22, 2013. In 8 of the tweets, participants addressed only Youssef; in the remaining 34 tweets, participants addressed other Twitter users, too. The result is six small subgroup interactions that varied in length from 3 to 11 turns and in quality from mere *ad hominem* exchanges to serious justify-and-refute ones.

In his initial tweet, Youssef advanced what seems like an abstract opinion: "Inciting violence and sectarian strife is not freedom of expression but hate speech."[1] However, taking the context of the tweet into account, the abstract opinion can also easily be understood as a point of view concerning the latest developments in the Egyptian revolution that started in early 2011 and was still unfolding in mid-2013 when the exchange took place. The tweet came right after the army removed President Morsi from power and shut down four media channels that were considered the main media platforms for the Muslim Brotherhood to which the president belonged. In the context of the controversial measures taken by the army, Youssef's initial tweet can be seen as an argument in favor of the closure of the channels: The closed channels were inciting violence and sectarian strife and, therefore, they are guilty of hate speech, which justifies their closure. The tweet is, in that sense, an argument that supports two "supra-standpoints" that were left implicit: *The closed channels are guilty of hate speech* and *Their closure was the right measure to take.* These two supra-standpoints were indeed the subject of (dis-)agreement in most of the responses in the interaction (disagreement issue 1). The Twitter users who responded to Youssef also brought other (related) issues into the discussion: the performance of other (mainly liberal) media channels, namely whether or not they were also guilty of hate speech (disagreement issue 2); the credibility of Youssef, in particular his commitment to defending freedom of expression and his role in inciting violence (disagreement issue 3); and the issue of the legitimacy of removing Morsi from power (disagreement issue 4).

The majority of the participants addressed the first disagreement issue. Many of them also had positions in relation to one or more of the other issues. In this polylogical exchange, the multiple parties had complex positions, comprising their standpoints and arguments in relation to the several issues at stake. Despite the high level of polarization, which characterized the Egyptian scene in general and was clearly visible in the exchange at issue, there were disagreements within the same camp. For example, T8 (Twitterers will be referred to by number to preserve anonymity) was of the opinion that the closure of Muslim Brotherhood channels was not right because these channels were not guilty of hate speech and also of the opinion that liberal channels were guilty of that. T9, who like T8 disapproved of the closure of Muslim Brotherhood channels, did so mainly because the decision on whether or not these channels were guilty of hate speech should not have been taken by the military (but rather by the courts of law) and also claimed that Youssef was inciting violence. T11, who, like T8 challenged the claim that the closed channels were guilty of hate speech, did so because of the absence of clear-cut criteria that distinguish freedom of expression from hate speech and did not seem to consider Youssef or the liberal channels guilty of hate speech or incitement. The multiple issues addressed within the exchange, and the multiple positions taken by the participants regarding them, shaped the disagreement into a complex network in which distinct lines of disagreement in relation to different issues crisscross and overlap.

The technical design of Twitter was present in the way users managed their disagreement network. Users employed brief language and often left much of their position and argument implicit to cope with the 140-character limit. Tweets, often ambiguous, allowed multiple interpretations by the readers. Sometimes, the ambiguity was strategically employed to minimize disagreement with the readers. For example, at turn xii, T11 tweeted: "the problem is who determines the criteria for incitement?" With this ambiguous tweet, T11 could convey a challenge to Youssef's supra-standpoints without being committed to it (he could choose the most abstract interpretation of his question and avoid commitment to any specific opinion related to the closed channels).[2] When T14, who responded to T11 at turn xv, discussed the closed channels in particular, T11 employed humor in order not to express his opinion about that. The sub-exchange, which started as confrontational and quite rigorous, ended abruptly but friendly. This could be partly due to the fact that T11 is a public figure who would rather avoid a position in which he seems to be defending the Muslim Brotherhood and also partly because T14 and T11 are Twitter users with a good history prior to this exchange who disagree within the same camp, and who would rather not embarrass each other publically.

The abrupt ending is actually a characteristic of the whole exchange, which can be traced to the technological design as well as the different goals Twitter users have. In the case of this Twitter exchange, Youssef did not respond to any of the tweets that engaged his position. Instead, two hours after the initial tweet, he sent a new initial tweet. For a couple of hours after, responses to the old initial tweet kept coming, but they then stopped. On the one hand, the fast nature and high number of new tweets coming contribute to the short life of a Twitter exchange. On the other hand, the goals of the participants play an important role in determining whether an exchange of opinion develops into an argumentative exchange where opinions are discussed or remains at the stage of expressing opinions and taking position, only. Some Twitter users make it clear in their profile description that they are under no obligation to engage in any argumentative discussion and that they reserve the right to use their pages as venues for non-conflict oriented socialization.

Theoretical Implications

Many of these qualities have been observed in contexts other than Twitter, notably in the old Internet Relay Chat system, which affords similar patterns of multi-party, 140-character per turn, quick back-and-forth exchanges prone to irrelevance, incompleteness, and *ad hominem* attacks (Weger & Aakhus, 2003). But even such studies investigating the affordances and constraints of online argumentation do not fully embrace the new theorizing about the networked public sphere that has since become prominent. Networked communication through digital media calls for a new conceptual paradigm partly grasped in the current cluster of "networked" concepts: from big notions of "networked society" (Castells, 1995), "networked self" (Papacharissi, 2011), "networked public sphere" (Benkler, 2006), to more concrete and argumentatively relevant analyses of "networked issues" (Marres, 2006) and "networked publics" (Varnelis, 2008). Our own claim is more circumscribed: Through radically changed conditions for argumentation over computer networks, argumentation itself becomes different. In particular, argumentative contributions to such a network are significantly different from contributions to public speaking before big audiences and to enclosed interactions between two, or very few, interlocutors. In order to outline these differences, we start from the distinction between "technological networks" (e.g., the Internet), "social networks" (e.g., one's group of friends), and "argumentation networks" which render the discursive manifestations of networked relations.

We propose that "argumentation networks" can be analyzed through the notion of *polylogue*. In the simplest definition, a polylogue is a form of dialogue that involves more than just two speakers (Kerbrat-Orecchionni, 2004). However, *argumentative* polylogues are best defined through a much broader set of definitional qualities than just many-to-many interaction (Lewiński, 2012, 2013a, 2013b; Mohammed, 2013a, 2013b). They involve *multiple parties*, that is, (often collective) agents with distinct positions on an issue; by definition, then, argumentation and counter-argumentation revolve simultaneously around *multiple positions* (rather than just two, e.g., simple pro and con) on a single issue, or indeed around *multiple issues*; arguers are attentive to achieving *multiple* argumentatively-relevant *goals* and to managing *multiple* levels of *addressees*. As a result, argumentative polylogues may lack a fixed focus for (counter-)reasoning: They are constantly open to expansions of complex disagreement networks in various directions distinct parties find relevant to the issues discussed. In all these senses, polylogues are quite unlike closely regimented discursive procedures between the proponent and opponent focused on one issue – typically imagined to be the loci of rational public argument.

What does it amount to in practice? Our analysis of Twitter messages exhibits some crucial features of polylogues. To start with, disagreement, rather than revolving around a unitary *space* delineated by a single speech act (Jackson, 1992), develops into a complex and open-ended *network*. Online discussants extend their arguments for and against the multiple issues and positions debated in a polylogue in various directions. As a result, different lines of discussion crisscross and overlap. This happens in instance when subgroups emerge to (simultaneously) discuss particular points. Moreover, many tweets (at least potentially) contribute to more than one such discussion. Some interpretive ambiguity (possibly used strategically) can aid in this goal. Finally, the notion of an addressee of a message becomes quite complex: Through the technological affordances of Twitter, discussants can explicitly address multiple (layers of) recipients; contribute to a chosen #hashtag; and speak to, in our case, the global and no doubt heterogeneous audience of Arabic speakers who easily can and do speak back.

Overall, polylogues carried over communication networks such as Twitter depart in many crucial respects from what we typically take to be a reasonable public argument, whether approached dialectically or rhetorically. Internet users quickly adapt to the new affordances and constraints of networked argumentation and, without much concern for the theoretical complications this entails, they continue engaging in a public argument – at times reasonably, at times hopelessly disappointingly. In our view, such practices of networked argumentation are yet to be properly appraised, beyond the classic accounts offered by dialectic and rhetoric.

Notes

1. The tweets in the interaction analyzed are all in Arabic except one. They were translated for the purpose of this study by the second author.
2. The need to be brief can of course also hinder the development of a rational argumentative exchange. Twitter users often find themselves in need of clarifying their positions after they have been misinterpreted. Some of the users, such as T18, post two or more tweets in a quick sequence to convey their idea properly and avoid that.

References

Benkler, Y. (2006). *The wealth of networks: How social production transforms markets and freedom*. New Haven, CN: Yale University Press.

van Benthem, J. (2009). Foreword. In I. Rahwan & G. R. Simari (Eds.), *Argumentation in artificial intelligence* (pp. vii–viii). Dordrecht, NL: Springer.

Blair, J. A. (2012). Rhetoric, dialectic, and logic as related to argument. *Philosophy and Rhetoric, 45*, 148–164.

Bou-Franch, P., Lorezo-Dus, N., & Garcés-Conejos Blitvich, P. (2012). Social interaction in YouTube text-based polylogues: A study of coherence. *Journal of Computer-Mediated Communication, 17*(4), 501–521.

Castells, M. (1995). *The network society*. Oxford, UK: Blackwell.

van Eemeren, F. H., & Grootendorst, R. (2004). *A systematic theory of argumentation*. Cambridge, UK: Cambridge University Press.

Hamblin, C. L. (1970). *Fallacies*. London, UK: Methuen.

Hample, D., Jones, A. K., & Averbeck, J. M. (2009). The rationality engine: How do arguers deal spontaneously with fallacies? In S. Jacobs (Ed.), *Concerning argument* (pp. 307–317). Washington, DC: National Communication Association.

Herring, S. C. (1999). Interactional coherence in CMC. *Journal of Computer-Mediated Communication, 4*(4). Retrieved from http://jcmc.indiana.edu/vol4/issue4/herring.html

Hsu, C. I., & Park, H. W. (2011). Sociology of hyperlink networks of Web 1.0, Web 2.0, and Twitter: A case study of South Korea. *Social Science Computer Review, 29*(3), 354–368.

Jackson, S. (1992). "Virtual standpoints" and the pragmatics of conversational argument. In F. H. van Eemeren, R. Grootendorst, J. A. Blair, & C. A. Willard (Eds.), *Argumentation illuminated* (pp. 260–269). Amsterdam, NL: SicSat.

Jackson, S., & Jacobs, S. (1980). Structure of conversational argument: Pragmatic bases for the enthymeme. *Quarterly Journal of Speech, 66*(3), 251–265.

Johnson, R. H., & Blair, J. A. (1977). *Logical self-defense*. Toronto, ON: McGraw-Hill Ryerson.

Kerbrat-Orecchioni, C. (2004). Introducing polylogue. *Journal of Pragmatics, 36*(1), 1–24.

Krabbe, E. C. W. (2000). Meeting in the House of Callias: Rhetoric and dialectic. *Argumentation, 14*(3), 205–217.

Lewiński, M. (2012). Public deliberation as a polylogue: Challenges of argumentation analysis and evaluation. In H. J. Ribeiro (Ed.), *Inside arguments: Logic and the study of argumentation* (pp. 223–245). Newcastle upon Tyne, UK: Cambridge Scholars Publishing.

Lewiński, M. (2013a). Debating multiple positions in multi-party online deliberation: Sides, positions, and cases. *Journal of Argumentation in Context, 2*(1), 151–177.

Lewiński, M. (2013b, May 22–26). Polylogical fallacies: Are there any? In D. Mohammed & M. Lewiński (Eds.), *Virtues of Argumentation. Proceedings of the 10th International Conference of the Ontario Society for the Study of Argumentation (OSSA)* (pp. 1–18). Windsor, ON: OSSA.

Marres, N. (2006). Net-Work is format work: Issue networks and the sites of civil society politics. In J. Dean, J. Asherson, & G. Lovink (Eds.). *Reformatting politics: Networked communications and global civil society* (pp. 3–17). London, UK: Routledge.

Mohammed, D. (2013a). Hit two birds with one stone: Strategic manoeuvring in the after-Mubarak era. In A. L. Sellami (Ed.), *Argumentation, Rhetoric, Debate and Pedagogy: Proceedings of the 2013 4th International Conference on Argumentation, Rhetoric, Debate, and Pedagogy* (pp. 95–116). Doha, January 11–13, 2013.

Mohammed, D. (2013b). Pursuing multiple goals in European parliamentary debates: EU immigration policies as a case in point. *Journal of Argumentation in Context, 2*(1), 47–74.

Papacharissi, Z. (Ed.) (2011). *Networked self: Identity, community, and culture on social network sites.* New York: Routledge.

Spranzi, M. (2011). *The art of dialectic between dialogue and rhetoric: The Aristotelian tradition.* Amsterdam, NL: John Benjamins.

Varnelis, K. (Ed.) (2008). *Networked publics.* Cambridge, MA: MIT Press.

Weger, H., & Aakhus, M. (2003). Arguing in Internet chat rooms: Argumentative adaptations to chat room design and some consequences for public deliberation at a distance. *Argumentation and Advocacy, 40*(1), 23–38.

Wenzel, J. W. (1990). Three perspectives on argument: Rhetoric, dialectic, logic. In J. Schuetz & R. Trapp (Eds.), *Perspectives on argumentation: Essays in honor of Wayne Brockriede* (pp. 9–26). Prospect Heights, IL: Waveland.

45

CONSTITUTING INCLUSIVITY AT THE EXPENSE OF INCLUSIVENESS

The economic realities of local food

Jessica M. Prody

ST. LAWRENCE UNIVERSITY, USA

I purchase shares of community supported agriculture (CSA), shop at farmers' markets, and belong to a food cooperative. I am also White, with an income significantly above the poverty line. I enjoy knowing the farmers who grow my food, and I believe my actions can make a positive impact on the environment and community. I fit neatly into the local food movement narrative. Alison Hope Alkon and Julian Agyeman (2011b) contend, however, "such a consistent narrative, along with the movement's predominantly white and middle-class character, suggests that [the movement] may itself be something of a monoculture" (p. 2). This essay explores how this "monoculture" is constituted through local food movement arguments and how the arguments may be reshaped to incorporate class-based concerns. I analyze Barbara Kingsolver's (2007) *Animal, Vegetable, Miracle* and Bill McKibben's (2007) *Deep Economy* to identify possibilities for increasing the inclusivity of the movement's constitutive arguments. I contend arguments built on complex historical narratives have potential to incorporate class-based concerns and expand movement participation, constituting a larger food movement that could have greater impact on our food production and consumption systems than the current movement.

Constituting Local Food Identities

The local food movement has been criticized by many, particularly those in the food justice movement, for excluding low-income individuals by privileging environmental concerns over those of food access (e.g., Alkon & Agyeman 2011a, 2011b; DuPuis & Goodman, 2005; Winne, 2008). My analysis exists alongside these critiques but deviates by going beyond critique to explore openings in the local food movement's arguments to address class issues. I ask how arguments might constitute a more inclusive movement so that wider participation can have a greater impact on environmental, economic, and food access issues than if the food movements remain distinct.

Kingsolver and McKibben both advocate local food consumption, though only Kingsolver has been cast as a voice of the movement. Kingsolver documented a year in which her family lived on local food; McKibben used local food as a model for reconstituting local economies, which he contended will address the environmental, health, and economic failures of the current system. I have chosen to analyze their texts because they are representative of dominant local food arguments, and the differences in their arguments provide critical insight into how reshaped arguments may increase movement inclusivity.

Maurice Charland's (1987) constitutive rhetoric has three ideological effects: (1) it constitutes a collective subject, (2) it positions that subject in an historical narrative, and (3) the narrative contains an illusion of freedom. The narrative must allow "its embodied subjects to act freely in the social world to affirm their subject position" (p. 141). Ashli Quesinberry Stokes (2013) found that local food arguments contain Charland's constitutive effects and are powerful because of their ability to define the movement, identify with movement outsiders through narrative, and model a lifestyle that appears possible. All three of the abilities identified by Stokes are present in the texts I analyze.

First, the constitutive identity of the movement is defined by individualism. Whether McKibben's contention that individuals must begin "a quiet revolution" (p. 3) or Kingsolver's do-it-yourself mentality, the identity of the local food movement is defined as that of an individual whose actions, in combination with others, can create social change.

Second, the authors identified with readers through a narrative of "conversion that ultimately results in an act of recognition of the 'rightness' of a discourse and of one's identity with its reconfigured subject positions" (Charland, 1987, p. 142). The authors demonstrated how they became local foodies by offering their own conversions to readers. Kingsolver (2007) saw the production and consumption of local food as a spiritual practice, one she compared to religious dietary limits. McKibben wrote (2007) that the effort spent eating locally earns one a "payoff" of connections to humans and environment (p. 94). The efforts of gathering and preparing food are time for contemplation and care, giving the food greater meaning. Like religious practices of praying, devotion, or spiritual work, the practices of local food produce understanding and connectedness. By modeling their conversions, the authors demonstrated the third ability of local food discourse, suggesting that anyone willing to undertake the practices of local food could achieve the belonging that comes with the identity. Constitutive narratives are powerful because they position readers in a broad historical narrative and encourage those who adopt the constituted identity to complete the story in ways that reinforce the narrative's ideologies. But not everyone can participate in this local food identity.

Exclusive Narratives

Kingsolver's (2007) narrative traced the loss of local food culture in the United States. She placed some blame on big agribusiness and government subsidies that have made it difficult for small, diverse farms to survive. But the social shift toward sex equality is her primary culprit. She wrote, "I belong to the generation of women who took as our youthful rallying cry: Allow us a good education so we won't have to slave in the kitchen" (p. 126). Kingsolver's narrative pinpointed the moment women left the home for the workforce as the beginning of a decline in food knowledge and culinary arts. Many will bristle at this connection, but arguing against the historical correctness of her statement is difficult. U.S. food culture shifted as the concept of a liberated woman was defined in contrast to the domestic housewife (Hollows, 2006, pp. 100–102; Pollan, 2013, pp. 2–3). Criticisms about placing blame on women for the loss of food culture are mitigated in part by Kingsolver's solution, which insisted food culture must be reclaimed in a way that exhibits sex equality, but even as she accounted for sex her solution omits issues of class.

Kingsolver touted that her family was able to live a local lifestyle on a "modest academic salary" (p. 70). Eighty percent of professors earn between $30,720 and $130,510 (Bureau of Labor Statistics, 2012). To call a salary in this range modest demonstrates ignorance of economic reality. The median annual income in the United States is $50,054 (DeNavas, Proctor, & Smith, 2012) and would be a sufficient salary for a local food diet, but this number doesn't illustrate the whole picture. The mode household income is between $10,000 and $14,999 annually. Approximately 7,127,000 households fit in this income bracket (U.S. Census Bureau, 2012), but Kingsolver writes from a class position that prevents her from accounting for low-income individuals.

Nearly 45 million people are on the Supplemental Nutrition Assistance Program (SNAP) (more commonly referred to as food stamps), with the average monthly benefit for an individual being $134 (Building a Healthy America, 2012). Consuming local food on this budget often is difficult because of location, cost, and cultural connotations. Food purchased locally is not more expensive across the board, but the produce sold at these places are typically not foods designed to last, to be stored, or to feed multiple people on a few cents. Nor are they always culturally relevant to racially and ethnically diverse low-income individuals whose food preferences may differ from those of "an educated, white clientele" (Winne, 2008, p. 140). Constitutive arguments that don't speak to such concerns limit movement participation.

This exclusion is compounded when Kingsolver argued local food consumption is economically reasonable when one buys in bulk and prepares food for later use. The do-it-yourself model is what Jesse McEntee (2011) called "traditional localism," which includes activities like canning, gardening, and hunting. Such an approach is less exclusionary than the "contemporary localism" of farmers markets and CSAs, but the upfront costs and time involved in such endeavors must still be accounted for. Kingsolver's arguments assumed that people have the money, time, and space to participate in things such as canning, freezing, or growing food. Many people don't have the upfront money available to buy food in the summer that won't be used until winter. Even if some low-income families could find extra money to buy 30 pounds of tomatoes, potatoes, or apples, many won't have the large freezer or closet space to store them.

Time also must be a consideration when determining who is capable of adopting the local food identity, particularly the acts of traditional localism. Kingsolver (2007) stated, "I think of my canning as fast food, paid for in time up front" (p. 201). In the United States, 7,123,000 people hold more than one job. That is 4.9 percent of the total U.S. labor force. Of these individuals, 3,704,000 work a part time job in addition to their full time job and 191,000 have multiple full time jobs (Bureau of Labor Statistics, 2013). In each case, the amount of free time for leisure is limited.

Kingsolver made valid arguments for why the identity she is advocating is one the majority of U.S. people could adopt; however, her lack of consideration for the income, space, and time required for this life ensures that a large minority of individuals are excluded from the identity. By comparing Kingsolver's constitutive narrative with McKibben's more complex history, the possibilities for more inclusive arguments are illuminated.

McKibben's (2007) narrative stems from his use of local food as representative of local economies generally and from using food as a jumping off point to discuss the much grander concern he identified as the culprit of modern day problems: hyperindividualism. McKibben acknowledged that individualism produced great changes throughout history, primarily in the realm of civil rights, but argued it has led us to forget that community provides valuable assets that individuals cannot. In McKibben's words, "We don't *need* each other for anything anymore. If we have enough money, we're insulated from depending on those around us – which is at least as much a loss as a gain" (p. 117).

McKibben did not shy away from class issues as they pertain to food economies. He detailed how the current economic system creates poverty and only benefits those who are already in top income brackets. He examined how the current system makes "*communities suffer*" (p. 107) and produces global inequality. He contended, "A large part of the problem, of course, is that growth is producing wild inequities around the developing world. *Nations don't get richer; people in them do, and often not very many of them*" (p. 195). He suggested that if individuals are willing to adopt community-centered identities, ones that involve producing and consuming local food, a more beneficial social structure could be created. By using food, a universal necessity, to illustrate the types of communities McKibben would like to see, his solution of localism appears universal.

McKibben argued hyperindividualism can be countered by constructing local economies within which each locality may identify its needs and resources (including local food) and determine a way of living that is beneficial to people and the planet. This suggested conclusion to the narrative can be empowering because it provides local autonomy, something those working toward food justice argue is essential to incorporating low-income individuals into the local food movement (Alkon & Agyeman, 2011a). There is no prescribed way of living, rather an invitation to participate in forming a strong community where one resides.

However, this emphasis on autonomy needs further development to open the local food movement to low-income individuals. McKibben's solution isn't immediate, so the relief those harmed by the wealth gap produced by hyperindividualism might feel in a system of local economies is a long time coming. His solution also omits the problem of agency needed to participate in the constituted local identity. Many in the food justice movement have detailed the lack of resources (material, economic, and political) needed to create McKibben's change. Recent partnerships have developed between the dominant local food movement and those who are food activists for civil rights reasons, but the food justice movement has been critical of the lack of concern the local food movement has given to issues of race and class. Alkon and Agyeman (2011b) explained, "Communities of color and poor communities have time and again been denied access to the means of food production, and, due to both price and store location, often cannot access the diet advocated by the food movement" (p. 5). Even access to traditional localism is limited for low-income individuals, particularly those of non-dominant races and ethnicity. For some the limitation is cultural. Julie Guthman (2011) explained the idea of "getting one's hands dirty" in a garden isn't a dream for everyone. She wrote, "For African Americans, especially, putting your hands in the soil is more likely to invoke images of slave labor than nostalgia" (p. 276).

In addition to cultural views of local food, governmental limitations can prohibit low-income individuals from enacting the agency needed to assume a local food identity. Through legislation, indigenous hunting and gathering practices have been erased or limited (Norgaard, Reed, & Van Horn, 2011). Immigrants have faced legal consequences for relying on traditional farming practices that exchange labor instead of wages (Minkoff-Zern, Peluso, Sowersine, & Getz, 2011). Global trade policies have forced farmers to migrate to other countries as their properties are seized for global corporations (Brown & Getz, 2011). And historical regulations, such as zoning and bank redlining, have contributed to a lack of capital investment in many low-income neighborhoods that has led to limited food access for current residents (McClintock, 2011). Local food arguments that don't account for these limitations fail to grasp the complexity of constituting an inclusive local food community.

Conclusion

The local food movement needs to be willing to grapple with class issues if it hopes to become large enough to make a significant economic and environmental impact. Food justice critiques and the analysis offered here demonstrate the lack of attention to class in local food movement arguments. Beyond critique, however, this analysis suggests there is space in existing local food movement arguments to account for class concerns. By filling in existing omissions, opportunities for greater partnerships between the local food movement and other food advocates emerge. To conclude this essay, I provide some initial suggestions for how local food arguments may be expanded to produce a more inclusive constituted identity and movement:

1. *The local food movement's arguments must acknowledge that the meaning of food is cultural.* As Alkon and Agyeman (2011a) stated, local food advocates must "create a more open dialogue about the various meanings people assign to the foods they consume" (p. 335) and begin to take those cultural understandings into account when advocating for local food practices (including those accessible to low-income individuals, such as hunting and gathering rights).
2. *Local food arguments should advocate for the broadening of offerings and accessibility.* Farmers markets and CSAs need to begin including more culturally diverse offerings that speak to food traditions beyond wealthy, White consumers. A discussion of alternative food offerings and broader acceptance of alternative payments, such as food stamps, is essential.
3. *Local food advocates must shift away from individualism in their arguments.* Local food can become a reality for many when the movement emphasizes the connections between local food and other social issues, as well as connections beyond farmer and consumer. A more inclusive movement can be achieved when discussion of fair wages, land use protections, and economic incentives for urban and rural food production are part of the narrative (McClintock, 2011).

Both Kingsolver and McKibben missed opportunities in their constitutive arguments, but McKibben's emphasis on local autonomy and positioning local food arguments in a broader social context illustrated the space available in local food movement arguments for more inclusivity of class-based concerns. Accounting for class in local food arguments may allow for the development of a polyculture in the local food movement that brings together knowledge, practices, and motivations not included in its current "monoculture" state (Alkon & Agyeman, 2011b). This diversification is essential if food movement practices are to have a significant impact on our environment, economy, and issues of food access.

References

Alkon, A. H., & Agyeman, J. (2011a). Conclusion: cultivating the fertile field of food justice. In A. H. Alkon & J. Agyeman (Eds.), *Cultivating food justice: Race, class, and sustainability* (pp. 331–347). Cambridge, MA: MIT Press.
Alkon, A. H., & Agyeman, J. (2011b). Introduction: The food movement as polyculture. In A. H. Alkon & J. Agyeman (Eds.), *Cultivating food justice: Race, class, and sustainability* (pp. 1–20). Cambridge, MA: MIT Press.

Brown, S., & Getz, C. (2011). Farmworker food insecurity and the production of hunger in California. In A. H. Alkon & J. Agyeman (Eds.), *Cultivating food justice: Race, class, and sustainability* (pp. 121–146). Cambridge, MA: MIT Press.

Building a healthy America: A profile of the supplemental nutrition assistance program. (2012). Washington D.C.: United States Department of Agriculture, Food and Nutrition Service: Office of Research and Analysis.

Bureau of Labor Statistics. (2013). Economic news release: Table A-16. Retrieved from http://www. bls.gov/news.release/empsit.t16.htm

Bureau of Labor Statistics, U.S. Department of Labor. (2012). Occupational outlook handbook, 2012–2013: Post-secondary teachers. Retrieved from http://www.bls.gov/ooh/education-training-and-library/postsecondary-teachers.htm

Charland, M. (1987). Constitutive rhetoric: The case of the *peuple Québécois*. *Quarterly Journal of Speech*, *73*(2), 133–150.

DeNavas-Walt, C., Proctor, B. D., & Smith, J. C. (2012). *Income, poverty, and health insurance coverage in the United States: 2011.* Washington, D.C.: U.S. Census Bureau, Current Population Reports, U.S. Government Printing Office.

DuPuis, M.E., & Goodman, D. (2005). Should we go "home" to eat?: Toward a reflexive politics of localism. *Journal of Rural Studies, 21*, 359–371.

Hollows, J. (2006). Can I go home yet? Feminism, post-feminism and domesticity. In J. Hollows & R. Moseley (Eds.), *Feminism in popular culture* (pp. 97–118). New York, NY: Bloomsbury Academic.

Kingsolver, B. (2007). *Animal, vegetable, miracle: A year of food life.* New York, NY: HarperCollins Publishers.

McClintock, N. (2011). From industrial garden to food desert: Demarcated devaluation in the flatlands of Oakland, California. In A. H. Alkon & J. Agyeman (Eds.), *Cultivating food justice: Race, class, and sustainability* (pp. 89–120). Cambridge, MA: MIT Press.

McEntee, J. C. (2011). Realizing rural food justice: Divergent locals in the northeastern United States. In A. H. Alkon & J. Agyeman (Eds.), *Cultivating food justice: Race, class, and sustainability* (pp. 239–259). Cambridge, MA: MIT Press.

McKibben, B. (2007). *Deep economy: The wealth of communities and the durable future.* New York, NY: Henry Holt Company, LLC.

Minkoff-Zern, L., Peluso, N., Sowerwine, J., & Getz, C. (2011). Race and regulation: Asian immigrants in California agriculture. In A. H. Alkon, & J. Agyeman (Eds.), *Cultivating food justice: Race, class, and sustainability* (pp. 65–85). Cambridge, MA: MIT Press.

Norgaard, K. M., Reed, R., & Van Horn, C. (2011). A continuing legacy: Institutional racism, hunger, and nutritional justice on the Klamath. In A. H. Alkon & J. Agyeman (Eds.), *Cultivating food justice: Race, class, and sustainability* (pp. 23–46). Cambridge, MA: MIT Press.

Pollan, M. (2013). *Cooked: A natural history of transformation.* New York, NY: Penguin Press.

Stokes, A. Q. (2013). You are what you eat: Slow Food USA's constitutive public relations. *Journal of Public Relations Research, 25*(1), 68–90.

U.S. Census Bureau. (2012). Current population survey: Table HINC-06. Retrieved from http://www.census.gov/hhes/www/cpstables/032012/hhinc/toc.htm

Winne, M. (2008). *Closing the food gap: Resetting the table in the land of plenty.* Boston, MA: Beacon Press.

46

OPPOSING THE ALREADY OPPOSITIONAL

The Westboro Baptist Church, counter-protests, and the limits of controversy

Brian J. Schrader

REGIS UNIVERSITY, USA

John J. Rief

UNIVERSITY OF PITTSBURGH, USA

Matthew P. Brigham

JAMES MADISON UNIVERSITY, USA

The Westboro Baptist Church (WBC) is infamous for its protests, often at sensitive events like funerals and against the LGBTQ community, as well as its efforts to attach sexual politics to military deaths in Iraq and Afghanistan (Brouwer & Hess, 2007; Schrader & Rief, 2012). Previous scholarly work has investigated reactions by the Supreme Court to WBC protest strategies (Schrader & Rief, 2012) as well as the "vernacular responses" of counter-protesters (Brouwer & Hess, 2007); however, significant work remains to understand the WBC's role in U.S. culture. Importantly, unpacking how the WBC has been counter-protested remains a largely unfinished task that may highlight what the WBC's wider rhetorical context can tell scholars about the study of public argument.

The WBC has been counter-protested since the group emerged into the national spotlight during the tumultuous events following the murder of Matthew Shepard, a gay college student, in Laramie, Wyoming, in 1999 (Hudson, 2011). In particular, members of a group, "Angel Action," donned large wings and blocked WBC protesters during the trial of Shepard's murderers (Orr, 1999; Patterson, 2011). LGBTQ groups and their supporters have continued to protest the WBC, focusing on the offensiveness of its message and attempting to block it (Brouwer & Hess, 2007; Patterson, 2011; Nussenbaum, 2013). Here, we focus on another set of counter-protests that pose important questions with implications for current scholarly understandings of public controversy – those initiated by celebrities in response to WBC protests at their events.

Our work proceeds in two parts. First, we highlight the critical tools used in our analysis of celebrity-based counter-protests of the WBC, specifically the notion of "oppositional argument" (Olson & Goodnight, 1994). We then analyze two such instances of protest by the musicians of the Foo Fighters and by the filmmaker, Kevin Smith, in order to investigate how opposing already oppositional forces implicates the development of oppositional contestation. We argue that the celebrity-driven counter-protests of the WBC we focus on here complicate the meaning and scope of the term *oppositional* and indicate the multi-directional trajectories of protest along the axes of style and substance. In particular, we suggest that the Foo Fighters and Smith called forth "emergent collective[s]" (Asen, 2000, p. 438–439) to oppose the WBC at staged and mediated events. While doing so, they simultaneously craft messages for both their specific contexts and for mainstream U.S. culture.

The WBC and Its Opponents: New Challenges and Opportunities for the Study of Controversy

In his keynote address at the 1991 Alta conference, G. Thomas Goodnight initiated a call for more "theoretical reflection" (p. 3) about the meaning of controversy. Developing such inquiry, Goodnight and others have challenged colloquial definitions of controversy (e.g., point-counterpoint, argument-refutation), contrasting them with "oppositional arguments" that feature contestation over often implicit communicative norms (Asen, 2000; Asen & Brouwer, 2001; Fraser, 1992; Fritch, Palczewski, Short, & Farrell, 2006; Harr-Lagin & Palczewski, in press; Olson & Goodnight, 1994; Palczewski, 2002; Palczewski, 2010; Pezzullo, 2003). As Olson and Goodnight (1994) argued, oppositional argument occurs when "arguers criticize and invent alternatives to established social conventions and sanctioned norms of communication" (p. 249). In these early expositions of the concepts of controversy and oppositionality, there is no indication that exhibiting an oppositional *ethos* requires a progressive or liberatory *telos*; however, oppositional argument has most often been ascribed to the systematically disempowered (see e.g., Asen & Brouwer, 2001; Fritch, Palczewski, Short, & Farrell, 2006; Olson & Goodnight, 1994; Pezzullo, 2003). Despite this trend (also noted by Asen, 2009), there is increasing awareness of the importance of oppositionality as a rhetorical tactic used by conservatives and progressives in ways that ultimately serve privilege and domination (Asen, 2009; Fraser, 1992; Palczewski, 2010; Pezzullo, 2003), a claim that could easily be made of the WBC. In addition, some scholars have noted that major performative transformations occur when opposition is oriented not toward the state or institutions but rather, for example, toward other activist groups (Harr-Lagin & Palczewski, in press; Palczewski, 2010). Our argument focuses on a different inflection of countering the already "counter" than has been raised in the literature briefly glossed here: that is, celebrities cultivating collective action in response to a marginal and trenchantly radical, religious, and conservative group: the WBC. Our examples open up space for critical reflection about the ways in which oppositionality can work in multiple directions, from the periphery to the center of power (Asen & Brouwer, 2001; Fraser, 1992; Mansbridge & Morris, 2001). We investigate the consequences of this oppositional multi-directionality in the next two sections.

The Foo Fighters: Using Musical Performance to Counter the WBC

On September 16, 2011, the WBC staged a protest in reaction to the rock band, the Foo Fighters, and a promotional music video for their summer concert tour entitled "Hot Buns" (Michaels, 2011). This video depicted the band members "dressed up like hillbilly cowboys" eating at a truck stop ("Foo Fighters," 2011) and was likely targeted because it included suggestive scenes of the band members showering together nude ("Foo Fighters," 2011). For the WBC, the Foo Fighters' video exemplified the entertainment industry's wanton disregard of the importance of faith (Michaels, 2011). The WBC has argued that "musical writers and performers use their God-given talents to rebel against their Maker" and that "nearly all of their lyrics, rhythms and melodies are designed . . . to draw the mind away from serious consideration of God's law" ("Music," 2013).

In response, the Foo Fighters staged a counter-protest (Hartman, 2011), performing their song, "Keep it Clean (Hot Buns)," which has been described as "a gay love song" (Michaels, 2011) and contains themes of openness, kindness, and patriotism (foofighters, 2011). For example, at one point, the chosen lyrics for this performance embrace a diversity of sexual identities. This pluralism is woven into a larger articulation of sexual difference (and difference as such) at the heart of American identity (see Michaels, 2011). In our view, the performance of this song during the counter-protest represented an attempt to negotiate between the competing poles of difference and unity, that is, sexual difference and diversity on the one hand and unity despite difference in American culture on the other.

Crucially, the counter-protest was not limited to singing the song. The Foo Fighters performed on the back of a truck driven between WBC protestors and the venue for their upcoming concert (foofighters, 2011; Michaels, 2011). The truck was decorated with U.S. flags and hay bales, and band members wore their "hillbilly cowboy" costumes from the "Hot Buns" video ("Foo Fighters," 2011; Michaels, 2011). Not only did their singing drown out shouts from the WBC protestors, but the truck also created a physical barrier blocking the church members' message. Video also shows acrimonious exchanges between WBC members and people on the street that abruptly ended upon the band's arrival as attention shifted to the makeshift stage. The WBC members seemed confounded, and dissenters mostly took to cheering on the band.

Choosing to sing the song being protested by the WBC represented a clear enactment of the Foo Fighter's refusal to be silent. In this way, the band negated the WBC's attempt to interrupt the space of their concert venue by staging their irreverent performance directly in front of them. Furthermore, the Foo Fighters ironic appropriation of stereotypical country dress, in clear contradiction with their song lyrics and message, served to challenge the assumption that rural conservative Christian groups would necessarily support the WBC's views. The costumes drew upon the stereotypical association between "hillbilly cowboy" ("Foo Fighters," 2011) culture and conservative perspectives on issues like homosexuality and marriage, while the lyrics of their song celebrated diversity and openness, particularly in terms of sexual orientation. This contradiction does its work enthymematically, requiring observers to interpret the performative elements and infer from context the meaning of the counter-protest. The visual cues that the Foo Fighters relied upon are widely shared "visual archetypes" (Birdsell & Groarke, 2007, p. 105) that circulate in a uniquely U.S. "visual culture" (Birdsell & Groarke, 1996; Finnegan, 2005), including most notably the band's costumes and the presence of hay bales and U.S. flags. The Foo Fighters also challenged the WBC's condemnation of the United States by including multiple U.S. flags on their make-shift stage (Michaels, 2011), thus contesting and challenging the WBC's perspective about the country (sinful, immoral, wicked, etc.) while performing the band's affirmation of a vision of American-ness that respects openness and diversity.

At the level of their audience, the Foo Fighters deployed counter-protest strategies embedded in their past performances that potentially fall outside dominant modes of public argument. However, when their methods are combined with their overall message, it becomes clear that the Foo Fighters also attempted to speak to a larger community – U.S. popular culture. They drew on symbols (the flag) and arguments (for diversity, equality, and respect) that might be viewed as more widely shared than (and potentially at odds with) the performative tactics they utilized. In short, this example suggests that when responding to an already oppositional group, counter-protests may end up calling upon a variety of rhetorical tactics, some oriented toward their specific audience, others oriented toward a larger culture.

Kevin Smith: The Inventive Opportunities of "Wit"

In 2011, independent filmmaker Kevin Smith released his self-described "horror" film, *Red State*, (Falsani, 2011), featuring characters based loosely on the WBC (Godfrey, 2011). The film premiered at the Sundance Film Festival to critical acclaim and WBC picket signs (Orr, 2011). Smith issued a playful press release announcing his intention to protest the WBC and inviting his fans to join him, using the moniker "The Harvey Boys," the name Smith gave to the production company behind *Red State* (Advocate.com, 2011; Godfrey, 2011). As with the Foo Fighters, Smith's strategy was to challenge the church at the level of both their message and their tactics:

> The Harvey Boys are seeking the aid of the Mighty Thor, hoping he'll lay down his hammer and instead pick up a protest sign on our behalf, in a Park City battle of the mega-gods . . . For thirty minutes of fun-filled photo-opportunities, the Harvey Boys will peacefully counter-protest the WBC Eccles Theater Protest. All are welcome. Wear YOUR dopey sentiments nobody gives a shit about on a sign of your own making, as you stand shoulder-to-shoulder with the folks who've mastered the art of writing utter horseshit on cardboard! BYOS (Bring Your Own Sign) . . . Remember: this is a PEACEFUL protest. The only venom you bring is printed on a placard, your only weapon: wit.
>
> *(The Harvey Boys, 2011)*

Smith indicated here that calling on God is no different from calling on Thor or Zuul, thus undermining the religious foundations of the WBC's arguments. In addition, Smith made clear that the counter-protest would be peaceful in nature. Accordingly, the "only weapon" that could be used in the counter protest is "wit," an entirely different approach from the radical offensiveness of the WBC. Thus, "wit" is contrasted in the press release with descriptions and inferences about the WBC's picket slogans that are indirectly described as "venom[ous]," "dopey," and "utter horseshit."

In making these claims, Smith invoked common oppositional strategies. His call to undermine religiously based protest through "wit" functions much like Olson and Goodnight's (1994) notion of "blocking enthymemes" (p. 273). The WBC's position relied on a specific understanding of faith as a validation for their actions, represented enthymematically by the constant evocation of God in their protest materials. Smith blocked these evocations by deploying "wit" to render absurd any appeals to the divine. Furthermore, Smith not only attacked the message of the WBC but also its communicative tactics (e.g., yelling and offensive speech). His strategy was the use of "wit" as a counter-communicative norm.

This press release is clearly aimed at Smith's fans, especially those who enjoyed his rousing criticisms of the Catholic Church in *Dogma* (1999) and are already primed to view religious arguments skeptically. Additionally, the use of "wit" to criticize those who take life and politics too seriously is a common trope in most of his films. However, in his call for non-violence,

Smith might be arguing against the extreme from the mainstream, as concerns about violence as substitutes for peaceful protests are routinely deployed against oppositional groups (such as more radical civil rights activists). In so doing, Smith re-inscribed norms with which denizens of dominant U.S. culture would likely identify in a way similar to that chosen by the Foo Fighters, although much less obvious given the lack of primary symbols like the U.S. flag.

Implications

It may be profitable to deploy the imagery of center-periphery in order to determine the status of counter-protesters. Given the overwhelming disdain for the WBC in U.S. culture, scholars could identify them as inhabiting a space at the periphery (e.g., as "oppositional" or "counter"). In opposing a movement that is on the periphery, counter-protesters could challenge the WBC from another point on the periphery, seeking to undermine the WBC's message without occupying the space of a dominant culture. Such counter-protesters could alternatively move toward the center, challenging the WBC from more commonly shared norms. Our examples show how counter-protesters may at times destabilize categories of center/periphery by calling on a multiplicity of resources for the invention of argument, some that call on the attention of specific collectives of fans, others that call on the broader culture. The argumentative strategies of the Foo Fighters and Kevin Smith embody tendencies that might be classified as oppositional but simultaneously reach out for wider acceptance using well-established symbols and communicative norms.

More specifically, the Foo Fighters and Kevin Smith have cultivated their own celebrity communities with fans and followers who have extant strategies for counter-protesting (e.g., musical performance and "wit") that are not necessarily consonant with dominant modes of public argument. Thus, they have oppositional tendencies. However, their counter-protests also play on more dominant visions of appropriate public argument, one rooted in affirming a version of U.S. identity that may too easily mask the larger heteronormative and exclusionary practices of its dominant culture (the Foo Fighters), the other in the valuation of peaceful protest which can be used to denigrate more radical efforts to achieve social change (Kevin Smith). While another study has shown that military-linked counter-protesters utilize different, even contradictory, ideological resources in responding to the WBC (Brouwer & Hess, 2007), we have shown that a similar process can occur in specifically progressive counter-protests. Finally, our examples suggest that opposing the already oppositional from a progressive standpoint might mean that otherwise oppositional activities, when deployed both toward another opponent at the periphery and toward a larger audience, end up tapping into societal *doxa*, both about appropriate rhetorical activities and particular social/political views, thus resulting in a more centrist argumentative performance overall.

References

Advocate.com Editors (2011, January 20). WBC protest to be picketed. *Advocate.com*. Retrieved from http://www.advocate.com/arts-entertainment/entertainment-news/2011/01/20/wbc-red-state-protest-be-picketed

Asen, R. (2000). Seeking the "counter" in counterpublics. *Communication Theory* 10(4), 424–446.

Asen, R. (2009). Ideology, materiality, and counterpublicity: William E. Simon and the rise of a conservative counterintelligentsia. *Quarterly Journal of Speech*, 95(3), 263–288.

Asen, R., & Brouwer, D. C. (2001). Introduction: Reconfigurations of the public sphere. In R. Asen & D. C. Brouwer (Eds.), *Counterpublics and the state* (pp. 1–32). Albany: State University of New York Press.

Birdsell, D. S, & Groarke, L. (1996). Toward a theory of visual argument. *Argumentation and Advocacy, 33*, 1–10.

Birdsell, D. S, & Groarke, L. (2007). Outlines of a theory of visual argument. *Argumentation and Advocacy, 43* (Winter and Spring), 103–113.

Brouwer, D. C., & Hess, A. (2007). Making sense of "God Hates Fags" and "Thank God for 9/11": A thematic analysis of Milbloggers' responses to Reverend Fred Phelps and the Westboro Baptist Church. *Western Journal of Communication, 71*(1), 69–90.

Falsani, C. (2011, September 9). Kevin Smith's "Red State": Masterful, spiritually powerful [Web log message]. *The Huffington Post (The Blog).* Retrieved from http://www.huffingtonpost.com/cathleen-falsani/kevin-smith-red-state_b_952907.html

Finnegan, C. A. (2005). Recognizing Lincoln: Image vernaculars in nineteenth-century visual culture. *Rhetoric & Public Affairs, 8*(1), 31–58.

Foo fighters "hot buns" video: Band nude in the shower (nsfw video). (2011, October 29). *Huffington Post.* Retrieved from http://www.huffingtonpost.com/2011/08/29/foo-fighters-hot-buns-video_n_941033.html

foofighters. (2011, September 17). Foo Fighters – Keepin it clean in KC [Video file]. Retrieved from http://www.youtube.com/watch?v=6e5hRLbCaCs

Fraser, N. (1992). Rethinking the public sphere: A contribution to the critique of actually existing democracy. In C. Calhoun (Ed.), *Habermas and the Public Sphere* (pp. 109–142). Cambridge: MIT Press.

Fritch, J., Palczewski, C. H., Farrell, J., & Short, E. (2006). Disingenuous controversy: Responses to Ward Churchill's 9/11 essay. *Argumentation and Advocacy, 42*, 190–205.

Godfrey, A. (2011, September 23). Kevin Smith hits out at Harvey Weinstein, critics, and rightwing bigots. *The Guardian.* Retrieved from http://www.theguardian.com/film/2011/sep/24/kevin-smith-red-state

Goodnight, G. T. (1991). Controversy. In D. W. Parson (Ed.), *Argument in controversy: Proceedings of the 7th SCA/AFA Summer Conference on Argumentation* (pp. 1–13). Annandale, VA: Speech Communication Association.

Harr-Lagin, K., & Palczewski, C. H. (2013). Pledge-a-picketer, power, protesting and publicity: Explaining protest when the state/establishment is not the opposition. In C. Foust, K. Rogness, & A. Pason (Eds.), *Social movements and counterpublics.* Tuscaloosa: University of Alabama Press, in press.

Hartman, K. I. (2011, September 21). Westboro church serenaded by the Foo Fighters at counter-protest. *Digital Journal.* Retrieved from http://www.digitaljournal.com/article/311773

Harvey Boys. (2011, January 19). The Harvey boys will picket the Westboro Baptist Church picket of the screening of "Red State" at the Eccles Theatre, Sunday, January 23rd [Press release]. Retrieved from http://viewaskew.com/kevin/HarveyBoysPressRelease.pdf

Hudson, W. (2011, October 12). Remembering Matthew Shepard: 13 years later [Web log message]. *The Huffington Post (Huffpost Gay Voices, The Blog).* Retrieved from http://www.huffingtonpost.com/waymon-hudson/matthew-shepard_b_1006878.html

Mansbridge, J., & Morris, A., eds. (2001). *Oppositional consciousness: The subjective roots of social protest.* Chicago, IL: University of Chicago Press.

Michaels, S. (2011, September 19). Foo fighters sing back at Westboro Baptist Church. *The Guardian.* Retrieved from http://www.theguardian.com/music/2011/sep/19/foo-fighters-westboro-baptist-church

Music. (n.d.). Retrieved from http://www.godhatesthemedia.com/music-index.html

Nussenbaum, K. (2013, September 3). Anti-gay rally sparks community response. *The Brown Daily Herald.* Retrieved from http://www.browndailyherald.com/2013/09/03/anti-gay-rally-sparks-community-response/

Olson, K. M., & Goodnight, G. T. (1994). Entanglements of consumption, cruelty, privacy, and fashion: The social controversy over fur. *Quarterly Journal of Speech, 80*, 249–276.

Orr, A. M. (2011, January 25). Sundance 2011: Kevin Smith's *Red State* and the Westboro Baptist Church. *Blogcritics.* Retrieved from http://blogcritics.org/sundance-2011-kevin-smiths-red-state/

Orr, B. (1999, October 12). Angels again take action against hate message. *Wyoming Tribune-Eagle,* p. A1.

Palczewski, C. H. (2002). Argument in an off key: Playing with the productive limits of argument. In G. T. Goodnight (Ed.) *Arguing Communication and Culture: Selected Papers from the Twelfth NCA/AFA Conference on Argumentation* (pp. 1–23). Washington, DC: National Communication Association.

Palczewski, C. H. (2010). Reproductive freedom: Transforming Discourses of Choice. In S. Hayden & D. L. O'Brien Halstein (Eds.) *Contemplating maternity in an era of choice: Explorations into discourses of reproduction* (pp. 73–94). Lanham, MD: Lexington Books.

Patterson, R. (2011, March 4). Let Westboro have their hate speech. We'll smother it with peace. *Washington Post*. Retrieved from http://www.washingtonpost.com/wp-dyn/content/article/2011/03/04/AR2011030402461.html

Pezzullo, P. C. (2003). Resisting 'National Breast Cancer Awareness Month': The rhetoric of counter-publics and their cultural performances. *Quarterly Journal of Speech, 89*(4), 345–365.

Schrader, B., & Rief, J. (2012). Between free speech and public debate: An analysis of *Snyder v. Phelps*. In R. C. Rowland & J. Howell (Eds.), *Reasoned argument and social change: Selected papers from the 17th Biennial Conference on Argumentation* (pp. 647–654). Washington, DC: National Communication Association.

47

DISTURBING BLACK NATIONALISM

The minor rhetoric of Drew Ali

Scott J. Varda

BAYLOR UNIVERSITY, USA

In the urban north during the 1920s, an important debate played out over the appropriateness of Black Nationalism as both a political strategy and cultural identity for Black Americans. Two schools of thought primarily shaped the contours of this argument: the integrationists (largely mobilized around the economic assimilationism of Booker T. Washington) and the Black Nationalists (favoring a separatism from White America, as enunciated by Marcus Garvey and his Universal Negro Improvement Association). These intellectual camps focused on the possibility of disturbing the oppressive and dehumanizing vision for Black America contained within hegemonic discourses that circumscribed the possibility of Black citizenship. Following Washington's death and Garvey's deportation, a new vision of Black Liberation appeared in the urban North that troubled the conception of Black identity as forwarded by each of these competing discourses. Drew Ali and his Moorish Science Temple of America (MSTA) constructed a vision of Black identity – Moorish Americanism – that simultaneously appropriated *and* upended central argumentative tenets of thought contained within integrationist and separatist discourses.

Drew Ali's argumentative practices are important to analyze in order to better understand the construction of Black public culture in the United States. Contemporary historian Michael Gomez (2005) explained, "By virtue of his disproportionate impact," Ali should be understood as "a principal architect of early-twentieth-century black social thought and movement" (p. 214). In addition to laying the foundation for establishment of the Nation of Islam, Drew Ali constructed a vision of race, religion, and nationality that, to this day, can be seen in numerous religious orders as well as contemporary hip hop groups associated with the Five Percent Nation, including Wu-Tang Clan, Nas, and Public Enemy. To understand Ali's persuasive, and pervasive, impact, this essay reads his argumentative tactics as a *minor rhetoric* of Black Nationalism. Following a brief introduction to minor rhetoric, I introduce the MSTA, followed by an analysis of the central argumentative tenets Ali appropriated and reconfigured to fashion Moorish American identity. I demonstrate that the concept of minor rhetoric can be productively mobilized to investigate argumentative attempts to craft identity. In short, the MSTA's arguments constructed an identity that traversed the dichotomous positions offered by integrationists and Black Nationalists. I conclude by asserting that the concept of minor rhetoric can be profitably extended to argumentative analysis to demonstrate the constitution of a Black identity simultaneously opposing hegemonic norms and prior responses to those norms.

Minor Rhetoric

Premised on Gilles Deleuze and Felix Guattari's (1986) minor literature, *minor rhetorics* are discursive practices forwarded by "a minor rhetorician for a minority people, a people to come" (Zhang, 2011, p. 216). Especially important given the theme of this conference, minor rhetorics disturb dominant discourses when they "use the language of the majority in such a way as to make that language stutter" in order to interrupt "the displacement" minorities are subjected to within dominant publics (Deem, 2002, p. 447). Zhang explains several rhetorical figures who embody his construction of minor rhetoricians, including Martin Luther King, Malcolm X, Friedrich Nietzsche, and Franz Kafka. In other words, minor rhetoricians disturb the existing social order.

Implicit in the formulation of minor rhetoric as proposed by Zhang and Deem, however, is the idea that minor rhetorics ought to be understood as primarily antagonistic with dominant discourses, while simply communicating with other minor rhetorics. This assumed binary construction (minor vs. major) posits the minor as always already against, and only against, the major. This juxtaposition flattens the argumentative understanding that can be gained by analyzing competing minor organizations and their argumentative endeavors. Instead, minor rhetoric should be understood not as something simply employed by a minor rhetorician, but rather as a tactic that can cut against other minor rhetorics and/or oppose the major culture. Considering minor rhetoric through the lens of argument facilitates this mode of thinking given argumentation's ability to evaluate tensions between competing claims. This essay demonstrates the productive possibilities of just such an approach by analyzing the argumentative appropriations of Drew Ali from integrationists and Black Nationalists. In all, this analysis offers a fledgling attempt to trouble our current understanding of minor rhetoric and to expand the explanatory power of the study of argumentation.

Drew Ali and the MSTA

The MSTA, a proto-Islamic religious and cultural order, emerged in the early 1920s and quickly spread throughout the urban North. Headed by Drew Ali, the organization boasted tens of thousands of members prior to Ali's untimely death in 1929. Positing the true name for Asiatics (Ali's catch-all for people of color) as homage to their majestic Moorish roots, Moorish Americanism was a preordained identity simultaneously describing one's religion, race, and nationality. Deploying his own vision of Islam, most publicly through his own *Circle Seven Koran*, Ali reconfigured the argumentative force contained within a wide variety of sources – Christianity, Islam, Garveyism, Freemasonry, and nineteenth century Pan-Africanism – to construct a new identity that rearranged religion, race, and national identity into a cohesive whole (Turner, 2003). These efforts displayed a path to affirm a unique set of beliefs about religion, race, and nationality. Ali's construction of identity reworked competing racial narratives of the day to argue for a middle path between separation and assimilation.

Ali's Argumentative Appropriation

Analysis of key arguments Ali borrowed from Booker T. Washington and Marcus Garvey furthers understanding of the MSTA, the means by which Ali constructed a new identity for

Moorish Americans, and the process by which minor rhetoric can be extended to better understand argument construction. Here, I explain how these appropriations both shaped the contours of Moorish American identity and demonstrate how Drew Ali's tactics subsumed and inverted key arguments and practices of other minor rhetorics.

Ali borrowed heavily from the argumentative work of Booker T. Washington. While there are numerous similarities in thought between Ali and Washington, two stand most prominently: Ali's appropriation of Washington's emphasis on "upright moral behavior" (Remnick, 1999, p. 130) and Washington's inadvertent blueprint for successful passing. Washington attained a national prominence previously unmatched by any Black American by the time of his death (Riley, 1916, p. 213), and is perhaps is the best representative of integrationism during this historical period. Washington publicly proclaimed emancipation was assured only by education, industriousness, and virtue. In *Up from Slavery* (1901), Washington explained his views on uplift suggesting that Black self-improvement would eventually result in a gain in political rights. For Washington, the demonstration of an appropriate code of conduct was a prerequisite to civil and political equality.

Ali's argument for appropriate conduct was highly reminiscent of that articulated by Washington. *How* Ali suggested these norms of conduct be performed, however, illustrates an important understanding of minor rhetorical appropriation. Borrowing Washington's claim regarding the importance of demonstrating "upright character" (Bieze, 2008, p. 241), Ali substantially altered the warrant underlying the logic of this move. Ali constructed symbols of character distinct from those preferred by Washington by encouraging markers of difference that set Moorish Americans apart from other Black Americans and demonstrated "upright character." To denote a vision of upright character, Ali encouraged male MSTA members to sport beards and wear fezzes, demarcating MSTA members from other Black Americans (Nance, 2002, p. 623). This particular display of facial hair and headwear was both reminiscent of the Black Shriners and an effort to bolster the dominant culture's view of MSTA members as respectable by drawing upon positive notions the public might associate with Morocco, Islam, and, more generally, royalty (Nance, 2002).

A second reconfiguration of Washington's argument for integration can be located in Ali's retelling of Washington's tale of the Moroccan traveler. In *Up from Slavery*, Washington relayed to his readers the difference between White attitudes toward Black bodies perceived as American and those perceived as foreign. Conveying a story describing the difficulty a "dark-skinned" "citizen of Morocco" had acquiring a hotel room, until "it was learned that he was not an American Negro," Washington (1901) revealed a vital lesson about U.S. culture (p. 103). Namely, White American antipathy was grounded in an understanding of Black bodies as American Negros. Conversely, "all the signs of indignation disappeared" (Washington, 1901, p. 103) if those same bodies were read as foreign. As understood by Washington, this account illustrated that perceived skin color was not what troubled White America, but rather the constructed notion of American blackness. Black Americans, so Washington urged, ought to alter American blackness to better match White Americans' notion of respectability. Ali, however, redeployed this narrative to demonstrate that Black Americans could work the argumentative logic of American racism against itself. In short, Ali coopted the argumentative force of Washington's anecdote but altered the grounds upon which Black Americans might be afforded their proper treatment.

Ali similarly appropriated aspects of Marcus Garvey's rhetorical arsenal to construct Moorish American identity in line with, but distinct from, Black Nationalism. In so doing, Ali constructed an argument for Moorish Americanism warranted by practical necessity and divine authority. Garvey's Universal Negro Improvement Association (UNIA) was a racial uplift organization promoting African unity. Central to Garvey's political philosophy was a pan-African ethic partially represented by his Back-to-Africa plan, a symbolic program for repatriation to Africa (Vincent, 1971, p. 16). Despite his deportation after a mail fraud conviction, Garvey remained a highly popular figure in the Black community (Cronon, 1955, p. 50). As the most prominent voice for Black Nationalism during this period, Garvey's argumentative tactics almost inherently opposed Washington's integrationism.

Ali's transformation of Garvey's transnational model for Black political community not only warranted Moorish Americanism, but bridged the argumentative divide between assimilation and separation. Garvey's model of a transnational Black political community celebrated an African homeland while Ali argued Moorish Americanism around a constructed notion of the Orient in the United States. Garvey's Pan-African Black Nationalism centered about a figurative repatriation owing to the belief that the United States was an unsuitable home for Black Americans. For example, in debates against assimilationist positions, Garvey (1923/1986) argued that the "humanity of white America . . . will seek self-protection and self-preservation, and that is why the thoughtful and reasonable Negro sees no hope in America" (p. 40). Grounding this claim in historical examples, Garvey concluded the "Negro in America" was ultimately "doomed to extermination" (p. 54). For him, Africa was the only reasonable solution for Black American freedom. Garvey sought to mobilize "brotherly co-operation which will make the interests of the African native and the American and West Indian Negro one and the same" to better construct "a common partnership to build up Africa in the interests of our race" (p. 70). For Garvey, "the progressive Negro who wants a society and country of his own" (p. 122) was to adjust their horizon toward Africa.

Drew Ali adopted the claims Garvey urged but changed both the nature of transnational political community and the resultant locale to which Black Americans were to set their sights. Ali was not merely "inspired" or "inflected" by Garvey's rhetorical practices, as Zhang's (2011, p. 226) analysis might argue. My analysis, however, reads Ali's efforts as opposing the warrant to Garvey's vision. Seen in a number of Ali's various proclamations, it is most apparent in analysis of the MSTA-supplied "Nationality and Identification Card." The card announced the holder honored "all the Divine prophets, Jesus, Mohammad, Buddha, and Confucius," and concluded with the exhortation "I AM A CITIZEN OF THE UNITED STATES" (as cited in Lincoln, 1961, p. 53). Ali's transnational community was premised around a majestic identity of Asiatic origin, rather than upon racial brotherhood, per se. Ali's argumentative construction of an invented Orient cohered his congregants within a community in, but not of, the United States. In this way, Ali coopted the essence of the UNIA but altered Garvey's suggested destination through the construction of an Asiatic homeland in the United States. Rather than centering their identity in Africa, Moorish Americans instead needed to embody their Asiatic inheritance in America.

Implications

Twenty-five years into the last century, Black America largely faced two opposing notions of how to best proceed toward liberation. With Washington deceased and Garvey deported, two of the most prominent voices in this debate were silenced. Drew Ali opened a new chapter in the debate over the direction of Black public culture by using argumentative tactics to posit Moorish Americanism as an identity capable of bridging the divide between these competing visions. To wit, Ali used argumentative tactics that borrowed, inverted, and opposed the claims of other prominent figures in Black public culture in order to disturb dominant conceptions of Blackness. In this sense, Ali's rhetorical tactics can be read as minor rhetorical arguments.

This essay suggests that the constitution of a people through minor rhetoric is largely accomplished through arguments. Generally, minor rhetoricians are understood as disruptions to the existing order. Minor rhetorics, then, constitutively "call into being" a people whose resistance resides "in the inventive articulation of new possibilities of life" (Zhang, 2011, p. 226). Whether that interpellation is premised in a religious call from authority, a secular appeal for pragmatism, or a radical cry for nationalism, it is made through argument. In this way, the concept of minor rhetoric can be productively marshaled to analyze community-wide arguments. Using argument as a tool to cultivate our understanding of minor rhetoric suggests that our current conception of minor rhetoric should be expanded. Drawing from Deleuze and Guattari's minor literature, both Deem and Zhang focus on minor rhetoric to understand how resistance is mobilized. As this essay has demonstrated, the concept of minor rhetorics can be productively extended into the study of argumentation by considering the way in which minor rhetorics shape resistance. Such an approach encourages scholars to attend to minor rhetorics not as emanating from historical figures or as overarching systems, but rather as rhetorical tactics manifested through arguments.

In addition, this analysis suggests that minor rhetoric can be expanded to illustrate how minor rhetorical tactics need not be simply oppositional to a larger culture but can juxtapose themselves to other minor rhetorics. As made plain in this analysis, Drew Ali inverts the dominant discourse's desire for Black Americans to "act appropriately" (thereby surrendering their efforts to object to racist treatment) by constructing a Moorish American identity whose own insistence on appropriate moral codes allowed adherents to demand their rights as U.S. citizens. Rather than direct their freedom efforts in a symbolic image of Africa, as Garvey posited, Ali urged Moorish Americans to demonstrate their fitness for U.S. citizenship. Here, Ali's appropriation neatly fits the description of minor rhetoric: Ali makes the major language "stutter." However, in Ali's appropriation of Washington's argument against mistreatment of Black America (as illustrated though his story of the Moroccan visitor), his minor rhetoric inverted and opposed the argumentative tenets of another minor rhetoric. Similarly, Ali co-opted Garvey's notion of transnational brotherhood. The argumentative force of that negotiation simultaneously challenged the dominant view of Black inferiority as well as the Washingtonian view that high character be demonstrated only through terms set by the dominant culture. This analysis troubles the notion that minor rhetorics merely disturb the language of the major culture. More pointedly, Ali's argumentative tactics indicate that minor rhetorics can invert the evidence, warrants, and goals of particular discourses – both major and minor – through appropriation and alteration of the arguments undergirding those discourses. As Palczewski (1997) has persuasively explained, arguments mark bodies in particular ways. Relatedly, bodies can be marked to function as arguments. In this instance, Drew Ali inscribed the bodies of Moorish Americans in a way that functioned as an argument against the dominant understanding of Black Americans, the integrationist drive for assimilation, and the Black Nationalist call for separation.

Warranting his advocacy for adoption of Moorish Americanism, Ali borrowed from the discourses of the majoritarian culture and competing minor rhetors to construct a new vision of Islam. These argumentative tactics helped construct a new identity for Black America that simultaneously challenged the arguments underpinning the logic of integrationism and Black Nationalism. This identity critiqued the hegemonic notion of Black inferiority and appropriated and reconfigured the arguments of rhetorical communities constituted by Christian churches, projects begun by Washington, and competing Black Nationalist organizations. Ali coopted and altered major and minor discourses not merely to build his ethos, but as a critique of the opposing argumentative solutions proffered for Black Americans. Ali's difference from other minor discourses, as well as from major discourses that disdained the potential of the Black subject, was fundamentally grounded in his rearticulation of the United States as a promised land for Moorish Americans. In relationship to Washington's vision of assimilation and Garvey's insistence on Black emancipation, Ali averred that Moorish Americans must accept their divinely revealed identity and conduct themselves in a fashion correspondent to those origins. For Ali, the enactment of Moorish American identity demonstrated for Black America a way to simultaneously be, and not be, Black Americans – deserving of their rights as U.S. citizens while retaining their majestic Asiatic roots.

References

A black Moses and his dream of a promised land. (1921, March). *Current Opinion*, 328–331.

Bieze, M. (2008). *Booker T. Washington and the art of self-representation*, New York, NY: Peter Lang Publishing

Cronon, E. D. (1955). *Black Moses: The story of Marcus Garvey and the Universal Negro Improvement Association*. Madison: University of Wisconsin Press.

Deem, M. (2002). Stranger sociability, public hope, and the limits of political transformation. *Quarterly Journal of Speech, 88*, 444–454.

Deleuze, G., & Guattari, F. (1986). *Kafka: Toward a minor literature* (D. Polan, Trans.). Minneapolis: University of Minnesota Press.

Garvey, M. (1923/1986). *Philosophy and opinions of Marcus Garvey, or, Africa for the Africans* (Reprint), A. Jacques-Garvey (Ed.). Dover, MA: Majority Press.

Gomez, M. A. (2005) *Black crescent: The experience and legacy of African Muslims in the Americas*, New York, NY: Cambridge University Press.

Grant, C. (2008). *Negro with a hat: The rise and fall of Marcus Garvey*. New York, NY: Oxford University Press.

Nance, S. (2002). Respectability and representation: The Moorish Science Temple, Morocco, and Black public culture in 1920s Chicago. *American Quarterly, 54*, 623–659.

Palczewski, C. (1997). Bodies that argue: Power, difference, and argument. In J. F. Klumpp (Ed.), *Argument in a Time of Change: Definitions, Frameworks, and Critiques* (pp. 179–84). Annandale, VA: National Communication Association.

Remnick, D. (1999). *King of the world: Muhammad Ali and the rise of an American hero*. New York, NY: Vintage Books.

Riley, B. F. (1916). *The life and times of Booker T. Washington*. Chicago, IL: Fleming H. Revell Company.

Turner, R. B. (2003). *Islam in the African-American experience*. Bloomington: Indiana University Press.

Vincent, T. G. (1971). *Black power and the Garvey movement*. Berkeley, CA: Rampart Press.

Washington, B. T. (1901). *Up from slavery: An autobiography*. New York, NY: A.L. Burt Company.

Zhang, P. (2011). Gilles Deleuze and minor rhetoric. *ETC: A Review of General Semantics, 68*, 214–229.

48

DISTURBING COMMUNITY

Conflicting identities and citizenship in Japanese American concentration camp newspapers during World War II

Kaori Yamada

UNIVERSITY OF WISCONSIN – MILWAUKEE, USA

The Japanese attack on Pearl Harbor on December 7, 1941, catalyzed a radical increase in anti-Japanese sentiment in the United States. Resident Japanese Americans were designated "enemy aliens," although such labels were never applied to resident Germans or Italians (Thiesmeyer, 1995, p. 321). With the increasing sentiment against Japan, the U.S. government eventually decided to forcibly remove Japanese people living on the West Coast, arguing such action was a "military necessity" (Ng, 2002, p. 13). As a result of the evacuation program, approximately 120,000 people moved to 10 internment camps. Japanese Americans, especially Nisei (second generation Japanese Americans who were born and raised in the United States) were forced to grapple with their identities as U.S. citizens of Japanese descent.

To understand the rhetoric of civic identity among Japanese American internment camp residents, I examine the two Japanese newspapers distributed in the Heart Mountain camp, *The Rocky Shimpo* and *The Heart Mountain Sentinel*. *The Rocky Shimpo*, published in Denver, was the only newspaper that explicitly opposed the evacuation program. *The Heart Mountain Sentinel*, which was published in the Heart Mountain camp, reflected a pro-government perspective by arguing the resisters were "trouble-makers" (Muller, 2001, p. 81). Although *The Shimpo* was published in Denver, it was distributed to all the concentration camps including the Heart Mountain camp. Despite both papers being products of Japanese Americans, the two newspapers generated two different definitions of citizenship. My analysis underlines how definitional argument functions as an important way of understanding citizenship and civic identity. Minority identity is particularly complicated, and by focusing on the case study of Japanese internment, I argue that definitional argument allows minorities to negotiate their place in a civic space that appears to exclude and reject them.

This essay proceeds as follows: First, I provide contextual research on the draft resistance by Japanese Americans and the two community newspapers. Second, I argue definitions are arguments that create value hierarchies. Third, I reveal two different definitions of citizenship that entail different value hierarchies through analyzing the two community newspapers. My contention is that the citizenship defined in *The Sentinel* entails a value hierarchy of

317

duties over rights while the citizenship defined in *The Shimpo* entails a value hierarchy of rights over duties. The editorials of *The Sentinel* and *The Shimpo* generated different definitions of citizenship, and each entailed different, conflicting value hierarchies. Lastly, I offer a conclusion and implications, suggesting that definitions of citizenship can be negotiated and contested within and outside of a community. The contested definitions of citizenship also disturb what citizenship means in the United States.

Japanese Americans as Outsiders: Historical Contexts

Even as the government forced Japanese Americans to move to concentration camps under the guise of an evacuation program, the U.S. War Department organized a segregated combat team for Nisei Americans who wished to volunteer (Muller, 2001, p. 410). In 1944, the War Department formally announced its new policy of drafting the interned Japanese Americans, and young men in the camps were compelled to enrolled in the military by force of law (Muller, 2001, p. 64).

Little record of public discussions concerning the draft of Japanese Americans exists. However, several groups of Japanese Americans rejected the draft. Internees at the Heart Mountain camp established an organization called the Fair Play Committee (FPC) and protested against the draft by publishing and circulating anti-draft bulletins in the camp, refusing to report for physical examinations, and walking out of the camp's front gate without a pass (Muller, 2001, p. 90).

Although the FPC organized in one of the 10 internment camps, it reached Japanese American audiences across the country because of strong editorial support by Jimmie Omura, an editor of *The Rocky Shimpo*. Omura ran editorials and news items that reported favorably on the FPC's activities. These pieces bolstered the credibility of the FPC in the eyes of many camp residents (Muller, 2001, p. 82). With Omura's support, the FPC's messages were distributed to concentration camps across the country. The purpose of *The Heart Mountain Sentinel*, on the other hand, was "keeping the residents advised of W[ar] R[elocation] A[uthority] policies and of maintaining morale in the center" ("Heart Mountain," 2013).

The two community newspapers defined citizenship differently and created different value hierarchies. The next section overviews the argumentative nature of definitions in order to unpack how citizenship is addressed in the newspapers.

Definitions are Arguments

Definitions are "rhetorically induced," and direct and deflect people's understanding of the world (Schiappa, 2003). As Zarefsky (1997) contended, "while there might be limits, still the ways in which we define our terms affects [*sic*] the way we think, talk, and act about the realities for which they stand" (p. 4). Definitions frame a situation, while identifying causes, posing remedies, and inviting moral judgments about circumstances or individuals (Zarefsky, 1997, p. 5). In this sense, definitions can be powerful instruments for argument (Walton & Macagno, 2008, p. 83).

My analysis hinges on a connection between definitional argument and value hierarchies. Value hierarchies are established by "the intensity with which one value is adhered to as compared to another" and indicate "which value will be sacrificed" should the two values come into conflict (Perelman & Olbrechts-Tyteca, 1969, pp. 81–83). Perelman and Olbrechts-Tyteca (1969) claimed that a single abstract principle, capable of repeated application, can establish hierarchies (p. 80). For example, repeated circulation of the principle "freedom" in the United

States could establish a value hierarchy that prefers individual's choices over control by authorities. Given the argumentative nature of definitions, one can interpret a single word in different ways, depending on his or her persuasive goals. Therefore, value hierarchies engendered through definitions can also function as persuasive devices. By presenting a definition that entails a particular value hierarchy, a rhetor can lead audience members to a certain direction.

I argue that an analysis of definitions can be integrated with a value analysis. My analysis suggests each of the two community papers crafted a different definition of citizenship undergirded by the value pair of rights and duty. Each definition directed undecided internees' understanding of the draft and reinforced each newspaper's persuasive goals. Specifically, the definition of citizenship in *The Heart Mountain Sentinel* disparaged rights and created a hierarchy of duty over rights. That definition fit the goal of *The Sentinel*, supporting the U.S. government and justifying the draft. The definition of citizenship in *The Rocky Shimpo* acknowledged rights and created a hierarchy of rights over duty. That definition fit the goal of *The Shimpo*, arguing against the U.S. government's infringement of Japanese Americans' human rights.

Citizenship Defined as an Enactment: Duties over Rights

The citizenship defined in *The Sentinel* emphasized duties of citizens over rights. Moreover, citizenship was understood as an action rather than a status. Such understanding of citizenship encouraged Japanese American internees to enact citizenship (Asen, 2004) by fulfilling duties. An individual would not be considered as a citizen without acting in line with becoming a citizen. Through analyzing the editorials in *The Sentinel*, I argue citizenship as duty entailed (1) personal sacrifice in the military and (2) valuing the nation as more important than individuals or community.

Although citizenship was understood as an enactment, in *The Sentinel* only military service was considered an act of citizenship, while resistance was not. For example, one editorial cited Judge Kennedy's, an associate justice of the Supreme Court, statement on citizenship: "if they are truly loyal American citizens, they should, at least when they have become recognized as such, embrace the opportunity to discharge the duties of citizens by offering themselves in, [sic] the cause of our national defense" (as cited in "Editorial: Years," 1944, para. 5). This statement reinforced the definition of citizenship as duty-driven. Moreover, the duties were "opportunities," which have positive implications. The military duty was defined not as an obligation that the government compelled Nisei internees to fulfill, but opportunities that they were supposed to be willing to embrace. An individual's will was emphasized by this word choice. To be recognized as a loyal U.S. citizen, one must be willing to fulfill duties for the nation.

The Sentinel further attempted to persuade readers to understand citizenship as an action rather than a status. One must do something to obtain citizenship. Citizenship was not understood as a status, which was given to anyone when s/he was born. *The Sentinel* praised Nisei who had served in the military because they "proved" their loyalty. An editorial noted "the majority strongly feels that it must be taken in stride as our part in the war effort and that we must go even farther in proving our records as good citizens" ("Editorial: Two Objectives," 1994, para. 4). That implied citizenship is not taken for granted without proving it by enacting duties.

The Sentinel accused Nisei who were eligible for military service but did not answer the call of being "whimpering weaklings who were afraid to prove themselves, and who were calling to an unanswering, unconcerned source for rights and privileges they have never before sought so fervently" ("Editorial: Provocateurs," 1944, para. 13). The editorial suggested that resisters were not real men and, thus, were not worthy of full citizenship because they did not perform military service.

The Sentinel described Japan as an enemy nation. However, not only the Japanese government but also the Nisei themselves were responsible for the hardship they were experiencing according to *The Sentinel*. One editorial stated: "The burden of proof does not lie with the [U.S.] government or any agency but with the Nisei themselves" ("Editorial: Provocateurs," 1944, para. 11). Moreover, it continued: "We know by past experiences that we never were accepted too readily even in our own communities, or states. How we will be accepted after the war has much to do with our behavior now" ("Editorial: Provocateurs," 1944, para. 12). Japanese Americans were not accepted in the past, and the responsibility was on Japanese Americans themselves. *The Sentinel* did not blame the U. S. government or the U.S. public. To achieve citizenship, as defined in the newspaper, Japanese Americans should have taken actions that fulfill duties for, that serve, the country, while ignoring their own rights. This definition of citizenship privileged military service and duty to nation, not the rights of individuals.

The opportunity to prove citizenship was available, but the rights and status of U.S. citizens were not given to Nisei Americans. *The Sentinel* did not mention the rights of Japanese Americans as U.S. citizens, nor did it consider if the government infringed on the rights of Japanese Americans with its removal policy and the draft. Rather, *The Sentinel* justified the evacuation as part of Japanese Americans' duty. The definition of citizenship in *The Sentinel* seemed to direct readers to believe they must serve the nation to be recognized as U.S. citizens, regardless of whether the nation violated their rights as citizens. The definition of citizenship also made *The Sentinel* able to argue that the resisters were disloyal and unworthy because they were not serving the nation.

The analysis of the expectations of duty reveals that (1) citizenship was not universally attainable and necessarily excluded those who did not or could not fulfill military duties, and (2) acceptance of the evacuation program and the draft was justified in the Japanese American community as a way to enact citizenship.

Citizenship Defined as Status: Rights over Duties

While the citizenship defined in *The Sentinel* was duty-driven, citizenship was defined in *The Shimpo* as rights-driven and valued status over acts. Omura, the editor of *The Shimpo*, insisted that Japanese Americans were U.S. citizens whose human rights should be protected under the Constitution, and the U.S. government infringed on their rights. In *The Shimpo*, citizenship was understood as a status rather than action. Citizenship was granted by the Constitution to all Nisei Japanese Americans regardless of their actions. Citizenship as status entailed arguments that (1) citizenship is a given, (2) rights are a prerequisite for military sacrifice, and (3) democracy trumps the government's policies.

Citizenship was defined as status in *The Shimpo*. It asked for "authentic and authoritative clarification of the legal status of the Nisei as citizens" ("Editorial: The Rocky Shimpo" 1944, para. 10). *The Shimpo* emphasized that rights are given, not something people need to earn. It further stated: "We should at all times stand firm on our God-given rights" ("Editorial: Let Us Not," 1944, para. 7). In *The Shimpo*'s logic, citizenship should be given regardless of people's performance of citizenship and cannot be taken away.

The vision of citizenship in *The Shimpo* created a hierarchy of rights over duty. It insisted that rights should be recognized and granted before one is obligated to fulfill duties as a citizen. This rights-over-duty value hierarchy was clarified: "We further agree that the government should restore a large part of those rights before asking us to contribute our lives to the welfare of the nation – to sacrifice our lives on the field of battle" ("Editorial: Let Us

Not," 1944, para. 5). *The Shimpo* did not completely deny Nisei's duty to serve the country, however. It granted that Nisei should participate in military service when necessary. It argued Nisei's rights granted in the Constitution should have been protected before the government asked them to sacrifice in the military ("Editorial: Let Us Not," 1944, para. 5).

Defining citizenship as rights over duties, *The Shimpo* illustrated the resisters as freedom fighters. Instead of duties for military service, *The Shimpo* argued democracy should come first. In *The Shimpo*, the blame was on the U.S. government, not the Japanese government or Nisei Americans as *The Sentinel* argued:

> Democracy is not only a form of government, but it is also a spirit. If there is no spirit of democracy in our governmental leaders, we would not have democracy in action. Let us therefore not condemn democracy but the men who manipulate public affairs and the masses who sympathize and condone undemocratic ideals.
>
> *("Editorial: Let US Not," 1944, para. 6)*

The U. S. government was blamed for its undemocratic actions. The draft resisters were fighting against the government to achieve democracy, which guarantees equal status of all citizens including Nisei Americans. *The Shimpo* problematized the unprivileged status of Nisei Americans as U.S. citizens as a violation of democracy. In the logic of *The Shimpo*, fighting for democracy at home was more important than fighting for democracy abroad as a result of a service demand by the government.

The analysis of citizenship as status clarifies why (1) citizenship should be universally attainable to anyone with a legal status of citizenship, (2) the evacuation program and draft were criticized in the Japanese American community and became a controversy that disturbed the unity of the community, and (3) democracy was represented as a natural and neutral ideal beyond all components of identities such as ethnicity and gender.

Conclusion and Implications

Through analyzing the two community papers circulated among Japanese American internees in the Heart Mountain camp, my essay identified two conflicting definitions of citizenship. In *The Sentinel*, the definition of citizenship created the hierarchy of duties over rights, while the vision of citizenship in *The Shimpo* privileged rights before duties. Tied with its definition of citizenship, each paper constructed persuasive arguments that intended to achieve its rhetorical goal. For *The Sentinel*, the goal was to persuade undecided Japanese American internees to follow the U.S. government. For *The Shimpo*, the goal was to persuade undecided internees to fight to secure the rights they deserved.

Moreover, *The Sentinel* and *The Shimpo* described the draft resisters differently. While *The Sentinel* represented the resisters as shameful deviants, *The Shimpo* framed the resisters as extreme but heroic figures fighting for equal treatment. Each argument drew on different definitions of citizenship based in differing values, enforcing the hierarchy of duty over rights in *The Sentinel* and rights over duty in *The Shimpo*.

The two conflicting definitions of citizenship tell us that definitions are negotiated and contested within and outside of a community. While Japanese American internees shared a sense of community based on their national origin, the conflicting definitions of citizenship disturbed the unity of the community. Given the unique situation of being excluded from the body politic while being asked to fulfill duties to the government, the contested definitions of citizenship also disturbed what citizenship means in the United States. Although both rights and duties might be considered to be components of citizenship, the different value hierarchies lead to different results and actions.

The historic debate over citizenship informs contemporary remembering and forgetting. In the National Japanese American Memorial for Patriotism during World War II, for example, the citizenship that values duties over rights seems dominant. A stone wall at the center of the Memorial inscribes the names of the military dead in order to honor their patriotic acts; the Memorial does not include any names and/or stories of the resisters. Today in the United States, citizenship is presented as proven by patriotic military acts. However, a group of Japanese Americans called "Japanese American Voice" proposed that the Memorial should memorialize the resisters. Definitions of citizenship are still negotiated and contested.

For future studies, the value hierarchies in the term *citizenship* should be investigated in other crisis contexts to understand what actions are called for under the name of citizenship. For example, George W. Bush encouraged U.S. citizens to consume domestic products to sustain the country after 9/11. Consumption was a valued action under the name of citizenship. Definitions function as persuasive arguments by preferring a certain value hierarchy. Although a definition can be dominant in a community, as my analysis suggests, dominant definitions can be challenged by another definition that entails another value hierarchy.

References

Asen, R. (2004). A discourse theory of citizenship. *Quarterly Journal of Speech, 90,* 26–49.

Editorial: Let us not be rash [Editorial]. (1944, February 28). *The Rocky Shimpo.* Retrieved from http://www.pbs.org/itvs/conscience/resistance/rocky_shimpo/01_rash.html

Editorial: Provocateurs [Editorial]. (1944, March 15). *The Heart Mountain Sentinel.* Retrieved from http://www.pbs.org/itvs/conscience/resistance/crackdown/06_provocateurs_i.html

Editorial: The Rocky Shimpo affirms its stand [Editorial]. (1944, April 7). *The Rocky Shimpo.* Retrieved from http://www.pbs.org/itvs/conscience/resistance/rocky_shimpo/05_affirms_i.html

Editorial: Years of uselessness [Editorial]. (1944, July 1). *The Heart Mountain Sentinel.* Retrieved from http://www.resisters.com/documents/HMS_YearsOfUselessness.htm

Heart Mountain Sentinel (newspaper). (2013). *Densho Encyclopedia.* Retrieved from http://encyclopedia.densho.org/Heart%20Mountain%20Sentinel%20(newspaper)/

Muller, E. L. (2001). *Free to die for their country: The story of the Japanese American draft resisters in World War II.* Chicago, IL: University of Chicago Press.

Ng, W. (2002). Japanese *American internment during World War II: A history and reference guide.* Westport, CT: Greenwood Press.

Perelman, C., & Olbrechts-Tyteca, L. (1969). *The new rhetoric: A treatise on argumentation* (J. Wilkinson & P. Weaver, Trans.). Notre Dame, IN: University of Notre Dame Press.

Schiappa, E. (2003). *Defining reality: Definitions and the politics of meaning.* Carbondale: Southern Illinois University Press.

Thiesmeyer, L. (1995). The discourse of official violence: Anti-Japanese North American discourse and the American internment camps. *Discourse and Society, 6,* 319–352.

Walton, D., & Macagno, F. (2008). Reasoning from classifications and definitions. *Argumentation, 23,* 81–107. doi: 10.1007/s10503-008-9110-2

Zarefsky, D. (1997). Definitions. In J. Klumpp (Ed.), *Argument in a Time of Change: Definitions, Frameworks, and Critiques: Proceedings of the Tenth NCA/AFA Conference on Argumentation* (pp. 1–11). Annandale, VA: National Communication Association.

49

DRONES

Argumentation in a communication control society

G. Thomas Goodnight

UNIVERSITY OF SOUTHERN CALIFORNIA, USA
SENIOR SCHOLAR AWARD WINNER

Gordon R. Mitchell

UNIVERSITY OF PITTSBURGH, USA

The Obama administration accelerated the war in Afghanistan in 2009, increasing troops and shifting use of Remote Piloted Aircraft – drones – from surveillance to targeted killing. Regarding intensification of drone strikes, no official policy was stated, although leaks to the U.S. press played up the flashy, new technology as the number of targeted kills mounted. The Bureau of Investigative Journalism (2012), an independent organization, reported that drone strikes had killed 2,562–3,325 people in Pakistan, of whom 474–881 were civilians. *The New York Times* reported, "drones have replaced Guantanamo as the recruiting tool of choice for militants" (Becker & Shane, 2012). A crisis calling for presidential address appeared to loom in 2012, when UN High Commissioner for Human Rights Navi Pillay called the attacks "indiscriminate" human rights violations (as cited in Agence France Presse, 2012). It was left to Attorney General Eric Holder to justify attacks on U.S. citizens and to presidential advisor John Brennan to specify conditions for extending cross-border attacks.

The Holder and Brennan speeches formed a one-two punch, the first asserting the legality of drone policy from the perspective of sovereign presidential power and the second articulating publicly a defense of targeted killing. This essay shows how speeches from administration advocates filled the gap, until President Obama delivered a belated, post-election speech that strove to normalize policy. Our analysis explores ways the Obama administration strategically blended Bush justifications for preventive warfare while concomitantly purporting to dismantle the war on terror. More broadly, we illustrate how the executive branch of government strategically works public address to conceal, leak, announce, and confirm policy while presidential initiatives build, peak, and unwind – with the president entering in to strategically define policy at the end. Argumentation is viewed as tactical collaboration for buying time and co-opting criticism, with uncertain strategic outcomes.

From Surveillance to Disposition

The U.S. military initially deployed drones as surveillance tools that could unobtrusively relay information that would make fighter jet airstrikes more precise, later evolving into a dazzling weapon with the addition of Hellfire missiles (Keller & Mitchell, 2006, p. 11). At first, U.S. targets for lethal drone attacks were drawn from "kill lists" developed separately by the Pentagon and CIA. The need to bring drone decision making under more systematic institutional control led to development, around 2010, of a "disposition matrix" for vetting and approving new targets, which "functions like a funnel, starting with input from half a dozen agencies and narrowing through layers of review until proposed revisions are laid on Brennan's desk, and subsequently presented to the president" (Miller, 2012). Invention of the disposition matrix supported efforts to legitimate the drone program in the face of mounting criticism, enabling officials to claim, as we demonstrate in the following sections, that lethal drone strikes are carefully limited and painstakingly controlled.

The Resilience of Imminence

Speaking to an audience at Northwestern University, Holder (2012) refined and extended the George W. Bush administration's rationale for preventive warfare, arguing, "international law recognizes the inherent right of national self-defense." Yet Holder extended the so-called Bush doctrine, asserting that such a doctrine confers legal authority for the state to execute lethal drone attacks against an enemy, "even if that individual happens to be a U.S. citizen." "We are a nation at war. And, in this war, we face a nimble and determined enemy that cannot be underestimated," the attorney general argued. Just as enemy tactics vary, so Holder argued, war requires expanded use of authority: "Our legal authority is not limited to the battlefields in Afghanistan. Indeed, neither Congress nor our federal courts has limited the geographic scope of our ability to use force to the current conflict in Afghanistan. We are at war with a stateless enemy, prone to shifting operations from country to country." Holder was quick to point out that pursuit of leadership is not "assassination" but rather that the "use of lethal force in self-defense against a leader of al Qaeda or an associated force who presents an imminent threat of violent attack would not be unlawful – and therefore would not violate the Executive Order banning assassination or criminal statutes."

The traditional standard of imminent attack by another sovereign power authorizes self-defense as a rationale for war. In this case, the prospect of a lethal strike by a non-state actor justifies crossing sovereign boundaries to prevent or retaliate against such groups or individuals. Such considerations constitute due process, even if extra-judicial: "The U.S. government has determined, after a thorough and careful review, that the individual poses an imminent threat of violent attack against the United States; second, capture is not feasible; and third, the operation would be conducted in a manner consistent with applicable law of war principles" (Holder, 2012). Although Holder did not invoke by name the administration's disposition matrix, his comments mobilized the argumentative potential of the construct, framing the drone strike policy as limited, humane, proportional, and, most of all, driven inexorably by military necessity.

In the end, Holder assembled a hodge-podge of criteria that serve as stasis points for drone strike justification. Rules of war include: (1) ethical standards – necessity or military value, (2) distinction – that is only lawful targets, (3) proportionality – collateral damage must not be excessive, and, (4) humanity – which means that weapons should not inflict unnecessary suffering. Adherence to ethical norms renders legal standards beside the point. "The

Constitution guarantees due process, not judicial process," Holder (2012) said. "The unfortunate reality is that our nation will likely continue to face terrorist threats that – at times – originate from our own citizens." Legal processes require time. "In this hour of danger, we simply cannot afford to wait until deadly plans are carried out – and we will not." Abroad or at home, targeted killing must to be entrusted to the executive branch of government.

Holder's address was followed shortly after by Obama administration counterterrorism advisor John Brennan's (2012) appearance at the Woodrow Wilson Center. Brennan worked for the CIA during the George W. Bush administration, and his defense of drone policy was characteristic of the military's institutional approach to the old war on terror. "The American people expect us to use advanced technologies, for example, to prevent attacks on U.S. forces and to remove terrorists from the battlefield. We do, and it has saved the lives of our men and women in uniform," argued Brennan. Such expectations were legally established in the 2001 Congressional Authorization for Use of Military Force which enables the president to protect the nation from any imminent threat of attack and "to use all necessary and appropriate force" against those nations, organizations and individuals responsible for 9/11 (Brennan, 2012).

Following the Holder and Brennan appearances, there appeared to be an emerging gap between whom the administration claimed to be the target of strikes and those actually killed. The New America Foundation reported on drone strikes in Pakistan: "Under Bush, about a third of all drone strikes killed a militant leader, compared to less than 13 percent since President Obama took office" (Bergen & Braun, 2012). The administration claimed that, by definition, there were no accidental strikes and no collateral damage. Of course, it was difficult to say just who and how many were destroyed by putting together body parts. Just as the Bush policy was tarnished by what it called enhanced interrogation at black sites, so the Obama administration's claim to the high ground was subject to tarring by news coverage of kill sites.

Drone policy initially targeted al-Qaida leadership. These "personality strikes" posed a limited number of targets and strict standards of corroborating proof. "Signature strikes" (Heller 2012) eliminated the need for confirmation by intelligence and assessed targets based on behavioral profiles. Thus, the target population was widened and collateral damage eliminated. Locals did not report it this way. Zenko (2012) wrote:

> For instance, do legitimate targets include children, individuals attempting to rescue drone strike victims, and the funeral processions of deceased militants? U.S. drones have reportedly targeted all three on multiple occasions. Presumably, the United States deliberately targets these groups, but when asked, U.S. officials will not acknowledge such practices.

The incidents were met with flat denials, save where 9 Pakistani soldiers were mistakenly killed.

During the 2012 election campaign Obama did harvest credit for leadership strikes: "22 out of 30 top al-Qaida leaders who have been taken off the field," he said (as cited in Condon, 2011). At the same time as claiming victory, sources quoted Osama bin Laden's order for leadership to fly to remote areas. This was translated in terms of widening the hunt to Africa. The National Director of Counterterrorism told the American Bar Association at the end of 2012: "Even as al Qaeda's leadership in Pakistan struggles to remain relevant, the terrorist threat we face has become more diverse" (Olsen, 2012). An international network crosses sovereign borders. "Al Qaeda has turned to other groups to carry out attacks and to advance its ideology. These groups are based in an array of countries, including Yemen, Somalia, Nigeria and in Iraq" (Olsen, 2012). Policy clean up was left until after the election.

Presidential Concessions

By 2013, the Holder and Brennan explanations and justifications of drone policy had whetted the appetite of those in Congress always looking for a fight or scandal. In February 2013, "both Republicans and Democrats on the House Judiciary Committee ... denounced President Barack Obama's administration for refusing to share key documents or details of the armed killings by armed, robotic aircraft" (Agence France Presse, 2013). Senator Rand Paul (R-KY, 2013) called attention to the policy by filibustering Brennan's CIA nomination, asking, "The President says, I haven't killed anyone yet. He goes on to say, and I have no intention of killing Americans. But I might. Is that enough?" Soon thereafter Amnesty International joined with the coalition of Democrats and Republicans raising similar, pointed questions (Associated Press, 2013).

President Obama's (2013) speech at the National Defense University addressed the exigence created by the clamor, asserting that, on the whole, the trajectory of his regime has been progressive: "We unequivocally banned torture, affirmed our commitment to civilian courts, worked to align our policies with rule of law, and expanded our consultation with Congress." Of course, the failure of the administration to set policy publicly and the rubber stamp qualities of the secret FISA court system were not mentioned. In his defense of drone strikes, he argued "we are still a nation at war." Yet, total war is not an option. Thus, the United States must continue to "dismantle networks that pose a direct danger to us." The core has been disassembled because "their remaining operatives spend more time thinking about their own safety than plotting against us." The nature of the threat has changed, mostly to locally inspired violence, but it is still capable of circulation through the splinter influence of extremism. As extremists seek more exotic places for safety and training, pursuit requires even greater reach, with fewer risks to U.S. soldiers and less self-risking escalation entailed with boots on the ground. The bin Laden strike was not the norm, the president warned the public. Drones are the future.

Even while affirming policy success, Obama then proceeded to make concessions in order to preserve legitimacy by co-opting opposition. He argued "use of force against terrorists" will have clear guidelines. These include: (1) a preference to capture not kill terrorists, (2) a commitment to consult partners and respect state sovereignty, (3) a pledge to only act against those who "pose a continuing and imminent threat to the American people" and to secure careful support for reaching that decision. Thus, Obama articulated justifications and criteria for use of lethal force begun at a lower administration level the year before.

As for the targeting of U.S. citizens, Obama (2013) conceded that unilateral judgments of force are not legitimate. Therefore, "I've insisted on strong oversight of all lethal action" taken outside of Iraq or Afghanistan. "Every strike" was brought to Congress, including U.S. citizen Awlaki, said the president. The resulting standard is a "high threshold that we've set for taking lethal action" that applies to "all potential terrorist targets, regardless of whether or not they are American citizens. This threshold respects the inherent dignity of every human life." The speech ended with further promises to consult Congress and engage in diplomacy, even while the connections between domestic and international terror networks were posited as a continuing target for intervention.

Obama here attempted to unwind the perceived policy overreach of the early "kill lists," in the process clearing rhetorical space to couch drone policy in a rhetoric of possibility, gesturing toward a contingent future in which the "war on terror" can be shelved and drone strikes will no longer be compelled by military necessity. Yet the disposition matrix's institutional momentum may not be so easy to ratchet down with words and promises. The list of targets may shrink for a time, only to be expanded again by the next burst of incriminating intelligence vacuumed up by the U.S. government's massive surveillance dragnet. "The problem with the drone is it's like your lawn mower," Bruce Riedel, a former Obama adviser, told the *Washington Post*; "You've got to mow the lawn all the time. The minute you stop mowing, the grass is going to grow back" (as cited in Miller, 2012). Furthermore, the matrix's limiting principles, touted so prominently by Holder, Brennan, and Obama, could artificially prolong the drone strike program by providing excuses for decision makers to avoid facing the really tough questions about the wisdom of remote control killing. "Institutionalization of anything entails a bias toward its indefinite continuation, and maybe even its expansion," explains former intelligence official Paul Pillar (2013). Group think could follow. "By routinizing and institutionalizing a case-by-case set of criteria, there is even the hazard that officials will devote less deliberation than they otherwise would have to such larger considerations because they have the comfort and reassurance of following a manual" (Pillar, 2013).

This deliberative stall could prevent U.S. planners from coming to grips with one of the drone's most insidious aspects – its tendency to spark imitation. Following the U.S. lead, scores of other states now seek their own remote strike capability (Zenko, 2012). Non-state actors have begun to mimic the unique brand of humanitarian "stand your ground" self-defense logic presented to justify U.S. drone strikes. During his 2012 trial, in which Anders Behring Breivik was convicted of murdering 69 teenagers, he defended his use of force as a "preventive attack in defense of Norway's indigenous people, ethnic Norwegians, and our culture" (Breivik, 2012a), later claiming a mandate to do so based on "universal human rights, general international law and the right to self defense that gave me mandate to perform this preventive attack" (Breivik, 2012b). Should U.S. officials decide one day to make good on President Obama's promise to eventually shut down their own drone disposition matrix, they may discover that it is difficult to put toothpaste back into the tube.

President Obama's address is surely one of the oddest in U.S. history. Rarely does a president adapt legal standards, admit to killing four U.S. citizens without trial, strive to dismantle over a decade-long global war on terror, while articulating a need for network policies that use information to target specific splinter factions of influence. This is the policy that finally was articulated after years of pursuit, informal leaks, executive office defenses, and calls for public explanation. It extends the principles and holdings of surrogate discourses justifying drone policy. The same "imminent" and "continuing" logic of war by choice that animated the Bush administration continues to fund Obama even in the moment of purporting to limit such policy and foresee an end to limitless war.

Our case study illustrates one avenue regarding how presidential persuasion now becomes institutionally grounded and strategically deployed over time. In the past, moments of foreign policy have invited presidential addresses. Great speeches create great drama. No-drama Obama delayed his own public association with policy until the 2012 election was over, subordinates could test the water, strategies of co-optation of criticism could be developed, and the policy was in a wind-down phase. Studies of presidential address generally feature the executive office as engaging in acts of policy address and public persuasion. The conditions of network warfare and declining state sovereignty modify this rhetorical situation. The Obama policy achieved ostensible success, even though its strategies of argumentation remain open to question.

References

Agence France Presse. (2012, June 7). US drone attacks in Pakistan: UN backs probe into civilian casualties. *International Herald Tribune*. Retrieved from http://tribune.com.pk/story/390225/us-drone-attacks-in-pakistan-un-backs-probe-into-civilian-casualties/

Agence France Presse. (2013, February 27). White House stonewalling drone investigation say lawmakers. Retrieved from http://www.google.com/hostednews/afp/article/ALeqM5hiKv_eLCofND848tjkYdubEzv-Fw?docId=CNG.9cb5874de752c338bd36923b848726ac.301

Associated Press. (2013, May 22). Amesty International protests U.S. drone killings. *CBS News*. Retrieved from http://www.cbsnews.com/8301–202_162–57585822/amnesty-international-protests-u.s-drone-killings/

Becker, J., & Shane, S. (2012, May 29). Secret "kill list" proves a test of Obama's principles and will. *New York Times*. Retrieved from http://www.nytimes.com/2012/05/29/world/obamas-leadership-in-war-on-al-qaeda.html?pagewanted=all

Bergen, P., & Braun, M. (2012, September 5). Drone is Obama's weapon of choice. *CNN*. Retrieved from http://edition.cnn.com/2012/09/05/opinion/bergen-obama-drone

Breivik, A. B. (2012a, April 17). Anders Behring Breivik court statement [Opening statement]. The Breivik Archive. Retrieved from https://sites.google.com/site/breivikreport/documents/anders-breivik-court-statement-2012–04-17

Breivik, A. B. (2012b, June 22). Anders Behring Breivik court statement. The Breivik Archive. Retrieved from https://sites.google.com/site/breivikreport/documents/anders-breivik-court-statement-2012–06-22

Brennan, J. O. (2012, April 30). The efficacy and ethics of U.S. counterterrorism strategy. Address at the Wilson Center. Washington, D.C. Retrieved from http://www.wilsoncenter.org/event/the-efficacy-and-ethics-us-counterterrorism-strategy

Bureau of Investigative Journalism. (2012). Covert war on terror—the datasets. Retrieved from http://www.thebureauinvestigates.com/category/projects/drone-data/

Condon, G. E. (2011, December 8). Obama hits back with bin Laden killing at Republicans' charge of appeasement. *National Journal*. Retrieved from http://www.nationaljournal.com/whitehouse/obama-hits-back-with-bin-laden-killing-at-republicans-charge-of-appeasement-20111208

Heller, K. J. (2012). "One hell of a killing machine": Signature strikes and international law. Journal of International Criminal Justice, Forthcoming. U of Melbourne Legal Studies Research Paper No. 634. Retrieved from http://ssrn.com/abstract=2169089

Holder, E. (2012, March 5). Attorney General Eric Holder speaks at Northwestern University School of Law. U.S. Department of Justice website. Retrieved from http://www.justice.gov/iso/opa/ag/speeches/2012/ag-speech-1203051.html

Keller, W. W., & Mitchell, G. R. (2006). Preemption, prevention, prevarication. In W. W. Keller & G. R. Mitchell (Eds.), *Hitting first: Preventive force in U.S. security strategy* (pp. 3–26). Pittsburgh, PA: University of Pittsburgh Press.

Miller, G. (2012, October 23). Plan for hunting terrorists signals U.S. intends to keep adding names to kill lists. *Washington Post*. Retrieved from http://articles.washingtonpost.com/2012–10-23/world/35500278_1_drone-campaign-obama-administration-matrix

Obama, B. (2013, May 23). Remarks by the President at the National Defense University. Retrieved from http://www.whitehouse.gov/the-press-office/2013/05/23/remarks-president-national-defense-university

Olsen, M. (2012, May 16). The evolving terrorist threat and the NCTC mission. Remarks at the American Bar Association. NCTC website. Retrieved from http://nctc.gov/press_room/speeches/20120516_Director_Olsen_ABA_Remarks.pdf

Paul, R. (2013, March 6). Sen. Rand Paul filibuster of Brennan nomination. Unofficial transcript. Senator Rand Paul website. Retrieved from http://www.paul.senate.gov/?p=press_release&id=727

Pillar, P. (2013, January 20). The assassination manual. *National Interest* online. Retrieved from http://nationalinterest.org/blog/paul-pillar/the-assassination-manual-7992

Zenko, M. (2012, July 24). Collateral damage: The dangerous precedents of America's drone wars. *World Politics*. Retrieved from http://www.worldpoliticsreview.com/articles/12195/collateral-damage-the-dangerous-precedents-of-americas-drone-wars

50

DON'T FEAR THE REAPER

The disturbing case of how drones reconfigure technologies of deliberation

Heather Ashley Hayes

WHITMAN COLLEGE, USA

In the midst of a presidential campaign labeled "one of the nastiest and most personal of modern times" (Cordes, 2012, para. 2), so bad that it will "take time and great effort for the winner to drain the poison from the system" (Balz, 2012, para. 9), the 2012 presidential candidates were able to find some agreement when Governor Mitt Romney was asked about President Obama's drone policy:

> It's widely reported that drones are being used in drone strikes and I support that entirely and feel the president was right to up the usage of that technology and believe that we should continue to use it, continue to go after people who pose a threat to this nation and to our friends.
>
> *("Transcript and Audio," 2012, 1:09:35)*

The overt agreement on drone use, in the midst of a contentious presidential election cycle, points to a trend articulated by political scientist Richard Jackson (2005):

> Governments have to regularise and institutionalise the practice of war, especially when it appears likely to last for many years . . . The process of inducing consent . . . requires . . . the remaking of the world and the creation of a new and unquestioned reality in which the application of state violence appears normal and reasonable.
>
> *(p. 1)*

The execution of the drone program has allowed the application of state violence, in the form of technological surveillance and targeted killing, to appear normal and reasonable, such that the fiercest of political foes agree on the program's necessity. To date, even voices critiquing the drone program often dwell upon questions of the program's legality, domestic use, or its effect on U.S. citizens. This severely narrows the possibility for meaningful deliberation about the program's violent consequences for Muslim populations around the globe.

In this essay, I argue that the core of the U.S. drone program is rooted in a technical sphere of argument in a way that chills deliberative debate. Newly articulated forms of technical

329

argumentation have foreclosed deliberative processes, generating a new technology of deliberation with dangerous consequences. In proving these claims, this essay examines the central technology of the U.S. drone program: the disposition matrix, the sole resource for determining the use of drones for targeted killing in any given case. I articulate the unique form of technical argument generated by the matrix's central role in the drone program in two related ways. First, the notion of what constitutes technical experts has been not only vastly restricted, but also has detached from, human expertise. Second, the technological activity of the disposition matrix becomes understood as its own site of knowledge, creating invisible logics inaccessible to scrutiny. In this way, the disposition matrix's violent work becomes self-fulfilling. As Goodnight and Farrell (1981) noted, "So long as the assumptions, procedures, expectations, and formats of technical communication and surrogate discourse operate within undisturbed patterns, they are virtually self-fulfilling" (p. 79).

In building these claims, this essay unfolds in three stanzas. First, it offers a brief history of U.S. drone technologies and their deployment. Next, it demonstrates the ways that the drone program has foreclosed deliberation in favor of technical argument by looking to the work of the disposition matrix. Lastly, it concludes by expanding Goodnight's (1982) call for the need to "uncover . . . and critique . . . those practices which replace deliberative rhetoric by substituting alternative modes of invention and restricting subject matter" (p. 227). By understanding this vital component of the U.S. drone program for its newly insidious mode of invention, scholars can better confront the techniques of deliberation functioning to articulate certain bodies as killable within the global war on terror.

Buzzing the Public Sphere: The Global War on Terror and a New Era of Drone Deployment

Chief Washington correspondent for *The New York Times* David Sanger (2012) wrote, for the Obama administration, drones "are the perfect tools for an age of austerity – far cheaper than landing troops in remote deserts and mountains, and often more precise" (p. 243). The hundreds of billions of dollars authorized for wars against Afghanistan and Iraq in early 2002 gave birth to a new era of armed drone production. New drones were commissioned including the powerful 40-foot long Reaper model and production schedules were escalated for the two existing models deployed throughout the 2000s, the 38–inch long Raven and the 27-foot long Predator with Hellfire missile capacity. In early 2011, Secretary of Defense Robert Gates proclaimed that the newest generation of fighter jet, the F-35, would be the Pentagon's last manned fighter aircraft.

Even with this increased development, the current drone program would not come to fruition until the 2008 election, largely as a result of the Bush administration's misgivings about the technology. Richard Clarke (2012), White House counterterrorism adviser to three presidents, described the resistance met upon suggesting expansion of drone use in the early 2000s:

> We found bin Laden in October 2000 . . . There was, however, no such thing then as an armed Predator, so we saw him but could not kill him . . . After that experience, orders were given to create an armed drone, quickly. When President George W. Bush came into office, the CIA and DOD refused to fly the armed Predator, including balking at a cabinet level meeting on Sept. 4, 2001 . . . Once in office, Obama had no such hesitation.

(para. 5–8)

Since 2008, U.S. drone operations have increased forty-fold, primarily targeting Pakistan, Yemen, and northern Afghanistan. In Pakistan alone, nearly 329 strikes have killed between 1,910 and 3,228 people, an estimated 400 to 900 of which were civilians (New America Foundation, 2012).

Once the Obama administration bought into drone technology, it has been all-in on its outcomes. As a result of the program's speedy development and rapidly evolving technological capability, the infrastructure of the drone program traverses borders, including drone pilots in Air Force bases from Nevada to Virginia "operating the Predators and Reapers with joysticks while viewing live images beamed back from the drones' sophisticated camera systems" (Sanger, 2012, p. 249) and mechanical crews working on drone bodies throughout Afghanistan, Somalia, Pakistan, and beyond. This enhanced infrastructure called for new rationalities of governance.

Arguing Drones: Reconfigured Technologies of Argument and the Disposition of Terrorist Bodies

The capture and kill list was the first document generated by the Obama administration to catalogue possible terrorist targets around the world and determine when an armed drone would be deployed (Miller, 2012). The list was just that: a physical list, to which targets' names would be added and removed as deemed appropriate in security strategy meetings. As a result of the increasing technological burden of integrating drone body maintenance, drone pilot readiness, and administrative tracking and oversight, the capture and kill list evolved between 2008 and 2010, replaced by the "disposition matrix." Almost no information about the matrix has been declassified, so the best intelligence about the database stems from exposé style journalism or inferences from recent statements and documents from the Obama administration, including President Obama's 2013 National Defense University address and the declassified Department of Justice White Paper concerning the drone program's targeting of U.S. citizens.

In journalistic discourse, the matrix has simply been described as the lynchpin in the drone program "playbook" created by CIA Director John Brennan. News reports described the disposition matrix as containing "the names of terrorism suspects arrayed against an accounting of the resources being marshaled to track them down, including sealed indictments and clandestine operations" (Miller, 2012, para. 2). One reporter described the matrix this way:

> The matrix is more than . . . a capture-or-kill list. It is a sophisticated grid, mounted upon a database that is said to have been more than two years in the development, containing biographies of individuals believed to pose a threat to U.S. interests, and their known or suspected locations, as well as a range of options for their disposal.
>
> *(Cobain, 2013, para. 9)*

Discussed as a technical database, administration officials have argued, "The database is designed to go beyond existing kill lists, mapping plans for the 'disposition' of suspects beyond the reach of American drones" (Miller, 2012, para. 2).

This matrix, and a map of its features, is a key exemplar of a new technical sphere of argument by which the state identifies certain targets for attack and death. Even after the Obama administration's declassification of information about drone strikes in the wake of the Defense University address, the disposition matrix still remains markedly outside of public deliberation about the drone program. As best as can be surmised:

> The "playbook," as Brennan calls it . . . will cover the selection and approval of targets from the "disposition matrix," the designation of who should pull the trigger when a killing is warranted, and the legal authorities the administration thinks sanction its actions in Pakistan, Yemen, Somalia and beyond.
>
> *(DeYoung, 2012, para. 2)*

It appears from these same accounts that Brennan and Obama alone often make decisions regarding strikes, informed by the logics of the matrix. The field of experts charged with authorizing the disposition matrix's decision to strike is widely considered to be no more than two or three individuals, none of whom are known outside of Obama and Brennan.

The technical sphere of argument is marked by three distinctive components (Rowland, 1986). First, it focuses on questions of fact as opposed to value or policy. Second, its audience is comprised of specialized scientific communities. Third, the technical sphere focuses on issues in the technical arena. As a result of these criteria, calls have been made to "identify standards that can be used to determine when it is appropriate for members of the public to defer on factual claims concerning issues of public concern to the technical sphere" (Paliewicz, 2013, p. 233). Some suggestions for these criteria include finding consensus among scientific experts and ensuring scientific experts "produce research uncontaminated by insincere motives" (Paliewicz, 2013, p. 233). By producing a logic authorizing the certainty of particular names, locations, technical capabilities, and chance of kill success, the matrix has overtaken the work of human experts by generating a new logic of technical argument near impenetrable even by the few humans with whom it is intended to interact. The technology itself generates its own motives and manufactures its own consensus.

This visible work of the matrix points to its function as a new technology of deliberation. As Greene (2009) noted, "the materiality of rhetoric as a 'technology of deliberation' [informs] governmental judgments to remake reality" (p. 50). Those technical arguments generated by the disposition matrix have the effect of identifying "particular populations, behaviors, and situations" as "visible for the purpose of intervention and calibration" (p. 52). The most dangerous consequence of this particular technical form of argument is that it authorizes the subjection of Muslim populations for interventions that end their lives, and often the lives of those around them.

The articulation of particular populations as killable permeates the Obama administration's defenses of the drone program and news accounts of the matrix. Representing the administration's approach to drones, Clarke's position is representative of the Obama administration more generally. Clarke's claims are expanded in the declassified Department of Justice White Paper (2013), one of the few open documents produced by the administration concerning drones. It noted:

> As detailed in this white paper, in defined circumstances, a targeted killing of a U.S. citizen who has joined al-Qa'ida or its associated forces would be lawful under U.S. and international law . . . Were the target of a lethal operation a U.S. citizen . . . that individual's citizenship would not immunize him from a lethal operation.
>
> *(para. 2–3)*

The paper expanded the killable terrorist body beyond bounds of citizenship.

In addition to these administration defenses of drones, President Obama has dodged significant opportunities to expand deliberation about the program. In his National Defense University speech in May 2013, he noted:

I've asked my administration to review proposals to extend oversight of lethal actions . . . the establishment of a special court to evaluate and authorize lethal action has the benefit of bringing a third branch of government into the process, but raises serious constitutional issues about presidential and judicial authority . . . the establishment of an independent oversight board in the executive branch . . . may introduce a layer of bureaucracy into national security decision-making, without inspiring additional public confidence in the process . . . despite these challenges, I look forward to actively engaging Congress to explore these and other options for increased oversight.

Although Obama noted the need for amorphous "oversight" of the drone program, the matrix is invisible in his discourse. While technical decisions perhaps used to butt up against public argument, in this case no argument is authorized, or able, to occur. Rather, the processes of producing logics that are ongoing are assumed to be deliberative when they are merely overseen, rarely held accountable, or interrupted by competing logics. Obama's statements are based in an assumption of need for quick action rather than deliberative decision making.

The Dawn of a New Era in Technical Argument: Drones and the Foreclosure of Dissent

In his original formulation of the spheres of argument, Goodnight (1982) noted the need for critique of alternative modes of invention in argument. For Goodnight, the primary focus of argument and the potential for democratic deliberation lie in the public sphere, a forum to which all citizens have access and "share in the construction of the future" (p. 214). The technical sphere, in contrast, evokes expectations of a limited community of experts who can advance special types of understanding. Here, I have argued that the disposition matrix, existing in the technical sphere of argument, represents one of the most limited forms of technical argument to date as a result of both the extremely limited human expertise it utilizes and the new technology of deliberation it imposes, always with life-ending consequences for those deemed disposable. As a result, it represents a significant threat to public deliberation on the issue of drone use in the global war on terror.

The disposition matrix functions not only to avoid deliberation about the ethics of drone use (which would be typical of technical arguments generally) but also, more importantly, to materially deploy circumstances of violence without either public deliberation over ethics or human expert consensus. The matrix does its work by aligning a number of categories and producing a judgment that is then accepted or rejected by a remarkably small number of human interlocutors. These human assessors (most often Obama and/or Brennan) do not constitute deliberators in the process, but are relegated to judges of the argument skill of the matrix itself, dramatically limiting expert disagreement within the technical sphere. The sole purpose of human experts becomes verification, rather than invention, of argument. To our current knowledge, the matrix's logics are rarely, if ever, rejected.

E. C. White (1987) described *kairos* as "a passing instant when an opening appears which must be driven through with force if success is to be achieved" (p. 13). Perhaps no better description could be made of what the administration seeks to achieve with the technical work of the disposition matrix. Understood as an active database tracking a kairotic intersection between a target, a place, a time, and a technological action, the matrix functions as a technical subject that not only makes its own arguments, but manufactures the parameters of human consent within its logics. We are to assume that technical consensus has been achieved when the matrix verifies someone as killable. The work of the matrix here is self-fulfilling; it has come to have its own subjectivity in which it stands as its own arguer, its own dissent, and its own warrants and impacts. The matrix's existence as a purely technical mode of argument is further demonstrated through its continued classification and its invisibility in the public discourse of the administration.

The rising uncertainty expressed in Western journalism about the legality of the drone program has at its center one prominent argument, primarily about the killing of U.S. citizens without due process of law guaranteed by the U.S. Constitution. This heavily restricted public discussion avoids the ethical problem of a new technical normalization (via the disposition matrix) that functions by documenting subjects as killable, surveilling them, and ultimately disposing of them in a kairotic fashion – relying on its technical assessment of that kairotic moment as its strongest warrant for foreclosing dissent. Examining the processes of technical argument associated with the disposition matrix, critics can begin to map the dynamic process by which productive work may occur in empowering deliberation in the public sphere about drone use. This work points us to the ways in which argument scholars must remain vigilant in closely examining, and perhaps creating, new avenues of deliberation within the global war on terror.

References

Balz, D. (2012, August 15). President Obama, Mitt Romney running a most poisonous campaign. *Washington Post Politics Online*. Retrieved from http://www.washingtonpost.com/politics/a-most-poisonous-campaign/2012/08/15/16715a08-e6e7-11e1-8f62-58260e3940a0_story_1.html

Clarke, R.A. (2012, December 2). Give drones a medal. *New York Daily News*. Retrieved from http://www.nydailynews.com/opinion/give-drones-medal-article-1.1211249

Cobain, I. (2013, July 14). Obama's secret kill list – the disposition matrix. *The Guardian*. Retrieved from http://www.theguardian.com/world/2013/jul/14/obama-secret-kill-list-disposition-matrix

Cordes, N. (2012, August 15). What substance? Campaign attacks get nastier than ever. *CBS News Online*. Retrieved from http://www.cbsnews.com/8301-18563_162-57494114/what-substance-campaign-attacks-get-nastier-than-ever/

DeYoung, K. (2012, October 24). CIA veteran transforms U.S. policy. *The Washington Post, National Security*. Retrieved from http://www.washingtonpost.com/world/national-security/cia-veteran-john-brennan-has-transformed-us-counterterrorism-policy/2012/10/24/318b8eec-1c7c-11e2-ad90-ba5920e56eb3_story.html

DOJ released white paper (2013, March 7). *NBS News*. Retrieved from http://msnbcmedia.msn.com/i/msnbc/sections/news/020413_DOJ_White_Paper.pdf

Goodnight, G. T. (1982). The personal, technical, and public spheres of argument: A speculative inquiry into the art of public deliberation. *The Journal of the American Forensic Association, 18*, 214–227.

Goodnight, G. T., & Farrell, T. B. (1981). Accidental rhetoric: The root metaphors of three mile island. *Communication Monographs 48*(4), 271–300.

Greene, R. W. (2009). Rhetorical materialism: The rhetorical subject and the general intellect. In B. L. Biesecker and J. L. Lucaites (Eds.), *Rhetoric, materiality, and politics* (pp. 43–65). London, UK: Peter Lang.

Jackson, R. (2005). *Writing the war on terrorism: Language, politics, and counter-terrorism*. Manchester, UK: Manchester University Press.

Miller, G. (2012, October 23). Plan for hunting terrorists signals U.S. intends to keep adding names to kill lists. *The Washington Post*. Retrieved from http://www.washingtonpost.com/world/national-security/plan-for-hunting-terrorists-signals-us-intends-to-keep-adding-names-to-kill-lists/2012/10/23/4789b2ae-18b3-11e2-a55c-39408fbe6a4b_story.html?hpid=z1

New America Foundation Counterterrorism Strategy Initiative. (2012, December 1). The year of the drone. *New American Foundation Online*. Retrieved from http://counterterrorism.newamerica.net/drones

Obama, B. H. (2013, May 23). Remarks at National Defense University. Text from *The American presidency project*. Retrieved from http://www.presidency.ucsb.edu/ws/index.php?pid=103625&st=&st1=#axzz2i5jBdBnf

Paliewicz, N. S. (2012). Global warming and the interaction between the public and technical spheres of argument: When standards for expertise really matter. *Argumentation and Advocacy, 48*, 231–242.

Rowland, R. C. (1986). The relationship between the public and technical spheres of argument: A case study of the Challenger Seven disaster. *Central States Speech Journal, 37*, 136–146.

Sanger, D. E. (2012). *Confront and conceal: Obama's secret wars and the surprising use of American power.* New York, NY: Crown Publishers.

Transcript and audio: Third presidential debate. (2012, October 22). *National Public Radio Politics Online.* Retrieved from http://www.npr.org/2012/10/22/163436694/transcript-3rd-obama-romney-presidential-debate

White, E. C. (1987). *Karionamos: On the will to invent.* Cambridge: Cambridge University Press.

51

DRONES, BIOPOLITICS AND VISUALITY

The aestheticization of the War on Terror

Megan D. McFarlane

UNIVERSITY OF UTAH, USA

In March 2012, U.S. Attorney General Eric Holder defended the use of drones, including those that target U.S. citizens, claiming that the president has the authority to kill anyone he deems an enemy of the state. Holder's defense occurred around the time it was discovered that President Obama had "deployed drones against terrorism suspects in an unprecedented way" (Johnson, 2012, para. 3). Holder explained that the United States' "legal authority is not limited to the battlefields in Afghanistan," but rather anywhere the United States is given consent or deems the nation "unable or unwilling to deal effectively with a threat to the United States" (Johnson, 2012, para. 14).

Pir Zubair Shah (2012) recently offered insight into U.S. influence in other nations via drones in his *Foreign Policy* article titled "My Drone War." Shah has covered the drone war for about six years, first for *Newsday* and then *The New York Times*. He described how the drone attacks are part of the "most secret of wars across northern Pakistan" (para. 6) and how "283 drone strikes had occurred in the Afghanistan-Pakistan border region since 2004, [but] Obama never even publicly acknowledged them until this past January [2012]" (para. 5). Shah's account is important because he grew up in Waziristan, Pakistan, and has firsthand knowledge and understanding of the region, the language, and the people.

Shah (2012) discussed the tension drone attacks have caused in Pakistan as the landscape was turned into a "war zone" (para. 21), emphasizing the fact that the attacks were so secretive that no one ever knew the true story – including who ordered the attack, who implemented the attack, and how many were killed. The ambiguity of the information, as well as the lack of any acknowledgement of who was actually being killed and who was doing the actual killing, indicated that in the minds of those ordering the attacks, some lives count and some do not. The secrecy of the attacks created two populations: one visible and one invisible.

To analyze the rhetoric of visibility and invisibility of certain populations described in Shah's essay, I draw from Mirzoeff's (2011) theoretical construct of the *complex of visuality*. I argue that the War on Terror is aestheticized through the complex of visuality, which functions to make the war more palatable, renders certain people invisible, and therefore perpetuates disturbing aspects of biopolitical U.S. ideology through the practices of classification, separation, and aestheticization. I begin with an overview of Mirzoeff's definition and discussion of visuality, and then apply his concepts to Shah's article, examining how the rhetorical employment of visuality creates an atmosphere where the U.S. government participates in biopolitics to justify and aestheticize death. I further argue that Shah's essay is not an isolated case, but rather sheds light on the larger problems surrounding the United States, the War on Terrorism, visuality, and biopolitics. By making the victims of the drone strikes visible, Shah's account, and others like his, demystify the drone strikes and move the U.S. public to encourage needed policy changes.

Visuality

Visual studies and discussions of visual argumentation have long concerned themselves with the political implications of images (e.g., Barbatsis, 1996; Birdsell & Groarke, 1996; Blair, 1996; Fleming, 1996; Lake & Pickering, 1998; Palczewski, 2005; Shelley, 1996). Importing Mirzoeff (2011) into these studies adds his unique interpretation of visuality as "both a medium for the transmission and dissemination of authority, and a means for the mediation of those subject to that authority" (pp. xv). Visuality is authority's worldview, what Mirzoeff called a "complex of visuality," which is composed of three practices: classifying, separating, and aestheticizing (pp. 3–4). Ultimately, authority seeks to naturalize and aestheticize its perspective of classifying and separating the social order. Authority classifies by "naming, categorizing and defining" who is visible and who is invisible, and then separates the classified groups for social organizational purposes, dictating participation and drawing clear lines of inclusion and exclusion (Mirzoeff, 2011, p. 3). Then, authority aestheticizes, which:

> makes this separated classification seem right and hence aesthetic . . . such repeated experience generates an "aesthetic of respect for the status quo," the aesthetic of the proper, of duty, of what is felt to be right and hence pleasing, ultimately even beautiful.
>
> *(Mirzoeff, 2011, p. 3)*

The separated classification tends to go unnoticed because it appears to be right and therefore good.

Mirzoeff (2011) asserted that visuality is a limited construction of reality that must be resisted by alternative "countervisualities" which allow for the "right to look" and the right to be seen (p. 1). Using this framework, I argue that U.S. cultural texts engage in visuality's aestheticized classifications and that Shah's essay on the drone war makes evident the contours of visuality in operation. Essentially, simultaneously looking at the visual and the verbal through Mirzoeff's framework illuminates how verbal rhetoric can impact the visual realm by influencing political subjectivity in addition to providing context for pictures or other images.

Classifying and Separating: Construction of the Primitive Other

One of the prominent realms where classification and separation function is in the us/them binary used to distinguish, and visualize the relationship, between the United States and other nations. Differentiating and/or dehumanizing other people, cultures, or nations can serve two strategic purposes. First, the oppositional us–versus–them binary shifts attention away from U.S. motives and interests and instead onto the enemy. Second, by dehumanizing and labeling the other as evil, users of the binary define the United States as a moral agent and state or imply the other is the opposite (Esch, 2010; Ivie & Giner, 2009; Said, 1979). Through such discourse, a communal and political enemy can be created, granting the United States a specific purpose: naming and defining an identity (Mbembe, 2003, p. 16).

Often this defining consists of constructions of the primitive other. By classifying some non-U.S. countries as primitive – in either a moral, political, or militaristic sense – their citizens are dehumanized and made invisible. Separating these populations from the field of visibility, the U.S. public is allowed to ignore military actions in other countries, seeing only demonized entities instead of populations of people.

Visuality, and specifically the practices of classification and separation, is problematized in Shah's narrative. The drone attacks caused confusion in Pakistan because no one knew who was ordering the attacks (the United States or Pakistan) or who was being killed (civilians or militants). Shah (2012) explained that when a drone fragment was discovered imprinted with the words "Made in the U.S.A.," the villagers realized the United States was sending the drones (para. 8). Yet, despite this finding, in 2010 Wikileaks revealed that the Pakistani government had actually been complicit with the attacks (para. 30), implicating both the United States *and* Pakistan. Consequently, Shah "soon learned that the official version of the story was usually the least reliable" (para. 22).

The multiple entities involved and the rhetorical strategies employed contributed to the difficulty of obtaining an accurate understanding of who sent the airstrikes and who was killed. For example, Shah (2012) explained:

> The Taliban started adapting, too. The militants had come to realize that the increasingly effective drone strikes made them look weak, and they began getting rid of the evidence as fast as they could. After every attack they would cordon off the area and remove the bodies of the dead, making it difficult to verify who and how many people had been killed.
>
> *(para. 23)*

Because so many different groups were involved (the Pakistani government, the U.S. government, and the Taliban), in addition to the inaccessibility of the terrain where the attacks were taking place, the war has been elusive, if not invisible. People have disagreed over the classification of who has been killed by drone attacks, with some estimating that 70% of those killed by drones were militants and others arguing that mainly civilians have been killed (Inskeep & Shah, 2012, para. 1). Without knowing who has actually been killed, certain people have been rendered invisible in the complex of visuality. As Martin (2009) explained, "What cannot be seen cannot be counted" (p. 188). Therefore, the people killed by U.S. drone strikes will continue to remain invisible.

If the secrecy of the drone attacks creates an invisible population that is not named, acknowledged, or counted, this population does not matter or even exist politically. This contributes to what Rancière (2009) called a police state, in which visibility is only given to the dominant powers. Drawing from Mbembe's (2003) *necropolitics* – or the politics of death – Mirzoeff (2011) called this type of governance "necropolitical regimes of separation" in which "counterinsurgency classifies and separates by force to produce an imperial governance that is self-justifying because it is held to be 'right,' a priori and hence aesthetic" (p. 278).

Aestheticizing: Biopolitics and Necropolitics

This aestheticization of the War on Terror has been legitimized by dehumanizing the other through the employment of biopolitics and necropolitics. Introducing biopolitics, Foucault (2003) explained, "The right of [18th century] sovereignty was the right to take life or let live. And then this new right is established: the right to make live and to let die" (p. 241). Whereas the focus used to be on taking life and the right to kill, the current biopolitical era involves intervention to "make live" (Foucault, 2003, p. 248).

However, Foucault argued that even wars could be explained in light of biopolitics. As the United States finds itself in an ongoing war in the Middle East, how can it reconcile the concept of biopolitics? Are biopolitics only domestic, whereas sovereignty is still internationally dominant? But this still would not explain why U.S. citizens voraciously defend some countries and ignore or fight against others. Mbembe (2003) argued that necropolitics explains this tension between biopolitics' "making live" and the fact of killing in war.

Mbembe (2003) expanded on questions posed by Foucault, reflecting:

> Is the notion of biopower sufficient to account for the contemporary ways in which the political, under the guise of war, of resistance, or of the fight against terror, makes the murder of the enemy its primary and absolute objective?
>
> *(p. 12)*

He further lamented that "'peace' is more likely to take on the face of a 'war without end'" as people continue to embrace the aestheticization of war (Mbembe, 2003, p. 23).

Building on Mbembe's idea of necropolitics, Murray (2006) discussed what constitutes a human being and the interrelationship between what it means to be human (and the dehumanizing that often takes place), as well as how it is linked to concepts of life, death, voice, and visibility (p. 191). Murray explained, echoing Foucault (1976/2003), that it is possible to live in a world that upholds both biopolitics and necropolitics, using the example of the seeming hypocrisy of a pro-life country that is also committed to capital punishment. In this case, the prisoner's death is justified because it will prevent future harm/death to the living, and therefore the death penalty is founded in a biopolitical mentality. Clearly, classifications have been established based on the values related to life. In the name of biopolitics, even death and killing can be justified. Biopolitics and necropolitics are two sides of the same coin, so it is through biopolitical arguments that the United States engages in what would otherwise be considered necropolitical behavior.

In neocolonialist necropolitical fashion, drones have become part of the everyday rhetoric of those in Waziristan. As drones are woven into the fabric of the culture, by becoming incorporated as a naturalized and normal part of the common vernacular, the drone attacks are being aestheticized. Shah (2012) elaborated:

> Taliban fighters speaking a Waziri dialect of Pashto call the drones *bhungana* – "the one that produces a bee-like sound." Their local adversaries call them *ababeel* – the name of a bird mentioned in the Quran, sent by God to defend the holy city of Mecca from an invading army by hurling small stones from its mouth.
>
> *(para. 16)*

This passage shows the local vocabulary reflects both sides of the war within Waziristan and how both sides aestheticize the classification and separation occurring due to the presence of the drones. In a somewhat alarming statement, Shah (2012) wrote:

> Among Waziristan's residents, "I will drone you" has by now entered the vocabulary of day-to-day conversation as a morbid joke. The mysterious machines buzzing far overhead have become part of the local folklore. "I am looking for you like a drone, my love," goes a romantic Pashto verse I've often heard the locals recite. "You have become Osama; no one knows your whereabouts."
>
> *(para. 29)*

The incorporation of the word "drone" into the everyday vocabulary is the culmination of the complex of visuality. The word has been appropriated, and therefore aestheticized and deemed "right" (Mirzoeff, 2011, p. 278). This war permeates all areas of life and, as Shah (2102) conceded, drones are "now a fact of life in a secret war that is far from over" (para. 38). In the drone attacks, the U.S. public is hearing euphemisms such as "targeted killing" or "use of force" to keep the details of the drone attacks hidden. These moves rhetorically aestheticize the attacks (which could be construed by many as terrorism) by making them seem "right" (Mirzoeff, 2011, p. 287).

Conclusion

Importing Mirzoeff's visuality framework extends the conversation in visual argumentation. Analyzing verbal rhetoric within this framework, such as the vernacular of Waziristan residents, displays how the ongoing drone strikes have been situated and framed. This adds a new dimension to visual studies because not only can images be analyzed, but the visibility and invisibility of certain populations that result from verbal rhetoric can also be interrogated.

The U.S. drone strikes in Pakistan have become part of the continual biopolitical effort to "make people live" through the employment of the three practices of visuality: classifying, separating, and aestheticizing. Countries are classified and separated based on prevailing moral assumptions communicated by the U.S. government and military that demonize other nations as primitive entities and render their populations invisible. This allows for the legitimation of the drone strikes as a way to protect U.S. citizens and "make people live." The biopolitical reasoning enables the aestheticization of drone strikes, justifying them as right.

With the visibility of the drone attacks becoming more prominent due to articles like Shah's, there is a glimmer of hope that recognition of the complex of visuality will be achieved, the disturbing aestheticization of the drone attacks and the wars will be questioned, and policies may be changed. However, the difficulty with visuality is that it plays off of values and beliefs ingrained in culture – those with the status of what is common sense or deemed right. What articles like Shah's might do is "disclose some secret connection of things hidden behind everyday reality" (Rancière, 2009, p. 41), functioning both to persuade and argue for the recognition of populations that have been rendered invisible in this war and revealing disturbing practices (Blair, 1996).

These articles, as well as other criticisms of the drone strikes, may be working. Woods, Serle, and Ross (2013) reported, "civilian deaths fell sharply in Pakistan in 2012," with the estimate that "a minimum of 2.5% of those reported killed were civilians – compared with more than 14% in 2011" (para. 1). The authors argued that perhaps this significant change can be attributed to "sustained criticism" of the drone attacks (para. 1). However Woods et al.

argue there is still more progress needed in terms of policy, given "the details of those killed" still "remain classified" or invisible (para. 5).

Shah's (2012) article served to argue for countervisuality, or the right to look. People who were not, or are not, visible must be made visible if anything is going to change. To quote Murray (2006), "We must press forward into such a discourse, toward new mythographies, perhaps, or toward a postnational and postsovereign understanding of human relations" (p. 211). Instead of always lauding the United States as the world's biopolitical leader, fighting to "make people live," perhaps it is time to take into account its necropolitical actions, as well. Adding conceptual frameworks like Mirzoeff's visuality to current frameworks of visual argumentation may allow critics to make this next step, both in the academy and in policy.

References

Barbatsis, G. (1996). "Look, and I will show you something you will want to see": Pictorial engagement in negative political campaign commercials. *Argumentation and Advocacy, 33*(2), 69–80.

Birdsell, D. S., & Groarke, L. (1996). Toward a theory of visual argument. *Argumentation and Advocacy, 33*(1), 1–10.

Blair, J. A. (1996). The possibility and actuality of visual arguments. *Argumentation and Advocacy, 33*(1), 23–39.

Esch, J. (2010). Legitimizing the "War on Terror": Political myth in official-level rhetoric. *Political Psychology, 31*(3), 357–391. doi:10.1111/j.1467–9221.2010.00762.x

Fleming, D. (1996). Can pictures be arguments? *Argumentation, 33*(1), 11–22.

Foucault, M. (2003). 17 March 1976. In D. Macey (Trans.), *"Society must be defended": Lectures at the Collège de France, 1975–1976* (pp. 239–264). New York, NY: Picador.

Inskeep, S., & Shah, P. Z. (2012, February 29). Drone strikes tracked near Afghan-Pakistan border. *NPR.org*. Retrieved from http://www.npr.org/2012/02/29/147621396/journalists-tracks-drone-strikes-near-afghan-pakistan-border

Ivie, R. L., & Giner, O. (2009). More good, less evil: Contesting the mythos of national insecurity in the 2008 Presidential Primaries. *Rhetoric & Public Affairs, 12*(2), 279–301.

Johnson, C. (2012, March 6). Holder spells out why drones target U.S. citizens. *NPR.org*. Retrieved from http://www.npr.org/2012/03/06/148000630/holder-gives-rationale-for-drone-strikes-on-citizens

Lake, R. A., & Pickering, B. A. (1998). Argumentation, the visual, and the possibility of refutation: An exploration. *Argumentation, 12*, 79–93.

Martin, R. (2009). Mass customization: Corporate architecture and the "end" of politics. In B. Hinderliter, W. Kaizen, V. Maimon, J. Mansoor, & S. McCormick (Eds.), *Communities of sense: Rethinking aesthetics and politics* (pp. 172–193). Durham, NC: Duke University Press.

Mbembe, A. (2003). Necropolitics. *Public Culture, 15*(1), 11–40. doi:10.1215/08992363–15–1–11

Mirzoeff, N. (2011). *The right to look: A counterhistory of visuality*. Durham, NC: Duke University Press.

Palczewski, C. H. (2005). The male Madonna and the feminine Uncle Sam: Visual argument, icons, and ideographs in 1909 anti-woman suffrage postcards. *Quarterly Journal of Speech, 91*(4), 365–394. doi:10.1080/00335630500488325

Rancière, J. (2009). Contemporary art and the politics of aesthetics. In B. Hinderliter, W. Kaizen, V. Maimon, J. Mansoor, & S. McCormick (Eds.), *Communities of sense: Rethinking aesthetics and politics* (pp. 31–50). Durham, NC: Duke University Press.

Said, E. W. (1979). *Orientalism* (1st Vintage Books ed.). New York, NY: Vintage.

Shah, P. Z. (2012, April). My drone war. *Foreign Policy*. Retrieved from http://www.foreignpolicy.com/articles/2012/02/27/my_drone_war

Shelley, C. (1996). Rhetorical and demonstrative modes of visual argument: Looking at images of human evolution. *Argumentation and Advocacy, 33*(2), 53–68.

Woods, C., Serle, J., & Ross, A. K. (2013, January 3). Emerging from the shadows: US covert drone strikes in 2012. *The Bureau of Investigative Journalism*. Retrieved from http://www.thebureauinvestigates.com/2013/01/03/emerging-from-the-shadows-us-covert-drone-strikes-in-2012–2

52

AFTER HONOR

On drones and the distinguished warfare medal controversy

William O. Saas

THE PENNSYLVANIA STATE UNIVERSITY, USA

Military commentators commonly cluster the domains of drone activity into "the three D's: the dull, dirty, and dangerous" (Tice, 1991). When considering the role of aerial drone operators, the three D's each refer to distinctive, and distinctly unpleasant, modes of labor. *The dull*: Routine ISR (intelligence, surveillance, and reconnaissance) missions fly in 8 to 12 hour shifts (Hart, 2010, p. 24), rarely requiring much from the operator beyond "babysitting the automation" (Cummings, Mastracchio, Thornburg, & Mkrtchyan, 2012, p. 24). Drone operators commonly experience melancholy and boredom (Hurwitz, 2013). *The dirty*: This ostensibly refers to the utility of drones for entering spaces into which humans *could not* enter without incurring serious physical injury, including death. "Dirty," however, just as easily describes the too frequent imprecision of so-called surgical drone strikes and the tragic extent to which drone attacks have contributed to the piles of collateral damage – i.e., murdered innocents and traumatized populations – accumulated in the numerous dirty wars that comprise the ongoing war on terror (International Human Rights, 2012). *The dangerous*: Drone technologies offer surrogates for situations into which humans would *rather not* enter. In addition to the danger felt daily by civilians in foreign countries routinely surveilled and fired upon by U.S. drones, drones are also hazardous to the health of the people behind the controls. A recent study showed that drone operators are as likely as their boots-on-the-ground counterparts to experience post-traumatic stress disorder (Dao, 2013).

I propose adding two more categories to fill out the description of the drone operator's plight. In addition to being dull, dirty, and dangerous, drone labor is also a largely *derided* affair, insofar as the drone has lately been the object of much criticism in U.S. media. The blurred lines between quasi-legal targeted killings and legally sanctioned military drone strikes doubtless contribute to the apprehension generated by drone-centric headlines. Neither are there any particularly redemptive accounts of drone operator actions readily accessible to the popular imaginary. When successful drone strikes *are* reported, credit is attributed diffusely to something called the "intelligence community" (Obama, 2011). Add to the list, then, the *dehumanized* character of drone labor – that operators are not publicly recognized for their work, that they are forbidden to give unsanctioned interviews, and that their faces are usually obscured or directed away from the camera when photographed – and you have the perfect description for a perfectly unrewarding line of work. Dull, dirty, dangerous, derided, and dehumanized. And still the ranks of drone operators across the armed forces are projected to swell exponentially in years to come, even as the U.S. military shrinks to a "leaner" size (Obama, 2012).

This essay outlines the institutional controversy (Goodnight, 1991) that emerged when U.S. Secretary of Defense Leon Panetta proposed a means by which to redeem and humanize the drone operator. On February 13, 2013, in one of his final acts as Department of Defense (DoD) chief, Panetta announced the creation of the Distinguished Warfare Medal (DWM), a military-wide honor designed to reward "extraordinary achievement, not involving acts of valor, directly impacting, through any domain, combat operations or other military operations." The memo did not clarify which "technological advancements" or "domains" the Secretary had in mind for recognition, but his comments in a press conference the next day provided some clarity when he specifically remarked "I've seen first-hand how modern tools like remotely piloted platforms and cyber systems have changed the way wars are fought" (Panetta, 2013b). The DWM, he said, reflected "the reality of the kind of technological warfare that we are engaged in in the 21st century." As for the medal's rank, a list of criteria attached to the memo specified that the medal would be placed "immediately following the Distinguished Flying Cross" – in other words, just below the Silver Star, and immediately above the Purple Heart and the Bronze Star.

Within two months of Panetta's announcement, the DWM was revoked before it could be awarded. Having widely interpreted the DWM as a medal intended for drone operators, veterans groups and current service members vehemently argued that the DWM's placement above awards for valor effectively devalued the medals system. By April, the vocal opposition successfully pressured Panetta's successor, Chuck Hagel, to replace the DWM with a commendation of lesser rank.

In answering Mitchell's (2009) call to examine the arguments that comprise official policy, historicizing the DWM controversy will show how the institutional policy of a progressive military technocracy was reversed by the arguments of a conservative and entrenched opposition. Additionally, this study expands the object domain of argument studies to include military medals, specifically, and the numismatic, broadly. The military medal system, I argue, is best viewed as an economy of honor, its medals functioning as so many more or less precise attempts to articulate the boundaries of, and to maintain public trust in, the political currency of valor. As happens in a money economy, any change or supplement to the honor economy not only signals a shift in valor's relative use-value, but also calls into question the cultural and political purchase of honor itself.

Pro-DWM Arguments: The New Reality and Responsibility Theses

Few arguments were given in support of the DWM, as initially proposed, in the weeks and months following Panetta's announcement. Arguments offered by the Secretary and his supporters tended to promote two theses.

First, *the new reality thesis*: The nature of combat is changing, and the military awards system should be adjusted to better reflect the nature and implications of these changes. This echoed a complaint articulated by Major Brent A. Clemmer (2011), who argued that the reality of combat in the war on terror called for an overhaul of the military awards system. For Panetta, the DWM represented a necessary adjustment to the medal system in response to a specific contemporary exigency, namely, the lack of a means to recognize the operators of the drone and cyber systems that have come to play vital roles in the war on terror. The new reality thesis called for two forms of recognition: recognition of a new kind of warfare and recognition of those on the front lines of this new kind of warfare.

In a press release for the DWM from the Office of the Secretary of Defense (U.S. DoD, 2013), both Panetta and Joint Chiefs of Staff Chairperson General Martin E. Dempsey clearly articulated the new reality thesis. The release quoted Panetta's press conference remarks about how "remotely piloted platforms and cyber systems have changed the way wars can be fought." General Dempsey was more direct: "This new medal recognizes the changing character of warfare and those who make extraordinary contributions to it."

The new reality thesis also hinged on the enthymeme of "after 9/11," a claim for which the missing premise was that the terror attacks of September 11, 2001, marked a new era in U.S. political and military cultures. Panetta (2013a) argued in his memo announcing the DWM that "Since September 11, 2001, technological advancements have, in some cases, dramatically changed how we conduct and support combat and other military operations." In March, newly appointed Secretary of Defense Chuck Hagel (2013a) echoed this element of the new reality thesis in a letter addressed to Senator Pat Toomey: "The DWM reflects the evolving nature of warfare."

Second, *the responsibility thesis*: A medal for drone operators would reward and encourage responsible drone operation. This argument was compatible with the new reality thesis insofar as it turned on the premise that the nature of combat had changed to such an extent that a revision to the awards system was urgently needed. More than simply recognizing that a change had occurred, though, the responsibility thesis called for the establishment of a new model for combat morality to incentivize sober soldiering on the frontlines of the new reality. For proponents of the responsibility thesis, medals provided an ideal medium for such a model because the publicity of the medal system renders awards as forms of both recognition *and* evaluation. A medal for drone operators was thus framed as both a politically justified means of recognition and as a morally expedient system of accountability.

The first articulation of the responsibility thesis came in the May/June 2012 issue of the *Air & Space Power Journal*. An essay by Major Dave Blair of the U.S. Air Force parsed emergent conventions of the global war on terror with the "conventional wisdom" regarding what ought to count as combat. The latter he called the "concept of 'combat risk,'" a model that defines "combat" narrowly to describe situations wherein "lives [are] at stake in the face of enemy fire" (p. 62). Against the notion of face-to-face physical risk as the primary requisite for combat recognition, Blair proposed the concept of "combat responsibility" as a more fitting rubric for determining combat versus non-combat roles:

> An individual holds combat responsibility if his or her choices may directly result in the saving of friendly lives or the taking of enemy lives. In other words, if individuals immediately cue, fire, or guide weapons or if they are directly entrusted with the lives of Soldiers, Sailors, Airmen, or Marines going into harm's way, then they are in combat.
>
> (p. 64)

Flattening the distinction between drone pilots and soldiers on the ground was the fact that each engage with the enemy at one causal remove, insofar as they both "cue, fire, or guide" their weapons against their respective targets. Whether separated by 10 inches, 10,000 feet, or 10,000 miles, under the aegis of combat responsibility the decisive attributes of combat are not spatial and physical but causal and temporal.

Though Blair's argument focused on redefining combat in such a way that drone operators could qualify as combatants and, by extension, be eligible for combat awards, implicit in his argument for "combat responsibility" was the notion that combat medals should valorize responsible rather than overtly risky combat. This line of argument was made explicit in August in an essay by Jamie Holmes (2013) of the Future Tense project that argued a medal for drone operation could "help address, rather than exacerbate, a popular concern: that drones diminish accountability." Rather than emphasize the causal role of drone operators in combat, as Blair had, Holmes argued that the DWM would provide a means by which to codify morality into the standards for drone combat. After all, Holmes asked, "Don't we want drone pilots to be aware of their great responsibilities and to be rewarded for exercising them honorably?"

In the post-9/11 era, the new reality and responsibility theses argued, leading-edge technologies like aerial drones and cyber-defense systems precipitated the need for a more expansive combat morality that would duly reward the non-valorous labor of the military *avant-garde*. The high order of precedence given the DWM was at once a reaction to and symbol for the waning use-value of traditional notions of valor in contemporary U.S. warfare.

Anti-DWM Arguments: In Defense of Valor

Even though anti-DWM arguments were considerably more common and made more frequently than those in favor of the DWM, the central claims of anti-DWM arguments can be reduced to two main critiques.

First, *the devaluation critique*: The DWM's proposed order of precedence effectively devalued the economy of honor. This line of argument issued from both leaders of veterans' groups and members of Congress. These critiques acknowledged the new reality thesis and even assented to the argument for a drone operator medal, but they outright rejected the notion that such a medal should receive honorific priority over medals awarded to soldiers who risked their bodies on the battlefield.

One day after the DWM announcement, John E. Hamilton (2013), national commander of the Veterans of Foreign Wars, said "The VFW fully concurs that those far from the fight are having an immediate impact on the battlefield in real-time, but medals that can only be earned in direct combat must mean more than medals awarded in the rear." On February 15, the Military Order of the Purple Heart (2013) argued:

> To rank what is basically an award for meritorious service higher than any award for heroism is degrading and insulting to every American Combat Soldier, Airman, Sailor or Marine who risks his or her life and endures the daily rigors of combat in a hostile environment.

Accordingly, the Order urged the DoD to "reconsider the precedence of the Distinguished Warfare Medal or develop another way to recognize the achievements" of drone and cyber warriors.

The devaluation critique was taken up in late February and early March by Congress members and adapted into legislative proposals in both chambers. In a letter (Office, 2013) sent to Hagel, the Senate bill sponsors intoned, "While we support the Defense Department's decision to authorize a new decoration . . . as a way to recognize silent warriors, such as drone pilots and cyber warriors, we adamantly oppose the decision to elevate the award above those earned in direct combat."

Second, *the WTF critique*: The very idea of a medal for drone operators is absurd. Announcement of the medal and its order of precedence elicited, as one writer at *Stripes.com* called it, "an avalanche of Whiskey Tango Foxtrots" in the military community (Hlad, 2013). Anger and confusion over the DWM led some to invent alternative names and designs thought to better reflect the form and purpose of the DWM. Highlights include the "Purple Buttocks" award, the "geek cross," the "Distinguished Joystick Award," and the "Nintendo Medal." One commonly circulated visual mockup for the award displayed a golden X-Box controller suspended from a Distinguished Flying Cross ribbon (MOTHAX, 2013). Common to each oppositional iteration of the DWM was a biting sarcasm that simultaneously diminished the role of the drone operator and parodied the authority of the DoD to mint medals on a whim. At a deeper level, this line of argument exhibited a familiar anxiety over the role of remote technologies in modern warfare (see Mitchell, 2001, pp. 125–127).

Together, the devaluation and WTF critiques called into question the wisdom of altering the United States' honor economy to accommodate the new reality of responsibilized combat. While acknowledging the value of the drone operator's supporting role in combat operations, the DWM's many critics reasserted the rubric of traditional combat morality – premised on immediate and embodied risk – as a means to diminish the relative value of "non-valorous," or dis-embodied, combat.

Conclusion

On March 12, less than a month after the medal was announced, Hagel appeased critics by declaring that the DWM would be placed under review by the Joint Chiefs of Staff (Lyle, 2013). In an April 15th memo reporting on the committee's findings, Hagel (2013b) suggested that "misconceptions regarding the precedence of the award were distracting from its original purpose," and so the committee "recommended the creation of a new distinguishing device that can be affixed to existing medals to recognize the extraordinary actions of this small number of men and women." Thus, the Distinguished Warfare Medal was demoted, no longer distinguished but "distinguishing," no longer a medal but a "device"– loose change in the military's economy of honor.

To date, no such device has been created. Drone labor remains a dull, dirty, and dangerous affair, with scant hope for redemption through public recognition. Still, the Pentagon's response to the controversy offers much to argument scholars interested in the strategic maneuverings of government policy – here, military policy in the war on terror. Specifically, Hagel's argument that the DWM was revoked due to "misconceptions" – a lack of understanding on the part of the DWM's critics – reads less as a concession of defeat than a strategic refusal to continue engaging publicly with unreasonable interlocutors. Neither the new reality nor the responsibility theses were disavowed. The lesson learned at the Pentagon must have been this: With regard to remote warfare, when responsibility rather than valor is at a premium, less publicity is better publicity. Thus it appears that the DWM – a heroic currency for a post-valorous age – was designed for the very audience that ultimately rejected it.

References

Blair, Maj. D. (2012). Ten thousand feet and ten thousand miles: Reconciling our Air Force culture to remotely piloted aircraft and the new nature of aerial combat. *Air & Space Power Journal, 26,* 3, 61–69.

Clemmer, Maj. B. A. (2011). Challenges for this kind of war: Modifying army awards for a new century of conflict. *School of Advanced Military Studies*. Retrieved from http://www.hsdl.org/?view&did=698573

Cummings, M. L., Mastracchio, C., Thornburg, K. M., & Mkrtchyan, A. (2012). Boredom and distraction in multiple unmanned vehicle supervisory control. *Mit.edu*. Retrieved from http://web.mit.edu/aeroastro/labs/halab/papers/BoredomDistraction_SEP2012.pdf

Dao, J. (2013, February 23). Drone pilots are found to get stress disorders much as those in combat do. *New York Times*. Retrieved from http://www.nytimes.com/2013/02/23/us/drone-pilots-found-to-get-stress-disorders-much-as-those-in-combat-do.html?_r=0

Goodnight, G. T. (1991). Controversy. In D. W. Parson (Ed.), *Argument in Controversy: Proceedings of the Seventh SCA/AFA Conference on Argumentation* (pp. 1–13). Annandale, VA: Speech Communication Association.

Hagel, C. (2013a, March 7). Letter to Pat Toomey. Retrieved from www.stripes.com/polopoly_fs/1. . ./Hagel%20Drone%20Medal.pdf

Hagel, C. (2013b, April 15). Statement by Secretary of Defense Chuck Hagel on the Distinguished Warfare Medal [Press release]. Retrieved from http://www.defense.gov/releases/release.aspx?releaseid=15934

Hart, C. S. (2010). *Assessing the impact of low workload in supervisory control of networked unmanned vehicles* (Master's thesis). Retrieved from http://web.mit.edu/aeroastro/labs/halab/papers/Hart-Thesis-2010.pdf

Hlad, J. (2013). Troops use humor to disparage new medal. *Stripes.com*. Retrieved from http://www.stripes.com/blogs/stripes-central/stripes-central-1.8040/troops-use-humor-to-disparage-new-medal-1.208114

Holmes, J. (2012, August 2). Why drone pilots deserve medals. *Slate.com*. Retrieved from http://www.slate.com/articles/technology/future_tense/2012/08/drone_pilots_deserve_military_medals.html

Hurwitz, E. S. (2013). Drone pilots: "Overpaid, underworked, and bored." *MotherJones.com*. Retrieved from http://www.motherjones.com/politics/2013/06/drone-pilots-reaper-photo-essay

International Human Rights and Conflict Resolution Clinic at Stanford Law School, Global Justice Clinic at NYU School of Law. (2012). *Living under drones: Death, injury, and trauma to civilians from US drone practices in Pakistan*. Retrieved from http://livingunderdrones.org/wp-content/uploads/2012/10/Stanford-NYU-LIVING-UNDER-DRONES.pdf

Lyle, Amaani. (2013, March 12). Hagel directs review of distinguished warfare medal. *Defense.gov*. Retrieved from http://www.defense.gov/News/NewsArticle.aspx?ID=119507

Mitchell, G. R. (2001). Placebo defense: Operation Desert Mirage? The rhetoric of Patriot missile accuracy in the 1991 Persian Gulf War. *Quarterly Journal of Speech*, 86, 2, 121–145.

Mitchell, G. R. (2009). Higher-order strategic maneuvering in argumentation. *Argumentation*, 24, 319–335.

Military Order of the Purple Heart. (2013, February 15). Military Order of the Purple Heart opposes precedence of new Defense medal [Press release]. *Purpleheart.org*. Retrieved from http://www.purpleheart.org/News.aspx?Identity=238

MOTHAX. (2013). About that new "Distinguished Warfare Medal" for drone pilots. *Burnpit.legion.org*. Retrieved from http://burnpit.legion.org/2013/02/about-new-distinguished-warfare-medal-drone-pilots

Obama, B. (2011, September 30). Remarks by the President at the "change of office" Chairman of the Joint Chiefs of Staff Ceremony. *Whitehouse.gov*. Retrieved from http://www.whitehouse.gov/the-press-office/2011/09/30/remarks-president-change-office-chairman-joint-chiefs-staff-ceremony

Obama, B. (2012, January 5). Remarks by the President on the Defense Strategic Review. *Whitehouse.gov*. Retrieved from http://www.whitehouse.gov/photos-and-video/video/2012/01/05/president-obama-speaks-defense-strategic-review#transcript

Panetta, L. (2013a, February 13). Distinguished warfare medal [Memorandum]. *Defense.gov*. Retrieved from http://www.defense.gov/news/distinguishedwarfaremedalmemo.pdf

Panetta, L. (2013b, February 14). Defense Secretary Panetta remarks [Video]. *Defense.gov*. Retrieved from http://www.c-spanvideo.org/program/310984-1

Office of Joe Manchin. (2013, March 8). Manchin, Rockefeller bipartisan group protect rank of Purple Heart, Bronze Star [Press release]. Retrieved from http://www.manchin.senate.gov/public/index.cfm/2013/3/manchin-rockefeller-bipartisan-group-protect-rank-of-purple-heart-bronze-star

Tice, Captain B. P. (1991, Spring). Unmanned aerial vehicles: The force multiplier of the 1990s. *Airpower Journal*. Retrieved from http://www.airpower.au.af.mil/airchronicles/apj/apj91/spr91/4spr91.htm

U.S. Department of Defense. (2013, February 13). DOD announces the Distinguished Warfare Medal [Press release]. Retrieved from http://www.defense.gov/releases/release.aspx?releaseid=15817

Veterans of Foreign Wars. (2013, February 14). VFW wants new medal ranking lowered [Press release]. *VFW.org*. Retrieved from http://www.vfw.org/News-and-Events/Articles/2013-Articles/VFW-WANTS-NEW-MEDAL-RANKING-LOWERED/

53

MOTHERLY INSTINCT

Disturbing the demarcation of expertise

Lauren Archer

UNIVERSITY OF WASHINGTON, USA

Experts rely on communication to convey their specialized information to non-specialists. Around public issues, when experts often must compete with other experts for recognition, rhetoric and argumentation offer important tools for persuading listeners to pay attention. First surfacing in 1998, the autism vaccine controversy (hereafter AVC) highlights issues of expertise in public deliberation. The debate over a purported connection between childhood vaccines and autism brings scientific and medical experts into conversation with parents of autistic children, parents who claim an experience-based expertise of their own. While scientific research has failed to find evidence supporting a causal link between vaccination and the onset of autism, anecdotal evidence from parents reporting their experiences continues to circulate, keeping the issue alive in the public sphere.

Whidden (2012) noted a recent rise in discourse that frames motherhood as a type of expertise. She stated:

> Nowhere is this phenomenon of maternal expertise clearer than in the MMR-autism controversy in which a number of celebrities join other mothers to advance the idea that a mother's personal experience with her child is stronger evidence than research validated by the standards of the technical sphere.
>
> *(p. 251)*

Advocacy rhetoric represents the most vocal aspect of this mother-as-expert discourse, and celebrity Jenny McCarthy has become one of the most widely recognized parents contributing to such discourses (Greenfield, 2010; Shapiro, 2011; "There Isn't," 2011).

In this essay, I explore the rhetorical strategies used to declare the experience of motherhood as a disruption of traditional claims of expertise based on scientific evidence and technical arguments. My analysis centers on McCarthy's advocacy work, exploring her establishment of "motherly instinct" (p. 159) as a form of expertise on par with, and in ways superior to, the expertise of medical practitioners and scientific researchers. I argue that the narrative in McCarthy's (2007) book, *Louder Than Words*, aimed to establish the validity of her motherly instinct, as bodily experienced, as a means of knowing that challenges and potentially disrupts the hierarchy of expertise in the modern world.

I analyze how McCarthy (2007) promoted maternal instinct, first by establishing its strength and then by demonstrating its reliability as a means for decision making. She did this by recounting events in which her embodied experience – what she termed a reaction by her instincts or "motherly gut" (p. 67) – aided her in knowing what was happening with her son. Using these experiences as evidence and her gut as the warrant, McCarthy built what might be termed an argument *ad intestinum* (thanks to Leah Ceccarelli for her suggestion of this term). McCarthy used this argument to present her case that mother (not doctor) knows best, presenting motherly instinct as an epistemological challenge to science. I end with a brief discussion of what this case study offers in terms of understanding the role of experience-based expert discourses in public debates over the claims of medical science.

A Rhetorical Perspective on Expertise

In *The Rhetoric of Expertise*, Hartelius (2010) made a case for a rhetorical perspective on expertise, a point of view that recognizes that expertise comes from more than technical expertise. Without embracing a rhetorical perspective per se, other scholars have similarly discussed the importance of recognizing experience-based expertise in addition to technical expertise. Wynne (1989) argued for acknowledging the expertise associated with local knowledge that comes from spending a significant amount of time in a particular region or completing a particular task. He claimed such knowledge should be considered a type of expertise even though it is not gleaned from technical training. Similarly, Collins and Evans (2007) argued that a person without technical training in a particular domain could develop "interactionary expertise" (an ability to understand and participate in the discourse of that domain) as a result of extended exposure (p. 30). Additionally, Collins and Evans claimed judgments of expertise should be based not just on technical credentials, but also on experience (p. 68).

While these views recognize the specialized knowledge that comes from exposure and practice, Hartelius (2010) enlarged this embrace of experience-based expertise by noting the expertise that comes from having access to an embodied moment that not all share (p. 123). Experiencing such moments creates expertise because, as Hartelius explained, "Being an expert means having the right to a certain chunk of human experience. It means one's version of that experience is recognized as authentic, one's perspective is acknowledged and believed" (p. 14). The witness to a historical event and the patient suffering from a disease (two examples that Hartelius explored in her book) represent experts because they can bear witness to a lived moment that others cannot. McCarthy grounded her own expertise in this type of lived experience, arguing for the epistemological validity of motherly instinct by offering up moments of her embodied experience as evidence. Her expertise regarding her son comes not from the extended time she has spent with him or the skills she has developed in caring for him, but from a bodily connection she has with him because she is his mother.

Establishing the Existence of Motherly Instinct

McCarthy first engaged the vaccine issue in her 2007 book, *Louder Than Words: A Mother's Journey in Healing Autism*. In the book, McCarthy wove a narrative that leads readers through her experience of learning that something was wrong with her son Evan, through a long diagnosis process to conclude that he was autistic, and through a frustrating treatment period that slowly allowed Evan to make progress. Throughout the book, McCarthy juxtaposed her own maternal instinct with the knowledge and efforts of the medical establishment in responding to her son's health problems. Through this juxtaposition, she portrayed her own knowledge as not just on par with the technical training of medical professionals but as superior to it. McCarthy built this argument through a highly descriptive narrative that illustrated the bodily experience of her motherly gut to demonstrate how it allows her to be more in tune with her son than the doctors treating him while showing how often the medical complex falls short in effectively helping her son. McCarthy's gut not only lets her know when something is amiss with her child, but also provides a means for evaluating the information presented by various medical experts. Offering these events as evidence, McCarthy constructed an argument *ad intestinum* that attempted to establish the epistemological superiority of her motherly gut as compared to the science-based research and medical treatments offered by traditional Western medicine.

McCarthy (2007) began her argument for the unique perspective her maternal instinct offers with the opening line of her story. She recounted, "The moment I opened my eyes that morning, I had an uncomfortable feeling. It was as if my soul had the flu" (p. 1). She then explained why her soul felt that way, telling the story of finding Evan having a seizure. According to her story, her own physical symptoms increased as she got closer to Evan, and through her highly detailed account, she showed readers what her concern, fear, and panic felt like. With this opening anecdote, McCarthy established not only the existence but also the strength of her connection to her son and her ability to know, in her soul, when something is wrong with him. This connection defines the core of her maternal instinct.

McCarthy (2007) continued to demonstrate the power of this connection to her son, recounting a time when, while working on the road, she became physically ill at the same moment that her son was having a seizure in another location. McCarthy stressed her bodily experience when relating the event:

> Less than five minutes into working, my heart started beating unusually fast. I began to feel dizzy and became very nauseated. I had never felt anything like this before … I looked up at my sister Joanne, who was with me, and said, "Something is wrong with Evan. I know it. I feel it."
>
> *(p. 132)*

McCarthy immediately called home and discovered that Evan was having a seizure. Despite the distance, the strength of her connection to her child – her motherly instinct – allowed her to know something was wrong. Even McCarthy expressed a bit of initial incredulity:

> I couldn't believe I was physically feeling what he was feeling. I've heard about moms knowing something is wrong with their children when they are far away from them, but I had never felt it before. It was and is very real.
>
> *(p. 132)*

Through each anecdote, McCarthy further constructed an argument that motherly instinct is something real, even if beyond logical explanation, and that it offers insights beyond what any doctor can learn in a book. While she may not be able to explain how or why it works, she made a case for recognizing its power by not just telling readers about it but by demonstrating this instinct at work. McCarthy referred to this connection as her "motherly instinct" (pp. 20, 30, 40, 49, 53, 159), "mommy radar" (p. 81), "motherly gut" (pp. 30, 49, 67), and "emotional guidance system" (pp. 30, 40, 65, 83), but her argument remained the same – it allowed her to know things about her son that no one else was able to discern.

Establishing the Superiority of Motherly Instinct

In contrast to the strength of McCarthy's motherly instinct, most medical practitioners that McCarthy encountered seem ill-equipped to effectively care for Evan. Regarding one of their hospital stays, McCarthy (2007) remarked, "This was supposed to be a well-respected hospital, and I felt like we were in a Third World country, being cared for by 13 year olds" (p. 23). This comment underscored how inadequate the medical establishment proved itself to be. McCarthy's less than positive view of the medical establishment came through in various ways, such as when she referred to doctors as "poking" and "pinching" as if they were not quite sure what to do (p. 6). She repeatedly referred to one of the neurologists as "brain-dead" (pp. 40, 47, 52), and she made clear how illogical the recommended treatments seemed, such as when the hospital decided to treat Evan for meningitis even though the test results were negative (p. 8). When not critiquing medical practitioners for being incompetent, McCarthy critiqued them for being absent. During another seizure episode, McCarthy expressed her anger at having to wait over a day to see a neurologist, despite the fact that her son kept having seizures (pp. 25–26).

McCarthy's (2007) argument came full circle when she juxtaposed her own motherly instinct with these shortcomings, such as when McCarthy discussed the second time Evan started seizing. McCarthy described herself as standing with a group of doctors, answering a list of questions she had already answered. Although surrounded by a number of highly trained medical practitioners, it is McCarthy who first noticed that her son was having another seizure (p. 19). During this same incident, these doctors (who happened to be interns) decided to run a test for meningitis – an invasive test that Evan had just undergone three weeks earlier, with negative results. McCarthy stated, "I felt like everyone was looking in all the wrong directions. I've always had very good instincts, and I knew the interns weren't going to find anything" (p. 19).

McCarthy (2007) similarly relied on her motherly instinct as a means for evaluating the information and advice offered by doctors. Initially doctors diagnosed Evan as epileptic. McCarthy told readers about hearing the diagnosis:

> I sat back and felt relieved to have a label I could hold on to – something I could research and learn about. My relief lasted only a second, though. My emotional guidance system didn't agree. I blurted out, "That just doesn't seem right. Other doctors from the last hospital said that epilepsy usually runs on one side of the family. That's why everyone kept asking me that question over and over again. It feels like we're missing something." Honestly it was my maternal gut instinct that epilepsy was not the end of this road.
>
> *(p. 30)*

Readers learn later that this diagnosis was wrong. Evan was not epileptic; he was autistic (with which seizures are sometimes associated). Thus, readers see McCarthy's gut feeling validated, adding to its persuasive potential. Furthermore, upon finally hearing the autism diagnosis, McCarthy recalled instinctually knowing that it was right, even though she did not want to believe it (p. 65). Her motherly instinct enabled her to evaluate and accept the correct diagnosis.

McCarthy (2007) also conveyed her motherly instinct as providing a way of knowing which treatments to try. During one exchange about switching medications, "The doctor said, 'You need to relax and trust me.' I did trust him. My motherly gut said, 'Trust this man,' so I planned on doing everything he said" (p. 67). Her gut did not rest though, so that even when discussing treatment options with doctors she trusted, McCarthy still relied on her motherly gut to guide her, which sometimes meant rejecting the recommended treatment and creating her own approach (p. 139). Given Evan's progress, the reader is led to believe that McCarthy made the right choices – guided by her motherly gut – to heal her son.

Through recounting each of these experiences and offering them as evidence, McCarthy (2007) argued for trusting one's motherly instinct as a means for making evaluations of technical medical information. She claimed that this instinct enabled her to determine which diagnosis was right or which treatments were appropriate. McCarthy did not ignore technical information; in fact, she was quite fond of doing her own research at the "University of Google" (p. 166). However, McCarthy ultimately relied on her motherly gut – that feeling she got, that embodied experience – to guide her in knowing which experts to trust, which diagnoses to believe, and which treatments to pursue. Furthermore McCarthy argued for all mothers to utilize this powerful tool. In the appendix, McCarthy encouraged readers to consult a pediatrician, but she also argued, "Most important, trust your instincts, and if something doesn't feel right, ask questions" (p. 195). By offering motherly instinct as a reliable means of evaluating scientific knowledge, McCarthy's argument potentially disrupts the hierarchy of expertise itself by positing motherhood as a type of expertise and the motherly gut as an epistemological guidance system that provides the necessary knowledge to sit in judgment of, not deference to, medical experts.

Discussion

From a theoretical perspective, it is not difficult to assess the limitations of McCarthy's argument *ad intestinum*. If classified as an argument by example, McCarthy offered only her own experience and thus fails to provide a sufficient number of examples to support her claim that mothers should trust their gut instincts. Alternatively, one might consider McCarthy's case an argument by sign, but then it fails because alternative explanations exist for the seemingly supernatural connection McCarthy claims to have with her son. Although McCarthy's argument does not present much of a challenge to argumentation scholars seeking to critique it, an issue arises when engaging in discussion with someone making such an argument, such as in public discussions surrounding the AVC. How does one respond in public to an argument based primarily on embodied experiences? Are there any responses available that do not devolve into the realm of *ad hominem* attacks? After all, as Hartelius (2010) pointed out, people making such arguments represent experts because "they know what an experience *feels* like . . . reporting on one's own experience does not require special training" (pp. 117–118). At the same time, the evidence offered – the embodied experience – is unverifiable because no one else can attest to exactly what that experience was like for that body. Although everyone may have the ability to communicate these experiences, when such experiences become the basis of advocacy discourse, a conundrum arises because they are not open to being tested by others.

Brody (2013) tackled this question when responding to an argument from Leon Kass, a bioethicist who argued against human cloning based on an instinctual knowledge that pursuing such technology is undesirable. In much the same way that McCarthy offered her motherly gut as the grounds for her argument, Kass presented one's gut as a means for making ethical decisions regarding technology. Brody claimed Kass's argument fails because it possesses an *ad hominem* quality by offering no reasonable means for responding without dismissing someone else's feelings and by implying that anyone who has a different gut reaction is less sensitive to the moral ill of the issue under consideration.

While Brody makes a valid point about the deliberative dilemma posed by the argument *ad intestinum*, I would argue there is something more at play here. For McCarthy at least, the argument is not one that forces all people without the gut feeling to find it or admit their lack of sensitivity. Rather, it establishes the uniqueness of mothers in their possession of this sixth sense. McCarthy made it clear that Evan's father lacks this instinct, just as the doctors fail to have it. Thus, McCarthy's argument seems aimed at establishing this type of expertise in mothers and making a case for its legitimacy. By demonstrating the power of her motherly gut through her narrative, McCarthy created space for mothers to make arguments *ad intestinum* as a means for challenging scientific or medical authority.

As an experience-based expertise that grounds itself in embodied moments, the maternally inflected argument *ad intestinum* presents an argumentative challenge. Other types of experience-based expertise develop through long-term exposure or practice resulting in unique knowledge or skills. In these cases, claims to expertise can be countered by considering the amount or relevance of the experience. However, argumentative claims based on a mother's gut feelings leave little room for such counterarguments. While theoretically the limitations of such arguments may be clear, in public debate one declaring such maternally-inflected arguments *ad intestinum* logically flawed risks being construed as arrogantly dismissing a mother's bond with her child. Those engaging with such arguments in public discourse will need to consider carefully how to respond to claims of motherly expertise without resorting (purposely or not) to ad hominem attacks.

References

Brody, H. (2013). Bioethics, economism, and the rhetoric of technological innovation. In M. J. Hyde & J. Herrick (Eds.), *After the genome: A language for our biotechnological future* (pp. 177–191). Waco, TX: Baylor University Press.

Collins, H., & Evans, R. (2007). *Rethinking expertise.* Chicago, IL: University of Chicago Press.

There isn't enough science in the world to debunk anti-vaccine quackery for some people [Editorial]. (2011, January 17). *NY Daily News.* Retrieved from http://www.nydailynews.com/opinion/science-world-debunk-anti-vaccine-quackery-people-article-1.154665

Greenfeld, K. T. (2010, February 25). The autism debate: Who's afraid of Jenny McCarthy? *Time.* Retrieved from http://content.time.com/time/magazine/article/0,9171,1968100,00.html

Hartelius, E. J. (2010). *The rhetoric of expertise.* Lanham, MD: Lexington Books.

McCarthy, J. (2007). *Louder than words: A mother's journey in healing autism.* New York, NY: Dutton.

Shapiro, N. (2011, June 14). The anti-vaccine epidemic. *Seattle Weekly.* Retrieved from http://www.seattleweekly.com/2011–06-15/news/the-anti-vaccine-epidemic

Whidden, R. A. (2012). Maternal expertise, vaccination recommendations, and the complexity of argument spheres. *Argumentation and Advocacy, 48*(4), 243–257.

Wynne, B. (1989). Sheepfarming after Chernobyl: A case study in communicating scientific information. *Environment, 31*(2), 10–15, 33–39.

54

SCIENTIFIC COUNTERPUBLICS

In defense of the environmental scientist as public intellectual

Brett Bricker

UNIVERSITY OF KANSAS, USA

The environmental and health effects of stratospheric ozone depletion emerged as an issue of public concern in the United States in the early 1970s. Not surprisingly, "the initial public debate was polarized between those who predicted catastrophe and those who thought" that predictions of the threat to human health were "absurd" (Morrisette, 1989, p. 803). A range of voices debated the link between chlorofluorocarbons (CFCs) and ozone depletion and argued about regulation. Manufacturers of CFCs "opposed any effort to regulate" (Morrisette, 1989, p. 803); they claimed there was insufficient evidence to be certain that humans were negatively influencing the stratosphere. In opposition, a majority of the public was concerned with the effects of a growing ozone hole (Morrisette, 1989, p. 804). Politicians were torn between two powerful constituencies – a general population fearful of the harmful effects of CFC pollution and an influential group of businesses opposing costly regulations.

A corps of scientists, led by Frank Sherwood Rowland and Mario Molina, believed that regulation of harmful substances was necessary to reverse the growth of the ozone hole. Rowland and Molina dedicated themselves to making these concerns public by founding the Task Force on Inadvertent Modification of the Stratosphere to "develop a coordinated plan of action for federal agencies" (Morrisette, 1989, p. 804). These efforts were successful. In December 1978, the Environmental Protection Agency banned the nonessential use of CFCs. Ten years later, the Montreal Protocol, an international treaty designed to limit ozone depletion, was implemented. Compared to other environmental problems, the speed and scope of the response to ozone depletion was remarkable.

I argue that environmental scientists who made their findings public played a critical role in convincing the government to regulate CFCs. These scientists functioned as counterpublic intellectuals: by standing in opposition to a public of well funded and powerful industrial lobbyists, by constituting public discourse through task forces and government testimony, and by rhetorically participating in multiple (scientific and lay) publics.

Locating Counterpublicity

Contemporary public sphere theory can be traced to the influential works of Jürgen Habermas. For Habermas (1989) the public sphere was a single realm founded on the "principle of universal access" (p. 85) that challenged the power of the state through formation of public opinion. Each individual, given certain educational and financial privileges, was able to make private interests public through "rational-critical debate" (pp. 142, 178). Importantly, Habermas did not concern himself with identity differences of members within the public sphere and instead assumed that "general interest" (p. 87) applied universally and equally throughout "bourgeois society" (p. 79). Because of these criteria, Habermas's interpretation of the public sphere left little room for competing publics.

In response to Habermas's monolithic definition of public, competing interpretations developed. A decade following the German publication of *Structural Transformation*, Negt and Kluge (1993) popularized the term "proletarian public sphere" as a place where workers can resist "their bourgeois opponent" (p. 93). Negt and Kluge imagined multiple competing publics based on class difference – an important transition in the development of counter-public theory. They characterized the proletarian public as *counter* to bourgeois interests, emphasizing "autonomous communication of the proletariat," "an expression of the self-organization and unfolding interests of the workers," and a "self-defence organization of the working class" (Fuchs, 2011, p. 296). The members of the proletarian public produced counter-ideas, counter-products, and counter-media (Fuchs, 2011, p. 296–297).

Fraser (1990) similarly criticized Habermas for failing to examine "other, nonliberal, nonbourgeois, competing public spheres" (p. 75). She found multiple "counter" (p. 75) civil societies based on exclusions intrinsic to Habermas's conception of publicity. She challenged the "bourgeois, masculinist" (p. 76) conception of Habermas's public sphere – both because of its false claim to universal access and its exclusive reliance on rational-critical discourse. Her criticism of the singular, universally accessible, rational public sphere centered on "the fact that it [was] exclusionary toward subordinated social groups such as women, workers, people of color, and gays and lesbians" (Zuidervaart, 2011, p. 102). Fraser's attention to historically oppressed peoples was foundational to the development of counterpublic theory. But, counterpublicity can be applied to populations that may not face oppression based on race, class, gender, sex, or sexuality.

This extension has already begun. For example, Hess (2010) broke from tradition in his description of scientific minority opinions as "scientific counterpublics" (p. 5). In doing so, he broadened the definition of "subaltern" (p. 3) to include minority opinions in any social field. "Rather than assuming that the counterpublic is limited to a social category marked by race, class, gender, or sexuality as an historically dominated or oppressed social category" (p. 3), Hess found that oppositional counterpublics may also arise in the "problematization of scientific authority" (p. 4). A scientific counterpublic, for Hess, arose when a group of scientists who were "located in subordinate positions in their respective research fields" (p. 4) made their findings public.

Extending Hess's interpretation of scientific counterpublics, I argue that environmental scientists who participated in the ozone debates the 1970s and 1980s constituted an influential counterpublic. Specifically, they performed the "key communication dimensions" (Brouwer, 2006, p. 195) of counterpublicity by:

- expressing opposition to a powerful public – in this instance, influential business interests disseminating anti-science propaganda;

- opening discursive space by making their comments public through task forces and government testimony; and
- rhetorically participating in multiple publics simultaneously – the scientific public demanded by their profession and the lay public demanded by their participation in activities of the public sphere.

Because this public debate pitted powerful industry, with strong ties to media, against a group of scientists who were rhetorically constructed as representing a minority opinion, analyzing scientific public intellectuals' arguments as an example of counterpublic discourse provides important practical and theoretical insights.

Ozone Debates and Policy Formulation

The development of CFC-ozone science was far from public. Rowland and Molina were torn between their scientific commitments and their desire to make their findings public; "recognizing the grave significance of their results, Molina and Rowland waited for the paper to appear before discussing it publicly" (Parson, 2003, p. 31). Even after they published their initial hypothesis tying CFC emissions to ozone destruction in *Nature*, "there was no response from the scientific world" (Royal Society of Chemistry, n.d., p. 2). This was troublesome because, as Rowland (1995) noted, once they "realized that this was not just a scientific question . . . but a potentially grave environmental problem" (para. 21) the need to be heard at higher levels of the government became evident. Rowland and Molina targeted a "strong, hard-working group of postdoctoral and graduate student research associates" to advance their research and build a base of "specialists" (Rowland, 1995, para. 22) that could expose the CFC-ozone link. Fearing that their findings would go unheard, they made their theory "public" (Royal Society of Chemistry, n.d., p. 2) at the American Chemical Society meeting in September 1974. From their research, an international discourse about the link between CFCs and ozone started to circulate. By 1976, the link between CFCs and ozone depletion was confirmed. A "major study" (Mullin, 2002, p. 209) done by the National Academy of Sciences found that six to seven percent of the ozone would soon deplete without further regulation. These two independent findings helped this theory find "wide support" (Masters, 2004, p. 1) in the scientific community.

Rowland, in particular, took an "unusually public stance" ("Obituary," 2012, para. 5) for scientists at the time: attending and speaking at legislative hearings, being the subject of extensive media coverage, and undergoing a "much heavier travel schedule" ("Obituary," 2012, para. 4) than his previously private scientific life demanded. After countless trips from Irvine to Washington, D.C., he became a true "citizen-scientist, in that it seemed to come quite naturally to him to report on the results of his work out in the public sphere" (Shahan, 2012, para. 6). By standing in opposition to the dominant public of the CFC industry, he created the foundation for a counterpublic of environmental public intellectuals.

This epistemic community "drafted documents and reports" and "organized scientific panels" while simultaneously pressuring policy-makers to apply these scientific findings to policies (Haas, 1992, p. 194). In congressional testimony about the Montreal Protocol, Michael McElroy (Ph.D., applied mathematics) and Rowland argued for a substantial reduction of CFC use. The *Boston Globe* covered this testimony, and published particularly accessible quotations. For example, McElroy argued that "there is no longer reason to doubt that industrial gases containing chlorine are responsible in large measure for dramatic, large-scale change in the stratosphere" (as cited in "Even Stronger," 1987, p. 3). In agreement, the article cited Rowland's claim that "we have to reduce emissions drastically and soon" (as cited in "Even Stronger," 1987, p. 3). By using accessible language, testifying at congressional hearings, circulating findings at large international conferences, and publishing bulletins, ozone scientists found "national and international media coverage" (Haas, 1992, p. 194-195). Scientists, in a sense, were speaking two languages. They were asked to simplify their scientific discourse and sacrifice their scientific identity when addressing a lay public. However, this sacrifice was necessary to achieve public influence.

Scientists who "articulated what scientific developments implied for policy" were a "potent political resource" for motivating domestic regulation and encouraging international cooperation for the Montreal Protocol (Haas, 1992, p. 196). Dr. Richard Benedick argued that CFC regulation "couldn't have occurred without" modern scientific methods, models, and projections applied to policy (as cited in Haas, 1992, p. 196). Although their academic background may not have qualified environmental scientists to participate in changing public opinion and drafting environmental policy, many chose to leave the laboratory and join the public discourse.

In the years following the initial reports, the science supporting the CFC-ozone hypothesis was met with extreme skepticism. John Ehrlichman, Nixon's chief of staff, rhetorically constructed Rowland and Molina's scientific findings as inconsistent with the rest of the scientific community. In particular, he argued that the White House was under no obligation to take the findings seriously because scientists themselves disagreed (Mullin, 2002, p. 210). Industrial backlash fed this opposition as well.

E. I. du Pont de Nemours and Company (DuPont) was the "worldwide leading producer and marketer" of CFCs, "controlling over 45% of the CFC market" (Risciotti, 1989, p. 42). DuPont faced the loss of a substantial market share and, thus, publicly opposed domestic environmental regulations and the Montreal Protocol. DuPont engaged the scientific debate, claiming that "no ozone depletion has been detected despite the most sophisticated analysis . . . all ozone depletion figures to date are computer projections based on a series of uncertain assumptions" (as cited in Rowlands, 1995, p. 50). This strategy was well-funded contrarianism; Dupont "spent millions of dollars running full-page newspaper advertisements defending CFCs in 1975, claiming there was no proof that CFCs were harming the ozone layer" (Masters, 2004, p. 2). DuPont's (1975) full-page *New York Times* advertisement stated: "You want the ozone question answered one way or another. So does DuPont . . . Before a valuable industry is hypothesized out of existence, more facts are needed." This statement not only posited DuPont and the larger population on the same side of the debate, but also co-opted the term *hypothesis* that had been consistently repeated by advocates of regulation.

Rowland, in particular, "found himself targeted by a $28-billion-a-year industry" that "spared no effort to rubbish his hypothesis" ("Obituary," 2012, para. 5). Rowland was met by a skeptical public at press conferences and "found himself peppered with hostile questions by industry representatives" in public settings ("Obituary," 2012, para. 5). The industry campaign questioned his sanity and even tied his campaign against CFCs to the Ministry of Disinformation of the KGB ("Obituary," 2012, para. 5). Other scientists, hoping to avoid public criticism, remained silent. Members of the CFC research team at NASA's Goddard laboratory "hoped to chart out a small inconspicuous research project" (Haas, 1992, p. 192) and, according to physicist Richard Stolarski, find a "quiet" area of study where "nobody would bother" them (as cited in Haas, 1992, p. 192).

The community of environmental scientists, circulating a counterpublic discourse in opposition to influential business interests, "prevailed over" (Benedick, 2000, p. 25) disinformation, anti-science propaganda, and hyperbolized claims of economic costs and "were pre-requisites to a political solution" (Benedick, 2000, p. 20). The Montreal Protocol may be the "forerunner" of an important "partnership between scientists and policy makers" as daunting environmental challenges of the 21st century unfold (Benedick, 2000, p. 25). In particular, the role of environmental scientists in the CFC-ozone debates provides an important model for changing public opinion and motivating policy changes to prevent the worst effects of global warming.

Environmental Scientists as Counterpublic Intellectuals

Given the similarities between the ozone debates and contemporary global warming debates, environmental scientists can use the ozone victory as a model for formulating a scientific counterpublic. First, environmental scientists must stand in opposition to public discourse dominated by well-funded industrial interests, conservative media, and exaggerated skepticism. Just as stratospheric ozone scientists formed a community based on shared discourse, contemporary environmental scientists must form a transnational counterpublic based on faith in the scientific method, concern for environmental harm, and the need for progressive environmental regulation. This oppositional stance is necessary, but not sufficient, for influencing public opinion and policy formulation; a more public representation also is needed.

Second, environmental scientists must constitute a public discursive space (Brouwer, 2006, p. 197). Currently, "researchers rarely communicate directly with the public" (Andresen, 2009, p. 9) and may have their goals better served by constitution of a public discourse of (and about) science. In doing so, they should publish in non-scientific disciplines, find alternative media outlets, and infiltrate discursive space dominated by industrial interests. If science is to overcome anti-intellectual biases among the broader public, "it is important that citizens get used to scientists arguing out controversial facts, theories, and issues" in public (Miller, 2001, p. 119). Instead of remaining "backstage," environmental scientists must "become more visible" if the general public, and policy-makers, are going to take their findings more seriously (Miller, 2001, p. 119). This move into the lay public sphere, requiring both sacrifice and vulnerability, means that scientists must participate in multiple competing publics simultaneously – the technical public where findings are produced and the lay public that demands a translation of scientific findings into an accessible vocabulary.

Third, to participate in multiple publics, scientists need to become rhetoricians – using persuasive tactics to represent their findings and convince the broader public and policy-makers of the need for progressive environmental regulation. The time in which science can be isolated "from society is clearly over" (Madsen, 2007, p. 170). Despite the historical, theoretical and practical divisions between scientific and lay discourses, environmental scientists must embrace the challenge posed by the inevitable intersection of the scientific sphere and public spheres and "establish meaningful communication across" these eroding "barriers" (Madsen, 2007, p. 165). To do so, environmental scientists must step out of the comfort of the laboratory and into "both worlds" of science and politics (Madsen, 2007, p. 166). As they do so, there must be recognition that new "demands for proof" and "forms of reasoning" (Goodnight, 1982, p. 219) will require adaptation and translation away from purely scientific discourse.

Understanding scientists as counterpublic serves two functions. First, it highlights the way in which industrial influence on government policy acts as a dominant and marginalizing force. Instead of understanding these forces as two equal publics, exposing the counterpublicity of environmental scientists acknowledges the power differential. Although an argument could be made that the CFC industry also laid discursive claim to counterpublicity, I am skeptical that treating them as such serves the critical project. Instead, taking a cue from Asen (2009) and Brouwer (2006), it may be more beneficial to look at intersections of discourse, materiality, and ideology to determine legitimacy. Second, it enlarges scholarly interpretation of marginalization. Too often, the focus on race, class, gender, sex, and sexuality overlooks other forms of marginalization, like the treatment of scientific opinion in a polity. Although not every marginalized public must be approached as counterpublic, Brouwer's working definition may provide guidance for application of counterpublic research beyond the norm.

References

Andresen, E. (2009). *Rhetoric of global warming: Multimodal arguments in scientific and public contexts.* (Thesis). Retrieved from http://www.wpi.edu/Pubs/E-project/Available/E-project-042909-005136/unrestricted/Rhetoric_of_Global_Warming.pdf

Asen, R. (2009). Ideology, materiality, and counterpublicity: William E. Simon and the rise of a conservative counterintelligentsia. *Quarterly Journal of Speech, 95*(3), 263–288.

Benedick, R. (2000). The improbable Montreal Protocol: Science, diplomacy and defending the ozone layer. *American Meteorological Society.* Retrieved from http://www.ametsoc.org/atmospolicy/documents/Benedickcasestudy_000.pdf

Brouwer, D. (2006). Communication as counterpublic. In G. Shepherd, J. St. John, & T. Striphas (Eds.), *Communication as . . . Perspectives on theory* (pp. 195–208). Thousand Oaks, CA: SAGE.

DuPont. (1975). You want the ozone question answered one way or another. So does DuPont. *New York Times.* Retrieved from LexisNexis

Even stronger protection needed for ozone layer. (1987, October 28). *Boston Globe,* p. 3

Fraser, N. (1990). Rethinking the public sphere: a contribution to the critique of actually existing democracy. *Social Text, 25/26,* 56–80.

Fuchs, C. (2011). *Foundations of critical media and information studies.* New York, NY: Routledge.

Goodnight, G. T. (1982). The personal, technical and public spheres of argument: A speculative inquiry into the art of public deliberation. *Journal of the American Forensic Association, 18,* 214–225.

Haas, P. (1992). Banning chlorofluorocarbons: Epistemic community efforts to protect stratospheric ozone. *International Organization, 46*(1), 187–224.

Habermas, J. (1989). *The structural transformation of the public sphere: An inquiry into a category of bourgeois society.* Cambridge, MA: MIT Press.

Hess, D. (2011). To tell the truth: On scientific counterpublics. *Public Understanding of Science, 20*(5), 627–641.

Madsen, C. (2007). When the dog must talk to the cat – Communicating science to politicians or science and politics – Thoughts about a complex relationship. In A. Heck & L. Houziaux (Eds.), *Future professional communication in astronomy* (pp. 161–170). New York, NY: Springer.

Masters, J. (2004). The skeptics vs. the ozone hole. *Weather Underground.* Retrieved from http://www.lpl.arizona.edu/resources/globalwarming/documents/skeptics-vs-ozone-hole.pdf

Miller, S. (2001). Public understanding of science at the crossroads. *Public Understanding of Science, 10,* 115–120.

Morrisette, P. M. (1989). The evolution of policy responses to stratospheric ozone depletion. *Natural Resources Journal, 29,* 793–820.

Mullin, R. (2002). What can be learned from DuPont and the Freon ban: A case study. *Journal of Business Ethics, 40*(3), 207–218.

Negt, O., & Kluge, A. (1993). *Public sphere and experience: Toward an analysis of the bourgeois and proletarian public sphere.* Minneapolis: University of Minnesota Press.

Obituary of Sherwood Rowland. (2012). *Telegraph.* Retrieved from http://www.telegraph.co.uk/news/obituaries/science-obituaries/9139284/Sherwood-Rowland.html

Parson, E. (2003). *Protecting the ozone layer: Science and strategy.* Oxford, England: Oxford University Press.

Risciotti, C. (1989). *DuPont and the ozone layer issue: Public relations as a source of media coverage.* (Master's Thesis). Retrieved from http://www.udel.edu/communication/web/thesisfiles/risciottithesis.pdf

Rowland, S. F. (1995). F. Sherwood Rowland – Autobiography. *Nobel Prize.* Retrieved from http://www.nobelprize.org/nobel_prizes/chemistry/laureates/1995/rowland-autobio.html#

Rowlands, I. (1995). *The politics of global economic change.* New York, NY: Manchester University Press.

Royal Society of Chemistry. (n.d.). Mario Molina (1943–) information sheet. Retrieved from http://www.rsc.org/learn-chemistry/content/filerepository/CMP/00/000/864/Mario%20Molina%20infromation%20sheet.pdf

Shahan Z. (2012). If the ozone hole were discovered today . . . We'd probably let it fry. *Planet Save.* Retrieved from http://planetsave.com/2012/03/20/if-the-ozone-hole-were-discovered-today-wed-probably-let-it-fry-us/

Zuidervaart, L. (2011). *Art in public: Politics, economics, and a democratic culture.* New York, NY: Cambridge University Press.

55

IGNORANCE, LESBIANS, AND MEDICINE

Disturbing the messages of safer sex

Valeria Fabj

LYNN UNIVERSITY, USA

Plenty of evidence demonstrates that lesbians are not immune to HIV. When the Lesbian AIDS project began in 1992 in New York City, "It started with a caseload of 30 women and by the end of two years had jumped to 400 HIV positive lesbians. Currently the Lesbian AIDS project serves more than 1,000 HIV positive lesbians" (Mbondgulo, 2009). In fact, from the early years of the pandemic, groups like the ACT UP/NY Women and AIDS Book Group (1990) called for lesbians to engage in safer sex practices to protect themselves from HIV and AIDS; their mantra was "It's not who you are that puts you at risk, it's what you do" (p. 114). More than two decades have passed since then and yet messages about the importance of using safer sex practices still are not reaching lesbians, many of whom consider themselves at very low or no risk of contracting HIV due in large measure to authoritative messages that drastically minimize the risks. This essay looks at the construction of safer sex narratives and the continuing assumption that lesbians do not need to take measures to protect themselves from HIV/AIDS unless they use injection drugs or have sex with men. Specifically, it looks at the ways in which even the most well-intentioned safer sex messages are disturbed by the argument strategies that have been used to reach what are considered high risk populations, but have the regretful side effect of deflecting the awareness of risk for lesbians.

Ignorance as Purposeful Deflection

To better understand the disturbance created by contradictory messages about low-risk groups and high-risk behaviors, this essay draws on Nancy Tuana's discussion of the relationship between knowledge and ignorance. Tuana (2006) explained:

> If we are to fully understand the complex practices of knowledge production and the variety of factors that account for why something is known, we must also understand the practices that account for not knowing, that is, for our lack of

knowledge about a phenomenon or, in some cases, an account of the practices that resulted in a group unlearning what was once a realm of knowledge.

(p. 1)

Medical research has made great strides in understanding HIV and HIV transmission since the beginning of the pandemic. Thus, it follows that lack of knowledge about woman-to-woman transmission must be the result of the choice to ignore this population and render it invisible.

Tuana (2006) also called for the contextualization of ignorance:

We need the ability partially to translate practices of ignorance among very different – and power-differentiated – communities. Ignorance, like knowledge, is situated. Understanding the various manifestations of ignorance and how they intersect with power requires attention to the permutations of ignorance in its different contexts.

(p. 3)

The next three sections of this essay highlight how the construction of ignorance serves as the foundation for arguments that disturb the awareness of risk among the lesbian population. These arguments include: 1) There is no evidence of HIV transmission among lesbians, therefore lesbians must be a low risk population. 2) Lack of knowledge about the nature of lesbian sex implies that concern about HIV transmission is not warranted. 3) The needs of high-risk groups justify the erasure of this population as the target of safer sex messages. These arguments are particularly troubling given that traditionally public health warnings are driven by political considerations in addition to scientific research, thus necessitating safety measures even when risk of transmission is suspected and not confirmed.

The Perception/Deception of Low Risk

When trying to understand the risks of contagion, many people rely on the reports of the Centers for Disease Control and Prevention (CDC). The CDC (2006) webpage on HIV/AIDS among women who have sex with women (WSW) opens with the following statement:

To date, there are no confirmed cases of female-to-female sexual transmission of HIV in the United States database (K. McDavid, CDC, oral communication, March 2005). However, case reports of female-to-female transmission of HIV and the well-documented risk of female-to-male transmission indicate that vaginal secretions and menstrual blood are potentially infectious and that mucous membrane (for example, oral, vaginal) exposure to these secretions has the potential to lead to HIV infection.

The page provides statistics that further minimize the problem by summarizing a 2004 study that stated that only a small minority of women infected with HIV reported having sex with women (7,381 out of 246,461). Of these, 534 reported having sex only with women but 91% had other risk factors (such as injection drug use). The minimization of the risk was overt: "As of December 2004, none of these investigations had confirmed female-to-female HIV transmission, either because other risk factors were later identified or because some women declined to be interviewed" (Centers for Disease Control and Prevention, 2006). The narrative continues:

A study of more than 1 million female blood donors found no HIV-infected women whose only risk factor was sex with women. Despite the absence of confirmed cases of female-to-female transmission of HIV, the findings do not negate the possibility. Information on whether a woman had sex with women is missing in more than 60% of the 246,461 case reports – possibly because the physician did not ask or the woman did not volunteer the information.

(Centers for Disease Control and Prevention, 2006)

Not until the bottom of the page is advice on prevention found. However, even this advice is previewed by the statement: "Although there are no confirmed cases of female-to-female transmission of HIV, female sexual contact should be considered a possible means of transmission among WSW" (Centers for Disease Control and Prevention, 2006). Therefore, three-quarters of the page is dedicated to stressing the low risk of transmission among WSW.

The argument that ignorance about HIV transmission among WSW is evidence that transmission is unlikely stems from the misleading data collection practices of the CDC. In fact, the CDC follows a hierarchy of risks, so that if someone belongs to a high-risk group, she or he automatically is categorized as having contracted the disease through such a risk factor (Kwakwa & Ghobrial, 2003). For example, lesbians who have, at some point, had sex with men are categorized under the heterosexual label because transmission from man to woman is considered at a higher risk than transmission from woman to woman. The same is true for women who have used injection drugs. No consideration is given to the fact that a long time might have passed between behavior and infection. Thus, a lesbian who had sex with a man or used injection drugs 30 years ago is considered to have contracted HIV through those behaviors even though it is highly unlikely that the virus would have remained dormant for all those years. Any woman who had sex with a man after 1978 is considered heterosexual (as far as risk factor). Furthermore, the CDC does not have an exposure category for sex between women when tracking HIV infection, so that self-reports of sex between women are categorized as "other." Such a choice of categorization is not politically neutral; it changes the terms of the debate:

While it is true that HIV transmission between women is likely to be low when compared to other population groups such as gay men, not including it has the effect of ensuring that there are no reliable statistics on the actual number of HIV cases that can be attributed to female-to-female transmission. This helps to sustain beliefs that lesbians are not at risk of HIV through sex with women.

(Power, McNair, & Carr, 2009, p. 68)

The result is that the CDC's message disrupts the notion of woman-to-woman transmission of HIV, constructing ignorance about its risks. Its highly authoritative message functions as a framework for much of the public discourse on the risks of HIV/AIDS transmission among lesbians.

A Google search of "Lesbians and Safer Sex" reveals similar strategies in most sources including those of well-known HIV/AIDS prevention organizations such as Poz and Avert. For example, the Avert HIVAIDS information webpage begins its instructions for lesbian safer sex practices with the following sentence: "Lesbian or bisexual women are not at high risk of becoming infected with HIV – the virus that causes AIDS – through woman to woman sex" (Lesbians, Bisexual Women and Safe Sex, 2013). A search of YouTube videos on lesbians and safer sex yields similar results, with all videos including some comment minimizing risk as rare or non-existent. As a result, very few messages validate lesbians' concerns of HIV transmission when having sex with women.

Obviously, neither the CDC nor AIDS organizations are trying to send the message that lesbians should not engage in safer sex practices. However, once ignorance about HIV transmission in WSW is used to position messages about safer-sex practices, the implicit argument becomes that lesbians are not at risk because there is no evidence that they are and thus action is not warranted. By stating that lesbians are at risk of transmission not by having sex with women but through other risk factors such as having sex with men, using injection drugs, or being artificially inseminated with infected sperm, these sources prioritize the notion that the risk of sexual transmission between women is minimal and give the impression that this is not something lesbians need to worry about. Thus, the construction of ignorance regarding the possible transmission of HIV in lesbian sexual practices deflects concerns about infection.

Invisible Minority and High Risk Behavior

Lesbians who seek sexual health advice from healthcare professionals often find unexpected obstacles. In fact, disturbing evidence exists of physicians' ignorance about lesbians and HIV. This is not surprising given the discourse that stresses the lack of reported cases of woman-to-woman transmission and the limited research on lesbian sexual health (McNair, 2005). Physicians are trained to focus on gay men and sometimes on heterosexual men when it comes to HIV. They know to ask injection drug users about safer sex practices. But they are, for the most part, dismissive of women and especially lesbians. Whereas gay men are often provided safer sex information when visiting physicians, women, and lesbians in particular, are not. Furthermore, most physicians are not even aware of their female patients' sexual practices and many lesbians choose not to share their sexual histories with physicians:

> For many women, as soon as you tell your doctor you have sex with women, a certain line of questioning stops. Many people – even within the health care and lesbian communities – still think that lesbians aren't supposed to get HIV/AIDS and that woman-to-woman sex poses no HIV transmission risk. This hobbles HIV testing efforts among lesbians, who often conclude that they aren't part of the at-risk population. It may also keep doctors from helping HIV-positive lesbians protect themselves from other sexually transmitted infections.
>
> *(Pechman, 2009)*

Added to the perception that lesbians are at low risk of HIV is the still held belief that lesbian sex is not "real" sex, "contributing further to the lack of information available about the pleasure or risk associated with SMW [sexual minority women] sexual practices and expressions" (Mautner Project, n.d.). When health care professionals avoid discussion of high-risk behaviors such as penetrative practices (i.e. anal or vaginal use and sharing of sex toys) or even non-penetrative practices (i.e. oral sex), and are dismissive of sex between women, lesbians' sexual practices become invisible and their sexual health care needs are ignored (Marrazzo, Coffey, & Bingham, 2005).

Even lesbians who speak to their physicians about safer sex often face resistance. In an article on the POZ website, Rachel Pachman (2009) explained:

> Vanessa Campus has never had trouble discussing her sexuality . . . She's not afraid to talk with her doctor about being a lesbian either – but he doesn't seem to share

her comfort level. "He doesn't talk about [my risk of] transmitting HIV to my partner," Campus says. "It seems like it's taboo for him to even bring it up."

Clearly, the purposeful deflection of risk can have very negative consequence for lesbians who may not be tested for HIV and delays treatment if they are positive. The ignorance of physicians is translated into the implicit argument that lesbian sex does not warrant concern about HIV transmission and leads to missed opportunities for safer sex messages to reach lesbians:

> A lot of assumptions about risk are made when lesbians are told not to concern themselves with HIV. Rough unprotected toy play is cited as the first "lesbian only" (no other risk factors identified) transmission cited by the CDC in 2003, but there are lesbians with HIV reported as early as 1984. This is not surprising considering risk follows behavior not identification. Lesbians may have unprotected sex, may have anal sex, may have oral sex, may have sex with a man, may not have been monogamous, may have injected drugs intravenously, may have artificially inseminated without testing, and/or exchanged bodily fluids (cum, blood, and milk).
>
> *(Rogers, 2011)*

The reality that, for many, lesbian identity is more than a sexual identity complicates matters further. Ana Oliveira, CEO of the New York Women's Foundation and former director of GMHC explains, "When a woman identifies as a lesbian, it doesn't mean that she only has sex with women or doesn't engage in other risky behaviors" (as cited in Eve for Life, 2010). The perception of being at low or no risk of contracting HIV can be devastating for lesbian and bisexual women. In fact, "Women who identify as lesbian or bisexual and have sex with men may be at higher risk for HIV than heterosexual women" (Eve for Life, 2010). When seeking information about safer sex, for example, lesbian women who sometime have sex with men and bisexual women are able to find information about safety when having sex with men but little or no information when having sex with women (Namaste et al., 2007). Furthermore, if infected, they are more likely to infect their female partners because they believe transmission between women is unlikely.

HIV and AIDS as a Male Issue

The majority of messages about HIV and AIDS continue to focus on males as the primary carriers/spreaders of the disease, paying particular attention to gay men and anal sex. As a result, much of the research on safer-sex practices has been done on gay men and heterosexual men. The penis remains central to most discussions of safer sex and the use of male condoms is hailed as the best solution for preventing the spread of the disease. The almost universal connection between penile penetration and HIV/AIDS leads many lesbians to be alienated from the majority of safer sex messages. Absent the penis, the need for safer sex becomes irrelevant. In fact, "Any type of sex not involving penetration with a penis – such as massage, kissing, body rubbing, mutual masturbation, digital penetration – is presented as a safer way to have sex. This information indirectly constructs lesbian sex, which does not involve a penis, as safe sex" (Power et al., 2009, p. 75). As such, lesbians become invisible in safer sex messages and deaf to them.

The only parallel to the condom argument is the suggestion that lesbians should use dental dams. Many of the messages targeted at lesbians, although dismissive of the risk of HIV transmission, do recommend dental dams for protection during oral sex. Even if lesbians ignore the argument that they are at low risk of HIV, their exposure to safer sex messages aimed at the general population makes them suspicious of the need for dental dams, given no similar messages are targeted at men who have oral sex with women (Power et al., 2009). The alienation from popular safer sex messages further solidifies the notion that lesbians do not need to engage in safer sex. Thus, the construction of ignorance surrounding the risk of HIV transmission among lesbians disrupts the possibility of global safer sex messages that might reach this population.

When lesbians look for safer sex messages aimed at their population, the messages are dismissive. When they turn to health care professionals, they often are invisible. When lesbians are exposed to safer sex messages aimed at the general population, they cannot find self representations and cannot identify with such messages. As a consequence, they assume that safer sex messages do not apply to them.

The construction of ignorance surrounding lesbians and HIV transmission has very serious consequences and disturbs warnings about risks, which is especially troubling as it is contrary to accepted public safety practices. Public health crises warrant actions even when there is no hard evidence to prove a particular population is at risk. In fact, mere suspicion warrants action. Although there are no officially documented cases of HIV transmission among WSW, the knowledge that HIV is transmitted through sharing of bodily fluids means that any behavior that results in such sharing has the potential to lead to the spread of the virus. Unfortunately, arguments based on ignorance about lesbian risk of transmission, lesbian sexual practices, and effective ways to reach this audience interfere with the collection of meaningful data, hinder HIV prevention, and justify inaction. These arguments need to be reframed so that the call for safer sex practices among lesbians is no longer seen as contingent upon the evaluation of this population as being at high risk of contracting the disease.

References

ACT UP/NY Women and AIDS Book Group. (1990). *Women, AIDS & Activism*. Boston, MA: South End Press.

Centers for Disease Control and Prevention. (2006). HIV/AIDS among women who have sex with women. Retrieved from http://www.cdc.gov/hiv/topics/women/resources/factsheets/wsw.htm

Eve for life: Supporting women and children living with HIV and AIDS. (2010). Women and HIV/AIDS. Retrieved October 20, 2012, from http://www.eveforlife.org/Lesbians-and--HIV---AIDS.html

Kwakwa, H. A., & Ghobrial, M. W. (2003). Female to female transmission of human immunodeficiency virus. *Clinical Infectious Diseases, 36*, e40–e41.

Lesbians, bisexual women and safe sex (2013). Retrieved February 18, 2013, from http://www.avert.org/lesbians-safe-sex.htm

McNair, R. (2005). Risks and prevention of sexually transmissible infections among women who have sex with women. *Sexual Health, 2*(4), 209–17.

Marrazzo, J. M., Coffey, P., & Bingham, A. (2005). Sexual practices, risk perception and knowledge of sexually transmitted disease risk among lesbian and bisexual women. *Perspectives on Sexual and Reproductive Health, 37*(1), 6–12.

Mautner Project (n.d.). Sexual health. Retrieved April 7, 2013, from http://www.mautenerproject.org/health_info/sexual_health.cfm

Mbondgulo, Z. (2009, April 9). Are lesbians free from contracting HIV/AIDS? *The SOP.* Retrieved from http://thesop.org/story/health/2009/04/09/are-lesbians-free-from-contracting-hivaids.php

Namaste, V., Vukov, T. H., Saghie, N., Jean-Gilles, J., Lafreniere, M., Leroux, J., Williamson, R., Leclerc, N., & Monette, A. (2007). HIV and STD prevention needs of bisexual women: Results from Project Polyvalence. *Canadian Journal of Communication, 32*, 357–381.

Pechman, R. R. (2009, June). The L+ Word. *POZ*. Retrieved February 20, 2013, from http://www.poz.com/articles/lesbians_hiv_risk_2331_16600.shtml

Power, J., McNair, R., & Carr, S. (2009). Absent sexual scripts: Lesbian and bisexual women's knowledge, attitudes and action regarding safer sex and sexual health information. *Culture, Health & Sexuality, 11*(1), 67–81.

Rogers, K. (2011, October 19). Should lesbians care about HIV. *The L Stop.* Retrieved October 15, 2012, from http://thelstop.org/2011/10/should-lesbians-care-about-hiv/

Tuana, N. (2006). The speculum of ignorance: The women's health movement and epistemologies of ignorance. *Hypatia, 21*(3), 1–19.

56

RATIONALITY AND RISK

A pragma-dialectical assessment of Bernardo DeBernardinis's public statement on earthquake risk in L'Aquila

Eileen Hammond

FLORIDA ATLANTIC UNIVERSITY, USA

David Cratis Williams

FLORIDA ATLANTIC UNIVERSITY, USA

On April 6, 2009, a magnitude 6.3 earthquake devastated the rural village of L'Aquila, Italy. L'Aquila is in one of the most seismically dangerous regions of Italy, but the events leading up to this particular quake were anything but typical. Resident and retired lab technician Giampaolo Guiliani predicted a major earthquake would strike based on increasing levels of radon gas, but measuring radon gas is not a scientifically accepted method for predicting future seismic events. Giuliani was officially silenced by an order from Italy's Civil Protection Agency on March 30, 2009, but residents were still unnerved by the predictions and the nonstop onslaught of minor seismic tremors – a phenomenon referred to as swarming (Hall, 2011). In order to calm the public, the Civil Protection Agency called an emergency meeting of top scientists on March 31 to determine the level of risk that a major quake would strike in the near future. The meeting adjourned after only one hour of discussion, and the Deputy Technical Head of the Civil Protection Agency, Bernardo DeBernardinis, made public remarks to a news reporter on broadcast television to relay the findings of the meeting. In his interview, DeBernardinis (2012) said that the recent swarming tremors were a positive sign of continuously discharging energy and that the residents of the area had nothing to fear. However, the scientists' actual conclusion was that while a major earthquake was unlikely, it could not be ruled out (Trapasso, 2010). Less than one week later, on April 6, the now-pacified town of L'Aquila was devastated by an earthquake that destroyed 20,000 buildings and killed more than 300 people (Hall, 2011). Influenced by DeBernardinis's casual attitude and confident public statement presumably based on scientific data, many residents, who historically would have vacated their homes after even a slight tremor, were reassured and remained in their homes, leading to a devastating loss of life. Three years later, six scientists and DeBernardinis were convicted of manslaughter and sentenced to six years in prison for negligence (Maloney & Wang, 2012).

A pivotal moment in the sequence of events was DeBernardinis's statement to the press. After the earthquake struck, residents of L'Aquila referred to DeBernardinis's words of reassurance as their reason for not evacuating their homes. When DeBernardinis addressed the reporter, he invoked his public authority to informally debrief the residents of L'Aquila about the outcome of the meeting of scientists. Under the guise of risk assessment, he pandered to the public's need for reassurance and grossly misrepresented the facts of the case as recorded in the official minutes of the meeting (Trapasso, 2010). Our task is to analyze his statement to discover what argumentative moves DeBernardinis made, what fallacies he committed, and what other rhetorical moves he used to represent the resolution of the facts of the case in the light most favorable to his purpose. The application of pragma-dialectics illuminates how the flawed argumentation derailed substantive risk communication and ultimately led to public outrage. By reconstructing the arguments dialectically and evaluating the overarching rhetorical moves, we argue that the statement was effective rhetorically but flawed argumentatively.

Method

The pragma-dialectical approach to argumentation is a comprehensive research program initiated in the 1970s by Frans van Eemeren and Rob Grootendorst, who sought to combine the descriptive dimension of pragmatics with the normative dimension of dialectics. Based on a critical-rationalist philosophy of reasonableness which assumes that reasonableness depends on compliance with critical testing, they developed a theoretical model of a critical discussion by which argumentation is tested and evaluated. The model of a critical discussion has four stages – confrontation, opening, argumentation, and concluding – and each stage includes certain types of speech acts. The two parties proceed through the four stages of argumentation with the goal of resolving the difference of opinion on the merits. The pragma-dialectical approach to argumentation also offers an analytic component, in which real-life argumentation is reconstructed by performing an analytic overview to identify and organize only the argumentative moves that contribute to the resolution of the difference of opinion on the merits. By reconstructing argumentation, one can evaluate the argumentation based on its adherence to the model of a critical discussion (van Eemeren et al., 1996).

Because argumentative reality includes both dialectical and rhetorical dimensions, van Eemeren and Houtlosser (2001) later introduced the extended model of pragma-dialectics, which incorporated the rhetorical dimension of argumentation through the concept of strategic maneuvering. In *Strategic Maneuvering in Argumentative Discourse*, van Eemeren (2010) defined strategic maneuvering as "the continual efforts made in all moves that are carried out in argumentative discourse to keep the balance between reasonableness and effectiveness" (p. 40). In argumentative discourse, strategic maneuvering occurs at every stage because there is always a tension between maintaining reasonableness and effectiveness, but the strategic maneuvers must still remain within the dialectical boundaries of the critical discussion.

Pragma-dialectics also redefines fallacies within the model of a critical discussion. Because certain argumentative moves should be made in each of the four discussion stages, it follows that certain other moves should not be made. In the standard theory of pragma-dialectics, van Eemeren and Grootendorst (2004) established a code of conduct, composed of ten rules, for conducting a critical discussion to resolve a difference of opinion on the merits. Any violation of one of the ten rules is therefore a fallacy. In the extended theory of pragma-dialectics, van Eemeren (2010) warned that fallacies can be difficult to detect because strategic maneuvering may obfuscate the line between a sound move and a fallacious move. In *Strategic Maneuvering in Argumentative Discourse*, van Eemeren (2010) put it clearly: "All derailments of strategic maneuvering are fallacies in the sense that they violate one or more of the rules for critical discussion and all fallacies can be viewed as derailments of strategic maneuvering" (p. 198).

We face a unique challenge in our analysis of DeBernardinis's statement because it is not explicitly dialectical. One of the most fundamental qualities of a critical discussion is that it is a dialogue; therefore, it requires the presence of two voices. Without the alternating moves for and against the standpoint at issue, the difference of opinion cannot be resolved on the merits. DeBernardinis's statement to the media was technically a dialogue between himself and the reporter, but it was situated within a much broader argumentative context. The events leading up to the statement suggest that DeBernardinis was making arguments against Giampaolo Giuliani, the community scientist who had been predicting a major earthquake would strike and who (authorities feared) was inciting panic among the people. Moreover, the structure of his statement most closely resembles a monologue, in which only the standpoint of the speaker is represented and the other party is passive. Our pragma-dialectic reconstruction of DeBernardinis's part of the argument assumes this broader context.

In the next section, we provide a reconstruction and analysis of the statement based on the four stages of the pragma-dialectical model of a critical discussion. Then, we offer an analysis of those aspects of the discourse that are excluded from the model of a critical discussion because they do not contribute to a resolution of the difference of opinion on the merits.

Analysis of the Critical Discussion

In the confrontation stage, the protagonist asserts a standpoint and the antagonist expresses doubt about that standpoint and may also assert a counter-standpoint. The confrontation stage manifests in any part of the discourse where a clear standpoint is asserted. We identify five standpoints that DeBernardinis advanced throughout his statement: (1) this event [the swarming of tremors] is a normal phenomenon, (2) we need to live with this territory, (3) we must maintain a state of vigilance without anxiety, (4) there is no danger, and (5) we have to be one population. Each of these standpoints will be contextualized in the argumentation stage.

In the opening stage, the parties explore material and procedural starting points for conducting the discussion. DeBernardinis (2009) advanced his intended material and procedural starting points in the beginning of the interview, after the reporter asked, "I do not ask you to do the miracle of reassuring us, because nobody can, neither you nor others, right?" The reporter was giving DeBernardinis an opportunity to admit that the scientists could not rule out the possibility of a major earthquake. However, DeBernardinis took advantage of the reporter's uncertainty to make a bold opening statement of reassurance even though a magnitude 4.0 tremor had already hit the nearby town of Sulmona. He said:

> I have already said, on Sunday, to the mayor of Sulmona, who I personally called in order to let him know that all of us were present in sharing their sorrow, not only monitoring, watching, together with the "INGV" and all the other institutes, and evaluating the situation, but we were also there as the Civil Protection Agency next to the mayors *in order to face and reassure the population* [emphasis added].
>
> (DeBernardinis, 2009)

DeBernardinis mentioned the tremor that hit Sulmona to implicitly acknowledge the common point of agreement that a tremor did strike after Giuliani predicted it, his material starting point. Then he explicitly stated that his intended procedure was "to face and reassure the population." Because Giuliani had established some surface level of credibility when Sulmona was shaken by a 4.0 tremor shortly after one of his predictions, simply silencing him would not pacify the local residents. The officials had to discredit Giuliani or override his authority. So, the government agency convened an *official* meeting of *real* scientists to "assess the risk," when in reality they were dialectically reacting to Giuliani's public warnings.

In the argumentation stage, the parties advance argumentation in support of their standpoints. The structure of DeBernardinis's arguments in favor of his five standpoints is illustrated below. The standpoints are listed at the first level with the arguments listed at the second level. After each argument, we briefly describe some of the strategic maneuvering at play and the fallacies present.

1. This event is a normal phenomenon.
   1.1 Seismic phenomena are expected in this area.

DeBernardinis implicitly challenged Giuliani's credibility here: If something is a normal phenomenon, predicting it takes no special skill. He also addressed the public's panic by reminding them that tremors in L'Aquila are not out of the ordinary. This argument amounted to the same thing as the standpoint and is therefore fallacious. It violated rule six of the code of conduct for conducting a critical discussion, which states that a party may not falsely present a premise as an accepted starting point (van Eemeren et al., 1996).

2. We need to live with this territory.
   2.1 This territory is composed of landslides, floods, and seismicity.

Standpoint 2 referred to the public's reaction to the tremors, whereas standpoint 1 referred to the tremors themselves.

3. We must maintain a state of vigilance without anxiety.
   3.1 There are many people ready to intervene and give the maximum support.
   3.2 I am a part of the community and prepared to face the situation.

By saying that we must maintain a state of vigilance, DeBernardinis implied that the people were already in a state of vigilance. In reality, the people were in a state of panic, so this maneuver worked to convince the people that vigilance is the normal state of affairs and that they should be vigilant, not panicked. DeBernardinis evaded the burden of proof by enveloping the proposition in a presupposition. This maneuver is fallacious because it violated rule six of the code of conduct for conducting a critical discussion. Argument 3.2 attempted to persuade by means of authority, which violated rule four of the code of conduct and is therefore also a fallacy. Rule four states that a party may defend a standpoint only by advancing argumentation relating to the standpoint (van Eemeren et al., 1996).

4. There is no danger.
   4.1 Scientists say this is a favorable situation.
       4.1.1 There is a continuous draining of energy.
   4.2 We have seen little damage.

In standpoint 4, DeBernardinis claimed that there was no danger of major damage or injury should an earthquake hit. According to argument 4.1, the *real* scientists' opinion should override the community scientist's opinion. Argument 4.1.1 is a sub-argument in support of argument 4.1; the scientific explanation of continuously draining energy directly refuted Giuliani's radon gas argument. It should be noted that there is no record of any scientist actually saying this during the meeting. In argument 4.2, DeBernardinis assumed that because they had seen little damage yet, there would not be a major earthquake in the near future. This is fallacious because it violates rule eight of the code of conduct for conducting a critical discussion. Rule eight states that a party may only use arguments that are logically valid (van Eemeren et al., 1996).

5.   We have to be one population.

This standpoint does not have any clear supporting argumentation. However, it reinforced DeBernardinis's overall purpose of calming and reassuring the population; a united population is a calm population.

   There is no true concluding stage in this argument because both parties are not present to agree on the outcome of the critical discussion. DeBernardinis did not have to answer any objections, so he finished his statement as though the difference of opinion was resolved in his favor.

Analysis of Other Appeals

The pragma-dialectical theory of argumentation is concerned with the practice of argumentation as a means of resolving a difference of opinion on the merits. In the extended pragma-dialectical model, strategic maneuvering offers a rhetorical insight into the argumentative moves of a critical discussion, but strategic maneuvering applies only to those moves within the critical discussion made to resolve a difference of opinion on the merits. By the pragma-dialectical analytic reconstruction process, anything that does not contribute to the resolution of the difference of opinion on the merits is deleted from consideration (van Eemeren, 2010, p. 13). However, not all rhetorical moves can be considered strategic maneuvering. Outside the framework of the critical discussion, rhetoric can also be used to induce the audience to accept an arguer's conclusion regardless of the merits. These rhetorical moves are not ethical or unethical in and of themselves; it depends on the context and outcome of the discourse.

   DeBernardinis relied heavily on the use of ethos to persuade his audience, but his ethical appeals did not clearly fit into any of the four stages of a critical discussion, nor did they purport to contribute to the resolution of the difference of opinion on the merits. DeBernardinis had to project a level of credibility greater than Giuliani's in order to calm the public, but he did not actually have the knowledge to refute Giuliani's predictions, nor did he truly demonstrate goodwill towards the citizens.

   DeBernardinis made several rhetorical moves to enhance his perceived expertise and trustworthiness. In the beginning of the statement, DeBernardinis (2009) pointed out that he "personally called" the mayor of Sulmona "in order to let him know that all of us were present in sharing their sorrow." Later, he mentioned his connection to the mayor of Sulmona again when he said, "I personally told the mayor of Sulmona" that there was no danger. DeBernardinis was setting himself up as equal to the mayor in a governmental hierarchy of authority. He admitted that he had "already abandoned the scholarly hat," but as an "operator," or public official, he had the positional authority to report on the findings of the meeting of scientists. Just after this turn in the interview, the reporter addressed him as "professor," underscoring the fact that while he was no longer a scholar, he had been at some point. DeBernardinis needed to build up this kind of positional authority to challenge and undermine the surface validity of Giuliani's prediction of the Sulmona quake.

DeBernardinis also enhanced his ethos through identification with the people of L'Aquila. He talked about how the beauty of the region was part of "my own memory when I was a child" (DeBernardinis, 2009). He mentioned that his great-grandfather "used to tell me about the seismicity, about the events and how they were ready to face them and how they remembered the stories from their own parents." By tracing his roots back several generations, DeBernardinis cemented himself as a true local who is trustworthy by association. On top of that, he attempted to flatter the audience by marveling at the beauty of the region and recommending a regional wine: a glass of Montepulciano for the residents now at ease. By pandering to the public in this way, DeBernardinis was attempting to lower their defenses and make them more susceptible to his weak arguments.

Conclusion

When the Civil Protection Agency called an emergency meeting on March 31, 2009, top government scientists gathered to discuss the risk of a major earthquake striking in the immediate future. DeBernardinis spun the outcome of the meeting to suggest that he was presenting the conclusion of robust scientific argument, but the overlying motive structure illuminates the real truth: He presented a sham recapitulation of a risk assessment that underscored a predetermined conclusion based on the sanctity of the authority of the system. Faced with the argumentative predicament, DeBernardinis completely tipped the delicate balance between reasonableness and effectiveness by advancing fallacious arguments. He used his authority, positionality, and credibility to publicly discredit Giuliani, regardless of the merits of the case. In the context of risk assessment, his use of fallacious arguments undermined the reasonableness of his position, resulting in a catastrophic loss of life. If he had fully appreciated his burden of responsibility to the residents of L'Aquila, he would have recognized that risk communication cannot be falsified to achieve secondary political aims. DeBernardinis's statement helps us better understand risk communication in real situations and the need to remain within the boundaries of the argumentative framework.

References

De Bernardinis, Bernardo. (2012, September 25). Statement (2009, March 31). In *Requisitoria Scritta Del Pubblico Ministero* 46–47. (M. De Tollis, trans.). L'Aquila, I: Procura Della Repubblica presso il Tribunale di L'Aquila. Retrieved from http://www.fondazionegiuliani.it/Foto/RequisitoriaCGR.pdf

van Eemeren, F. H. (2010). *Strategic maneuvering in argumentative discourse: Extending the pragma-dialectical theory of argumentation.* Amsterdam, NL: John Benjamins Publishing Company.

van Eemeren, F. H. van, & Grootendorst, R. (2004). *A systematic theory of argumentation: The pragma-dialectical approach.* Cambridge, UK: Cambridge University Press.

van Eemeren, F. H., Grootendorst, R., Snoeck Henkemans, A. F., Blair, J. A., Johnson, R. H., Krabbe, E. C. W., Plantin, C., Walton, D. N., Willard, C. A., Woods, J., & Zarefsky, D. (1996). *Fundamentals of argumentation theory. Handbook of historical backgrounds and contemporary developments.* Mahwah, NJ: Lawrence Erlbaum.

van Eemeren, F. H., & Houtlosser, P. (2001). Managing disagreement: Rhetorical analysis within a dialectical framework. *Argumentation and Advocacy, 37*(3), 150–157.

Hall, Stephen S. (2011, September 14). Scientists on Trial: At Fault? *Nature, 477,* 264–269. doi:10.1038/477264a

Moloney, L., & Wang, S. (2012, October 22). Court Convicts 7 for Inadequate Warning of Quake Risk. *The Wall Street Journal.* Retrieved from http://online.wsj.com/article/SB10001424052970203 63060457807278135727300.html#

Trapasso, P. (2010, March 31). 31 Marzo 2009: L'intervista Video a De Bernardinis, il Verbale Della Commissione Grandi Rischi. *6aprile.it.* Retrieved from http://www.6aprile.it/non_ dimentichiamo/2010/03/31/31-marzo-2009-lintervista-video-a-de-bernardinis-il-verbale-della-commissione-grandi-rischi.html

57

"TRUE" LOVE WAITS

The construction of facts in abstinence-until-marriage discourse

Casey Ryan Kelly

BUTLER UNIVERSITY, USA

The National Abstinence Clearinghouse (2011) emphatically declared their support for sexual purity through "the distribution of age appropriate, factual and medically-referenced materials" (para. 1). Similar abstinence organizations, including the National Abstinence Education Association, True Love Waits, and Independent Women's Forum, argue that the best public health data indicate that abstinence education is responsible for a decline in teenage pregnancies; condoms do not prevent sexually transmitted infections (STI's); HPV vaccination causes promiscuity; and premarital sex is the leading cause of mental illness, low self-esteem, depression, crime, poverty, and welfare dependence. Despite the abstinence movement's secular embrace of *logos*, the Sexuality Information and Education Council of the US (2008) reported that "there are no published studies in the professional literature that show that abstinence-only programs will result in young people delaying sexual intercourse" (para. 5). Instead, "these programs include negative messages about sexuality, distort information about condoms and STDs, and promote biases based on gender, sexual orientation, marriage, family structure, and pregnancy options" (para. 4). Studies published in the *American Journal of Public Health, Journal of Adolescent Health*, and *Pediatrics* found that condoms and birth control are actually highly effective against pregnancy and STI's, abstinence pledgers were no more likely to refrain from premarital sex but were less likely to use contraception, and that no medical data support the efficacy of abstinence-until-marriage programs (Bersamin et al., 2004; Bruckner & Bearman, 2005; Rosenbaum, 2009, 2006). Even though abstinence organizations stress the importance of facts, facts are where their public campaign unravels.

Yet, the abstinence movement continues to attain substantial victories in public policy. Since 1981, more than $1.5 billion in federal grants have been committed to abstinence-only education (SIECUS, 2013). Despite the Obama Administration's diversion of federal money to comprehensive sex education, Congressional Republicans reintroduced abstinence through an amendment to the Affordable Care Act, which includes $50 million through 2014 (Kopsa, 2011). Virginity advocates have also successfully lobbied to make marriage training a central component of HIV/AIDS prevention initiatives in Sub-Saharan Africa as well as a precondition for social services (Valenti, 2009). Moreover, abstinence groups boast over 2.5 million teenage abstinence pledges since 1993 (Bearman & Bruckner, 2001).

What explains the success of a campaign lacking substantive data and expertise? Recently, a number of scholars have inquired into the kinds of rhetorical strategies and deliberative environments that enable groups traditionally opposed to scientific reasoning and expertise to gain public legitimacy (Banning, 2009; Ceccarelli, 2011; Fritch, Palczewski, Short, & Farrell, 2006; Kelly & Hoerl, 2012). These scholars attend to how public controversies are manufactured to create the illusion of an ongoing, intractable, and indecisive debate where there actually is expert consensus. This scholarship demonstrates the status of facts in public culture is precarious, destabilized by rhetorical campaigns that suggest that there are not only different interpretations of scientific data, but that stakeholders are entitled to their own facts.

In this essay, I argue that abstinence advocates *manufacture logos*, translating an advocacy that was once based in Evangelical morality into a secular language of evidence, facts, and data. Whereas abstinence advocates are guided by a Biblical notion of universal truth, they view secular epistemologies with skepticism and are inclined to select and arrange evidence to reaffirm their own beliefs. As Kelly and Hoerl (2012) observed, "fundamentalist movements have adapted their foundational narrative texts to the formal and aesthetic conventions of secular society to establish their public legitimacy" (p. 127). For Evangelical abstinence advocates, scientific facts are only found where data intersect religious truth. Abstinence advocates churn out pseudo-scientific reports and analysis of scientific data to establish their legitimacy as stakeholders in a technical controversy over abstinence. I argue that manufactured logos builds from the misconception that because secular reasoning allows for revisions based on new evidence, successful arguments are just arrangements of facts in a preferred pattern. I conclude that manufacturing logos constructs dangerous information silos where facts are dictated by emphatic belief.

Just the Facts

Abstinence advocates are fond of one truism: Sexual abstinence is the only 100 percent proven method to prevent pregnancy and STIs. A tautology *par excellence*, this statement is incontestable and painfully obvious. No public health expert would expend energy contesting a self-evident claim. In public policy, the central question is not whether abstinence works but whether *promoting* abstinence is effective. This truism exemplifies how abstinence advocates present facts in a perfunctory arrangement of common sense wisdom and self-evident claims that begin and end with the same conclusion: Abstinence works. To retain a foothold in public policy, abstinence advocates can no longer structure their arguments solely around religious and moral appeals (Gardner, 2011). Instead, they must contend with the growing medical evidence that many pro-abstinence policies have failed. An analysis of the abstinence movement's public health strategy reveals an ornamental use of facts taken out of context of scientific reports, mixed with refutational arguments derived from pseudonymous think tanks. Advocates sift through scientific data, winnowing facts based on their comportment with religious values.

Perelman (1982) distinguished between points of agreement between rhetor and audience that converge based on reality, "facts, truths, and presumptions," versus the preferable, "values, hierarchies, and the *loci* of the preferable" (p. 23). Adherence to facts is a subjective reaction to the objective conditions that equally bind all regardless of acknowledgment. Rhetoric *of* facts is distinct from rhetoric *about* facts. Whereas the former is a language for communicating observed data and verifiable conditions that structure material existence, the latter communicates attitudes toward those conditions. Rhetoric *about* facts should be distinguished from rhetorical propositions that mobilize facts to build a persuasive case or rhetoric that contests facts through procedural processes. Rhetoric about facts establishes criteria for judgment that guide interpretation of evidence. But, because rhetoric about facts communicates and cultivates attitudes toward material conditions, it can be subject to Perelman's description of the preferable. And when the preferable is shaped by transcendent values, rhetoric about facts can be marshaled as a sieve that filters out unwanted messages that do not align with a desired belief structure.

The term *manufactured logos* names the rhetorical practice of political convenience in which a rhetor arranges selected facts to support what s/he already believes is a foregone conclusion. This rhetorical practice is bolstered by the belief that all information is subjective and deliberative reasoning is speculation. Manufactured logos also is dependent on the proliferation of information silos where individuals can self-select facts to confirm preexisting beliefs. Rather than arguing from the same set of information, stakeholders in public controversies become entitled to their own facts. Moreover, if an expert consensus emerges, the existence of a vocal minority can be used to suggest that facts are less reliable than intractable certainty in one's personal beliefs (Banning, 2009; Ceccarilli, 2011). Manufactured logos constructs what Hoerl and I have argued is "a closed, anemic system of pleasing appearances" (p. 140). Further, manufactured logos is also girded by a what Cloud (2003) called an "affected public" (p. 125), whose attitudes toward facts are shaped by discourses that structure public culture around emotional attachments to political ideals rather than shared reasoning. In the affective mode, facts are questions of feeling and intuition, dictated by what is self-evident, and susceptible to sentimental appeals to transcendent truths (e.g., religion, nationalism). This explains why "some attachments are held in the face of contrary evidence simply out of unreasoning blindness" (Cloud, 2003, p. 131). Manufactured logos is employed when mounting uncertainty about the truth of people's convictions conflicts with what they feel to be true in their hearts. Affected publics are instructed to trust their feelings and ignore their shared interests.

The Facts of Life

The National Abstinence Clearinghouse (NAC) is the hub of the contemporary abstinence movement. It is a center for abstinence-until-marriage curricula, resources, peer networking, conferences, and lobbying. They boast supporting a national advisory council comprised of 40 renowned abstinence educators and 60 health professionals who proudly refuse to dispense contraception to unmarried teens (NAC, 2012d). Replete with confusing citations, chains of hyperlinks, and decontextualized medical information, the NAC website illustrates the rhetorical features of manufactured logos.

First, manufactured logos relies on cherry-picked data and out of context references to expert opinion. Citing a report from the National Institutes of Health (NIH, 2003), the NAC (2012e) declared: "the truth" is that "condoms fail to prevent exposure to HIV/AIDS" and that "there is no scientific evidence that condoms prevent transmission of chlamydia, trichomoniasis, herpes, syphilis, chanchroid or human papilloma virus (HPV)" (para. 4). This citation creates the impression that public health officials concede that condoms are ineffective. But, an examination of the original source reveals that the NIH simply resolved to collect more data so that it can make more definitive claims about condom efficacy. The NIH (2003) report stated that condoms have "significantly reduced the risk of HIV infection in men and women" (p. ii). The NAC ignored the NIH's plea that the report "not be interpreted as proof of the adequacy or inadequacy of the condom to reduce the risk of STDs other than HIV transmission in men and women and gonorrhea in men" (p. ii). The NIH indicated that public health professionals support condom usage but seek greater claim validity.

Another example shows how decontextualized information is used to attribute success to abstinence policies. In an article on low birth rates, the NAC (2012a) argued:

> The Center [*sic*] for Disease Control, CDC, has reported that 2010 has seen historic lows in teen birth rates in the United States. Among the contributing factors for this trend, we need to give credit to: Abstinence education in schools and churches, Parents raising the bar, Purity Balls, God, Mom & Me Teas, Father/Son Time Outs.
>
> *(para. 1)*

Here, the NAC creates the impression that the CDC supports ritualized virginity pledges and abstinence-only education, even attributing low birth rates to abstinence programs; however, the CDC report is silent about virginity pledges and purity balls. Other data from the CDC indicated that the key factors that explain teen birth disparities are demographic, including income and education (Matthews, Sutton, Hamilton, & Ventura, 2010). Casting more doubt on the NAC's claim, a CDC-funded study of virginity pledges found that pledgers were no less likely to delay sexual intercourse, but were less likely to use contraception (Brücker & Bearman, 2004).

Elsewhere, the NAC (2012e) referenced a different CDC report, saying "a recent study by the Centers for Disease Control confirms what we already know – sex outside of marriage is not safe" (para. 1). They even encouraged readers to "take a look at the following article to see just what a disservice to our youth we are doing by handing out condoms in schools" (para. 2). An examination of the report in question casts doubt on whether the NAC even reads their sources. The CDC report (2012) encouraged health professionals to find ways to encourage teens to delay sexual activity but does not promote abstinence. The study found that many teenage parents held misconceptions about contraception and human sexuality. The report actually defended "providing access to contraception and encouraging use of more effective methods plus condoms to protect against both pregnancy and sexually trans-mitted infections" (p. 27). This seemingly deliberate misreading of CDC reports creates the appearance of concordance where there is profound disagreement.

Second, manufactured logos is cultivated in information silos. Even though I followed the hyperlinks, nothing on the NAC website encourages readers to actually analyze the original scientific reports without their guidance. The "clearinghouse" is less of an archive than an interpretive filter, a sieve that fences readers within their preferred news silo as they navigate a maze of hyperlinks that divert readers to abstinence organizations to interpret health reports for them. For example, in a synopsis of data about cohabitation before marriage, the NAC (2012b) argued: "the statistics are not in their favor. Forty percent of couples who cohabitate never get married and those who do decide to tie the knot are 50–100% more likely to get a divorce" (para. 1). The hyperlink they provide does not go to the University of Virginia report, but instead to a *Washington Post* "guest voices" blog for faith-based perspectives that eventually links to the original report. While a recent National Center for Health Statistics (NCHS, 2012) study found that the link between cohabitation and marital instability has weakened, the NAC argued emphatically that there is no evidence for that position. The NAC is able to keep their readers from examining such reports by providing links to intermediary sources that either divert readers or instruct them about how to dismiss scien-tific data. In this case, the NAC outsourced its indictment of the NCHS to *The Baptist News*, in which a Focus on the Family affiliate provided an amateur critique of the report's meth-odology. If readers eventually reach these reports, they are armed with extreme skepticism. This hyperlink network keeps casual readers within the abstinence information silo where evidence contrary to their beliefs are less likely to enter. The NAC (2012b) lamented: "of course the mainstream media won't recognize the importance of purity education, but we know it changes lives, and we've seen the proof in the testimonies of youth and young adults. Keep up the good work!" (para. 1). Put differently, no matter what the health experts report, it pales in comparison to the personal testimonials available throughout the NAC website. Readers are valorized for trusting their gut and dismissing the experts.

Finally, manufactured logos relies on tautologies, circular reasoning, and false causation. The NAC routinely conflated its premises with its conclusion, placing abstinence beyond skepticism. Consider claims such as "it's no secret that in recent years the family structure that our grandparents knew so well and fought so hard for has really taken a turn for the worst [*sic*]" (NAC, 2012e, para. 1). While these statements appear authoritative, the extensive work of researchers like Stephanie Coontz (2000) and Susan Douglas (2004) showed that such claims are rooted in nostalgia for a family structure that never existed except on television. Divorce rates actually peaked in 1945, during the period idolized by the NAC (Coleman, Ganong, & Warznik, 2007, p. 27). The NAC (2012c) even acknowledged the demographic factors (e.g. education, income) linked to high divorce rates while in the same breath proposing that "marriage preparation" courses would lessen the "financial burden to taxpayers" and create a "healthy society as a whole" (para. 1). In another case, the NAC (2011a) provided a hyperlink to an article that they explicitly acknowledged makes the case for increased government support for single mothers but then defiantly suggested "but we believe that marriage preparation and support for healthy marriages is the best solution" (para. 1). These rare moments of lucidity are cut short by quick reversals to dogmatic beliefs. This obstinate certainty that marriage classes are the solution to a problem the NAC acknowledges is material demonstrates how abstinence advocates frequently conflate emphatic conviction with truth.

Conservative World Making

While many groups dispense with inconvenient facts, manufactured logos appears in discourse communities that are resistant to change, skeptical of expertise, and opposed to secular values. Particularly in conservative religious communities, God dictates facts, human reasoning is imperfect, truths do not change, and tradition is exalted. Although some may deliberately distort the truth, others manufacture logos to reconcile their traditional beliefs with modernity. When faced with overwhelming evidence that a long-held belief is faulty, many conservative communities seek out only the evidence that reconstructs the world in which those beliefs remain intact. Manufactured logos is not just about arranging facts to support a desired truth, but fortifying a desired world against new knowledge. Unfortunately, trusting intuition cannot help people solve the public health crises of the future.

References

Banning, M. E. (2009). When poststructural theory and contemporary politics collide: The vexed case of global warming. *Communication and Critical/Cultural Studies*, *6*, 285–304.

Bearman, P. S., & Brückner, H. (2001). Promising the future: Virginity pledges and first intercourse. *American Journal of Sociology*, *106*, 859–912.

Bersamin, M. M., Walker, S., Waiters, E. D., Fisher, D. A., & Grube, J. (2004). Promising to wait: Virginity pledges and adolescent sexual behavior. *Journal of Adolescent Health*, *35*, 428–436.

Brückner, H., & Bearman, P. (2005). After the promise: The STD consequences of adolescent virginity pledges. *Journal of Adolescent Health*, *36*, 271–278.

Ceccarelli, L. (2011). Manufactured scientific controversy: Science, rhetoric, and public debate. *Rhetoric and Public Affairs, 14,* 196–228.

Centers for Disease Control (2012). Prepregnancy contraceptive use among teens with unintended pregnancies resulting in live births. *Morbidity and Mortality Weekly Report,* 61, 25–39. Retrieved from http://www.cdc.gov/mmwr/pdf/wk/mm6102.pdf

Cloud, D. (2003). Therapy, silence, and war: Consolation and the end of deliberation in the "affected" Public. *Poroi: Electronic Journal in Communication Studies, 2,* 125–142.

Coleman, M., Ganong, L. H, & Waznick, K. (2007). *Family life in twentieth-century America.* Westport, CT: Greenwood Publishing Group.

Coontz, S. (2000). *The way we never were: American families and the nostalgia trap.* New York, NY: Basic Books.

Copen, C. E., Daniels, K., Vespa, J., & Mosher, W. D. (2012). First marriages in the United States: Data from the 2006–2010 National Survey of Family Growth, *National Health Statistics Reports, 49,* 1–21. Retrieved from http://www.cdc.gov/nchs/data/nhsr/nhsr049.pdf

Douglas, S. (2004). *The mommy myth.* New York, NY: Free Press.

Fritch, J., Palczewski, C. H., Farrell, J., & Short, E. (2006). Disingenuous controversy: Responses to Ward Churchill's 9/11 essay. *Argumentation and Advocacy, 42,* 190–205.

Gardner, C. J. (2011). *Making chastity sexy: The rhetoric of Evangelical abstinence campaigns.* Berkeley: University of California Press.

Kelly, C., & Hoerl, K. (2012). Genesis in hyperreality: Legitimizing disingenuous controversy at the Creation Museum. *Argumentation and Advocacy, 48,* 123–141.

Kopsa, A. (2011, December 22). Abstinence-only: It's baaaack. *Ms. Magazine.* Retrieved from http://msmagazine.com/blog/2011/12/22/abstinence-only-its-baaack/

Mathews, T. J., Sutton, P. D., Hamilton, B. E., & Ventura, S. J. (2010, October). State disparities in teenage birth rates in the United States, *NCHS Data Brief, 46,* Available at http://www.cdc.gov/nchs/data/databriefs/db46.htm

National Abstinence Clearinghouse. (2011a, May 10). Divorce costs. Retrieved from http://www.abstinence.net/library/studies-and-statistics/divorce-costs/

National Abstinence Clearinghouse. (2011b, May 4). Single parenthood on the rise. Retrieved from http://www.abstinence.net/library/studies-and-statistics/single-parenthood-on-the-rise/

National Abstinence Clearinghouse. (2012a, February). Record low teen birth rates in 2010. Retrieved from http://www.abstinence.net/library/studies-and-statistics/record-low-teen-birth-rates-in-2010-2/

National Abstinence Clearinghouse. (2012b, May 23). Cohabitation: The facts. Retrieved from http://www.abstinence.net/library/cohabitation/cohabitation-the-facts/

National Abstinence Clearinghouse. (2012c, April 24). Intro to fatherhood. Retrieved from http://www.abstinence.net/our-blog/the-culture/intro-to-fatherhood/

National Abstinence Clearinghouse. (2012d, May 23). About us. Retrieved from http://www.abstinence.net/about-us/

National Abstinence Clearinghouse. (2012e, May 23). Abstinence is the answer. Retrieved from http://www.abstinence.net/library/studies-and-statistics/abstinence-is-the-answer/

National Institutes of Health. (2000). Workshop summary: Scientific evidence on condom effectiveness for sexually transmitted disease (STD) prevention. Retrieved from http://www.niaid.nih.gov/about/organization/dmid/ documents/condomreport.pdf

National Marriage Project. (2012). Social Indicators of marital health and well-being: Trends of the past four decades. Retrieved from http://stateofour unions.org/ 2010/si-cohabitation.php

Perelman, C. (1982). *The realm of rhetoric.* South Bend, IN: University of Notre Dame Press.

Rosenbaum, J. E. (2009). Patient teenagers?: A comparison of the sexual behavior of virginity pledgers and matched nonpledgers. *Pediatrics, 123,* 110–120.

Rosenbaum, J. E. (2006). Reborn a virgin: Adolescents' retracting of virginity pledges and sexual histories. *American Journal of Public Health, 96,* 1098–1103.

SIECUS. (2008). Abstinence-only-until-marriage, Q & A. Retrieved from http://www.siecus.org/index.cfm?fuseaction=page.viewpage&pageid=522&grandparentID=477&parentID=523

SIECUS. (2012). A history of Federal funding for abstinence-only-until-marriage programs. Retrieved from http://www.siecus.org/index.cfm? fuseaction=page.viewPage&pageID=1340&nodeID=1

Valenti, J. (2010). *The purity myth.* Berkeley, CA: Seal Press.

58

STANDARDS FOR SCIENTIFIC ARGUMENTATION IN THE JAMES ZADROGA 9/11 HEALTH AND COMPENSATION ACT

Marcus Paroske

UNIVERSITY OF MICHIGAN-FLINT, USA

Science regulation and bureaucratic policymaking have recently drawn the attention of argumentation theorists (McKenzie, 2009; Von Burg, 2010; Rehg, 2011). I have offered a critical perspective to examine one specific set of arguments that occur within scientific regulatory contexts. The *presumptive breach* is a moment during the development of a scientific regulatory controversy where policymakers believe that a remedy is required for some problem and yet they are unable to craft a traditional argument to overcome their burden of proof (Paroske, 2012). This results in a disconnect between the public's, and often the policymakers', desire for speedy action and the requirements imposed on the science regulators by their authorizing statutes and the demands for argumentative rigor imported from the technical scientific fields of the object of regulation. Presumptive breaches are especially likely to emerge when bureaucrats cannot meet their burdens of proof because sufficient scientific evidence does not exist. When forced to meet a predetermined burden of proof for which the proper type of evidence is not forthcoming, crafting needed regulations requires inventive thinking by the policymaker. These moments of argumentative problem solving in a presumptive breach invite analysis.

This essay offers a development of the presumptive breach, in this case surrounding the question of whether to cover certain cancers under the James Zadroga 9/11 Health and Compensation Act of 2010. The Zadroga Act, named after a New York police officer whose death was attributed to respiratory ailments caused by the toxic dust kicked up by the collapse of the World Trade Center towers, created a World Trade Center [WTC] Health Program that was to analyze which conditions could be causally linked to 9/11 and draft regulations extending federal health benefits to eligible survivors and first responders who contracted those conditions.

The passage of the Zadroga Act required effort from outside Washington, as opponents were demanding spending cuts to offset the additional cost. A campaign sparked by 9/11 survivors, and championed by the influential television program *The Daily Show,* elevated public awareness of the bill. Its eventual passage was heralded as a national expression of goodwill to those who put their lives on the line in the immediate response to the tragedy. That goodwill soon soured as the administrator of the program first declined to add any cancers to the list of covered conditions, only to reverse himself some months later. To see how public pressure and scientific evidence interacted to craft a solution to this presumptive breach, I first examine the statutory requirements of the Zadroga Act and why they were likely to create an impossible hurdle for regulators. The essay then turns to the rationale for the initial finding of insufficient evidence, followed by the public backlash against that policy decision. The essay then examines how the WTC Health Program argued its way out of the predicament before drawing conclusions about the role that argumentation theorists can play in determining best practices for writing administrative statutes.

Context of Argumentation Under the Zadroga Act

The Zadroga Act itself explicitly names over 25 conditions covered by legislative fiat. To understand the argumentative constraints placed on the administrator of the WTC Health Program by the Zadroga Act, I look specifically at the stipulations set forth in the statute about how health conditions can be added to the approved list.

A two-tiered process was established for new conditions to be named to the list. The first (paragraph five) dealt specifically with cancers:

> (5) CANCER-
> (A) IN GENERAL – The WTC Program Administrator shall periodically conduct a review of all available scientific and medical evidence, including findings and recommendations of Clinical Centers of Excellence, published in peer-reviewed journals to determine if, based on such evidence, cancer or a certain type of cancer should be added to the applicable list of WTC-related health conditions.
>
> *(James Zadroga 9/11 Health and Compensation Act of 2010,*
> *42 U.S.C. 6A, XXXI, B, 1, 22, 5(A))*

The second procedure (paragraph six) dealt with the addition of conditions other than cancers:

> (6) ADDITION OF HEALTH CONDITIONS TO LIST FOR WTC RESPONDERS –
> (A) IN GENERAL – Whenever the WTC Program Administrator determines that a proposed rule should be promulgated to add a health condition to the list of health conditions in paragraph (3), the Administrator may request a recommendation of the Advisory Committee or may publish such a proposed rule in the Federal Register in accordance with subparagraph (D).
>
> *(James Zadroga 9/11Health and Compensation Act of 2010,*
> *42 U.S.C. 6A, XXXI, B, 1, 22, 6(A))*

Paragraphs five and six differ in two significant ways. First, paragraph five, explicitly applying to cancer, prescribes that only evidence published in peer-reviewed journals can be used to add conditions to the approved list. Paragraph six, apparently dealing with all conditions other than cancer, is silent on the type of evidence required to justify expanding the list of covered conditions. Second, paragraph five requires the administrator to make the decision alone, whereas paragraph six allows the administrator to request an advisory committee to prepare a recommendation.

Paragraph five is more restrictive in both the types of evidence permissible and the diversity of perspectives that participate in the policy-making process. Under such restrictive conditions, a presumptive breach is possible if stakeholders view the regulators as acting too slowly, even if the conditions of argumentation make swift action impossible. Indeed, the inherent latency period for the development of cancers almost guarantees an unpopular delay in policy in this case. The peer-review requirement in paragraph five failed to take into account that there are often years, or decades, between exposure to carcinogens and the development of cancer. Furthermore, peer-reviewed studies that could show a causal link between an event and cancer have a further waiting period as surveillance is performed and the studies are then drafted and reviewed. For a body of peer-reviewed studies to emerge that conclusively prove a link between 9/11 and cancer could take quite a long time. This is little comfort for the patients whom the act was supposed to help by providing health benefits. They are the data points necessary to create the peer-reviewed studies, but their health care is not covered in the law until the studies are completed.

Within this evidentiary Catch-22, WTC Administrator John Howard was required by law to produce his first findings on cancer no less than 180 days after enactment of the Zadroga Act. No one was happy with the result.

First Finding

In July 2011, Howard found that insufficient evidence existed to include any cancers on the list of approved health conditions. To explain the reasoning behind his finding, Howard noted how the Zadroga Act required the agency to weigh evidence in making the determination to add cancers to the list of approved ailments: "**All** available scientific and medical evidence is a broad category, but the Act narrows the broad category to include **only** the scientific and medical evidence that is published in peer-reviewed journals" (U.S. Department of Health and Human Services, 2011, p. 29; emphasis in original). He noted that this constraint is not always the case in law governing health administration. For example, in the federal law extending health benefits to those who contracted medical conditions during the Persian Gulf War, the agency's decision on which conditions to treat must be "based on sound medical and scientific evidence that a positive association exists between specified exposures and an illness in humans" (U.S. Department of Health and Human Services, 2011, fn 7). This "positive association" standard requires that all the available evidence supporting a link between the war and an illness outweigh the evidence against such a link. Cancers for 9/11 survivors had to meet the much higher standard of proof of utilizing only evidence from peer-reviewed publications under the Zadroga Act's paragraph five.

The report examined all peer-reviewed studies of cancer in 9/11 victims and found that "Only one peer reviewed article (on any type of cancer) has been published to date" (U.S. Department of Health and Human Services, 2011, p. 39). Moline et al. (2009) found eight cases of multiple myeloma, a cancer of plasma cells, among first responders and urged clinicians to screen others for the disease. The small study could not be used to draw any larger causal claims according to the Zadroga Act standards. Howard also referenced two modeling studies, both of which actually anticipated a minimal risk of increased cancer for those exposed to Ground Zero. Howard anticipated that future peer-reviewed studies of cancer would be forthcoming, but in the end concluded that a single extant study, contradicted by two modeling studies, could not demonstrate a link between 9/11 and cancer under the conditions of proof contained in the statute.

The presumptive breach is at work here. Howard reminded readers at the end of the report that the absence of data showing a causal link is not a reason to believe there is no causal link. He simply lacked the evidence to meet the burden of proof in the statute. In these cases, wanting to make policy does not justify that policy. Still, in the case of 9/11 in particular, this structural barrier to a solution did not stop many from criticizing Howard's finding.

Public Reaction

Condemnation of the ruling was swift and severe. It came from several fronts. Elected officials from New York came together to release a statement:

> As the sponsors of the Zadroga Act, we are disappointed that Dr. Howard has not yet found sufficient evidence to support covering cancers. This is disappointing news for 9/11 responders and survivors who tragically have been diagnosed with cancer since the attacks and are suffering day-to-day and awaiting help.
>
> *(Nadler, 2011)*

They expressed personal disappointment in the WTC Health Program administrator himself for not finding sufficient evidence. Later in that statement, lawmakers asserted that the link will be found anyway: "We are confident that studies on the effects of toxins at ground zero . . . will ultimately prove the scientific evidence that Dr. Howard needs to make this determination" (Nadler, 2011). The sense of urgency is palpable, as current cancer patients cannot wait for more evidence to emerge before they receive health benefits.

Another, more strident set of voices critiquing Howard came from first responders and survivors themselves. The New York tabloid the *Daily News* developed a cottage industry in collecting expressions of anger and frustration aimed at the administrator. John Feal, a high profile advocate for 9/11 victims and champion of the Zadroga Act, directly attacked the necessity of using scientific expertise to make the cancer link: "I don't care how many years of college you have, I will argue with you that the reality is people are dying from cancer and they got it from breathing the air down there" (as cited in Gendar, 2011). New York Police Commissioner Raymond Kelly deployed personal anecdote to justify his belief that his men and women were dying of cancer because of 9/11: "Based on the knowledge I have, 46 of those 49 died as a result of cancer . . . So at least from a layman's [sic] view, there certainly looks like there is a nexus, there a connectivity there" (as cited in Doyle, Prendergast, & Hutchinson, 2011). The head of a police officer's union noted "logic and common sense dictates [sic] that cancer should be included under the Zadroga Law. These men and women are sick and dying today. They cannot wait for science to catch up with common sense" (as cited in Parascandola, 2011).

This sense of urgency, offered by the lawmakers and advocates for the sick, is exactly the sort of vexation caused by a presumptive breach. In the minds of critics, this is not merely a methodological debate over the quality of extant scientific evidence, but it is the result of an intransigent bureaucracy hiding behind intellectual double speak. Doing so is killing brave survivors of a horrific attack, and will do so for the scores who will inevitably contract the same cancers in the future. From this perspective, waiting for the burden of proof to be met was unacceptable.

Some months later, a new cancer study was published in the *Lancet* (Zieg-Owens et al., 2011). The researchers found a modest increase in the incidents of cancer for firefighters on the scene versus firefighters who were not exposed. The authors argued that, while there was not enough scientific evidence to link the toxins of 9/11 to these cancers, there is a stronger case to link those toxins to conditions like microbial infections, chronic inflammation, and auto-immune diseases. These conditions were known to be oncogenetic, and through them the researchers made a case for the biological plausibility of a link between 9/11 and cancer. The study did not purport to be a definitive causal analysis, but it did add a further data point.

Members of Congress used the *Lancet* study to ask Howard to reconsider his finding. Howard needed a way to close the presumptive breach. His strategy is an exercise in creative argumentation to overcome public policy challenges.

Second Finding

The second report was printed directly into the Federal Register as a proposed rule. Howard now argued that the more expansive rules of evidence contained in paragraph six of the Zadroga Act, the clause that had been separated from cancer in the law, could actually be used to justify the listing of cancers:

> Unlike the explicit language in Title XXXIII, § 3312(a)(5)(A) of the [Zadroga] Act, which prescribes the standard to be used in the periodic reviews of cancer, § 3312(a)(6) does *not* specifically limit the type of sources upon which the Administrator may base his or her determination to propose the addition of cancer or types of cancer to the List of WTC-Related Health Conditions.
>
> *(World Trade Center Health Program, 2012, p. 35577)*

There is textual evidence in another section of the Zadroga Act to support Howard's interpretation. After the list of conditions pre-approved by Congress to be included is the following clause: "(D) ADDITIONAL CONDITIONS – Any cancer (or type of cancer) or other condition added, pursuant to paragraph (5) or (6), to the list under this paragraph" (James Zadroga 9/11 Health and Compensation Act of 2010, 42 U.S.C. 6A, XXXI, B, 1, 22, 3(D)). The clause reads like a typographical error, given paragraphs five and six make a hard distinction between cancer and other conditions. Howard, though, utilized the ambiguity to justify application of the paragraph six procedure to review cancer.

Doing so included soliciting the opinion of the WTC Health Program's Science and Technical Advisory Committee [STAC]. The STAC members were not only scientists and health researchers, but lay representatives of survivors and first responders. It also had the latitude to consider evidence not published in peer-reviewed studies; that restriction only applied to the paragraph five procedure. This allowed the STAC to consider unpublished reports from private contractors and government reports to predict what exposure rates likely were, as opposed to direct physical evidence of what they actually were. After making an assumption that the general exposure raised the likelihood of cancer in individuals, the STAC then detailed the types of cancer caused by known chemicals released when the Towers fell. Because it was likely that someone exposed to those chemicals could develop cancer, it was therefore permissible to list them under the Zadroga Act even though no peer-reviewed research had made this case. The result:

Although acknowledging some lack of certainty in the evidence for targeting specific organs or organ site groupings as WTC–related, the majority of the committee agreed that recommending the specified cancer sites and site groupings was based on a sound scientific rationale and the best evidence available to date.

(Ward, 2012, p. 7)

Based on the "best evidence available" (perhaps the paradigmatic phrase of those within a presumptive breach), the committee recommended that 23 categories of cancer be added to the approved list. Howard concurred, and the rule was published much to the relief of patients and the public.

Conclusion

While there are a number of lessons to draw from this case, let me focus on one in the space provided here. There is little reason to believe that Congress wanted to make it so difficult to include cancer in the list of WTC conditions that it wrote a purposefully impossible burden of proof. The move to require peer-reviewed literature seems on its face to be in the interests of sound scientific reasoning, an "evidence-based" approach. In this case, though, the statutory prescription that a certain type of evidence be used to justify a regulatory decision perversely prevented an evidence-based decision. Indeed, it prevented any decision at all. A more diverse set of inputs, and more flexibility in the decision-making process, can make the policymaking apparatus more amenable to the public will and more responsive to emerging problems.

Thinking through the conditions of argumentation that are outlined within a statute helps prevent presumptive breaches from opening. Argumentative flexibility as a criterion for evaluating the quality of legislation is an area where experts in argumentation should be able to improve the ability of policymakers to solve pressing issues.

References

Doyle, J., Prendergast, D., & Hutchinson, B. (2011, July 28). Commish Kelly disagrees with Zadroga doctor. *Daily News*, p. 4.

Gendar, A. (2011, July 27). Evidence doesn't show 9–11 dust and cancer link – Doc. $2.8B Zadroga bill won't compensate families of thousands sickened from towers' collapse. *Daily News*, p. 4.

James Zadroga 9/11 Health and Compensation Act of 2010, 42 USC § 300m *et seq.*

McKenzie, K. (2009). The public presentation of a hybrid science: Scientific and technical communication in "Iraq's weapons of mass destruction: The assessment of the British government." *Journal of Technical Writing and Communication, 39*(1), 3–23.

Moline, J., et al. (2009) Multiple myeloma in World Trade Center responders: A case series. *Journal of Occupational and Environmental Medicine, 55*(12), 896–902.

Nadler, J. (2011, July 26). Statement of Zadroga Act authors on 9/11 cancer decision [Press release]. Retrieved from http://nadler.house.gov/press-release/statement-zadroga-act-authors-911-cancer-decision

Parascandola, R. (2011, August 21). For many, battle still rages. Now enemy isn't the terrorists, it's cancer & the gov't. *Daily News*, p. 18.

Paroske, M. (2012). Overcoming burdens of proof in science regulation: Ephedra and the FDA. *Rhetoric and Public Affairs, 15*(3), 467–498.

Rehg, W. (2011). Evaluating complex collaborative expertise: The case of climate change. *Argumentation 25*(3), 385–400.

U.S. Department of Health and Human Services, National Institute for Occupational Safety and Health. (2011). *First periodic review of scientific and medical evidence related to cancer for the World Trade*

Center Health Program. (DHHS, NIOSH Publication No. 2011–197). Retrieved from http://www.cdc.gov/niosh/docs/2011-197/pdfs/2011-197.pdf

Von Burg, R. (2010). Cinematic genetics: GATTACA, essentially yours, and the rhetoric of genetic determinism. *Southern Communication Journal, 75*(1), 1–16.

Ward, E. (2012). WTC STAC recommendation on petition 001. Retrieved from http://www.cdc.gov/niosh/topics/wtc/pdfs/WTC_STAC_Petition_001.pdf

World Trade Center Health Program: Addition of certain types of cancer to the list of WTC-related health conditions, 77 Fed. Reg. 114, 35574-35615 (2012, June 13).

Zeig-Owens, R., et al. (2011). Early assessment of cancer outcomes in New York City firefighters after the 9/11 attacks: An observational cohort study. *Lancet, 378,* 898–905.

59

SYNECDOCHE AS ARGUMENTATION STRATEGY IN THE RHETORIC OF AN AUTISM ADVOCACY GROUP

Vesta T. Silva

ALLEGHENY COLLEGE, USA

Rachel Avon Whidden

LAKE FOREST COLLEGE, USA

Since 2000, the number of children with autism has jumped from 1 in 150 to 1 in 88, prompting many to declare an autism "epidemic" (Baio, 2012). Although there is no consensus in the scientific community concerning what causes autism (Anderson, Jacobs-Stannard, Chawarska, Volkmar, & Kliman, 2007; Frans et al., 2013; Noh et al., 2013; Robinson, 2012), there is widespread agreement among doctors that no causal link exists between vaccines and autism. Parents who claim to know that vaccines (often coupled with antibiotics or other environmental toxins) caused their child's autism often report being dismissed by their doctors when they make these claims and inquire about alternative treatments. The lack of support such parents feel has directly contributed to the rise of groups of parents who come together to share stories of injury, champion the use of (often) medically-derided interventions to address autism, and mobilize in an effort to reform the government vaccination program.

The expansion of the Internet and social networking affords parents in search of a supportive community an unprecedented ability to connect with each other. With a simple Google search, parents can easily find dozens of autism organizations (e.g., Age of Autism, Autism One, Talk About Curing Autism, and Generation Rescue) whose agendas move beyond the support of further research and more extensive support services. These groups, which we refer to as *counter-mainstream*, promote views of autism as a human-induced illness from which many children can recover and position themselves as ideologically opposed to mainstream medicine and science. Parents with easy access to Internet technologies can now generate their own content related to diagnosis, causes, treatments, or advocacy to share with like-minded others. As J. A. Muir Gray (1999) noted over a decade ago, "Medicine [used to be] based on knowledge from sources from which the public was excluded – scientific journals, books, journal clubs, conferences, and libraries . . . The World Wide Web, the dominant medium of the post-modern world, has blown away the doors and walls of the locked library" (p. 1552).

For parents in these counter-mainstream groups, the science on autism does not reflect their personal experiences. Statistics and studies denying a vaccine/autism connection seem irrelevant or even deceptive to the mother who witnessed a change in her child's behavior hours after receiving a shot, and data indicating that dietary changes do nothing for autistic children are dismissed by the father who sees a gluten/casein-free diet helping his child. Every story of the success of an alternative therapy strengthens the view among like-minded members that "what science says" and "what I know" are incompatible. As they see it, mainstream science is making its claims about autism without including their stories – stories of injury and healing – that counter the scientific evidence on which autism treatments and vaccination policy are based. In this essay we argue that one counter-mainstream autism advocacy group, The Thinking Moms' Revolution (TMR), has, through accident or design, hit upon a unique rhetorical strategy utilizing the trope of synecdoche such that personal narratives can serve the dual purpose of validating the individual while amassing data to fuel a revolution.

Synechdoche as Proof

Burke (1969) defined synecdoche as "part for the whole, whole for the part, container for the contained, sign for the thing signified . . ." (p. 508). Synecdoche is a trope of representation, but importantly this representative relationship is dual-directional. That is, all synecdochic conversions "imply an integral relationship, a relationship of convertibility, between the two terms" (Burke, 1969, p. 508). The perfect synecdoche is one that works in both directions, where the whole represents the part and the part represents the whole. Foss and Domenici (2001) explained, "Either side of the equation is taken as a sign, symbol, or symptom of the other, capturing, naming, or summing up the essence of the situation" (p. 243). For example, an army represents its soldiers, and the soldiers represent an army. When employed as a rhetorical strategy, synecdochic constructions can define, maintain, and even heighten public controversies (Foss & Domenici, 2001; Moore, 1993, 1994, 1997, 2003, 2009).

In the case of TMR, their organizing slogan of *revolution* and the individual stories of each child pursuing recovery outside of the medical mainstream exist in a synecdochic relationship. TMR builds a community of "revolutionaries" by providing a space for parents to share their unique personal journey and have their counter-mainstream beliefs validated. Each individual child's story represents a distinct part of the revolutionary movement, while *revolution* condenses the whole range of TMR's goals and ideological positions. The members' experiences – anomalies of the prevailing scientific evidence – function as authoritative and substantiated proof to create what Kuhn (1982) called a crisis, which would lead to a paradigm shift or scientific revolution and, in turn, a necessary change in vaccine policy and accepted treatments. Their already revolutionary thinking, once packaged as quantifiable and undeniable data, propels their social and political agenda.

Collective Acts of Change and the Rise of the Revolution

TMR was born out of a Facebook group started by parents seeing the same homeopath. "It was the Internet that was their lifeline," wrote Ann Dachel (2013) of Age of Autism, providing "the education they needed" and allowing them to build a group identity by sharing experiences of injury and paths to healing. Unlike many Facebook or Internet-only groups, however, digital communication was only the beginning of what has become a far-reaching, politically motivated group. TMR launched their website and blog in November of 2011 with a single post titled "Revolutions Never Go Backwards." Though the blog did not really take off until February of 2012, within the next 16 months TMR would maintain their highly active Facebook page; post 552 blog entries on www.thinkingmomsrevolution.com; guest blog at Age of Autism, Generation Rescue, and other sites; design and post dozens of TMR Facebook memes; create numerous web videos; design and market t-shirts and buttons; attend multiple conferences; appear on several local television programs; publish a book, *The Thinking Moms' Revolution: Autism Beyond the Spectrum: Inspiring True Stories from Parents Fighting to Rescue Their Children*; and embark on a multi-nation book tour. Across all these media, their core strategies and messages remained the same, with the synecdochically linked revolutionary personal narratives at the center of all their outreach and advocacy efforts.

The term *revolution* works on multiple levels for the group; a revolution is always a collective act of change, it fundamentally alters the rules of the game, it progresses and grows over time, and it relies on the selfless acts of revolutionaries. In the introduction to the book, Conroy (2013) wrote, "Nothing brings about change like a group of dedicated parents who are fighting for their own children" (p. ix). These aspects of revolution are evident from the first blog post and are expanded throughout TMR's (2012) messages, most overtly in their "Declaration of Independence from Medical Tyranny, Institutional Corruption, and Medical Apathy." This Declaration marked a formal secession from mainstream views. They pledged "to dissolve the political bands" and "declare the causes which impel them to the separation." Thus, each new member must tell her story in a way that supports the revolutionary whole. Adding each story elevates the credibility of the group and legitimizes the movement not just as desirable, but necessary, and the movement snowballs. Explaining how to join the revolution, TMR member noahspins (2012) wrote:

> Here's how you join. TELL EVERYONE IN YOUR WORLD, YOUR STORY! Tell your doctor, your neighbor's [*sic*], your friends . . . your friend's friends, your mechanic, your banker and the guy at the gas station. We are speaking out. We are telling everyone what happened to our kids, letting them know it did not have to happen and WE CAN ALL DO SOMETHING ABOUT IT.

In the blog post "Why you have to tell YOUR story," The Rev (2013) explained that storytelling "leave[s] an imprint of our collective purpose (healing and SAVING children) on the minds of those we engage." Having heard the experiences of a mother of an autistic child, mommy-blogger Jessica Gianelloni (2013) wrote, "Her story broke my heart and I felt a compassion I had never felt before for a fellow mom. I had a desire to fight for the truth for her and her son. I had to tell her story." Thus, each telling of each story functioned as a unique part that nonetheless invoked the whole, collective purpose – the revolution.

With a collection of such stories, people can work together to change the rules of the game in which they find themselves. For TMR, the rules that need to change are those of mainstream science and profit-driven medicine. In her account of her twins' vaccine injury, Twonk (2013) lambasted the pediatrician who recommended she vaccinate her children, describing her as "part of a machine – a cold-hearted, narrow-minded, bought-and-paid-for medical establishment – and she didn't even know it. But, based on the advice of this assumed superior intellect, I obediently led my lambs to the slaughter" (p. 5). Poppy (2013) wrote that after learning the "truth" about autism, "I felt like I was in a bad conspiracy theory movie . . . I was a new kind of mother. No more blindly trusting the doctors" (p. 32). TMR continually urged its members and readers to question, think, research and read – to engage in insurrection – not just buy into accepted medical doctrine.

In order for such individual actions to change medical doctrine, however, they still have to engage with it. They need their reports and stories on the record in ways that might be heard by those with the power to change law or policy. Following the November 2012 Congressional Hearings on the Federal Response to the Rise in Autism Rates, TMR member LuvBug (2012) gave readers a "To Do List," which urged readers to "document [their story] so it can be submitted to the official congressional testimony" and supplied a hyperlink to the Oversight Committee's Facebook page.

TMR positioned the *documented* stories as official evidence – the revolution has to move beyond neighbors, friends, or even individual doctors to address the larger system in terms that it may understand: documented testimony. Again, the stories are the primary means of revolution, but the revolution is more than any one story. The stories now function as both the argument for change *and* the evidence that change is needed.

Revolutions in Motion

Because a revolution cannot, by definition, be static, TMR's arguments (as well as the individual children's stories) often included a narrative of growth and progress. One version of the group's progression is told by Founding TMR President Goddess in her blog post "Accidental Activist." Although "the original idea [for founding TMR was one of support," she and the other TMR members now felt it was their "mission" to prevent the damage and pain of autism from happening to others (Goddess, 2012). With that realization, Goddess (2012) explained they realized they had to reach more people "so, we thought, we'd write a book." Thus, TMR moved as a group from providing localized and contained support to pursuing the wider goal of protecting others. Their multi-nation book tour has enlisted new members, not all of whom are parents of autistic children. Again, however, the telling of their stories is the key means for achieving their revolutionary aims.

The book collected the stories of all 23 of the original TMR members as a concrete and material manifestation of the revolution and its progress – the force of the whole became visible through the compilation of the stories into the single volume. Although all the TMR members had told their stories online, some in multiple venues, the move to the book helped to reinforce the synecdochic relationship between the parts (each story) and the whole (the revolution) by making that relationship physically visible in a new way. While the online stories were scattered somewhat over time and across venues, the book allowed for a powerful symbol of the building force of multiple stories *documented* in a single location. As the reader moves through the book, the weight of each new story of injury and healing contributes to a cumulative sense of evidence and a mounting sense of urgency and the need for radical change. TMR urged people who buy the book to use it as motivation or opportunity to write and tell their own stories – and thus contribute to the power of the revolution. With each reader who adds her own story, the revolution gains more members, more force, and moves forward. The whole is embodied in each part and in every retelling the part invokes the force and power of the whole.

Conclusion

While there are hundreds of autism support groups in which members share their stories, and at least dozens that are calling for changes in current medical understandings of the disorder, the rhetorical force of The Thinking Moms' Revolution is unique. By constructing a powerful synecdochic relationship between their guiding term *revolution* and the personal narratives of all those trying to recover their children, TMR has found a way to build and expand their group (through narrative identification) while simultaneously reaching audiences beyond that group (through the weight of collective evidence). Separating the revolution from the stories of those fighting it robs the term of any mass appeal and guts efforts at larger advocacy goals. Telling the stories of individual families and children without linking each one to a larger picture makes the stories little more than isolated moments of hope or sadness. The synecdochic relationship creates a constant interplay between the collective revolution and the individual stories that simultaneously validates the individual and links that individual into rising tide of evidence for revolutionary change.

References

Anderson, G., Jacobs-Stannard, A., Chawarska, K., Volkmar, F., & Kliman, H. (2007). Placental trophoblast inclusions in autism spectrum disorder. *Biological Psychiatry, 61*(4), 487–491.

Baio, Jon. (2012). Prevalence of autism spectrum disorders – Autism and Development Disabilities Monitoring Network, 14 sites, United States, 2008. *Surveillance Summaries, 61*(SS03), 1–19.

Conroy, H. (2013). Introduction. In H. Conroy, R. Sears, & L. Goes (Eds.), *The thinking moms' revolution.* New York, NY: Skyhorse Publishing.

Dachel, A. (2013, April 18). Book review: The Thinking Moms Revolution. *Age of Autism.* Retrieved from http://www.ageofautism.com/2013/04/book-review-the-thinking-moms-revolution.html/

Foss, K. A., & Domenici, K. L. (2001). Haunting Argentina: Synecdoche in the protests of the mothers of the Plaza de Mayo. *Quarterly Journal of Speech, 87*(3), 237–258. doi:10.1080/00335630109384335

Frans, E. M., Sandin, S., Reichenberg, A., et al. (2013). Autism risk across generations: A population-based study of advancing grandpaternal and paternal age. *JAMA Psychiatry, 70*(5), 516–521.

Getting Personal. (n.d.). The Thinking Moms' Revolution. Retrieved from http://thinkingmoms-revolution.com/getting-personal/

Gianelloni, J. (2013, August 26). My three days with the Thinking Moms Revolution [Web log message]. The Gianelloni family. Retrieved from http://gianelloni.wordpress.com/2013/08/26/my-3-days-with-the-thinking-moms-revolution/

Goddess. (2012, April 4). The accidental activist [Web log message]. The Thinking Moms' Revolution. Retrieved from http://thinkingmomsrevolution.com/the-accidental-activist/

Kuhn, T. (1982). *The structure of scientific revolutions.* Chicago, IL: University of Chicago Press.

LuvBug. (2012, December 5). Let's get it on [Web log message]. The Thinking Moms' Revolution. Retrieved from http://thinkingmomsrevolution.com/lets-get-it-on/

Media Kit: Q & A with TMR. (n.d.). The Thinking Moms' Revolution. Retrieved from http://thinkingmomsrevolution.com/media-kit/#video_page_qa_with_tmr

Meg F. (2013, February 13). Dear medical experts: We regret to inform you [Book review of *The Thinking Moms' Revolution*]. *Amazon.com.* Retrieved from: http://www.amazon.com/The-Thinking-Moms-Revolution-Inspiring/dp/1620878844

Moore, M. P. (1993). Constructing irreconcilable conflict: The function of synecdoche in the spotted owl controversy. *Communication Monographs, 60*(3), 258–274. doi: 10.1080/03637759309376312

Moore, M. P. (1994). Life, liberty, and the handgun: The function of synecdoche in the Brady Bill debate. *Communication Quarterly 42*(4), 434–447. doi: 10.1080/01463379409369948

Moore, M. P. (1997). The cigarette as representational ideograph in the debate over environmental tobacco smoke. *Communication Monographs, 64*(1), 47–64. doi: 10.1080/03637759709376404

Moore, M. P. (2003). Making sense of salmon: Synecdoche and Irony in a natural resource crisis. *Western Journal of Communication, 67*(1), 74–96. doi: 10.1080/10570310309374759

Moore, M. P. (2009). The Union of Concerned Scientists on the uncertainty of climate change: A study of synecdochic form. *Environmental Communication: A Journal of Nature and Culture, 3*(2), 191–205. doi: 10.1080/17524030902916657

Muir Gray, J. A. (1999). Postmodern medicine. *Lancet, 354,* 1550–1553.

Noahspins. (2012, February 12). Re: Getting personal [Web log message]. Retrieved from http://thinkingmomsrevolution.com/getting-personal/

Noh, H., Ponting, C., Boulding, H., Meader, S., Betancur, C., Buxbaum, J., Pinto, D., Marshall, C., Lionel, A., Sherer, S., & Webber, C. (2013). Network topologies and convergent aetiologies arising from deletions and duplications observed in individuals with autism. *PLOS Genetics*, *9*(6), e1003523. doi:10.1371/journal.pgen.1003523

Poppy. (2013). Poppy flips autism the bird. In H. Conroy, R. Sears, & L. Goes (Eds.), *The Thinking Moms' Revolution*. New York, NY: Skyhorse Publishing.

Quantumerik. (2011, May 10). EBCALA (Elizabeth Birt Center for Law and Advocacy), Press Conference [Video file]. Retrieved from http://youtube/zo3fONPmD08

The Rev. (2012, July 12). Declaration of independence from medical tyranny, institutional corruption, and government apathy [Web log message]. The Thinking Moms' Revolution. Retrieved from http://thinkingmomsrevolution.com/the-thinking-moms-declaration-of-independence-from-medical-tyranny-institutional-corruption-and-government-apathy/

The Rev. (2013, June 7). Why you have to tell YOUR story [Web log message]. The Thinking Moms' Revolution. Retrieved from http://thinkingmomsrevolution.com/why-you-have-to-tell-your-story/

Revolutions Never Go Backwards – Wendell Philips. (2011, November 10). The Thinking Moms' Revolution. Retrieved from http://thinkingmomsrevolution.com/the-times-they-are-a-changing/§hash.lfyVZaYd.dpbs

Robinson, J. (2012, May 21). Ultrasound and autism: A connection? *Psychology Today*. Retrieved from http://www.psychologytoday.com/blog/my-life-aspergers/201205/ultrasound-and-autism-connection

Twonk. (2013). Twonk: Into the fire. In H. Conroy, R. Sears, & L. Goes (Eds.), *The Thinking Moms' Revolution*. New York, NY: Skyhorse Publishing.

60

ANTIDEPRESSANTS AND IATROGENIC SUICIDALITY

Disturbing arguments in the politics of the supplement

L. Paul Strait

UNIVERSITY OF SOUTHERN CALIFORNIA, USA

G. Thomas Goodnight

UNIVERSITY OF SOUTHERN CALIFORNIA, USA
SENIOR SCHOLAR AWARD WINNER

In this essay, we review a case in which disingenuous interlocutors created a public scientific controversy and invested it with enough ambiguity to delay the reformation of consensus for decades. Specifically, we examine the controversial link between antidepressant medication and suicidality. We read the antidepressant-suicidality controversy in two interconnected ways: first, as an instance where tactical institutional discounting of arguable effects produced state-of-the-art rationales for needed research while publically stigmatizing criticism and its engagement; second, as the strategic management of the ambiguous tensions between depression and sadness, lifestyle-enhancing drugs and disease-treating medication, and the division of risk-management labor entailed in a system in which prescription-only medication is directly marketed to potential patient-consumers.

Accordingly, our inquiry examines the dynamics of pseudo-controversy within a constellation of concerns we label the *politics of the supplement*, by which we mean a field of contestation concerning the risks and benefits of new technologies of the self aimed at redressing defects in one's human nature. *Supplements* are material and symbolic surpluses that promise to: overcome lack through improving the security of living, aid in coping with chronic impairment, or retard undignified outcomes of mortality. The politics of the supplement fit into the larger category of what Giddens (1991) called life politics, "a politics of self-actualization in a reflexively ordered environment, where that reflexivity links self and body to systems of global scope," in which the meaning of risk and its associated burdens of proof are contested, and where market forces, scientific expertise, and other intersecting institutional influences "intrude deeply into the reflexive project of the self" as it is carried out at the material level (p. 214). We argue that the politics of the supplement rhetorically entwine desire, risk-engagement, and satisfaction in individual and collective contexts of morbidity and mortality. In the following section, we provide an overview of the antidepressant-suicidality controversy and the historical and institutional contexts in which it developed. We then take up the question of whether the debate should be understood as an example of pseudo-controversy. Finally, we resituate the (pseudo-)controversy in terms of the politics of the supplement and show that the peculiar dynamics of the controversy are structured around a logic of risk-management that appears in a wide variety of contemporary argumentative contexts.

Antidepressants and Iatrogenic Suicidality

When antidepressants were discovered, it was well known in the medical community that antidepressants could induce suicidal thoughts, but this was not seen as especially problematic because the patients were all severely ill and closely monitored (Loomer, Saunders, & Kline, 1957). Indeed, the behavioral side effects were documented before the antidepressant main effects were discovered. Before medical researchers noticed the antidepressant effects of isoniazid (a tuberculosis medicine), a case report appeared describing a patient who became violently suicidal. There was "unequivocal evidence" of a causal relationship, "including a fairly sudden onset after a period of drug therapy . . . [that] rather quickly cleared up as soon as the drug was discontinued" (Pleasure, 1954, pp. 315–316). In the paper announcing the discovery of the first tricyclic antidepressant imipramine, Roland Kuhn (1958) warned of an "increased risk of suicide" during the early stages of treatment, leading him to suggest as a reasonable precaution that psychiatrists "commit [their patients] to an institution" before beginning treatment (p. 464). Four months before the first commercially successful antidepressant (amitriptyline) was approved by the Food and Drug Administration (FDA), William Sargant (1961) presciently raised concerns about the "intensive advertising of the new antidepressant drugs for cases of depression in which they may be quite unsuitable, and if used can only increase the grave risks of suicide always present in severe depressive illnesses" (p. 225).

Institutional amnesia about this link 30 years later coincided with the immense popularity of the selective serotonin reuptake inhibitor (SSRI) fluoxetine (branded Prozac). Noted for its relatively favorable side-effects profile, Prozac quickly achieved superstar status, appearing on the front covers of *Newsweek, Time,* and *New Yorker,* in the play *Prozac Sisters,* the video game *Virtual Prozac,* and in psychiatrist Peter Kramer's (1993) best-selling *Listening to Prozac: A Psychiatrist Explores Antidepressant Drugs and the Remaking of the Self.* Celebrated in the popular press as a "happy pill," a "wonder drug," and "the feel-good pill," Prozac had by the mid-1990s become the most well known brand name in psychiatric medicine (Montagne, 2001, p. 1267). The emerging concept of "cosmetic pharmacology," by which psychiatric medication could be used to change patients "not just away from illness but toward some desirable psychological state," inspired suggestions that all sorts of non-depressed people might benefit from trying Prozac as a "personality enhancer" (Cowley & Springen, 1990, p. 38).

Physicians generally do not try to conceal or downplay the risks of modern pharmaceuticals. Far from threatening the institutional legitimacy of modern medicine, these risks provide a justification for prescription-only arrangements that make physicians into the exclusive gatekeepers of regulated pharmaceuticals. Surprisingly, then, psychiatrists were quick to discount the reports (Gorman, Liebowitz, & Fyer, 1987; King et al., 1991) of suicidality as an adverse effect of fluoxetine. The first paper establishing a pattern of suicidality over multiple cases described patients with relatively mild symptoms of depression suddenly fantasizing about "killing themselves with a gun . . . [or dying] in a gas explosion or car crash," leading the clinical psychologists who authored the study to comment that "it was remarkable how violent these thoughts were" (Teicher, Glod, & Cole, 1990, pp. 209–210). In response, a *Time* magazine story in July 1990 quoted Paul Leber, director of the FDA's neuropharmacology division, arguing that people should not be "scared away" from this "wonder drug," as "the evidence linking Prozac to suicidal behavior is tenuous and relies mostly on anecdotal histories" (Toufexis & Purvis, 1990, p. 54). The *British Medical Journal* published a large meta-analysis of data involving thousands of patients, in which all mentions of suicide were recoded as symptoms of a depressive episode; having made this methodological move, the authors concluded that there was no link between fluoxetine and suicide (Beasley et al., 1991). After pontificating that evidence-based medicine should trump anecdotal clinical wisdom, one of the study's authors remarked: "I doubt if there is any study that could be done that could possibly demonstrate a relationship between fluoxetine and suicidality" (*Deposition of John Heiligenstein*, 1994). This hypothetical epistemic limitation stems from the apparent difficulty in distinguishing suicidality caused by depression from suicidality caused by treatment. Similarly, several defenders of fluoxetine argued that by effectively treating depression, fluoxetine lowered the overall risk of suicide (Jick, Dean, & Jick, 1995; Nakielny, 1994).

Against this entrenched view, evidence to the contrary slowly began to emerge over the following decade. For example, David Healy (2000) conducted a study with sertraline, another SSRI, on healthy volunteers, two of whom became suicidal within two weeks, a finding that is statistically significant at the level of $p = 0.0000005$. After more studies of this nature began to accumulate, the FDA in October 2004 issued a public warning about the risk of suicidality (in children and adolescents) being treated with SSRIs. Inverting the epistemic priority of quantitative data over clinical observation established by Leber and Heiligenstein, the institutional response was to suggest that research protocols are complicated and that this was "an instance where clinical wisdom surpasses evidence-based medicine" (Rihmer & Akiskal, 2006, p. 10). Not persuaded, the FDA in 2007 completed its own meta-analysis of data from trials conducted from 1988 to 2006, concluding that while the benefits of SSRI therapy most likely outweigh the risks, recipients of SSRIs (vs. placebo) were twice as likely to exhibit suicidality. Consequently, the FDA (2010) required that prescribing and patient information sheets for all antidepressant medications carry an expanded "black-box warning" disclosing information about an increased risk of suicidal symptoms in young adults aged 18 to 24.

Pseudo-Controversy?

Pseudo-controversy, characterized by the false representation of expert dissensus in the public sphere, is a burgeoning area of research in argumentation studies (Banning, 2009; Ceccarelli, 2011; Dreier & Martin, 2010; Fritch, Palczewski, Farrell, & Short, 2006; Kelly & Hoerl, 2012; Murray, 2007). In a typical pseudo-controversy, "commercial and political entities labor to generate a perception of widespread debate among a scientific community where instead there is a strong agreement" (Banning, 2009, p. 287). One might see this case as the same phenomenon in reverse. But as we have shown, the antidepressant-suicidality link was first documented in the 1950s and did not become controversial for more than three decades. When the link was first contested, the new controversy was immediately characterized as a pseudo-controversy by the same disingenuous actors who were responsible for its existence. That they were disingenuous is now beyond question, as investigators have published internal memos between pharmaceutical executives and the scientists who contested the link, revealing that Eli Lilly was aware of the side-effect years before Prozac came to market, and that the various data-analysis strategies and talking-points that were deployed to discount concerns about the risks were planned in light of legal liabilities and PR imperatives (Healy, 2004).

Yet in contrast to a pseudo-controversy in which an asymmetrical debate is made to appear symmetrical, this debate actually became asymmetrical and remained so until the evidence became overwhelming, illustrating perhaps the extent of influence the pharmaceutical industry maintains with psychiatric opinion-leaders. The ambiguities and paradoxes inherent in the politics of the supplement help to explain the peculiar trajectory of this pseudo-controversy. A risk society manages the anxieties that it creates by identifying perceived deficiencies that can be ameliorated through supplementation. When supplementation fails, there is uncertainty about whether the supplementation was insufficient or excessive. The anxieties of risk management are only intensified by an awareness that the most serious risks we face as a society are those we created (e.g., nuclear war, climate change, economic depression). As serious as these impersonal risks are, the risks entailed in the reflexive projects of the self pose existential threats to the individual person in a way that is uniquely and profoundly disturbing.

The discursive framework in which individual subjects regard their own human nature as incomplete is a distinctive feature of late modernity. As Lyotard (1991) argued, "[that] children have to be educated is a circumstance which only proceeds from the fact that they are not completely led by nature, not programmed. The institutions which constitute culture supplement this native lack" (p. 3). The self is always an incomplete reflexive project. As a "surplus or supplement whose political force derives from the sense in which it evades recuperation by instrumental use or determinate meaning" (Carroll, 2008, p. 178), the antidepressant transcends the technical milieu in which its use is managed by experts, becoming a technology of the self. The signifier *anti-depressant* contains a referent to yet another supplement, the diagnosis of depression, by which psychiatry medicalizes human misery. Yet the meaning of *depression*, as with that of the implied non-depressed healthy state, is no less elusive. The spontaneous emergence of violent fantasies, sometimes leading to suicidal acts, activates the deepest anxieties one can have concerning a mood supplement. As Derrida (1974) explained:

> When the supplement accomplishes its office and fills the lack, there is no harm done. The abyss is the chasm which can remain open between the lapse of Nature and the delay of the supplement ... The play of the supplement is indefinite. References refer to references ... This play of the supplement [entails] the always open possibility of a catastrophic regression and the annulment of progress.
>
> *(p. 298)*

The reflexive project of the self is not simply side-tracked, but completely derailed with the auto-destruction of the self. This is why iatrogenic suicidality is so profoundly disturbing.

All state-of-the art institutional practices involve a balance of risk and uncertainty. The contested framing of the risks of state-of-the-art practices occurs at "a crucial nexus between the scientific and public spheres [which] exists precisely at those points where scientific theories and research programs have implications for prevalent world views, ideologies, and practical social policies" (Czubaroff, 1997, p. 52). Despite the pervasive presence of antidepressant drugs in the popular imaginary, the public is woefully misinformed about their mechanisms of action and the array of potential benefits and risks (Blease, 2013; Glazer, 2013; Lacasse & Leo, 2005). If judgments about the risks and benefits of medication are to be informed by public deliberation, the potential for that deliberation to be distorted by pseudo-controversy constitutes a threat to public health. But the politics of the supplement call into question the categories of health and illness in the first place. With approximately 70% of people in the United States consuming at least one prescription medication every day (Zhong et al., 2013), health is not the normal or typical condition of the body but rather an ongoing but incomplete project that always ends in failure. The antidepressant-suicidality controversy arises from the ambiguities, tensions, and slippages in the meanings assigned to diagnostic and therapeutic concepts, which together constitute the polysemic grounding for the neurotic fascination with the possibility to reshape our human nature pill-by-pill. Even its status as a (pseudo-)controversy is ambiguous. Health controversies get hashed out in this discursive environment, and the semiotic ambiguity that runs through the biomedical conceptual corpus also permeates our words for contesting uncertainty and risk.

Our reading of the antidepressant-suicidality controversy reveals the techniques of institutional self-protection manifested by the discounting of standing research and by associating criticism with illegitimate, non-scientific research. The linguistic turn in this kind of argument thwarts the transparent practice of science through subordinating uncertainty to the interests of money and power. By linking a biomedical technology to the reflexive project of the self, disingenuous scientific actors were able to convert consensus into controversy and finally pseudo-controversy, as concerns about the safety of a commercial product were experienced as disturbing threats to the self-identity of both the psychiatrist as physician and the patient as health consumer. Antidepressants treat a disease defined (in part) by an elevated risk of suicide and suicidal ideation. By packaging depression as a risk disorder and marketing Prozac as its remedy, the terms of the debate were so infused with doubt that it became difficult to discuss the increased risk of suicidality as an adverse effect without a high degree of causal uncertainty. Consequently, it took nearly two decades to untangle the risks that had actually been well documented decades before the first Prozac prescription was ever filled.

References

Banning, M. E. (2009). When poststructural theory and contemporary politics collide – The vexed case of global warming. *Communication and Critical/Cultural Studies*, 6(3), 285–304.

Beasley, C. M., Dornseif, B. E., Bosomworth, J. C., Sayler, M. E., Rampey, A. H., Heiligenstein, J. H., . . . Massica, D. N. (1991). Fluoxetine and suicide: A meta-analysis of controlled trials of treatment for depression. *British Medical Journal*, 303, 685–692.

Blease, C. (2013). The duty to be *Well*-informed: The case of depression. *Journal of Medical Ethics*. Published Online First: April 26, 2013, 1–5. doi:10.1136/medethics-2012-101122

Carroll, J. (2008). The limits of the sublime, the sublime of limits: Hermeneutics as a critique of the postmodern sublime. *The Journal of Aesthetics and Art Criticism*, 66(2), 171–181.

Ceccarelli, L. (2011). Manufactured scientific controversy: Science, rhetoric, and public debate. *Rhetoric & Public Affairs*, 14(2), 195–228.

Cowley, G., & Springen, K. (1990). The promise of Prozac [Cover story]. *Newsweek*, 115(13), 38.

Czubaroff, J. (1997). The public dimension of scientific controversies. *Argumentation*, 11(1), 51–74.

Deposition of John Heiligenstein. (1994, April 27 and 28). In *Fentriss v. Eli Lilly*, Jefferson Circuit Court. Retrieved from http://www.healyprozac.com/Trials/Fentress/Depositions/Heiligenstein%20JH.txt

Derrida, J. (1974). *Of grammatology*. Baltimore, MD: The Johns Hopkins University Press.

Dreier, P., & Martin, C. R. (2010). How ACORN was framed: Political controversy and media agenda setting. *Perspectives on Politics*, 8(03), 761–792.

Food and Drug Administration. (2010). Antidepressant use in children, adolescents, and adults. *U.S. Food and Drug Administration: Drug safety and availability*. Retrieved from http://www.fda.gov/Drugs/DrugSafety/InformationbyDrugClass/ucm096273.htm

Fritch, J., Palczewski, C., Farrell, J., & Short, E. (2006). Disingenuous controversy: Responses to Ward Churchill's 9/11 essay. *Argumentation and Advocacy*, 42(4), 190–205.

Giddens, A. (1991). *Modernity and self-identity: Self and society in the late modern age*. Stanford, CA: Stanford University Press.

Glazer, W. (2013). Scientific journalism: The dangers of misinformation. *Current Psychiatry, 12*(6), 33–35.

Gorman, J. M., Liebowitz, M. R., & Fyer, A. J. (1987). An open trial of fluoxetine in the treatment of panic attacks. *Journal of Clinical Psychopharmacology, 5*, 329–332.

Healy, D. (1997). *The antidepressant era*. Cambridge, MA: Harvard University Press.

Healy, D. (2000). Antidepressant associated suicidality. *European Neuropsychopharmacology, 10*(Supplement 3), 260.

Healy, D. (2004). *Let them eat Prozac: The unhealthy relationship between the pharmaceutical industry and depression*. New York: New York University Press.

Jick, S., Dean, A. D., & Jick, H. (1995). Antidepressants and suicide. *British Medical Journal, 310*, 215–218.

Kelly, C. R., & Hoerl, K. E. (2012). Genesis in hyperreality: Legitimizing disingenuous controversy at the creation museum. *Argumentation and Advocacy, 48*(3), 123–141.

King, R. A., Riddle, M. A., Chappell, P. B., Hardin, M. T., Anderson, G. M., Lombroso, P., & Scahill, L. (1991). Emergence of self-destructive phenomena in children and adolescents during fluoxetine treatment. *Journal of the American Academy of Child, 30*(2), 179–186.

Kramer, P. (1993). *Listening to Prozac: A psychiatrist explores antidepressant drugs and the remaking of the self*. Bloomington: Indiana University Press.

Kuhn, R. (1958). The treatment of depressive states with G 22355 (imipramine hydrochloride). *The American Journal of Psychiatry, 115*, 459–464.

Lacasse, J. R., & Leo, J. (2005). Serotonin and depression: A disconnect between the advertisements and the scientific literature. *Public Library of Science Medicine, 2*(12), 101–106.

Loomer, H. P., Saunders, J. C., & Kline, N. S. (1957). A clinical and pharmaco-dynamic evaluation of iproniazid as a psychic energizer. *Psychiatric Research Reports, 8*, 129–141.

Lyotard, J. F. (1991). *The inhuman: Reflection on time*. (G. Bennington & R. Bowlby, Trans.). Stanford, CA: Stanford University Press.

Montagne, M. (2001). Mass media representations as drug information for patients: The Prozac phenomenon. *Substance Use & Misuse, 36*(9 & 10), 1261–1274.

Murray, B. (2007). Manufactured arguments: Turning consensus into controversy does not advance science. *British Journal of Sports Medicine, 41*(2), 106–107. doi:10.1136/bjsm.2006.030106

Nakielny, J. (1994). The fluoxetine and suicide controversy: Correspondence. *CNS Drugs, 2*(3), 252–254.

Pleasure, H. (1954). Psychiatric and neurological side-effects of isoniazid and iproniazid. *Archives of Neurology and Psychiatry, 72*(3), 313–320.

Rihmer, Z., & Akiskal, H. (2006). Do antidepressants t(h)reat(en) depressives? Toward a clinically judicious formulation of the antidepressant-suicidality FDA advisory in light of declining national suicide statistics from many countries. *Journal of Affective Disorders, 94*, 3–13.

Sargant, W. (1961). Drugs in the treatment of depression. *British Medical Journal, 1*(5221), 225–227.

Teicher, M. H., Glod, C., & Cole, J. O. (1990). Emergence of intense suicidal preoccupation during fluoxetine treatment. *American Journal of Psychiatry, 147*(2), 207–210.

Toufexis, A., & Purvis, A. (1990). Warnings about a miracle drug. *Time, 136*(5), 54.

Zhong, W., Maradit-Kremers, H., Sauver, J. L. S., Yawn, B. P., Ebbert, J. O., Roger, V. L., . . . Rocca, W. A. (2013). Age and sex patterns of drug prescribing in a defined American population. *Mayo Clinic Proceedings, 88*(7), 697–707. doi:10.1016/j.mayocp.2013.04.021

61

DEBATING TECHNICAL RHETORIC IN THE PUBLIC SPHERE

Statistical forecasting and science denial in the 2012 presidential election

Benjamin R. Warner

UNIVERSITY OF MISSOURI – COLUMBIA, USA

Over the previous four years, Nate Silver's election forecast model has correctly predicted the Electoral College winner in 99/100 states and the outcome of 100/105 Senate elections. Silver was not the only election forecaster to succeed. Sam Wang, Drew Linzer, and Simon Jackman all developed election forecast models that predicted essentially the same outcome in the 2012 presidential election. In spite of this consensus among election forecasters, many in commercial print and broadcast media portrayed the election as a tossup. Some pundits even participated in a vocal backlash to the forecasts. Peggy Noonan, former communications director for Ronald Reagan and columnist for *The Wall Street Journal*, reacted to Silver's forecast by arguing that "nobody knows anything" about who would win; David Brooks of *The New York Times* proclaimed that election forecasters lived in "silly land;" and Jennifer Rubin of *The Washington Post* tweeted that polling averages were "junk" (as cited in Bartlett, 2012, para. 7). Joe Scarborough, former U.S. House Representative and host of *Morning Joe* on *MSNBC*, argued that the race was a tossup and anybody suggesting otherwise, Nate Silver included by name, "should be kept away from typewriters, computers, laptops, and microphones for the next ten days because they're jokes" (Scarborough & Ridley, 2012).

Mainstream criticism of Silver echoed a full-throated rebuttal to forecasting that was especially prevalent in online media during the final weeks of the 2012 election. This essay examines the rebuttal as a special case of science denial in which empirical claims were engaged by lay critics and dubious standards of evaluation were used to discount technical knowledge. I identify three dominant argumentative strategies used by forecast deniers: First, election forecasting was personified and presented as the subjective opinion of one person; second, the judgments of the forecaster were attributed to partisan bias; and third, uncertainty was cultivated through selective attention to data. These strategies combined to reframe the grounds of the conversation from one about empirical estimations of probable election outcomes to one about competing partisan guesses. I describe this shift as a mechanism deniers used to reduce the burden of proof on lay arguers who challenge technical knowledge in the public sphere. In the sections that follow, I review the tension between technical and public argument spheres, analyze each of the three argumentative strategies used by forecast deniers, and consider the implications for technical knowledge.

Technical Knowledge and Science Denial

The status of technical knowledge in the public sphere was a feature of Goodnight's (1982) essay on spheres of argument. At that time, he was concerned that the technical sphere would dominate and stifle public debate. When revisiting his essay, he recently observed a different problem – while technical discourse is highly accessible, the status of technical knowledge has been diminished by manufactured controversies. Technical knowledge, he argued, needs to "find productive entry into public communication" (Goodnight, 2012, p. 265). The relative prominence of science denial in the form of the anti-vaccine movement (Whidden, 2012), the HIV/AIDS pseudo-controversy (Ceccarelli, 2011), the evolution debate (Ceccarrelli, 2011), and climate denial (Ceccarelli, 2011; Paliewicz, 2012) all suggest that technical knowledge, far from supplanting public debate, may not receive appropriate deference.

While this essay seeks to understand how opponents engage technical claims in the public sphere, the analogy to science denial is imperfect. Most science denial involves public critics manufacturing controversy and uncertainty by cherry-picking data, misconstruing the nature of scientific doubt, recruiting dissident experts, and manipulating the norms of free expression and balance in media coverage (Ceccarelli, 2011). The burden of proof is different for those who seek to challenge the validity of election forecasts because, while forecasting is based on fairly settled norms of statistical inference, the actual models are not subject to peer review or replication. Because the claims come from a few statistical forecasters rather than a vast corpus of scientific research, challengers do not need to cast doubt on an entire body of research. Thus, the election forecasting debate is a unique instance of technical knowledge in the public sphere and presents an opportunity to examine how technical knowledge that is outside of the scientific community is debated.

To determine how critics in the public sphere evaluated the technical claims advanced by election forecasters, I analyze a series of dominant forecast denial texts. These texts were the most prominently referenced, linked, and shared instances of what came to be known as "Silver Trutherism." The central texts were an article by Dylan Byers (2012) in *Politico*; a piece published in *Examiner.com* by Dean Chambers (2012), the man who became infamous in 2012 for "unskewing" the polls; a *BuzzFeed* article by Rosie Gray (2012); a *National Review* editorial penned by Josh Jordan (2012); Matt Lewis's (2012) *Daily Caller* article; and two blog posts from the conservative journalist/pundit Robert McCain (2012a, 2012b).

Make Forecasting Subjective

Forecast deniers' first argumentative strategy was to transform the technical claim from an empirical result to the subjective judgment of an individual. Although four prominent forecasting models predicted essentially the same results, Silver's received exclusive attention. His predictions were presented as opinion rather than the statistical output of a forecasting model. This was primarily accomplished by suggesting that the weighted poll averages used in Silver's model were a function of his judgment rather than a regression trend line, the observed house effects of each poll, and the past performance of each polling firm. For example, in describing

Silver's weighted polling average, Chambers (2012) explained that, "he appears to look at the polls available and decide which ones to put more 'weighting' on" (para. 4). In misreading the house effect adjustment, Chambers (2012) told his readers that Silver "labels some polling firms Republicans, even if they over sample Democrats in their surveys, apparently because he doesn't agree with their results" (para. 4). Agency is assigned to Silver and the procedures are presented as individual decisions. Lewis (2012) made the same attribution when he suggested "Silver can just 'adjust' his numbers in, say, early November – if he senses an Obama defeat" (para. 12). The implication is that Silver manipulated data, making his projections a function of his will rather than the data itself.

McCain (2012a) dismissed the data more freely than most, saying the projection was "based on . . . what? I dunno. I'm not an expert with a New York Times column or anything, much less a Magical Forecasting Model™" (para. 2). McCain's characterization of forecasting as magic is representative of his broader dismissal of the forecast as subjective interpretation. "The plural of 'anecdote'" he argued "is data" (para. 6). He would go on to suggest that "Nate's just pulling his 'data' out of his ass and wishcasting" (para. 8) and clarified "I have no definite reason to accuse Nate Silver of deliberate fraud, and it's entirely plausible that he's just the victim of his own erroneous faith in statistical modeling" (para. 9).

While McCain's initial post did not echo the poll-weighting critique, his follow-up described the weighting as purposeful, conscious, and a function of Silver's preferences (McCain, 2012b). Jordan (2012) argued that Romney lagged in forecasting models because, "in Silver's opinion" (para. 7), he would have trouble winning 270 electoral votes. In trusting the polling data from battle-ground states, according to Jordan, Silver was exercising his opinion. Hence, "the real problem with Silver's model" is that the "weighting he puts into state polls gives an edge to Obama, and the distribution of that weighting is highly subjective" (Jordan, 2012, para. 7).

Jordan (2012) thus compared the regression weights applied to polls to the unskewed polls produced by Chambers, suggesting that Silver's method is "just a more subtle" (para. 8) version of data manipulation. Indeed, Jordan presented the model weights as "what you think of the pollster and the results" rather than "what is actually inside the poll" (para. 13). He suggested that Silver "walks a very thin line between forecasting and cheerleading" (para. 13) and even conflated a blog in which Silver characterized a Gallop poll as a likely outlier with a decision to exclude it. The data is thus personified and presented as subjective opinion, no better or worse than that of anyone else. The probabilities produced by the model are not data-driven empirical predictions; they are the mere opinion of a *New York Times* blogger.

Make Partisanship Salient

By creating the impression that election forecasts showing Obama as the favorite were actually Silver's subjective judgment, the debate about the accuracy of the prediction was moved from a technical evaluation of forecasting models to an assessment of Silver's opinion. The second set of arguments advanced by forecast deniers sought to cast doubt on Silver by implying his judgments were a function of his partisanship. Making Silver's worldview salient could contextualize his subjective judgments about the polling data. This is implicit when McCain (2012a) called the model "wishcasting" (para. 8) and when Chambers (2012) referred to it as "cheerleading" (para. 13). Each of these authors also foregrounded Silver's partisanship for their readers. In the opening to his article, Chambers (2012) placed Silver's analysis in partisan context: "While many conservatives look to former Clinton political consultant Dick Morris to understand the polls and political surveys on elections, or even a site like

UnSkewedPolls.com, those on the left look to *New York Times* blogger Nate Silver" (para. 1). Silver therefore appeared to provide the same service for liberals that pundits on the right did for conservative readers. McCain (2012a) opened by telling his readers, "Nate Silver continues to lead the Democrat Graveyard Whistling Choir" (para. 1). Again, Silver is introduced via his partisan orientation.

Though not all forecasting deniers introduced Silver as a partisan, his partisanship was never absent. Gray (2012) suggested that Silver was the most trusted name in polling "if you're an Obama supporter" (para. 7) and pointed out that "Silver is a declared liberal who privately reviewed Obama campaign polling in 2008" (para. 13). Jordan (2012) also implied that Silver's writing was primarily consumed by Democrats and observed, "Nate Silver is openly rooting for Obama, and it shows in the way he forecasts the election" (para. 5). Lewis (2012) wondered if Silver's predictions were "wishful thinking," pointing out "Silver was up front about being an Obama supporter in 2008, and it's hard to blame conservatives for wondering if he might be working the refs" (para. 10). Byers (2012), for his part, did not include reference to Silver's partisanship though he did advance a weaker version of the partisanship argument by suggesting that Silver's forecasts were sedatives for nervous liberals whose "heart rates continue to fluctuate with the release of every new poll" (para. 1).

Cultivate Uncertainty

If the first component of forecast denial was to move the prediction from an empirical estimate of probable outcomes to the subjective judgments of the forecaster, the second was to reframe the judgments so they were interpreted through a partisan frame. Argued this way, Silver could be thought of as one voice among many partisan pundits. To complete the denial, the third argumentative strategy illustrated why Silver's partisan guessing should be discredited. Forecast deniers borrowed a trope from the argumentative arsenal of science denial: cherry-pick data to portray empirical uncertainty. The 2012 election provided a unique opportunity for forecast deniers because Romney fared much better in national polling averages than in polls of battle ground states. Sean Trende (2012), the senior elections analyst for *Real Clear Politics*, even suggested that the national and state polling told fundamentally different stories about the election. The forecast models, by including both state and national polls, successfully predicted the election outcome in spite of this apparent discrepancy. Nevertheless, the availability of credible national polling provided a reasonable-sounding empirical basis to dismiss Silver. Gray (2012) argued that "his forecasts are the answer to a welter of conflicting national poll results and a Republican insistence that Mitt Romney is, in fact, winning" (para. 4), and Byers (2012) contrasted Silver's prediction with "this year's polls" which "suggest a nailbiter" (para. 2). Lewis (2012), meanwhile, admitted that an Obama victory was "entirely possible," but guessed "right now, it's probably a 50–50 proposition" (para. 5), and argued "empirical evidence suggests the race is actually close" (para. 6). Following this logic, Jordan (2012) insisted that the race was much closer than Silver's projections implied because the "incumbent president is stuck at 47 percent nationwide, the odds might not be in Obama's favor, and they certainly aren't in his favor by a 67–33 margin" (para. 6). This variation on the national polling argument invoked the myth that an incumbent president with less than 50 percent approval will lose because undecided voters will break for the challenger. The empirical record suggests no support for this incumbency myth (Silver, 2012).

While most of the forecast denials portrayed a close and uncertain race, Chambers (2012) and McCain (2012a) argued that the objective evidence suggested a decisive Romney win.

McCain (2012a) dismissed systematic evaluation of data because "events cannot be predicted by polls and all we can do (unless we wish to make a claim to Special Expertise) is watch the trend and keep an eye out for the anecdotal evidence that might indicate which way the trend will go in future days" (para. 10). The anecdotal evidence he saw suggested a Romney victory. For example, the number of yard signs and rumors about Obama's campaign decisions suggested he would lose Virginia (McCain, 2012a). Furthermore, a national poll showing Romney leading among independents caused McCain (2012b) to conclude that "we're gonna be looking at an all-out Republican romp Nov. 6" (para. 6). Chambers (2012) employed much the same tactic, cherry-picking polls to argue against Silver:

> He still has Obama winning Virginia and Colorado even though the most recent and credible polls in those states show Romney winning them. He gives Obama a 73.4 percent chance of winning Ohio, which is downright absurd, as Rasmussen has the candidate tied in Ohio, which really means the undecided voters tip the state of Ohio to Romney.
>
> *(para. 3)*

Favorable results for Romney were highlighted and combined with selective applications of anecdotal observations. Similarly, a majority of Jordan's (2012) article is filled with polling minutiae reinterpreted to appear favorable to Romney.

Lessons from Forecasting Denial

The forecasting denials analyzed here are a special case of science denial. Although an enormous body of scientific literature does not need to be refuted as is the case with climate, vaccines, the HIV/AIDS conspiracy, and evolution, public critics still must dispute empirical claims that they may not be qualified or motivated to evaluate on technical grounds. So, as with denials in other contexts (Ceccarelli, 2011), public critics seek to cultivate controversy. If controversy is present – if smart people simply disagree about a complicated question – audience members are free to pick a side and believe as they please. Disagreement with technical knowledge presents a different burden of proof. Those who disagree must overcome the presumption of the empirical record and justify why the claims they challenge are either a result of a faulty procedure or why the case being examined will deviate from the laws or theories associated with the technical field in question. The forecasting denials analyzed here attempted to shift the grounds of debate by portraying empirical prediction as subjective judgments made by an avowed partisan in the face of national uncertainty. The burden of proof for their arguments was thus reduced; it was a debate between partisans in the public sphere rather than a challenge to empirical knowledge. Election forecasting denial illustrates the argumentative strategies used to shift spheres of argument and the consequences of this shift on the burden of proof.

The objective of this essay is not to imply that election forecasts should be accepted uncritically. Low probability events happen frequently. There will surely be an election in the future that is too close to predict with high confidence. It is possible that social changes will advance more quickly than polling procedures and Dewey will once again defeat Truman. All of these are reasons to maintain a healthy amount of skepticism regarding election forecasting. However, healthy skepticism should not be conflated with science denial. Technical claims supported by rigorous procedures and empirical data were dismissed through argumentative manipulations of the burden of proof. Transforming the grounds of debate from the technical sphere to the public sphere reduced the debate to a disagreement between partisans. These arguments did not diminish the reliability of the technical claims. Instead, they were little more than public spectacle for an audience seeking reasons to doubt empirical evidence they found unpleasant. As Goodnight (2012) pointed out, technical knowledge is more available now than at any time in recent memory. It is incumbent upon scholars of public argument to understand and evaluate the conditions under which this knowledge is introduced into the public sphere, for these conditions may influence things more important than who is better at guessing the outcome of an election.

References

Bartlett, T. (2012, November 7). The poll quants won the election [Web log message]. *The Chronicle of Higher Education*. Retrieved from http://chronicle.com/blogs/percolator/the-poll-quants-won-the-election/31722

Byers, D. (2012, October 29). Nate Silver: One-term celebrity? [Web log message]. *Politico*. Retrieved from http://www.politico.com/blogs/media/2012/10/nate-silver-romney-clearly-could-still-win-147618.html

Ceccarelli, L. (2011). Manufactured science controversy: Science, rhetoric, and public debate. *Rhetoric & Public Affairs*, *14*, 195–228. doi: 10.1353/rap.2010.0222

Chambers, D. (2012, October 25). The far left turns to Nate Silver for wisdom on the polls. *Examiner.com*. Retrieved from http://www.examiner.com/article/the-far-left-turns-to-nate-silver-for-wisdom-on-the-polls?cid=db_articles

Goodnight, G. T. (1982). The personal, technical, and public spheres: A speculative inquiry into the art of public deliberation. *Journal of the American Forensic Association*, *18*, 214–227.

Goodnight, G. T. (2012). The personal, technical, and public spheres: A note on 21st century critical communication inquiry. *Argumentation and Advocacy*, *48*, 258–267.

Gray, R. (2012, October 29). Why liberals cling to Nate Silver. *BuzzFeed*. Retrieved from http://www.buzzfeed.com/rosiegray/why-liberals-cling-to-nate-silver

Jordan, J. (2012, October 22). Nate Silver's flawed model. *The National Review*. Retrieved from http://www.nationalreview.com/articles/331192/nate-silver-s-flawed-model-josh-jordan

Lewis, M. K. (2012, October 19). Nate Silver vs. the world. *The Daily Caller*. Retrieved from http://dailycaller.com/2012/10/19/nate-silver-vs-the-world/

McCain, R. S. (2012a, October 23). Signs and omens: Obama's fading hope and the graveyard whistling choir. *The Other McCain*. Retrieved from http://theothermccain.com/2012/10/23/signs-and-omens-obama-campaign-and-the-graveyard-whistling-choir/

McCain, R. S. (2012b, October 26). Are you a "Nate Silver Truther?" *The Other McCain*. Retrieved online: http://theothermccain.com/2012/10/26/are-you-a-nate-silver-truther/

Paliewicz, N. S. (2012). Global warming and the interaction between the public and the technical spheres of argument: When standards for expertise really matter. *Argumentation and Advocacy*, *48*, 231–242.

Scarborough, J., & Ridley, J. (2012, October 29). [Television series episode]. In C. Licht (Executive producer), *Morning Joe*. New York, NY: MSNBC.

Silver, N. (2012, July 22). Do presidential polls break toward challengers? [Web log message]. *Five Thirty Eight*. Retrieved from http://fivethirtyeight.blogs.nytimes.com/2012/07/22/do-presidential-polls-break-toward-challengers/

Trende, S. (2012, October 31). What's behind the state-national poll divergence? *Real Clear Politics*. Retrieved from http://www.realclearpolitics.com/articles/2012/10/31/whats_behind_the_state-national_poll_divergence_115979.html

Waldman, P. (2012, November 1). Show us your model: Explaining Nate Silver trutherism and the real reasons liberals lean on the election's star blogger. *The American Prospect*. Retrieved from http://prospect.org/article/show-us-your-model

Whidden, R. A. (2012). Maternal expertise, vaccination recommendations, and the complexity of argument spheres. *Argumentation and Advocacy*, *48*, 243–257.

62

CULTURAL PEDAGOGY AS MOTIVATION AND THE ROLE OF "INSTITUTIONAL AGENTS" IN INTERCOLLEGIATE DEBATE

Luis M. Andrade

CALIFORNIA STATE UNIVERSITY, FULLERTON, USA

Jon Bruschke

CALIFORNIA STATE UNIVERSITY, FULLERTON, USA

Cultural pedagogy is an umbrella term for a style of education that incorporates minority members' lived experience into the way knowledge is understood. Cultural pedagogy affirms diverse cultural experiences, centers on students' experiential learning, and encourages educators to affirm distinct students' cultural and personal strengths. For example, a traditional study of U.S. history might emphasize democracy and economic progress and treat the genocide of indigenous people as a tragic footnote. A cultural pedagogy approach would reject any claim to a neutral history, explore how the genocide was the product of specific cultural assumptions, and review alternative cultural beliefs – overlooked by a dominant reading of history – as valuable alternatives. It would explore how contemporary institutions might still bear the mark of historical inequity. While traditionalists view cultural pedagogy as a supplement (largely driven by special interests and fringe cases) to academic content, cultural theorists view culture as central to knowledge production, which is never free from cultural influence.

Research has demonstrated that across academic fields cultural pedagogy motivates students to persist in school (Pew, 2007), especially in higher education (Hacket, 2003), and has been linked to retention and student success (Ambrosio, 2003; Stipek, 2002; Weinstein, Curran, & Tomlinson-Clark, 2003). Communication scholars have noted the usefulness of cultural pedagogy in the classroom (Allen, 2010; Alvesson, Ashcraft, & Thomas, 2008; Warren, 2001).

Despite these findings, a conservative backlash from academic institutions, politicians, and officials exists to censor cultural pedagogy (Calafell & Moreman, 2009; Delgado, 1998; Flores, 2000; Giroux, 2012; Holling, 2002). The most visible form of backlash has been the de-institutionalization of ethnic studies programs in Arizona's educational institutions.

Educators serve an important role in resisting censorship and practicing cultural pedagogy, yet their role is under-theorized (Bensimon, 2007; Martínez Alemán, 2007; Stage & Hubbard, 2007). Bensimon (2007) noted that educators:

> possess an expertise that enables them to be responsive to marginal and marginalized students. These individuals are not only knowledgeable in their subject matter or areas of specialty, but they also have the capacity to respond to students in ways that make them feel valued, worthy, and respected.
>
> *(p. 463)*

This essay seeks to explore the way these trends embody themselves in intercollegiate policy debate. Broadly speaking, a group is seeking to integrate cultural pedagogy into the argumentative lexicon, other forces are seeking to exclude it, and educators are the key agents who can embrace or reject this component of the curriculum. Specifically, we advance the following interconnected claims. First, women and minorities are under-represented in academic debate. Second, the content of debates plays a significant role in this exclusion. Third, the content of debates is largely determined by judges/coaches, and their decision to grant or deny credence to framework arguments can expand or contract the presence of arguments based on cultural pedagogy. Finally, we contend that cultural pedagogy, and not critical theory, presents content that can address demographic exclusion.

Demographic Exclusions

The first point, that demographic exclusion exists, we take to be beyond dispute. Several studies have explored sex equity in debate and *all* studies have found it wanting (Matz & Bruschke, 2006). Women are under-represented in debate compared to overall university enrollment and the differences are stark: Women comprise roughly 60% of the college student population, but only about 40% of the national-circuit competitor pool. No more than about 20% of highly successful college debaters are female. This pattern is persistent and there is no clear, rapid progress toward alleviating it. Evidence on racial minorities is much spottier, but extant data suggest that racial equity lags to even greater degrees (Allen, Trejo, Bartanen, Schroeder & Ulrich, 2004). All empirical data indicate a major under-representation problem in intercollegiate debate.

Content as a Contributor to Exclusion

Commentators have noted that the apparatus of traditional debate – including its content – plays a role in demographic exclusion. Rogers (1997) documented a bias, especially by judges, toward White male competitors and Hill (1997) similarly expressed concern over "traditional forensics models" that squelch the motivation of students of color. While space prevents a full exposition, we believe content plays a prominent role. Demographic exclusion is not a problem intercollegiate debate inherits from high schools, where women and minorities are *over*-represented in forensics teams (McRee & Cote, 2002). It can hardly be simply a recruiting problem given Urban Debate Leagues (UDLs) have now introduced literally hundreds of thousands of students to the activity. We do not believe that the coaches themselves hold individual racist beliefs or intentionally try to exclude women and minorities from their squads. This process of eliminating explanations leaves few remaining candidates.

We believe the cultural studies lesson from other areas of the academy probably holds true in debate; minority participants are generally less motivated to engage ideas that present themselves as culturally neutral but instead encode a dominant and largely White perspective (as Hill has noted), and are generally more willing to engage with ideas that embrace culture and connect themselves to the lived experience of minority participants. We take it as telling that the most diverse squads – for example, Louisville, Fullerton, Towson, and Emporia – share a common commitment to a culturally relevant argument style.

Educators as Agents of Change and Gatekeepers of Content

There is almost no central authority capable of wielding juridical power in intercollegiate debate. Official organizing bodies establish eligibility rules and calendar structures, but almost never attempt to regulate argument content. Codified rules are generally years behind practice. This is not meant as a criticism of these organizations or their structure; national forensic organizations that govern least may indeed govern best. But any serious examination of power in the debate community must look beyond official organizations.

Informal power is directly linked to argument practice and is apportioned on the basis of tournament success due to judges' ballots and legitimization of dominant arguments. Teams that do well because of judges' votes are heavily scouted; the arguments they advance and the authors they read become the focus of the research efforts of their opponents. In addition, winning arguments gain credibility because of judges' votes. If a team wins a national-circuit tournament early in the season by reading Nietzsche as an author, it is harder for a judge two tournaments later to dismiss a Nietzsche-based argument as too esoteric or poorly explained.

The judge's ballot has social significance. Judges hold the power to make arguments popular. If judges repeatedly vote against a specific argument, the popularity of such literature wanes. Cultural pedagogy, in this case, is marginalized if critics expel such literature in the name of dominant frameworks, including policy-making arguments that view such literature as unpredictable and impractical in comparison to legislative action.

As institutional agents, judges resemble Foucault's specific intellectual, "one whose radical work of transformation, whose fight against repression is carried on at the specific institutional site where he [*sic*] finds himself [*sic*] and on the terms of his [*sic*] own expertise, on the terms inherent to his [*sic*] own functioning as an intellectual" (Lentricchia, 1983, pp. 6–7).

The Content of Debate as it has Emerged

What is dominant today was once innovative; tracing the history of the content in policy debate can help explain current trends and provide valuable lessons for contemporary innovation. In the 1950s, the intercollegiate debate community struggled with developing proce dures to assess commonplace argumentative practices, resulting in paradigms to evaluate or regulate debate rounds. Debaters advanced paradigms for debate bearing names such as *tabula rasa*, hypothesis testing, game theory, and policy-making. Paradigms served as super-metaphors that directed how individual arguments would be evaluated.

Argument development followed a pattern of innovation followed by incoherence followed by normalization. Argumentative innovations were characterized by a period of initial incoherence; opposing teams did not know how to respond to the new ideas and judges did not know how to evaluate them. The innovators then offered criteria, and for a period debaters would spend the vast majority of their allotted speaking time arguing for the legitimacy of, and criteria for, their strategies. Newly popular forms of argument would win out and become so accepted that debaters no longer needed to substantiate them; debaters could simply reference buzzwords the judge understood. By 1990, initial innovations had become normalized.

Any ideas were allowed, but they generally had to be filtered through the dominant criteria of a policy framework. Debate became a self-referential, critical thinking game played around the content of policy studies literature.

The introduction of critical arguments tested the dominant policy framework as new philosophical trends became popular in academic circles outside and inside of debate. For instance, a set of ideas bearing the loose title postmodernism were emerging in the academy marked by Jean-Francois Lyotard's publication of *The Postmodern Condition: A Report on Knowledge* in 1979. Sim's (2001) brief history explicates: Saussure's structural study of language gave way to Barthes's skepticism and finally Derrida's deconstruction. Foucault linked the pursuit of knowledge to power, paving the way for feminists such as Irigaray to critique patriarchal power structures. Inspired by Heidegger, Lyotard pronounced a supreme distrust of technology. Liberal democracy and Marxism were well flayed by Baudrillard, Laclau, and Mouffe. The academic underpinnings of collegiate debate – stable political structures and established fields like international relations – were called into crisis.

These ideas worked their way into collegiate debate before 1990 when feminist criticism emerged during the free speech topic in 1987. In 1990, the University of Texas became a key player in using critical theory. By the 2005 NDT, teams in the elimination rounds divided into three groups; one issuing exclusively critical arguments, one issuing exclusively traditional policy arguments, and one capable of doing either successfully.

Important developments quickly followed. First, critical arguments became ubiquitous. While in 1997 few teams carried more than a single file to deal with all critical topics, by 2006 almost all teams had thick files on Heidegger, Nietzsche, Spanos, Derrida, and others. Critical theory had won its way into the intercollegiate debate canon as firmly as any policy argument. Second, once a corpus of great books concerning critical theory developed, sophisticated debaters from large schools read the books and co-opted critical argument into their strategies. Thus evolved a form of the critical argument that had all the technical sophistication of the traditional policy debates but was simply focused on subject matter similar to a graduate seminar in literature or criticism. Third, non-critical teams eventually settled on what would be called framework arguments. The framework argument outlined a vision of what debate was (almost always some version of the established policy-making paradigm with a defense of the merits of switch-side debating) and attempted to justify the approach with traditional appeals to argumentative ground and the use of some quotations from policy-oriented sources.

The last few developments created a split on what would be called performance lines – some teams wished to advance critical arguments in a traditional debate style while others wanted to directly call issues of presentational style into question. The performative set drew on a body of literature common in communication studies (e.g., *Text and Performance Quarterly*). Their performances ranged from the use of poetry and videos as evidence to a variety of visual presentations, hand-puppet shows, humorous prose readings, dances, skits with props (including a skeleton), and references to zombies, to name just a few examples. The worst were silly; the best were the serious expositions of important philosophical and cultural points that explored the interplay between form and content.

Within the performative camp emerged specific teams that focused on cultural pedagogy. For example, the all-Latino Fullerton team of Brenda Montes and Luis Magallon used arguments that celebrated Latino culture and communication and rejected cultural commodification of their narratives by mainstream and educational spheres. At times they would debate entirely in Spanish. Each finished in the top 11 speakers at the 2007 NDT. Similarly, the all African-American team at Towson University won the 2008 CEDA Nationals using Black aesthetics literature. Other advocates of cultural pedagogy came from Louisville (the African-American team of Liz Jones and Tanya Green reached the quarterfinals of the 2004 NDT), Idaho State, and West Georgia. Emporia was the first African-American team to win the NDT and CEDA using quare, or Black gay liberation, theory and cultural pedagogy. Despite the success of performance teams and their cultural consciousness-raising in debate, they remain exceptions and the most common strategy against them is still the framework argument.

Performance and Cultural Pedagogy as Content That Resists Normalization

The fourth purpose of this essay is explaining why the success of critical arguments has not addressed demographic exclusions. The key distinction between cultural pedagogy and critical arguments is the relationship to normalization. The philosophical arguments followed the same innovation-incoherence-normalization pattern as all the arguments that came before them. The critical innovation created incoherence as nobody was sure how to judge the arguments, a framework was developed for assessing them, and they subsequently became normalized. This explains why the emancipatory potential of the ideas failed to address the material exclusion of under-represented people. As critical theory arguments that exposed structural oppression became normal, routine, and popular, they became less revolutionary.

The power of the performative approach is precisely its inability to be normalized into an argument set that successful traditional debaters can co-opt. Arguments from cultural pedagogy are not repeatable because of the embodied performances of the debaters. The key maneuver that resists co-option is the insistence on the lived experience of minority debaters as a valuable source of knowledge apart from and not subordinate to expert or academic forms of knowledge. A sophisticated debater can learn Lyotard and beat a minority competitor in a technical debate; it is a far more tenuous task, however, for a debater to replicate the lived experience of the minority debater and appropriate it for his or her own use.

Viewed this way, performative arguments based on lived experience can be understood as an exercise of cultural pedagogy, and framework arguments that insist that such knowledge is outside the purview of college debate are attempts to de-institutionalize such knowledge. The analogue to the ethnic studies programs in Arizona is clear.

A Call to Judges and Coaches

The main conclusion offered here is that institutional agents should affirm a critical cultural pedagogy in debate. We ask for three specific practices. First, judges should show a greater skepticism toward framework arguments. An analogy to topicality is apt; while most judges are willing to vote on topicality in rare cases, critics generally do not want to let negative teams use topicality arguments as a way to systematically avoid the substance of the topic. In the same way, judges should look unfavorably on framework arguments that are used as a tool to forever shield competitors from having to read and engage cultural pedagogy. Second, coaches should encourage their own students to make arguments based on cultural pedagogy literature and treat that literature as a valuable source of knowledge. Third, in their post-round comments, judges should affirm the value of cultural pedagogy arguments. Even when a judge votes against a team on a framework argument, they can state that they value the content of the literature and help the teams find ways to make their arguments more relevant. Such practice is common on all other arguments of substance.

To the extent these institutional agents place importance on the cultural backdrops that help students express their identities, desires, and motivations, we can expect growing participation from minority students. To the extent these institutional agents dismiss such viewpoints, we can expect demographic exclusions to persist. In a nutshell, if judges exclude the identity performances of minority competitors, it should be no surprise to discover that such competitors do not participate in large numbers.

There are now more than 60 years of empirical proof that debating in the dominant framework actively excludes under-represented groups and women. There are good theoretical reasons to believe that cultural pedagogy can be an effective remedy that will improve minority retention and success.

References

Allen, B. A. (2010). Critical communication pedagogy as a framework for teaching difference and organizing. In D. Mumby (Ed.), *Organizing difference: Pedagogy, research, and practice* (pp. 103–126). Thousand Oaks, CA: Sage.

Allen, M., Trejo, M., Bartanen, M., Schroeder, A., & Ulrich, T. (2004). Diversity in United States forensics: A report on research conducted for the American Forensic Association. *Argumentation and Advocacy, 40*, 173–184.

Alvesson, M., Ashcraft, K. L., & Thomas, R. (2008). Identity matters: Reflections on the construction of identity scholarship in organization studies. *Organization, 15*(1), 5–28.

Ambrosio, J. (2003). We make the road by walking. In G. Gay (Ed.), *Becoming multicultural educators: Personal journey toward professional agency* (pp. 17–41). San Francisco. CA: Jossey-Bass.

Bensimon, E. M. (2007). The underestimated significance of practitioner knowledge in the scholarship on student success. *The Review of Higher Education, 30*(4), 441–469.

Calafell, B. M., & Moreman, S. T. (2009). Envisioning an academic readership: Latina/o performativities per the form of publication. *Text and Performance Quarterly, 29*(2), 123–130.

Delgado, F. P. (1998). When the silenced speak: The textualization and complications of Latina/o identity. *Western Journal of Communication, 62*(4), 420–438.

Flores, L. A. (2000). Constructing national bodies: Public argument in the English-only movement. In T. A. Hollihan (Ed.), *Argument at Century's End: Proceedings of the 11th SCA/AFA Conference on Argumentation* (pp. 436–453). Annandale, VA: National Communication Association.

Giroux, H. A. (2012, Feb. 8). Book burning in Arizona. Retrieved from http://truth-out.org/news/item/6548:book-burning-in-arizona

Hackett, T. (2003). Teaching them through who they are. In G. Gay (Ed.), *Becoming multicultural educators: Personal journey toward professional agency* (pp. 315–340). San Francisco, CA: Jossey-Bass.

Hill, S. K. (1997). African American students' motivation to participate in intercollegiate debate. *Southern Journal of Forensics, 2*(3), 202–235.

Holling, M. A., (2002). Transformation and liberation amidst racist-assimilationist forces. *The Review of Communication, 2*(4), 387–391.

Lentricchia, F. (1983). *Criticism and social change.* Chicago, IL: University of Chicago Press.

Martínez Alemán, A. M. (2007). The nature of the gift: Accountability and the professor-student relationship. *Educational Philosophy and Theory, 39*(6), 574–591. DOI: 10.1111/j.1469-5812.2007.00307.x

Matz, I. S., & Bruschke, J. (2006). Gender inequity in debate, legal, and business professions. *Contemporary Argumentation and Debate, 27*, 29–47.

McRee, N., & Cote, R. (2002). Does college debate inherit a lack of diversity from high school debate? *Contemporary Argumentation and Debate, 23*, 28–44.

Pew, S. (2007). Andragogy and pedagogy as foundational theory for student motivation in higher education. *Student Motivation, 2*, 14–25.

Rogers, J. E. (1997). A community of unequals: An analysis of dominant and subdominant culturally linked perceptions of participation and success within intercollegiate competitive debate. *Contemporary Argumentation and Debate, 18*, 1–22.

Sim, S. (2001). Postmodernism and philosophy. In S. Sim (Ed.), *The Routledge companion to postmodernism,* (pp. 3–14). New York, NY: Routledge.

Stage, F. K., & Hubbard, S. (2008). Teaching Latino, African American and Native American undergraduates: Faculty attitudes, conditions, and practices. In M. Gasman, B. Baez, & C. Turner (Eds.),

Interdisciplinary approaches to understanding minority-serving institutions (pp. 237–256). Albany: SUNY Press.

Stipek, D. (2002). *Motivation to learn: Integrating theory and practice* (4th ed.). Boston: Allyn & Bacon.

Warren, J. T. (2001). Doing whiteness: On the performative dimensions of race in the classroom. *Communication Education, 50*, 91–108.

Weinstein, C., Curran, M., & Tomlinson-Clarke, S. (2003). Culturally responsive classroom management: Awareness into action. *Theory Into Practice, 42*(4), 269–276.

63

SPECTRUM OF INTERROGATION

Developing a new vocabulary for affirmative cases in intercollegiate policy debate

R. Jarrod Atchison

WAKE FOREST UNIVERSITY, USA

Edward Panetta

UNIVERSITY OF GEORGIA, USA

In *Navigating Opportunity: Policy Debate in the 21st Century* (Louden, 2010), the working group on controversies in debate pedagogy outlined a disagreement over the role that the annual resolution should play in informing the practice of contest debating. In that essay, two competing perspectives on the role of a resolution are outlined for the reader. For traditional policy debate advocates, the annual resolution serves as a point of rhetorical stasis and argumentation proceeds from the resolution. For others, a critical perspective of debate portrays the contest as a site where competitors are not tethered to the resolution as the controlling focus for argument (Panetta & Mosley-Jensen, 2010). These competing visions of the role a resolution plays in debate often result in contests with little or no argumentative clash between teams.

The communicative divide found in contemporary debate does not occur in a vacuum; it reflects the practice of argument found in U.S. public life. Political pundits of the left and right both regularly speculate on the seemingly incommensurable worldviews that divide the United States into red and blue. Communities of political partisans identify rhetors who deliver self-affirming appeals to believers in an environment often undisturbed by genuine argumentative clash (Dionne, 2012). Opposing viewpoints can be dismissed as dated, radical, or both and orthodoxy is confirmed. In the case of policy debate, all too often contests are decided by the predispositions of the critic selected to adjudicate debates between policy and critically based teams.

Although we have argued in the past that the benefits of debate are best maximized when both teams agree to debate the question of the resolution, our goal in this essay will be not to render judgment on the affirmative cases, but to initiate an organizational schema which we hope will produce a vocabulary to help debaters and coaches in their discussions on the practices of intercollegiate debate. We established a lexicon of the spectrum of interrogation after reviewing the range of affirmative cases deployed by teams in recent years. This spectrum includes five recurrent tactics used by teams: the case studies approach, the resolutional play approach, the controversy area approach, the micro-political approach, and the change through contest debate approach.

In order to establish a continuum of approaches – the spectrum of interrogation – we examined the 2010-2011 policy resolution and highlight a recurring pattern of affirmative choices. By mapping a range of plausible affirmative interpretations, our hope is to disturb the argumentative binary currently dominating the policy debate community. We need a vocabulary to begin transitioning from debates that devolve into topicality or framework contests to ones that consider ways in which distinctive affirmative approaches open distinctive lines of argument. As in any attempt to catalogue argument practices, these categories are fluid and there is room for definitional disagreement. It is important to start a dialogue that will allow debate theorists to move beyond the current dichotomous characterization of an affirmative proposal as either "topical or not."

The Annual Resolution: A Traditional Dividing Ground

For many participants and coaches, the Cross Examination Debate Association's (CEDA's) annual announcement of the resolution is one of the most exciting days on the debate calendar. This announcement represents the culmination of hundreds of hours of work by debaters, coaches, and CEDA officers. The process of selecting the resolution has undergone several revisions and the current process is the most open in the history of the organization. The process provides multiple points of input by any interested party, including open access to the topic committee discussions, open submission for resolution wording suggestions, and voting privileges for every institutional member of CEDA.

For most policy debate history, the announcement of the resolution has been met with great anticipation because it signals the start of a new season with the resolution serving as the point of stasis. Identifying a point of stasis, the turning point or focus of a dispute, has been a defining characteristic of argumentation and debate since classical antiquity (Thompson, 1972). A point of stasis is the site where a group believes that argument should begin. A point of stasis can be the result of a set of laws or customs that operate in a discourse community. The stock issues era of the 1950s and 1960s provided participants and judges with a ready-made set of stasis points. A negative team would test the harm, inherency, solvency, and cost of an affirmative case. Each of these categories was treated as a discrete point of stasis and a negative team could present arguments that might seemingly contradict when viewed through the lens of contemporary policy debating.

While debate has moved away from this paradigmatic approach, the resolution has remained a stasis point. When policy making replaced stock issues analysis as the model used for the assessment of debates, the resolution continued to direct the research focus of college debaters towards literature surrounding complex and controversial policy questions. The affirmative team has been defined in opposition to the negative by its responsibility to argue on behalf of the resolution.

Debaters cannot, however, focus solely on one side of the resolution. The practice of switching sides to defend both sides of the resolution requires debaters to examine and research diverging viewpoints on the proposition. Coaches have trumpeted the pedagogical benefits of switch-side debate for more than 50 years. Although there is a large, and growing, literature on the benefits and disadvantages of switching sides, the tradition of assigning one side the affirmative and the other to the negative is still a defining characteristic of intercollegiate policy debate (Atchison 2011; Greene & Hicks, 2005; Harrigan, 2008; Young 2011).

While there have been periods when affirmative teams argued broadly on behalf of the resolution, in recent years they have defended narrower case studies. In this model, the negative can use topicality to argue that the affirmative's proposal is not an example of the resolution and therefore violates the assumed agreement that the resolution is the point of stasis. Writing in 2004, Tim O'Donnell described the role of the resolution as follows: "The idea that the affirmative begins the debate by using the resolution as a starting point for their opening speech act is nearly universally accepted by all members of the debate community" (p. 4). According to O'Donnell, the explanation had less to do with pedagogy and more to do with competitive success. His blunt assessment was that "affirmative teams that have ignored the resolution altogether have not gotten very far" (p. 4).

A Shifting Tide: Patterns of Argument Ground in Current Policy Resolutions

Our survey of the intercollegiate affirmative cases from the 2010–2011 debate season found at http://opencaselist.wikispaces.com suggests that O'Donnell's description of affirmative argument practice is dated. Debate theorists need to move beyond the current dichotomous characterization that an affirmative proposal is either "topical or not" to expose the possibilities of shared argument ground which has some relationship to the national resolution and could lead to spirited debates.

Immigration was selected as the 2010–2011 intercollegiate controversy area, winning the balloting by a single vote over an international treaties topic. After a second round of voting, the 2010–2011 CEDA resolution was selected by the community: "Resolved: the United States Federal Government should substantially increase the number of and/or substantially expand beneficiary eligibility for its visas for one or more of the following: employment-based immigrant visas, nonimmigrant temporary worker visas, family-based visas, human trafficking-based visas." This topic wording sidestepped the long-standing controversy in the larger societal debate: the state of undocumented workers. And, one is left to question whether the resolution addressed the question raised in the topic paper: "Who should and should not be a part of our country?" In the next section, we outline the spectrum of how affirmative teams engaged the diverse areas of scholarship embedded in the resolution.

Our review of the 2010–2011 caselist quickly resulted in an identification of the traditional approach to defend the resolution by deploying a *case-study approach*. Teams from Emory, Harvard, and Northwestern defended case studies that expanded agricultural visas, capped H-1B visas, and expanded T visas intended to protect victims of organ trafficking. These case studies attempted to answer the question of the resolution in the affirmative. Although current debate practitioners characterize these affirmatives as "traditional", in the not so distant past, these affirmative cases would have been deemed too narrow. It is difficult to mark the exact date of this transition, but anecdotal evidence suggests that many of the earliest intercollegiate debate competitions focused on the resolution broadly rather than allowing the affirmative to choose to defend a single example of it. More recently, affirmative teams have been able to pick very specific examples of the resolution rather than having to defend its overall claim. Assuming that both teams in a debate agree to this practice, the negative team has the option of proving the affirmative proposal is not topical – not an example of the resolution. Topicality is essentially a test of whether or not the affirmative has met the agreed-upon point of stasis for the debate by defending a proposal that is an example of the resolution.

Whether an affirmative team defends the resolution as a whole, or a specific case study within it, the practice of using the resolution as the point of stasis for debate has been the dominant practice in intercollegiate debate circles since its inception in 1892 (Ringwalt, 1897). Resolution-based cases anchor one end of the spectrum of interrogation and are exemplars of the orthodox approach to affirmative construction. Programs with a long-standing history and resource base often gravitate to this approach, although not all such teams do.

A number of teams debating in 2010–2011 elected to defend the resolution via a second approach we have labeled the *resolutional play approach*. Located at a point of the spectrum closest to the case study approach, these teams engage the resolution without assuming the burden of affirming the question posed by it. Under this approach, teams often utilize the resolution rather than take a position on the question posed by it. The resolution is a problem area that serves as a device to limit the research area. In the current topic selection process, limiting research is the role that the vote before the topic meeting serves for participants.

We identified affirmatives deployed by Kansas State, Idaho State, and Towson that demonstrated that the resolution was important, but did not focus on the possible enactment of policy by the United States Federal Government as the central question of the affirmative case. These teams queered the resolution with a performance of fractured identity, advocated the topic as a site to avow the middle passage as the United States' first immigration policy, and affirmed the resolution as a site of rejection of the exclusionary practices of the United States' immigration system.

In these instances, the participants utilized the resolution to accomplish something broader than the case study approach allows. Although these affirmative teams do not debate the traditional point of stasis by answering the policy question posed by the resolution, the resolution does serve as a focal point of their cases. This approach allows the affirmative to avoid a number of the procedural or process-oriented argument strategies deployed by a negative against the case study model. Teams using the resolutional play approach also are positioned to avoid language-based kritiks of the topic wording.

We label the third approach identified in our review of the 2010–2011 resolution the *controversy area approach*. An increasing number of teams engage the controversy area but do not defend the use of the United States Federal Government. Although these affirmative cases do not take the literal question of the resolution as their point of stasis, they engage the controversy in which the resolution operates. For example, Fullerton affirmed the "politizen" as a political disruption of whiteness and White supremacy inherent in U.S. citizenship. Rather than relying on the question of the resolution, the debaters argued that the debate should be adjudicated based on which team provided the best methodology to challenge White supremacy in the construction of citizenship. The University of Oklahoma asked judges and opponents to rethink terrorism through the prism of the visa. And, Emporia State University argued that debate participants are obligated to engage in discussions that allow for the interrogation of the ways the resolution functions and, in turn, the ways participants interact with it.

Each of these cases interrogated crucial components of the controversy area but did not assume the obligation of defending the resolution. The strategic benefits of this choice become clear when viewed beside the literature of the argument controversy. A broad and less defined point of stasis provided the affirmative with a wider range of rhetorical choices. A broader controversy allows the affirmative to more easily make the debate a conflict over terminal values rather than over distinct approaches to a shared end.

Unlike other cases further along on the spectrum of interrogation, the controversy area affirmative cases are broadly tied to the controversy at hand. The cases demonstrate that the controversy area can include a wide variety of affirmative arguments ranging from the historical construction of citizenship to "possibilities of being." These affirmatives also highlight that once the obligation to affirm a particular side of a controversy is removed, the point of stasis becomes more difficult to determine; the affirmative team can defend "disruption" and "contemplation" which do not directly translate into policy advocacy on behalf of a controversy's side.

The fourth approach identified in the spectrum of interrogation is that of *micro-political resistance*, a significant move on the spectrum in which affirmative teams begin to engage the practice of debate itself. This shift represents one of the most important controversies in contemporary debate: What is the role, if any, for individual debate rounds in challenging broader issues within the debate community? These micro-political affirmative cases are generated out of the resolution's controversy area and challenge the debate community to consider its relationship to that controversy. This approach forces the negative to defend the history and real-world practices of the debate community. Argumentatively, the affirmatives often outline an ideal vision of community that many find compelling and inclusive. The negatives are left to defend the flawed discourse practices of a community.

Cases presented by Liberty University, the New School, and the University of Vermont in the 2010–2011 debate season highlighted the connections between the immigration controversy and the current practice of intercollegiate debate. Liberty called for a rewriting of immigration history with the inclusion of slavery to help deconstruct White supremacy, the New School called for centering political alternatives on the violence that immigrants undergo to better their material realities, and Vermont asked debaters to reflect on the work done by attendants who service debaters at tournament hotels.

In these micro-political affirmative cases, the central question of the debate relates to the practices of the debate community as informed by the controversy area. Unlike the previous category, which uses the controversy area to dictate a point of stasis, these affirmatives include an explicit call for the judge to evaluate the current practices of the debate community. Although the controversy area helps focus the affirmative's engagement with the community practices in question, a negative argument about whether or not the federal government should increase visas cannot be responsive to the affirmative case. The controversy, therefore, provides analytic tools for criticizing the debate community, but ceases to serve as the debate's point of stasis. This can often leave the negative in an argumentatively untenable position. The debate community, like many academic enclaves, suffers from a history of homophobic, racist, and sexist behavior. Current debaters who find themselves in these debates are left with the unenviable task of defending a history which neither they, nor in some cases their schools, were participants when exclusionary practices were operating largely unchecked in the community.

The *change through contest debate approach* is the affirmative category most removed from the case study approach. Affirmative cases clustered here do little to engage the resolution or the controversy area. Their consistent theme across these affirmatives is a call to use the individual debate contest as a site for engaging a broader debate practice. The University of Louisville has employed this method for several years. In the 2010–2011 season they articulated a mission statement calling for the use of debate to improve decision-making in a multicultural democracy. In this case, the resolution had a minimal role in providing a point of stasis. There seemed to be little effort to tie multiculturalism to immigration. Rather, these teams addressed the location of an African American co-culture in our country's larger political milieu. At this end of the spectrum debaters rarely attempt to feign a connection between the debate's central question and the resolution voted on by the debate community.

Conclusion: Searching for Common Ground

The Controversies in Debate Pedagogy working group set the parameters for one of the most important questions facing the debate community today: What role, if any, should the annual resolution serve in the practice of competitive debate? In our opinion, the conversation over this fundamental question has utilized a limited vocabulary that focuses on hypothetical extremes with little concern for the actual practices of affirmative teams. In this essay, we have attempted to outline a spectrum of interrogation that will help stakeholders approach the controversy with a greater understanding of the diversity of approaches to the resolution. Hopefully, reflecting on an argument continuum like the spectrum we propose will allow debaters and coaches to identify and evaluate the argument ground that derives from competing approaches. Our goal here is to initiate a discussion over an appropriate point of stasis for contemporary debate by outlining the spectrum of cases along a continuum of interrogation which represents the current practices of debate.

References

Atchison, J. (2011). Who cares?: Learning perspective taking through stakeholders. *Contemporary Argumentation and Debate*, 32, 79–84.

Dionne, E. J. (2012). *Our divided political heart*. New York, NY: Bloomsbury USA.

Greene, R. W., & Hicks, D. (2005). Lost convictions. *Cultural Studies*, 19, 100–126.

Harrigan, C. (2008). Against dogmatism: A continued defense of switch side debate. *Contemporary Argumentation and Debate*, 29, 37–66.

Louden A. (Ed.). (2010). *Navigating opportunity: Policy debate in the 21st century*. New York, NY: International Debate Education Association.

O'Donnell, T. (2004). And the twain shall meet: Affirmative framework choice and the future of debate. In S. Bauschard & J. P. Lacy (Eds.), *Blue helmet klues: United Nations peacekeeping and the United States* (pp. 1–12). Winston Salem, NC: Debater's Research Guide.

Panetta, E. M., & Mosley-Jensen, W. (2010). Controversies in debate pedagogy: Working paper. In A. Louden (Ed.), *Navigating opportunity: Policy debate in the 21st century* (pp. 211–235). New York, NY: International Debate Education Association.

Ringwalt, R. (1897). Intercollegiate Debating. *Forum*, 22, 633.

Thompson, W. N. (1972). Stasis in Aristotle's rhetoric. *The Quarterly Journal of Speech*, 58, 134–141.

Young, K. (2011). Impossible convictions: Convictions and intentionality in performance and switch side debate. *Contemporary Argumentation and Debate*, 32, 1–44.

64

DISTURBING CATEGORICAL REASON IN MORAL ARGUMENTATION

Ryan Gillespie

UNIVERSITY OF SOUTHERN CALIFORNIA, USA

> I cannot see how to refute the arguments for the subjectivity of ethical values, but I find myself incapable of believing that all that is wrong with wanton cruelty is that I don't like it.
>
> Bertrand Russell (1999, p. 165)

Imagine a child, C, who likes to kill spiders. Soon unsatisfied with squishing, C takes to picking the spiders up with tweezers and pulling off their legs. But the event is placid. So C moves on to cats, and then to dogs. The child's parents are aghast, and try reasoning: harming animals is wrong, inflicting pain intentionally is wrong, would you like that if someone did it to you?, it is bad for your soul to commit such acts. Unfortunately, C is a clinical psychopath, and none of these appeals works or even makes sense. Tragically, C grows up and moves from de-limbing animals to humans. C's explanation for this behavior is straightforward: Tearing limbs is jolly good fun! When counterarguments are given, C dismisses them all as irrational: "Morality proper is logically inconclusive because reason is simply instrumental. The tearing of limbs is actually quite rational given my desires; in fact, I have a reason to tear limbs and no reason not to."

It seems that C is acting immorally, and dedicatedly so. C is conscious of the actions, and willfully rejects not just an ethic but morality in general. The subject under scrutiny here is not the existence of the moral realm, universal vs. particular moral reasoning, or the logical validity of ethics. The primary issue raised in this essay is: Although people might be willing to admit that C has an apparent reason to tear limbs, they probably also want to say that C has another reason, a real reason, a better reason, or a normative reason, not to tear limbs. This other reason I call a categorical reason. But is there really such a thing? And, more saliently, does C indeed have – *is C in possession of* – this reason?

A *categorical reason* is a reason that applies to all agents, regardless of their desires, ends, or other commitments. In Shafer-Landau's (2009) words, categorical reasons are "reasons that obtain independently of their relation to an agent's commitments" (p. 189). In this view, categorical reason has both epistemological and ontological elements. Epistemologically, categorical reasons are true reasons for action in the same way that "the world is not flat" is true, no matter who you are or where you are from. The ontological claim is that categorical reasons do not depend for their existence on agents' psychology or any relationship between ends and states of affairs per se; they exist mind-independently.

In antiquity, particularly in Aristotle's (trans. 1984) *Nicomachean Ethics*, reason establishes objective and true moral ends and actions. This is a process of discovery. But objectivity and categoricity are out of favor in ethics in argumentation theory. McGee's (1985) Alta keynote adequately summed the trajectory and widespread sentiment of the field: "Above all, I hope to live in a community where reality is lived, truths are made, and facts are used. I tire of discovery. Let's create something" (p. 12). How did we get to a point where ethics moved from discovery to creation? In other words, what disturbed the view of categorical morality, and why? In this essay, I look specifically at the notion of moral reasons, and categorical reason in particular, especially given that categorical reasons are understudied in argumentation theory. (Though terminology varies, searching <categorical reason> in the "Communication and Mass Media Complete" database yielded zero results).

While elements of the story in which categorical reason is disturbed from its place in moral discourse and practice might be familiar, I also argue that categorical reason still disturbs contemporary moral argumentation. "Disturbing categorical reason," thus, is a double entendre: Moral argumentation and practice over the last few centuries has disturbed the existence and status of categorical reason, and contemporary moral argumentation and practice (rightfully) continue to be disturbed by the concept of categorical reason.

Commands of Reason: Categorical and Instrumental

An essential question in moral argumentation is whether moral normativity is reason-based or desire-based. This question gets to the heart of the case of C: Does C have a (categorical) reason not to act? A simple desire-based normative theory (DBN) would say "no," whereas a reason-based normative (RBN) theory says "yes." Put baldly, RBN claims that reason does, and ought to, govern moral discourse and practice. DBN claims that desires and commitments do, and ought to, govern moral discourse and practice. Reason still plays a significant role in DBN, but it is a different type of reason (a noncategorical reason). But, in both cases, reason still commands action.

Formally, there is a triple ordering <R, X, A>, where R represents a reason, X an agent, and A an action. That reason commands certain actions is uncontroversial for both views. But what it commands is not. That is, there is a distinction in moral argumentation between categorical and instrumental reason. The distinction is often put in terms of the categorical and the hypothetical. The version presented here conflates the hypothetical and instrumental, though sophisticated Hypotheticalism (e.g., Schroeder, 2007) is sensitive to the instrumentalist charge, and accounts for reasons all agents might have.

In the case of the categorical, R is a reason for X to A regardless of whether or not it satisfies desires. The idea is that categorical reasons command action; they are agent-neutral and community and context free. That is, no matter who you are, where you are from, and what you believe, R is a reason for X to A. Put in the imperative form:

(1) You ought to help starving children in Africa.

This imperative has normative force due to its connection with categorical reason, in this case, alleviating human suffering.

In the case of the instrumental, R is a reason for X to *A* if R satisfies a desire. This is characteristic means–ends rationality, in which the end is the product of desires. In other words, the end is not established by reason per se but by desire. Reason commands the relationship between the given – between the antecedent and the consequent. So, in an instrumental formulation, (1) becomes:

> (1⋆) If you want to reduce human suffering, you ought to donate money to starving children in Africa.

The difference that concerns me here is neither the surface formulation nor the moral content but rather what ultimately has authority. In (1), the reason to act is a categorical reason that exists and applies regardless of the agent's psychology or community, whereas, in (1⋆), reason only commands based on given elements. The simplest way to see how the latter runs into problems is to imagine an interlocutor who responds:

> (2) Well, I am not interested in reducing human suffering.

Given rejection of the end (the antecedent), the consequent does not follow, and, hence, no command of reason is present. So, in the instrumentalist view, there are no reasons for or against certain desires: "One just has them or one doesn't" (Dancy, 2000, p. 33). This is the case with C, who just doesn't desire to respond to other people's interests or views of morality. More strikingly, while instrumentalism shows you how to get what you want, it doesn't establish what you ought to want in the first place (Millgram, 1997, p. 2). That is, to the person who utters (2), people probably want to say:

> (3) But, you should be interested in reducing human suffering!

And with this, a moral argumentation problem flairs: How is it possible to convince interlocutors of the right moral action in a given context? That reasons must be furnished is universally agreed, but the normativity of reason is precisely what is at question here. That is, does reason command categorically, or does reason command only in means–ends relationality?

The command of categorical reason in moral matters likely will be greeted with a smirk by the contemporary argumentation scholar. The next section briefly explains how and why categorical reason is disturbed from its authoritative position.

Disturbing the Status of Categorical Reason in Morality

There are a number of reasons for the disturbance of categorical reason in morality. The three most important are: (1) logical argument; (2) analyses of power as undergirding language and sociopolitical structures; and (3) modern socio-politico-economic arrangements, namely, (a) the establishment of moral pluralism in liberal democracies, and (b) the forces of globalization. As these reasons are familiar, brief summaries hopefully will suffice.

The case for (1), logical argument, works as follows. From one angle, the objectivity of morality is apparent: People say "wanton cruelty is wrong" in a propositional manner, and propositions are capable of being judged true or false (either "wanton cruelty is wrong" is true or it isn't). But what is it that would make this statement true or false? In the reference theory of descriptions, a proposition like "it is sunny outside" is judged true or false given whether or not it really is sunny outside. What confirms facts of the moral variety?

Hume (2006) famously noticed this problem, often called Hume's Law, or the Is/Ought Problem: One cannot get from a description about how the world is to a logically necessary moral thought or action (p. 77). There is a divide between empirical facts and morality. Morality is not, so to speak, part of the world. This problem is expressed poetically in *Hamlet* (2.2): "for there is nothing either good nor bad, but thinking makes it so" (Shakespeare, 2008 version). Thus, inside of morality the matter seems objective, but, it is claimed, this is an illusion. Morality is just an agent's desires or the conventional standards of the agent's community. Logic does not, and cannot, prove categorical reason, or the substantive truth of ethics; and so, morality becomes the domain of passions, or, in Russell's (1999) view, subjective preferences.

The case for (2), ethics as preferences, works as follows. If there is no moral reality, then moral expressions are really just expressions of arbitrary will. This arbitrary will, however, is always someone's will, and thus is, essentially, the will of the most powerful. In this view, morality and moral language are but expressions of power. As MacIntyre (1984) memorably put it: "The moral utterance provides a possible mask for almost any face" (p. 110). This view is traceable from Nietzsche and Marx to Foucault, Derrida, Deleuze, and much of contemporary rhetorical studies, as crystalized in McKerrow (1989).

The case for (3), moral pluralism, works as follows. Moral pluralism can be understood in terms of both liberal democratic and globalization structures and forces. The establishment of modern liberal democracies was, in many ways, the establishment of a separation between the state and morality. The state does not, and shall not, define the Good Life for its citizens. Hence, moral pluralism is enshrined in the structure of contemporary constitutional democracies. Moral pluralism is largely inconsistent with categorical reason. Similarly, globalization has shrunk the world, putting diverse societies into closer contact with each other. One of the initial impetuses for community relativism as a moral (and not just a descriptive) position came from anthropologists in the early 20th century (Gowans, 2008). Globalization intensifies this position, as the possibility for categorical reasons is made all the more challenging in the face of competing ethical systems.

These are three ways of disturbing categorical reason as a category and a way of conducting moral inquiry and practice. But, as the example of C illustrates, categorical reason is not easily defeated.

Categorical Reason as Disturbing Pluralistic Moral Thought and Practice

Categorical reason, as a concept, persists in contemporary moral inquiry and practice. One possible explanation is the Nietzschean one: We simply have not fully achieved enlightenment, and need to shake the chains of moral universalism. A more Marxist explanation would posit that society and institutions move slowly, and are built and carried through with the materials of the past. Indeed, MacIntyre (1984) saw moral judgments writ large as but "linguistic survivals from the practices of classical theism which have lost the context provided by those practices" (p. 60). But, there are substantial arguments in favor of categorical reason. In this sense, then, one can think of categorical reason as returning the favor to instrumentalism and pluralism by disturbing *them* as concepts and practices.

Two arguments seem unshakeable in this regard. The first I call the *Better Argument*, drawing on Parfit (2011), and the other, the *Blameworthy Argument*, drawing on Shafer-Landau (2009). The idea is that common concepts like *better* and *responsibility* need at least one categorical reason to remain coherent.

Calling X *better* than Y presupposes a standard of judgment, and without an ideal on one end of the spectrum, *better* is rationally unintelligible. The idea that something is better than something else – e.g., that not exploiting the poor is a better reason to ban human organ sales than individual property rights is to allow sales even if they exploit the poor – means that such a reason is the reason agents have more reason to have under RBN. Contrastingly, in narrow DBN, what is rational, what counts in favor of some act, is that it fulfills a desire. So if I have a desire to maintain individual property rights, but you insist that it is better to help the poor, it is, in one sense, more rational for me to prefer my position; after all, one of those things is internal (my desires entail reason) and the other is external (your reasons, or reasons "out there.")

But this elevation of individual preferences is, in Parfit's (2011) words, "much of what went wrong in the moral philosophy of the mid twentieth century" (p. 373). Parfit's overarching position is a defense of categorical reason and RBN. Parfit argued that it is mistaken, for example, to even *say* that C has a reason to tear limbs, or that it is more rational for me to prefer to exploit the poor, because the preference given by normative truth – and not individual desires or commitments – is the most rational one. This is because "when we have more reason to have some preference, that is not an empirical fact that causes us to have this preference, but an irreducibly normative truth" (p. 373). In order to call some reasons better than others, there must be a standard, a target at which to aim, and so (at least one) categorical reason must exist. Our everyday language of *better reasons* reinforces as much. The language of reasons is sufficiently ecumenical to accommodate that preferences entail reasons to act, and hence the real vs. apparent reasons distinction ought to be dropped. So C has a reason to act. The objection is to C's reason-entailing desires and the categorical reason not to act being somehow equal. C has a reason to tear limbs, but C also has a (weightier) categorical reason not to do so. So goes the Better Argument.

Finally, categorical reasons are necessary to the very concept of holding agents responsible for their actions. Typically, people are not culpable for actions beyond their control. The very possibility of being blameworthy entails that an agent could have acted otherwise. But, on a strictly instrumental account, the agent would not have had this reason to act differently. Consider C, the dedicated immoralist: The *reason* to hold C responsible is not part of the content of C's (a) morality and commitments. C has no desire or interest in my or your or anyone else's morality; morality is not a category, not a concept for C. Holding C responsible nevertheless is precisely to say that C has a reason to act (otherwise), regardless of C's commitments (desires, ends). And so, there is at least one categorical reason. So runs the Blameworthy Argument.

The Mutual Disturbance of Categorical Reason

In summary, there is a mutual disturbance at work in moral argumentation: Scholars continue to try to disturb the concept and processing of categorical reason, and categorical reason continues to disturb scholars. There are shifts in categorical reason's status, namely, from its hegemony in antiquity to its destabilization in the Enlightenment to its dismantling post-Enlightenment.

These shifts are due to a number of factors, but Toulmin (1964) was keen to note a key underlying factor: rhetoric. While there is always an element of rhetoric in logical argument, the shifts are less about logical establishment or critique than they are about finding "some argument which would replace the current feelings against reform by others in favor of it" (Toulmin, 1964, p. 196). The contemporary moment is perhaps best characterized as having a disturbed feeling toward categorical reason: It is something from which one recoils and, simultaneously, something which one also requires, if not demands, when considering and evaluating human action.

More work is needed in argumentation studies to explain and understand the character of moral argument, including the relationship between reason and emotion generally, and the function, force, and status of categorical reason in particular. Simply attributing categorical reason to rhetorics of power will not do. Additionally, something might be made of persistence, the sort of perennial, seemingly unshakeable nature of certain concepts, as an argument category, and as perhaps a (non-decisive) kind of evidence.

In conclusion, categorical reason is a disturbing and disturbed concept, having been disturbed by logical argument, analyses of power, and modern sociopolitical arrangements, and yet continuing to disturb all of the above, particularly moral discourse and practice. As a student of argument, it is disturbing that categorical reason cannot be proven. But as a human being, contemplating categorical reason's nonexistence, and saying that C *has* no reason to stop de-limbing, is even more disturbing.

References

Aristotle. (1984). Nicomachean ethics. (W. D. Ross & J. O. Urmson, Trans.). In J. Barnes (Ed.), *The complete works of Aristotle* (Vol. 2, pp. 1729–1867). Princeton, NJ: Princeton University Press.

Dancy, J. (2000). *Practical reality*. New York, NY: Oxford University Press.

Gowans, C. (2008). Moral relativism. *Stanford encyclopedia of philosophy*. Retrieved from http://plato.stanford.edu/entries/moral-relativism/

Hume, D. (2006). A treatise of human nature. In G. Sayre-McCord (Ed.), *Moral philosophy* (pp. 12–184). Indianapolis, IN: Hackett.

McGee, M. C. (1985). The moral problem of *argumentum per argumentum*. In R. J. Cox, M. O. Sillars, & G. B. Walker (Eds), *Argument and Social Practice: Proceedings of the Fourth SCA/AFA Conference on Argumentation* (pp. 1–12). Annandale, VA: Speech Communication Association.

MacIntyre, A. (1984). *After virtue* (2nd ed.). Notre Dame, IN: University of Notre Dame Press.

McKerrow, R. (1989). Critical rhetoric: Theory and praxis. *Communication Monographs*, 77, 91–111.

Millgram, E. (1997). *Practical induction*. Princeton, NJ: Princeton University Press.

Parfit, D. (2011). *On what matters* (Vol. 2). New York, NY: Oxford University Press.

Russell, B. (1999). *Russell on ethics*. London, England: Routledge.

Schroeder, M. (2007). *Slaves of the passions*. New York, NY: Oxford University Press.

Shafer-Landau, R. (2009, August). A defence of categorical reasons. *Proceedings of the Aristotelian Society*, 109(2), 189–206.

Shakespeare, W. (2008). *Hamlet*. New York, NY: Oxford University Press.

Toulmin, S. (1964). *Reason in Ethics*. Cambridge, England: Cambridge University Press.

65

RETHINKING THE HISTORY OF THE JAPANESE–U.S. EXCHANGE TOUR

Early tours, early topics, and early traffic

Brian Lain

UNIVERSITY OF NORTH TEXAS, USA

In the summer of 2013, the National Communication Association's (NCA) Committee on International Discussion and Debate (CIDD) engaged in the 38th debate exchange tour between the United States and Japan (S. Howell, personal communication, June 6, 2012). While international exchanges between the United States and other countries date at least to 1922 (Hall & Rhodes, 1972; Woods & Konishi, 2007), Japan and the United States began official exchanges in 1969 (Ellis, 1968). Scholarly investigations of a recent rise in Asian debate notwithstanding (Jarvis, 2010), the U.S-Japan exchange debates are the longest standing relationship between any U.S. debate community and an Asian debating society. However, scholars have relatively little information on the history of the tours.

Scholars have noted both the inadequacy and the difficulty of gathering historical materials from these exchange tours (Aonuma, 1989; Suzuki & Matsumoto, 2002; Woods & Konishi, 2007). Even though scholars have done little to historicize the tours, participants and other stakeholders have evinced continual interest in historicizing debate practices *in Japan* (Davidson, 1976; Inoue, 1996; Klopf, 1975; Suzuki & Matsumoto, 2002), including the CIDD cataloging the exchange tours. Suzuki and Matsumoto (2002) as well as Inoue (1996) have argued that sending U.S. debaters to Japan has had a large impact on the development of debate practices in Japan; however, the specific contributions of particular exchanges between U.S. debaters and Japanese hosts is lacking. These histories, though important, are incomplete because they tell only one side of the exchange: the influence of U.S. debaters on Japan. However, 13 of the 38 exchange tours have involved Japanese debaters traversing the United States, debating in English to a wide variety of audiences. The importance of this side of the tour is often underexplored, despite the fact that Japanese debaters performing in front of U.S. audiences constitutes an important part of the exchange

Woods & Konishi (2007) do the best to try to rectify this. They examined past tour reports and conducted oral history interviews with past participants in order to conclude that the CIDD-Japan tours have had a lasting impact on the two argument cultures. They cite

426

exchanges on issues related to cultural interaction, gender, debate theory, and other topics as evidence that the exchanges left a positive impact on participants. While trying to explain the dual features of the past CIDD-Japan exchanges, however, the context in which the tours took place is eliminated. Participants from across 50 years of CIDD-Japan debates are compared to assess the overall importance of the exchange. There is little consideration of the cultural context in which each exchange took place. It is as if the debates and the exchange tours by both U.S. and Japanese citizens occurred in a vacuum. Whether it is the CIDD report of the U.S. debaters' travels in Japan or the oral history of the Japanese debater who traveled the United States, the circumstances under which the tour took place are not included. That is unfortunate because the history of this exchange is marked by cultural politics affecting the tour. While the discipline of communication evinces a strong regard for the importance of context in public discussion, we have failed to appreciate the cultural politics of these debate tours. What are the cultural circumstances that led up to these international debates, and how do the politically charged climates inform the exchanges themselves?

The 1969 tour by Japanese citizens debating in the United States, the first official exchange between the two, highlights the necessity of not only considering the tour's effects on the United States' side, but also of taking seriously the context in which the tour takes place. In this essay, I attempt to historicize this exchange by understanding the contentiousness of the tour itself, reading it within the politics of the late 1960s turmoil. What has been elided by incomplete and acontextual histories is that these tours are themselves produced in a political crucible of their times, and international debate itself is a product of its cultural context. I begin by examining why the CIDD engaged in this particular tour and why it almost ended before it began. Then I discuss the importance of two international crises that directly affected the exchange debates because of connections to the topic and team debated: Vietnam and Okinawa.

The Tour That Almost Wasn't

The 1969 Japanese debate tour of the United States must be understood in relation to events going on within the CIDD and the Speech Association of America (SAA, the NCA's precursor). Individual colleges and universities originally arranged international debates. The first is generally recognized as the Bates College-Oxford 1922 contest (Hall & Rhodes, 1972). According to a report published by the Committee on International Debating, between 1922 and 1928 colleges and universities held approximately 400 international debates (Hall & Rhodes, 1972). In 1929, at the National Convention of the American Association of Teachers of Speech (which eventually became the National Communication Association), a motion was made to establish a formal committee charged with organizing and administering tours among U.S. universities and tours of U.S. teams abroad; the Committee on International Discussion and Debate was formed.

By 1967, the CIDD had scheduled hundreds of debates in the United States featuring debaters from other countries, but almost all visiting debaters were from English-speaking countries (England, Scotland, New Zealand, Australia, etc.), the notable exception being the University of the Philippines which toured in 1928 (Hall & Rhodes, 1972). The zenith of the CIDD was probably in the early 1960s when memos indicate over 200 applications by U.S. universities to host during a single British tour. However, hosting the tours was costly and visiting debaters straining hosts' budgets caused a number of problems. Hall and Rhodes (1972) argued that "capricious actions" by British debaters and "irate host institutions," likely related to the capricious actions, pushed the committee to find new partners

(p. 19). Personal correspondence between Robert Hall, Glenn Capp, James McBath, and Fergus Currie also suggested the CIDD faced increasing difficulty keeping the international debates under its control. Several universities threatened to go it alone and set up separate hosting arrangements to invite British debaters to U.S. colleges (McBath, 1963). This represented a threat to the monopoly the CIDD had on foreign debaters visiting the United States. With an increasing demand by U.S. host colleges to see foreigners visit, and the possibility that if the CIDD could not provide acceptably gracious debaters (those that respected their hosts in the United States) U.S. colleges would make independent arrangements, the CIDD tapped its membership to search for new debaters to come to visit the United States.

The SAA contacted members in other countries in an effort to expand the pedagogical reach of the tours. Among these, Dean Ellis of the University of Hawaii suggested that Japanese debaters were ready to visit the United States. Ellis had become aware of a rise of debating in English in Japan since 1953, especially with the Sophia University Invitational Debate Tournament (Ellis, 1968). Ellis noted in correspondence with Hall that the director of debate at Sophia, Father John Nissel, was interested in an exchange. In 1967, the CIDD extended an invitation to Father Nissel to select a Japanese Team to tour the United States.

CIDD members shared a widespread concern about the language facility of the Japanese debaters and their ability to put on good contests in front of native speakers. Father Nissel had alleviated this concern by using a topic for the Sophia tournament that mirrored the tour topic (Nissel, 1968).

The plan was to utilize the Sophia Invitational Debate Tournament to select the competing team; the tour of the United States would be awarded to the first place team. This plan added to the credibility of the Sophia tournament as a "Japanese Nationals" and established a selection process that the CIDD supported (competition). However, Sophia University was unable to hold its 1968 tournament due to student sit-ins, protests, and marches challenging government policies. Without a competition, any team selected would have no experience on the topic. The exchange was nearly canceled and CIDD members expressed concern as they received handwritten letters from Nissel saying there was no electricity on his campus and he was unable to get to his own office.

Despite the cancelled tournament, Nissel selected two debaters to continue the planned tour: Yuji Endo, a Sophia junior, and Masahiro Hosoya, a Sophia graduate student. They embarked on the planned tour, which took place February 20 – April 3, 1969, visiting 25 colleges and universities. Before the Japanese debaters even arrived in the United States, political contentiousness affected the tour; it prevented the original selection process and thus dictated which students could attend.

Timely Topic: Vietnam

Debate topics need to be timely enough to create interest for audiences and allow ample ground for both sides. The 1969 topic that Sophia debated was exceptional and the choice of topic itself is worthy of discussion. For the spring tour, both the CIDD and Father Nissel agreed that the topic would be: Resolved, that the U.S government should withdraw all direct economic and military assistance to the Far East.

The U.S. public already was debating about the withdrawal of economic and military forces from Asia in 1969. With Vietnam War protests in full swing, the summer of 1968 had seen a wave of marches, rallies, sit-ins, and demonstrations across the United States. The draft added to resistance among U.S. audiences to what they perceived to be an unnecessary and increasingly violent war. The Japanese tour actually took place on the one-year anniversary of the My Lai massacre, an event about which U.S. media reported that 60–70 U.S. infantrymen destroyed a small village, killing women and children in the process of looking for enemy soldiers. Student protests were already becoming quite large by 1969. Before the tour had started, in reaction to demonstrations in December, San Francisco State University president S. I. Hayakawa banned all speeches, marches, rallies, and disruptive events and threatened to arrest students who participated in protests ("California College Braces," 1969). Interestingly, Hosoya and Endo debated at the University of San Francisco, near Hayakawa's campus, at the end of the tour on April 1.

In the middle of the tour, the *Monmouth Oracle*, a college newspaper, described one of the debates between the Japanese team and a U.S. college team on the withdrawal of military assistance topic. In their account, the paper reported that the Japanese "contended that American aid had succeeded only in spreading conflict," and that military policy "had not succeeded in the policy of containment" ("Japanese Debaters," 1969). Read within the politics of late 1960s protest and resistance, the debate itself is an instance of public deliberation heavily politicized by events outside the doors of the debate.

Events related to military and economic assistance to the Far East frame the tour itself. The week before the Sophia University debaters arrived in the United States, California Governor Ronald Reagan declared a state of emergency due to the massive student protests at the Berkeley campus. Officials would not regain control of the campus until later ("Reagan Declares an Emergency," 1969). The day after the Japanese debaters departed, April 5 (the one year anniversary of the assassination of the Rev. Dr. Martin Luther King, Jr.) the nation saw speeches, picket lines, and other demonstrations in remembrance of Dr. King ("A Nation Recalls," 1969). Discussion over military assistance in the Far East was at a high point. Indeed, debates held in cities like Pittsburgh, New York, Dallas, and San Francisco were not only timely, but even potentially incendiary given the climate.

Viewing the 1969 Japanese tour not simply as the first exchange debate, but as a tour that began with a state of emergency in California and ended with the memorialization of Dr. King, himself a critic of foreign intervention, politicizes the very history of the tour itself. Between those two markers of late 1960s resistance and memorialization, two Japanese debaters engaged the topic of United States' military and economic withdrawal from the Far East in 22 different public debates. This historic framing has been lost in our understanding of international debates.

Timely Topic: Okinawa

Not only was U.S. military policy in the Far East broadly under the microscope during the spring of 1969, but U.S-Japanese relations were also particularly strained. The tour planners had no way of knowing about the evolving problems in Asia in the years prior to this first tour, nor that difficulties in the U.S-Japan security treaty were brewing. Just days before the tour started, Professor Nobumoto Ohama, president of Waseda University and keynote speaker for the Japanese-United States Kyoto Conference on Asia and Okinawa, announced the results of the Kyoto conference's discussions concerning the U.S-Japan relationship. According to Professor Ohama, the United States' unrestricted use of its base on Okinawa Island and positioning of atomic weaponry on B-52 bombers so close to Japanese cities posed a threat to continued relations. According to Ohama, Okinawa was a "malignant tumor" which would have to be removed before it proved fatal to Japanese American relations (as cited in Oka, 1969a). Two days after Ohama delivered this closing speech, 10 radical Japanese students breached the U.S. Embassy in Tokyo and unfurled banners from the roof which read,

"Withdraw B-52 Bombers from Okinawa," "Crush U.S.-Japan Security Treaty," and "Carry out a general strike in Okinawa and crush U.S. imperialism" ("10 Who Breached," 1969). While the tour was ongoing, the topic of withdrawal became particularly pointed. On March 9, 1969, while the Japanese debaters prepared for their debate against Saint Cloud State the next day, the Okinawa Base Problem Study Committee released its report that detailed the problems with the Okinawa base, urging Premier Sato to call for removal of all U.S. forces by 1972 (Oka, 1969b).

In 1969, Japanese students offered official declamations and protests over Okinawa and people in the United States also were divided on the issue. When a newly inaugurated President Nixon made his first visit to the State Department in January of 1969, according to *The New York Times*, he asked a top-level diplomat at the first meeting: "What are we going to do about Okinawa?" (as cited in Smith, 1969). *The New York Times* reported about a division among the Joint Chiefs of Staff as to whether Okinawa should be returned or the United States should continue to enjoy the exceptions afforded by the base agreement. While the U.S. base in Okinawa continues to be a source of anxiety in the present era (Fackler, 2012), 1969 marks the beginning of this conflict.

During this period, President Nixon failed to name a new ambassador to Japan. That is perhaps a metaphor for the Nixon administration's relationship with Japan during this time: uncertainty. The tenuous relationship between the United States and Japan from the Okinawa situation informed the tour in which debaters discussed withdrawal of U.S. aid to the Far East. Given this backdrop to the tour, the topic choice posed a number of challenges for all sides involved in these debates.

Toward a New Debate History

The 1969 Japanese debaters' tour of the United States started as a move to diversify the CIDD's longstanding history of international debate. Political turmoil affected the debate exchange before the Japanese debaters were chosen and the tour was conducted in a time when social controversy connected explicitly to the tour itself. During the 46 days that Endo and Hosoya traveled to 30 different U.S. cities, protests over Vietnam and proclamations concerning Okinawa challenged all tour participants to carefully consider U.S. military and economic withdrawal from the Far East. While the CIDD-Japan exchange tours have most certainly had an impact on the two argument communities, the political context in which past tours have operated has affected that contribution greatly. Intercultural debates are inherently politicized by their cultural and social context. In order to fully understand the history of the international debates, further contextualizing of the exchanges is required.

References

10 who reached U.S. Embassy held. (1969, February 4). *New York Times*, p. 18. Retrieved from http://www.proquest.com

A nation recalls Dr. King's Death a Year Ago. (1969, April 5). *The New York Times*, p. 1. Retrieved from http://www.proquest.com

Aonuma, S. (1989, April). *American debate practice: Reflections of a Japanese exchange debater.* Paper presented at the Central States Communication Association Annual Convention, Kansas City, MO.

California college braces for new strife; Picketing restricted 15 demands made tough new rules prescribed for reopening Monday. (1969, January 5). *The Washington Post*, p. 3. Retrieved from http://www.proquest.com

Davidson III, J.P. (1976). Debater as pedagogue: The first United States-CIDD debate tour of Japan. *Speaker and Gavel, 14*, 2–9.

Ellis, D. S. (1968). Debate in Japan. *Journal of the American Forensic Association, 5,* 95–98.

Fackler, M. (2012, February 14). Amid image of ire toward U.S. bases, Okinawans' true views vary. *The New York Times.* Retrieved from http://www.nytimes.com/2012/02/15/world/asia/okinawan-views-on-us-military-presence-are-nuanced.html?

Hall, R. N., & Rhodes, J. L. (1972). *Fifty years of international debate 1922–1972.* New York, NY: Speech Communication Association.

Inoue, N. (1996). Tradition of "debate" in Japan. *Bulletin of the Graduate School of Social and Cultural Studies, Kyushu University, 2,* 149–161. Retrieved from http://www.flc.kyushu-u.ac.jp/~inouen/deb-trad.html

Japanese debaters contend American aid in Orient is counterproductive. (1969, March 13). *Monmouth Oracle, 72*(19), p. 1. Retrieved from http://www.access.newspaperarchive.com

Jarvis, J. (2010). The growth of Asian debate: Implications for America. In A. D. Louden (Ed.), *Navigating the opportunity: Policy debate in the 21st century* (pp. 357–360). New York, NY: International Debate Education Association.

Klopf, D. (1975). Forensics in Japan. *Journal of the American Forensic Association, 9,* 212–215.

McBath, J. (May 31, 1963). Letter to Judith Sayers. Inventory of the National Communication Association, msCollection MS0673, Box 35. Marriot Library, University of Utah, Salt Lake City, UT.

Nissel, J. (May 3, 1969). Letter to Robert Hall. Inventory of the National Communication Association, msCollection MS0673, Box 35. Marriot Library, University of Utah, Salt Lake City, UT.

Oka, T. (1969a, February 1). Okinawa Issue called a "tumor" afflicting Japanese-U.S. Ties. *New York Times,* p. 11. Retrieved from http://www.proquest.com

Oka, T. (1969b, March 10). Report asks Okinawa's return by 1972. *New York Times,* p. 2. Retrieved from http://www.proquest.com

Reagan declares an emergency in Berkeley campus disorder. (1969, February 6). *The New York Times,* p. 28. Retrieved from http://www.proquest.com

Smith, H. (1969, March 31). U.S. perplexed by Okinawa issue. *The New York Times,* p. 2 Retrieved from http://www.proquest.com

Suzuki, T., & Matsumoto, S. (2002). English language debate as business communication training in Japan. In. J. E. Rogers (Ed.), *Transforming debate: The best of the International Journal of Forensics* (pp. 51–70). New York, NY: IDEA Press.

Woods, C., & Konishi, T. (2007). What has been exchanged?: Towards a history of Japan-US debate exchange. In T. Suzuki, T. Kato, & A. Kubota (Eds.), *Proceedings of the 3rd Tokyo Conference on Argumentation: Argumentation, the Law & Justice* (pp. 271–280). Tokyo: Japan Debate Association.

66

REVISITING THE U.S. FOOTPRINTS

A critical exploration of interscholastic/intercollegiate policy debate in post-world War II Japan

Satoru Aonuma

TSUDA COLLEGE, JAPAN

Junya Morooka

RIKKYO UNIVERSITY, JAPAN

Kazuhiko Seno

THINKHARD, INC. JAPAN

The purpose of this essay is to offer a critical-synoptic history of the U.S.-style debate in post-World War II Japan. Although the U.S. debate community has recently discovered that the "fastest growing region in the world for debate is Asia" (Jarvis, 2010, p. 357), modern Japanese forensic practice has been under U.S. influence since its inception. *Kaigiben*, the first debate textbook published in Japan, was a translation of a 1855 U.S. publication: *The American Debater, Being A Plain Exposition of the Principles and Practice of Public Debate* by James N. McElligott (Branham, 1994; see also Ohno, 2003). All through the post-World War II period, the powerful presence of U.S.-style debate has persisted on Japanese soil. Presently the United States and Japan are among the very few nations where switch-side, cross-examination team debate using policy topics is one of the prominent styles of competitive, interscholastic debating.

Updating Ellis's (1968), Ishii and Klopf's (1975), Davidson's (1977), Becker's (1983), and Inoue's (1996) earlier studies on Japanese forensics, as well as extending Woods and Konishi's (2008) more recent studies on the history of the U.S.-Japan student debate exchange, this essay will discuss some of the notable transmutations that this U.S.-grown educational technology has gone through on Japanese soil at the turn of this century. Sketching what has happened in the Japanese debate community after World War II, we specifically engage our analysis on the following recent developments: (1) the crisis in traditional intercollegiate policy debate and (2) the growth of debate events and venues alternative to, and outside of, traditional college debate.

College Policy Debate on the Rise

At the century's turn, saying that there is no place for debate in Japan or that Japan lacks an argument culture sounds anachronistic. Debate is no longer considered obscure or foreign on Japanese soil, to say the least. First, with both positive and negative connotations, the term debate has now become part of Japan's household vocabulary. As Inoue (1996) maintained, "The accommodation of debate in Japanese society is undergoing a rapid change now. Popularity of debate in education and media is increasing people's familiarity with the [Japanese] word *dibeeto*" (Section 5, para. 2). Second, and perhaps more important for the present study, "the earliest extensive use of the word *dibeeto* would be found among people who practiced debate under the influence of American speech education" (Inoue, 1996, Section 4.1, para. 1). These people were members of so-called English Speaking Societies (ESSs), popular extracurricular clubs where college students learned practical English through public speaking, discussion, drama, and debate. Long before enjoying any national recognition, debate had already been well recognized and rather popular on college campuses because of the strong presence of English-language debate.

Debate in this last sense is basically a post-World War II Japanese appropriation and adaptation of the U.S. way of debating. As Japanese college debaters have been actively engaged in "imitation pedagogy" in a rather positive sense (c.f., Clark, 1956; Vandenberg, 2011), what they do in the name of debate bears a strong resemblance to U.S. college debate. Right from its start, college debate in Japan uses policy propositions. For instance, the first national topic (drafted for the inaugural national intercollegiate English-language debate tournament held in 1950) was: Resolved: That Japan should rearm in order to defend itself from invasion. Over the course of a half century since then, Japanese college students have debated propositions ("List," n.d.) that require intensive and extensive research on national policy issues, just as their U.S. counterparts.

Another Japanese appropriation of U.S. debate can be found in the debate format and tournament structure. The primary form of collegiate policy debate in Japan is switch-side, team debate. During the 1950s through the 1970s, there existed some variances in team formation. While many tournaments adapted the traditional two-person format from the United States, others used a three-person team format, and still some others used a rather innovative five-person team debate for competition. By the mid-1980s, however, most collegiate tournaments adopted the two-person team, cross-examination format used by the United States' Cross Examination Debate Association (CEDA) and National Debate Tournament (NDT) competitions. Japan's organization of tournaments has also become similar to its U.S. counterpart. In early days, a typical tournament organized competition in a series of single elimination rounds. Currently, most, if not all, college debate tournaments feature multiple and power-matched preliminary rounds followed by elimination rounds, with the exception of some round robins that are typical in the U.S. debate circuit as well.

Finally, as Japanese college debaters have been actively copying U.S. policy debate, argumentative strategies and terminologies used in competition have become very similar to the ones found in CEDA/NDT or high school policy debates. Japanese students imported classic U.S. debate textbooks, such as *Argumentation and Debate, Basic Debate, Strategic Debate,*

Argumentation and Advocacy, and *Contemporary Debate*. Photocopies of periodicals like *Debate Issues*, the *Journal of the American Forensic Association* (now *Argumentation and Advocacy*), and even debate-related essays printed in the Alta Conference proceedings were widely circulated among college debaters and they frequently test-ran arguments based on these readings (e.g., better definition topicality, counterplan permutation, two-constructive development of negative disadvantages, counterwarrants, etc.). In addition, to further study and better copy the U.S. way of debate, these Japanese debaters have taken the opportunity to participate in student debate exchanges. For instance, in the past Committee on International Discussion and Debate (CIDD) Japan tours, the Japanese debate community has welcomed the U.S. national teams not only as their peers and friends but also as their model debaters and debate teachers (Davidson, 1977; Woods & Konishi, 2007). Conversely, a Japanese participant in the 1977 U.S. tour, Shigeru Matsumoto, learned a new affirmative case strategy; after coming back home, his team ran that case and won a national championship.

The Japanese appropriation of U.S. policy debate reached its heyday during the 1980s through the early 1990s. Becker (1983), a debater-turned Fulbright scholar visiting Japan, observed, "Debate in Japan has grown from a handful of 'eggheads' in Tokyo in 1950, to several dozen schools in the sixties, to over a hundred schools and thousands of students in the eighties" (p. 146). This is far from exaggeration. For instance, to compete in the 1985 All Japan Debate Tournament for the Prime Minister's Cup, the Japanese equivalent of the NDT at that time, a total of 182 teams from 103 college ESSs entered and debated at district qualifying tournaments held nationwide ("Report," 1985, p. 5). The National Association of Forensics and Argumentation (NAFA), the country's largest student-run debate organization, started two regional tournaments, one in the Kansai (western) region, the other in the Tohoku (northeast) region, in addition to its annual national championship. Replacing the contract-based home-to-home debate exchanges, tournaments that allowed multiple team entries from different college ESSs were created. One result was a drastic increase in local competitions for novice and less-experienced debaters.

The Crisis, Alternatives, and Change

Policy debate in Japan has certainly seen better days. Once enjoying a strong presence on college campuses nationwide, this U.S. implantation now fails to attract students interested in English and speech communication. First, just as in the United States, the number of college policy debaters has decreased considerably; accordingly, the national collegiate debate circuit had shrunken drastically. As mentioned above, in 1985 a total of 182 teams entered the annual All Japan Debate Tournament; in 2005 it only had 42 entries (Japan Debate Association, 2005). More disturbingly, in 2012 no women's colleges entered the district qualifiers for the All Japan. This is truly unfortunate given that in 1985 five out of the top 32 teams that competed in the national tournament were from women's colleges. Many local and regional tournaments, notably the ones in Hokkaido (the northern main island) and Kyushu (the southern main island), ceased to exist most likely because they failed to secure enough entries to sustain competition.

Second, and equally unfortunately, college policy debate in Japan has degenerated in terms of theory and practice as we entered the new millennium. Put simply, it has become too conservative and self-contained. For one thing, debaters stopped using imitation pedagogy and refused to import new arguments from the United States. In addition, as national topics became narrower to accommodate the needs of busy college students, the research-intensive nature of policy debate faded. For instance, the 2013 national college topic was Resolved:

That Japan should abolish the death penalty. Compare the narrowness of the 2013 topic to the 1992 topic: Resolved: That the Japanese government should adopt a program to eradicate unfair commercial practices inside Japan carried out by private corporations or public organs. Taken together, narrow topics and the resistance to new argument forms discouraged students from researching policy on the broader scale, limited the room for argumentative innovation, and allowed them to recycle the same and old stock arguments from previous years' files.

While the college policy debate community in Japan is in critical condition, it is interesting to note that the diversity in debating styles and the demography of debaters has increased. One such development is the rise of U.K.-style parliamentary debate. While parliamentary debate had been known to the Japanese for quite some time (first introduced to Japan by a Shakespeare scholar named Peter Milward in the 1970s), its presence as a potential alternative to policy debate became evident with the inauguration of the Japan Parliamentary Debate Union (JPDU) and the English Speaking Union of Japan (ESUJ) in the late 1990s. At first glance, the attractiveness of parliamentary debate is rather obvious to English-learning college students in Japan: slower speech with less or no debate jargon, less research-intensive topics, etc. In addition, compared to policy debate, parliamentary debate is more international in scope, as students can travel overseas or invite non-Japanese college teams to Japan to debate.

Because of these features, the number of college students who participate in parliamentary debate competition is growing. At the same time, however, this U.K.-originated debate is yet to fully replace the switch-side, policy format informed by the U.S. tradition. For instance, despite its relatively low entry barrier, the number of college debate squads that actively participate in parliamentary debate competition does not seem to exceed that of policy debate squads: The JPDU currently has 40 institutional members (Japan Parliamentary Debate Union, 2013) whereas NAFA, a policy debate organization, has 42 (National Association of Forensics and Argumentation, n.d.). Additionally, the international feature of parliamentary debate does not seem attractive to many potential college debaters. Namely, given college ESSs, of which parliamentary or policy debate teams are a part, are not school-funded (they are entirely student-run, student-funded clubs), not many can afford to travel overseas on their own and participate in international tournaments. Just as in Japan's real-life national parliament, where many of its members are from economically well-off families or families of career politicians, to compete internationally in parliamentary debate may be premised upon the wealth and affluence of students.

Besides the emergence of parliamentary debate, other interesting developments that relate to policy debate can be found in the high school debate scene. Particularly notable is the growing popularity of Japanese language debating. In 1996, the National Association of Debate in Education (NADE) was established by a group of educators and professionals. Wishing to promote the use of debate in secondary education, the NADE launched the national high school debate championship. Called the Debate Koshien, this annual event has been sponsored jointly by the NADE and Yomiuri Newspaper Company to date. The current membership of the NADE's board of directors includes former English-language college policy debaters; the NADE's topic committee has also featured those who used to be active in the college policy debate circuit.

The Debate Koshien has been a huge success. Using a policy topic similar to the one used in college debate competition (this year's Debate Koshien topic is on political/electoral system reform calling for the introduction of the direct election of the country's Prime Minister), it has succeeded in expanding the high school debating circuit nationwide and attracting hundreds of high school students, a large potential pool for would-be college policy debaters.

Despite that, however, the Japanese-language college debate community still remains quite small. Only a few tournaments are held at the varsity level every year with a very limited number of teams entering; only 18 teams competed in the 2011 All Japan Intercollegiate Debating Championship hosted by the Collegiate Debate Association (CoDA), the national organization for Japanese-language college debate. The low number of teams entering these tournaments indicates that the majority of high school students quit debating once they have entered college. Against this backdrop, it is hardly surprising that, unlike their U.S. counterparts, no colleges in Japan host a high school debate tournament. And it is rare that those who debated policy at the Debate Koshien choose to join a college ESS and participate in English-language debate competition, either policy or parliamentary.

We should note another interesting, and perhaps more remarkable, recent development in the high school debate scene. With the incorporation of the All Japan High School English Debate Association (HEnDA) in 2006, presently many high school students throughout the nation participate in competitive debate using English. In the words of Yano (2013), a former CIDD tour participant and the immediate past president of the Japan Debate Association (JDA), "English debates at the high school level have been spreading at an explosive rate." The 2012 HEnDA national tournament featured 64 schools from no less than 33 prefectures; about 250 schools participated in local qualifying tournaments, a seven-fold increase from the first tournament (Yano, 2013).

To the college debate community, the success of the HEnDA is indeed significant and potentially relevant. In the first place, in the HEnDA circuit, high school students debate policy propositions. For instance, the topic for its inaugural tournament was Resolved: That Japan should make English its Second Official Language. In 2013, they are debating whether or not Japan should lift the tariff on imports of agricultural produces. Second, an increasing number of high schools have become involved in the CIDD Japan tour. For instance, only two high school debate programs hosted the U.S. team in 2005; in 2012 and 2013, the number has increased to nine and five, respectively (individual high schools and regional high school debate associations combined). And given that ESS debaters and their organizations wishing to host the U.S. teams are currently few, perhaps we can say that the time has come for English-speaking high school policy debaters to engage in imitation pedagogy, learning directly from their English-speaking elders with more experience and knowledge in the practice and theory of competitive policy debating. As most of the high schools with strong English-language debate programs are top-notch schools that send a large number of their students to prestigious colleges in Japan, there is a possibility that some HEnDA-trained students will choose U.S. colleges instead and debate competitively in the CEDA/NDT circuit, leaving behind the weakened college debate community in Japan.

Implications

Revisiting the post-WWII U.S. footprints on Japanese soil, we hope our brief narrative will help our colleagues in the world get at least some sense of what is going on in and around the Japanese policy debate community. We hope our discussion will also help our friends and comrades in the U.S. policy debate community engage in critical self-reflection on their own practices for a better future both within and across their national borders. Just like its U.S. counterpart, policy debate in Japan suffers from multifaceted problems. While the term *dibeeto* has become part of Japanese public culture, we fail to attract as large a body of college students as we did in the past. It is our observation that English-language college policy debate in Japan has now reached a critical stage.

Yet, given neither parliamentary debate nor the Japanese-language CoDA can fully be a viable alternative to the traditional policy competition, our only remaining option may be to revitalize this Japanese-appropriated U.S. implant. Once again following U.S. footsteps, perhaps we should try new things. For instance, the Japanese debate community has yet to incorporate the activist turn of U.S. policy debate into its practice, one argumentative innovation worth testing. Or, to further strengthen ties and foster more vibrant exchange with its U.S. counterpart, the Japanese college community *could* use a national topic in an area similar to the NDT/CEDA topic as they did in the past. During the 1955 season, for instance, U.S. and Japanese college students debated the same topic concerning the diplomatic recognition of Communist China. It is useful to remember that U.S. and Japanese policy debaters using a cross-examination team format are a peculiar and endangered species in the world. If the CIDD-sponsored debate exchange has promoted friendship and produced significant collaborative scholarship between the two countries (Woods & Konishi, 2007), perhaps we could make a case that the creation of such a trans-Pacific policy debate community (with the same policy topic and debate activism at the both ends of the Pacific) freed from the constraint of national-congressional or parliamentary discourse would be exciting and effectively disturb the power of politico-economic-juridical borders.

References

Becker, C. B. (1983). The Japanese way of debate. *Forensic Journal, 1*, 141–147.

Branham, R. J. (1994). Debate and dissent in late Tokugawa and Meiji Japan. *Argumentation and Advocacy, 30*, 131–149.

Clark, D. L. (1956). Imitation: Theory and practice in Roman rhetoric. *Quarterly Journal of Speech, 37*, 11–22.

Davidson, III, J. P. (1977). Debater as pedagogue: The first United States-CIDD tour of Japan. *Speaker and Gavel, 14*, 2–9.

Ellis, D. S. (1968). Debate in Japan. *Journal of the American Forensic Association, 5*, 95–98.

Inoue, N. (1996). Tradition of "debate" in Japan. *Bulletin of the Graduate School of Social and Cultural Studies, Kyushu University, 2*, 149–161. Retrieved from http://www.flc.kyushu-u.ac.jp/~inouen/deb-trad.html

Ishii, S., & Klopf, D. (1975). Differences between American and Japanese forensics. *Speaker and Gavel, 13*, 12–13.

Japan Debate Association. (2005). Retrieved from http://japan-debate-association.org/tournament/05.htm

Japan Parliamentary Debate Union. (2013). Retrieved from http://www.jpdu.org/?page_id=103

Jarvis, J. (2010). The growth of Asian debate: Implications for America. In A. D. Louden (Ed.), *Navigating the opportunity: Policy debate in the 21st century* (pp. 357–360). New York, NY: International Debate Education Association.

List of propositions for intercollegiate English debate contests/tournaments in Japan. (n.d.). Japan Debate Association. Retrieved from http://japan-debate association.org/propo/p-list.htm

National Association of Forensics and Argumentation. (n.d.). Retrieved from http://nafadebate.org/nafa/members/

Ohno, H. (2003). Adapted debate in Japan: An analysis of debating textbooks with a focus on Kaigiben. *Speech Communication Education, 16*, 1–18.

Report on All Japan Debate Tournament. (1985). *PRESS, 5*, 4–6.

Vandenberg, K. M. (2011). Revisiting imitation pedagogies in composition studies from a Girardian perspective. *Contagion: Journal of Violence, Mimesis, and Culture, 18*, 111–134.

Woods, C., & Konishi, T. (2007). What has been exchanged?: Towards a history of Japan-US debate exchange. In T. Suzuki, et al. (Eds.), *Proceedings of the 3rd Tokyo Conference on Argumentation: Argumentation, the Law & Justice* (pp. 271–280). Tokyo: Japan Debate Association.

Yano, Y. (2013, February 18). The growing popularity of high school English debates in Japan: Current conditions and issues. *The Japan News.* Retrieved from http://www.yomiuri.co.jp/adv/chuo/dy/opinion/20130218.htm

67

WHAT IS EDUCATIONAL DEBATE FOR?

An analysis of high school and college debate in Japanese popular culture

Noriaki Tajima

KANDA UNIVERSITY OF INTERNATIONAL STUDIES, JAPAN

Although its objectives, goals, and visions may vary in time, space, and culture, educational debate has most strongly emphasized participants' skills of elocution, argumentation, public advocacy, evaluation, and judgment. Nourishing these skills, among others, has been the primary objective of the activity and the chief means to financially sustain debate events. Advancing these skills may even be the *raison d'être* for many argumentation scholars and pedagogues (e.g., Rieke, Sillars, & Rai, 2012; Ziegelmueller & Kay, 1997).

This process of justifying debate education insinuates that the technology of debate has had a good affinity with how the society has dealt with the exchange of arguments, that is, the status of what Tannen (1998) famously called "argument culture" in a certain society. Specifically in the United States, argument culture and debate education have been wed together very well: The culture of argument has made debate education possible and meaningful, while the long history of debate education has nourished the culture and enabled it to grow up in a civil way.

This cultural tendency to appreciate the exchange of argument has produced a variety of popular media outlets that feature U.S. debate, and this tendency has seemingly become more noticeable in the last decade or so. For instance, debate stories have been told focusing on: the rights of minorities and their advocacy (Whiteley, 2007; Winfley, et al. & Washington, 2008), school romance (Dornbusch & Greenspun, 2006; Gordon & Stewart, 1989), adolescence and human development (Bregman & Stephenson, 2005; Fine, 2001; Welch & Blitz, 2007), and even the pathological aspect of the U.S. culture of competition and oral combat (Tolchinsky, Ward & Tolchinsky, 2011; Walling & Robbins, 2008). Some of these examples present debate as an integral part of the story, others just as a character device; some fictionalize debate to project a utopian vision, other documentary films are very real. In general, however, all these debate films "incorporate [debate] as an important plot device" (Sears & Chung, 2008, p. 198).

These artifacts imply that, good or bad, debate reflects U.S. culture. Whether the United States is defined by its democracy, diversity, adult development, or pathology, debate has been an important part of U.S. culture. To me, the main characteristic of these films is that their plots can proceed without bastardizing what debate is or without devaluing the meaning of the activity itself. It is true that some of these movies project debate, especially intercollegiate competitive debate, in negative ways. Yet, these negative projections – such as being elitist, chauvinistic, White-centric, and hyper-competitive – are also represented as one aspect of the entire U.S. culture in each of these artifacts. In this way, debate movies epitomize the United States' political and cultural struggle by and through the representation of debate.

These movies take what Stuart Hall (1998) understood as the *popular*. Hall (1998) argued that the power of the popular is found in "[t]he capacity to constitute classes and individuals as a popular force that is the nature of political and cultural struggle: to make the divided classes and the separated peoples . . . into a popular-democratic cultural force" (pp. 452–453). For these movies and TV programs, debate has been the means to mobilize larger citizens as "a popular-democratic cultural force." With the role of U.S. debate movies described with Hall in mind, this essay attempts to review a mirror case of the debate movies from Japan.

Once, Japan was described as "harmonious," in contrast to being an argument culture, in that it prioritizes silence and maintains established social relations rather than contextualizing individual public claims (Condon & Saito, 1974, 1976). Along the same line, Western rhetorical scholars described Japan as a "rhetorical vacuum" (Morrison, 1972, p. 89), barren of the art of public argumentation.

However, it is well known among argumentation scholars that this foreign perception was not necessarily true. For instance, Kanke and Morooka (2012) have shown that Japanese college students organized "youth clubs" in order to debate important public issues of the time in the Meiji, Taisho, and early Showa eras (1868–1936); Inoue (1994) reported that, in the post-WWII period, many English Speaking Societies (student unions of Japanese universities) made tremendous efforts to incorporate the methods of policy and parliamentary debate from U.S. counterparts and develop their own version of debate. More recently, Woods and Konishi (2008) have demonstrated the robust tradition of exchange debate tours between the United States and Japan.

As in the case of the United States, Japan has its own popular culture genres, and each has its own audience expectations attached to it. In terms of the social recognition of debate, debate is less recognized by the Japanese public even though it has an increasing presence in the educational context. Therefore, it is difficult to find movies and films about debate. However, debate materials do appear in genres targeting youths – novels and manga comics. In what follows, I investigate the representations of debate mainly from these artifacts and analyze what it means for argumentation and debate scholars and educators.

Altered by Secondary Objectives: Light Novels and Promotion Phrases

In 2010, a novel about a high-school debate club was released and it was feverishly welcomed by high school and college competitive debaters. The novel, *Kanojo O Iimakasu Nowa Tabun Muri*, or *I Can't Beat Her in Debate, Perhaps*, has been serialized in four volumes (Urema, 2010–2012). In the genre of what Japanese call *raito noberu*, or light novels, it is an easy-reading novel primarily targeting middle and high school students. Typically, light novels are between 40,000–50,000 words long, as long as novellas in U.S. publishing terms, and rarely exceed 200 pages. However, *Kanojo* was as long as 300 pages per volume. Yet, *Kanojo* shared a similar tendency with many other light novels. Episodes advanced with a consistent hero and a beautiful heroine: Yuya, a thin, craven, and modest first-year high school boy, and Aira, an aggressive and assertive second-year high school girl with an outstanding talent for debate.

Volume 1 featured three debate rounds with other debate team members, one as a club practice and the other two in assemblies in front of the whole school. The topics of the debates
were all quite familiar with Japanese high school debaters: "The cat-roid robot from the
future is harmful"[1] (pp. 46–57); "Supermarkets should charge the price of plastic bags on
consumers" (pp. 102–112); and "The Japanese government should prohibit the use of private
motor vehicles" (pp. 232–263). Volume 1 of *Kanojo* described the growth of both Yuya's
debate skills along with the romantic sentiments toward Aira. In this sense, Volume 1's plot
developed like the U.S. movies *Listen To Me* (Gordon & Stewart, 1989) and *Rocket Science*
(Welch & Blitz, 2007), with its taste of adolescent high school culture.

Volumes 2–4 of *Kanojo* receded from featuring debate. They had fewer debate rounds and
less description of Yuya's growth through debate practices. Volume 4, the last volume, featured
two debate rounds. The first one was to decide whether the club should visit a beach for a
summer vacation (pp. 65–92), which was the main scene of this Volume. The second debate
occured toward the end in a hospital room between Yuya and Aira, who is sick with a high
fever and temporary memory disorder, over the fact proposition: "sentiment is not delivered
without words" (pp. 241–265). Even though the novel called this extemporaneous exchange
a debate, it was more a performance of Yuya's personal sentiment toward Aira. In the middle
of this exchange, the one-on-one debate is suspended as soon as Aira's memory is back and
Yuya confesses his feelings and they are not reciprocated.

In my understanding, this way of concluding the entire four-Volume novel is symptomatic
of the way debate is evaluated by the Japanese general public. As *Kanojo* proceeded across
Volumes, debate is overshadowed by high school romance. Even though debate and romance
are nicely integrated in the climax of Volume 1, by Volume 4 debate is a mere pretext of
beginning and maintaining the romantic conversation. Partly for this very reason, *Kanojo* lost
the attention of many high school and college debaters.

Prioritizing other objectives – such as romance and friendships – is not something that
happens only in light novels. In English-speaking high school national policy debate tournaments, for instance, the individual competencies of oral performances and decision making
are recognized as secondary benefits. In the tournament, all participants reiterate a "make-
friends pledge" to give testament at the opening ceremony every year, which reads:

> I will strive to develop my integrity as I work with others to inquire into the wisdom
> and skills of debate. . . . I accept that *the most important goal of this tournament is* not to
> win or lose but *to make friends*.
>
> *(emphasis added)*

No further description of the "wisdom and skills of debate" is offered in the pledge. Benesse
(2009), the sponsor of the tournament, described its goals for the debate tournament this way:
"the educational value of English debate is on improving English skills, . . . But the true value
of the activity . . . rests on making debate friends in this tournament site." At the high-school
level, the value of debate education is overshadowed by the state demand of promoting
English proficiency while also maintaining the harmonious social status quo.

At the college level, the standards for evaluating the value of debate education are
somewhat different but, again, the "wisdom and skills of debate" are not emphasized. For
instance, the National Association of Forensics and Argumentation (NAFA, 2013), the
biggest tournament host for English-speaking intercollegiate policy debate, promoted
itself on the top page of its website: "What is necessary to be a human *resource needed* in the
world? English, logical thinking, and speech skills – English debate has them all"; "Debate

X Career – NAFA knows thousands of former debaters working in the world, and we can show what kind of working careers become available after debate" (emphasis added). In such promotions like NAFA's, debate is not directed toward democratic deliberation and equal possibilities of participation. Instead, it is the skill of neoliberal citizenry and of entrepreneurship, the skill to be a leader of the free world and of a market-fundamentalism, which now determines democratic attributes, characteristics, and norms (cf., Brown, 2003; Greene & Hicks, 2005, p. 113).

All these examples do not prioritize the skills of argumentation, advocacy, public deliberation, and democratic participations that are harnessed in debate. Instead, they deflect it in favor of romance, dwindle it to English proficiency, and prioritize survival in the economic world. In these representations of debate, the merits of debate education that we argumentation scholars think of as essential seem to be dissolved in the specific cultural contexts.

Taken Over by Weirdos: Manga Comics

In addition to Urema's novel, I would like to introduce another debate artifact from Japanese popular culture: a series of Hongo Shimoyoshida's two volume manga comic *Dibeitian* (2012), or *Debate-ian*, featuring a high-school debate team. The title comes from a Japanese direct translation of debate (*dibeito*) with a suffix meaning profession or expert (-ian, like rhetoric*ian* or histor*ian*). Shimoyoshida crafted the story after careful observation of actual high school debate practices, including several visits to high-school policy debate tournaments (and perhaps for this reason, a few major characters resemble coaches and debaters actually participating the tournaments).

Distinctive in this comic is its description of debaters as being weird. Typically, debaters may be described as being cunning, fiendish, and foxy; other times, they are esoteric and nerdish. But, throughout the two volumes until the end of the story, Shimoyoshida's description of debaters is far more than that. For instance, the beginning of the story has a scene with two debaters, Mr. Hiruma and Mr. Kurisu, organizing a booth in front of their clubroom to recruit first-year high school students. They successfully recruit one, Mr. Takeda, and the skills of debate were just nominally exhibited there. That is, in the course of conversation, Mr. Hiruma set Mr. Takeda's concern in the form of debate proposition, that "Which is a better club, debate or soccer?," and they overwhelm Mr. Takeda's naïvete with a tsunami of arguments "tagged" with such terms as "1NR" through "2AR." Drawn into an argument and then brainwashed, Mr. Takeda signs his name on the form with an expressionless, blank look on his face (Vol. 1, pp. 16–22). Throughout the rest of the story, Mr. Takeda is depicted as having become one of the weirdos, like a member of a cult religion. In the rest of the story, Shimoyoshida (2012) consistently described debaters as weird. Debate is the cause of their wicked, malevolent, and mesmerizing ethos, and the characters, throughout the story, are described from an outsiders' viewpoint.

To be precise, manga comics are a genre in which readers expect an overemphasis of characteristics – caricature – in order to create humor, and I suspect that the high school community tolerated and acknowledged Shimoyoshida's freedom of expression. Still, Shimoyoshida's characterization of debaters epitomized the present barrier between the debate culture and the public in Japan. As noted above, in recent years advocates have promoted the benefits of debate, especially on the high school level. Unfortunately, however, once those interested in debate visit actual tournament sites, debate rounds occur at an unintelligible speed with terminologies unfamiliar to a lay audience to the point that it appears to be funny to them.

Summary

In the first section, I observed that present debate education is itself within the realm of political, educational, and cultural hegemony in Japan. In the second section, I confirmed that norms of policy debate have their own obstacles. In Japan, one of the struggles in letting the public acknowledge debate culture is found in popular culture depictions. Even though promoters of debate eagerly spread their ideas, several factors – such as debate theories, actual debate performances at tournaments, and the time and energy necessitated to participate – tend to make debate culture inaccessible and mysterious to a larger audience.

Therefore, I argue that debate needs to take an educational turn in order to be better situated within the society (e.g., Keith, 2010; Woods and Konishi, 2008). But the educational turn in this case is a daunting task: Debate needs to be made widely open to the public and inviting to lay audiences, while at the same time being sufficiently honorable to high school and college students. In this sense, it is perhaps quite hard for the Japanese culture of argument to be as mature as the U.S. culture of argument. Yet, I am still encouraged by an increasing visibility of educational debate in popular artifacts such as light novels and manga, high school curriculum, and TV programs in Japan. Because, as Giroux (2000) explained, culture "deploys power in its connections with the realm of . . . identifications and subject positions through the forms of knowledge, values, ideologies, and social practices" (p. 10), I hope that the formation of debate culture in the popular culture realm will attract the attention of more citizens and eventually mature its civic orientation. Once, Fine (2001) claimed that the high school debate culture, even though it does not deal with real-world issues, is quite meaningful to participants (p. 185). Like Fine warm-heartedly aligned the meaning of students' high school debate culture with their futures, I would like to see the present treatment of debate education align with the future Japanese culture of argument.

Note

1. Due to the wide popularity of *Doraemon* for over 30 years in manga comics and TV animation, the topic has been familiar to Japanese people across generations.

References

Benesse. (2009, February 7). Eigo dibēto o tōshite zenkoku ni hirogaru yūjō no wa [Nation-wide circles of friendship through English debate]. *Benesse*. Retrieved February 22, 2013, from benesse. jp/berd/center/open/kou/view21/2009/02/07view_report1_01.html

Bregman, A., & Stephenson, B. (Producers). (2005). *Thumbsucker* [Motion picture]. USA: Sony Pictures Classics.

Brown, W. (2003). Neoliberalism and the end of liberal democracy. *Theory and Event*, 7(1), 1–43. Retrieved from Project Muse.

Condon, J. C., & Saito, M. (Eds.). (1974). *Intercultural encounters with Japan*. Tokyo, JP: Simul Press.

Condon, J. C., & Saito, M. (Eds.). (1976). *Communication across culture for what?* Tokyo, JP: Simul Press.

Dornbusch, J. K. (Producer & Director), & Greenspun, A. (Producer). (2006). *Thanks to gravity* [Motion picture]. USA: Voyage Entertainment.

Fine, G. A. (2001). *Gifted tongues*. Princeton, NJ: Princeton University Press.

Giroux, H. (2000). *Impure acts*. New York, NY: Routledge.

Gordon, D. (Producer), & Stewart, D. D. (Director). (1989). *Listen to me* [Motion picture]. Los Angeles, CA: Colombia Pictures.

Greene, R. W., & Hicks, D. (2005). Lost convictions. *Cultural Studies*, 19(1), 100–126.

Hall, S. (1998). Notes on deconstructing "the popular." In J. Storey (Ed.), *Cultural theory and popular culture* (pp. 442–453). Harlow: Pearson/Prentice Hall.

Inoue, N. (1994). *Ways of debating in Japan* (Doctoral dissertation, University of Hawaii). Available from ProQuest Dissertations and Theses database. (UMI No. 9519451)

Kanke, T., & Morooka, J. (2012). In search of an alternative history of debate in early modern Japan. *Journal of Argumentation in Context, 1*(2), 168–193.

Keith, W. (2010). Keynote address: A new golden age. In A. D. Louden (Ed.), *Navigating opportunity: Policy debate in the 21st century* (pp. 11–26). New York, NY: International Debate Education Association.

Morrison, J. (1972). The absence of a rhetorical tradition in Japanese culture. *Western Speech, 36*, 89–102.

NAFA. (2013). Retrieved from http://nafadebate.org/

Rieke, R. D., Sillars, M. O., & Rai, T. (2012). *Argumentation and critical decision making* (8th ed.). Boston, MA: Pearson.

Sears, W., & Chung, S. (2008). Review: Representation of debate in film. *Contemporary Argumentation and Debate, 29*, 197–206.

Shimoyoshida, H. (2012). *Dibeitian* [*Debate-ian*]. Vols 1–2. Tokyo, Japan: Kōdansha.

Tolchinsky, D. (Director & Producer), Ward, R., & Tolchinsky, D. (Producers). (2011). *Fast talk* [Motion picture]. USA: Cross-X Productions.

Urema, S. (2010–2012). *Kanojo o iimakasu nowa tabun muri* [*I can't beat her in debate, perhaps*]. Vols 1–4. Tokyo, JP: Smash Bunko.

Walling, J. (Producer), & Robbins, D. (Director). (2008). *Debate team* [Motion picture]. San Mateo, CA: Green Lamp Picture.

Welch, S. (Producer), & Blitz, J. (Director). (2007). *Rocket science* [Motion picture]. USA: HBO Films.

Whiteley, G. (Producer & Director). (2007). *Resolved* [Motion picture]. USA: One Potato Productions.

Winfley, O. et al. (Producer), & Washington, D. (Director). (2008). *The great debaters* [Motion picture]. New York, NY: The Weinstein Company.

Woods, C., & Konishi, T. (2008, August 8–10). *What has been exchanged?: Toward a history of Japan-US debate exchange.* Paper presented at the Third Tokyo Conference on Argumentation, Tokyo, Japan. Tokyo: Japan Debate Association.

68

SHOUTING, CLAPPING, AND LAUGHING WITH THE MONKS

Toward a boisterous, cosmopolitan argumentation pedagogy

Don Waisanen

BARUCH COLLEGE, CITY UNIVERSITY OF NEW YORK, USA

Contrary to expectations based on stereotypes, Tibetan monasteries are actually full of playful, boisterous, highly physical argumentation (see Drepung, 2009). Tibetan monks could be described as "first and foremost *homo disputans*" (Dreyfus, 2003, p. 204), having adopted and adapted Indian philosophical debate in their seventh century turn to Buddhism (Perdue, 2008). Unfamiliar observers often describe the format as mesmerizing to watch; one Westerner even thought he was watching some type of new, emerging genre like "Tibetan Socrates meets Jerry Springer" ("Tibetan Monks," 2007, para. 2).

I stumbled upon this remarkable practice during a fellowship exploring Himalayan art and culture. The shouting, clapping, and laughing in the format drew my interest, as did possible implications for the study and teaching of argumentation. In a globalizing planet where the possibilities for incommensurability loom large, Liu (1999) has urged scholars to examine novel, productive intercultural debate practices like "cross-arguing," where "two contending sides . . . each try to justify [their] position in the other party's terms" (p. 309). Combs (2004) has further described many differences between holistic, polysemous traditions of Daoist debate and Greek traditions; such contrasts in argumentative style and assumption are well worth parsing out.

Intracultural traditions can provide new deliberative forms that can be adapted for inter-cultural engagement. Hicks (2002) called for such "interactive" and "emergent" models of public argument (p. 256), while Bohman (2000) argued that:

> for all their talk about deliberation, few theorists or philosophers describe it at all, and few of those who describe it do so in sufficient detail to make clear why it is democratic, [and] what putting it into practice would mean.
>
> *(p. 17)*

Habermas and others have also continued to explore religious models that could point the way toward useful deliberative norms (see Goodnight, 2007, p. 103).

For these reasons, this study examines the practices of Tibetan debate to construct new perspectives for argumentation. I inputted the search term "Tibetan Debate" on *YouTube* and then conducted a close reading of the 583 video search results (excluding redundant or non-related materials), while working through links and other sources provided. These videos and other sources provided a range of perspectives on Tibetan debate – from first-person footage to engaging lectures around the world on the topic. Given obvious difficulties in language translation and context, I also searched for and threaded together extant literatures on Tibetan debate.

In the following section, my goal is less to cover all the intricacies of this debate form than to construct and distill several themes from these data with implications for the theory, practice, and especially the teaching of argumentation. Based upon this analysis, this essay concludes with a classroom exercise that may be implemented in argumentation or deliberation courses.

Combining Status and *Stasis*

The unequal postures between arguers constitute one of the most striking features of Tibetan debates. In its most basic form, one person *stands* and walks around as a questioner, while the other *sits* on the ground ready to defend a position (Perdue, 1992, p. 28). The overarching spirit of these debates is highly egalitarian ("Great Debates," 2011), but also is aimed at sharpening the mental capacities of both debaters by assigning height, movement, and "presence" (Perelman & Olbrechts-Tyteca, 1969) to the questioner, while the questioned assumes a more meditative, still position. Typically, novices are assigned to the sitting position while more experienced teachers or students stand.

Tibetan debate defines *stasis* as independent from equal status. As much as figures like Habermas (1985) emphasized that *ideal speech situations* should maintain equality between participants, for pedagogical purposes this does not always need to be the case. Both participants exhibit respect toward one another – indeed, differences in beliefs and attitudes are revered in this tradition ("Great Debates," 2011) – but for the sake of learning, debaters play higher and lower statuses to increase the intensity of questioning, answer giving, and audience involvement.

Those standing pose a question on a particular topic and the person sitting responds with a thesis; finding some initial agreement has historically been a way to provide some equal grounding for monks meeting from different sectarian traditions (Dreyfus, 2001a, para. 3). Debate then proceeds, with those standing using boisterous movements to enliven their arguments. Those sitting start at a physical disadvantage, which calls for heightened, intense concentration toward the incoming questions.

A major goal of this format is as much to become more aware of the limitations of one's own understanding (Dreyfus, 2003, p. 269) as to discover or generate knowledge. Participants are asked to become as comfortable raising their status as lowering it – cultivating the ability to play both for a short-term win in the debate competition while accounting for long-term needs for the relational and individual growth provided by the exercise.

Shifting, Improvisational Coalitions

Compared with Oxford and other debate styles where arguers focus on a resolution and audiences may vote at the end ("Great Debates," 2011), in Tibetan debate audiences are far more involved and even enter the forum themselves as argumentation proceeds. Any topic can be debated ("Tibetan Debate," 2006), with debates becoming increasingly collective ("Great Debates," 2011). The videos and talks evidence background observers suddenly joining in so that, for instance, two defendants of a thesis become seated while one questioner stands. At other times two questioners argue with one person sitting. Combinations of any number of debaters are possible to the point where entire cohorts can be seated or standing against other players. A group versus group format can also develop.

These practices demonstrate a procedure where audience members are allowed to change their minds over the course of a debate and need not decide a position and stick with it ("Highlights," 2011). In general, the goal is to start with rules and procedures but move to a point where participants can go beyond "set formulas" ("Highlights," 2011, 5:25). It is not uncommon for the initial debaters to eventually switch roles in the course of a session given the debates tend to continue for hours at a time (Dreyfus, 2001b). These practices teach that debaters and audiences should not necessarily remain polarized or come into the debate with inviolable *a priori* commitments; instead, Tibetan debate focuses students on open-ended investigation.

Tibetan debates highlight pluralism and human processes involving multiple interpretations on matters of wisdom or truth. Monks recognize that "the hold of tradition cannot be too tight; otherwise tradition would be unable to cope with ever changing circumstances" (Dreyfus, 2008, p. 44). Underscoring the expansive goals of the form, Geshé Rabten argued that "after developing his [sic] intelligence and discriminatory powers in this way, a monk is able to apply as many as twenty or thirty logical approaches to each major point of teaching" (as cited in Cabezón, 2008, p. 3).

Games of Consequence

Tibetan debates are quite similar to Socratic methods of argument but also surpass such methods in several respects. Some of the format's features could be characterized as games of consequence. Questions and answers generally follow an enthymematic line of reasoning, collapsing syllogistic logic into single thesis sentences like "the subject Socrates is mortal because of being a man" ("Great Debates," 2011, 7:30), which quickly allow the debates to take off in numerous directions.

From the thesis statements, Tibetan debates follow an argument-from-consequences structure. Other debating forms tend to adhere to probative structures, which aim "to establish a true thesis to an audience that does not yet know it to be true," while consequences models aim "not to establish a point but merely to draw the consequences of previous statements and bring out the contradictions or absurdities entailed by these statements" (Dreyfus, 2008, p. 47). Respondents are expected to provide fast answers to questions, following one of three/four general responses: I agree, I disagree, this is a fallacy, or by trying to turn the question back on the questioner ("Buddhist Monks," 2011). In general, respondents' main method is to draw distinctions about their topics to prevent contradictions (Dreyfus, 2001a).

An informal spirit guides these formal procedures. Tibetan debate should be seen as a game like chess, where each move has numerous implications ("Great Debates," 2011, 38:35). The rules are not completely strict and many rhetorical elements such as humor can contribute to making the debates more lively and involving (Dreyfus, 2008). In the same way that Palczewski (2002) described argumentation built upon metaphors of play as offering more expansive, productive possibilities for debate, fun is meant to be a part of the exercise. Debate in Tibet is, as one observer described, "a mental sport [that] has the advantage of being most useful and delightful" (Sierksma, 1964, p. 140).

Animated Sounds and Physicality

The aural and kinetic dimensions of these debates challenge simple, "talking heads" conceptions of argumentation. Indian culture, from which Tibetan debate developed, placed more emphasis upon oral communication than just about any other ancient culture (Kennedy, 1998, p. 172). Outside observers sometimes wrongly assume that there is a great deal of anger present among debaters (see Sierksma, 1964, p. 140); yet, far from some scholastic exercise (see Stein, 1972), these debates evidence useful intellectual *and* emotional activity (Dreyfus, 2008).

Several physical characteristics stand out. Debaters usually start in low vocal tones, which rise progressively to animate arguments. The questioner's clapping invokes a specific Buddhist ritual, with the right and left arms representing a joining of "method" and "wisdom" ("Great Debates," 2011, 5:05). Gestures like stomping also have Buddhist overtones, indicating the avoidance of rebirth in a lower dimension, with the hope that rigorous debate will lead to emancipation (Cabezón, 2008, p. 4). Another practice involves the questioner wrapping a robe around his or her waist to signal "understanding and control" with "forceful sweeping gestures" ("Tibetan Monks Debate," n.d., para. 4). Gestures not only help stage the debates, but bring a focus on clear expression that mobilizes both debaters and audiences (Dreyfus, 2008, p. 50).

These practices direct our attention to how argumentation can incorporate more sound and movement than has been the case in many Western traditions. Such an approach comports with tested educational programs integrating "multiple intelligences" in curricula (Gardner, 2006). Moreover, deliberation scholarship has perhaps overstated needs for civil language and behaviors; as Ivie (2002) suggested, more rowdy conceptions of deliberation could be warranted in public argument. Respectful communication remains an ideal, but Tibetan debate invites us to consider how civil rhetoric can perhaps be more emotional and embodied than has been thought possible.

Outdoor Argumentative Spaces

Different than many educational institutions, monasteries do not have any classrooms. Instead, the academic space is an outdoor courtyard, which is primarily designed for debate. The courtyard space is important for argument in a few respects. As demonstrated in the videos, this context permits debaters to argue in a louder and more energetic style than an indoor setting allows. Additionally, given the external interferences of nature and, often, fellow monks debating all over the courtyard, questioners and defenders are challenged to bring force to their arguments.

These spaces also are designed as distinct zones for failure. The courtyard is considered by monks "a separate arena where embarrassments and even humiliations are seen as part of the learning process. Hence, no stigma is attached to one's mistakes" (Dreyfus, 2003, p. 197). There are plenty of times and places in everyday life when people are subject to structures of hierarchy and perfection (see Burke, 1966). But in Tibetan debate, the courtyard is a place to free individuals from social demands and expectations that might normally hinder generative argumentation.

Conclusion and Exercise

Tibetan debate can advance the study and practice of argumentation. The form is currently practiced in some Indian middle schools (Learning, 2009), but as Perdue suggested, "there is this potential for adaptation" in the format (as cited in "Great Debates," 2011, 47:00). Others have proposed that it could be used in undergraduate education ("Great Debates," 2011, 48:00), but specific instructions are needed. Toward this end, I built from the previous analysis to construct the following exercise.

First, instructors should draw students' attention to the topic of intercultural argumentation. At a point in the semester when students have covered more Western understandings of debate, perhaps through the practice of policy or parliamentary debate, instructors can segue to how comparative cultural forms support or challenge extant understandings of argumentation. I would advise showing a six-minute "Highlights" (2011) video, which provides both a context for Tibetan debate and demonstrates how it is typically conducted. Other short videos (e.g., Drepung, 2009) can provide more direct examples of actual Buddhist monks debating. These segments should lead to discussion – given where classes are at this point in the semester, what do students make of the monks' styles, etc.?

Second, after discussing the videos, teachers should cover the five aforementioned approaches in Tibetan debate: the combining of status and *stasis* in debaters' verbal and nonverbal orientations, the shifting improvisational coalitions that can be built over the debate's progression, the games of consequence format that focuses logical procedures, the animated sounds and physicality that are available as rhetorical resources, and the ways in which having an outdoor space can contribute to the argumentative encounter.

Last, instructors should explain that course members will engage in a few, adapted rounds of Tibetan debate in an outdoor space on campus. The exercise can start with two individual volunteers, one the standing questioner and one the sitting defender. Debaters should start with a handshake to signal respect toward each other. Although just about any topic is fair game for the format, I recommend starting with a philosophical or religious topic, like most Tibetan debates. Topics should be somewhat accessible, such as: Does truth exist? Is religion good for society? Are the lives of animals equal to or less than human lives? The respondent should provide a thesis statement answering the question so the debate can proceed.

Instructors should remind students of several expectations. The questioner should generally only ask questions, trying to draw out the consequences of the respondent's statements to point out potential contradictions. Respondents, in turn, should respond to answers as quickly as possible. The questioner should start to use energetic movements and heightened vocal gestures (as respectfully as possible) to make her or his points. After the first few minutes, audience members should begin to join one of the sides, putting their hands up if they think they have additional points to help either the defender or questioner. The first time the debate takes place, the instructor should let the students know she or he will be facilitating at various points to help the process run more smoothly. For teaching purposes, I recommend that the instructor calls time and uses the number of students who have shifted to each side to determine which side won. At other times, an ending will emerge more organically, such as when a questioner is no longer able to prod forward with a line of questioning.

Once this example debate has occurred, a variety of formats can be used, such as pairing every student with debate topics chosen by the instructor. Alternatively, a two-on-two or five-on-one debate can be formed. Providing these variations should allow for repetitions of the exercise to keep students interested. Once the exercise is completed, instructors should debrief with the class: Did they find their debating skills sharpened? What areas for improvement did it help them identify in their argumentation? What did they learn about themselves in this process? To finish on an encouraging, positive note, the instructor should identify best practices and anything noteworthy observed during the debates. Overall, there is much to be gained from such argument traditions. Following the Tibetan monks, this training can sharpen students' skills, enlarge their outlooks, and, hopefully, inspire them toward a reasoned and reasonable way of life.

This project was supported by a Baruch-Rubin Museum Project Grant to Integrate Arts across the Curriculum.

References

Bohman, J. (2000). *Public deliberation: Pluralism, complexity, and democracy.* Cambridge, MA: MIT Press.

Buddhist monks. (2011, April 22). Buddhist monks. A Socratic debate [Video file]. *YouTube.* Retrieved from http://www.youtube.com/watch?v=moJpZC5IN-k

Burke, K. (1966). *Language as symbolic action: Essays on life, literature, and method.* Berkeley: University of California Press.

Cabezón, J. I. (2008) *The life of a Sera Monk.* Retrieved from http://www.thlib.org/places/monasteries/drepung/essays/

Combs, S. C. (2004). The useless-/usefulness of argumentation: The Dao of disputation. *Argumentation and Advocacy, 41,* 58–70.

Drepung debates [Video file]. (2009, September 7). *YouTube.* Retrieved from http://www.youtube.com/watch?v=z4Lsy5aj3fw

Dreyfus, G. B. (2001a). Procedures and rules of debate. Drepung Monastery. Retrieved from http://www.thlib.org/places/monasteries/drepung/essays/#!essay=/dreyfus/drepung/monasticed/s/b41#ixzz21r0gD1Qv

Dreyfus, G. B. (2001b). Examinations and the organization of debate. Drepung Monastery. Retrieved from http://www.thlib.org/places/monasteries/drepung/essays/#!essay=/dreyfus/drepung/monasticed/s/b44#ixzz22CvXxXIs

Dreyfus, G. B. (2003). *The sound of two hands clapping: The education of a Tibetan Buddhist monk.* Berkeley: University of California Press.

Dreyfus, G. B. (2008). What is debate for? The rationality of Tibetan debates and the role of humor. *Argumentation, 22,* 43–58.

Gardner, H. (2006). *Multiple intelligences.* New York, NY: Basic Books.

Goodnight, G. T. (2007). The engagements of communication: Jürgen Habermas on discourse, critical reason, and controversy. In P. Arneson (Ed.), *Perspectives on philosophy of communication* (pp. 91–110). West Lafayette, IN: Purdue University Press.

Great debates: Tibetan debate. (2011, April 29). *Asia Society.* Retrieved from http://asiasociety.org/video/countries/great-debates-tibetan-debate-complete

Habermas, J. (1985). *The theory of communicative action* (Vol. 1, T. McCarthy, Trans.). Boston, MA: Beacon Press.

Hicks, D. (2002). The promise(s) of deliberative democracy. *Rhetoric & Public Affairs, 5,* 223–260.

Highlights – Tibetan Debate. (2011, April 29). *Asia Society.* Retrieved from http://asiasociety.org/video/countries/highlights-tibetan-debate

Ivie, R. L. (2002). Rhetorical deliberation and democratic politics in the here and now. *Rhetoric & Public Affairs, 5,* 277–285.

Kennedy, G. A. (1998). *Comparative rhetoric.* New York, NY: Oxford University Press.

Learning Tibetan debate at TCV [Video file]. (2009, September 20). *YouTube.* Retrieved from http://www.youtube.com/watch?v=O1OGbl0Ryhs

Liu, Y. (1999). Justifying my position in your terms: Cross-cultural argumentation in a globalized world. *Argumentation, 13,* 297–315.

Palczewski, C. H. (2002). Argument in an off key: Playing with the productive limits of argument. In G. T. Goodnight (Ed.), *Arguing communication and culture* (pp. 1–23). Washington, D.C.: National Communication Association.

Perdue, D. (1992). *Debate in Tibetan Buddhism.* Ithaca, NY: Snow Lion Publications.

Perdue, D. (2008). The Tibetan Buddhist syllogistic form. *Chung-Hwa Buddhist Journal, 21,* 193–211.

Perelman, C., & Olbrechts-Tyteca, L. (1969). *The new rhetoric: A treatise on argumentation.* (J. W. Wilkinson & P. Weaver, Trans.). Notre Dame, IN: University of Notre Dame Press.

Sierksma, F. (1964). rTsod pa: The monachal disputations in Tibet. *The Indo-Iranian Journal, 8,* 130–152.

Stein, R. A. (1972). *Tibetan civilization*. Stanford, CA: Stanford University Press.

Tibetan debate [Video file]. (2006, March 2). *Google Tech Talk*. *YouTube*. Retrieved from http://www.youtube.com/watch?v=O5D1O7eb_H4

Tibetan monks . . . you can't be closer to this [Video file]. (2007, October 2). *YouTube*. Retrieved from http://www.youtube.com/watch?v=OTTlRjYP1DM

Tibetan monks debate. (n.d.). *Snow Crest Inn*. http://www.snow-crest-inn-dharamsala.com/tibetan-monks-debate.html

Traditional Tibetan debate – at Jonang Monastery Kathmandu Nepal [Video file]. (2011, September 22). *YouTube*. Retrieved from http://www.youtube.com/watch?v=2KfD1uRJsDs

PUBLICATION INFORMATION

This selected works volume represents the best of the scholarship presented at the 18th National Communication Association/American Forensic Association Conference on Argumentation. Also known as the Alta Argumentation conference, given its locations in the mountains of Alta, UT, the conference happens every other summer and brings together a lively collection of argumentation scholars from a range of disciplinary approaches and a variety of countries.

Papers, abstracts, and panels submitted to the conference underwent a rigorous review process. Two members of the editorial board and the conference director reviewed, rated, and ranked every conference submission. The acceptance rate for conference submissions was 75%. Of all the presentations at the conference, only seven (the six spotlight papers and the keynote), were invited. All the rest underwent a double-review process: once for selection for presentation, another for inclusion in the selected works.

Once accepted for presentation, authors were given the option of submitting their papers for consideration for inclusion in the selected works volume for the conference. Again, every submission was reviewed by a member of the editorial board and the conference director. Papers rated and ranked in the lower half of submissions were reviewed by at least two more editorial board members and discussed by a core group of six members of the editorial board in order to provide editorial feedback and to make decisions about which essays would be included in the selected works. A number of essays underwent a revise and resubmit process prior to acceptance; all essays received editorial suggestions and underwent various degrees of revision. The acceptance rate for the selected works was 70%. The acceptance rate calculated by counting all conference submissions in relation to those essays accepted for publication was 36%.

The end result of this process is a collection of well written, tightly argued, and engaging essays.

Catherine Helen Palczewski, PhD
Conference Director and Editor of the selected works volume